❧ THE SECRET WITHIN

THE SECRET WITHIN

HERMITS, RECLUSES, AND SPIRITUAL OUTSIDERS IN MEDIEVAL ENGLAND

WOLFGANG RIEHLE

Translated by Charity Scott-Stokes

CORNELL UNIVERSITY PRESS
Ithaca and London

This translation was prepared with the kind assistance of the Austrian Fund for the Promotion of Research and of the Austrian government of Styria.

Der Wissenschaftsfonds.

Originally published as *Englische Mystik des Mittelalters,* copyright © Verlag C.H. Beck oHG München, 2011.
First published 2014 by Cornell University Press
First paperback printing, 2018
Printed in the United States of America

Library of Congress Cataloging-in-Publication Data

Riehle, Wolfgang, 1937– author.
  [Englische Mystik des Mittelalters. English]
  The secret within : hermits, recluses, and spiritual outsiders in medieval
England / Wolfgang Riehle ; translated by Charity Scott-Stokes.
      pages cm
  Includes bibliographical references and index.
  ISBN 978-0-8014-5109-6 (cloth : alk. paper)
  ISBN 978-1-5017-2516-6 (pbk. : alk. paper)
  1. Mysticism—England—History—Middle Ages,
600–1500. 2. English literature—Middle English,
1100–1500—History and criticism. 3. Christian literature, English
(Middle)—History and criticism. I. Scott-Stokes, Charity, translator. II.
Riehle, Wolfgang, 1937– Englische Mystik des Mittelalters. Translation of:
III. Title.
  BV5077.E54R5413   2014
  248.2′209420902—   2013027551

Cornell University Press strives to use environmentally responsible suppliers and materials to the fullest extent possible in the publishing of its books. Such materials include vegetable-based, low-VOC inks and acid-free papers that are recycled, totally chlorine-free, or partly composed of nonwood fibers. For further information visit our website at www.cornellpress.cornell.edu.

In memoriam Wolfgang Clemen

Quid enim habet aliquis quod non accepit?

Aelred of Rievaulx, *Institutio inclusarum*

✄ Contents

ILLUSTRATIONS

 PREFACE

More than thirty years have passed since I published my book *The Middle English Mystics,* which focused on mysticism's metaphorical language. In the meantime, the study of—and appreciation for—mystical literature have taken new turns. Not surprisingly, as interest in mysticism has grown, we have seen some confusion as to exactly what the term "mysticism" means. Now more than ever there is an urgent need for clear definitions. For Kurt Ruh, whose work on the history of mysticism has been essential to my own, mystical literature is characterized by its focus on the knowledge of God through experience of the divine, succinctly expressed by the scholastics' *cognitio Dei experimentalis.*[1] Such a distinction allows for the inclusion of works by authors who write about mystical experience and knowledge of God without necessarily claiming to have been granted such experience themselves. Scholars nowadays generally avoid getting caught up in trying to decipher the *ineffability* of mystical experience itself, preferring instead to focus on the circumstances and extent of its occurrence, and in particular with the way in which mystical language is intended to make perceptible by concrete linguistic means what it is that transcends (however briefly) everyday experience.

In a parallel enterprise to Ruh's history of mysticism, the theologian Bernard McGinn set out to define mystical experience as "presence of God," even choosing this phrase as the overarching title of his four-volume work.[2] Foregrounding the mystic's experience of God's presence, rather than that of knowing God, is a more modest and more realistic target for the scholar of mysticism. Consequently for McGinn, "union with God is not the most central category for understanding mysticism," and he has no objection to classifying as mystical a merely meditative text that aims to encourage devotion and absorption in the deity; the Christian tradition had always regarded meditation as a valid preparation for mystical experience.

McGinn goes on to argue that to use "experience" of the presence of God as a heuristic principle is imprecise and ambiguous because, for the mystic, God's *presence* may in fact alternate with suffering from his *absence.* To get around this problem McGinn adopts the term "consciousness": consciousness of the presence of divine transcendence becomes the subject matter of mystical texts. The presence of God is felt in a manner "both subjectively and objectively more direct, even at times as immediate," which distinguishes it from "other forms of religious consciousness." While I appreciate the distinction McGinn is making, I do not consider the term "consciousness" entirely satisfactory; it refers too strictly to the intellect and fails to encompass fully the *existential* experience of the divine, which touches the whole human being.

How was mysticism spoken of in the Middle Ages? The correct answer would be: by using the Latin word *contemplatio,* or—as a less common alternative—the Greek word *theoria.* John Lydgate, for one, neatly describes Richard Rolle as "contemplatif of sentence" (author of mystical texts), famous for having considered it his task to instruct and guide his readers toward *contemplatio,* the desired beholding of God granted by divine grace. This leads McGinn to insist that mysticism should not be seen as an isolated phenomenon but rather as one manifestation of the Christian religion or religious practice, the implication being that the mystics are not the only ones who cherish the prospect of seeing God. Ordinary Christians do, too, even if their only hope to experience it is after death. Both mystics and ordinary Christians are *in via,* on a pilgrimage from earthly "exile" in a *regio dissimilitudinis* to the celestial *patria.* It is not surprising, therefore, that a mystical text such as Hilton's *Scale of Perfection* shares structural similarities with other, more mundane works of didactic theology such as the rambling allegorical epic *Pèlerinage de l'âme,* which tells of the soul's wanderings on its path to the vision of God in the next world and the final attainment of God's peace in the heavenly Jerusalem. Works that cover some but not all stages of mysticism are more aptly classified as "spiritual" than "mystical." Likewise, there is not always a clear distinction between pastoral, devotional, and mystical literature. A number of mystical works can be attributed to their authors' involvement in pastoral care, which may impart a certain mystagogical character.

Medieval mystical texts were thus not thought of as forming a genre of their own, as recent work on mystical literature has rightly acknowledged. It is well worth considering Nicholas Watson's more inclusive term, "literature of interiority."[3] This term, currently in vogue, draws attention to the need to go beyond a merely literary approach to mystical texts, in order to grasp their theological scope and their relation to tradition, and it prompts hermeneutic investigation of the *theological* constituents of interiority. Literary consideration of mystical texts has to be complemented by an interdisciplinary theological perspective.

One of my aims in writing this book on the mystics of medieval England is to give their texts the kind of attention they deserve, which means interpreting them according to the authors' own express intentions. To do this it is essential to step outside the limits of philological analysis and consider the texts as works of literary and theological significance. Bearing fully in mind the inadequacy of considering mystical texts as a distinct genre, I have nonetheless chosen to focus mainly on the canon of five mystical authors: Richard Rolle, the anonymous author of *The Cloud of Unknowing,* Walter Hilton, Julian of Norwich, and Margery Kempe. For reasons that will become clear, it will also be necessary to consider first the *Ancrene Wisse,* a rule of life for three young recluses, and later *The Mirror of Simple Souls,* an English version of Marguerite Porete's *Mirouer des simples âmes.* By adding these works as well as the Wooing Group, *A Talkyng of þe Loue of God,* and the Meditations of the monk of Farne to the established canon, it is hoped that this book nonetheless presents an expansive picture of the rich variety of English mysticism.[4]

Another goal of this book is to bring a comparative perspective to the subject by considering mystical activity on the Continent, which strikes me as indispensable for a full understanding of English mysticism. The briefest comparison between English and German mysticism immediately shows that it is no longer possible to agree unreservedly with Ruh's claim that "mysticism really comes into its own only in the vernacular languages."[5] In England such a conclusion is refuted especially by the case of Richard Rolle, who wrote the majority of his mystical works in Latin, works that were quite similar thematically to his English work. In *Melos amoris* his mystical theme evolves in a highly original linguistic structure that was possible only in Latin (the language preferred by Walter Hilton, too, for many of his texts). Moreover, *Incendium amoris* is explicitly intended to address uneducated as well as educated readers, and Rolle anticipates female addressees even for his highly complex *Melos amoris.*[6]

Mysticism scholarship has made significant strides in recent years, but in my view it has sometimes ended in a cul-de-sac. This can be seen in research that starts from the cognitive assumptions of our own times, projecting those assumptions onto the mentality of medieval people, an approach that is not likely to yield convincing results because it neglects the wide historical gap that separates us from the Middle Ages.[7] Having said this, I too must admit that, in the course of writing this book, I have had to revise and correct some of the views I expressed and conclusions I reached in my earlier book. This applies particularly to the chapter on Margery Kempe. I used to endorse the once prevalent view that she was largely an eccentric figure in terms of her spiritual life pattern and that therefore she should be numbered among the English mystics only in the broadest sense. After the passage of several decades, new research and my own consideration of the theological background of her work have brought me to a far more positive view of this late medieval "pious woman," who, incidentally, has a surprise in store for today's readers: she knows very well that in distant times there will be people (whereby she means, of course, men) who will set out to slander and condemn her—but she forgives them. It is humbling to have to include myself in this number, suddenly brought into a relationship with a woman who lived six hundred years ago, and it has sharpened my awareness of the obligations we have as modern readers of her work. This brief spotlight on a medieval woman who "prophylactically" cuts down to size her critics in a future age illustrates the fallacy of any sense of superiority with regard to the "dark" Middle Ages. We have far more in common with those times than the Enlightenment could sweep aside.

❧ Acknowledgments

This work is based on the book *Englische Mystik des Mittelalters,* which I published in Germany in 2011. Various people and circumstances have helped to make it a reality. The impetus came from Kurt Ruh, who suggested that I should flesh out my earlier work on medieval English mysticism with a new history of the major works, and that this should form a supplement to his four-volume *Abendländische Mystik des Mittelalters*—volumes that have proved very useful to me. Through Kurt Ruh I came into close contact with Germanist research on mysticism. I am also glad to be able to mention my academic mentor Wolfgang Clemen, who not only taught me the vital importance of close reading for the assessment of the intrinsic quality of a literary text, but who also recommended the field of medieval English mysticism to me as a young scholar. I therefore dedicate this translation to his memory.

From the time of my youth up to the present day I have often had the good fortune to be placed in circumstances particularly favorable to the study of mysticism, which have provided stimuli from Catholic as well as from Protestant sources. I recollect with gratitude the formative years spent in the theological seminary, rich in tradition, in the former Cistercian monastery of Maulbronn, which is now part of the World Cultural Heritage. That time spent within the walls of well-preserved Cistercian architecture nurtured my interest in this particular order's contribution to the shaping of medieval mysticism. During my student years, I was given a place at the University of Durham in the north of England, a city of great importance for the study of mysticism. Much later in life, during a period of preparatory research for the present study spent in Durham, I received valuable help and advice from Dr. A. I. Doyle. Most recently I have benefited with great thanks from the (Catholic) New Theology of Eugen Biser, professor emeritus of the University of Munich, which I find very illuminating, and which, I believe, has sharpened my perception of several aspects of medieval English mysticism. Like myself, he seeks to combine the study of literature with theology.

I also owe thanks to my colleague in Graz, musicologist Rudolf Flotzinger, for having pointed out salient features of late-medieval music. Furthermore, I thank my first reader, Klaus Bitterling, for his knowledgeable specialist assessment of the work. It is a pleasure to acknowledge with great thanks the very useful suggestions I have received from Peter Potter, editor-in-chief of Cornell University Press; with his expert contributions he has intensified and rounded off my discussion of the early English mystics.

My very special thanks are due to Dr. Charity Scott-Stokes for taking on the difficult task of translation. I was very fortunate that after some hesitation she accepted the challenge. Her patience with successive revisions to the text and her easygoing cooperation were indeed remarkable and encouraging. As a critical reader and competent scholar in the field, Charity made perceptive suggestions of various kinds, for which I am also most grateful.

I should point out that the English version does not correspond in every detail to the original German text. Some sections needed to be shortened, because they contained material likely to be familiar to an Anglophone readership, while other sections required further clarification for the new readers. I am grateful to the German publishing house of C. H. Beck for their readiness to pass on the translation rights for the original German version. I also want to take this opportunity to express my gratitude for the various permissions readily granted for the reproduction of illustrations.

For generous financial support of the translation I am greatly indebted to the Austrian Fund for the Promotion of Research (FWF) and to the Austrian government of Styria ("Das Land Steiermark"). Gratefully I recall the support of the British Library, Durham University Library, and the staff of Graz University Library (especially those responsible for loans from other libraries). Finally, I give heartfelt thanks to my wife and my whole family for the help and understanding with which they have supported and accompanied my work on English mysticism.

Wolfgang Riehle
Stattegg bei Graz

THE SECRET WITHIN

CHAPTER 1

The Development of Eremitical Mysticism in the British Isles

The beginnings of vernacular mysticism in England, as on the Continent, can be traced back to the decisive transformations in theology, intellectual history, and the history of mentalities that have long been associated with the "twelfth-century Renaissance."[1] During this period, which can actually be said to begin around 1050, historians have noted an emerging interest in the question of what constitutes human individuality.[2] Yet how can a new understanding of human identity be grasped and described centuries after the fact? Can one speak of isolated individuals "emerging" from community bonds, insisting on self-determination and on being their own person independent of external support?

Rather than dwelling *in extenso* on this much discussed problem, we need only mention the name of Abelard to illustrate the point. The case of Peter Abelard (1079–1142), the brilliant scholastic philosopher and theologian whose affair with his student Heloise ended tragically, shows how the theme of love as *the* great existential human experience gained unprecedented explosive force in the twelfth century. Of course, we shouldn't forget that writers and artists in Greco-Roman antiquity had already explored the ennobling power of love, even if only from man to man, with or without the inclusion of Eros. Yet in the twelfth century we see something genuinely new: women being idealized as the goal of erotic passion, a development that soon would have the effect of depriving ennobling love of innocence.[3]

Indeed, it is impossible to speak of the obsession with love during the twelfth century without noting that, for the first time, women dared to articulate and satisfy their emotional and spiritual needs, as the example of Heloise most aptly demonstrates. In the unconditional yet passionate love between Abelard and Heloise we see a new expression of human experience: passionate love in feminine form.[4] Texts of literary fiction, especially courtly lyric and romance, turned to this theme on a grand scale, even if giving shape to this new experience of *fin'amor* (fine love) frequently led to sublimation and renunciation of ultimate fulfillment of desire; the beloved was close in thought, but unattainably distant nonetheless. Even if there is still scholarly disagreement as to the exact origins of courtly lyric, the parallels between the cult of the lady and the cult of Mary are fascinating indeed, and out of Marian devotion came a whole retinue of female saints as Christianity began to "veer toward an appreciation of feminine values."[5]

Not surprisingly, the twelfth century also saw a revival of interest in the erotic poetry of Roman antiquity, including that of Ovid, whose sophisticated portrayals of pagan sensuality, libidinous and gratified, were enormously popular—especially his playful instructional guide, *Ars amatoria* (*The Art of Love*). Countering this fascination with poetry's power to evoke passionate love between the sexes, some writers began focusing on a different love—love between the individual soul and God, or Christ. It was above all the Cistercians who, through their attention to love, granted the individual an interior space in which to experience subjectively the self and God. They responded especially to women's need for a spiritual life of their own. With their predilection for allegorizing the *Song of Songs,* the Old Testament book with its rich imagery of love, they, and Bernard of Clairvaux in particular, were influenced by the great church father Origen, who had already interpreted it as an allegory of the *unio* of God and the bridal soul, and whose commentary on the *Song of Songs* had made him the "creator of Christian bridal mysticism."[6] As Bernard McGinn has aptly observed, Origen viewed the Song of Songs as the place where "scripture reveals the heart of its message about the love of the descending Christ for the fallen soul," and from there it was not far to go to find in the erotic language of the Song of Songs the "deepest inscription of the mystical message."[7]

This link between the erotic and the mystical can be seen, for example, in the great Cistercian theologian William of St. Thierry, who opens his famous work *De natura et dignitate amoris* (*On the Nature and Dignity of Love*) with the sentence, "The art of arts is the art of love," and initiates the projection of this existential human experience onto the passionate *spiritual* union of the human being with God.[8] Here again there is good reason to speak of a kind of sublimation. But in mystical love, unlike courtly love, the ultimate union is not denied; rather, it is experienced as a specifically mystical paradox, "sensually spiritualised." For William this means a transformation from *amor* to *caritas*.[9] At the same time, one often finds in mystical texts a conscious relinquishing of terminological differentiation, and *amor* is spoken of in the secular as well as in the spiritual contexts, precisely to arouse awareness that in mystical as in human love a passionate *fire* burns.

The Cistercians will play a key role in this book. Indeed, one of my central claims is that the Cistercians of the twelfth century provided a necessary backdrop for the specific affectivity of mystical experience in England. This fact, which has yet to receive the scholarly attention it deserves, will be demonstrated in several ways.[10] Because the Cistercian order believed that it was returning to a true observance of monastic life as the desert fathers had practiced it, and because English mysticism of the late Middle Ages also followed clear eremitical tendencies, our story begins with a brief survey of the development of anchoritic spirituality up to the time of the Cistercians.

Eremitical Beginnings

The earliest anchorites dwelling in Britain wanted to renew the *vita apostolica* (apostolic life) by means of an ascetic lifestyle of the utmost simplicity and poverty, appealing to the authority of the New Testament and the early church fathers. Many of them chose the harshest form of life conceivable, far from the noise and external constraints of society, because they did not believe they could put into practice the ideal of radical devotion to God in any other way. Rather than being regarded as pitiful outsiders, they often were held in high esteem; even abbots and kings sought them out in order to obtain their advice.[11] The term "anchorite," which comes from the ancient Greek verb meaning "to withdraw," originally was used to refer to a range of individuals who withdrew from secular society, including hermits and recluses, but a distinction must be made between hermits, who were not necessarily confined to a single dwelling place, and recluses, who took radical rejection of the world to the extreme by spending their days in complete isolation, walled up in a cell and given over entirely to silence.[12]

We find the first Christian "dropouts" from society as early as the third century in the desert landscape of Egypt, not far from Alexandria, as well as in Asia Minor.[13] Dissatisfied with the social and religious life of the city, individual inhabitants launched into a solitary existence in the desert. Since ancient times, the desert had been regarded as the archetypal site for liminal experience and the attempt to find oneself; with its hot days and cold nights it presupposed the highest degree of readiness to undergo ascetic hardship. In this process, the desert corresponds on a spatio-sensual level to an inner "evacuation," *vacatio* or *kenosis,* the experience of total freedom as the indispensable prerequisite for a direct encounter with the divine. In their wish to expose themselves to this liminal experience the desert fathers appealed to the authority of the Bible above all, where the desert is a frequently recurring motif.[14] One need only think of the forty years' exile of Israel or of Jesus's "analogous" forty days in the desert.

The most famous of the desert monks was St. Antony, "the Great" (251–356).[15] His biographer Athanasius emphasizes particularly his ascetic severity and the fight against demons and grave temptations during his twenty years of solitary life in Egypt. Athanasius recounts the interesting detail that toward the end of Antony's long life a group of like-minded monks gathered around him and chose him as their spiritual leader, thus giving rise to the early form of a monastic community, a *coenobium.*[16] A survival strategy led the early desert hermits to live at such a distance from one another as permitted them to be within reach and, if necessary, help one another in times of bodily or spiritual need. They also lived sufficiently close to urban centers to be able to influence by example the adherents to the Christian faith, providing a model of a life pleasing to God.

Another important figure in this early period was Pachomius (292–348), generally considered the founder of Christian cenobitic (communal) monasticism. While Pachomius had lived as a hermit for a time, he is best remembered for establishing multiple communities in upper Egypt filled with like-minded persons, who followed a rule of life that imposed poverty, humility, and obedience. These communities were similar in some respects to later monasteries, but the eremitical influence was still quite evident: monks and nuns lived in individual cells. By the year 350 the anchoritic and the cenobitic ways of life were both being practiced. It is also worth noting that from the very beginning there were female as well as male anchorites, including the by-now well-known example of Thais, who acquired latter-day fame as an operatic heroine; she was first a prostitute, but was then converted to become an anchorite. *Ancrene Wisse,* the guide for recluses, mentions two of the desert mothers by name.

Even if the anchoritic idea gave rise to later forms of communal monasticism (as is indicated by the word formation "mon-achos"), it would be overly simplistic to say that one gave way to the other. Both Jerome and Cassian remained convinced that the *hermit* represented the highest rung on the ladder of perfection, for which reason life as a monk could only be seen as preparation for the eremitical life. Their view—that every monk should eventually become a hermit, because only the hermit can attain the highest form of contemplation—was taken up and put into practice at various times by isolated individuals throughout monastic history, but it never gained wide acceptance.[17]

Soon, news of the ascetic way of life, in both solitary and communal forms, spread beyond the eastern Mediterranean. Indeed, monks and nuns would play a critical role in the diffusion of Christianity into Europe. Nowhere was this more evident than in Ireland. While it is still not clear exactly how Christian teaching reached the Emerald Isle, we know that Irish society converted to Christianity sometime between the fifth century and the time when the Vikings arrived, around the year 800. During this period, anchorholds (the dwelling place of anchorites) were founded on the islands off the west coast of Ireland. Not surprisingly, in such a setting the sea took over the role of the desert. Celtic monks, notably the famous Columba, or Columcille (521–597), traveled by sea as missionaries to the Hebridean island of Iona, to Scotland, and to England.[18]

These Irish monks and anchorites would exert a powerful influence on Anglo-Saxon England. This is perhaps most evident in Bede's admiration for them in his *Ecclesiastical History of the English People,* where otherwise he is mostly interested in the cenobitic life. Another impressive example is St. Cuthbert, the patron saint of northern England.[19] Born in Northumbria circa 634, Cuthbert is best remembered for his life as a monk and hermit, having been inspired by the Irishman St. Aidan, founder of the monastery on the island of Lindisfarne (known as "holy island"). Because of his exemplary qualities Cuthbert became prior of the Lindisfarne abbey after the Synod of Whitby in 664. In spite of Lindisfarne's remoteness (it could be reached from the mainland with dry feet only at low tide), Cuthbert was drawn to yet greater solitude, to the totally inhospitable island of Farne, farther out at sea, where he sang psalms in all weather. While he would be recalled to serve as bishop of Lindisfarne for a short time, he finally withdrew for good to Farne, to a life in prayer and contemplation of visions; he died soon thereafter, in the year 687.

Gradually the Celtic influence on anchoritic life in England receded as Benedictine monasticism became more and more firmly established. And yet the eremitic tradition of the desert fathers would continue to be discernible, as is evident in the eighth-century *Life* of St. Guthlac by the monk Felix. According to Felix, who modeled his portrait on the *Lives* of Antony and Cuthbert (d. 714), Guthlac lived for some time in the Benedictine monastery at Repton in Derbyshire before moving to a hermitage on a bend in the river Welland in the Fens, where he lived an even harsher ascetic life.[20] But it would be the tenth century that would see the beginnings of a remarkable upsurge of interest in the anchoritic life in England, which scholars have observed as part of a more widespread flowering of the eremitical movement in the eleventh and twelfth centuries throughout Western Europe.[21] A leading figure in this movement was Peter Damian (d. ca. 1072), the reforming monk from Italy, who once wrote,

> O eremitic life, you are the soul's bath, the death of evildoing, the cleanser of filth; you make clean the hidden places of the soul, wash away the foulness of sin and make souls shine with angelic purity. The hermit's cell is the meeting-place of God and man, a cross-roads for those who dwell in the flesh and heavenly things. For there the citizens of heaven hold intercourse with men, not in the language of flesh, but by being made manifest, without any clamour of tongues, to the rich and secret places of the soul. The cell knows those hidden counsels which God gives to men.[22]

The eremitical ideal would also prove to be a defining feature of the incipient new monastic orders, above all the Cistercians and Carthusians, as well as the Premonstratensians and Camaldolese, who separated from the Benedictines in the wake of the Cluniac reform. As contemplative orders, they all absorbed eremitical characteristics. Thus Cistercian history begins with a group of recluses who settled in Molesme, and then grew rapidly as hermitages scattered throughout France became affiliated with the new center in Cîteaux. The Carthusian order, founded as early as the eleventh century by Bruno of Cologne, attempted to combine the secluded eremitical way of life with the cenobitic ideal, inasmuch as the monks lived in individual cells and only came together for liturgical purposes and for communal recreation. The *vita solitaria* became a serious alternative version of the true *vita religiosa,* and presented a constant challenge to the cenobitic life.[23] Not surprisingly, scholars have noted a crisis of sorts within cenobitic monasticism during this period as these new *monachi peregrini* sought to return to the roots of monasticism in the desert fathers. For them salvation was to be found not in the religious community but in the hermit's cell, far away from human beings, alone with God.

It is in the context of this revival of eremiticism that the origins of the specific reforming order of the Cistercians—of particular interest for the present study—should be viewed. Cistercian spirituality consciously absorbed recollection of the mysticism of the desert fathers, as is beautifully attested in the *Golden Epistle* of William of St. Thierry, which ends with the words of Isaiah 24:16, succinctly formulating the individual's relationship with God: "Secretum meum mihi, secretum meum mihi [My secret is mine, my secret is mine]."[24]

Wulfric of Haselbury, Godric of Finchale, and the Rise of Affective Spirituality

Two impressive English figures from the twelfth century may be taken to represent the many. One is a recluse and anchorite who, like Julian of Norwich at a later date, lived in a cell built onto the wall of a parish church—Wulfric of Haselbury. The other is a solitary who tended the hermitage he had created at a bend in a river—Godric of Finchale.

Nearly everything we know about Wulfric (ca. 1090–1154) comes from a single surviving biography penned by John, prior of the Cistercian abbey of Forde in Devon.[25] John tells us that Wulfric was born of modest (*mediocris*) English stock in the village of Compton near Bristol. John was clearly fascinated by Wulfric, collecting stories about him after his death. The picture that emerges of Wulfric in John's account is that of a man astonishingly open to the world. Although he became a priest at a relatively young age, he continued to indulge his passion for hunting and hawking alongside his ministry in his first parish. Soon, however, a conversion experience took him back to Compton, where he "died to the world" and became a recluse in an anchorhold at the church of St. Michael and All Angels in Haselbury. This anchorhold consisted of an inner room for Wulfric and an outer room for a servant and even occasionally a scribe. He received visitors, commoners and nobility alike, through a shuttered window and could enter the church to pray and celebrate Mass. Altogether, Wulfric would spend nearly thirty years at Haselbury. John describes in loving detail the simplicity of his devotion and mystical love, drawing on the imagery of the Song of Songs, even depicting the holy man as the bride of Christ.

Godric of Finchale (ca. 1065–1170) was born in Walpole in Norfolk, the son of poor parents.[26] After a period as an itinerant hawker he felt the irresistible pull of the sea. He bought a share in a ship and, drawing on his knowledge of winds and tides, became steersman. Although he earned his livelihood "trading in diverse wares," he never hesitated to interrupt his voyages in order to visit churches and saints' shrines. Yet what fascinated him most of all was the holy island of Lindisfarne, where St. Cuthbert had lived and worked, and—not surprisingly—the even lonelier Inner Farne. His seafaring life had lasted sixteen years when he resolved to follow the example of St. Cuthbert. Of his own free will, and not because he had no other option, he chose the quite different world of silent, inward-looking spirituality. After deciding to live the life of a hermit he gained the minimal education required for liturgical prayer at a school in Durham. In what is still a delightful setting on a bend of the river Wear at Finchale, not far from the city of Durham, Godric found a sheltered site for the hermitage in which he would spend the next sixty years living under harsh conditions, entirely dictated by nature, as was thoroughly in keeping with his own robust nature.

According to Reginald, it took Godric forty of those years to conquer his passions and attain peace in his new life. Central to his devotion was his focus on the experience of Jesus's humanity. In a vision with strong Cistercian resonance, he saw the Christ child emerge from the lateral wound on the crucifix in his cell, which caused him to weep tears of joy.[27] By means of prayers, some he composed himself, he attained a high level of contemplation, with visions of the mother of God and several saints. The following verse to Mary, which Reginald records, served him as protection against the devil's temptation:

> St. Mary, the Virgin
> mother of Jesus Christ of Nazareth,
> receive, defend and help your Godric
> (and) having received (him), bring (him) on high with you in the
>   Kingdom of God.
> St. Mary, chamber of Christ,
> virgin among maidens, flower of motherhood,
> blot out my sin, reign in my heart,
> and bring me to bliss with that self same God.[28]

As with Wulfric, Godric received visitors in search of spiritual counsel. One of these was the Cistercian Aelred of Rievaulx in Yorkshire. We do not know what advice Godric gave Aelred, nor can we assess the depth of spiritual insight this hermit gained during the sixty years he spent living the solitary life, but we do know that the two men became friends.[29] Godric died at Finchale in the year 1170.

These brief portraits of Wulfric and Godric point to an aspect of the spirituality of both men that recent scholarship has shown to have been an increasingly pronounced feature of Christian devotion, in England and elsewhere, during the twelfth century. Wulfric's love of imagery from the Song of Songs and Godric's visions of the child Jesus can be seen as part of a growing affective spirituality that was especially prevalent among the contemplative orders. For instance, we know that the Cistercians were particularly fond of maternal imagery when talking about male figures (e.g., Mother Jesus).[30] Mary, the mother of Jesus, was also the focus of renewed attention, specifically her part in the work of salvation.[31] This turn toward what might be called feminine aspects of Christianity can be seen as part and parcel of the new esteem accorded to women more generally, of which mention was made at the start of this chapter.

The impact of these developments on female spirituality was also quite profound, as growing numbers of women found themselves drawn to a life of spiritual devotion. They wanted to preserve their virginity for love of God, and this meant departing from the world.[32] But where could they go? Demand for the monastic life among unmarried women was greater than the number of monasteries. The new orders were not yet in a position to satisfy the need for a *cura monialium* (care of nuns). Indeed, they hesitated to have anything to do with this problem; for instance, it would take until the end of the century for the Cistercians to begin founding a significant number of women's houses.[33] On the Continent the lay religious communities known as beguines offered a solution, but in England this form of shared living hardly existed. With few options at their disposal, therefore, a not inconsiderable number of unmarried women found that their only solution was the life of a recluse, cut off from the world by the enclosing walls of a small cell, as a way of surviving in a world full of dangers.[34]

In monastic theory, of course, the recluse as a form of life was considered exceptional, reserved for only a select few religious men and women who had passed through the cenobitic school. Monastic statutes made it possible for a spiritually ambitious nun to transfer from the convent to the more radically enclosed anchoritic life.[35] Since a recluse of this kind had already been trained as a nun, it was thought that there was no risk of her lapsing into heterodoxy. Yet, in practice, this prerequisite for the life of a recluse was often dispensed with, not least because there were very few convents, which led considerable numbers of women to opt for the recluse's cell without a preliminary period as a nun, a tendency that began in the eleventh century.[36] Lay people— and in England predominantly aristocratic women—bought their way into such cells by means of gifts, and dedicated themselves to religious activity under the patronage of the monastery, but without losing touch with the lay world outside.[37] There is a surprising spread of cells in the twelfth and thirteenth centuries, scattered throughout the medieval countryside and mainly occupied by women.[38] In truth, it was much more difficult for women to live as unprotected hermits, for they had to maintain their position in society.[39] Admittedly, on the Continent there is evidence of hostility toward recluses and hermits, sometimes from the church but also from the laity, because of the exclusiveness of this form of life. They were often reproached for taking an interest only in self-sanctification, motivated ultimately by egoism.

The clergy also interpreted the hermits' and recluses' totally nonattached status as a lack of willingness to obey superiors, and as a tendency toward unbridled self-indulgence.[40]

On the other hand, the life of a recluse entailed particularly severe hardship. For some aristocratic women with sponsors willing to make generous donations, a cell might include several small rooms with servants and a little garden, but the fact is that they were shut off from the outside world. The institution of enclosure consisted in the "walled-up" recluse being, as it were, buried alive in the eyes of the world, for which reason her ceremony of enclosure included a recitation of the Office of the Dead. In many cases the bishop himself celebrated the enclosure. One can imagine the torments these women endured. Not only was the procuring of food frequently a problem; they were also subjected over the years to an array of temptations, not to mention illnesses. The unchanging pattern of the day, always the same spiritual exercises, prayers, meditations, and activities that led to no concrete outcome, was a grave trial for the none-too-stable human disposition. We know of one aristocratic woman, Eve, who during the late eleventh century lived under the protection of the royal monastery at Wilton but took an enormous risk when she fled to Angers to live under even stricter conditions as a recluse, relinquishing her friendship with her abbess, St. Edith, and her spiritual guide, Goscelin of St. Bertin. Nevertheless, a testament to the great strength that this woman must have possessed is the fact that in 1082 Goscelin wrote for her a book of consolation, or rule of life, the *Liber confortatorius,*[41] which made the greatest demands on her—equal to those made on men—in the fight against temptations, well knowing that she was able to meet them.[42] Incidentally, on the Continent several letters to recluses from bishops and other clergy have survived;[43] it seems that the recluses could maintain certain epistolary contacts. Some sermons, too, delivered on the occasion of the *obstructio* of a recluse, convey a vivid and detailed picture of the conditions of enclosure.[44]

Christina of Markyate: Paths to Female Liberation

We have an unusual amount of information about the English recluse Christina of Markyate (born between 1096 and 1098), from the fragmentary *Life* written by a monk of St. Albans who knew her.[45] This *Life* betrays a remarkable ambivalence on the holy woman's part—a fact that has recently received the attention of scholars. It begins very much in the manner of a typical saintly biography with a portent-prophecy that prepares Christina's mother during her pregnancy for the fact that her child will be one of the elect.

A dove is said to have remained with her for seven days—a sign that the child would attain sanctity in body and soul, and find peace in the contemplation of higher things through renunciation of the world.[46] It was also a sign that later in her life Christina would enjoy the special protection of Mary. Indeed, Mary and Christ determine the course of her frequently perilous life. She is given the name Theodora ("gift of God"), after the early Christian martyr—an indication that her parents are prepared to respond to the prophecy of election and to govern their lives accordingly. They undertake a pilgrimage to the famous Benedictine monastery of St. Albans with their daughter—still a child, but of exceptional piety.[47] So impressed is she by the monks that she makes a promise to God of virginity and lifelong devotion. She changes her name to Christina (even though she already has a "pious" name), presumably an expression of her new devotion to Christ. With the sign of the cross incised into the church door with her fingernail, she betroths herself to Christ.[48]

Christina would grow up to become a beautiful woman, and we learn that her parents want her to marry. Considering the respect accorded by society to the parents of a daughter whom portents have shown to be the chosen bride of God, it is hardly comprehensible that they made such strenuous efforts to have her married.[49] In time, however, she aroused the sensual desire of a clerk (who subsequently became bishop of Durham). He attempted to seduce her in his own bedchamber, but had to brook the humiliation of her flight. Thereupon he urged Christina's parents to force her to get married. They determined to break their daughter's resistance by any means, including violence, and the formal betrothal took place. Christina, however, sought to escape the approaches of the spouse and finally won his agreement to a chaste marriage. Eventually, she succeeded in fleeing in male clothing to the hermitage at Flamstead, where she spent two years. When a change of location was deemed necessary, she moved to Markyate to be with the hermit monk Roger, who had previously refused to accept her. They lived together in holy love, it is said; yet after some time the aged Roger made her spend her days locked in a cell beside his hermitage; lovingly he called her "myn sunendaege dohter" (my Sunday daughter) and functioned as her spiritual guide. For four years she endured this life of extreme hardship, until he died. After her marriage had been annulled, she lived for some time with a clerk, whereby both had to contend with great bodily temptation. Christina admitted having felt the heat of desire so acutely that she believed the clothes on her body had caught fire. She learned a lesson from this and resolved from then on—for ever, as her biographer assures us—to renounce erotic desire. Finally she took over Roger's abandoned hermitage in Markyate. After some time a small group of women hermits gathered around her, including her own sister.

Christina's emotional life was to be aroused once more, however, in an unforeseen manner. Some years after his appointment as abbot of St. Albans, Geoffrey de Gorran got to know Christina. Soon a spiritual friendship developed between them. Yet because of his regular visits, evil gossip was not long in coming. Without doubt these two had to grapple with the problem that their mutual affection could not be entirely confined to a platonic relationship. In 1145, one year before Geoffrey's death, the settlement of women hermits, whose patron he had become, was officially transformed into the priory of Markyate, dedicated to the Trinity. Around 1131 Christina finally chose to become a nun and made her profession in St. Albans (see figure 1); thereafter she lived for another twenty-five years.

In the most striking manner, Christina's extreme insistence on virginity is repeatedly subjected to dangerous tests by her friendships with men. Others have wondered, with good reason, why her biographer emphasizes so strongly her sensual passion for the clerk, whose identity may not be revealed. Her feelings for Abbot Geoffrey, too, clearly exceed mere friendship. She admits to thinking of him day and night, and calls him her lover. And he addresses her as his beloved girl; it is hard to find a parallel in the *Lives* of the mystics, men or women. During the Christmas liturgy, while Christina seems to abandon herself to the birth of Christ, to whom she is actually promised as *sponsa* (bethrothed), she nonetheless cannot suppress her sensual desire for her beloved friend Geoffrey.

All this deserves mention because it rounds out our picture of women in the twelfth century, who made up a large proportion of the "mystical" public. The woman is no longer seen as seducing the man; rather, she is accorded her own capacity for passionate love.[50] Of course, Christina triumphs in this battle. Yet the emotional intensity of her spirituality, clearly depicted in her spiritual love for Roger, is reminiscent of the mysticism of Aelred, and of the Cistercians as a whole.[51] In fact, one could even say that Christina and Geoffrey had the kind of emotional and spiritual attachment that Aelred describes in his famous tract, *Spiritual Friendship,* to be discussed later—ultimately they are *friends in Christ*.[52] Moreover, Christina's orientation in her devotional practice comes from the Cistercian understanding of meditation. Her spiritual life takes shape in visions, some of which have mystical implications.[53] She is allowed to touch the baby Jesus to overcome her sensuous yearnings, a widespread and all too familiar experience in late-medieval women's biographies; yet we are also reminded of Godric. While she is rapt in trance during a celebration of the Christmas liturgy, Jesus appears to her, and then vanishes, in the manner described by the Emmaus disciples. Another time he pays

FIGURE 1.   Possibly Christina of Markyate, followed by the monks of St. Albans, pleading for mercy before Christ. St. Albans Psalter. Dombibliothek Hildesheim, HS St. God. 1 (property of the Basilica of St. Godehard, Hildesheim). Copyright © Dombibliothek Hildesheim.

a surprise visit as a pilgrim to Christina and her sister, and the two behave like Mary and Martha—a further Gospel reminiscence, brought into the present, as it were, or enacted anew, whereas more frequently the woman mystic is *transposed* directly into the original event. Of particular note is Christina's vision of the Trinity, which grants her a brief anticipatory fulfillment of the mystics' yearning to see God.[54] Overall it is astonishing to observe the degree to which Christina as a "breakaway" figure anticipated by several decades the tendencies of the women mystics, or beguines, of Flanders, of whom much more will be said.[55]

In this brief survey I have attempted to show that the anchoritic form of life was a well-developed phenomenon in the British Isles, even before the period under study in this book. It should be added, of course, that the phenomenon was also widespread on the Continent. Yet I would argue that the anchoritic idea exerted an exceptionally intense influence in England, which produced, for instance, such works as *The Cloud of Unknowing* and the writings of Walter Hilton, which were specifically addressed to anchorites (not to mention some of Richard Rolle's works). In the High Middle Ages, mystical spirituality in England had its focal point in Northumbria, in the county of Yorkshire, before it shifted southward in the late Middle Ages. This geographical distinction is important, I believe, in that it is in the north where the Cistercians, with their sympathy for the eremitical idea, developed their activities most strongly. This is where the great Cistercian abbot Aelred of Rievaulx lived and worked, and it is no accident that Godric of Finchale was his friend, because in many ways both figures embody the new spirit of the twelfth century.

❦ CHAPTER 2

Early Cistercian Theology in England

The presence of the Cistercians in medieval England remains powerfully visible today in the ruins of the great Cistercian abbeys of Yorkshire, especially Fountains (1131), Rievaulx (1131), and Byland (1135). Visitors to those abbeys, however, may not fully appreciate the enormous impact that the Cistercians had on English spirituality in the Middle Ages. Nor, for that matter, are they likely to realize the critical role that England played in the formative years of this order of reformed Benedictine monks, which traces its origins back to the village of Cîteaux, near Dijon in eastern France.[1] Although a complete history of the Cistercians in England is beyond the scope of the present book, this chapter offers a brief overview of the subject, focusing on key figures and ideas that will be important for the subsequent history of English mysticism. The story begins with Stephen Harding, a great Englishman of distinguished ancestry and a decisive figure in the founding of the order.

Stephen was born around 1060 in Merriott, Somerset, and was sent as a child to the Benedictines of Sherborne, not far away. After leaving the monastery for reasons unknown, he traveled to Scotland and Ireland and then France, where he studied at the cathedral schools of Reims, Laon, and Paris. Later he made a pilgrimage to Rome with a friend, and on the return journey he visited the hermit communities of Camaldoli and Vallombrosa. In 1085 he joined the Benedictine monastery in Molesme, where he assumed the name Stephen. Molesme, which had been founded in 1075 in the wave of enthusiasm for monastic renewal, was led by its founder, the resolute abbot Robert. Unfortunately, the spirit of enthusiasm would soon fade in Molesme (as it would elsewhere). Becoming fed up with the growing laxity of the community, Robert and Stephen left the monastery, accompanied by a number of other like-minded monks. The result was the founding of Cîteaux Abbey in 1098, which would become the mother house of the Cistercian order. Robert was Cîteaux's first abbot, but he would not retain that position very long. The following year he returned to Molesme, when the monks there repented of their sins and pleaded with the pope to recall him as abbot. The Cîteaux foundation was then taken forward by the new abbot Alberich and then by Stephen Harding, who became the third abbot after Alberich's death in 1108.

Stephen's influence would prove essential in shaping the Cistercian order. He is generally credited with writing the first version of the *Carta caritatis* (Charter of Charity), the constitutional document that set forth the administrative principles of the order, including the system of general chapters and regular visitations. Stephen's special share in this was the idea that the entire organization should be based on, and bound together by, love (*caritas*).[2] He also helped to instill one of the most important features of Cistercian spirituality—its deep reverence for the Bible. Remarkably, he was even responsible for a new and, by the standards of the day, more reliable text of the Hebrew Old Testament. Sometimes called the Stephen Harding Bible, it was produced in the Cîteaux scriptorium after Stephen had discovered transmissional variants in the Vulgate manuscripts. His *monitum* tells us that in striving for authority he even turned directly to certain Jews who were experts in their language—that is to say, to rabbis—for elucidation of divergent Old Testament readings caused by the use of part-Hebrew, part-Aramaic exemplars. Such an effort to produce an authoritative text is quite extraordinary for its time (actually, quite modern) and shows the degree to which Stephen Harding was indeed an original thinker.[3] Yet his profound respect for the Bible is characteristic of the whole order and, as we shall see, of English mysticism in general.

The twenty years of Cistercian history following Stephen's death in 1134 bear the indelible stamp of Bernard of Clairvaux, probably the outstanding personality of his age. Born of a noble Burgundian family, Bernard might just as easily have become a knight or a prelate had he not chosen the monastic life. Instead he sought admission into the Cistercian order and entered Cîteaux in 1113, bringing with him some thirty of his friends and relatives from Burgundy. Stephen was abbot of Cîteaux at the time, and it was Stephen who in the summer of 1115 sent Bernard, age twenty-five, to found a new abbey eighty miles north in a place that would become known as Clairvaux, the "Valley of Light." Bernard was a remarkably eloquent and persuasive advocate of the Cistercian way of life, especially in his sermons. A good example of this comes from one of Bernard's many trips, during which he stopped in Paris to preach a sermon to a crowd of learned clerics. Hoping to persuade his listeners, men of birth and intelligence, to leave behind their vain studies for the worship of true wisdom, he pleaded with them to reject the thinking of men such as Peter Abelard, who rely utterly on the powers of reason and logic, and instead "convert to their hearts."[4] He invited them to come to Clairvaux, "the place of the wonderful tabernacle, where men eat the bread of angels" and "discover the paradise of pleasure planted by the Lord." And lest they somehow missed his point, he went on to explain, "You must not suppose this paradise of inner pleasure is some material place: you enter this garden not on foot but by deeply-felt affections.... There eagerly we have a foretaste of the incomparable delights of charity."[5] Here Bernard's words echo Stephen Harding's message of a community bound together by *caritas*.

Through Bernard the biblical orientation of the Cistercians would also gain ever greater currency throughout Europe. This can be seen above all in the allegorical exegesis of the Song of Songs undertaken by Bernard and other early Cistercians. Bernard's decision to compose his exegesis of this Old Testament love poem not as a commentary but in the form of sermons was an innovation with far-reaching consequences. According to Kurt Ruh, Bernard's sermons represent a high point in Western mysticism, an achievement made possible by a master preacher using the sermon format to its fullest effect. Indeed, Bernard is able to establish a powerful sense of intimacy with his reader by directly addressing the soul (*anima*) of the monk, who in turn is invited to identify with the Beloved (*sponsa*).[6]

In these magnificent sermons the theme of human likeness to God is absolutely essential.[7] Indeed, the ultimate goal for Bernard is to restore this likeness; and the force driving us toward restoration is love—love of God, to which end we love ourselves and our neighbor, and love of self, which presupposes self-knowledge. Then he strongly emphasizes the revelation of divine love through Christ's Passion. His famous confession in Sermon 43, "My highest and innermost philosophy is to know Jesus, and him crucified," alludes to Paul's statement in 1 Cor 2:2 that "I decided to know nothing among you except Jesus Christ and him crucified," a good indicator of why Bernard was regarded in his own day as a second Paul.[8]

Bernard, however, dwells less on the bodily torments of the Passion and more on the *spiritual* love of God and the joy resulting from this *inner* experience. Following Origen (and ultimately the Gospel of John), he calls Christ the Word (*logos*), which kindles his love; and the language of his response, replete with erotic metaphor, has a captivating and unique sensual fluidity and an astonishingly "feminine" feeling. In Sermon 15, for instance, we find Bernard's joyous exultation that his experience of Christ is like "honey in the mouth, song in the ear, and jubilation in the heart" (*mel in ore, in aure melos, in corde iubilus*), a line that has become proverbial, eventually earning him the distinction *doctor mellifluus* (honey-sweet doctor). He recognizes the need for moderation and order in love (*caritas ordinata*), and yet the love of God knows no measure; it is of the very greatest intensity and vehemence (*amor praeceps, vehemens, intemperans*). Nor is this love a one-sided matter, for not only does the soul direct a cry of longing to God; God himself longs for the soul. Moreover, it is no surprise that Bernard also infuses his sermons with imagery of Mary, the mother of God and chief patron of the order, for ultimately Mary is the common thread that ties together all of Bernard's thinking. Indeed, the theme would reverberate throughout Cistercian spirituality, reaching a bold climax in the later Middle Ages in the legends of Bernard receiving milk from Mary's breast (figure 2).[9]

Sadly, Bernard would never completely finish his exegesis of the Song of Songs. At his death in 1153 he left behind a fragmentary series of eighty-six sermons, but other prominent Cistercians would be moved to carry on Bernard's project. Gilbert of Hoyland (d. 1172), abbot of Swineshead, added a further forty-eight sermons composed in Bernard's spirit. After Gilbert's death, another 120 sermons were added by John of Forde (d. 1214), abbot of Forde in southwest England. The whole series is thus rounded into an impressive unity.[10]

It is difficult to overestimate Bernard's influence on those around him and on those who would succeed him. This is not to say that he was a man without his flaws, for in many ways Bernard was an ambivalent figure, even with some irreconcilable contradictions.[11] He took great care of the monks in his charge, yet he could be unapproachable and unsympathetic in the extreme, most notably in his conflict with Abelard, in whose philosophy he saw no benefit for individual spiritual life, and in his own enthusiastic preaching on behalf of the Second Crusade.

Still, any review of early Cistercian history will show that the most significant figures were connected to—and deeply influenced by—Bernard. Take, for instance, William of St. Thierry (d. 1148), perhaps the greatest theologian of his time. A close friend of Bernard, William wrote a number of important works. No one has written more fervently on the desire of the mystic soul than did William, and he is best remembered for the impressive tract, *On*

FIGURE 2. According to legend, Bernard of Clairvaux had an ecstatic vision while praying before a statue of the Virgin Mary in her *lactatio*. As he prayed "Monstra te esse Matrem" ("Show yourself the mother"), he was blessed with shooting milk from the Virgin's breast. The legend has a long iconographical tradition. This fifteenth-century engraving (32 × 24.1 cm), by an unknown Netherlandish master, also illustrates the idea that Bernard's preaching and eloquence were "sweet as milk."

the Nature and Dignity of Love, and probably his most cherished work, *The Golden Epistle,* a letter addressed to the Carthusian brothers of Mont-Dieu.

Another example is Guerric of Igny (d. 1157). Guerric was born probably at Tournai and studied there at the noted cathedral school. He then visited Clairvaux, where Bernard persuaded him to become a monk. He would eventually be elected abbot of Igny, a daughter house of Clairvaux, where his lasting legacy would be his liturgical sermons. One particularly noteworthy sermon was delivered on the feast of the Annunciation in which the angel Gabriel announces to the Blessed Virgin that she will conceive and become the mother of Jesus. In it Guerric elaborated the remarkable tradition of God's birth in the soul, drawing an analogy between spiritual motherhood and the phases of bodily pregnancy.

> O faithful soul, open wide your breast, enlarge your desire so that you do not become too narrow within; conceive him whom no creature is able to contain! Open the ear of your hearing to the Word of God. This is the way of the Spirit conceiving in the womb of the heart; for "this reason the bones of Christ" (that is, the virtues) "are knit together in the womb of the pregnant woman."[12]

A common theme running throughout Guerric's sermons is that of the divine light. For example, in his first sermon for the feast of the Purification of Mary he talks about the "lovely custom" in the church of bearing lights on this feast day (commonly called Candlemas) and graphically interprets it in terms of "the Word clothed in flesh as the candle-flame is cupped in wax."[13] Generally speaking, the theology of light is part of the very essence of Cistercian spirituality, as is the admiration of beauty.

I would be remiss if I did not mention, if only in passing, the important affinity between the Cistercians and the so-called Victorines, an influential group of mystical writers associated with the Augustinian abbey of St. Victor near Paris. Suffice it to say that the Victorines flourished in the twelfth century, tracing their ideas back to William of Champeaux (d. 1121), head of the cathedral school at Paris and bitter foe of Peter Abelard, his pupil.[14] William left his position at the school in Paris in 1108 and moved to the abbey of St. Victor, where he continued to lecture. One of William's pupils there was Hugh of St. Victor (d. 1141). Generally regarded as the founder of the Victorines, Hugh is best remembered today for his *Didascalion,* which offers a unique vision for the integration of all human knowledge; but his treatise *De laude caritatis* (In praise of love) is an important work that belongs very much in the Cistercian tradition of meditations on love. Richard of St. Victor (d. 1173), who succeeded Hugh as master of the school, would also write works such as *The Twelve Patriarchs* and *De quattuor gradibus violentae caritatis* (The four degrees of fervent love), which considerably influenced the medieval mystics.

Aelred of Rievaulx

Above all, it was Aelred who enabled the Cistercian order to flower in England and who furthered its influence. Under him, the Cistercian abbey of Rievaulx, a daughter foundation of Clairvaux not far from York, became a stronghold of spiritual life and the center of Cistercian piety in the north of England (see figure 3).[15]

Aelred (1110–67) came from a priestly family in Northumbria, at a time when celibacy had not yet been imposed on the priesthood. In his youth he spent ten years at the court of the Scottish king David and served as master of the household. During a grave crisis, to which impressive sermons and Augustine's *Confessions* must have contributed, he was seized by a violent antipathy toward his worldly way of life, especially the sins of his youth, and by yearning for God. On a royal mission to Archbishop Thurstan of York he learned that the new Cistercian order had already established a daughter foundation nearby called Rievaulx (Lat. *Rievallis* = Rye valley). He was sufficiently interested to visit this monastery, still in its early days, and was so attracted by the spirit that prevailed there, and especially by the new teaching,

FIGURE 3. The ruins of Rievaulx Abbey in Yorkshire, where Aelred was abbot from 1147 until his death in 1167. His biographer Walter Daniel claimed that the number of inhabitants at Rievaulx rose to about 650 during his abbacy. Photo by John Armaugh.

that he broke off his return journey to the king of Scotland and, after hesitating briefly, decided to join the order in Rievaulx.

He spent the first eight years as a simple choir monk, during which time monks from Clairvaux, above all Abbot William, instructed him in the Cistercian spirit. When he was sent to Rome in 1141 by the abbot, in connection with a nomination to the episcopate in York, he traveled via Clairvaux, where he met the great Bernard. Unfortunately we know nothing of their encounter, but after his return to Rievaulx in 1142 he was appointed master of novices. Less than a year later he was elected abbot of the new Cistercian foundation of Revesby in Lincolnshire. In 1147 he became abbot of the English mother house, Rievaulx, and retained this position for almost twenty years. According to his biographer, Walter Daniel, the abbey flourished under Aelred's leadership.

The key to Aelred's success, according to Walter Daniel, was that he made his monastery into a place of peace for all who entered it. "Who ever came to Rievaulx crippled in spirit and did not find in Aelred a loving father, and all they needed of comfort in the brethren?" It was especially important to him that he conduct his own life in such a way that he served as a model for others; he endeavored to suffer human weakness with compassionate kindness and to be considerate of others' needs while, at the same time, never losing sight of his own inadequacies, weaknesses, and passions. Perhaps his most striking characteristic was a readiness to adjust to each individual according to temperament, character, feelings, and intellectual level. He was capable of a high degree of intuition and empathy, as is most evident in his treatise *Spiritual Friendship,* where he writes, "Thus praying to Christ for a friend and desiring to be heard by Christ for a friend, we focus on Christ with love and longing. Then sometimes suddenly, imperceptibly, affection melts into affection, and somehow touching the sweetness of Christ nearby, one begins *to taste* how dear he is and experience *how sweet* he is."[16] Schooled in the ancient view of the ennobling power of love, especially as found in Cicero, he distinguishes between the charity that links him to his fellow human beings and the sublime spiritual love of individual friends.[17] He is convinced that the human being is good in his deepest self.[18]

In the course of time the cold, damp climate took a toll on Aelred, such that during his last ten years he was nearly incapacitated by arthritis. Walter Daniels describes one scene in which monks carried Aelred away from his bed on a linen sheet so that he might relieve himself. Finally, the general chapter of abbots at Cîteaux made provision for him to eat and sleep in the infirmary and otherwise reduce the burdens of his office, but, finding such concessions "hard to bear," Aelred had a hut built for himself close to the infirmary. There he continued to radiate a benign influence up to the end of his life. Brethren would gather by him daily, "twenty or thirty at a time, and sit discussing the spiritual delights of the Scriptures and the observance of the monastic life.... They walked and lay about his bed, talking with him as a child will prattle to its mother." Throughout his final days he displayed his emotional love for his brothers, which was most impressively returned. He died at night with "the great gathering of his sons" by his side.

The Mirror of Charity

Aelred's earliest and most famous work, *The Mirror of Charity (Liber de speculo caritatis)*, written between 1142 and 1143 when Aelred was still a young man in his early thirties, penetrates to the very core of Cistercian spirituality, even if it does not yet reflect his own *experience*.[19] Written at the behest of Bernard of Clairvaux, it is part of a rich tradition in the Middle Ages of *speculum* texts. The word *speculum* means mirror or reflection, and the point of a *speculum* text is to encourage the reader to delve deeply into a particular subject in order to see greater truths. Such texts are characterized less by logical reasoning than by their didactic and edifying quality.[20] In *The Mirror of Charity* Aelred conveys the full range of his intellectual interests, his emotional disposition, and literary influences. Yet it is even more important to recognize its great significance as an exemplar of twelfth-century spirituality as a whole, with its emphasis on the individual's affective relationship with God—a God who reveals himself as a human being, loving and suffering for man, rather than as the omnipotent ruler of the world, who demands obedience and fulfillment of his commandments. The believer, in turn, revels in his place as created being and gladly offers beloved devotion to God. Such a view of God's relationship with man requires a theory of love, one that guides the individual believer while fulfilling the broader vision of the Cistercian order as set forth in Stephen's *Carta caritatis*.

Accordingly, Aelred sees the uniqueness of God's love manifested in the six days of his creation, perfect in every respect, but especially so in the seventh day, the day of God's rest, which represents the key to the divine mystery:

> But what about the seventh day, the Sabbath that saw the completion of God's handiwork? To us the Sabbath brings perfect rest when the work of all the virtues is completed. And this completion of their work is found in charity, which affords refreshment for our souls and the perfect attuning of our lives to God. With charity as their root all the virtues grow to perfection, until on the seventh day charity refreshes us with God's grace. (I: 21)

Here Aelred is picking up the thread of early Christian interpretation of the Sabbath and makes it a central concept, used especially to express the soul's capacity to reach "the fullness of peace" through devotion to Christ and ultimately to divinity itself, when it liberates itself from everything and, above all, forgets itself; for such a soul experiences the dawning of the Sabbath of Sabbaths.[21] Man, however, distanced himself from his original unity of love with God, chose another path, and became a wanderer in a *regio dissimilitudinis* ("a place of unlikeness"), a concept borrowed from book 7 of Augustine's *Confessions*.[22] His return is possible only through love of God made man, Christ. On earth, of course, the return will remain incomplete, since the goal is reached only in beholding God.

Aelred's attempt to develop a "theory of love" and plumb its depths by inquiring into its prerequisites and early forms is a significant achievement when considered in the broad sweep of the history of mentalities. It is not possible here to do more than touch briefly and selectively on his success in generating an individual affective doctrine that encompasses all stirrings of the will, but it is important to follow his train of thought in order to avoid simplistic reiteration of his mysticism as "affective."[23] For him *affectus* is a "spontaneous inclination of the soul" that can be "spiritual, rational, or irrational." As such, it might be grounded in nature, for instance in relationships with friends or family, or it might be aroused "carnally" by outer appearance or bearing (III: 11). Aelred, of course, accords the highest value to the love that comes from God. "The soul," he writes, "is moved by a spiritual attraction when in some mysterious and unexpected way the Holy Spirit comes to it, giving a taste of that sweetness which comes to us in our love for God and for our fellow men" (III: 11).

The soul, however, can be misguided or succumb to temptation. Thus, even good attraction can be turned by a man to his own ruin. On the other hand, bad attraction can ultimately be turned into a trial that makes good men stronger so that they can resist evil in the future (III: 16). Natural affect, therefore, must be accompanied by reason; for without it, affect is merely an animal sensation. On the importance of reason, Aelred writes,

> Even though we may not feel a great deal of love towards our fellow men, or even towards God, reason insists that we make the necessary effort to love. Reason convinces us that we must so act not only because it is to our advantage or use, but because God and our neighbor are worthy of our love. . . . If we accept these truths, even in our minds only, and without the full consent of the heart, desire for God [*affectus*] will grow even in our hesitant love." (III: 17)

Aelred's complex discussion of *affectus* is of the greatest importance, for it points far into the future; indeed, it is the most significant Cistercian attempt to define more precisely the quality of love between God and man. The intensity of this love surpasses every other affect because in Jesus Aelred finds "my one delight and joy" (I: 1). This emphasis on *joy* as a consequence of mystic union will become a special characteristic of later English mysticism.

Furthermore, for Aelred love also inclines toward beauty; beauty, too, is something good, and will always be so. This has rightly been seen as one of the foundations of Aelred's humanism.[24] For the Cistercians in particular, beauty is one of God's attributes, and this generates joyful feeling. Aelred also refers to the beauty of art, and to emotional responses to tragedy and romance. As a lover of literature he perceptively observes that art, through fiction, has great power to touch, even if it merely offers a world of appearances.[25]

Spiritual Friendship

Spiritual Friendship (*De spiritali amicitia*) was almost certainly Aelred's most popular and influential spiritual treatise throughout the Middle Ages.[26] Although he wrote it late in life (between 1164 and 1167), his thinking about friendship went back much further, as he explains in the prologue:

> While I was still a boy at school, the charm of my companions gave me the greatest pleasure. Among the usual faults that often endanger youth, my mind surrendered wholly to affection and became devoted to love. Nothing seemed sweeter to me, nothing more pleasant, nothing more valuable than to be loved and to love. Wavering among various loves and friendships, my spirit began to be tossed this way and that and, ignorant of the law of true friendship, was often beguiled by its mirage. At last a volume of Cicero's *On Friendship* fell into my hands. Immediately it seemed to me both invaluable for the soundness of its views and attractive for the charm of its eloquence. Though I considered myself unworthy of such friendship, I was grateful to find a model to which I could recall my quest for many loves and affections. (Prol: 1–3)

That Aelred admired the stylistic elegance of Cicero's *On Friendship* (*Laelius de amicitia*) is clear: he even incorporated one-third of this famous treatise into his own text. But Aelred proved himself to be a master of prose in his own right, striving for just the right word and displaying a knack for combining inner content with outer form. It is his most personal book, composed in dialogue form as a conversation between an abbot and three monks.

Not surprisingly, Aelred sees love as the fundamental prerequisite for friendship. Yet for him there is also love without friendship, namely instinctual love, love from a sense of duty, from reason, or emotion (III: 3). Friendship actually arises through an *affectus rationalis* (reminiscent of Bernard's *amor rationalis*). Aelred agrees with Cicero that the friend is the other self whom one must love as one loves oneself.[27] But Aelred wants to elevate antiquity's humanist understanding of friendship to a Christian plane: the link between love of self and love of one's neighbor is possible only with the help of divine grace. So powerful is his experience of inner friendship that he adds an erotic coloring to overflowing union. In book III he recounts a moment at the monastery when he saw the brothers "sitting in a most loving circle," causing him to marvel as though he were in paradise. "Finding not one soul whom I did not love and, I was sure, not one soul by whom I was not loved, I was filled with a joy that surpassed all the delights of the world. Indeed, as I felt my spirit flowing into them all and the affection of all coursing through me, I could say with the prophet, 'See how good and how pleasant it is for brethren to live in unity'" (III: 82). This intense experience is at once transformed and sublimated. According to Aelred it deserves to be called "holy" because it widens to encompass God: ultimately Christ is the goal of the love with which—with resonances of mystical language—the friend is loved. When the friendship between two people is grounded in Christ and directed entirely toward God, and the two who have united as friends are sunk in contemplation of God, they receive its true reward (II: 60).

Spiritual Friendship reaches a climax with Aelred's claim that by rising above the holy love of friendship, with which we embrace our friend, to the love with which we embrace Christ, we are able to "take the spiritual fruit of friendship fully and joyfully into the mouth while looking forward to all abundance in the life to come" (III: 134). As Aelred boldly puts it, "God is friendship" (I: 69), and in human friendship there is a reflection of divine friendship. The work ends brilliantly, as Aelred employs erotic language to show that true spiritual friendship reaches its conclusion in "friendship with Christ, and, through him, friendship with God."[28]

Particularly striking is the freedom with which Aelred relates corporeality and spirituality, as when he speaks of the kiss.[29] At one point he reproaches himself for understanding love in too carnal a manner, but then he diversifies the intimacy of the kiss, even distinguishing three distinct kinds of kiss: physical, spiritual, and intellectual (*osculum corporale, spirituale, intellectuale*); whereby the aim—entirely in the Cistercian tradition—is to proceed from the physical to the spiritual, and finally to the divine. The *osculum spirituale* finds fulfillment in the *coniunctione animarum,* whereas the *osculum intellectuale* signifies the highest experience of union, possible only through the spirit of God and infusion of grace, *infusione gratiarum* (II: 24). In Aelred, and in Cistercian mysticism as a whole, mystical experience must be understood as spiritualized bodily feeling, and tasting of the inner *spiritual* senses, as will be investigated in more detail below. With Bernard of Clairvaux and others, Aelred made a substantial contribution to the growth of sensual intensity in twelfth-century mystical diction, an intensity that would prove long lasting.[30]

Rule of Life for a Recluse

It is beyond the scope of this book to discuss all of Aelred's writings, but there is one work in particular, his *Rule of Life for a Recluse* (*De institutione inclusarum*), that merits special attention for its striking originality and lasting influence on English mysticism. At first glance, *Rule of Life for a Recluse* might appear to be an unexceptional document, but in fact it was far ahead of its time in envisioning a form of monastic training through meditation that is most often associated with the affective spirituality of the later Middle Ages. Aelred wrote it in the early 1160s at the request of his older sister, who had decided to live the life of a recluse. We do not know much about the sister (her name is never mentioned in the text, and we do not know whether she decided on life as a recluse at an early age, or whether she was first a nun), but from what Aelred says in the *Rule* itself, she was most likely well educated, with a good command of Latin, and was able to read the Bible and study it herself.[31] Aelred speaks to her directly in his opening address:

> For many years now, my sister, you have been asking for a rule to guide you in the life you have embraced for the sake of Christ, to provide spiritual directives and formulate the basic practices of religious life. How I wish you had sought and obtained this from someone wiser than myself, someone whose teaching was based not on mere conjecture but on personal experience. Yet by birth and in spirit I am your brother and unable to refuse any request you make. I shall do as you ask then, and endeavour to draw up a definite rule for you, selecting from among the various regulations of the Fathers those that appear most useful in forming the exterior man. I shall add some details suited to your particular circumstances of time and place, and, wherever it seems helpful, blend the spiritual with the corporal.[32]

The *Rule* falls into three parts, the first of which addresses the physical and material circumstances of the recluse's life: "rules for bodily observances by which a recluse may govern the behavior of the outward man" (33). In the second part Aelred begins to turn to the "inner man": first, he teaches his sister how to beware of the devil's temptations and to preserve her chastity "in the practice of virtue" (21); then he instructs her how to lead a life of charity, as far as love of one's neighbor is concerned, and here he draws upon the famous Mary-Martha episode from the Gospel of Luke. In the third part Aelred focuses particularly on nourishing the love of God through medita- tion. In considerable detail, he sets forth a "threefold meditation" for the recluse to observe: "So if the sweet love of Jesus is to grow in your affections, you need a threefold meditation, on the past, the present, and the future that is to say, you must call to mind what happened long ago, experience the pres- ent and look forward to what lies in the future" (29). He urges his sister to remember Jesus's life, especially his act of love in suffering and dying. This is the meditation on what is past. Next, there is meditation on the present, which involves examination of one's conscience. Finally, meditation on the future encourages thoughts of one's own (welcome) death and the Last Judg- ment. All three kinds of meditation are meant to intensify human *affectus,* and therefore also the capacity for love.

As Aelred's teaching on meditation has seldom been fully appreciated, it is worth taking a closer look at it, specifically his meditation on what is past—Christ's Passion and resurrection—which is where he spends most of his time.[33] Kurt Ruh has pointed out that the *memoria* of Christ's life, suffer- ing, and death as a special type of meditation developed in the late eleventh century. Bernard was a forerunner, but, as Ruh observes, Aelred was the first to create the intense *memoria* of Christ's life and Passion, which would cul- minate in the Franciscan *Meditationes vitae Christi,* one of the most influential devotional texts of the later Middle Ages.[34] However, these observations do not encompass fully the decisive aspect of Aelred's new and groundbreaking achievement.

At the heart of Aelred's teaching on meditation is the principle of remem- bering (*dulcis memoria*). This remembering is a continuation of reading (*lec- tio*), which is in effect the subject matter of the meditation. Aelred not only recounts for his sister the essential stations of Christ's suffering, but also presents them in a way that implants in her the seed of intense emotional love. To this end he makes the decision to *stage* the stations of Christ's life, directing his sister to become a participant in the events she is meditating upon. So, for instance, he tells her,

> First enter the room of blessed Mary and with her read the books which prophesy the virginal birth and the coming of Christ.... Next with all your devotion accompany the Mother as she makes her way

to Bethlehem. Take shelter in the inn with her, be present and help her as she gives birth, and when the infant is laid in the manger break out into words of exultant joy together with Isaiah and cry: "A child has been born to us, a son is given to us." Embrace that sweet crib, let love overcome your reluctance, affection drive out fear. Put your lips to those most sacred feet, kiss them again and again. (29)

Aelred goes on to follow Christ in his footsteps from his childhood to his death on the cross and resurrection. His "performance" of the Passion presents it vividly to the imagination, and involves the reader much more than does simple *memoria;* rather it results, as in the case of the meditation on the twelve-year-old Jesus, in a *spectaculum* of the kind produced in the late Middle Ages by the great mystery plays. The sister-reader is *transposed* into the center of the action, with Aelred himself serving not simply as a narrator but as the director of the play.[35]

The high point of the meditation comes with the "staging" of the crucifixion followed by the encounter between Mary Magdalen and the risen Christ. Aelred first urges his sister to observe the "narrated" events, revealing that he himself is deeply moved. He wishes her to see with her inner, spiritual eye what those who were there at Golgotha were able to witness in person. To this end Aelred employs brilliantly persuasive rhetoric, and the suggestive power of his extraordinary psychological skill seems positively modern: "Heaven is aghast, earth marvels. And what of you? It is not surprising if when the sun mourns you mourn too, if when the earth trembles you tremble with it, if when rocks are split your heart is torn in pieces, if when the women who are by the Cross weep you add your tears to theirs" (31).[36]

This staging of Christ's Passion is a powerful means of generating the kind of deep emotional empathy (*affectus*) in the reader that Aelred describes in *The Mirror of Charity.* He addresses Mary Magdalen, too, and asks about her feelings when she encountered the risen Jesus, and her bitter tears when he commanded her not to touch him (*"Noli me tangere"*). Temporarily transformed into Mary Magdalen, he turns directly to Jesus, desiring to hear from him the reason for this rejection. While he receives no answer, Mary Magdalen continues with pressing questions as to why she may not touch Jesus, but gradually the thought of her as speaker dissipates, and her place is taken by Aelred's sister. The whole episode is skillfully structured, effectively reenacting the biblical narration in the here and now.

Aelred's staging of Christ's life so that his readers could become virtual participants in the events as they are being narrated, is a literary device most often associated with the Franciscan *Meditationes vitae Christi.*[37] Indeed, it is the Franciscans of the fourteenth century who immediately spring to mind today when we think of graphic depictions of Christ's Passion and resurrection. Aelred, however, wrote *Rule of Life for a Recluse* in the twelfth century, which suggests the need to rethink our understanding of the sources of the affective spirituality depicted in *Meditationes vitae Christi*. Given the widespread influence of *Rule of Life for a Recluse,* it is hard not to see a connection between the two documents, indicating at the very least that the Cistercian roots of Franciscan affective spirituality are deeper than many have acknowledged.[38]

It must be noted, however, that while Aelred uses nuptial imagery and speaks of the crucified Christ inviting embraces and kisses, he stops short of the explicit sexual analogies—for example, *unio passionalis* with the suffering son of God—that would become commonplace in the later Middle Ages. Of the wounds of Christ Aelred says, alluding to the imagery of the Song of Songs, that his sister will be welcomed, "like the dove in the hollows of the rock" (31), but this does not yet compare with the rather later wish to penetrate Christ through these wounds. Even the occasional metaphor drawn from the Song of Songs is immediately allegorized.[39] The text concludes, in keeping with mystical tradition, with a hymnic prospect of the saved soul reaching God, combined with expectation of the ultimate beholding of God, no longer "in a mirror, dimly" (*per speculum in enigmate*), but knowing him "as he is" (1 Cor 13:12; 1 Jn 3:2). The soul's yearning finally to embrace her spouse intensifies this desire (33).

The recluse's devotion culminates in the complete silence of prayer. Like John in the Gospel, she rests her head on Jesus's breast and is inebriated by the experience of his divinity (figure 4). If she cannot attain the higher levels of knowledge, and cannot approach Christ more closely, she is advised to be satisfied with the milk that flows from the breasts of his humanity. Here Aelred is making a deliberate play on gender boundaries, as Christ "naturally" encompasses maleness and femaleness in equal measure—on the one hand as son of God, and on the other as mother.[40] There is also a play on gender boundaries within the human plane: within the recluse's cell there is a crucifix on the wall flanked by images of Mary and St. John—the "virgin mother" and the "virgin disciple"—signifying "how pleasing to Christ is the virginity of both sexes" (26)

The recluse could thus assume her right to identify entirely with John, resting in contemplation on Christ's breast. Perhaps not surprisingly, the English mystics, both male and female, sensed an especial affinity with St. John, and it is even possible that the "prototype" of the sculptures of

FIGURE 4. Sculpture of Christ and John, Oberschwaben, around 1320. Note how the artist has shaped John as a markedly sexless figure. Skulpturensammlung und Museum für Byzantinische Kunst, Staatliche Museen zu Berlin / Inv. No. 7950. Copyright © bpk / Skulpturensammlung und Museum für Byzantinische Kunst, SMB.

Christ and John came from England.[41] The creation of these touching sculptures owes much to the influence of the Cistercians with their emphasis on love, and also to some extent to Anselm of Canterbury's *Orationes sive meditationes*. Optically these sculptures convey a deep spirituality, a contemplative union of God-Man with the favorite disciple; this has the effect of a stream of energy flowing through the bodies of Christ and John via their joined hands and arms. The clasped right hands are analogous to the linking of the two right hands (*dextrarum junctio*) in the official marriage ceremony of the Middle Ages.

The Hymn *Dulcis Iesu memoria* by an Anonymous Cistercian

Perhaps more than in any other twelfth-century text, Cistercian spirituality resonates in the impressive poetic diction of the famous hymn *Dulcis Iesu memoria,* a great lyric meditation on the soul's intense desire to be united with Jesus. The poem was long ascribed to Bernard, and mistakenly called his *Jubilus*.[42] Recently, Continental Cistercian scholarship has returned to the earlier thesis that the hymn was composed in England, possibly by Aelred of Rievaulx; yet this has not been proven, even if it now seems more likely.[43] Be that as it may, the author of this remarkable poetic composition was certainly an English Cistercian.[44] The entire hymn has between forty-two and fifty-three stanzas, depending on the manuscript. Parts of it were used in the Liturgy of the Hours (Divine Office) on the feast of the Holy Name of Jesus, and it was later set to music, most notably in the seventeenth and eighteenth centuries by baroque composers, and even Johann Sebastian Bach may have become familiar with it. It is worth reflecting on the *prooemium* (stanzas 1–2):

Iesu, dulcis memoria,	Jesus, the very thought of Thee
dans vera cordis gaudia:	With sweetness fills the breast!
sed super mel et omnia	Yet sweeter far Thy face to see
ejus dulcis praesentia.	And in Thy Presence rest.
Nil canitur suavius,	No voice can sing, no heart can frame,
nil auditur jucundius,	Nor can the memory find,
nil cogitatur dulcius,	A sweeter sound than Jesus' Name,
quam Iesus Dei Filius.	The Saviour of mankind.[45]

The whole poem is, in effect, an act of "remembering" (*memoria*) of Jesus as the "King most wonderful" and "Conqueror renowned." Having gained victory on the cross for man, he is the hero who has earned the praise of heaven and earth and "rules in peace." In accordance with a tradition reaching back to antiquity, personal recollection of the hero's *name* guarantees his fame, enabling him to outlast the ages. Now this tradition is transformed, for praise of the divine name yields in importance to personal experience of his "sweetness" (*dulcedo, dulcor*), an essential aspect of English mysticism in general. This hymn's remembrance is sweet because for the speaker it means, above all, *private* meditative visualization of Jesus; it seeks him especially in the bed (*lectulo, cubiculo*) of the heart. Christ appears "more lovable than any other"; for the soul, there is no real alternative. Words are inadequate; hence the multiple attempts to convey the yearning for the one and only love.

The use of repetition with mono-rhyming stanzas should not be seen as a sign of inferior writing, as has sometimes been suggested, but rather as a deliberate stylistic means of encouraging meditation. The poet sings of Christ's love not only as a delight but also as an experience that never quite fulfills his longing.[46] Moreover, in a manner characteristic of Cistercian sensual spirituality, love activates all the senses by recalling favorite biblical exhortations such as "O taste and see that the Lord is good" (Ps 34:8). Taken individually, the metaphors are not new, yet cumulatively and in clusters they acquire originality. The traditional, ultimately biblical image of divine fire is employed with the utmost intensity, and is reminiscent of Bernard; not only is love a consuming fire, but also—paradoxically—sweetly invigorating and refreshing. Like the first-person narrator of secular love poetry, the speaker confesses unreservedly that fire is consuming him totally (*totus ardeo*), reminiscent of a line in the famous *Carmina Burana* lyrics, *Iam amore virginali totus ardeo* (I am burning all over with first love).[47] The poem speaks, too, of the lovesickness caused to the mystic soul by love's withdrawal (*amore langueo*). Of such intensity is the soul's insatiable longing for love that it is raised to delirium or inebriation: *Quem tuus amor debriat.* The powerful desire for a privileged place in heaven anticipates one of Richard Rolle's motifs: may we be granted a seat with him in heaven (*ut nos donet celestibus / cum ipso frui sedibus*). Mystical love is extolled as unearthly and hence indescribable in song—*in aure dulce canticum* (= celestial *canor*). This poetry runs the whole gamut of sensual/spiritual experience that gives Cistercian diction its unmistakable fluidity, the quality referred to by Bernard as *eloquii suavitas* (delightful eloquence).[48]

In order to appreciate this fully, we have to bring into play an important influence on which Bernard and his friends could draw, namely Origen's allegorizing of the erotic love of the bride and groom (*sponsus* and *sponsa*) in the Song of Songs. This was possible for him because he had ventured to take a fresh view of the body. According to him, the body is by no means a prison for the soul, as the Platonic tradition had taught. Origen takes his lead from Paul, who had already accorded more value to the notion of the body as a temple: "Do you not know that your body is a temple of the Holy Spirit within you, which you have from God? (1 Cor 6:19). Man no longer simply has a body, he *is* a body—an extraordinarily new view of the human being in which corporeality and spirituality cannot be separated from one another.[49] Both are linked to form one whole, and thus Paul rejects a strictly dualist way of thinking. For Origen, the soul is the vital midpoint between body and spirit, which creates a choice for the human being as to whether he will be fleshly or spiritual.[50] In this Origen takes over from Clement of Alexandria the idea that the human being has not only corporeal but also spiritual senses. Denying the human being the gratification of the outer bodily senses, by means of asceticism, sets it free for the delight of spiritual sensuality. "The spirit must learn to 'burn' in its deepest self."[51]

There are good reasons, therefore, not to reduce Cistercian images of spiritual sensuality to mere metaphor. Bernard of Clairvaux, too, considers the body as good; spiritual experience cannot simply be separated off from the physical.[52] Indeed, one can speak of a common Christology that runs from Origen through Bernard to Aelred. And this fresh praise of spiritual sensuality accounts for the powerful influence of *Dulcis Iesu memoria* both in England and on the Continent.[53] With its intensity of feeling it may justly be acclaimed as *the* essential exemplar of Cistercian mystical language. Moreover, its linguistically skillful affective intensity explains why *Dulcis Iesu memoria* exerted a profound influence in England, as on the Continent. For instance, the poet John of Howden (d. 1275) was clearly inspired by the hymn, incorporating whole stanzas into his long Latin poem *Philomena*.[54]

The Wooing Group—Cistercian Spirituality Transmuted into the Vernacular

By the late twelfth and early thirteenth centuries we can see manifestations of this particularly Cistercian spirituality beginning to be "transposed" into the vernacular texts of the so-called Wooing Group and the related *Ancrene Wisse*.[55] The Wooing Group is a collection of Middle English texts written by an unknown author as meditations aimed at a group of women living as anchoresses and recluses; it takes its name from the longest of these texts Þe Wohunge of Ure Lauerd (*The Wooing of Our Lord*). In each of these texts *anima* functions as the first-person speaker, usually to be understood as an enclosed recluse, who begins with meditative recall of the incomparable, longed-for beloved. For instance, in the meditation titled "Lofsong of Ure Lauerd" (Lovesong of our Lord), *anima,* most probably a woman recluse, remembers how Jesus as her only friend and savior changed her life. Not only do these Wooing Group texts adopt the human adoration and devotion expressed in the sensual Cistercian language of *Dulcis Iesu memoria;* they also add the visualization of the divine lover's Passion in the meditative tradition of Anselm, and especially of Aelred. As in that tradition, the speaker longs for divine embraces, allegorizing a familiar verse from the Song of Songs, and yet we still do not see the eroticism of later devotional writings—for example, Christ on the cross with outstretched arms is portrayed as a mother wanting to embrace her child, avoiding any suggestion of *unio passionalis.*

The focus of meditative recall is at first less on the hideous torment of the Passion than on the sweetness of the countenance that arouses ardent yearning. In full awareness that it is not possible for mankind to behold the face of God on earth, the two texts, "Ureisun of Ure Louerde" (Orison of our Lord) and "Ureisun of God Almihti" (Orison of God Almighty), both to be understood as prayers, begin emphatically with a glowing visualization of the indescribable radiant beauty of his countenance. His uniqueness is evoked by one synonym after another, for instance by the grandiose hyperbole that his face puts even the radiance of the sun "in the shade." One could imagine any number of stimuli for such metaphors of light—including St. John the Evangelist—but we would certainly not go astray in pointing to the Cistercian predilection for light imagery, as seen in Bernard of Clairvaux and Guerric of Igny, among other prominent Cistercians. The imagery also brings to mind Abbot Suger of St.-Denis, whose concept of architecture as carried out in Gothic cathedrals is predicated on the architectonic directing of light. Indeed, one could even say that equating beauty with brightness and light was a central theme of the twelfth century as a whole.

The most important text in the Wooing Group is also the longest one, *Þe Wohunge of Ure Lauerd* (*The Wooing of Our Lord*). The work is structured as a monologue spoken by a young woman addressed to a partner who excels beyond all other suitors because of his unique qualities. The young woman, who is of marriageable age (although it is not certain if she is a virgin), wonders which suitor she should prefer, even if she has already decided on the life of a nun or, more probably, a recluse, and has detached herself entirely from the world.[56] In an amazingly realistic manner, she compares the virtues of all imaginable earthly lovers with Jesus, and finds essential deficiencies in them, on which she comments, one by one. They have to do with beauty, wealth, generosity, wisdom, strength, nobility, humility, kindness, gentleness, kinship. All of these she can find in Jesus, in "ideal-typical" perfection. Since she observes that no suitor is more deserving to be termed "gentle" than Jesus, who outshines everything in his beauty, and he also excels in other courtly values, it is likely that she herself is of noble birth.

The influence of Aelred's type of meditation is clearly discernible in *Wohunge*. It is Christ's prior love for the human being that determines this love relationship, and therefore, as in Aelred, the speaker's actual activity consists entirely in her visualization and *recollection* of this act of love ("munegunge," l. 4) while "performing" the text of *Wohunge*—reading aloud, in an act of aurality.[57] And in this recollection of the incomparable love of Jesus shown to the soul, the *Wohunge* converges with *Dulcis Iesu memoria*. The wealth and generosity of the lover elevate the speaker and make her "lady" (l. 84) of the whole world. Through accepting human flesh Jesus is "related" to the human being, for which reason it would be a veritable perversion of nature not to love him as a kinsman (l. 230). Of course, for this the speaker had to accept rejection by her brothers in the flesh (lines 244–45). The text's line of argument will also be given great weight in Julian of Norwich.

When the speaker's thoughts begin to focus on the Passion there is an enormous heightening of affect. As in contemporary Cistercian illuminations, the crucified body appears to her streaming in blood (ll. 479ff., 517, as can be observed also in all the other Wooing Group texts; see figure 5). Blood oozes from all the wounds inflicted by the crown of thorns—just as it does in a vision shown to Julian of Norwich. As the meditation progresses, the "mode" moves to the present—as prescribed by Aelred's "threefold" meditation. The speaker's *compassio* reaches such a degree of intensity that her heart seems to break and her eyes flood with tears. From this point she follows Christ's sufferings with complete empathy and experiences the Passion as an event in the here and now: "Ah, what shall I do now?" (ll. 488–89). The separate stages are introduced each in the same manner, by spontaneous reaction at the moment of speaking, again as Aelred recommended. A link is intimated between the blood and water flowing from the wound in Christ's side and the sacraments of Eucharist and baptism.[58] Then the speaker turns to Mary with a strange mixing of modes—on the one hand, she recalls the pain felt at that moment by the mother of God, on the other hand, she wants to abandon herself to weeping with her.

Then the speaker turns again to Jesus. Her cell is the chamber where she may kiss and embrace her beloved, yet this part is introduced by her expression of joy that he has led her from the world to the chamber of his birth (ll. 573–74); he is newly born in her soul. Here there is at least a suggestion of Origen's motif of the birth of God in the soul,[59] very rare in English mysticism, but interpreted, with such originality, in Guerric of Igny's previously mentioned sermon. From this it follows that the eroticizing of

FIGURE 5. St. Bernard and a Cistercian nun with the crucified Christ with blood streaming down his body, Rhineland, 1301/1500, Museum Schnütgen, Cologne. Copyright © Rheinisches Bildarchiv Köln, RBA 94 813.

the love relationship between the soul and her beloved, suggested only in this passage, is void of any sexual association; the author is simply alluding to a verse from the Song of Songs, and immediately adds that from this union the soul derives "spiritual" pleasure (11. 376–377).[60] Even when the speaker in *Wohunge* compares Christ with the young candidates for secular marriage, she avoids giving expression to sensual yearning.

Then follows the great climax of this text. Although she does not say so directly, the speaker is well aware of the famous "Improperia," Jesus's lament over the soul that is dilatory in recompensing his act of love; with the psalmist she asks how she can thank and "repay" him (11. 581ff.). She provides the answer herself, exclaiming "My body shall hang beside your body nailed to the Cross." This image of the speaker hanging with Christ on the cross represents the physical reenactment of his experience of suffering, radicalized by the simultaneous longing to die with him, in ultimate *imitatio.*

Despite all this, the speaker envisions a God who is not only loving but irate and vengeful; in spite of a love relationship defined in personal terms, there is fear of the dreadful day of wrath and judgment, as Aelred had described it to his sister in *Rule of Life for a Recluse.* Still, she finds solace in the thought of the all-important "sweet grace" of God, which makes her salvation possible. In her certainty of salvation she can look forward to the Day of Judgment; love has overcome fear of punishment. It will become apparent that the theme of naked fear of the Last Judgment is a powerful factor in English mysticism. Yet the more valid tradition is a different one that is already articulated clearly in the *Rule* of St. Benedict and on which the first letter of John is based, whereby the fear of God, if not eliminated, is *overcome* by the love of God (1 Jn 4:18).[61]

Overall, the *Wohunge* bears the stamp of Cistercian spirituality. It is a Passion meditation on a lofty theological plane, comparable in design to Aelred's *Rule of Life for a Recluse,* which predates it by several decades. At the same time it recalls the intense and sensual poetic language of *Dulcis Iesu memoria.*[62] The author operates skillfully with the technique of comparison and intensification and succeeds in creating a powerful and moving text that meets the individual needs of private devotion—which suggests that the work did not arise spontaneously but with a high degree of artistic awareness. As in the other texts belonging to this group, the author effectively uses rhetorical devices, including frequent alliteration, occasional rhyme, intensifying anaphora with end-weighting, parallelism, cumulative questions, sequences of apostrophe and apposition, building to a climax, and doublets, all of which help to establish an effective rhythm. In this meditative structure there is also a repetitive tendency,[63] manifested in a short prayer used as structural refrain to express the speaker's lasting constancy in love, and then, especially, in reiterated recollection of Christ's salvific act. In short, *Wohunge,* like the related smaller texts, deserves to be regarded as a persuasive, skillfully original prose composition, with some genuinely lyrical elements.[64]

Were all these texts written for a specific group of readers? This does seem to be the case, perhaps with the exception of "Lofsong," yet at the time of writing the author (or authors) seems to have had a wider readership in mind as well.[65] Moreover, the texts contain various tantalizing indications that they were intended to meet the specific needs of *female* readers. This, of course, has led to speculation that the texts might have been written by a woman.[66] While this is not inconceivable, we have yet to see persuasive proof, and in the absence of such proof it is safer to assume that the texts of the Wooing Group were composed, like most written works, by a cleric or secular priest, initially for a female reader or circle of readers.[67] This is indicated by the final remark of *Wohunge,* that the author wrote this book for his "dear sister" (11. 645–46), which reminds us very much of the genesis of Aelred's *Rule,* which he wrote for his sister.

✍ CHAPTER 3

Ancrene Wisse

A Magnificent Exemplar of Early English Mysticism

We now turn to *Ancrene Wisse,* a pinnacle of early Middle English prose and, in recent years, a major focus of scholarly attention. *Ancrene Wisse (AW)*, which means "guide for anchoresses" in Middle English, was written sometime in the late twelfth or early thirteenth century to meet the religious needs of three young sisters, who had chosen the recluse's extreme form of life in a solitary cell.[1] The author, who is unidentified, probably knew them personally. Diverse allusions to the three sisters' former station in life indicate that they were young and came from a wealthy background; the earliest manuscript calls them "gentle."[2] On the Continent, too, the life of a recluse was largely the prerogative of aristocratic women. Without question, it was the firm intention of these young women of the gentry class to match their exclusive position in society with inner nobility of soul, and with ambition to achieve spiritual perfection in a decidedly singular way. The text tells of their unconditional dedication to passionate love of God, in radical, frugal seclusion from the world. The author was psychologically sophisticated enough to know that even the most powerful love cools with time, and therefore he takes effective steps to guard against this danger and accords them twofold merit: on the one hand, he recalls that Christ himself dwelt in a cell, namely in his mother's womb; on the other hand, he assures them in a nice pun that as *anchorites* they act as a stabilizing *anchor* for the church (with its nave!) to which their cell is attached (figure 6).

Figure 6. A recluse immured in her cell. The Pontifical of Richard Clifford, Parker Library, Corpus Christi College, Cambridge (CCC MS 79, fol. 96r). By permission of the Master and Fellows of Corpus Christi College, Cambridge.

The three recluses did not remain in isolation for very long. Soon, additional women decided to seek enclosure in the vicinity and to follow the same pattern of life, with female messengers providing links between them. In time the group of recluses grew so large that an expanded guidebook was required.[3] This new version of AW refers to some twenty women and to the convent of a "motherhouse" from which other houses evolved and a "movement" spread throughout England.[4] The coming together of the recluses caused an institutional change from an anchoritic (solitary) to a cenobitic (communal) form of life.[5]

Only recently have the mystical aspects of AW been generally acknowledged, even though it is difficult to escape mystical themes. For instance, the first part of the text alludes to Christ asking to enter the young women's hearts, which he has dilated so that they may embrace him and be "ravished" by him.[6] Moreover, favorite Bible passages are referred to, which have inspired mystical metaphor since ancient times; and Bernard of Clairvaux's mystical teaching shines through.[7] This experience is conjoined with the sisters' liturgical "performance" of prayers of the hours, penitential psalms, antiphons, parts of the Office of the Virgin and the Office of the Dead, and various further liturgical texts.[8]

Moreover, AW establishes a direct link between the newly prevalent desire in the twelfth and thirteenth centuries for anchoritic solitariness and the first Christian hermits. It recalls explicitly not only the fathers in the deserts of Egypt and Asia Minor, but also the desert mothers, too often overlooked, and implies that the three sisters, and others like them, are seeking to resume the threads of this early spirituality, even more than the Cistercians, who were influenced by the early hermits. It is therefore likely that the positioning of the individual cells of our three sisters consciously imitated the organization of the early anchorites' cells: they are close enough for contact by messenger, and for mutual help when required,[9] and they are reminded that they have returned to the *source* of monasticism. In the European High Middle Ages the desert was replaced by the wilderness, especially by the primeval forest, which the AW author uses with allegorical or typological force, rather than as an actual symbol.

The Letter of James as *Ancrene Wisse's* Basic Authority

The anonymous author of the AW consciously sets up the desert fathers and mothers as a model for the three sisters to follow—in effect, an external manifestation of their inner purpose, a life enabling direct, mystical experience of God. Although they receive twelfth-century monastic theology for their guidance, the sisters are not asked to follow any established *order*.[10] On the contrary, the author seems to hold himself somewhat aloof from the religious orders as institutions, and he advises the sisters to call themselves members of the "order of James" after the apostle James (*AW,* 49–50). They would not need a black or white habit because they were already black on the outside like the bride of the Song of Songs ("I am dark [*nigra sum*]," Sg 1:5), burnished by Christ's radiant splendor; while their virginal purity made them white on the inside and therefore beautiful ("*sed formosa*"). They are at first a private community, which does not require official monastic support. By "order" he means the religious rule of life established by James in the letter that bears his name.

That these noble ladies should "submit" to the apostle James should come as no surprise, since James was a patron saint for twelfth- and thirteenth-century courtly culture. Indeed, the author of *AW* refers to him in such a way that it seems clear that he expected his readers to be familiar with him. In the Middle Ages it was not common to distinguish between James "the Greater," the apostle and brother of John, and James "the Lesser," brother of the Lord and reputed author of the biblical Letter of James. His alleged grave in northwestern Spain became a place of pilgrimage, and the cathedral built in his honor in Santiago de Compostela developed into a famous pilgrim destination, not least for the twelfth-century English nobility. He was also invoked as aide-de-camp and knight, and revered as *miles Christi* (soldier of Christ).[11]

It is not difficult to see that James was a "suitable" patron for these young recluses from the gentry class inasmuch as they are on a lifelong pilgrimage in the sense described by the apostle Paul; their pilgrimage *in via* ends only in heaven—*in patria* (*AW,* 176–78). In mystical writings, and particularly in *AW,* the idea of Christian life as pilgrimage is often reinforced by the popular verse from the letter to the Hebrews: "For here we have no lasting city, but we are looking for the city that is to come" (Heb 13:14). This speaks to all the faithful and is one of the reasons for *AW*'s subsequent appeal to the laity. The *AW* author presents a practical theology as *foundation* for the recluses' inner, spiritual pilgrimage; as members of the symbolic order of James they bind themselves to the rule of life of the "canonical epistle" of St. James, who defines true "religiun" and "riht ordre" (*AW CC,* 3.98–100). The Letter of James is referred to several times (including a gloss on it). It calls to mind the transience of our existence, comparing it to a fleeting puff of smoke (Jas 4:14). The recluses have taken their decision and bid farewell to wealth (2:5–6; 5:1) and worldly temptations, in order to lead a radically different life (*AW,* 110). They comply systematically with James's requirement to keep themselves "unstained by the world" (Jas 1:27), in order to attain sanctity and perfection (1:4); for friendship with the world means "enmity with God" (4:4). Of course, such compliance involves considerable difficulties, especially for beginners.

The biblical Letter of James was composed precisely with the problems of "new converts" in mind. It anticipates doubts over the choice that has been made and focuses on decisions required by the radical antagonism between God and world.[12] To make the recluses members of a symbolic order of James, with the Letter of James as their rule of life, was an intriguingly original idea on the part of the *AW* author. Thus the Letter of James provides spiritual guidance for the young recluses' novel sociological situation, which is not one of total isolation, but of the interesting social experiment, the coexistence with neighboring cells. James quotes from Leviticus Jesus's central command: "You shall love your neighbor as yourself: I am the Lord" (Lv 19:18), which is most easily implemented in small groups of equals. The recluses are to behave with kindness and love toward one another, as the early Christians are said to have done, who were "of one heart and soul" (Acts 4:32; *AW,* 140). Furthermore, James describes the commandment to love as the "law of freedom" or the *"royal* law" (Jas 1:25, 2:8); it is obeyed through the curbing of desire and passion. This results, according to James, in the *"dignity* of a human being destined for perfection and *freedom* [emphasis added],"[13] and *AW* also insists on the inviolability of "dignete" (*AW CC,* 55.312; *AW,* 101).[14] And just as humility emerges in the Letter of James from the commandment to love, so also it is emphasized in *AW* (149).

The *AW* author continues to take his lead from the Letter of James when he seeks to enhance the recluses' shared life, in which "probity and peaceableness" are particularly important.[15] Safeguarding communal life involves overcoming destructive manifestations of *affect,*[16] in which the five external senses play a crucial part, and about which Aelred had written with such sensitivity. This detailed discussion has biblical roots, especially in James (1:26, 3:5, 3:8, 5:11), where reference is made to the "evil effects that can emanate from the tongue, the smallest and yet at the same time the most powerful and most dangerous limb of man,"[17] which must be held in check—as must the whole person. The *AW* author sharpens this admonition in the astonishing and psychologically profound statement: "The word kills more than the sword" (*AW,* 75; with wordplay on the similar sounds *word—sweord; AW CC,* 30.397). As in James, there is a warning against backbiting and envy, quarrelsomeness, and, particularly, anger.[18] The anonymous author has perceptively discerned that the Letter of James pays special attention to the power of the *word.*[19] Following this lead, and with direct reference to Bernard of

Clairvaux, the author speaks of God as the eternal *verbum,* through which we were created. Our life should be understood as response to this word (*AW,* 77; with another wordplay on *word—andweord,* "answer"). Everyday speech, by contrast, should be characterized by simple and sparing utterances (*AW,* 72–78; Jas 5:12: "Let your 'Yes' be yes and your 'No' be no"); bodily gestures and contortions as means of achieving emphasis should be avoided (89), as should exaggeration (a theme picked up later especially by the *Cloud* author). For a long while, *AW* is concerned with the human heart as seat of the emotions, a "very wild animal" (66) driven by desire. Everything depends on a pure heart—a motif that recurs throughout the work.

The text talks less of the feminine soul and more of the grammatically neuter heart, an almost omnipresent term, which suggests that *unio* of love is not intended to be an exclusively female prerogative, and that *AW* does not envisage a quasi-sexual relationship with God;[20] the appeal can also be felt by a male reader, as God's partner in love.[21] *AW* is directed not only to the three young women, but also *expressis verbis,* to a wider public of women *and* men, in fact to any Christian of a contemplative disposition, and this again serves to explain the text's popularity in the late Middle Ages.

Another major theme in the Letter of James, and a further important stimulus for *AW,* is "conduct in the face of temptation."[22] The letter talks of the manifold temptations caused by the affect of desire (Jas 1:2), which must be met with patience (1:3–4, 5:7); when it defines the problem of temptation in sexual terms (2:11, 4:4), *AW* follows suit. Our author shows great understanding of human weakness, and outlines a remarkable psychology of temptation. This is not only basically rooted once more in the Letter of James (1:12–14), but also represents a modified Augustinian "doctrine of the stages of sin" that was particularly powerful in the twelfth century, emanating from a general intensification of concern with sin and conscience.[23] First comes *suggestio* as temptation to sin, then *delectatio* as pleasure in sin, then *consensus* as consent to its enactment, and finally the transformation of sin into habit (*consuetudo*).[24] A direct reference to Bernard shows that this was a topical theme: Bernard is reported to have said that initial "cogitation," in which evil thoughts do not yet cause any harm, is followed by "affection" (as synonym for *delectatio*), the desire to give in, and finally by "consent" to sin (153).

It is interesting to note the difficulty of the battle against sensuality for the author of *AW.* He has evidently experienced it himself, and is well versed in the psychology of sexual seduction; he expects that the anchoresses will need to confess sensual misconduct, in spite of their renunciation of the world (165–66). However, this does not mean that they are constantly (any longer) attached to the world;[25] rather, they consciously take the suffering of this battle upon themselves through "evocation of sensuality, which must be staged in all its seductiveness."[26] Rather than taking St. Antony as model for his female readers, the *AW* author chooses a woman, the desert mother Sara, who is said to have fought against sexuality for thirteen years (134).[27]

Incidentally, there is quite a bit of discussion in *AW* of sexual temptations, which suggests among other things that the author had a wider readership in mind. Tangentially he informs his readers that God allows temptations, and that the possibility cannot be excluded that he himself could appear as tempter, as Origen had already ventured to argue. The next chapters of *AW* concentrate on penance and confession. The author characteristically interweaves his own line of argument with abundant references to Old and New Testament passages, at times letting the Bible interpret itself by itself. Such detailed discussion has, however, little to do with the frequently cited institutionalization of confession brought about by the Fourth Lateran Council of 1215. The council made it obligatory for lay people to confess *once a year*, whereas in *AW* confession features of course much more powerfully, since the sisters must confess *at least once a week*.[28] This in turn is much closer to the Letter of James, where the order's members are required to engage in *correctio fraterna* very frequently—"Therefore confess your sins to one another, and pray for one another" (Jas 5:16)—in order to remain *unsullied* in confronting the world. With his customary empathy, the *AW* author elaborates on the need for the women to augment love of their neighbor by epistolary means, as well as awareness of their own sinfulness. And the extended Corpus Christi MS version recommends Dominicans and Franciscans as confessors. The sixth chapter tells the recluses that they should regard their entire life as penance. Although they are dead to the world and suffer loss of social standing, the certainty promised in the Letter of James (1:12) lives within them, namely that they will be *crowned* by their beloved Lord after the battle, and that one day they will be allowed to *sit with him* in judgment over mankind. Many mystics, male and female (*AW*, 180), in particular Rolle, cherished the hope of being rewarded with this promised crown.[29]

Thus the author has indeed founded a small Jamesian community as a kind of private "order." In fellowship his recluses practice love of their neighbor, and comply with James's recommendation to live in a *small community* "through the ethical norms that God as 'lawgiver' has prescribed; that is the community of James."[30] The *AW* author derives his authority from God, as bestowed on him in the New Testament epistle. It is highly interesting that the Letter of James has received long-overdue reevaluation in recent theological research and is now considered "in its ethics...to be the centre-piece of the New Testament...[for] no other New Testament author has interpreted the commandment to love so unambiguously as an obligation to treat all people equally."[31] The author of *AW* came to the same conclusion eight hundred years ago!

It would be a mistake to think that medieval knowledge of biblical texts was merely sporadic, or partial.[32] In the Middle Ages the Bible itself was read as well as the traditional patristic theology. Of course, the fathers themselves—one need only think of Origen and Augustine—demonstrated a particular reverence for *sacra pagina*. As Origen put it, "[Knowledge of scripture] is the art of arts and the science of sciences,"[33] and "the scripture of the old and new testament is woven together from all kinds of variegated thoughts."[34] The *AW* author must have been deeply impressed by the Letter of James, for he emphasizes its theological significance and authority most strikingly: he says it is the work of the James who was called "God's brother" because of his exceptional sanctity. It succinctly draws together important aspects of the Christian faith and therefore offers a foundation for the discussion of direct experience of God that follows in *AW*.[35] As a highly educated master of divinity, the *AW* author often includes further biblical, patristic, and monastic allusions; thus the question of which orders, if any, he was following becomes fairly irrelevant.

Christological Intensification

Martin Luther called the Letter of James an "epistle of straw" because in it Christ's work of salvation, though tacitly assumed, is not proclaimed. *AW* fills this theological "lacuna" by recalling important aspects of Pauline Christology, selected from a mystical perspective. The author combines Christology with allegorical interpretation of the Song of Songs, making astonishingly varied use of the new Cistercian allegorizing that flourished in the twelfth century,[36] and culminated in the work of Bernard of Clairvaux. It is incorrect to say that *AW* is "not...a self-contained work."[37] Its "exegesis" of the Song of Songs with its central theme of bridal love overarches as it were the Jamesian theology, which is based on the law of love; and *love* is at the heart of *AW*.

The very beginning of *AW* makes an intriguing connection between the Song of Songs and the Letter of James; the introductory quotation "*Recti diligunt te*" (Sg 1:3) alludes in particular to Bernard's fascinating 24th sermon on the Song of Songs ("The righteous love you"), which has not been observed hitherto. With his typical subtlety Bernard exploits the multiple meanings of the term *rectus*. He appeals to those who "direct" their gaze upward with upright gait and are not buckled by egocentricity (not *curvati*), and who are at the same time "right" (in the sense of just, *rectificati*) and live according to the *regula* in "right" love with a pure heart (*recto corde*), following the ethics outlined by James and elaborated in detail by *AW.* This is distilled in the commandment to love God and one's neighbor, including one's enemy (but without mention of self-love). Thus the opening of *AW* already alludes to the Cistercian theme of *rectitudo.*[38] Yet, however much the author was influenced by Bernard's interpretation,[39] and also by other authorities, the work's theological complexity is his own achievement.

In the course of what follows the readers are told in great detail *how* God wishes them to love him (cf. Bernard's *On Loving God*), as the *sponsus* of the Song of Songs who demands the utmost intensity of love. What is required of them is the self-knowledge so crucial for mystical texts, and expressed in similar terms by Bernard. *AW* follows his interpretation of the Song of Songs,[40] in which the bride is reproached for lack of self-criticism, and for letting fleshly desires distract her from her lover (*AW,* 85). In response to the Song of Song's invitation (5:2), the bride should embrace Christ in the chamber of her heart, experience Eucharistic communion as ecstatic *unio,* entirely oblivious of the world, and "leave behind" her own body (*AW,* 59). Early on, the mystical union with God frequent in women's mysticism is experienced as *unio sacramentalis.*[41] The following description is well-known: "After the kiss of peace when the priest consecrates the host, forget all the world, be wholly out of your body, embrace in shining love your lover who has alighted into the bower of your heart from heaven, and hold him as tight as you can until he has granted all you ever ask" (59).

The author links this with the Pauline motif of "Christ in you" and "you in Christ." The moment of *unio,* which the happy recluse (*"seli ancre," AW CC,* 44.946) experiences, is felt with indescribable sweetness in the kiss of God, a gestural visualization of the perfect concord of divine and human will. But *AW* is also familiar with the well-known, pseudo-Bernardine *amplexus* motif of Christ stretching out his arms to his beloved and inclining his head to kiss her. It is difficult to understand the view that in *AW* the soul is deficient in mystical devotion.[42] The wounds of Christ, so widespread a theme in high-medieval spirituality and mysticism, also receive interesting treatment in *AW.* The theme was promoted by Bernard, who, in his 45th sermon on the Song of Songs, allegorically interprets the dove dwelling in the cracks of the rock face as the soul longing for Jesus's wounds, then sojourning in the wounds in all humility, dwelling there, and letting contemplation arise.[43] In *AW* the wounds are opened in token of Jesus's great love;[44] yet interestingly there is no suggestion of quasi-sexual *unio.*

The fourteenth-century redaction of *De institutione inclusarum* goes an important step further, with "the dramatic representation of the recluse hiding inside Christ's bloody wound and revelling in his blood."[45] Without question, this can be regarded as "gendered erotic language," but it is important that, at the same time, a theological theme is being articulated as powerfully as possible, namely, personal experience of God incarnate, who suffers a bodily wound and proffers it to man. Imposing this theological significance on the wound "disembodies" it at the same time and turns it into purely spiritual symbol; it can also be interpreted as the place of origin of the church,[46] or of the two main sacraments of baptism and Eucharist, as water and blood flow out of the wound.[47] All this must be taken into account when an attempt is made to discover a new sexualizing tendency of the female anchorites.

In the seventh part of *AW* the author joins mystical love with a succinct and also competent outline of Christology, although there is no "clear overall structure."[48] This chapter bears the stamp of the apostle Paul's *theologia crucis,* as mediated by Bernard. Since Christ's death is to be understood as atonement for the sin of man, man in response is called upon to shape his life as thanksgiving. All human activity must arise from love of God, who, according to the First Letter of John, is himself love and who first loved us, as Bernard emphasizes time and again. The recluses have been exhorted, especially in *AW* chapter 6, to regard their enclosed life as an uncompromisingly bold attempt to implement in their bodily lives a core message of Pauline theology, namely *imitatio Christi* (as well as James's "law of love"). Their way of life, their ascetic practice as set up by Aelred for his sister in *De institutione inclusarum,* is virtually equated with Christ's suffering and dying on the cross, equivalent to martyrdom—*mortificatio* (*AW,* 177–78).

The virgins' yearning to die "in God and on God's cross" (179) signifies for them, by mystical paradox, the height of bliss, as is already intimated in the first chapter's prayer: "grant me to die with him and rise up in him" (61). They can apply to themselves the words of Paul, "For you have died, and your life is hidden with Christ in God" (Col 3:3), "and it is no longer I who live, but it is Christ who lives in me" (Gal 2:20; *AW,* 177).[49]

In typically Cistercian language the five human senses are featured in detail with reference to Jesus's Passion. Although *AW* usually speaks of *the* senses, it differentiates between outer senses and inner, spiritual senses, following Origen's very influential theory.[50] The function of the inner senses is thought to be just as "real" as that of the outer senses, and references to them are not simply metaphorical. Here the sense of touch comes last, since it is our most important one and since, under secular conditions, it allows the

most intense experience of God. It is said that Christ wanted to suffer the
agony of his Passion through this sense, thought of as participating in the
perceptions of the other senses (89), in order to console us in our own suffering.

Since for the author of *AW,* as for the later English mystics, the spiritual
senses have unquestioned reality, he shares Origen's conviction that any experience of God must draw on man's sensual nature: man must be grasped as
one person in physical-spiritual wholeness ("The soul and the body make
but a single person, and to both of them comes a single judgment. Will you
divide in two what God has joined as one?" *AW,* 117), for which reason God
assumed human nature. The author even speaks of *love* between body and
soul (193), of the marital oneness of the two entities joined by God.[51] Admittedly, in an Augustinian sense *AW* attaches little value to the corporeality of
man, since it is there that sin arises and the soul or spirit is diverted from its
divine orientation. On the other hand, the body also participates in resurrection; the miraculous transfiguration of all resurrected bodies, shining more
beautifully and with greater clarity than the sun, is a prospect anticipated
beyond all doubt (*AW CC,* 136, 163–75), as was later the case for Rolle, the
Cloud author, and Walter Hilton.

The sensual Cistercian language is reinforced in *AW* by metaphors of fire,
widespread in Christian mysticism. Christ himself, *AW* says, did everything
in order to kindle *fire* in the heart of his beloved (195).[52] The fierce flame of
this mystical love is compared with *real* fire.[53] While this notion is of course
of biblical origin,[54] the anonymous author exceeds traditional bounds. He
even has recourse to a drastic analogy with Greek fire (178), which could not
be extinguished by means of water—a highly effective piece of weaponry
in the High Middle Ages, used by the Muslim enemy in the Third Crusade
(1189–92).[55] Leaving aside a grotesque feminist interpretation referring it to
the female body, the uniqueness of this image deserves to be stressed: with the
utmost boldness the author ventures to relate an image from the genuinely
male world of the un-Christian Saracen enemy to the extremely contrasting subject matter of his female readers' mystical love of God, whereby the
tertium comparationis, what really matters to him, is the unquenchable quality
of this *incendium amoris.* However, the image *must* have perturbed the women
emotionally, and such a radical, unsettling effect was just what the author
intended.

AW reaches an impressive climax in the almost hymnic conclusion of the
seventh chapter. The author recommends to his readers: "Stretch out your
love to Jesus Christ, and you have won him. Reach for him with as much
love as you sometimes have for some man. He is yours to do all that you want

with" (197). It has on occasion been thought that he concedes to them the same sensual love that they might feel for a man they loved, even allowing them to woo him, but this is by no means the case. In context it is clear that the maidens' desire can only mean the whole person's unconditional self-abandonment to God in spiritual-sensual love (cf. 1 Cor 6:17). God as the great suitor loved them first; his wooing always precedes their love. Therefore, according to Bernard of Clairvaux, he must be loved for himself.[56] Bernard, the *"doctor mellifluus,"* goes on to emphasize that what God bestowed upon the soul with his most blissful embrace is "nothing other than sacred and chaste love, sweet and exquisite love, joyful because pure love, mutual love, intimate and strong, that unites two beings not in *one flesh,* but in *one spirit."*[57] *AW* follows the same Bernardine line of thought, alluding to this same *castus amor.* The text reaches such a pitch that God himself is declared subject to the power of Love personified, and powerless without her. He experiences love as binding power—*caritas ligans,* as Richard of St. Victor put it. Furthermore, the influence of the Cistercian William of St. Thierry, a great writer on love-longing, is evident.[58] *AW* goes so far as to speak of God's thirsting for the soul (91). Not even God can evade the compelling pressure exerted on him by love: "Love is his chamberlain, his counselor, his spouse, from whom he cannot hide anything, but tells all that he thinks" (198). Conversely, the soul has power over God, if she has the gift of tears (137). She ascends to God with utmost yearning, he draws her to himself and inclines toward her, and the conclusion of the seventh part of *AW* offers an excellent example of the "hallmark of 12th-century piety," namely "the reciprocal approach of human being and God," from above to below and vice versa.[59] Thus the seventh chapter is permeated by reminiscences of the great fathers' attempts to indicate in words, however cautiously, the mystery of mystical *unio.* It is therefore difficult to understand why scholars have repeatedly denied *AW* its ultimate purpose: appropriation of mystical spirituality as practiced by the Cistercians.[60]

The Anonymous Author and His Target Audience

The question may be asked: could the three aristocratic recluses' mystical intensity not have been achieved without the almost unimaginable hardships of their lives? The answer to this question lies in a point already mentioned that is fundamental to an understanding of the Middle Ages, and surely played a part in the choice of this path: the sisters see their lives not only as battle and even martyrdom, but also as spiritual "travail," for which they may expect a crown in heaven, as promised in the Letter of James. They choose an extreme form of Christian humility, but paradoxically they also lay claim to the impressive "power" of *serving* the triune God (56).

That *AW* should have been written in Middle English is by no means self-evident. Since French, or Anglo-Norman, was the official language of the English court, and Middle English was not highly regarded in aristocratic circles, the question has been raised as to why only two French versions and far more English versions of *AW* have been handed down, and why it was presumably originally written in English, although the initial readers were brought up to be bilingual? Here a further point needs to be taken into consideration. As stated by the *AW* author himself, the text was intended also for a wider readership of "men and women," and this made English, "the language of the people," the preferable choice as linguistic medium.[61] It seems to me more important that the readers, whether female or male, should be able to absorb this intimate subject matter in their mother tongue.

What level of education could the author assume in the nobly born sisters? They were partly literate at least and can hardly be numbered among the *illiteratae*.[62] Their lofty ambitions make it likely that they knew some areas of theology, and some Latin. We remember that Aelred composed his sister's rule in Latin, and in *AW* it is striking that we not only find a Latin gloss (!), but occasionally also a mixed Latin-English discourse. Our author is also acquainted with some highly educated recluses whom he describes as "learned" (72).[63]

The individual identity of the three sisters, and the intriguing author of *AW,* is likely to remain forever obscure. They lived at the time when the beguine communities were emerging, probably a few decades earlier than the beguine Hadewych, who, on her own account, was in communication with nine perfect women in England.[64] Yet their life was very different from that of the urban beguines, and the recent attempt to establish connections between beguines and anchorites is not at all convincing.[65] According to Dobson, the cells of the three recluses were located in the West Midlands, close to the Welsh border, in the vicinity of the Augustinian abbey of Wigmore, a daughter foundation of the famous theological center of St. Victor near Paris. Dobson also sees good reason to associate the author of *AW* with Wigmore Abbey, which was dedicated to St. James, and owned the Corpus Christi *AW* manuscript in the fourteenth century. Even if many of *AW*'s themes, as we have seen, are reminiscent of the Cistercians, the recluses' spiritual guide and confessor was not a Cistercian monk himself; he had some experience of the world and was acquainted with its subtle seductions, although he belonged to an order. He is also familiar with various forms of misuse of the reclusive idea. His aloof tone in speaking of the Dominicans and Franciscans makes it unlikely that he was a member of either of these new orders.[66]

He expects the three sisters to address him as "master," an academic title that he very probably acquired in Paris, as Dobson surmised.[67] He deserves the title, for the text yields evidence of advanced theological scholarship, and he is most likely to have acquired his wide-ranging education from the Augustinian canons of St. Victor. Trained in evangelical-Christocentric spirituality, they were especially open to Cistercian theology.[68] The influence of the Victorine rule, *Liber ordinis,* on *AW* has been proven.[69] Speculative Victorine and Cistercian elements are juxtaposed in *AW,* and it is most probable that the author was an Augustinian canon.[70] The regular canons took their orientation especially from the apostolic life and were therefore particularly mindful of James as the first martyr. The author's demand that the sisters' lives should be as in the Acts of the Apostles, "of one heart and soul" (Acts 4:32), again points toward the Augustinians, for their monasticism institutionalized this form of life in the High and late Middle Ages, and from them it was *taken over* by the Dominicans.[71]

Whatever the sources or antecedents of *AW,* they do not explain what is so strikingly human, and original, in this work. These qualities may have something to do with the contact that the author maintained with the reality of life in the world, whereby he does not conceal a Francophile bias. On occasion he addresses his female reader as "bel ami" (freely using the masculine form of address, appropriate for a general readership); he mentions the French patron saint, St. Gilles (Aegidius) and the place that bears his name, an important station on the pilgrim route to Santiago de Compostela. His experience of the world may have derived from such a pilgrimage. Be that as it may, veneration of James appealed above all to knights, and members of the lower aristocracy.[72] The author explains to the three ladies the well-known theological doctrine that their life should be understood as an imaginary pilgrimage to their true home. William the Conqueror's niece and daughter, the recluses Salome and Judith (a frequent name for a recluse, as *AW* says), lived by the church in the Lower Bavarian village of Niederaltaich from 1068 until after 1079. They had asked to be received there, separately, as recluses on their return from a pilgrimage to the Holy Land.[73]

The easy flow of images and comparisons from everyday rural life suggests that the author was familiar with country life. He is well able to bring spiritual matters to the mind's eye with vivid sensual metaphor. For instance, he personifies physical sickness as a goldsmith who has the task of gilding the crown that is waiting in heaven. Of course, some images that now seem original may have been commonplace in the Middle Ages, or may derive from other sources.

Associations between birds and the spiritual world can be traced back to antiquity, and contemplation tends to be given the attribute of wings, which help, as Gregory the Great says, to lift us above and beyond ourselves.[74] The notion of the soul as a bird is an archetype; for the *AW* author the recluses are birds (97), and he finds several delightful ways to justify this. Job described the anchorite's cell as a nest (98), but God's true nest is her own heart (99). The author also cites the identification of the beloved with a dove in the Song of Songs, in order to make clear the recluses' exceptional state of mind and spirit. Although their present life is that of birds in a cage, yet they feel so free that they can soar up to the bliss of heaven or sit on the branches of green trees and await the joys of heaven; this concretizes the Pseudo-Dionysian ascent to the world of the divine, found also in Origen.[75] It appears to the author that the lightest birds fly best, which immediately conveys a spiritual meaning; they can reach the spiritual world in so light a fashion because they are least weighed down by their bodies. The head held low as they fly is expressive of their humility, while wings and body together form the shape of the cross that the recluses take upon themselves in *imitatio;* for this medieval author, everything in this world can refer symbolically to the world beyond, an idea that we already find in Origen.[76] Thus, time and again he demonstrates an originality that is still impressive today.[77]

No attempt to identify the author of *AW* as a person has resulted in a satisfactory conclusion. Like Aelred of Rievaulx, to whom he is related in spirit, he must have been a learned theologian with superb knowledge of the Bible and the fathers, as well as of monastic-scholastic theology. Unlike most medieval writers, he almost always identifies the authors of his numerous quotations. Yet he was not governed by intellect alone; he was of a winning, even humorous, disposition, and, above all, sensitive and capable of enthusiasm. He did everything possible to kindle in the aristocratic sisters the fire that he evidently felt within himself, and to make it blaze as brightly as possible. His empathy enabled him to put himself in their position, to be alive to their needs and to the dangers that threatened them—a gift that Aelred also had to a high degree. This tempered certain misogynous views that he held in common with his contemporaries. Again, like Aelred, he defined the human being as by nature tender (*"animal mansuetum natura,"* *AW CC,* 49.42), for which reason he was against exaggerated asceticism and self-castigation, and in favor of wise moderation (*AW,* 184), that is, the golden mean, which was fundamentally the courtly and the Benedictine ideal at the time.[78] In sum, he was very understanding, within limits.

"Within limits"—because he also reveals another trait. It was his clear intention to define God not only as love but also as the dreadful and wrathful judge at the end of time. His statement that he would rather see his three young friends dead than robbed of their virginity doubtless conforms to the mentality of his time. On one occasion, he has Christ woo the soul and most unexpectedly raise his sword and threaten her with death, should she not yield to his wooing (194). In this he reveals what might be called a "crusader mentality," like the equally refined Bernard of Clairvaux, who was able not only to preach inspirational and ardent sermons on mystical love, but also to sound a clarion call for a new crusade against the Muslims who denied the true faith (in Vézélay in 1146). It is therefore not surprising that the *AW* author uses the symbol of Greek fire drawn from the real world, and numbers among his acquaintances a knight in armor, and clarifies a theological matter by pointing out that a good soldier does not seek tranquillity during battle (179), entirely in line with the Bernardine temperament.[79] He is familiar with Bernard's *De laude novae militiae,* written in praise of the Templar order and on the problems of just war. As a Francophile he probably knew of the significant status accorded to the hermit in courtly romance, from Chrétien de Troyes's *Perceval* onward, with regard to a knight's spiritual education. *AW* impressively describes Christ himself to the aristocratic sisters as a knightly hero of courtly romance, who has undertaken his greatest *aventure,* death on the cross and the triumph of resurrection, for his beloved lady, the soul.[80]

The European Context: *Ancrene Wisse* and the *St. Trudpert Hohelied*

Hope Emily Allen, the great expert on English mysticism, dated the composition of *AW* to the first half of the twelfth century, expressing her conviction that it displayed the spiritual renewal of the twelfth century.[81] Moreover, it has long since been observed that no thirteenth-century text worthy of mention is cited in this text, despite its abundance of quotations.[82] Nonetheless, more recent research places *AW* and the texts associated with it in the first half of the thirteenth century, postdating the Fourth Lateran Council of 1215.[83] Yet, as we have seen, for *AW* the council was not a hugely significant event.[84] It would be ridiculous to think that the sisters needed to wait for this council in order to learn of the fundamental importance of penance and confession for their spiritual life. I therefore see no reason to assign the *genesis* of *AW* to the first half of the thirteenth century.

What is instead clearly discernible in *AW* is the spirit of the twelfth century, which can be seen by looking at other comparable texts of the period.

For instance, the first great Middle High German mystical text, a commentary on the Song of Songs inappropriately titled *Das St. Trudperter Hohelied* (St. Trudpert [commentary on the] Song of Songs), has gone largely unnoticed but demands to be compared and contrasted with *AW*.[85] Composed around 1150 (that is, at about the same time as Aelred's *Institutio inclusarum*), the *St. Trudpert Hohelied (TH)* is addressed to Benedictine nuns, perhaps those of the double monastery at Admont in Styria.[86] The author, who is clearly in the milieu of French Cistercian mysticism, adopts a different position from *AW* regarding the esteem accorded to recluses and nuns; he charges recluses with indulging too much in egotistic self-sanctification. Looking at both texts together, it is possible to read *AW* as an indirect defense of the reclusive life, perhaps even a *response* to the *TH* and its perceived attack on the eremitical life. Whereas *TH* was vehemently critical of those who withdraw from the monastic community to pursue their own salvation as recluses or solitaries, *AW* seems intent on refuting any such charge, by having the recluses live in neighboring cells in a small *community*, in order to achieve perfection by following the prescript of James's theology.[87] Yet, whatever their differences, with regard to Cistercian influence on mysticism, the two texts reveal a number of striking similarities, of which only a brief selection can be given here. Both texts warn against lukewarm love (*AW*, 195; *TH*, 158.1216); fire has a mystically uniting force;[88] both texts proceed from the ontology of the inner spiritual senses (*TH*, 28.51); soul and body are one whole, and the soul loves the body (*TH*, 80.82; "The soul loves the body very much indeed," *AW*, 193); not only does God dwell in the soul (*AW*, 59, 82, 99; "Christ in me," *AW*, 177; *TH*, 58, 60, and passim), but, conversely, God is the dwelling place of the soul (*AW*, 156, 158, 180; *TH*, 270).

   TH provides its own title: "A teaching of knowing God through love"— a Bernardine theme, but one that goes back to Origen[89] (cf. *TH*, 306), and which also determines *AW*'s line of thought, "to see him and to know him, and *through that knowledge to love him* [emphasis added] over all things" (82).[90] Like Bernard, the two texts describe love of God as boundless (*AW*, 195–98; *TH*, 687). In both, Christ as ineffably beautiful lover first loves the soul and woos her in courtly fashion (*AW*, 191–92; *TH*, 34). As in the Song of Songs, he lets her enjoy his kiss (*AW*, 86; *TH*, 34, 38, 40). The German commentary is at pains to prevent any misunderstanding and to exclude eroticism: "This kissing does not press fleshly mouths upon one another, but spiritual wills" (*TH*, 41). There is a clearly noticeable allusion to Aelred's threefold definition of the kiss; the kiss of spiritual friendship "does not occur through oral contact, but through movement of the soul, not through joining of the lips, but through mingling of the spirits."[91] Similarly, the *AW* author comments on the biblical "Let him kiss me with the kisses of his mouth" (Sg 1:2) with the words: "This kiss, dear sisters, is a sweetness and a delight of the heart so immeasurably sweet that every taste of the world is bitter compared with it" (86). At another point he comments further that sensual love makes a virgin into a woman, whereas spiritual love of God can turn a woman into a virgin once more (*AW,* 193). *TH,* incidentally, also envisages the possibility that the readers are not all virgins, but are nonetheless the virginal brides of Christ (*TH,* 40, and commentary, 565).

These correspondences—and the list is by no means complete—are significant; they show not only that *TH* is dominated by the new affective Cistercian spirituality, based on exegesis of the Song of Songs, but also that this applies very strongly to *AW,* which therefore needs to be situated within twelfth-century monastic theology. There is no need to argue in favor of an influence of modern sermon rhetoric. We have also seen that it is wrong to compare the urban beguines' liminal position between the laity and the religious with the decidedly religious status of the "retrospective" anchorites. These cannot be placed within a religious movement toward the later Middle Ages. The reason why *AW* was so very popular lies in the fact that it focuses on the core of Christian belief and that it provides the "mystagogic" possibility of a personal emotional sense of the divine.

Conclusion

From whatever perspective we look at *Ancrene Wisse,* it is a most remarkable work. Its contribution to the history of English prose has been amply discussed, and we need not reiterate that discussion here, but there is still much to be learned about its larger significance in the context of the clearly related smaller works of the Wooing Group and the Katherine Group.[92] I should like to make a case for the possibility that the smaller texts predate *AW.* Indeed, the author of *AW* points out to his readers that useful spiritual texts are available for their own religious lives, and names the life of St. Margaret (*Seinte Margarete*). There are also some indications in *AW* that the author is familiar with the longest Wooing text, *Þe Wohunge of Ure Lauerd,* including several instances of the (rare) motif of God as the wooer of the soul and the claim that Christ is superior to any worldly lover.[93] There is even a further echo of these minor works in part 7 of *AW.*[94]

That the remaining small texts of the so-called Katherine Group were composed before *AW* gains probability from the very useful stylistic analysis of Cecily Clark. She points to the highly artificial style of *St Marherete* and *St Katherine:* particularly that their alliterative prose style discloses their "retrospective" tendency and their intention to set these female saints in the tradition of "heroic virginity."[95] She does not consider the Wooing Group, yet despite their affectivity these texts are formally, rhythmically highly organized and patterned too. By contrast to these smaller texts, in *AW* (with its related subject matter) Clark discovers a more flexible, spontaneous, and relaxed manner, a language near to "the real language of men," "fresh and up-to-date" and reminiscent of personal, conversational communication.[96] I suggest that this may reflect a certain additional influence of the epistolary genre of the Letter of James, which means so much to our anonymous author. All this contributes to the assumption that *AW* is the last and most complex of these interrelated texts.

CHAPTER 4

"Female" versus "Male" Spirituality?

A Talking of the Love of God *and the Meditations of the Monk of Farne*

Remarkably, the flowering of religious prose in England that we have observed in previous chapters largely ceased after the middle of the thirteenth century. It would not be until the fourteenth century that England would again produce such an impressive body of writings, by the likes of Richard Rolle, *The Cloud of Unknowing* author, Walter Hilton, and Julian of Norwich. This "yawning gap," this absence of mystical prose texts during the later thirteenth and early fourteenth centuries, is astonishing, particularly if we consider the emergence of Franciscan spirituality in the thirteenth century. What we have are a few examples of affective and devotional poetry, some with echoes of the *Dulcis Iesu memoria* and some focusing on the Passion of Christ, which we shall not discuss further. Suffice it to recall one lyric poem, *Love Rune,* a work of considerable artistry composed sometime during the middle decades of the thirteenth century.[1]

The author of *Love Rune* states at the very beginning of the poem that he is a Franciscan friar named Thomas of Hales, writing "at the request of a young girl dedicated to God."[2] Distressed by the inconstant, chimerical character of the world, the young girl hears of famous unhappy pairs of lovers in literature—Paris and Helen, Amadas and Idoine, and Tristan and Iseult—but, like the speaking person of *The Wooing of Our Lord* (*Þe Wohunge of Ure Lauerd*), she turns her thoughts instead to Jesus as the ideal partner in love, and she is reminded of the importance of possessing the precious jewel of virginity. The poem's immediacy and simplicity of diction are impressive, notwithstanding the magnitude of the theme, and the poet skillfully mines themes and motifs in secular love poetry of the time.[3] The precise meaning of the term "love rune" (*luve ron*) is uncertain, but it is clearly meant to evoke the imagery of lovers secretly exchanging sweet words, as in a love song or a love letter. In this respect, *Love Rune* borrows a metaphor that we have seen already in both the Wooing Group and *Ancrene Wisse* (see chap. 2), that of the New Testament Gospels as Christ's love letter to the soul. So, while there is plenty to admire in *Love Rune,* there is little in it that is innovative and that would suggest therefore the need to look beyond the tradition of the Cistercians as a source of inspiration. Of course, *Love Rune* is a work of poetry. What about in the field of prose? Do we really have to wait until the fourteenth century to find renewed evidence of mystical spirituality?

Further Vernacular Literature for Recluses

If there is to be an affirmative answer to this question it would most likely be found by looking at the famous Vernon MS, the largest and most significant surviving manuscript from late medieval England. Now housed in Oxford's Bodleian Library, Vernon contains some 370 lavishly decorated and illustrated texts. Written in the dialect spoken in the English West Midlands during the late fourteenth century, it is, in effect, a large miscellany of poetry and prose for pious readers—probably nuns or a group of pious women organized in a semireligious manner—as suggested by the title on the opening page: "Salvation of the Soul" (*salus anime* in Latin; *sowlehele* in English).[4] Among its treasures are stories about the lives of saints, miracle stories, and narrative accounts of the life of Mary and the infancy of Christ. In addition to a number of poems, including *Piers Plowman*, Vernon features works by Richard Rolle and Walter Hilton, as well as a version of the *Ancrene Wisse,* indicating the interest this early thirteenth-century text continued to arouse in the later Middle Ages.

Of particular interest for our purpose here is the unique prose text in Vernon that prefaces *Ancrene Wisse,* titled *A Talkyng of þe Loue of God* (*A Talking of the Love of God*).[5] To appraise the significance of this text is certainly not easy. Its editor Salvina Westra dates *A Talking of the Love of God* to the late fourteenth century, based on a number of factors, including, perhaps most importantly, her judgment that it reflects the influence of the affective mysticism of Richard Rolle, and therefore it must postdate Rolle's death in 1349.[6] It could just as easily be argued, however, that *Talking,* with its clearly lyrical qualities, is reminiscent of *The Wooing of Our Lord,* which as we have already seen dates back to the first half of the thirteenth century.[7] *Talking* displays greater affective intensity than the earlier texts of the Wooing Group, it is true, but there is nothing new in tone or style, and it yields no evidence of a "new mysticism" in form or content. As in *Wooing,* so also in *Talking,* the central theme is the soul's love for her divine bridegroom and his yearning for her. It is therefore a priori more appropriate to surmise a date of composition rather closer to *Wooing* and *Ancrene Wisse,* especially since there are no linguistic objections to such a proposition. If this is correct, then the gap between the great prose texts of the early thirteenth century and the start of Richard Rolle's literary productivity in the fourteenth century would be narrowed.

At first glance, *Talking* appears to be little more than a compilation of several texts. For instance, the opening is strongly based on the Wooing Group text "Orison to God Almighty." The final part derives largely from *Wooing* plus an added "Prayer to Our Lady," with which the "Orison" similarly ends. There are also a few pieces for which no direct exemplar has been found—most notably, the middle section and an apparently independent conclusion.[8] In her analysis of the independent sections, Westra has observed echoes of Anselm's *Orationes sive meditationes* (*Prayers and Meditations*)—particularly the middle section.[9] While probably true to a certain extent, this claim deserves greater scrutiny. No doubt, *Talking* shares with Anselm an interest in the theme of God as wrathful judge, who demands satisfaction for Adam's fall through the sacrifice of his own son. But one must not overlook the fact that *Talking,* by its very title, is concerned above all with God's *love*—and here, again, *Talking* can be seen to recall *The Wooing of Our Lord,* where the wrath of God as judge is similarly invoked, but in the end it is definitively and triumphantly overcome.

Upon closer reading, one discovers that the author of *Talking* treats the problem of God's wrath versus his love more thoroughly and with greater subtlety than one would expect if the text were merely echoing Anselm. How can God be the railing judge, the author seems to be saying, if God is also the *father* of man and, through Christ's incarnation, his *brother*? (24). Indeed, in truly Cistercian manner, God is also the loving divine *mother.* With this in mind, the reader should take comfort in the realization that God will act not merely as a judge but as a family member. This goes well beyond Anselm's theological position—in fact, it is hard not to see in *Talking* a strikingly "modern" view of Christ's incarnation as an unprecedented act of *co-suffering* between God and man, rather than as sacrificing himself for the purpose of divine satisfaction. Be that as it may, these considerations suggest that to treat *A Talking of the Love of God* as essentially a "compilation" of disparate texts does not entirely do it justice.[10] While it may not be a work of great inspiration, there is enough evidence to suggest that considerable thought went into the composition of the work and the interweaving of the parts into a whole.

Following the middle section, with its "Anselmian" meditation, there is a deliberate new start with a fresh turning to Jesus in prayer that is clearly reminiscent of the Wooing Group's praise of Jesus, but in which the Cistercian sensuality of language is heightened and the narrator confesses that his or her heart is melting in longing for this beloved (26.20–21, page and line reference). The theme of partner choice that follows corresponds in broad strokes to that in *Wooing,* and the impression increases that the speaker is a woman. Consistent with this is the strong emphasis on the important ideal of poverty (40–44; there is a comparable emphasis in *Wooing*). This is followed by the thought that *imitatio Christi* implies not only acceptance of poverty but also endurance of ignominy and contempt. Then comes the meditative recollection of Christ's Passion, with such affective immediacy that the speaker thinks her heart is breaking asunder (50.16). As in *Ancrene Wisse,* Jesus now allows the beloved (the soul, *anima*) to gaze into his heart, so that she can see the love letters concealed there. As so often in mystical texts, the wound in Christ's side is linked with his heart as actual goal of yearning. Here *Talking* produces a particularly bold effect; the erotic analogy is only too clear, and exceeds what had previously been customary in comparable texts. In this instance it is indeed appropriate to talk of Franciscan emotionalism— through the images of sucking on the wound and of penetration as the goal of yearning desire. Nonetheless, I still maintain that a Cistercian tone of *Talking* continues throughout.

A new speech situation prepares the ground for a further prayer to Jesus, an unparalleled climax in this text: the meditating person lives like a bird in the cage (an image that also appears in *Ancrene Wisse*) and longs passionately for her lover, shedding hot tears of love. This unresolved tension finds release only in her succumbing to love's madness. There can be no doubt about the spiritual nature of the spellbindingly passionate tone. It is no wonder that the speaker loses control of herself, since she is attacked by Love personified, and leaps upon the beloved "al out of my self" (60.22–23), as the greyhound leaps upon the stag—a striking use of metaphor, without doubt.[11] We see her embrace the cross, suck on Christ's feet (a Cistercian motif), and kiss him like a madwoman. Her imagination turns the situation into such a real experience that she believes she is tasting his warm blood on her lips, and tangibly feeling his body. Here the exuberance of *Talking* is unparalleled, even though no actual *unio passionalis,* or consummation, occurs.[12] Finally the speaker returns to the here and now—that is, to the cell in which she is once more a bird in the beloved's cage. For Jesus the soul would like to sing enchantingly, and find the right response for him, who is her song (66.23–24).

Talking is also framed in an interesting manner by a prologue and a conclusion. While the prologue will be considered below, we here cast an anticipatory glance at the end, in which the editor could see nothing of note.[13] It gathers together the work's motifs and themes—but recapitulated at the highest emotional level. Like *Wooing*, *Talking* recalls that divine love *preceded* human love, which therefore sees itself as responding love. Nothing less is suggested than the possible *unio* of the soul with the beloved in the fulfilled experience of mystical "feeling" (68.16), which is by no means restricted, as has been supposed, to "consciousness."[14] The last section answers the question often put by the speaker in the course of the meditation, and familiar to us from *Wooing*, as to what she shall do herself in view of the superabundant flow of divine proofs of love (66.10–11), and provides closure. With the knowledge she has gained, she answers the question herself; now she knows what she wants to do (66.29–30). Of course, the text consciously restricts itself to love between the soul and God incarnate as spiritual "eroticism." The final step taken by Bernard of Clairvaux, moving forward through love of God's humanity to his love in the spirit, is no longer—or not yet—achieved in *Talking* (any more than in *Wooing*). One may see the beginning of a tentative attempt, but it falters (68.12–13).

Now to the highly original prologue. In its indication of themes (*materia, intentio, modus tractandi*) it conforms to the usual requirements of rhetoric. *Lectio* serves as preparation or stimulus for *oratio* and *meditatio*, following monastic tradition.[15] Of interest is the explicit recommendation that the text should not be read from beginning to end but rather in sections that have special appeal in particular situations. *Talking* sets out, as was so often the case, to incite devotion to Jesus—the main function of a meditative text. In order to do this, the anonymous author applies the technique that he himself labels as "cadence." The reader is specifically alerted to the fact that the text is correctly punctuated ("riht pointed"), and the Vernon MS does actually add punctuation throughout, but not consistently, and it therefore cannot be interpreted unambiguously.[16] However, it has been demonstrated that this was intended to divide a period into smaller units by the use of pauses, which gave heightened emphasis to phrase endings, and highlighted rhyme in particular.[17] Furthermore, the differentiated use of semicolon and inverted semicolon was intended to indicate intonation, for this system of punctuation evidently had a rhetorical speaking-cum-performing function rather than a grammatical one. Occasionally the "cadence" may also coincide with the Latin "cursus" tradition[18] (*cursus planus, tardus, velox*), although this vernacular text does not set out to adopt consistently a principle of style that belongs to sophisticated Latin prose.[19] By and large it may be said that "cadence" was used to establish a "rhythmic pattern,"[20] whereby rhythmic structure is important not for its own sake but in order to stress phrases of particular import, and to invite the reader to dwell on them in greater meditative depth. Affective intensification, so important in this text, which is both *meditatio* and *oratio,* is achieved with the help of various rhyming techniques and numerous repetitions combined with rhetorical figures. Although for a time it seemed to me that *Talking* should be interpreted as an early precursor of a prose poem, I no longer believe this to be the case, because a meditative dwelling on special points is the intended goal, rather than a "flowing" lyric effect; the divisions into sense units are intended to support the *ruminatio* of the text.

A Talking of the Love of God: A Text for Women Written by a Woman?

As the prologue and main text indicate, the work is intended for all contemplatively inclined readers, whether female or male; "man" is not used in a gender-specific way, but refers to "the human being." It is therefore not of great significance that grammatically masculine forms are retained, or that "child" becomes "son," and mention is made of a "brother." Rolle's English Psalter, although definitely written for women, often refers to "man" or "men." It should therefore not be concluded too hastily that *Talking* is addressed primarily to monks or friars.[21] More pertinent is the editor's considered view that the text was written "not exclusively for women." As we have seen on several occasions, both sexes could address Jesus as lover ("lemman" *anima, persona*), and long for him.

Yet there are indications in *Talking* that the author has in mind a specific circle of addressees.[22] As in *Wooing of Our Lord,* so also in the parts of *Talking* that are dependent on this earlier text, the first-person speaker should be thought of as a woman, who comes to recognize Christ as her ideal lover and partner. We must assume that she, like so many recluses, is a member of the aristocracy; numerous courtly terms confirm this. When she perceives herself as bird in a cage, this traditional image, which could of course be applied to a *nonna,* refers rather to the life-world of the *inclusa,* who is compared with birds several times in *AW;* a phrase such as "to wone wiþ þiself in þis holy place" (58) suggests the world of a recluse. It is also hard to imagine that a man would praise Jesus as "bird sweet as honey." If we assume a female speaker, then her resolve never to turn away from him, "for no mon" (66.29), should quite clearly be taken as a promise that she will not decide in favor of marriage to a "terrestrial" man.

This assumption is supported by the fact that the speaker evidently comes from a family with lofty religious ambitions; it seems that as a child she was already urged to make her marriage vow to Jesus, and this "at chirche dore" (66.34), that is, validated in ritual form at the entrance to the church, just as the wife of Bath in Chaucer's *Canterbury Tales* took her five husbands in marriage "at chirche dore."[23] It may perhaps mean that she was already entrusted to a monastery in childhood, or that she was first educated in a monastery school. One may call to mind, for instance, the thirteenth-century aristocrat Mechthild of Hackeborn (1241–98/99), author of the extremely popular *Liber specialis gratiae,* who entered a monastery at the age of seven, or Gertrud of Helfta (1256–1301/2), who also came from a high-ranking family and was entrusted to a monastery at the very early age of five.[24] We further recollect the good English example of Christina of Markyate: as a young girl she promised herself irrevocably to Christ before St. Albans church, by carving a cross into the church portal with her fingernail (also "at chirche dore"; cf. chap. 1).[25] The text of *Talking,* however, points rather to the conclusion that the speaker moved from the status of *nonna* to that of *inclusa,* in order to be able to devote herself with even greater intensity to her mystical love (being crucified with Christ [Gal 2:20], p. 10).

All this could also suggest that the text was composed entirely by the speaker herself; with her betrothal she would then have given us a relevant biographical detail, a kind of authentication. That she speaks of her "order" (4.62) could remind us of the fact that the three *AW* recluses also belonged to the fictitious "order" of James, whose definition of temptation is even referred to in the text (40). Whereas for the Wooing Group it was necessary to reject any assumption of female authorship, with *Talking* the situation may be exactly the opposite. Here a woman may have been inspired by the Wooing Group texts; not hesitating to take over whole sections, she might then have introduced her own thoughts and feelings, and have created a new work, which actually outstrips the earlier texts in its intensity of mystical devotion. It would be wrong to object that the language is too passionate for any assumption of female authorship, for there are striking examples of a similar sort, especially in the thirteenth century; one need only think of the beguines of Flanders or of Mechthild of Magdeburg, where tempestuous courtly love abounds, the heart hunts God in the chase, and love's desire is intensely passionate.[26] Moreover, it was entirely possible for a woman to acquire some familiarity with the basic concepts of the rhetorical "cursus."

If there is a possibility of female authorship *before* Julian of Norwich and Margery Kempe, then it is here, in the intriguing *A Talking of the Love of God.*

Scholars have considered *Talking* to be typical of fourteenth-century mysticism, and thus have sought to establish the influence of Richard Rolle, or indeed an imitation of his vernacular prose.[27] Now it is time to put the question the other way round: could not Rolle, conversely, have known *Talking* and been influenced himself by it? For instance, the whiteness of the eyes of the crucified Christ, which becomes visible when he sinks his head at the point of death (52.14), is a detail found only in *Talking* and at the end of Rolle's Passion meditation.[28] Rolle, however, especially in this meditation, employs additional, elaborate metaphor that goes beyond anything in *Talking,* making it in my view less likely that *Talking* was inspired by him. Then there is the matter of the strong formal and thematic link between *Talking* and the Wooing Group. The reception of late twelfth- and early thirteenth-century texts in *Talking* is so intense, in spite of the Franciscan element we could observe in one respect, that it needs to be understood ultimately as resulting from the direct *impact* of these Wooing Group texts. In the same vein, themes and language as well as the frequent addresses to Mary point to a strong influence of Cistercian spirituality.[29]

There are good reasons, therefore, to believe that *Talking* was in fact a continuation and final intensification of the Wooing Group, written probably in the first half of the thirteenth century, or a little later. The fortunate circumstance that it was still highly regarded in the late fourteenth century, when English mysticism was again flourishing, is something it shares with the rediscovered *Ancrene Wisse;* both contribute to the continuity of English mystical prose.[30] However, the possibility cannot be excluded that *Talking* was composed at much the same time as the works of Rolle and the monk of Farne.

The Monk of Farne and the "Sensuousness" of His Mysticism

There are thus good reasons for juxtaposing *A Talking of the Love of God* and the collection of meditations of the "monk of Farne," who can almost certainly be identified as John Whiterig.[31] He was educated in Oxford and later became a Benedictine novice master in Durham, until he exchanged this life for that of a hermit on Farne Island, where he died in 1371. There he composed his series of Latin *Meditationes;* it was recently said of them that they "aimed primarily in the Bonaventuran tradition to evoke pity for the sufferings of Christ."[32] Pantin, however, knew better and called him "a contemporary . . . of Richard Rolle, yet in some ways a link between the school of St. Bernard and the classic English mystics of the fourteenth century."[33] Bernard is indeed frequently brought to mind.[34]

First, it is hardly surprising that a solitary Durham monk on the island of Farne should direct a *meditatio* to St. Cuthbert; this saint, who fled from people and spent nine years in the island solitude of Farne, was surely a special model for him.[35] Of greater importance for him was St. John the Evangelist, to whom as his probable name-day saint he directed two meditations. John, who, as was wrongly believed, was granted the privilege of apocalyptic visions on the island of Patmos, is revered by both Rolle and the Farne monk. A major reason for the devotion to him is that he was thought to have preferred the sweetness of heavenly love to libidinous delight.[36] A formal example of the monk's originality occurs in his *Meditation on Abraham and David* where we encounter one meditation inset within another, when Abraham himself engages in meditative reflection (230). Most interesting of all is his very expansive *Meditacio ad crucifixum,* which may usefully be compared with *Talking.*

The first thing that strikes us is the close similarity between this text, primarily written for male monastic readers, and *Talking.* Both are affective prayers. The monk's Passion meditation is clearly conceived along the lines of Cistercian bridal-mystical exegesis of the Song of Songs. Thus familiar themes and motifs include the crucified Christ as *Deus desiderans* and jealous lover, awaiting the soul's devotion. As has been pointed out, this is anticipated in a shorter and simpler form in Anselm of Canterbury's Meditatio X.[37] The soul experiences most intense love-longing, which cannot be satisfied, not even by the sweetest sensuality of a tempestuous kiss. In a manner typical of the time, the text describes this love-longing as a kind of greed that may lead to madness, as in *Talking,* a madness from which not even God is exempt. This text, like *Talking,* is underpinned by Bernard's idea of love without measure, and words from one of his sermons on the Song of Songs spring to mind: "O love, you are indeed rash, violent, fragrant, impetuous, and brooking considerations of naught but yourself, you eschew all else and despise everything, content with yourself alone. You subvert order, disregard custom, recognize no measure. All that propriety, reason, self-respect, deliberation and judgement would seem to demand you triumph over" (102).

On several further occasions, the monk of Farne takes a surprisingly original turn, particularly when he successfully creates a climax in his discussion of mystical love. Intent on displaying the power of this love to the very end, he builds on the central verse of the Song of Songs, in which love is as strong as death ("fortis est ut mors dilectio," Sg 8:6), and love and death converge, as it were, into one. The monk has heard tell of the power of adulterous love, but intimates that such love dies from remorse. By contrast, for the mystic, death is the desired climax of the most intense devotion, because by dying he—in the words of the apostle Paul—will be with Christ (Phil 1:23;). Yet this is just a foretaste of the ultimate union with God.

Since the daring intensity of feeling in *Talking* and *Meditacio* is most strikingly similar, we do not find an answer to what constitutes specific feminine spirituality. It is true that the monk goes some steps further by his use of erotic metaphors, as when in the intoxicated yearning of love the *pudenda* lie entirely uncovered, a situation that recalls the drunken Noah (Gn 9:22; p. 189, 1957 ed., not translated into English); the erotic sensuality of imagery is indeed unparalleled. As in *Talking,* we also find in this intriguing *Meditacio* the motif of exchange of hearts, but with an idiosyncrasy typical of this author. He ventures to set a condition for Christ's winning of his heart: only if Christ bestows himself entirely upon him will he gain his heart.[38] As in *Talking,* and as in the Cistercian tradition, the soul is sucking at Christ's breast; yet unlike in *Talking,* the meditating subject is taken *into* the wound in Christ's side, but only after he has received the divine kiss he desired: "I open my side to draw thee into my heart after this kiss, that we may be two in one flesh";[39] nonetheless the idea of *penetration* is absent both in the *Meditacio* and in *Talking.*

The only really distinguishing quality that makes this text a specimen of male mysticism is the layer of learned theology, which de-sensualizes some of his metaphors. Several of his kiss images serve as metaphors for speaking of the mystery of the incarnation, by which God completely joined his divinity with the human flesh. The text's firm anchoring in scripture, the network of biblical references that pervades it, and at the same time the exegetical use of typology with an intensity rarely encountered elsewhere (many Old Testament figures serve as anticipatory types of Christ) are here distinctive features of an author well versed in the scholastic tradition. Surprisingly, learned allegorization *and* very intense, personal, emotional devotion merge into one another as if such sudden transitions were a matter of course. Christ's loving arms outstretched on the cross are simultaneously *interpreted* allegorically as the law and the prophets.[40]

A feature that immediately stands out is the comparison of the crucified Christ with an open book—a metaphor that will recur in Rolle's *Meditations on the Passion.*[41] The invitation to eat the volume (76) combines allusion to the Eucharist with consumption of the book in *Revelation.* Our author, well versed in Bernardine thought, knows that the *amor castus,* spiritual love independent from Christ's bodily Passion, has to be the ultimate goal of the soul's love. On the other hand, he calls to mind Christ's Passion with a high degree of realism, and he emphasizes, as does *Ancrene Wisse,* that Christ suffered the greatest pain in all five senses (45), which is elaborated in detail. His writing is then again suggestive of a male author when he tries to distinguish nine different forms of love; he fails, however, to develop a convincing classification. Instead, the very last type of love does not go beyond a strongly sensual character in that it is equated with inebriation. From the time of his physical birth, he tells us, he felt drawn toward his divine mother; therefore it is necessary for him to enter into the body of the Lord and be born there to eternal life (73); yet he also wants to be suckled by his God-Mother throughout his life. He, too, is not free from the "Anselmian" fear of damnation and God's wrath, yet he takes refuge and finds comfort in Christ's wounds and is aware of the promise to be given the form of God and to be made "*deiformis.*" Yet what he knows about the possibility of the knowledge of God is summed up by a statement that borrows from Gregory the Great: "The measure of your love is the measure of your knowledge."[42]

The monk of Farne's passionate intensity corresponds closely to the mystical discourse we encountered in *Talking.* On the one hand, the monk's glowing spirituality could be considered idiosyncratic; on the other, it reminds us of Richard Rolle, with whom, among other things, he shares his desire to be among the burning seraphim.[43] In the end, one can only conclude that the monk of Farne deserves greater acclaim than he has received up until now. He took the English, specifically Cistercian, tradition of mystical devotion to new heights.

✒ CHAPTER 5

Richard Rolle of Hampole

England's First Great Mystic

Richard Rolle seems to have been born in Thornton Dale near Pickering in north Yorkshire as son of a certain William Rolle, about whom no detailed information is available. He clearly came from a good, though not affluent, family.[1] His birth has usually been dated around the first year of the new century. His parents sent the highly gifted thirteen- or fourteen-year-old to study in Oxford, with financial support from the priest Thomas de Neville, later archdeacon of Durham.[2] For a depiction of Rolle's life we are dependent on the *Officium et miracula*, compiled after his death with the aim of canonization, which, however, was not pursued further after a formal submission made in the late fourteenth century. Some features of the *Officium et miracula* are reminiscent of the literary conventions of hagiography, such as Rolle's allegedly miraculous deeds.[3] Therefore it is often not possible to distinguish between truth and fiction in the account of his life. On the other hand, the "liturgical" language of the *Officium* conveys very well the special quality of Rolle's work. It is therefore reasonable to assume a valid core in the biographical details provided in the *Officium,* which are sometimes confirmed by Rolle's own works. Unfortunately it does not contain more information about his life.

It is doubtful whether he could have acquired all the scholarly and cognitive prerequisites for the exceptional quality of his works in Oxford, where, for instance, it was not easy to acquire a good knowledge of Latin.[4] Rolle, however, had at his disposal an enormous vocabulary with a unique breadth of expression. He must also have had some knowledge of Greek, not noted by scholars hitherto.[5] It would have been difficult for him to acquire such knowledge in Oxford. In theological matters, the Franciscan nominalism of a teacher such as William of Ockham did not appeal to Rolle's specifically mystical disposition. Moreover, his very special interest in music, in the compositions of *ars nova,* to which he alludes using detailed musical terminology, could not really have been satisfied in Oxford. Music was part of the quadrivium, but the musical enthusiasm that is discernible in his *Melos amoris* could hardly have been *inspired* in Oxford; rather, it points to Paris as its source, where he would also have been able to enrich decisively the full range of his spectrum of knowledge.[6]

Like the theological elite, the young Richard was probably drawn to Paris as a place to study. It is not my intention to reopen for discussion the account of his studies at the Sorbonne found in a seventeenth-century Paris compilation.[7] The argumentation with which such studies have been refuted seems tendentious. Scholars have been unwilling to acknowledge that the great English mystic Richard Rolle was exposed to non-English influences—but this is a quite unmedieval way of looking at things. The account actually seems well informed. What motivation might there have been to link Rolle with Paris, and the Sorbonne? The most cogent proof, which has not previously been adduced, lies in his own work. The argument has been put forward that Rolle's learning is not sufficiently comprehensive for a period of study at the Sorbonne to be likely,[8] but this needs to be contradicted most emphatically, because the situation is exactly the reverse. Rolle's learning is enormous. For example, when he doesn't understand a phrase in the Vulgate Psalter, he has recourse to the Greek Septuagint and finds its Greek equivalent.[9] However one interprets the existing testimony, the fact that his name does appear in the ambit of the Sorbonne cannot be attributed to chance or arbitrary whim.

His strict rejection of scholastic theology because of its unending *questiones* ("magnis theologicis infinitis quescionibus implicatis")[10] makes sense only if he had previously become familiar with this kind of study of theology in the Paris center of scholasticism; such rejection presupposes thorough knowledge. Above all, Rolle is probably speaking from personal experience when he describes running after *famous teachers* as a false form of study, and argues instead for the "inner teacher" (*Incendium amoris,* chap. 5, 240). We should also remember that, about a decade and a half prior to Rolle's probable studies in Paris, no less a person than Meister Eckhart had discussed his *Quaestiones* (1–3) there as "philosophical school questions."[11]

The significant first *quaestio* asked "whether being in God and knowing are identical."[12] In Paris, Eckhart gave knowledge precedence over love,[13] but Rolle explicitly rejects this stance and makes love, with which the whole of *Incendium amoris (IA)* is concerned, the sine qua non for knowledge and understanding.[14] Love is for him the only form of knowledge of God to which one may aspire, and Rolle refutes the "new doctrinal opinions" that unsettle the faithful with new "quesciones" and lead to heresy (*IA*, 160). This could be understood as evidence of the continuing impact of Meister Eckhart in Paris, and even as a "sideswipe" at this magister.

Those who are not willing to accept that Rolle spent a period of study in Paris must at least concede that he was familiar with the new philosophical and theological developments in Paris. Cultural transfer between the Continent and Britain took place more rapidly, and at a deeper level, than we can easily imagine.

Without having completed his studies, Rolle decided at eighteen years of age to turn his back on the university. One contributory factor would have been the conviction that the study of scholastic theology was useless and enhanced nothing but human vanity,[15] but disappointment over certain secularizing tendencies within the church would also have hastened his decision.[16] He was repelled by the spread of materialism in some priests, and also in monks,[17] but he must also have had a "conversion experience," of whatever sort, as did other mystics. The *Officium* records (probably correctly) that he was existentially affected by the threat to human life imposed by death and the imminent end of the world.[18]

After his departure, or flight, from Oxford, Richard presumably first returned home. There, out of two of his sister's garments and a rain hood belonging to his father, he fashioned for himself something like a hermit's habit (the *Officium* calls the result a "confusam similitudinem heremite," 24). To us this may seem comic, but Rolle, a "performer" by disposition, took this theatrical gesture very seriously, as an exterior sign of his new goal in life. His sister was horrified, thought he was mad, and took flight. He, however, withdrew to the solitude of nature, the *eremos,* and became a hermit, continuing a specifically English tradition in order to follow his spiritual vocation—a life in poverty.

Through this radical new beginning in his life, any expectations that the totally astonished father may have had for Richard's career in the world were dashed. As the *Officium* recounts, on one occasion he interrupted his solitary retreat in order to take part in a celebration for the vigil of the feast of the Assumption of the Virgin Mary in a church (probably in Pickering), where the wife of the squire John de Dalton, an official of the Earl of Lancaster, was accustomed to pray. In spite of his garb he was recognized by her sons, former fellow students at Oxford. The following day he took an active part in the feast day service, spontaneously donned a surplice, received the blessing of the priest, which he had requested, and delivered a sermon with emotionally stirring rhetoric that rendered the congregation contrite and tearful ("compuncta," *Officium,* 25), a fact of particular significance for the subsequent development of his mysticism. People agreed that they had never heard so gripping a sermon.

It was more than two and a half years later that Rolle had his first profound mystical experience. After John de Dalton, who was a friend of Richard's father, had been convinced of the rightness of Richard's decision to become a hermit, he provided him with lodging and food for a considerable time. Admittedly, Dalton was an avaricious parvenu, who made scant provision for Richard and evidently expected him to make himself useful as preacher, with a quasi-political slant.[19] It was probably during the period when Richard's mysticism was still developing that he felt himself compelled to leave Dalton; the latter lost interest in the not very affable hermit, who was also particularly sensitive to noise.[20] Moreover, Rolle had not refrained entirely from criticism of society; through his benefactor he came into contact with the world of the court and its ways, since the king quite frequently resided in Yorkshire, at no great distance.[21]

Rolle's break with his first benefactor could hardly be avoided, for a specific reason. His emotional balance seems to have been upset by an experience involving a young girl ("iuvencula") in Dalton's household.[22] He tells us that shortly after his conversion the devil appeared at night with the purpose of seducing him, in the shape of a beautiful young woman who had attracted his attention.[23] The name of Jesus and the sign of the cross, however, caused the beautiful figure to disappear. Interestingly, he experienced the same temptation as Bernard of Clairvaux, and Perceval in the so-called *Prose Lancelot,* who would have succumbed to the desire to enter into sexual union with the young woman already lying in his bed, had he not seen the red cross on the pommel of his sword and made the sign of the cross, whereupon the devil's chimera dissolved in smoke.[24] Rolle says that whereas previously he did indeed enjoy the bodily embraces of young women, from this moment on his only love was for Jesus, and the praise of his name.

As it was obviously very difficult for him to decide on total renunciation, a considerable time later he still had to fight vigorously against sexual temptations.[25] It is not enough for him to chastise himself as "lascivus"[26] and admit to having played and joked with girls. He, whose senses are particularly receptive to female beauty and who makes an impression on women—they commend his nice face and nice language (*IA*, 179), but also call him to account because his conduct betrays an interest in them—sees the temptation to sin and the great danger for the spiritual path, from now on, in the charm ("elegancia"),[27] beauty, and voluptuousness ("mollicies") of women. This should not be misinterpreted as misogyny on Rolle's part; it is in line with criticism, typical of the times, of women's fashions.[28]

In this context it is hardly possible to refrain from mentioning that in *Melos amoris* (*MA*) Rolle, unabashed, goes so far as to refer to himself surprisingly as "castratum."[29] Should this be taken literally? In his commentary on the Song of Songs he maintained in self-assured manner that the intensity of his love for God allowed him to linger "without danger" in the midst of beautiful women. But did this self-assurance last? It is important to remember that St. Matthew's Gospel already speaks of many "making themselves eunuchs" for the sake of the kingdom of God (Mt 19:12), a statement that Rolle cites, moreover, in the same context (*MA*, 77). In *IA* women scorn him as impotent; he just looks handsome and can talk well, but has nothing more to offer (179). Origen, of paramount importance as father of the church, was by no means hostile to the body, as has been amply demonstrated, yet he resolved to take this step of castration[30] in order to be free of libidinous urges when he fulfilled his task of imparting spiritual instruction to women. We cannot exclude this possibility in Rolle's case, since he speaks clearly in *MA* of a time when he was *still* physically capable of love ("aptus amori," 105). Now he warns men still in possession of their virility that they should not let the balance of their psyche be disturbed by women's breasts (*MA*, 65).[31]

Although the risk of feminine seduction may have been the immediate reason for Rolle's separation from Dalton, he changed lodging and benefactor several more times, and sometimes his benefactors were women, as is apparent from *IA*. We are not given any detailed information. He considered that he had the right to keep looking until he found external conditions for undisturbed solitude that were suitable for his mystical experience (see, for instance, the beginning of *Judica me* A), but this was not always understood, as we shall see. It would be wrong to picture Rolle as a man totally isolated from society, even if he compares himself to Cain, the restless wanderer, for he gained supportive approval from clergy and lay people, without whom his literary activity would have been inconceivable. Several of Rolle's works presuppose a special interest on the part of educated followers among the clergy,[32] and the hermit Richard was consulted personally by many people seeking counsel, which was a pleasure to him, as he observes in *Judica me*.[33]

We know that in later life Rolle spent some time in the vicinity of Richmond in the Yorkshire Dales. It seems certain that he took on the *cura monialium* of the Cistercian nuns (the Sanctimoniales in the *Officium*) of the convent at Hampole in this region. However, he could not carry out this task for long because he soon died—in September 1349—in Hampole, very probably a victim of the appalling black death epidemic (the *Officium* presumably refers to this with the play on words "mortis *pestis*," 80). One of these nuns, Margaret Kirkeby, who had lived in the convent since 1343 and was on friendly terms with him, had herself enclosed some time later in East Layton near Teesdale, in a cell that was only twelve miles away from his own hermitage. Evidently she followed the example of Richard's form of life, striving for particular sanctity. Toward the end of his life it seems that he felt called to act as her spiritual director. As rule for her new life he wrote the *Form of Living* in epistolary form, and probably his English commentary on the Psalms. Perhaps Margaret was the original recipient of Rolle's English treatise *Ego dormio*.[34] Presumably these texts were further used for the spiritual *cura* of the Cistercian nuns at Hampole. There his remains were buried, and his literary legacy was administered. It is likely that attempts were still being made to achieve Rolle's canonization in the 1380s, through composition of the *Officium*.

Rolle's Path to Literary and Theological Authority

Richard Rolle has too often been misunderstood as an unstable eccentric with a strong desire for an original lifestyle.[35] When he decided on the life of a hermit he did so in full knowledge of the fact that this was a form of life with a rich tradition of its own, and one of the possibilities open to religious. He must therefore be understood in the context described in chapter 1. Seen in this light, he moves within the framework familiar to us from other English and Continental hermits and anchorites, as prescribed in the *Regula heremitarum*,[36] to which we shall return. His "original" qualities should be seen as idiosyncrasies of his highly developed subjectivity.

Furthermore, in order to give Rolle due understanding, it is necessary to start from the fundamental prerequisite he shares with other hermits: absolute devotion to God in total solitude and quietness. For good reason, the verse poem *The Desert of Religion,* for instance, juxtaposes Richard Rolle and Godric of Finchale, although they are separated by two hundred years.[37] The comparison is apt, because in many ways Richard still adheres to twelfth-century spirituality; we recall the crisis in cenobitic monasticism that resulted when the hermit life was institutionalized, and the rivalry that developed between the two, and the opposing points of view in the *St. Trudpert Hohelied* and *Ancrene Wisse*. Rolle, too, finds himself confronted with this unresolved conflict, and has to adopt his own stance. Quite radically, he stresses the absolute superiority of the eremitic life as compared with monasticism for pure *contemplatio,* which inevitably led to tensions. He alludes to some of his conflicts with monks; it requires some energy for him to ward off their attacks and defend the hermit life. He could have had recourse directly to Cassian's *Collationes.*[38] Instead, he refers to great biblical and non-biblical precedents: Job (whom he sees as an anchorite, in accordance with medieval understanding), Jeremiah, Enoch, John the Baptist, and Cuthbert, who, he says, exchanged the position of bishop for that of hermit (*IA,* 181). It is of some interest that the famous Eckhart follower and Dominican Henry Suso, who resembles Rolle in some respects, also felt an "inclination...toward the hermit life,"[39] but this was adamantly rejected by his teacher.

Usually hermits were placed under the patronage of a bishop, who was licensed to bless a life of this sort. But in isolated cases the anchoritic life was chosen without episcopal consent,[40] and this seems to have been the case with Rolle. He indicates unequivocally that in his total commitment to freedom he is not willing to bow down to any authority; he knows that he owes obedience to God alone. He is admirably consistent in his defense of the hermit's life as especially "suitable" for mystical contemplation, and even ventures to contradict the great archbishop Anselm of Canterbury in this regard. As the most self-assured of hermits, Rolle sounds a clarion call for insurgency against the highest clerical authority![41]

For his emphasis on obedience to God alone he could cite the authority not only of the New Testament (Acts 5:29), but also, especially, of the *Regula heremitarum* of the High Middle Ages: "To God alone must the hermit be obedient, because he is abbot, prior and superior of the cloister of his heart."[42] However, anchorites were widely criticized precisely for their refusal to submit to ecclesiastical authority, and this was also the reason why the church was mistrustful of the solitary way of life, as was the *St. Trudpert Hohelied.*[43] The familiar resentments of monks toward male recluses were particularly strong; it was said that the recluses turned out to be troublemakers and displayed "insufficient discipline and...dangerous casualness [*libertas*]." The anchoritic life might be good and holy, but it offered too much freedom and should therefore be avoided. If the enclosed anchorites were criticized on account of their "freedom," how much more so the hermits. They were accused of frequently changing their dwelling place and roaming as vagabonds and *girovagi* through the countryside, in order to discover the best places of entertainment, amusing themselves with girls, as certainly happened from time to time.[44] Such gyrovagues are criticized in the very first chapter of the *Benedict's Rule.*[45] Richard had to defend himself against this criticism in particular, as he recounts in his works (e.g., in *IA*, 183.16). His detractors, who included monks,[46] reproached him for his frequent change of location (as early as *Judica me*). As has rightly been pointed out, there are no indications that Rolle ever got into difficulties with official authorities;[47] but he was assailed by hatred and envy (*MA*, 143). On the other hand, we should not discount the possibility that he sometimes liked to exaggerate his conflicts with society in order to resemble biblical sufferers, especially the elegiac psalmist, for Rolle was evidently one of those who interpreted hostile acts on the part of society as a sign of special election.[48]

Rolle doubtless felt an urge to preach, as is vividly attested by his youthful address on the feast day of the Assumption. But even more powerful was his resolve to lead the life of a hermit, which excluded any activity in society. Evidently, two conflicting tendencies were at work within him. The problem was exacerbated by the need for a preacher to be ordained as a priest. It is therefore very interesting that with his early *Judica me* he composed a pastoral handbook for a priest who was a friend, obliged to preach ex officio, while Rolle himself is not as yet compelled to preach.[49] This leads us to assume that later on he did seek to acquire the official license to preach through ordination (the *Officium* plausibly calls him "Pater...heremita," 77). On the other hand, he probably became aware early on that it was possible to reconcile the conflicting tendencies within him without ordination by means of written communication, by composing sermons to be read, in the special guise of treatises, for which he gained legitimizing authority.[50] This compromise is clearly discernible, for instance, in his commentary on Job, where he equates writing with preaching (206).[51] A preaching intention also explains the "oral-performative" rhetoric of his works, entirely in the Bernardine tradition.[52] In this way he could fulfill his obligation to serve his neighbor without undermining his own *vita contemplativa*. Yet he did not interrupt his still and solitary devotion to God without need ("He who loves more is better than he who preaches more," as is said on one occasion, [*IA*, 205]).

Richard's early development toward contemplative eremitism had several "phases" that he describes in the famous fifteenth chapter of his *IA*. Two years and eight or nine months after his "conversion" he had his key mystical experience, a visionary gaze through the "opened door of heaven," to seek the beloved of his soul so that the two might enter into union. Almost a year later he experienced the intensity of God's love, while meditating in a chapel, as blissful, intense fire. Singing psalms nine months later in the same chapel, he received for the first time the gift of mystical *melos* or *canor*, an unearthly spiritual experience of sound with ineffably sweet "harmony."[53] In prayer directly afterward, he felt this music within himself; it continued without interruption, and he sought to "attune" his thinking and meditating to it.[54] Another four years were to pass before he reached full spiritual maturity.

Because of his visionary sight of heaven he felt called to undertake exegesis of essential biblical texts of the Christian faith, for which he sought to equip himself above all by intensive study of the Bible ("scrutinium," *MA,* 5.7), by perfecting his biblical scholarship ("scientia scripturarum").[55] This had already been pressingly recommended in Grimlaic's *Regula solitariorum.*[56] Rolle's studies enabled him to establish connections between biblical statements from the most diverse books, and to interpret such combinations;[57] in so doing he followed the age-old maxim that the Bible be allowed to be its own interpreter,[58] as implemented especially by Origen, suggested by Augustine (esp. in *De doctrina christiana*) and practiced much later by Bernard of Clairvaux. Rolle also meets the theological requirements imposed on exegetes of the High Middle Ages, as formulated especially by Bonaventure.[59] This, together with his familiarity with the exegetical tradition,[60] provides Rolle with an impressive degree of authority that he deploys in imparting effective spiritual instruction; it was also recognized by the church.[61]

However, he was firmly convinced that the real legitimation of his writing was bestowed upon him by the Holy Ghost; it is God who, as he says, unlocks the sense of a biblical text (its "secrets") to whomsoever he will. God teaches him through inspiration and the grace of mystical "amor," indeed through his entire mystical experience, what he should write ("what I teach I learnt from God, who found me worthy").[62]

Richard Rolle is by no means the only one to justify or legitimize his authority in this way. Rupert of Deutz offers an informative and surprisingly clear twelfth-century parallel; he declares "that God opened his book to him through visions and mystical experiences, and that his privileged access to scripture derives from these occurrences."[63] Rupert is "admitted to God's secrets and legitimated as authentic interpreter of God's scripture";[64] thereupon "interpretation of scripture becomes Rupert's actual task in life,"[65] and his themes are bridal mysticism (with a special commentary on the Song of Songs) and Passion mysticism. As for Rupert, so also for Richard, it is true that he "never ceased to be a biblical commentator"; therefore Moyes rightly concludes that to neglect Rolle's activity as exegete is to ignore what is probably the most important element of his literary activity.[66]

The self-assurance that Rolle displays as author and exegete is easier to understand when one considers that he saw his activity as a *vicarious* one; for he goes so far as to name God as the actual author, and wants to be understood simply as God's acknowledged servant;[67] God has taught him what he writes.[68] The thought of the divine *auctor* causes any claim to individual authorship to fade. It was widely held in the Middle Ages that it is God himself who speaks from a text, above all in the appraisal of women's mystical literature, for this "legitimized" women's literary activity.[69] To argue like this can, of course, be taken both to affirm and to belittle the author's self: on the one hand, Rolle repeatedly presents himself as one chosen to write, with great self-assurance; on the other hand, he retracts by referring to himself as a mere mouthpiece.[70]

At the same time, Rolle combines his exegetical activity with an attempt to present his own person to the reader as exemplum for a life in compliance with God's commands. In a manner difficult for us to comprehend today, he insists on the holiness of his life. It is possible to gain a true understanding of this claim only through taking into account the fact that the hermits defined their decision in favor of a life of constant devotion to God as a singular intention ("singulare propositum"),[71] a concept that includes their "legitimation." Furthermore, it should not be forgotten that the Bible knows the motif of saintliness during life on earth, and indeed the requirement to pursue it; Jesus himself admonishes his disciples: "Be perfect therefore, as your heavenly Father is perfect" (i.e., "saintly," Mt 5:48). Rolle makes an important distinction in his English Psalter: we are saints who are sanctified, while Christ is the sanctifying saint (311). Therefore *theologically* there can be no objection to Rolle on one occasion identifying with the psalmist, and declaring himself sanctified (Ps 86:2: "sanctus").

It would be wrong to derive from all this an ambitious penchant on Rolle's part for ecclesiastical canonization, even if his followers, male and female, sought to promote his canonization after his death. Nonetheless, Rolle displays a low level of "diplomacy" when he adds that he has to state his sanctity in the interests of truth. On other occasions he refrains from self-evaluation of this kind, and consciously no longer ventures to speak of his own sanctity. After all, in the Middle Ages, too, it was highly unusual to class oneself as saintly. It is not surprising that in his writings Richard repeatedly seeks to refute the charge of "arrogancia,"[72] and that during his lifetime he was already misunderstood on this knotty issue; then, as now, he was not given the benefit of a differentiated appraisal of his *sanctitas*. It is of incidental interest that for Rolle the theme of male virginity as prerequisite for sanctity is not of prime relevance. Even if he did not lead a life of sexual continence before his conversion, chastity consistently maintained could have earned him the title of virgin in later life, but this theme is never broached in his writings, as far as I can see.

Rolle's understanding of his role as author cannot compare with the elaborate self-dramatization, already indicative of the modern era, that an early humanist writer such as Petrarch could structure with such subtlety.[73] The most that can be said is that there are incipient traces of it. For in Richard the subjective gestures are still derived entirely from the Bible; appropriate to him is still the "verticality" of the upward gaze, to the grace of God, on which, as he knows, his whole authorial activity depends, and to which he still responds with the *humilitas* expected of him. A Continental parallel may be found in the self-understanding of Henry Suso, who portrays himself in great detail in his own *Vita*. This contains specially commissioned illustrations that display an astonishing point of agreement between the two mystics: each wears, for example, an "IHS" monogram on his breast.[74]

Essential Features of Rolle's Mysticism

For a long time there was a widely held view among Germanists that medieval German mysticism, or, to be more precise, Rhenish mysticism, reached its literary peak in vernacular rather than in Latin works, and that this could be observed most strikingly in Meister Eckhart. However, recent Eckhart research has paid more attention to the Latin works and has recognized their importance more fully. This has even resulted in a reappraisal of Eckhart as philosopher or theologian rather than mystic.[75] Like Meister Eckhart and Henry Suso, Richard Rolle is one of the bilingual authors of the Late Middle Ages; however, in his case it was never possible to conclude that only his *vernacular* texts excelled in quality. As an author with an unmistakable voice of his own, he is encountered above all in his Latin works, while the texts in his mother tongue do not achieve the breathtaking singularity attempted in *MA,* even if they are carefully organized and written in masterly artistic prose.[76] The actual reason why Rolle composed many of his works in Latin may be sought in his intention to carry forward a great tradition of mystical writing.[77]

As we have already seen, for Rolle the solitude and quietness of the *eremos* were the fundamental preconditions for mystical experience, although he does not make a clear distinction between the two forms of life, *vita contemplativa* and *vita activa,* and does little more than hint at the superiority of the contemplative life.[78] Notwithstanding the opinion of Watson and Baker, there is no unambiguous indication that he ever diverged from this position.[79] His paramount aim is expressed in familiar biblical language as being free for God ("soli Deo vacare," alluding to Ps 45:11) or as keeping the Sabbath of the mind ("sabbatizare in mente"),[80] as Aelred had taught, following Augustine.

In line with the well-known anchoritic rules of life (especially Aelred's *De institutione inclusarum*), Rolle gives preference to a sitting posture for meditation and contemplation. To describe his insistence on sitting as strange is wide of the mark, for his purpose is to choose an outer posture that matches the spiritual ("in gestu corporis...figuram...mentis"), and in so doing he anticipates an insight of modern semiotics.[81] This physical posture becomes the signifying type of the contemplative through allegoresis of diverse biblical narratives, especially of the seated Mary listening to the words of Jesus as opposed to the bustling Martha (occasionally Mary is replaced by Rachel, and Martha by Leah);[82] this also enables Rolle to achieve the freedom of "letting go," for he emphasizes in his commentary on Psalm 20 that sitting makes a person more free than running, walking, or standing. Ultimately, God himself is in this state of freedom, and so are the angels and saints. No wonder Rolle longs to be allowed to *sit,* here on earth, among the citizens of heaven.[83] In complementary fashion, the mystical presence of the divinity in man (Rom 8:10) is experienced in concrete form as God "taking his seat" in the soul.[84] So important is this contemplative sitting for Rolle that he abandons it, as he mentions on one occasion, only briefly for a sermon.[85]

Degrees of Mystical Experience and Definitions of "Love"

How does Rolle define the spiritual development of the mystical soul? He considers all the developmental stages customary from the time of Hugh of St. Victor onward, even if not in precise conformity to medieval gradualism (formulated by Guigo II). He begins with *lectio* and ascends via *meditatio* and *oratio* to *contemplatio,*[86] which, however, is frequently not described as such. The *lectio* of affective biblical texts is intended to incite the love of God,[87] which rises in *oratio* to yearning for God and leads to a new state of "consciousness."[88] *Oratio,* in Aelred's language a devout emotion of the soul directed toward God,[89] is also a preparation for *meditatio,* or it may coincide with *meditatio* (or indeed with *contemplatio*) and can even be described as "praise, hymn, spiritual beholding, extasy, admiration" (*laus, ympnus, speculacio, excessus, admiracio*).[90] *Meditatio,* to which "in the degrees of perfection... a firmly established rank" is assigned,[91] is directed especially toward God's incarnation and Passion; for the actual experience of God it has an adjuvant, mediating function;[92] the more devoutly one thinks of the Passion, the more rapidly one is elevated to behold the heavenly world. *Compassio* with the suffering deity is not explicitly demanded of the meditator, unlike in women's mysticism where it has a dominant role. In the best Cistercian tradition, Rolle favors meditations that let the more pleasing sweetness in God be felt most strongly, to which end intense dwelling on the name of Jesus seems especially conducive. Yet his own mystical texts are *explicitly* Christocentric only in part.[93] Nor does he distinguish strictly between *meditatio* and *contemplatio,* or between *oratio* and *meditatio.* For the process of mystical experience, prayer is undoubtedly of paramount importance.[94]

Only through grace can *contemplatio* be experienced in the actual sense of the word as vision. Still it is said, as in Paul's experience of ecstasy, that this earthly *visio* is merely for the moment and imperfect, for to behold God's essence is denied to man on earth; he sees him only "in a mirror, darkly" ("per speculum in enigmate," 1 Cor 13:12).[95] Therefore the wish for death occurs frequently in Rolle. He writes about *contemplatio* at length in his *Emendatio vitae (EV);* he says it is difficult to define, and equates it on one occasion with the *iubilus* with which the soul reacts to divine love, the sight of the heavenly world, and the angels' praises.[96] It is therefore understandable that he sometimes equates *contemplatio* directly with listening to the divine *canor,* and uses terms such as *invisiblis melodia, sonus coelestis, canticum spirituale* as synonyms.[97] At times he distinguishes another kind of *contemplatio,* rather loosely formulated, which incidentally occurs also in Bernard (in his 62nd sermon on the Song of Songs, and in Aelred):[98] *contemplatio* not only as vision of dwellers in heaven and heavenly things, but as direct awareness of divine love. Admittedly, he is often content to be a celestial *civis,* and confines himself therefore to describing how he belongs to the citizens of heaven, the "celicoli" (with recourse to Paul, in Phil 3:20, "But our citizenship is in heaven"); that is to say, he often practices his first form of contemplation. The term *contemplatio* is then usually equated with his *iubilus* response to the divine melody,[99] whereby the *memoria* of the name of Jesus often prompts the *iubilus.*[100] In this process, the experience of the divine therefore occurs for him, as in *Ancrene Wisse,* and later in the *Cloud* author and Hilton, more through the sensual mediality of *feeling* than through seeing.[101]

The great theme of Rolle's writings is love in its twofold manifestation as *caritas ordinata* and *amor sine modo.* Even if man's social relationships demand moderate *caritas ordinata,* yet mystical love of God cannot be regulated by any kind of moderation, as he states, entirely in keeping with Bernard of Clairvaux, other Cistercians, and the great Victorines, and the monk of Farne: "For the measure of love is without restriction, its grades are without grading, its order is without order."[102] "It is expressed through glowing in *calor,* feeling in *dulcor,* and jubilation in *canor.*"[103]

Rolle's English works, destined for female readers, contain only short definitions of love. In *Ego dormio* he offers a simple differentiation into three stages, which may be described, following Lehmann, as ethical, ascetic, and mystical.[104] Most widely known is his threefold division of love according to differing degrees of intensity,[105] *insuperabilis, inseparabilis, singularis,* which are discussed above all in his Latin *Emendatio vitae, and also* in *The Commandment, The Form of Living,* and *Ego dormio.* The love described as *amor insuperabilis* cannot be surpassed by any other stirring of the will; it wards off every temptation and knows only the fear of injuring or angering God. One may speak of the second degree of love, *amor inseparabilis,* when heart, soul, and spirit are directed entirely toward Jesus, especially toward his name.[106] Finally, *amor singularis* is experienced when all joy and consolation come only from God, through incandescent love that is as strong as death; when the loving one wants only what God wants and is prepared to suffer for him, and through this love all thought is transposed into music.[107] Rolle concludes his definition of love by pointing out that many achieve the first degree, very few the second,[108] and hardly any the third, for "the higher the degree of perfection, the fewer its followers" (euer þe more þat þe perfeccioun is, þe fewer folwers hit hath, 17). It has repeatedly been emphasized[109] that this division of mystical love is very close to Richard of St. Victor's fourfold love in his tract *De quattuor gradibus violentae caritatis;* there it is said, much as Rolle states, "Unsurpassable [is love] when it gives way to no other feeling; inseparable when it never ceases to remember [Jesus]; singular when it admits no other."[110] However, for Richard of St. Victor love culminates in the all-surpassing "insatiable love, when man cannot be satisfied."[111] It has become customary to suggest that this fourth degree of insatiable love is absent in Rolle for good reason, since "he already has what he desires."[112] The opinion prevails that Rolle feels his mystical experience to be a permanent state, and it has even been asserted that the hermit Richard Rolle, intent on the "sweet, solitary, enclosed life," eliminated the fourth degree of love because it does not accord with the "'gentle' emphasis in his writings," he himself being heir to the "gentleness of Francis and to the Jesus-devotion of Bernard."[113]

What an extraordinary misunderstanding of the mysticism of Richard Rolle and Bernard, what an idyllic-romantic portrayal of Rolle! *EV,* for one, provides manifold testimony of Rolle's wistful, languishing desire, repeatedly and restlessly seeking its ultimate fulfillment through the deity.[114] Evidently the fact has also been overlooked that in the treatise *Contra amatores mundi* (*CAM*) the "singularis" degree of love has not only been taken out of the triad and praised individually in anticipation of what is to follow,[115] but replaced by the epithet "insaciabilis"[116] borrowed from Richard of St. Victor— a further clear indication that Rolle is indeed familiar with the experience of insatiable love. Thus Rolle's triadic definition of love is not confined to his late texts. Just as important for his mystical understanding of love is the fact that in the conclusion of *CAM* as well as in *EV* he launches into a prose hymn to the "might" of mystical love directed exclusively toward God, in thoroughly Bernardine language: "O vehement, burning, strong, ravishing love, maintaining all of us in servitude and admitting no thought except of you" (*CAM*, 108.254–55); "O love, all-excelling and peerless, how powerful you are, how ineffable! You...compel God to man and draw man to God" (109.288–89).[117] That love through its might can even compel God to enter man ("Deum rapis ad hominem"), we read quite frequently in Cistercian texts and ones influenced by the Cistercians (*Ancrene Wisse* also praised love that can subjugate all).[118] Thus Rolle carries forward the powerful dynamics of the Cistercian view of love, in *CAM* and in *EV.*

Rolle concentrates entirely on the language of love and therefore does not attach great importance to reason on man's ascent toward experience of God. He does observe rather vaguely on one occasion that mystical ecstasy does not occur without involvement of *racio* and *intellectus* (*IA,* 241), and he is familiar with the traditional term *anima rationalis,*[119] and on one occasion grasps the essence of man—in an entirely Augustinian sense—as "substantia rationalis";[120] he talks of the human being as having, in a figurative sense, two eyes, a bodily and a spiritual one.[121] But Rolle offers no clear description of the rational nature of the soul, no precise definition of its rational capabilities, because for him *knowledge* of God and *love* of God are always identical;[122] *cognitio Dei* and *amor Dei* coincide (*IA,* 210; also in Aelred). In this he actually agrees entirely with William of St. Thierry's interpretation of the two inner eyes as yearning love and reason.[123] This is one of the points that make Rolle's mysticism a paradigm for the later English mystics.

Rolle's terms for ecstasy are *extasis* (only in *EV,* 64.72), *excessus mentis* (e.g., *Incendium amoris,* 255; also used by Bernard of Clairvaux), and *raptus* (e.g., *IA,* 253–57), whereby, interestingly, his preferred *raptus* or the verb *rapere* occur with the same frequency as in Bernard.[124] Furthermore, it is remarkable that he distinguishes between *raptus* as ecstatic rapture (as experienced by Paul, transported to the third heaven) and *raptus* as contemplative ecstasy (*IA,* chap. 37). In the first instance, the person does not know whether he was within his body or without. To be distinguished from this is the *raptus* in *contemplatio,* which is caused entirely by the tempestuousness ("uiolencia," *IA,* 255) of love, and is "contrary to nature."[125] He suggests that this ecstasy through contemplative love is to be valued more highly. The mystical experience of God, taking place in *anima, cor, mens* (*IA,* 254) is couched in the language of utmost spiritual-sensual intensity, embodied spirituality.

The *unio* experienced, rarely, and in the highest phase of *contemplation,* presupposes, as Rolle stresses most firmly (e.g., *IA,* 254), intense *purgatio.*[126] Like other mystics, he demands that beginners and advanced practitioners should busy themselves with penance and remorse, for *contemplatio* is associated with the immense labor (*EV,* 66.116) of long-lasting...spiritual exercises (64.75–76). Gertrud of Helfta, whose mystical language matches Rolle in some respects, wrote a whole book about such *Exercitia spiritualia.* In all his major works Rolle addresses the corrective function of conscience. This is very significant, because in so doing he picks up the interpretation of conscience (as does *Ancrene Wisse*) as a decisive element in the personal, responsible relationship of man to God, for which reason conscience was assigned a central Christian function in scholasticism by Thomas Aquinas. For Rolle, the great challenge is the work of ascetic cleansing (*IA,* 208). He even asks God for flagellation, in the face of judgment to come (e.g., *Expositio super novem lectiones mortuorum* 127); he also lies on a hard bed. Thus he himself does the work of penance (weeping and sighing over his own sins, e.g. in *EV,* 64) and asceticism, even if he sometimes relinquishes strict ascetic observance for a short time. At the same time, he does advise his female reader not to overdo her ascetic exercises.

Since Rolle is concerned primarily with spiritual experience at the highest level, *perfectio,* he naturally does not explore the details of penitential practices for their own sake; rather, he stresses, as does Bernard, that the fire of God's love consumes all impurity.[127] However, to conclude from this that penitential exercises had no meaning for him personally, since he was anti-penitential,[128] is entirely unfounded. Such an appraisal could only arise because Rolle does not adopt a rigorist position on the subject. While for Rolle, as for others, *purgatio* is very important as commencement of the mystical path, *illuminatio* is never discussed independently. It is alluded to only by the verb *illuminare* ("impura mens purgetur ac illuminetur"); the redeemed shall contemplate the heavenly citizens with a purified eye of the heart ("purgato cordis oculo," *EV,* 65.86–87).

Scholars have stressed further that certain themes are missing in Rolle's talk of mystical experience. He says hardly anything of God's "harsh withdrawal of vision," which every mystic suffers,[129] of the desolate experience of the absolute remoteness of God, of being thrown back into the dark night of the soul, or of the possibility that temptations may serve as prerequisite for spiritual growth.[130] Even if the opinion is widespread that his mystical experience occurs not *raptim,* but as a permanent condition, and he confirms this at least once,[131] Rolle is actually familiar with the experience of being borne aloft to God for a short time—which may be repeated often. We shall see that Julian of Norwich likewise talks of the constant and lasting indwelling of God in the soul. There is therefore no reason not to rate him a genuine mystic on these grounds. The great Continental mystics are granted the experience of *unio* on the one hand in brief ecstatic moments, but on the other hand they also talk of an experience of *having* God, or adhering to him in oneness of spirit, which implies duration. For Rolle, too, mystical union is not achieved as a matter of course; rather, as we have seen and as he often emphasizes, it requires long, hard, and penitential toil and divine grace.[132] Thus, scholars have not yet noted clearly enough all that is required for a differentiated and just assessment of Rolle's mysticism. One result of this is the frequently reiterated and, on the whole, superficial theological judgment that Richard remained a beginner in mystical spirituality.[133] This verdict is too harsh, or too much of a generalization, and must therefore be dismissed. McGinn is closer to the mark, when he follows Thomas Merton in characterizing him as "a different kind of mystic,"[134] constantly surprising—and therefore engaging.

Rolle's Major Textual Contributions to Medieval Mysticism

It is thanks to the admirable work of Hope Emily Allen that it is possible to speak today of a Rolle canon. There is general agreement that the canon comprises essentially the following texts: *Canticum amoris, Judica me Deus, Super apocalypsim, Incendium amoris, Melos amoris, Expositio super novem lectiones mortuorum, Super canticum canticorum, Contra amatores mundi, Super psalmum vicesimum, Emendatio vitae;* shorter texts: *Super threnos, Super magnificat, Super mulierem fortem, Super orationem dominicam, Super symbolum apostolorum, De Dei misericordia, Seven Gifts of the Holy Spirit;* in addition, the English works, *The Form of Living, The Commandment, Ego dormio,* several poems and *Meditations on the Passion,* and the shorter *The Bee, Ghastly Gladnesse, Desyre and Delit;* and an English and a Latin commentary on the Psalms (English Psalter, Latin Psalter). It is worth noting that for his biblical commentaries Rolle chooses texts that are highly rated for their literary quality as well as their theological significance; he is a great writer, and one with a highly developed sensitivity to literary quality.

Allen's essential criterion for a text's inclusion in the canon was that it should reflect the individuality of his mysticism; but to require that this condition be fulfilled in every controversial case necessarily led to distortion and misjudgment. One important motivation for Rolle's activity as a writer was pastoral-theological instruction, the *cura pastoralis.* Allen, however, started from the unsustainable premise that an author pursues much the same aims in all his works. Furthermore, her criterion of originality must be discarded as foreign to the Middle Ages. Therefore, at several points her Rolle canon is outdated; she did not succeed in determining it once and for all, as she intended.[135] It now seems certain to me that Rolle was the author of the didactic *Prick of Conscience,* very popular in the Middle Ages, as John Lydgate maintains. The evidence will be presented elsewhere in support of a previous article of mine;[136] suffice it here to point out that the correspondences are overwhelming, that the basic theme "conscience," contrary to what Allen says, was an important aspect of the life of faith, and thus occurs frequently in Rolle, too. The Rolle canon seems therefore incomplete without the *Prick of Conscience.* Yet this in no way diminishes the lasting relevance of Allen's monumental work to any scholarly study of Richard Rolle.

It is basically impossible to establish a convincing chronology of Rolle's works, since there are no reliable facts on which to ground such a chronology. When, for example, Rolle defines himself in his own texts as *puer* or *iuvenis,* such descriptions must be used with great caution because of their elasticity and possible semantic interference from theology. Any attempt to establish a chronology is also made more difficult by Rolle's practice of taking phrases and even extended passages from one text and incorporating them into another, which inevitably makes tracing the works' temporal sequence hazardous. Therefore, I deliberately refrain from suggesting a detailed chronology, and use aspects of internal evidence merely for approximate orientation.

One of the few chronological details that have indeed been transmitted from Rolle's life is that his "conversion" coincides with the feast of the Assumption of the Blessed Virgin Mary. This should perhaps be viewed in the context of the specifically Cistercian devotion to Mary.[137] Just as in Cistercian spirituality feelings toward women are sublimated above all in love of Mary, so also we read in *MA* that Rolle had loved Mary ardently as mother of mercy since the days of his youth, and the virginity of Mary, the "pulcherimma...puella" who inflames love in her friends, was for him the model for preservation of his own chastity.

The Early *Canticum amoris*

The *Canticum amoris* is Rolle's only work dedicated to Mary, not counting his commentary on the Magnificat.[138] It had perhaps been preceded by a disappointed youthful love, for his works contain indications of experiences with women. There is good reason to surmise that it stems from the time when Richard as a very young man had to contend most severely with sexual temptations.[139] It is therefore very striking that, rather than attempting to cultivate sublimation, he abandons himself in this "love poem"[140] to frankly unbridled sensuality.

In Rolle's poem she is not the Blessed Virgin, but the most beautiful maiden (*puella*) imaginable. Praise of her unparalleled beauty resounds in the spirit of rhetorical *effictio*, with deliberate echoes of the secular love lyric.[141] This immediately distinguishes Rolle's *Canticum amoris* radically from the usual Marian lyrics of late-medieval England, where Mary is, as it were, "disembodied."[142] Had he wanted to sing a song of praise to Venus, Rolle could not have configured it with greater sensuality. At the same time he applies the language of Cistercian mysticism to his love for Mary.[143] His heart is inflamed by the fire of love for her ("fervor," 104) with the utmost intensity. He experiences ineffable sweetness ("dulcor," 140); but at the same time he already speaks of the music he feels in his heart ("canor," 38, 113), which prompts him—in anticipation of his Christocentric mysticism—to start singing a "canor iubileus" (38). Moreover, his mystical love for Mary is reminiscent of the mystical marriage with the mother of God that occasionally occurs among the Cistercians.

Without question, there is something eccentric in Rolle's love for Mary, breathtakingly original, but theologically not unobjectionable; for in this early *Canticum amoris*[144] his love does not stop short of a kind of mystical *unio* with Mary, when he reveals to us that his heart is intimately joined to her ("in quam cor innexi," 88; see also *IA*, 201, where he speaks in similar terms of his love for Christ, and "innexi" is replaced by "infigi").[145] It is important to remember that he develops his love for Mary in the tradition of Mariological exegesis of the Song of Songs, which indirectly justifies the *sensuality* that he evokes.[146] It should be noted that, unlike in Rolle's *MA* (122.23) and English Marian veneration in general, Mary's intercession for sinful mankind—a major aspect of medieval veneration of Mary—does not feature in *Canticum amoris*.

This astonishing poem does seem to represent a key stage in Rolle's psychological development and theology. It evidently needs to be seen in connection with the account already mentioned of nocturnal temptation by a pretty girl he liked to look at. He wants to resist this temptation, but invoking Mary as *puella* could hardly have saved him from the sensuous longing aroused. When the girl climbed into his bed it was not to Mary that he cried for help, but to the crucified Christ, whom he loved from that moment on (*Super canticum canticorum,* 48, and *Officium,* 37). Thereafter, Mary perceptibly recedes into the background in Rolle's works.[147]

The Biblical Commentary *Super apocalypsim*

Super apocalypsim is an early and very characteristic example of Richard Rolle's great prose texts;[148] it demonstrates the extent to which his mysticism is shaped by the Bible, especially by the New Testament, and is indeed "generated" by scriptural texts. His experience of the door opening into heaven and of celestial vision was evidently preceded by reading texts that included the so-called Revelation of John (of course not written by the apostle, as was occasionally surmised in the Middle Ages). For Richard, the novice hermit, this last book of the Bible had especial relevance, for John was revered not only as Jesus's favorite disciple, who, resting on his breast, experienced *unio* with him (see figure 4), but also as the anchorite on the island of Patmos who beheld the mystery of God's ultimate intention for the world with his visionary gaze into the opened heavens; and he was regarded as the exemplary model, indeed as patron, of the hermits.[149] When Richard Rolle, *sitting* and *writing* in his hermit's cell, comments on John's vision of heaven in the book of Revelation (Rv 3:8 and 4:1), his own "comparable" visionary experience flows into the text, probably shaped in turn to a considerable extent by his *previous reading* of this biblical book. He himself draws attention to the analogy, and to that with the apostle Paul's mystical vision of heaven.[150]

The Revelation of John, with its bold apocalyptic wealth of images, has always made a special impact on receptive dispositions, and continues to do so.[151] In Rolle, too, one senses the particular fascination of this text. It would be very surprising if this were not the case, for the highly sensitive Richard probably read Revelation at a very early age and internalized the images of apocalyptic catastrophe, the fight with the dragon, Christ's victory, and the Last Judgment. These themes arouse great fear—a feature of Revelation that Martin Luther criticized.[152] In a number of Rolle's works one can see the intensity of the impression made on him by this threatening apocalypse. Since, unlike other English mystics male and female, he is convinced that he will live at the end of time, he believes that he has a prophetic calling to prepare his listeners or readers not so much for Christ's second coming as for the impending Last Judgment, and to move them to change their lives.

Chapters 4 and 5 of the book of Revelation must have made a particular impression on him, understandably, because chapter 4 contains the account of seven "uisiones."[153] He gazes into the celestial throne hall, and beholds the lamb that was slaughtered and led God to victory. It has redeemed mankind, but interestingly Rolle does not connect this explicitly in his commentary with the theme of Christ's *atonement* for mankind's sin; rather, he omits the Anselmian theory of satisfaction. Just as the prophet on Patmos receives his visions, so also Richard, afire with love, gazes through the opened door of heaven and receives the celestial gifts proffered.[154] His visionary experience is optically (through the visible "celestes ciues," 148) and acoustically (through *canor*) of equal intensity, and is thus at once *visio spiritualis* and *auditio spiritualis*. That Rolle's mysticism has a visionary dimension is no exception in medieval literature; there is no strict borderline between specifically mystical and visionary texts.[155] What he sees and hears in his vision is actually not entirely novel.

Richard hears Christ, as loving, incarnate God, beseech the soul to open her door to him; this inner door is intended to "correspond" in the Revelation of John to the door of heaven (Rv 3:20). Gazing into heaven, and looking within, together make possible a direct mystical experience, and may even be interchangeable.[156] In mystical language, spatial categories are in any case eliminated, or no longer valid, as the *Cloud* author will expound in detail. Moreover, where God is, in medieval thinking, there also heaven is. If God is in the soul, the soul receives something of the quality of heaven, and even expands into the heaven of angel choirs. Rolle speaks, as we already saw, not only of the *unio* of man with God or Christ, but also, above all, of *contemplatio* as life (*conversatio*) in the celestial city; *contemplatio* and *conversatio in caelo* become one.

Those elevated through *contemplatio* to heaven also enjoy heavenly delight and ineffable, if "unreal," euphony, that flows into them (140), and to which they respond with song (140), meditation, prayer, and jubilation. Rolle's particular experience of *unio* is already described at this point as a unique experience of sound. And there appears here, most strikingly, the Cistercian motif of veneration of the name of Jesus inscribed in the soul, which is explained by the fact that Rolle now comes across it as a major theme from the Revelation of John: "They do not cease to sustain my name in exultation within them, and they sing the joys of eternal love in my ears with ineffable chant" (130; see also the *Comment on the Canticles,* 40.)

Rolle's commentary on Revelation may be assigned a certain programmatic relevance for his entire work. Here we gain insight into the *emergence* of his mystical thought-world and its anchoring in the Bible.[157] I therefore surmise that this tract is his first work of biblical exegesis. That it remained a fragment may be explained by the possibility that he has already said what is important to him in his comments on the first five chapters. Characteristically, he laid aside his pen after interpreting the essence, as he saw it, of the book with seven seals. It was important to him to interpret the sevenfold sealed book as the holy scripture that had to be unsealed by him, Richard Rolle, with the assistance of the divine spirit. He does not concern himself with the events that follow in Revelation; he passes over the appearance of Antichrist and the final arrival of God in the world: "See, the home of God is among mortals" (Rv 21:3). There is no comment, either, on the woman upon the crescent moon, traditionally associated with Mary. The abrupt conclusion of his text also means that there is no statement that Christ will be victorious at the end of time, and will enter powerfully into his dominion.[158] We hear nothing of the "marriage of the lamb," the "new heaven," the "new earth," or the "new Jerusalem." Rolle concentrates on man's experience of God within, and the impending Last Judgment. As in many other mystics, Rolle's kerygmatic proclamation of the love of God also has an anagogical, and ultimately even eschatological, vein, combined with marked characteristics of the sermon.[159]

Another work of Rolle's youth is his commentary on Psalm 43, *Judica me Deus,* which neatly and informatively supplements what has been said so far about the emergence of Rolle's mysticism.[160] Here he is in a sense writing for a dual readership. He wants to clarify for a friend what it means to decide on the life of a hermit. Evidently the friend had suggested that he wanted to tread in Rolle's footsteps; but when the same friend, presumably, has become a priest, Rolle provides him with guidelines for his *cura pastoralis.*[161] This must have been a welcome opportunity for him to contribute to the training of a genuine priest, since he so often has cause to lament the worldliness of members of the priesthood. At the same time, the choice of this psalm shows the extent to which Rolle is dominated by the notion of God as judge—on the one hand, by the conviction that Christian souls will have to account for their deeds, but, on the other hand, by the hope that at the end of time they will be allowed to "sit in judgment" with God. The separate parts of *Judica me* are held together precisely by the different aspects of judging, which also pertain to his understanding of the sermon: the request at the beginning of the psalm to be *granted his just deserts* by God, and separated from the ungodly nation; then the discussion of Jesus's injunction not to judge one's neighbor, and the commandment to know (and judge) oneself; the priest's task of passing judgment on sins, and forgiving them; and finally the eschatological prospect, so essential to Rolle, of the Last Judgment.[162] Here he pays great attention to the examination of conscience as the central task of the priest's care of souls; he does this also in the knowledge that confession and penance as *purgatio* form the fundamental precondition for mystical ascent.

The *Incendium amoris*

The *Officium et miracula* says that *Incendium amoris* is Rolle's first "book"; but, for various reasons, this cannot be the case. *IA* is probably a relatively early work. For instance, Rolle wishes to impart mystagogical advice to a neophyte, which is sufficient indication of his own experience at that time, but he does not yet venture to preach, or compare himself with the saints (*IA,* 185). Watson may be closer to the mark in regarding this text as a work of the middle period, "finished before 1343."[163] Forty-two complete manuscripts have survived, with six fragments and three copies of a Middle English translation by Richard Misyn; nineteen of the "complete" manuscripts contain a shortened version.

This work provides a detailed discussion of Rolle's mystical concept of love, which we have already considered. It is of some interest to observe that Richard, whose human relationships were not always straightforward, also wishes to define love of one's neighbor in his own individual way. He uses the surprising argument that the love of God is already a form of neighborly love, since God is "all in all" (1 Cor 15:28).[164] Furthermore, he adds to his discussion of love the theme of friendship, and the manner in which he refers it back to God suggests that he is looking to Aelred's *De spiritali amicitia* for authority.[165] As Moyes noted, he extends the theme also to friendship between man and woman. Incidentally, Aelred's influence may also be discerned in his understanding of *amor* as a form of (Aelredian) *affectus,* which he regards as resulting from the will, and combines with voluntaristic ethics; that is, what counts for him is not the actual deed, but the will to act. "God, who looks into the heart, rewards the will more than the deed, for works depend on will" (*IA,* 205). Rolle also picks up the theme of man as the child of God (occasionally taken as far as "deification" of the human being), often forgotten in the history of theology. Once the divine original image has been restored, sinful man becomes a son of God through the power of *raptus* (*IA,* 255), a theological tenet we shall meet again in the later English mystical texts.

Overall, *IA* gives a first sample of Rolle's mature mysticism, attesting the importance he attached to picking up a great tradition begun in the twelfth century, and to focusing on interiority, to which the Cistercians had made a significant contribution. For Rolle as for Bernard of Clairvaux, love for the deity incarnate, Jesus—*amor carnalis*—is not the highest goal; rather, it needs to give way to *amor castus,* the pure, unconditional love of the spirit of God (see figure 7). A further "Bernardine" trait in Rolle is his insistence on individual *experience* as the precondition of mystical discourse. As Rolle tells us, the study of holy scripture has taught him that the most sublime love for God consists of *fervor* (or *calor*), *dulcor,* and *canor,* and he adds that he is speaking from his own experience ("hec tria ego *expertus* sum" [emphasis added], *IA,* 185).

Experiencing mystical love as fire is not a feature of Rolle's intensity of experience in particular, but rather a characteristic of Christian (especially medieval) mysticism in general, which has its roots in the Old Testament, and in the New. Repeatedly, from *Ancrene Wisse* onward, the mystics cite Jesus's

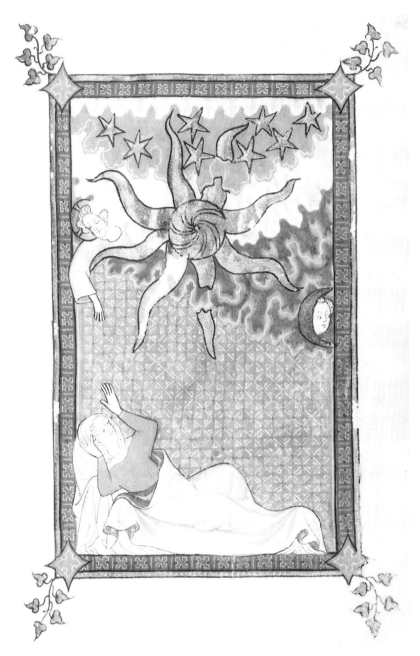

FIGURE 7. God and the loving soul in mystical union, symbolized by a love knot. The Rothschild Canticles (MS 404, fols. 65v–66r). By permission of the Beinecke Rare Book and Manuscript Library, Yale University.

words that he came in order to light a fire. For this glowing intensity, for the divinity's direct address of man with his fiery speech ("eloquium ignitum," *EV*), Rolle is receptive in the extreme; he experiences its transforming *calor.* Hence his pointed utterance "Love is fire" (*IA,* 156); hence also his proposition that the heart of the loving one is transmuted *entirely* into fire, though not into earthly conflagration (185). We should not take amiss Rolle's insistence that he experiences the mystical fire in reality ("uere non imaginarie," 145). Inasmuch as it burns sin and purifies the soul, it also has an ethical corollary.

Dulcor expresses what may be called an adjunct of mystical experience. It is ineffable bliss, "felt, but not grasped as a separate state. [It] seems to be very closely connected with *calor* and *canor,* yet is distinct from them,"[166] that is, *dulcor* is substantially determined *functionally,* since the sensation is occasioned by *calor* or *canor,* or may itself bring about these two (185).

By contrast, the *canor* Rolle heard appears to be the "last and concluding stage of the overall [mystical] experience."[167] This experience was first "mediated" to him by his own singing of psalms, which in a sense prepared him for it. He hears a "mystical resonance . . . that does not issue forth from the singer himself, but is heard 'above' him,"[168] and is therefore of supernatural character. As an element of the mystical meta-language, *canor* cannot take concrete shape in natural language, but can only be alluded to. Yet through grace the mystic is infused with divine music, and he answers, chanting and singing, with an intensity that seems to transmute him entirely into music. His song of praise becomes part of the angels' song, he joins with it in incomparable harmony. It has rightly been pointed out that *canor* is not simply a subjectively perceived process accompanied by self-glorification, "but the revelation of something divine in man,"[169] leading to the desire to glorify God. Of course, *canor* may vary in intensity depending on a person's mental state. In a sense, *dulcor* and *calor* prepare the way for it.[170] But these two can be effective only "according to the substance of the soul, not according to the mystical form of experience." It is not necessary for all three to be experienced simultaneously or to persist for the same length of time, whereby *fervor* is never experienced without *dulcor.*[171]

However, as has already been said, it would be a mistake to believe that this triad represents the full complexity of Rolle's mystical experience. For there is a further essential characteristic of Rolle's mysticism, the feeling of ineffable joy (e.g., *IA,* 158). This can on occasion be increased, as for other mystics, to a state of inebriation (151; *EV,* 59.76), a fact that resulted in the charge leveled against him that he was a befuddled drunkard (*MA,* 131).

The three terms, as already indicated, do not by any means always express just a single, individual experience; rather, one experiential mode is linked with others as adjuncts ("Fervor... et canor mirabilem in anima causant dulcorem," *IA,* 185; *fervor* precedes *dulcor* [*Super Cantica Canticorum,* 4]). Thus, a single state of mind cannot be consistently attributed to a single Rollean work; in other words, the single aspects of the "total mystical experience" cannot be made absolute, nor can they be isolated.[172]

Rolle's three central terms should rather be understood as attempts to capture in words the experience of mystical *unio,* which at bottom requires its own metalanguage. Kurt Ruh has commented aptly on this general problem.[173] He stresses the fact that the mystic is obliged to borrow images from concrete reality in order to render with clarity transcendental experiences for which there is no adequate language, so that his aim must be, with Henry Suso, to drive out images with images.[174] When Ruh defines the character of vivid mystical description as "diaphanous,"[175] he makes an important point, as is especially clear in Rolle's remarkable mystical self-characterization: "id quod sum dulcor ardor et canor sum."[176] This self-portrayal makes sense only when understood in a transparent way, as alluding to another, spiritual reality to which he belongs in entirety. Rolle himself talks of his figurative language as "metaphora" (*IA,* 146), meaning that it is diaphanous. These problematical issues were not always understood even by his contemporaries. It is well known that a certain Carthusian criticized Rolle's imagery for being false and seductive, because too earthly and real, whereupon the hermit Thomas Basset, one of Rolle's pupils, repudiated the accusations.[177]

All three terms, incidentally, are already contained in the Cistercian hymn *Dulcis Iesu memoria,* and combined with other graphic elements they form a kind of joint reference to Bernard of Clairvaux. For Rolle's language bears the stamp of the Cistercians down to the smallest detail, even if insufficient attention has been paid to this hitherto. This is attributable to the fact that it has become customary to characterize his spirituality without further reflection as "affective," which, however, is too superficial and vague a term to convey very much. What is needed is a sharpened awareness of the extent to which Rolle's mysticism takes its orientation from the Cistercians, supplemented by the Victorines, with regard to language. Rolle's texts are interwoven with words, sometimes newly coined formations, that match the honeyed sweetness of the "doctor mellifluus," as Bernard was called in his time, and are formed with the suffix "-fluus" (e.g., "mellifluus ardor," *IA,* 152).[178] They confer on the Cistercian language its distinctive blend of sensual experience and dynamic movement, with many characteristic intransitive verbs. Richard stresses the blissful sweetness of the experience of God almost more powerfully than his Cistercian models. At the same time, his language, like that of Bernard of Clairvaux, is shaped by the Bible;

sometimes whole biblical phrases flow into his text. In order to explain this influence, reference has been made to Bonaventure, and Franciscan spirituality in general.[179] But there is no compelling reason for this because there is such an obvious connection between Rolle's sensual language and that of the Cistercians.

That the text of *IA* contains many repetitions, sometimes verbatim, is a conscious principle of style on which Rolle comments several times, rather than a sign of authorial carelessness. The principle of "frequent repetition" (*crebra iteratio*) is a means of heightening expression—particularly with Bernard of Clairvaux.[180] *IA* is rhetorically composed, with considerable artistry,[181] and enriched by hymnic climaxes, as can also be observed in his great later texts. An effective contribution to the intensity of expression is provided by the use of alliteration, sometimes in cumulative sequences (e.g., 159), which provides a foretaste of *MA*, presumably written later.[182]

However, the book is held together by the central theme of love, which is discussed in one variation after another, functioning once more like a sermon written to be read ("predicandum in scripturis suis," *IA*, 206). As emerges from the informative foreword, and even indirectly from the very title *Incendium*, Rolle wants to "incite" his readers to love (*IA*, 147.241); this is the work's *materia* and *intentio*. In order to describe the structural peculiarity of *IA*, scholars have often had recourse to the term "rhapsodic,"[183] which, however, is lacking in precision. I would prefer to speak of a meandering process of association, for Rolle tries to shed light on the theme of love from one angle after another. It has also rightly been observed that, at times, several chapters are thematically bound together.[184] Thus the first chapters cohere consistently, as do those that form the last part (from chap. 31). Furthermore, a chapter may be devoted to a single subtheme, and seem thoroughly rounded in argumentation (e.g., the first chapter, which comments on "amor ordinatus"). Some single chapters could be independent treatises (e.g., chap. 28). At times Rolle feels the need to launch invectives against the impious. Incidentally, to speak of a cyclical return of the end to the beginning is justified in my opinion only in formal terms,[185] for we do not simply return to the beginning, but reach the end of a spiral ascent. In this, Rolle's recollection of the nightingale's song toward the end of the work plays a part; it has been interpreted hitherto as a covert allusion to John of Howden's great hymn, *Philomena,* and this poem has been considered as "an intermediary between the Cistercian literary milieu of the C12th and Rolle," yet without any cogent reason.[186] There is nothing that Rolle might owe to this hymn in particular that he could not have learned already from *Dulcis Iesu memoria.* His intention is entirely different, and he explains this very clearly. He introduces the Philomena motif by recalling his "conversion," when the wish arose in him to soar to heaven—like the nightingale seeking her partner with enchanting melody. With this beautiful image Rolle takes his leave of the reader, vividly illustrating his mystical "*canor* existence," and his desire to participate in the choir of the singing seraphim; among those who burn with fire, he, with flaming hair ("ignicoma," *IA*, 278), hopes to take his place, singing and praising. Interestingly, this particular nightingale image reveals a parallel between Richard Rolle's rather feminine sensitivity and the mysticism of Mechthild of Hackeborn; for Gertrud of Helfta says of her that she was allowed to add her voice to the great "choral symphony of praise" when Christ "welcomed her as his Philomena."[187]

Commentary on the Song of Songs (*Super canticum canticorum*)

In his *Commentary on the Song of Songs* (*SCC*) it emerges clearly that Richard Rolle bases his mysticism on the theology of the apostle Paul, which he reads as essentially mystical. He adopts Paul's desire to adhere to God, and to experience imminent death in order to be with him (*SCC*, 4). This experience is also suggested with remarkable frequency by dynamic images of melting and flowing, which refer to the soul and God, and were clearly inspired by the graphic and figuratively interpreted language of the Song of Songs. The soul melts, intoxicated by love ("cor in igne amoris divini liquefactum," 69.14–15); God flows into the soul ("deus se totum infundit in animam," 13.25–26). Then comes the magnificent theological notion that God achieves his true greatness only in man: "God becomes great not in himself but in us...because he shows himself at his greatest in that human soul, into which he flows more fully and more perfectly through his grace" (51.10–12, "Deus non in se set [*sic*] in nobis grandescat...quod in illa anima grandissimum se ostendit, in qua plenius et perfeccius se per suam graciam infundit").

As was only to be expected, in his *Commentary* Richard comes particularly close in content and language to Bernard of Clairvaux. One might say that in this particular text Rolle takes the quality of Cistercian language to extremes, adapting the well-known Bernardine statement that the name of Jesus is "in mente mea cantus iubileus, in aure mea sonus celicus, in ore meo dulcor mellifluus" (41.42). The *dulcor* or *dulcedo* granted by God pervades the entire work. There is a cumulation of images representing *dulcor*, as well as *calor* and *canor*. The manifold rays of divine light, to which the Cistercians were especially receptive, shine brightly through this text in particular (e.g., "permeated by the glow of eternal light," 66.21). But Richard's experience is described only by the *totality* of all the figurative phrases.[188] His gaze turns from within himself once more to heaven, where he hears the unending *canor* of the angel choirs. He wants to join in this *symphonia* with his own *iubilus*, which he sings at every possible opportunity (72.1).

The structure of the commentary is more successful than has been suggested.[189] The text is intended as a homiletic exegesis of biblical verses, produced with convincing complexity and compactness.[190] Structural coherence is achieved not so much by the recurrently biblical language[191] as by a network of multiple quotations from the Bible, on entirely Bernardine lines. Sometimes a quotation is supported by a further thematically related one, creating the impression that Rolle was working with a Bible concordance (which already existed in the Middle Ages). In each of the work's two parts, the recurrence of individual quotations increases the structural compactness. In Rolle's *SCC*, more than in any of his other texts, the effects of the medieval tradition of Bible reading as meditative *ruminatio* can be seen very clearly.[192]

It is worth looking closely at the final section. Rolle achieves a positively gripping climax, organized with great subtlety, by contrasting and simultaneously linking in brilliant exegesis the two parts of the canticle's verse "Trahe me post te" and "Curremus in odorem unguentorum tuorum."[193] The frequently evoked image of the soul languishing and *running* to God ("Curremus") is especially significant for the text's overall structure; it is introduced in preparation, long before Rolle embarks on exegesis of this verse. Added to this is the play on the reiterated *seeking*, failing to find, and eventual *finding* of the beloved ("quaesivi—inveni"). It is tempting to say that the theme of the soul's yearning haste in search of God is reflected in the hurried, urgent rhythm of the language. Bernard, too, exploited his linguistic brilliance to make vivid the urgent haste in the Song of Songs' "Curremus" verse (especially in his 23rd sermon). It is not surprising that Rolle's commentary, extant in fourteen manuscripts, exerted great influence; for especially in his exegesis of the verse "Oleum effusum nomen tuum," which was also translated into Middle English and was transmitted separately with the title of *Encomium nominis Iesu*,[194] the language achieves hymnic effects. Here, as elsewhere in the text, Rolle's language reaches a great climax; a multiplicity of rhetorical elements contributes to the intermittently lyrical character of the prose,[195] which can at times turn into rhythmical-ecstatic speech.

Thus, Rolle found a way of interpreting the "Oleum effusum nomen tuum" with great intensity, entirely in the spirit of the Cistercians, the hymn *Dulcis Iesu memoria*,[196] and Bernard's 15th sermon, as also of Anselm's *Meditationes*:

O holy Jesus, pour your oil into our viscera; write your name in our hearts... give us this oil to taste, to love, and to enfold; may this oil refresh us, this oil perfect us, this oil fatten us, this oil delight us. . . . This oil heals the sick, adorns the healed, refreshes the adorned, perfects the refreshed, leads the perfect to heaven, glorifies those led hither, and crowns the glorified with the vestment of immortality.[197]

One may assume that the linking of two successive words, by means of paronomasia and polyptoton, is intended to represent acoustically the onomatopoetic flowing of the oil, for texts were read "audibly" rather than visually ("Oleum egetos [sic for egrotos] sanans, sanatos adornans, ornatos reficiens, refectos perficiens, perfectos ad celum perducens, perductos glorificans, glorificatos immortalitatis stola coronans" [SCC, 40.1–3])

The popularity of Rolle's comments on the "Oleum effusum" verse, singly or in compilations, attests his practice of the cult of the name of Jesus, especially evident in his later works.[198]

There is a further point of interest in this allegorical interpretation of the "Oleum effusum" verse. Within it occurs the description already encountered of Rolle's nocturnal temptation by a girl in whom he thought he recognized the devil in disguise. Since he uses the name of Jesus as apotropaic protection, one may assume that, from this moment on, he intended to direct all his love toward Jesus. Interestingly, Rolle has paved the way in this commentary for his attempt to resist temptation with Jesus's help by stressing Jesus's femininity and motherliness. The reader has been invited to seek salvation at the breasts of Christ, his spiritual mother (33.19–20),[199] until such time as he is ready for solid spiritual food (alluding to Paul, 1 Cor 3:1–2). Rolle is evidently attempting to project the attractiveness of the feminine permanently onto an "androgynous" Christ, and thereby to sublimate it. In so doing, he has recourse not only to the notion of the spiritually nourishing breasts of Christ but also to the traditional identification of Christ with the biblical Sapientia, a tradition that can be traced back to the Sapiential books of the Old Testament (see figure 8). Christ in the "role" of Sapientia relates to Richard like a lover.[200] As a result of this allegoresis, Mary is relegated to the background, even if the flexible medieval technique of exegesis allows Rolle to see in "ubera tua" not the breasts of Jesus, but, fleetingly, those of Mary nursing the baby Jesus (SCC, 38.12–13). Now Rolle clearly distances himself from his youthful Marian mysticism, and directs his affective devotion from this time on solely to Christ himself.[201] In his maturity Richard Rolle will gain new interest in Mary, as embodiment of the spiritually ideal, strong woman, as "mulier fortis" with manly strength, praised as such in the Sapiential Book of Proverbs (Prv 31:10), on which he himself composed a small exegetical commentary.

FIGURE 8. Henry Suso, Christ as the "Ewig Weishait" (Aeterna Sapientia). Herzog August Bibliothek Wolfenbüttel. Cod. Guelf 78.5 Aug 20, fol. 97r. By permission of Herzog August Bibliothek
Wolfenbüttel.

Rolle turns once more to Christ's femininity in his treatise *Contra amatores mundi (CAM)*, where the speaker praises eternal Wisdom as friend and beloved in language that recalls the love lyric once addressed to Mary (she is "formosa," "pulcherrima," "amabilis," "preclara," 68.50).[202] Now Sapientia is the pearl of great price ("preciosa margarita," 68.54), found by the man in the Gospel parable. As Sapientia, Christ not only takes the place of Mary, whom Rolle once revered passionately, but also drives out the "mollicies" (73.37) of sensual female charms. Equating Christ, the mystical beloved, with Sapientia yields additional meaning at a higher level: Rolle alludes to the popular etymology of *sapientia* (from *sapere,* "taste") and, in line with medieval understanding, sees cognition as a sensual process, emphatically an experience that pervades the whole person; he extols total merging with the beloved (70.24). All the senses, external and internal, are now satisfied (88.189–90), and spiritual intoxication is strikingly frequent (e.g., 75.115–17). Certain instances of agreement between this rhetorically ambitious text and Rolle's magnum opus, *Melos amoris,* make it likely that the two were written at about the same time. Since Rolle indicates that he has already written a significant number of texts (80.91), both the treatise *CAM* and *MA* belong to the second half of his creative life. Because of its profound complexity and significance, however, consideration of the great Latin work—*Melos amoris*—will form the conclusion of this chapter.

Commentary on Job (*Expositio super novem lectiones mortuorum*)

Richard Rolle's most widely disseminated biblical commentary is his tract on Job, of which well over forty manuscripts are extant, as well as excerpts.[203] Admittedly, the *Expositio super novem lectiones mortuorum (NL)* does not offer a sequential interpretation of this magnificent Old Testament book, but a commentary on the nine lections for the Office of the Dead, the so-called *Dirige,* consisting in each case of several biblical texts, including one reading from the book of Job. Yet, without doubt, Rolle knew the entire Old Testament book. On one occasion he enters into a serious text-critical discussion as to which of two transmitted readings can claim greater authority.[204] This means that—consciously or unconsciously—he is continuing a tradition of biblical scholarship launched by the English Cistercian Stephen Harding. Since Rolle here refers to himself as a young exegete ("me iuvene"),[205] and also as a "modernus" (2:195.18), who must ask for lenience from his seniors in biblical scholarship, it is likely that *NL* is a relatively early text.

Most of the readings in the Office of the Dead (which was also read on the occasion of the enclosure of a recluse in her cell) were taken from the book of Job; the character of Job was thought in the Middle Ages to prefigure the anchorite, since he was a model of humility and patience in the most dire need and sickness, a man dead to the world, awaiting the Last Judgment in solitude.[206] Gregory the Great's complete exegesis, *Moralia in Iob,* was a "standard" theological text. As the title suggests, it launches a distinctive medieval moral-tropological exegesis, and to this Rolle's reception, if idiosyncratic, is no exception.

Rolle once more had a personal reason to turn his attention to this text. Whereas in *Super apocalypsim* he had been able to identify with John, the eremitical visionary who had retreated to the island of Patmos, now Job offers him a new possibility of identification. He makes a direct connection between this text and his own biography, and tells us that his decision to become a hermit and to fashion his own hermit tunic was taken not too long ago (2:196), to be followed by the painful experience that his friends turned into enemies (2:152). A distasteful erotic encounter in his youth seems to penetrate his consciousness once more; for when he alludes to women he does so with an image of misogynous vexation, seeing them as bees buzzing around men, with honey-sweet mouth and poisonous dorsal sting (2:265). This suggests that a negative experience with a woman could have played a part in Rolle's retreat from the world (in this context the term *meretrix,* "whore" occurs, 2:264.20); but caution is required, since the very same motif was traditional and can be traced back to Theocritus's Nineteenth *Bucolic.* The speaker in Rolle's text appropriates Job's wish to die (2:272) in order to be with Christ as soon as possible, and see him face to face. For Job, as for Richard, life runs its course toward death.

In *NL* we have to do with an eschatological text as well, for imagining death also provokes thoughts of the Last Judgment and personal sinfulness. Here, faced with the vision of assailing demons, snakes, and dragons, he consoles himself with the assurance that his pedagogical text scatters a positive *spiritual* seed for the young who are to receive instruction (2:283). As a medieval reader of *Job,* Rolle not only identifies with Job's exposure to contingent blows of fate; his fear of God's wrath and imminent judgment also increases, and he utters the fearful plea "Do not condemn me!" that is woven into the whole text like a refrain, and reinforced by the request to be spared.

Above all, Rolle takes up Job's great question, "What are human beings?" (Jb 7:17). Most insistently, he answers it in the spirit of *contemptus mundi.* He tries hard to make man's Janus-like existence starkly visible: God, on the one hand, created man in his own image ("ad ymaginem & similitudinem," 2:129);

on the other hand, he made him nugatory, vain, and therefore contingent and frail. Under the influence, especially, of Pope Innocent III's extremely popular text *De miseria condicionis humane*,[207] Rolle degrades man to the depths, although he is made in the image of God, as "a lump of rottenness" (*massa putredinis*, 2:129),[208] and "clod of earth" (*humus*, 2:130). Nothing filthier is imaginable than man born of woman, since he came into existence through her "voluptuousness" (*molli materia*, 2:207). Here there is no longer any question of seeking to reconcile body and soul; instead, a dualistic view of man has gained ground in this early fourteenth-century author. Paradoxically, the experience of unimpaired, pure corporeality is envisaged only in the next world, after the resurrection of the flesh.[209]

By using Job in a homiletic work on the subject of *purgatio*, Rolle is attempting nothing less than to defuse, or reinterpret, the gripping basic problem of this Old Testament text. However, Rolle's reading cannot achieve the aim he has set himself, of grasping the "author's intention" (*intentio auctoris*, 2:262), for under the influence of the Office lections, he takes into consideration only part of the great book of Job, only what can serve the purpose of his intended sermon; the original core of the text is entirely blanked out.

The disturbing basic idea of this great book is that Job quite *undeservedly* undergoes suffering. Since he was an irreproachable, god-fearing man, his proverbial series of misfortunes was bound to present difficulties to the medieval reader, inasmuch as the misfortunes expressly do not result from his sins. Therefore, in Christian readings, his suffering was justified by the notion that every man deserves sorrow and death because of the Augustinian doctrine of original sin. Rolle emphasizes that help comes only through understanding the necessity of suffering, undergone patiently and virtuously, combined with the consoling hope of eternal life. His exegesis is therefore largely of a tropological kind, which means that he uses the *NL* in the "obverse sense" to that intended by the text, theologically speaking, in order to create an interdependence of doing and being done by: since Job's own acts, like those of all men, are corrupted by original sin, he has "deserved" the misfortune that befalls him like everybody else (2:186).

Still more remarkable is the neglect of another theme of this great text. Sorely afflicted by his groundless series of misfortunes, the biblical Job even ventures to contend argumentatively with God. This, of all things, the medieval Rolle has to eliminate from the book of Job. In the Old Testament, Job even dares to inquire into JHWH's omnipotence, the origin of evil, and the existence of all-threatening chaos that has not been entirely subdued by God's creation, and against which JHWH conducts a battle, since he has repelled it but not vanquished it with creation. Evil, symbolized by hippopotamus (Behemoth) and crocodile (Leviathan), which cannot be over-come by man, is not simply ascribed to God, nor does it owe its existence exclusively to man.[210] Rather, Job comes to recognize that the position of man does not allow him to argue with God. It is more fitting for him to fear God, who answers human questions with a mighty storm. The biblical Job does indeed receive an answer, yet not in the hereafter, but, characteristically for the Old Testament, here on earth. How does the answer turn out? God allows Job to experience him, he lets him see his face, and not just hear him; he shows himself to Job *within his innermost self.* The biblical Job enters into the experience of divine reality, "that untransmutable and eternal truth of God...dwelling within man."[211] His vision of God causes him to become a different person. Yet this experience is granted only after his symbolic death, when "he has lost everything that he had and...[only after] his friends have already mourned [for him] as for one who has died."[212]

It is most surprising that in his commentary Rolle totally disregards this experience of God, which is mystical in a manner characteristic of the Old Testament. Rolle might (or perhaps should?) have esteemed Job's vision of God on earth as an exceptional gift of grace, since he insisted repeatedly that it could only be expected in the next world. It must have appealed to him, since he took Job to be a "hermit" (as was customary in the Middle Ages) and one of his own predecessors (*IA,* 182). It also seems strange that in this text Rolle articulates the Pauline theme of "God / Christ in us" only occasionally. Nevertheless, he preserves Job's statement of trust, "I know that my redeemer lives," which is incorrectly rendered in the Vulgate by the assurance of seeing God at some future time in the flesh (2:271; also used, incidentally, by Handel in his *Messiah*). Conforming entirely to medieval understanding, Rolle's comment on Job is: "Here is revealed what true faith the ancient fathers had with regard to the redemption of mankind and the resurrection of the flesh" (2:267). And in a manner not paralleled anywhere else in his works, he proceeds to describe in detail his notion of the resur-rected bodies, that suffer no defects, are of consummate beauty, and have hair like gold (2:271).

Not until the end does Rolle briefly confront the fascinating intellectual depth of the book of Job, when he takes up the challenge to provide his own response to Job's question at the beginning of the ninth lection, the question as to why God drew him from his mother's womb, "Quare de uulua eduxisti me?" (Jb 10:18). Like other mystics before and after him, Rolle finds himself face to face with the problem of theodicy. He is far removed from the kind of solution that Julian of Norwich will undertake; instead he resorts to uncon-ditional praise of God (2:275). For Rolle the actual question of why God created man, if he foresaw his damnation, is simply foolish ("stulta est ques-tio," 2:274–75), because it is not fitting for man to delve into the will of God.

In this commentary Rolle turns his attention to the passage of man from exile to home ("Transimus," 2:244.16–245.4); he sees no hardship in leaving the world, given the frailty of human existence, the threat of travail and danger, and the brevity of life. He does not speak only for himself, but wants to take the listener or reader with him, along the same line of thought, as befits the sermon genre, and in this he is exceptionally successful; treatise and sermon merge with one another.[213] His self-assurance has increased, and he frequently points out the boldness of this or that statement.[214] Moreover, this biblical commentary is in no way undisciplined or disorganized, but maintains thematic continuity between its different parts. The text "lives" through its meditative structure and its persuasive manner of speech, founded on religious experience,[215] marked by the associative inclusion of a large number of verses from the Bible (from Psalms, above all) and also by a convincing rhythm generated by forceful repetitions.[216] Here he consistently puts into practice what he had identified as essential for the purpose of intensifying meaning in his early commentary on Revelation, namely, frequent repetition ("crebra iteratio") as a stylistic principle. He shows sophisticated mastery of further rhetorical devices, and even takes up a position on questions of style (2:262), which underlines indirectly the profound existential *gravitas* of this text.

The Latin Psalter and the Commentary on Psalm 20

At different times Rolle composed a Latin and an English commentary on the Psalms; both are valuable and belong to his characteristic works,[217] even if they are firmly grounded in the patristic tradition. Fundamental qualities of this book of the Bible will be discussed in connection with the English Psalter (EP); a few remarks about the Latin Psalter (LP) must suffice at this point.[218] The LP owes a great deal to the Catena on the Psalms by Peter Lombard, who is one of the few authorities Rolle mentions by name. Furthermore, several scholastic reflections in this work led Allen to surmise that Rolle may have started his LP while still in Paris.[219] Although Rolle reveals himself to be a hermit, and we encounter once more the central aspect of his mysticism, the work also has a pastoral function, which means, among other things, that a lot of space is devoted to the necessity of activating the conscience (conscience being mentioned some forty times).

From the outset, Rolle's interpretation of the Psalms continues a well-established theological tradition, by finding in them prophecies of Christ.

At the same time, the commentary has ecclesiological relevance, because the Psalter, as Rolle specifically recalls, is used in the liturgy more than other biblical writings. In expectation of the second coming of Christ, he distinguishes between the *ecclesia militans* and the eschatological *ecclesia triumphans*. With regard to the form of this Latin commentary, it is interesting to note that it is hardly possible to discern when, or to what extent, Rolle incorporates himself into the first-person speaker of the psalms, who laments the hostility and persecution aroused for the sake of God—that is to say, to what extent Rolle exploits the psalmist as persona in order to make a personal statement of his own.[220]

Since Rolle's Latin writings also include an exegesis of Psalm 20 (21) that has survived in six manuscripts, the question arises as to why he responded to the appeal of this psalm in particular.[221] The very first verse is revealing: "The king shall joy in thy strength, O Lord; and in thy salvation how greatly shall he rejoice!" Rolle discusses true spiritual kingship in detail and distinguishes it from the bad regency of false earthly kings. While Rolle usually avoids taking a direct position on concrete contemporary situations, he clearly implies indirect criticism of the politico-social conditions of his time in his surprising commentary on Psalm 20. Allen rightly pointed out that Rolle will have heard tell of life at the court of his king, Edward II, since Edward often held court in Yorkshire and Rolle lived not far away.[222] So he will have heard of Edward's relationship with his favorite (and reputed lover) Gaveston, and of the adultery of Queen Isabel and Mortimer, and he probably launched into his lament on the moral decadence of kingship for this reason. However, Rolle goes no further than general criticism. The kings, he says, can rule neither themselves nor their subjects, and therefore plunge their people into ruin and come to an infamous end—as did Edward II, who probably met a violent death. And in both his psalters Rolle seems to allude to the outbreak of the war with France in 1337, which was to last one hundred years.[223]

Rolle's main interest, however, is in a *theological* interpretation of kingship. According to his Bible-based exegesis, every king who is able to control himself through love of God is worthy of coronation. A perfect king, on the model of Christ, conquers no less than four kingdoms, as shown in detailed allegoresis: the three kingdoms of the world, the flesh, and the devil, through voluntary poverty, prudent moderation, and patient humility; and finally the kingdom of heaven, through perfect love.[224]

Rolle's Rule of Life: *Emendatio vitae*

This fine rule of life has been taken since H. E. Allen's time to mark the beginning of Rolle's mature late phase and to be his last Latin work,[225] forming a kind of transition to his English writings; for Rolle used the *Emendatio vitae* as the basis for his Middle English rule for recluses, *The Form of Living.* The wide dissemination of the Latin text suggests that it was Rolle's most popular work in the Middle Ages; 108 manuscripts are known so far, along with 16 manuscript translations, the best known of which—as of the *IA*—is by the Carmelite Richard Misyn, who produced his translation in 1434 at the request of a recluse, "Syster Margarete" Heslyngton. The primary intention of this text is mystagogical, since it refers explicitly to a neophyte.[226] Although Rolle bids farewell to this person, he is not forthcoming with autobiographical information,[227] and only in a few places do we hear the voice of a first-person speaker. Rolle does let us know that he has not always been able to devote himself to the highest level of contemplation in utter solitude, because he has sometimes been obliged to preach for the edification of his fellows. Now, too, he does not wish to write only for the neophyte and other contemplatives, but addresses himself rather to lay people engaged in *vita activa* who are also interested in contemplation. Thus the thematic scope goes well beyond mysticism, or, to be more precise, special attention is paid to the first stage of *purgatio,* cleansing, purification from sin ("purificata mentis acie"[228]); we read of compunction, tears, sighs, and immense labors, as in *NL,* whereby conscience now takes on a positively central function (*EV,* 41). It is interesting that among Rolle's readers there are some who practice a *vita mixta,* but that he never refers to this form of spiritual life. What counts, once more, is to be entirely removed from the secular world, in order to achieve absolute freedom.[229] At the same time, he seems to tone down his earlier talk of his own sanctity, implying that he saw it as rather overexuberant;[230] at all events, he warns against striving for perfection in order to gain praise and recognition from society. At the very first glance, *EV* gives the impression of being a kind of summa compiled from all Rolle's earlier Latin texts; he has no qualms about quoting from them directly in several instances. Therefore, a brief commentary on some aspects of the work will suffice. The chapter headings are informative:

> This is a little book on reformation of life or rule of living. It is divided into twelve chapters: chap. 1, on conversion; chap. 2, on contempt of the world; chap. 3, on poverty; chap. 4, on the form of life; chap. 5, on tribulation; chap. 6, on patience; chap. 7, on prayer; chap. 8, on meditation; chap. 9, on reading the Bible; chap. 10, on purity of spirit; chap. 11, on love of God; chap. 12, on contemplation of God.
>
> (Hic est libellus de emendacione uite sive de regula uivendi. Et distinguitur in xii capitulis: primo, de conversione; secundo, de contemptu

mundi; tercio, de paupertate; quarto, de institucione vite; quinto, de tribulacione; sexto, de paciencia; septimo, de oracione; octavo, de meditacione; nono, de leccione; decimo, de puritate mentis; undecimo, de amore dei; duodecimo, de contemplacione Dei.) (*EV,* 33)

In these twelve chapters Rolle demonstrates his capacity for a systematic structuring that is on occasion missing in his works,[231] even if we sometimes discern once again an associative, meandering sequence of thoughts. Evidently, the structural principle of *EV* is *ascent;* Rolle ascends with the reader through the different stages leading to contemplation ("scalam celi scandimus," chap. 11, 62), as represented by the work's twelve chapters. It has been pointed out that the twelve stages may form segments of six or three, whereby each chapter has not only its own subject matter but also an individual style.[232] The last two chapters stand out not least on account of their length. Like the earlier *Ancrene Wisse,* Rolle builds up to an impressive climax in his penultimate chapter, with talk of the mystical love of God rising almost to hymnic levels. Again as in *Ancrene Wisse,* experience of God occurs principally as spiritual *feeling* ("For joy I can scarcely live, and I almost die; because I cannot bear the sweetness of such majesty in my corruptible flesh. For my heart...is turned entirely into fire of love"), and the notion of mystical *raptus* functions as a kind of leitmotif. Furthermore, he asks that consideration be given to the effect that the intensity of this love has on bodily movements, on the "gestum...corporalem" (67.153), so the mystical lover must accept that the world deems him a fool (line 151).

Furthermore, whereas in *NL* the fear of last things occupied a starkly threatening position in the foreground, now, with impressive serenity and calm, Rolle sets out to show a path bypassing fear for those who are *in via.* Now the idea of God as loving father is dominant, and the only remaining grounds for fear lie in the wish to avoid offending God.[233] In keeping with medieval mentality, reassurance is provided by a promise that is forcefully presented *ad oculos* by way of number symbolism; the work makes use of the holy number twelve as a structural principle, determined here in a particular way. Rolle cites the words of Jesus (Mt 19:28), which fascinate him in other tracts as well, whereby on the Day of Judgment the *perfecti* will judge the twelve tribes of Israel (*EV,* 40.54–55). The implicit notion is that Rolle's readers will achieve perfection by faithfully following the twelve chapters of his *EV,* which will "qualify" them in the course of time to sit in judgment on the twelve tribes of Israel. This strikes us initially as a preposterous idea; but it can already be found in *Ancrene Wisse* and derives ultimately from the New Testament, even if, there, the intended meaning is "to be lord over," rather than "to judge."[234] If one leaves aside this specifically medieval conceit, *EV* may be described overall as a major text, characterized by temperate level-headedness, indeed by "the maturity of advancing years."

Richard Rolle's Turn to the Vernacular

The question still needs to be resolved: for whom was Richard Rolle writing? In general, one may say that he primarily addressed religious, but then also all spiritually interested female and male readers. It is not easy to decide what led him to favor the Latin language. He certainly also had female readers in mind. In his *MA* he recalls the "moniales" at one point, that is to say, nuns in need of pastoral care (*MA*, 114.23), and he uses the form of address "vos religiose" (line 16). So he speaks to women, too, in a linguistically challenging Latin text. And on occasion he even addresses girls and young maidens in Latin (e.g., "domiselle," 114.11; "virgines," 79.17), and women who do not wish to relinquish their secular standing (line 13); they should scorn fleshly desires and seek Christ in love. In his Latin *IA* he turns his attention *expressis verbis* to the "uneducated and illiterate" (*rudibus et indoctis*).[235] Margery Kempe acknowledges the influence of this work in particular, but does not mention a single one of Rolle's English texts.

Yet his English works were written primarily for the spiritual care of nuns who were close to him, and for a recluse, and the works were shaped to some degree by this close association with women, as has been recognized. Since the vernacular works convey an impression of serene maturity, they should probably be attributed to Rolle's last years. Now and then, it is possible to see that he also had a wider public in mind. Here the choice of English is motivated exclusively by the fact that the women addressed had little or no knowledge of Latin. For further indications of a sociologically motivated choice of Latin or English, one may look to details of manuscript transmission, but these lead to the ultimately baffling conclusion that it is actually not possible to differentiate clearly between different groups of intended readers for the Latin and vernacular texts.

The English Psalter

Rolle's *EP* is an impressive vernacular commentary. It seems that he wrote both this work and the *Form of Living* for the recluse Margaret Kirkeby. The text is prefaced in one manuscript (MS Laud Misc. 286, Bodleian Library, Oxford) by a verse saying that it was written at Margaret's request. This piece of information is entirely credible, even if it was added many years later.[236]

However, the nuns of Hampole were assuredly also included in his intended audience. As a work of Rolle's mature years, it is far more interesting than his LP. Its popularity in the Middle Ages is impressively attested by the forty surviving manuscripts, which (in part) vary from one another very considerably. Furthermore, Rolle's EP foreshadows the debate over the legitimacy of vernacular Bible translation.[237] Unfortunately there is still no entirely reliable scholarly edition of the text.[238]

In the prologue Rolle declares his purpose to be mystical–contemplative exegesis of the Psalms, such as the Cistercian nuns of Hampole could expect.[239] In the language of the Song of Songs, he insists that the central theme of the Psalms is Christ as bridegroom of the church, or of the individual soul (4).

The Psalter, "the document of a long history of faith and prayer... was integrated into both the Jewish and the Christian Bible as Israel and the Church's book of prayer, lections, and life."[240] It is assigned a vital liturgical function in the church's Office of the Hours.[241] The spiritual significance of the Psalter was acclaimed early on by Evagrius Ponticus, for instance, who said that the singing of psalms calms the passions and brings tranquillity to the body's unsteadiness.[242] Rolle adopts this in his prologue, when he says that the book "distroys noy and angire" (3); prayer bestows in their place—in Cistercian terms—the sweet taste of honey (3). The Psalms' appropriateness for meditation is grounded also in their structure, for they are constructed on the poetic principle of "rhyming" thought and image, and therefore given to *repetition;* that is to say, what is said in one verse is reiterated through "parallelism of members" in a second verse, in varied form (or by antithesis or synthesis).[243] Thus, repetition as a principle of style, already acknowledged by Rolle on several occasions, occurs in the Psalms as a basic element of structure; it is helpful for meditation, and he welcomes it.

In the prologue to his EP, in which he gives rhetorically correct accounts of *materia, intentio,* and *modus tractandi,*[244] Rolle follows a tradition that divides the Psalms into 3 x 50, symbolizing the three most important stages in a Christian's religious life: first, penance (self-knowledge, examination of conscience, *purgatio,* served especially by the seven so-called penitential Psalms; second, life following the divine commandments ("rightwisnes"); third, love and praise, devotion to God, culminating in ultimate union with him ("louynge of endles lyfe," 4). The mystic's life is transformed into musical sound and joy ("in til soun & myrth of heuen," 3). The triple structure basically corresponds to the traditional division of contemplatives into *incipientes, proficientes,* and *perfecti.* Once more, Rolle includes an element of number symbolism, for the allusion to the Christian use of the number three is intentional. However, this should not obscure the fact that the Old Testament Psalter is divided by four recurring doxologies into *five* parts, which are intended to remind the Jewish devotee of the five books of the Torah; for the Jewish faithful, the Psalter is the singer's humbly loving response to the Law.[245] Rolle, however, rightly points out that the Psalter includes hymns that, from the outset, demand of the devout that they conduct themselves in a certain manner, singing God's praises, and, according to Rolle, such praise is sung in a state of yearning love. This, for him, is the essential state.

Rolle justly says of the Psalter: "This boke…is perfeccioun of dyuyne pagyne" (i.e., holy scripture, p. 4). Here he is entirely in agreement with Martin Luther, who greatly valued the book of Psalms, saying that it deserved to be called a little Bible because it contained almost "the entire summa of Holy Scripture."[246] Above all, Rolle is interested in the Psalter as prefiguring the New Testament, as he suggests in the prologue, "for it is a *prophetic* book" of the Old Testament, speaking of the expectation of the Messianic return of David and the "universal kingdom of JHWH,"[247] whereas the New Testament proclaims fulfillment through the anointed Christ. "The Gospels, especially the Passion narrative, present him as the paradigmatic reciter of psalms, who trod his path through life and death…reciting and contemplating the psalms of lamentation and trust, hoping also for the indestructible and redeeming fellowship with God that is expressed in these same psalms."[248] Thus it is not difficult to understand why the Psalter is the Old Testament book most frequently cited in the New Testament.

Rolle is fundamentally saying the same thing when, in medieval mode, he interprets the Psalms in many places according to their "fulfillment" in the New Testament ("that he hight [promised] in the alde testament he fulfils in the new," 395). His LP also had a Christological orientation, as has been shown. When the Psalms sing, as they often do, of the "anointed one," and the Vulgate adopts the Greek loan-word "Christos," Rolle leaves this term untranslated and uses it to designate the Christians' Messiah, thus forging a direct link to the New Testament.[249] A brief mention must suffice at this point of the fact that the motif of the divine name has essential significance in the Psalms; for a name still expresses the essence of the name-bearer. Through his subtle allusion to the Song of Songs, Rolle also creates a link to the Song's praise of the efficacy of the name of the Beloved, and therefore to the cult of the Name of Jesus. And, as has been shown, it is also possible to make a connection with the divine name in the Revelation of John; the three texts supplement one another in this regard, and therefore need to be viewed together.[250]

First, however, Rolle's concern is to translate the Vulgate text with the greatest possible care.[251] As the reader is told in the interesting foreword, he chooses for this purpose not an elaborate, elevated English ("straunge ynglis," 4), but the simplest and most popular style ("lyghtest and comonest," 4), with uncomplicated sentence structure. This shows that he seeks to alter his style from one work to another, and to adjust to his readers' needs. He tries, especially, to match his English translation to the Latin text—even to the extent of producing an aesthetically unambitious interlinear version. This strategy is intended to bring those ignorant of Latin as close as possible to the meaning of the text (with which they have been made familiar by the liturgy, at least in part), even retaining where necessary the original word order. When no English word occurs to him, he follows as closely as possible the intended meaning ("the wit of the worde," 5). Although Latin was not the original language of the Bible, yet he recognized its claim to spiritual authenticity and the authority of tradition, for which reason he had composed his most important works in Latin up to this point, including all the important works of biblical exegesis. The attempt to keep close to the Latin in his EP also sparks off linguistic creativity, for he sometimes uses a rare word or invents a new one—a process typical of the mystics—even if his loan-formations have usually not survived. Some of his formations never took root in English: for example, *susceptor* / "uptaker" (13); *circumdabit* / "sall vmgif" (25); *in opportunitatibus* / "in tydfulnesses" (32); *Dilatasti gressus meos* / "Thou made brade my gatis" (65–66). Sometimes doublets help him to approach the "original" as closely as possible. The consistent earnestness of Rolle's procedure, chosen with the intention of capturing precisely the meaning of the Latin Vulgate version, is appealing in spite of the objections that may be raised. Was he perhaps inspired by the translation technique of Robert Grosseteste? Grosseteste, for one, had reverted to Eriugena's word-for-word method in his translation of the works of Pseudo-Dionysius Areopagita, acknowledging the "venerability of his preaching" (*venustas sui sermonis*) and therefore imitating word-formation, Hellenisms, and peculiarities of style.[252] In this way Grosseteste had introduced the most stringent criteria of scholarly precision,[253] and Rolle followed them in his EP, whether consciously or not. When the meaning is obscure he even compares the Vulgate text with the Septuagint, making use, that is, of the Greek text. His concern for an exact text also again recalls the Cistercian Stephen Harding. Rolle translates this book of the Bible with great precision and, quite deliberately, without any attempt to produce a smooth stylistic effect. He sees the task of exegesis as "decoding" the text; he asks what meaning it conveys ("sygnifyd," 4).[254] However, he does not make do with exegesis of the Vulgate text, but enriches it by adducing supplementary passages from other parts of *sacra pagina,* thereby proving himself once more a biblical scholar as understood by medieval theology, far more so than in his L P. In the E P he refers from time to time to particular authorities.

A medieval author who undertook to comment on the Psalms was bound to follow in the path of Peter Lombard's Catena commentary.[255] Yet in spite of the help that he consciously sought, Rolle achieves something quite his own with this work; he uses Peter Lombard's commentary only where it offers him factual help. It is therefore unjust to describe his E P as an "abbreviated... version of Peter Lombard's standard Psalter commentary (with many characteristic Rollean additions)."[256] Watson's assessment in his Rolle monography is closer to the mark: "My impression is that Rolle is working with Peter Lombard's commentary at his elbow, but is referring to it more than copying it."[257] For one thing, the aim of his vernacular work is quite different from that of Peter Lombard's "classical" text, which is a commentary devoted entirely to explication, written in thoroughly factual language. Rolle also wants to encourage or ensure understanding of the Psalter, but everything is subordinated to his concern for pastoral *cura,* undertaken in order to inflame the love of God ("all my life [I] sall preche the luf of ihu crist," 250). We often encounter a call to penance and a focus on conscience; the image of God once found in man is in need of *reformatio* (17).

That Rolle interprets the Psalms entirely in the spirit of mysticism is made quite clear in the commentary on the very first psalm. For Peter Lombard, clearly following Augustine's fundamental idea,[258] the "blessed man" (*beatus vir*) addressed is exclusively Christ, whereas in Rolle he is the man who loves God.[259] In this text, more than in some others, Rolle articulates the need for unconditional love of God (as understood by Bernard of Clairvaux), and the duty to love one's neighbor and to perform good works. On the other hand, the motif of the boundlessness of the love of God is given rather less emphasis.[260] Nevertheless, it is affirmed that a life pleasing to God will make us similar to God ("we be like til god," 310; approaching the motif of *deificatio*). It is also noted that mystical experience depends on God's grace (232, 463), and that spiritual life absolutely demands the gift of "discretion" (170, 233). Rolle lets his readers feel the intoxication of the "wondirful swetnes of contemplacioun" (129); there is no trace of such ecstasy in Peter Lombard. Furthermore, we often encounter images for the indwelling of God in man, as when it is said in simple, yet powerful, mystical language that when the soul loves God, "then God is at home" (272) with the beloved; this is Rolle's contribution to the theme of God's *homeliness* in man, which later English mysticism will explore with delight.

One of the most famous psalms is undoubtedly Psalm 41 (42), "As a deer longs for flowing streams," where the image of the thirsting hart expresses the yearning for contemplation of God that fills all of man (153). That the Psalms often speak of the vision of God is explained by the fact that God is frequently seen in analogy to the king of the ancient Orient, who grants audience in his throne chamber and therefore lets his face be seen.[261] As a Christian exegete, however, Rolle usually interprets the vision of God as an epiphany that will gain actuality only in the life beyond. (This psalm is therefore sung at the Office of the Dead.) For this very reason, the second coming of Christ (68) is impatiently awaited (247). It is also striking that in his EP, more than in most of his other writings, Rolle calls to mind the church with its ceremonies of blessing and sacraments (so also in the LP). Psalm 21 (22) is famous because it can be read as anticipating the suffering and death of Christ, who himself appropriates on the cross the opening question: "My God, my God, why have you forsaken me?" In his commentary, however, Rolle alludes to the Passion several times with astonishing brevity, as in the rest of the EP and in most of his other works.

The hymnic quality of many psalms is identified by Rolle in his prologue; these hymns resound with the joyful praise of God, with which man gratefully submits to his creator. Martin Buber formulated what is perhaps the best and most apt characterization of the Psalms when he called them the "Book of Praises." Throughout the commentary, the speaker frequently refers to himself as one who loves and praises ("lufer & louer," 83); this is not a matter of two disparate states of mind, or actions, linked with one another by a play on words, by the assonance that both Rolle and Bernard favored; but rather, praise ("lof") is the natural consequence of love ("luf").

For Rolle, the highest form of praising God is music, and especially singing. Singing God's praises is what he actually does, in manifold ways; God's praises must be sung not only in the heart, but also in practical words and works, indeed in the whole conduct of life (Ps 46:6, "synge, that is, to life rightwisly," 334); in other words: a life pleasing to God *is* the best song of praise (334). Therefore, even the musical instruments named in the Psalms can acquire moral significance (334).

The Psalter had already been of outstanding importance to Richard in the days of his youth, when he had his first experience of mystical *canor* after singing psalms. This moved Watson to surmise that the Psalms "induce" *canor* in those who recite them contemplatively; a little later, he asserts that one may learn, through rejoicing in the Psalms, how they "turn into actual, experiential *canor*."[262] But Watson's understanding of the term *canor* is too wide, and actually equates it with contemplation. Rolle, however, uses it to mean the pure unearthly music that can only be experienced as a gift of grace. His experience of *canor* can only be conceived by one who has heard the celestial sound (96). In order to hear it clearly, he must remove himself from terrestrial liturgical music, which can only be an extreme disturbance at this point. When Rolle responds musically to the celestial music, his singing is of course not *canor,* but the exuberant rejoicing of the *iubilus,* which has a long patristic tradition. In Rolle it may combine with the *canor* descending from the transcendental Beyond, to form a "canora iubilacio" (301, 313) as inner, spiritual, ineffable song. In the EP there is rarely a form of words that could be taken to allude to specific *canor.* It does occur, for instance, in Rolle's exegesis of Ps 26:11, where he attests (assuredly with reference to himself) what we already know from his Latin texts, that the soul filled with the love of Christ is elevated to celestial music, and this flows into the soul. In the exegesis of Ps 12:6 he allows the nun to speak, who constantly experiences the name of Jesus as music, and feels herself raised "in the soun of heven" (47), whereupon she joins in praise of God with her song and with her whole life.

It is remarkable that Richard insists several times that the instrumental details found in Psalm 150 should all be understood "spiritually"—in other words, that he stresses the *spiritual* nature of music. While he could never do enough in his earlier writings to describe and laud mystical experience as spiritual *sensuality,* speaking for instance of the heat of *canor,* the whole commentary on the Psalter ends with emphatic repetition of the adjective "gastly" (ghostly). Altogether, the sensuality of the mystical language is somewhat toned down in the EP. If he still speaks "sensually" nonetheless of the experience of God, then, as in the Bernardine tradition, in essence the *calor* aspect predominates—the heat of the mystical fire of love, which is contained also in the Psalm texts, and which the female readers shall come to feel (more strongly than in the LP). And whereas the psalmist often feels within himself *iubilacio,* the affective prerequisite for the *iubilus,* as a manifestation of divine rapture, Rolle regularly makes do with the simple translation "joy" for terms from the semantic field of *iubilus.*[263] It has a powerfully expressive quality, nonetheless, for musical praise is combined with *joy* at the experience of God, which, as we have seen, is an essential characteristic of Rolle's mysticism.

The Form of Living and Ego dormio

The nuns of Hampole were assuredly foremost among the readers of Rolle's further vernacular and epistolary works.[264] A text that helps to forge the link already mentioned between his impressive Latin oeuvre and the English treatises is *The Form of Living (FL),* which consciously harks back to *EV.* Its very title indicates a bridging function with the Latin loanword "form," used here in the sense of conformation, norm, order, rule. The rule is presented as a letter addressed to Margaret Kirkeby, who embarked on the life of a recluse in Layton in 1349, the year of Rolle's death; it can therefore not have been written much earlier.[265] Unfortunately we are given few personal details regarding the addressee.[266] At least we learn that she is a young reader,[267] who can devote herself entirely to contemplation since she evidently has a maidservant. Yet the work is also intended for a wider circle of readers, since the opening of *FL* addresses "euery synful man and womman,"[268] even if, during the course of the text, an individual is often addressed familiarly as "þou." Occasionally Rolle speaks in his own voice.

None of Rolle's other English treatises met with such acclaim as *FL*, which even received a kind of theological authentication through being translated into Latin.[269] Although it is reminiscent of earlier rules for recluses, especially of Aelred's *Institutio inclusarum* and *Ancrene Wisse,* it offers no guidelines for the outer life. Like his predecessors, Rolle warns against every sort of excess in the spiritual-ascetic life (the *ne quid nimis,* "nothing to excess," of *Benedict's Rule*). Moreover it is interesting to observe the extent to which, in *FL,* the catalogue of sins (6), the discussion of penance and comparable themes, and the warning against the destructive power of the tongue recall *Ancrene Wisse.* As in his Latin writings, Rolle extends to his readers the prospect of attaining a state of sanctity; they are even animated to self-sanctification ("folow hit and be holy," 9) and may hope for the coveted coronation as virgin as their reward (5).

It is particularly relevant, in the context of the present study, that the primary recipient of the work was a Cistercian; the close connection with this tradition remains unbroken in *FL* and in the other vernacular texts, and there are specific references to Bernard of Clairvaux (4, 18). The reader's question as to *how* she should love God may at first seem puzzling, but Bernard begins his fundamental work on the love of God (*De diligendo Deo*) with this very question, and *Ancrene Wisse* follows suit.

Rolle gradually builds up to an unparalleled climax when he starts to answer the reader's series of questions on the essence of love. In a sequence of anaphoric sentences beginning "Loue is..." he encircles its mystery with one inspirational definition after another, designating love and God as fire, and evoking the ardor of the human and divine partner. Fire, Richard Rolle's basic mystical experience, characterizes and pervades this text even more than others, and is celebrated in a sequence of gerund constructions. The loving soul, or more precisely her heart, is transformed entirely into fire, as we already read in Rolle's Latin texts ("as hit were al fire," 20). It is admittedly not yet the fire of *unio,* but rather the yearning expectation of death (which is "swetter þan hony," 17), the prerequisite for contemplation of God. On occasion there is indeed a suggestion of *unio,* when in the final climax the contemplatives are promised that they will be ravished in Rolle's "singuler love" ("rauist in loue," 25). The yearning soul, however, is not only fire; if it is God's will, she experiences the unearthly song, the supernatural music (17): "the experience of love *is* supernatural sweetness and song, and . . . God . . . is experienced through music."[270]

The fact should not be overlooked that here, as elsewhere, Rolle, with his gift for empathy, dwells on particular forms of female spirituality, most likely to be expressed in revelations. He says that solitude is the important precondition for the experience of revelation, and cites John as an example, to whom God's mysteries ("pryuetees," 6) were revealed, and were interpreted by Rolle himself in his early commentary on the book of Revelation. In this connection he also speaks of the different kinds and qualities of dreams, a favorite topic in antiquity and in the Middle Ages. Some dreams may be attributed to physiological causes, and others should be interpreted as temptations of the devil, while others again result from prior thought processes; in the fifth kind of dream (as in biblical contexts), a "reuelacioun" of the Holy Spirit occurs, and may follow on from preceding meditative thoughts of Christ or the church (8).[271] Rolle surely did not integrate this identification of revelation and dream into a text addressed primarily to women without good reason. Together with the intense emphasis on joy and the "homeliness" of the soul with God (he is "homelier . . . þan broþer or sustre or any frend," 15), this allusion to divine revelations anticipates Julian of Norwich.

The stylistic level of the text is very well adjusted to its subject matter.[272] For instance, when Rolle comes to discuss the third and highest degree of love in *FL,* the style also reaches its most elevated intensity, with the help of the rhetorical techniques he favored, and employed lavishly in his Latin texts.[273] Here language becomes an "affective tool and . . . [a] sensual medium which can produce intimations of spiritual experience."[274]

A further Rollean text, the epistle *Ego dormio,* is a remarkable prose tract. The information that it was written for a nun of Yedingham makes good sense because the priory of Yedingham was close to a property owned by Rolle's patron, John Dalton.[275] Nevertheless, scholars have regarded this piece of information as erroneous on the grounds that Rolle was evidently writing for a reader who had not yet become a nun, and still needed to be persuaded.[276] I consider this view to be based on a serious misunderstanding. Without doubt, the young woman reader has already been introduced to contemplation, and there is hope that she will reach the height of perfection (26). The text begins with exegesis of the Song of Songs, and, even more astonishingly, Rolle proclaims not much later that he would like to arouse in her the wish to be received by the angels, especially the seraphim. This is an immensely powerful statement, for it articulates the highest mystical aim of Rolle's own love, and this means that the person addressed must have made substantial spiritual progress, and must already have been a nun. The warning against worldly desires has always been taken hitherto as an indication that she was still living in the world, but to assume this neglects the fact that such admonitions could very well be addressed to nuns or enclosed persons, as is clearly attested by the example of the three aristocratic ladies in *Ancrene Wisse,* who are warned even as recluses against worldly temptations (for instance in the form of indecent love-songs or dances), so that one might almost harbor the suspicion that they were able to leave their voluntary "prison" for short periods of time, or for a pilgrimage. Nor does *Ego dormio* exclude the possibility that the reader is no longer a virgin; she is told how she may dedicate herself entirely to God as bride even after the loss of virginity (*Rolle: Prose and Verse,* 29–30). Such provision is also made in the *St. Trudpert Hohelied* and in *Ancrene Wisse.*

We are doubtless taken by surprise at Rolle's suggestion to the "special" nun, to whom he is lovingly inclined, that he will woo Christ as proxy on her behalf (26) and lead her to his bridal bed. This erotically colored language is bound to be baffling, even if it is alluding to the Song of Songs. Needless to say, Richard does not see himself as pander;[277] rather he wants to offer his services for a mystical "marriage" by *preaching* (26). He implies that the nun has already attained the second degree of love ("inseparable love") and will therefore be able to relinquish all thought of worldly ties, every kind of bodily love, including love of parents and family, and to think only of Jesus and his love sacrifice, his suffering; in this, Rolle wishes to assist her especially with two moving poems. The first poem, "My kynge þe watyre grete, and þe blod he swete" (My king wept water and sweated blood),[278] is a Passion meditation moving into prayer, in which the love-yearning of the soul is expressed; it draws on Latin models and on Rolle's own *Incendium amoris.* Even more intense is the effect of the second poem, a love song composed for the reader, "My songe es in seghynge, my lif is in langynge" (My song is in sighing, my life is in longing).[279] The function of both poems is to heighten still further the emotional impact of the prose text into which they are integrated,[280] which marks a clear thematic and stylistic change as compared with his Latin works. The poem that he introduces as a song of sighing resumes important themes from the treatise, describing the love relationship.

These vernacular epistles have been shown to represent high points of late-medieval English prose, not least because of Rolle's use of persuasive rhetoric, tried and tested in his Latin texts. Moreover, Rolle is aiming for enhanced persuasiveness beyond the verbal power of words—suggestive, perhaps even rhapsodic.[281] Most convincing and mature among his vernacular texts is *FL,* through the balance of pastoral and lyrical-hymnic elements and through his skill in generating a lively prose rhythm.[282] For this lyrical prose Rolle could have recourse to, and carry forward, the great flowering of English spiritual-mystical prose embodied in *Þe Wohunge of Ure Lauerd,* the *Talkyng of þe Loue of God,* and *Ancrene Wisse.* However, by venturing on direct transitions at times from prose to lyric, and thus elevating the tone to a higher pitch,[283] he set new standards and transcended the literary achievements of his Latin texts. Gillespie's exemplary and detailed interpretations of the lyrics are particularly helpful.[284] Suffice it therefore here to say that these poems, surveyed as a whole, make manifest Rolle's great understanding of the close connection between rhythmic variation and intensification of states of consciousness, as well as an incantatory skill that may rise to rhapsodical levels. Without doubt, the poems are among the most outstanding lyrics of the English Middle Ages.[285]

The *Meditations on the Passion*

Very probably Rolle also wrote the *Meditations on the Passion* that have survived in two versions, A and B; they contain some Latin passages.[286] If space allowed, it would be possible to show that the poem "Ihesu swet, nowe will I synge"[287] is a transformation of *Meditation B* into a moving and skillful poem on the Passion. In both versions the sufferings of the crucified Christ are described very realistically, in order to convey vividly his love for mankind; the depictions recall Gothic painting, and also the mystery plays. Admittedly, Richard is not an author whose work we would immediately associate with Passion meditations. Some Passion meditations occur in his Latin treatises, but they are kept quite short.[288] Although they are not lacking in forcefulness, the element of the beholder's *compassio* with Christ's suffering on the cross, an important component of the vernacular texts, is almost entirely absent in the Latin works. What we do find is Rolle's penitential response to the events of the Passion: he sees Christ's Passion as compelling grounds for self-chastisement.[289]

In his late vernacular works, written primarily for women, there is a stronger focus on the Passion—deliberately continuing an earlier tradition.[290] Moreover, the fact that an author may change his interests and emphases to a certain degree makes it easier for us to regard the two English *Meditations on the Passion* as the work of Richard Rolle, given that they do contain genuinely Rolle-like qualities.

Although it has been shown that the substantially shorter *Meditation A* has occasional rhythmical merits,[291] *Meditation B* is especially interesting for the present study. In it Rolle achieves something that he does not achieve elsewhere. He carries forward an English tradition of Passion meditation that, as we saw, was started by Aelred of Rievaulx and brought to a vernacular high point in the Wooing Group, still with Cistercian imprint, and in *A Talking of the Love of God*. The Rollean meditations were presumably also written for the nuns entrusted to Rolle's care, so the first-person speaker is again a woman. She is absorbed in calling to mind (*memoria*) the suffering of Christ; but suddenly she sees how this is taking place before her inner eye with gripping immediacy,[292] and she feels an urgent desire to participate directly in what is happening. Particularly remarkable is the close correspondence between this meditation and Aelred. The meditating woman sees Jesus flowing with blood; in utmost sympathy she experiences his suffering and Mary's, and desires to follow him in his torment. Finally, like the speaker in *The Wooing of Our Lord*, she desires to hang with him on the cross. The climax of her bodily articulation of pain is reached when she longs to throw herself to the ground before the cross and bathe in Jesus's blood (p. 81.498–99).[293] There are ample parallels to this in Cistercian book illumination. The white of the eyes of the dying Christ becomes visible (82.543), providing a realistic detail that recalls directly the *Talking of the Love of God*, as we already saw in an earlier context. Furthermore, the frequent appeals to Jesus attest that the *meditatio* is cast in the form of a prayer; thus *meditatio* and *oratio* merge with one another.

It is interesting that in Rolle's vernacular texts, which were directed predominantly toward a female audience, the wounds of Christ are given far greater prominence than in his Latin works. The body of Christ is strewn with wounds as the heavens are with stars, an image followed by a sentence reminiscent of Rolle's Latin texts: a single wound of Jesus is sufficient to drive away the sinner's *clouds* and make his conscience *clear* (74.200–201). The wounds even acquire a dominant function: they are to be the focus of meditation, day and night (74.202–3). Furthermore they are compared to a net, a dovecote, a book written with blood,[294] a meadow full of flowers, and a honeycomb. The soul is to be caught in the net of his wounds and drawn to him, joined to him, and protected against temptation (74; the body of Christ "is given a function"). The foregrounding of the wounds through accumulation of metaphor is undeniably astonishing, but there is no reason to attribute it to rare Franciscan influence, for it is not used to achieve Franciscan heightening of affect. In spite of his insistence on the wounds, Rolle is far removed from the notion so emphatically discussed in the *Stimulus amoris*, that the soul desires to penetrate through the wounds into the heart of Jesus, and unite with him. Quite the opposite, he seems, surprisingly, to shrink from too much bodily closeness and intimacy—as may also be observed in Margery Kempe, who was influenced by him.

The Singularity of Richard Rolle's *Melos amoris*

Richard Rolle's *MA* is one of the most enigmatic and original texts of the entire Middle Ages. It therefore merits a special place in any consideration of his works, while at the same time it requires some familiarity with Rolle. Its "uncontrolled" exuberance, and the ambitious elitist urge to outdo others, prove that Richard must already have gathered considerable experience as a writer.[295] It is not possible to date *MA* precisely, because the text contains contradictory indications of his age. Closer scrutiny reveals that statements prevail presenting him as an aging man who, at the end of the book, not only yearns for death, but also hopes for the second coming of Christ in judgment, with striking recourse to the Revelation of John. It is as if he wanted to create a bridge reaching back to the work of his youth, the commentary *Super apocalypsim*. On several occasions he sets himself apart from his youthful self. On the other hand, there are contradictory utterances that undoubtedly stress Rolle's youthfulness (e.g., "iuvenculus").[296] Moreover, he calls himself inconstant and peripatetic ("de loco ad locum transeo," 11.32), but, then again, sees himself almost as a recluse (179.8–9). These contradictory descriptions could perhaps be explained by surmising that he wrote different parts of *MA* at different times. There is no denying that the text frequently calls to mind other Rollean works. Allen believed that he incorporated passages from *MA* in his later texts. I tend to agree with Watson that he did the reverse, namely that he included parts of preexisting works, especially of his commentary on the Song of Songs, in *MA*.[297] If this assumption is correct, then *MA* should be understood as a kind of summa. Admittedly, he cannot be said to have achieved serene maturity with this ebullient work; yet it seems particularly well suited for a concluding survey of his mysticism and the ambivalences in his personality, because it shows him at the height of his literary productivity.

MA is a highly demanding text, written in "medieval" Latin and with an immense vocabulary, sometimes including Greek words. It has been read in entirety by very few, and has hardly ever been the subject of detailed interpretation.[298] Since it has only survived in ten complete, or nearly complete, manuscripts, it cannot have achieved great popularity in Rolle's time either. As a rule, one outstanding feature of the text, namely its excessive use of alliteration and assonance, is all that has attracted scholarly interest. An overall account of this work with its wealth of surprises is therefore overdue.

MA essentially treats of the boundless love of God (145.27), which the mystic feels in the cloister of his heart (122.16). Even more than in his commentary on the Song of Songs, in *MA* Rolle lets himself be "carried away" and provides a highly affective interpretation of the Song, which once more breathes the spirit of the twelfth century. The tone becomes even more compelling and impatient than in the earlier work. Bernard had already recognized the uncommon boldness in the *Sponsa*'s demand of the lover, "Let him kiss me with the kisses of his mouth!" (Sg 1:2), given the extreme disparity between the love partners. Nevertheless, Bernard of Clairvaux allows the soul to love "self-consciously and unconditionally":[299] "Yearning compels me, not forethought. Do not accuse me of presumption, I beg, since loving feeling [*affectio*] drives me on . . . tempestuous love [*praeceps amor*] does not heed judgment, it cannot be tempered by counsel, reined in by shame, subjected by reason. I beg, I implore, I demand: 'Let him kiss me with the kisses of his mouth!' [Sg 1:2]."[300] Clearly Rolle sees himself, beyond the gender divide, as the *Sponsa* of the Song of Songs, as did the monastic listeners to Bernard's sermons on the Song of Songs.[301] Bernard goes on to explain how love "knows no difference between hearts that love one another perfectly. It does not distinguish between high and low, it not only makes them equal [*pares*], but makes them one [*unum*]."[302] Rolle follows Bernard when he draws attention to the presumptuousness of the soul demanding the kiss of God and lays claim to it himself, and when he defines love as "flaming, vehement, glowing, impetuous, invincible, inseparable, singular, drawing the whole man to himself," a love that binds to itself God, who cannot be grasped (*MA*, 159–60, 160.18–19). It is wrong to suppose that Rolle's "wild" love was inspired by Ovid, however widely read Ovid's works were; the twelfth century—Bernard's era—had seen a parallel intensity develop between secular Ovidian and spiritual Bernardine love.[303] The tempestuousness of mystical love competed with that of secular Ovidian love, and even exceeded it.

The parallel deployment of the mystical and secular language of love makes Rolle's style in *MA* more dynamic than ever before. It is heightened not only by images intended to convey Cistercian flowing of honey, but also by the intensifying use of verbs of movement and compound verbal constructions, and especially by cascades of alliterating phrases, which sometimes seem to enter Rolle's consciousness like automatic writing (71–72). The text is also pervaded by a rousing hymnic tone, intended to express the "canticum novum" of Ps 40:4.

Reading *MA* brings home the urgent need for a definitive answer to a question that research has not by any means clarified: What was Rolle's attitude toward the ineffability of *unio,* often stressed in mysticism, or how did he seek to put it into words?[304] Because Rolle himself does not adopt a clear position on this matter, a certain confusion has become widespread. There is some distortion in the statement that "Rolle's picture of eternal felicity is not one of absorption into God but of communal rejoicing in the heavenly court, and he is thus uninterested in imagery that has to do with the dissolving of the boundaries of identity."[305] The statement is inadequate because Rolle experiences God with all of his spiritual sensuality, as "offered" to him by the "sensuously flowing" language of the Cistercians. He stands so firmly in this tradition of allegoresis of the Song of Songs that he even experiences *unio,* as we have seen, as being imbibed ("ebibere," following Jb 6:4) and as complete liquefaction. Jesus, or God, is the longed-for goal of union (see esp. 141.26–142.14), to be experienced through total transformation into the fire-God's fire, or in transcendental music. Closely related to this, Rolle senses that God descends in his beauty into man,[306] and, above all, he emphatically resumes the Pauline mystical assertion of "God in you and you in God" (17).[307]

For Rolle it is also of paramount importance, as we have seen, that he favors a second definition of contemplation that is directed toward beholding the celestial world, which means that he often lingers in a visionary state, on the threshold of mystical *unio.* He wants to be in heaven, his *patria,* in the present moment, even if this is temporary. To a remarkable degree, he experiences heaven as a "supereelevated" terrestrial city. The richly differentiated vividness of his description of the Beyond comes about partly through the combination of relevant biblical motifs, partly through imaginative neologisms;[308] Rolle experiences heaven, in specifically medieval terms, first in the optically concrete form of a city with architectural features, but then above all in celestial music.

The Experience of Mystical *Unio* through the Medium of Medieval Music

The best description of this kind of contemplation in Rolle is "auditive" vision, as has already been suggested; for mystical experience and talk of such experience are regularly associated with music in his works. His heartfelt wish is to join the angel choirs and to be numbered among the singing and praising citizens of heaven, clothed in exquisite white raiment. When language fails, music speaks, even if it remains inaudible to the outer senses, as is beautifully conveyed by Mechthild of Magdeburg and Hildegard of Bingen.

A particularly close comparison can be made between Rolle's celestial experience of music and Hildegard of Bingen's visions.[309] Yet the fact that *canor* gained such significance for Richard Rolle's spiritual experience is surely grounded in the musical training that he received as part of the quadrivium, while he was studying theology; music mediated one form of knowledge of God.[310] He was familiar with Augustinian music theory, and with that of classical antiquity, handed down by Boethius (*De institutione musicae*). Since his detailed knowledge of music makes itself felt in many different ways in *MA*, it is not possible to make valid comments on the musical element in his mystical language without discussing some of the most important principles of music theory that differ from modern traditions.

In the early and High Middle Ages the ancient theory still prevailed that the entire cosmos (and the human microcosm) is constructed on harmonious proportions of measure and number. This harmony, not in the later sense of "euphony," but rather as "fitting together," is already music, as is expressed most clearly in the music of the spheres. Harmony is understood as a system of three intervals: fourth, fifth, and octave. Boethius mediates antiquity's famous distinction between three kinds of music: *musica mundana* (music of space, harmony of the spheres), *musica humana* (harmony of the soul, relationship between soul and body), and *musica instrumentalis* (music generated by instruments). The first two are not audible; for what was meant here by music is merely the potency of general, numerically fixed regularities in macrocosm and microcosm, space and mankind.[311] Only the *musica instrumentalis* is audible, the music generated by instruments, including the human voice. The entire universe, including the human soul, is organized according to numerical relationships. When man attempts to become aware of them, or experience them, he sets out on the path toward knowledge of God. Augustine's definition of music in his *De musica* set the standard for the Middle Ages: "Musica est scientia bene modulandi"[312]—music is the science of creating the right sound through or with numerical proportions that regulate the movements of melody. Shortly before 1330, coinciding quite closely with Rolle's period of literary productivity, Jacob of Liège expanded the threefold division of music by adding heavenly or divine music ("musica coelestis vel divina") in his *Speculum musicae;* for since music occurs wherever things are related to one another in any way, it is also present in the divine.[313] "The citizens of heaven devote themselves to this music, and its greatest *concordia* and *ordo* occur in the divine persons."[314] "The citizens of heaven see intuitively the organization and proportions of celestial things, that is, without mediation of the senses. It is music without sound, or prior to sound."[315] Here, numerical proportions still dominate the understanding of music. Yet Jacob also knows the *canticum* of the citizens of heaven, in which there is real sound, because they offer God real liturgical praise: "All the citizens of heaven share in this sound, they sing without end. . . . So this *musica coelestis* is on the one hand strictly speculative, without sound, while on the other hand it has the potential, at least, for real sound, as heavenly liturgy and real faith."[316] It is tempting to assume that the ubiquitous presence of heavenly music in Rolle was influenced by Jacob of Liège's new definition of heavenly music.

How can Rolle's understanding of music best be described against this theoretical background? He is still familiar with the idea that music consists of ordered numerical proportions. He is also familiar with Augustine's definition of music as the "scientia bene modulandi." Yet on the frequent occasions when he speaks of *modulari* (*MA,* 140.13, 141.5–6, 144.7–9, etc.), the term, for him, is actually synonymous with *canere* and *canor;*[317] he uses it in a practical sense. The surprising number of terms from musical practice in his works demonstrates the profundity of his knowledge of music.

Music, for Rolle, is preeminently vocal music of heaven, *musica coelestis.* The term used for celestial music as such is *melos,* or, far less frequently, *melum* and *melodia* (occasionally *melodema;* in Rolle, *melodima*). *Melos* signifies a *vocal* sound sequence as melody, which may also be audible on earth under certain circumstances. The music theorist Johannes de Grocheio, who attacked Boethius's triple taxonomy of music circa 1300 and contested the existence of any music of the spheres, expressly conceded that the inaudible angels' song could be experienced through divine "inspiration."[318] Rolle's joyful admission that he experienced the inaudible celestial *canor* (which is, in essence, angels' song), appeared entirely plausible to the medieval reader. In *IA,* for instance, it takes on concrete form as "tinnitus," for Rolle constantly hears it in his ear.[319] More than for any other mystic, as has been shown, music serves to express his mystical experience—which remains *ineffabile* nonetheless (147.3)—through concrete images, and this is particularly the case in *MA.* Thus he can speak of his innermost self as a "little bed of mystical sound" (lectulo contemplativi canoris, 140.21); "mens" is even transformed into "melos" (105.7). At the same time, the *melodia* of *canor* is "dulcis," as many authors point out, and of course the terms *melodia* and *melos* have been linked etymologically to "mel" (honey), because the dulcet tones of the angels' voices give rise to euphony.[320] Augustine had already drawn attention, in early Christianity, to the connection between music and the emotions.[321] It is of some interest that a twelfth-century two-part song from the Orkney Islands has survived with parallel voices at intervals of a third; later English music also has a predilection for thirds, and I would like to maintain that this underlines the music's intended *dulcedo*.[322] Under no circumstances can it be right to ascribe to celestial music a "violent, passionate, continuous, audacious nature," as Watson does.[323]

The Orkney Island composition also displays the organum form specific to the High Middle Ages. The term "organum," which is part of Rolle's musical terminology, has several meanings, including tool, instrument, guideline, rule, and above all *polyphonic singing,* though never the musical instrument "organ." Rolle often uses the verb *organizare* with reference to the practical performance of music. The main center of the practice of organum singing was Notre Dame in Paris.[324] In this connection, *organizare* designates organal *singing,* or more precisely "singing in the manner of instruments" (for Rolle, often, in the manner of the cithara). In Rolle's day this was usually two-part singing, in which the tenor of Gregorian chant was accompanied by a second voice ("vox organalis"). The tenor can be a bourdon-like ground interrupted by rests. Rolle refers to the "tenor" when he proclaims that, spiritually, he is himself his new ground melody, transformed from mourning into joy: "I dare to claim the tenor part: my mourning has become the cithara, and my weeping voice the organum" (*MA,* 74.2–3; Audeo asserere talem tenorem: conversus est luctus meus in citharam et vox flebilis in organum). When Rolle expresses his mystical experience "musically," he repeatedly returns to the concept of the organum. It is above all the angels who sing the organum (17.4; 7.12). He also knows the further term *neuma,* referring presumably to the alleluia *jubilus.*[325] The angels often appear with musical instruments in medieval iconography, but this does not indicate instrumental accompaniment, for the Middle Ages distinguished, as already mentioned, between "liturgical-sacral, vocal music, which is proclamation of the Word, and profane and instrumental music, not tied to words, which is itself, and purely musical."[326] This understanding predominates in Rolle (see figure 9). His most heartfelt wish is to be accepted among the heavenly *cives,* because he wants to take part in their angelic choral song ("choros concinencium," 28), add his voice to their organum ("in choro quo concinimus organizantes odas," 144.22), and join in their harmony ("celica… simphonia," 33.13).

He attaches the greatest importance to the seraphim, because, like the monk of Farne, he wants to be assimilated to them; their fire of love burns most brightly ("ut Seraphin assimilentur," 36.5).[327] According to the *Hierarchia caelestis* of Pseudo-Dionysius Areopagita, the seraphim are at the apex of the nine-choir hierarchy, followed by the cherubim. Being accepted as participant in the angel choirs and their liturgy gives reality, in anticipation, to what is foretold in the Revelation of John: "Cantabant sancti canticum novum *ante* sedem Dei," which he quotes in *MA* (drawing attention to

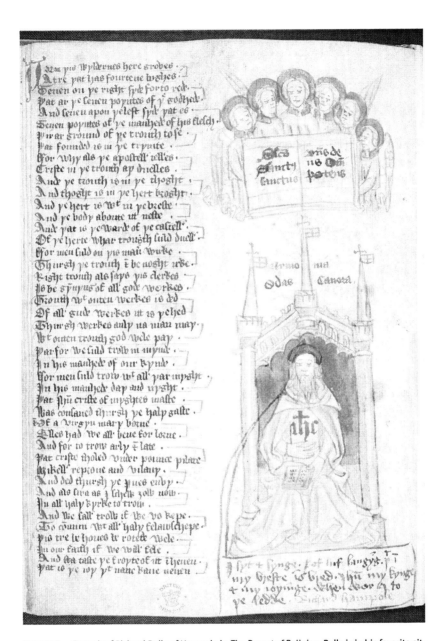

FIGURE 9. Portrait of Richard Rolle of Hampole in *The Desert of Religion*. Rolle is in his favorite sitting position and singing from his English lyrics; the Latin musical terms are reminders of the *Melos amoris,* and the central turret points fingerlike to the celestial choir Rolle wishes to join. British Library, MS Add 37049 (ca. 1460–70), fol. 52v. By permission of The British Library Board.

the past tense).[328] Theologically speaking, Rolle implements in an "outra-geously" radical manner the Pauline statement of man's citizenship of heaven (Phil 3:20).

It seems to me that, in *MA,* Rolle even made a very bold attempt to sug-gest an organum composition by linguistic means, and strove, drawing on late-medieval polyphony, to apply a *musical* structural principle to language. Rudolf Flotzinger drew my attention to a passage in Gerald of Wales that describes a two-part organum as follows: "In singing they employ harmony, but with differences of tone produced by two different voices and variations in modulation only, with one [voice] murmuring below, and another caressing and captivating [the ear] above." Giraldus Cambrensis is describing a bour-don chant, in which a deep voice sustains a root tone, interrupted by rests. Richard Rolle may have recognized the possibility of reproducing precisely, through alliteration, the two voices of the bourdon as described by Giraldus. The alliterating sounds are separated by the body of the word, and therefore always follow a "rest," thus producing or imitating the bourdon ground. The alliterating sounds can also be understood as the "tenor," while the remaining morphological components of the word form the upper voice, as it were, the *vox organalis.* However, this should not be understood as an attempt, on Rolle's part, to imitate mimetically mystical *canor,* or bring it down to earth, which is totally impossible in his view. His linguistic "analogy" aims only to *refer to* the celestial world ("per corporalia intelligi docens spiritualia," 139.13–14; Ps 150:3–5). Therefore I am unable to follow Watson's statement that "the text [of *Melos amoris*] is *canor,*"[329] or, put another way, "*Melos amoris* aims to represent *canor* verbally."[330] The alliterative, or "organal," style of *MA* does not by any means represent *canor* itself, and is not incantatory, though it may at times impel the reader toward a rhapsodic, ecstatic state.

This leads us to view quite differently the extreme abundance of allitera-tion in *MA,* which has regularly aroused great interest. Opinions differ as to how this should be assessed, especially with regard to the possible influence of native poetry or prose,[331] and association with the West Midland revival of the alliterative long line in late-medieval England.[332] Is the form of *MA* a Latin version of alliterative English prose, to be scanned as verse, as has often been suggested? Such a view can scarcely be sustained, for the reader or (medieval) listener does not perceive alliterative long lines. Nor does the interesting "Carmen prosaicum"[333] provide useful evidence on this point. It is the work of an anonymous reviser, who compiled a prose poem from a selection of pithy extracts from *MA;* yet whether the intention was to generate an alliterative verse pattern, as has been claimed, is questionable.[334] Be that as it may, it cannot be the effect that Rolle set out to achieve in *MA.*

His intention was to create an impression of continuously flowing euphony, more powerful than audible segments with two or four stresses. For Rolle, alliteration has a different function, and that is the crucial factor.

Richard Rolle is not the only one to believe that he hears unearthly music produced by angels. As has already been mentioned, Johannes de Grocheio spoke of this possibility. On the Continent, something similar was experienced by Douceline de Digne, who founded a beguine settlement in Provence in the mid-thirteenth century. She hears singing, but "not of this world, for no-one could distinguish the tones precisely, or understand the words."[335] The experience of heavenly *canor* does not mean participation in mystical *unio* with God himself, even if one might occasionally suspect that it should be equated with *unio*. Rather, Rolle seems to regard *canor* characteristically as a liminal experience, for his *contemplatio* embraces the entire celestial world.

It would be quite wrong to see in Rolle nothing more than a passive mystic and recipient of *canor*. He, for his part, responds with the ecstatic *iubilus,* a very early liturgical term indicating the onset of the irrational. It is a wordless "crying and singing in syllables of joy"[336] in the spirit of Augustine, for whom its justification lay in "acknowledging that one cannot express with words what one sings in one's heart.... The *iubilus* is a sound indicating that the heart is overflowing with what cannot be said...so that the heart may rejoice without words, and the infinite abundance of joys is not constrained by syllables."[337] And occasionally Rolle lets us know that, for him, *canor* and *iubilus* may merge into one another (e.g., in the phrase "canora iubilacio").

Rolle is known to have avoided church liturgy with its chants, because it was not helpful to his experience of celestial music. We may recall Origen's statement: "Singing of psalms is fitting for mankind, but the singing of hymns is fitting for the angels and for those who have the essence of angels."[338] It is therefore not surprising that Rolle, who is focused entirely on angel music, is fascinated especially by the genre of the hymn, and the Psalter contains hymns. The recurrence of Greek specialist terms also suggests that he even had a certain knowledge of the Byzantine hymn tradition.[339] He describes—interestingly, in the Latinized Greek terms current at the time—the activity of the music-making angels, singing in several parts, as "organizantes odas" (144.22); on one occasion we even find the more specialized lyric term "palinodias" (142–43). When he goes so far as to speak of hearing the angels' "odas olimpi" (135.28), we once more encounter his great boldness; he is alluding in a mystical context to the pagan Greeks, from whom so many musical terms are derived. Hymnic praise of love is in any case the appropriate tone for Rolle. In response to this, a new hymn in his honor is composed in *Officium et miracula,* beginning with the exhortation "Let us sing odes of praise" (Laudis odas decantemus).[340] According to Chrysostomus the cithara is a symbol of love, and Richard Rolle follows this interpretation when he calls God himself his "cithara," and wishes to suggest in so doing that it is the "love of God" that "causes sweet melodies to sound,"[341] and impels him dynamically to "gyrate" around his God ("girum gerens in Iesu generosum," 43.4–5), like the choirs of angels in Dante's *Commedia.*[342] Although Rolle does not have the outstanding figurative and poetic creativity of a poet such as Dante, his acoustic–optical realization of the celestial musical world is impressive, and attests particular imaginative power.

In order to complete the description of the mystical experience of *canor* it is necessary to add that Rolle attributes to it the utmost *clarity* (177.17–18), a quality that pervades his mysticism throughout, and that may ultimately be traced back to the transfiguration; other mystics, male and female, believed they experienced it, too. Thomas Aquinas stressed the prefiguring character of the transfiguration, indicative of future glory.[343] Of course, God himself remains concealed behind a cloud during the transfiguration; only his voice is heard. Jesus's transfiguration occurs on a high mountain, traditionally identified as Mount Tabor, which he has climbed with Peter, James, and John, as the synoptic Gospels all recount (Mk 9:2–9; Mt 17:1–9; Lk 9:28–36).

Richard Rolle's *Melos amoris* as Summa of His Life's Work

MA is directed so much toward the *perfecti,* and is permeated to such an extent by the celestial world and heavenly music, that one would hardly expect Richard Rolle to turn his attention as frequently as he does, in this work, to the godless and their terrible fate in hell, or that he would warn the reader most urgently against perversion of the divine will, or that chaos would be a frequently recurring motif. He tries to move the indifferent or godless, whom this chaos threatens, to change their ways: "We have written our book...so that they shall be converted, live anew, and be saved" (184.32–33). As has already been suggested, this text bears the stamp of the apocalyptic admonishments of the Revelation of John even more than Rolle's other works, including his early commentary on the Apocalypse. The reader is now made aware of these threats most compellingly by a large arsenal of images and themes. Rolle himself is evidently engulfed by fear of this event. Yet for the saved there is the prospect of witnessing the punishment of the *reprobi.* Furthermore, as previously mentioned, medieval readers were particularly stirred by the assurance, found several times in the New Testament, that the redeemed souls will sit with God in judgment over the godless, *wearing a crown,* the crown promised in the Letter of James and gained after suffering martyrdom.[344] Detailed instructions for *purgatio* practice are not given to those striving for perfection, because they have already left this stage behind them. Yet Rolle insists that ascetic practice without complete devotion does not achieve anything, nor does faith without works, following the Letter of James.

At the end of this text, which is so rich in themes and ideas, Rolle notes with satisfaction that he has achieved his dual aim of confronting the reader with both love and hate ("Amorem et odium utrumque *ostendi,*" 191.29). At the beginning and at the end of the book, its intention is clearly stated: to *attest* to others the divine love that he himself has experienced (*ostendens,* 3.5, 191.29), thereby contributing to their salvation. Thus in this text, as in others, he sees his writing as a form of *preaching.*

Did Rolle succeed in giving his exuberant *MA* a convincing structure? As with other Rolle texts, the structure has been much criticized, and associated with the "untidy mind" imputed to him;[345] or with his "natural impulsiveness" and "erratic temperament,"[346] but not all scholars agree.[347] The editor of *MA,* at least, was willing to understand the form of the text in the light of its genre, namely the "postil," or biblical commentary. In it, Rolle refers to himself as "probatus postillator" (69.1), and his *IA* and commentary on the Song of Songs also show evidence of this influence. *MA* consists of a series of postils commenting on biblical texts that are given coherence by the crusty, eccentric personality of the hermit Richard Rolle and the constant recurrence of his favorite themes.[348] The work's fifty-eight chapters often begin with a Bible verse, which, however, is often not actually interpreted, but taken rather as a cue for free association. It is therefore not surprising that some chapters begin without a Bible verse. Since exegesis of a quoted text may extend over several chapters, the impression sometimes arises that he wants to evade the postil genre and write the usual kind of tract. He sometimes links the quotations with verses from the Psalms, which strengthens the structure.[349]

F. Vandenbroucke, in particular, has tried to show that *MA* is not merely a series of ecstatic outpourings mixed with pastoral admonitions, but that it develops a line of thought. Of prime importance is his observation that Rolle "passe d'un thème à l'autre avec une aisance extrême tout comme d'une image ou d'un vocabulaire à l'autre," which reminds Vandenbroucke of modern cinematic techniques.[350] It is indeed possible to speak of frequent abrupt "cuts," which occur without any transition, as one range of images succeeds another. Even if Vandenbroucke's attempt to discern an overall plan that would manifest spiritual development is not entirely convincing, yet the sequence of postils is by no means arbitrary. This is apparent in the very first chapters, which return time and again to the great boldness of the *sponsa*, with which she ventures to implore God "O that he may kiss me with the kiss of his mouth." A comparable thematic link is created by the transformation of the heart into music, or fire. Especially clear is the cohesion of chapters 47–49, which focus on the singularity of eremitical solitude as precondition for the most intense mystical experience, whereby Rolle deliberately creates a transition to the theme of ordered love (155). And in *MA* as elsewhere, the frequent repetition of themes and motifs has a style-constituting function. Vandenbroucke is, to a certain extent, justified in seeing "réelle spontanéité" in this text.[351] Nevertheless, this is outweighed by the impression that Rolle wanted to present the treasure of his themes in appropriately sumptuous vesture ("sub ueste preciosa," *MA*, 146.7–9), in accordance with the principle of correspondence between form and content previously established in his commentary on Job (*Expositio*, 2:173.15).

It must also be said that at times Richard the hermit appears as the author personally onstage with quite deliberate theatricality, especially in *MA*, as in the wish-fulfilling "among the powers in paradise he will wear a most beautiful garment...woven with precious gems" (146.7–9). Recent research has reproached him, as already indicated in this chapter, for directing his "self-fashioning" toward egocentric self-sanctification, and even self-canonization. But what should be made of this? Did he scorn the Christian precept of humility? Once more we should recall that medieval religious decided on their strict, exclusive form of life in order to be *perfecti*, or even *perfectissimi*, that they were regarded as saints, and that Christians were challenged by Jesus himself to be perfect, or "holy." Bernard of Clairvaux was aware that the miracles he performed confirmed his sanctity.[352] Rolle's mystical experience did entitle him to the predicate of sanctity, but its self-referential use was not customary, because it simply cannot be reconciled with the precept of humility. Time and again he sees himself predestined by God to be the great preacher (for example in *MA*, 157), he retains his own understanding of sanctity, and, in order to present it in concrete iconic form, he develops his startling self-fashioning histrionics.[353] The actual theological motivation for this disconcerting conduct, especially pronounced in *MA*, lies in Rolle's biblical *imitatio*,[354] and especially in his *imitatio Christi* (175.29), undertaken in an unprecedented manner. His purpose, on this occasion, is no longer *imitatio* only of the Christ attested in the Gospels; rather, it extends to the eschatological Christ-in-Judgment of the book of Revelation, from whose mouth a two-edged sword goes forth. Since he is so fascinated by Christ's promise of permission to sit in judgment with him, he preempts, as it were, the fulfillment of the promise. Only in the light of imitation of the sword-bearing God and judge is it possible to understand Richard Rolle's own terrifying gesture with the sword, when he can no longer bridle his own temperament, and believes that he is called by God to punish with this powerful gesture the *perversos* who oppress him. God himself, as the real *auctor,* hands him the sword, "with which I stride, great, among the glorious ones, and wield the lance in order to pierce the tyrants who tormented tender youth, and it will exert power with which I shall punish the godless who oppressed me" (108.22–26). As we have already seen, he touchingly avoids this personal hatred in his EP, with the help of a maturity he did not yet have when he wrote *MA.*

Having reached the end of our investigation of Rolle's *MA,* we can gain an overview of its unique fascination. In addition to highly individual features, certain weaknesses also emerge very clearly. In some places it seems that he loses control of reason and sheers off into delusion, and feels this himself when he asks the reader not to consider him demented ("demens," 155.14). His excited manner of speech occasionally gives rise to senseless catachretic images, when the logic of Latin grammar also threatens to come totally adrift (e.g., 144.5–13). We see how, on occasion, he falls victim to a trance-like automatism in his writing. In many instances one also has the impression that he is operating, or indeed juggling, with terms and jargon not fully understood that are required by the alliterative pattern. Nevertheless, *MA* provides compelling proof of the vitality that the Latin language still has, in a virtuoso author who appreciates the beauty of this dead language, and its aesthetic norms. M. de la Bigne, the seventeenth-century editor of Latin texts by Rolle, noted that in all his texts Rolle was a masterful generator of *energia,*[355] who knows how to adapt his manner of writing to his subject matter, and to differentiate between the classical levels of style;[356] *energia* is achieved by an expressive, initiatory-persuasive use of rhetorical techniques,[357] which also brings about an attractive and very effective rhythm, as has often been noted.[358] In *MA* Rolle succeeds in imparting to his Latin the "flow" that is characteristic above all of Cistercian spirituality. Yet with the overall structure of the work he came to something of a dead end. He must have recognized that he reached only a few readers, and therefore failed to achieve his chief aim—not through inadequacy of form, but because of the exclusivity and difficulty of his style.

Some of the things we read in this text take us beyond Rolle's own time, and might even call to mind the consciousness of people born several centuries later. Yet the signs of "modern" subjective consciousness that point toward later times are for the most part incipient, and subdued, as has already been suggested. Richard Rolle is at all events a significant literary representative of the late Middle Ages, far above the distorting picture that shows him torn between "successes and failures... verbal sophistication and intellectual naivete, pastoral concern and personal egotism."[359] He could be identified more properly with his own statement: "The more a person loves, the more similar he is to God" (149.3–4). Rolle's great aim is the proclamation of divine love, beyond any gender boundary, in the realization of Pauline freedom, where "there is no longer Jew or Greek, there is no longer slave or free, there is no longer male and female" (Gal 3:28). It is incidentally very remarkable and indeed affecting that the greatest German poet was well aware of the specific spirituality of a hermit such as Richard Rolle. Although Goethe had problems throughout his life with Christian theology of the cross, yet he gave the Christian solitaries the most honorable place conceivable in *Faust*, his drama of humankind. Holy anchorites appear at the end of Part 2, where the scene is set as "Mountain ravines, forest, rock." Even if Richard Rolle was unknown to Goethe, Pater Profundus, Pater Seraphicus, and Pater Extaticus might well be identified with him. Goethe lets the anchorites add their voices to the praise of all-embracing, all-conquering, love divine; by this love they are profoundly moved and enthused in their very essence.

CHAPTER 6

Marguerite Porete's *Mirror of Simple Souls* and Its Reception in England

In 1310, about a decade after Richard Rolle's birth, a woman was sentenced to death at the stake in France because of her extraordinarily bold mystical text *Le mirouer des simples âmes anienties et qui seulement demourent en vouloir et desir d'amour;* twenty-one reputable theologians had condemned the work as heretical. Until the 1960s it was transmitted anonymously, and the author was unquestioningly assumed to have been a man; there are some reminiscences of Meister Eckhart, who may have read Marguerite's text or have heard of its tenets.[1] There are good reasons for devoting a whole chapter to it in a new history of English mysticism. First of all, a Middle English translation has survived, titled *The Mirror of Simple Souls,* which in turn provides vital information for establishing the French text. Second, the anonymous Middle English translator, M.N., introduces glosses that attest intensive reception of the *Mirouer* in England, and attempt to link it with the native mystical tradition. Manuscript transmission is a further justification for its inclusion: the English manuscript Cambridge, Pembroke College MS 221, contains a Latin translation by Richard Methley of both *The Cloud of Unknowing* and *The Mirror of Simple Souls;* and both *The Mirror of Simple Souls* and Julian of Norwich's *A Revelation of Love* were deemed worthy of inclusion in the famous Amherst anthology of contemplative texts (British Library, MS Add. 37790). Certainly, Marguerite's text fascinated readers, but at the same time it gave cause for them to guard against any suspicion of the incipient danger of heterodoxy.[2]

Marguerite Porete was a beguine, who lived in the vicinity of the Wallon city of Valenciennes (in Hainaut, close to the present-day Franco-Belgian border);[3] she is thus, after Hadewych and Mechthild of Magdeburg, "the third great beguine writer of vernacular female mysticism of the 13th century."[4] As an educated woman, familiar with the culture of the age, notably with courtly poetry, endowed with elite self-awareness and enormous self-confidence, she confronts us as a most exceptional figure of her time. How she acquired her education is unclear; possibilities include a Latin school in Valenciennes that was attended by boys and girls, and a *béguinage* that fulfilled an educational function. She was patently not a member of a religious order and did not choose a cloistered life. The possibility that she received private education has also been considered.[5] Evidently she had a wide-ranging knowledge of theology, although she never cites a single authority. Furthermore, her mysticism is suited only for a small elite of noble souls; she did not write for "asses."[6] Nevertheless she has exerted a lasting influence on the history of European spirituality; at different times she has been an inspiration to such important women writers as Margaret of Navarre and Simone Weil.[7]

Characteristics of the *Mirouer des simples âmes anienties*

The recent increase in feminist research has strongly encouraged scholarly interest in Marguerite's book, which may rightly be called one of the most original mystical texts of the Middle Ages. It is spellbinding on account of its radically uncompromising tone, its intellectual and spiritual qualities, and the individuality of language used in developing its specific mystical teaching. Some of its tenets, such as that God cannot be known in essence, that it is impossible to speak of him at all in any accurate way, that more lies are spread about him than truth, have caused scholars to attribute to it an apophatic or Pseudo-Dionysian "tendency."[8] Whereas the work may suggest a male mystic approach, some of the subject matter is very characteristic of female mysticism, such as the special interest in the dogma of the Trinity. There is, admittedly, a certain tension between this and the apophatic emphasis on the pure essence of God, about which no kind of definitive statement can be made. Reflections on the Trinity result in the attribution to God of certain qualities, namely power, wisdom, and goodness, each one of which "represents" one person of the Trinity, to which Marguerite then returns many times; she wishes God's goodness above all to make a strong impact on her readers. Her understanding of the dogma of the Trinity for the most part follows the Athanasian Creed, as is frequently the case with other mystics, such as Richard Rolle or Margery Kempe.[9] Beyond that it is also possible to discern the influence of Richard of St. Victor's *De trinitate*. With Richard as a model, her enthusiasm for the dogma of the Trinity is easy to understand: Richard argues that, since God is love, love must already be present in his essence, and this is conceivable only if he reveals himself as three persons joined with one another in love, in the familiar perichoresis; the uniting bond of love is the Holy Spirit. Similarly Marguerite Porete says:

> The Father is eternal substance, the Son is pleasing fruition; the Holy Spirit is loving conjunction. This loving conjunction is from eternal substance and from pleasing fruition through the divine love.... Divine love of unity generates in the Annihilated Soul...eternal substance, pleasing fruition, loving conjunction. From the eternal substance the memory possesses the power of the Father. From the pleasing fruition the intellect possesses the wisdom of the Son. From the loving conjunction the will possesses the goodness of the Holy Spirit. This goodness of the Holy Spirit conjoins it [the will] in the love of the Father and of the Son.[10]

She follows St. Augustine in recognizing man's likeness to God in the faculties of the human soul, which generate a created Trinity. For the *Mirouer* the definition of God, and of mankind's relationship to him, as love, is fundamental. It is love that renders the soul "transformed";[11] love is, as it were, the soul's "special" lover.[12] She knows that what "distinguishes" God as individual partner in love is contained in the paradox of the name that she gives him: "Loingprés" (*Mirouer,* 168), the distant-near one familiar to troubadour lyric poetry. Her ideal of love, *fin'amor,* is now transformed entirely into mystical chivalric love. Apart from occasional hints, such as the secret meeting of the lovers, this proceeds without explicit erotic analogies. Although love is experienced with great intensity, Marguerite has a "delicate restraint about making her relationship to God 'too intimate.'"[13] She knows that everything she has and is, is the grace of God.

Of course, love is often in conflict with reason in the *Mirouer;* reason represents intellectual thirst for knowledge and also the traditional teaching of the church.[14] Yet reason dies when the self is abandoned unconditionally to love. Marguerite makes this clear through allegorization of the birth of Benjamin, following Richard of St. Victor: the birth of Benjamin, who represents contemplative devotion, causes the death of his mother Rachel, who "signifies" reason.[15] Time and again Marguerite experiences mystical moments of most profound certainty, when she is united as by a flash of lightning or a "spark" with her God.[16] The "encounter of love"[17] does not entirely remove the distance between the soul and God; but she is allowed to behold the Trinity, even if only for a short time, and in the manner of a pledge ("erres," *Mirouer,* 178), which is rare with the medieval mystics. Especially because she was with God and loved by him even before the creation of mankind, from all eternity, her soul is even "transfigured" and chosen by him as dwelling place. Just as the sun derives its light from God, so the soul derives her existence from him *("Mirror,"* trans. Babinsky, 277), she lives from his substance; indeed, she has been linked to him by "something" ("le plus," *Mirouer,* 86) since the beginning of time.[18]

She includes the orthodox concept of *deificatio* of the individual, going back to the Greek fathers: "I am God, says Love, for Love is God and God is Love, and this soul is God by the condition of Love" (*"Mirror,"* chap. 21, 104).[19] Thus God is to be understood not only as being, but also as love, which furthermore may be experienced as tenderness, and which transposes the human being into a state of pure joy. Here we can see a highly interesting combination of two diverging and actually irreconcilable mystical approaches, namely of apophatic mysticism directed toward the unknowable Other, and personal love mysticism within the courtly culture of the High Middle Ages. Behind this lies a marked Cistercian influence through the definitions of love given by Bernard of Clairvaux and William of St. Thierry.[20] Therefore, transcendental experience occurs also with "Cistercian" sweetness.

In her book Marguerite structures the path to the most intensive experience of God possible on earth in seven stages, or modes of being. In this life it is only possible to reach the sixth stage, in which the soul is transfigured, liberated, and purified; its actual perfection as the goal of all striving is achievable, in her view, only in the life to come. The centerpiece of the book is actually the description of the fifth stage, for it is here that she experiences the freedom of the spirit, which was already important for the mystics so far discussed. Marguerite relates the (Pauline) notion of freedom entirely to the human will; her basic psychological understanding is voluntaristic. Since she speaks of the soul in terms of the will rather than of being, the intention to act counts as much as the act itself.[21] For Marguerite, God gave mankind free will in spite of his providential knowledge that the gift would be misused.[22] Therefore, since the human will usually leads to loss of freedom, Marguerite desires to demonstrate a path to complete freedom through radical renunciation of self-will. This involves abandoning all attachment to the individual "I" and to things of this world, since the person who wants to experience

God must relinquish and forget everything. Therefore, among the many names that can be attributed to the soul, none is so fitting as "Forgetting" ("obliance," *Mirouer*, 36). This calls for *mortificatio* of the flesh. The body is not simply rejected as sinful; the point is rather that its materiality is quite unfitted for experience of the divine. The soul becomes aware that she consists only of badness, that she is less than nothing ("vous estes moins que nient," *Mirouer*, 296). Only when she is ready to feel herself as nothing, to be annihilated,[23] can she experience God as All: there is a dialectic relationship between the human Nothing and the divine All.[24] She knows that she will never be able to melt entirely into God; not until she acts on her knowledge that God is the only working power within her (chap. 79) can she attain unlimited freedom and enjoy complete peace. Of course, this message is heard only by the great and noble souls who let themselves be transformed by divine love. Those who remain caught in their own will not only commit sin, they also deprive God of his own will—again, an original notion on the part of this daring woman.

The great multitude of souls who still cling to reason need Holy Church the Little, in order to be sure of her blessings and find their orientation in the words of holy scripture.[25] The noble souls, on the other hand, who succeed in submitting to the process of annihilation, belong to Holy Church the Great, and no longer need the blessings of *ecclesia minor*.[26] In Holy Church the Great, divine love alone prevails; only she is the true church. Since the noble souls no longer have any will of their own, the problem of sin has also become foreign to them; they no longer feel any discomfort on that account. This in itself suffices to make confession, indeed all sacraments, superfluous, which implies further setting aside of the mediating role of the church.[27] No longer is the soul concerned about honor or disgrace, salvation or damnation. Unfortunately the fact has almost always been overlooked that Marguerite, although she abandons her will to God, and relinquishes all thought, nonetheless recalls profoundly and frequently Christ's act of redemption in his suffering and death,[28] in other words, that the Christological aspect has not really disappeared from her mysticism.[29]

The lofty, nobly born soul who has noughted herself no longer needs spiritual rules of life, or a prescriptive, legalistic virtue system with detailed ascetic exercises; in fact, she is ready to send the virtues packing (chap. 6). Why? As one who has become totally free, she no longer needs to be at their service, as it were. Of course, her doctrine of radical relinquishing of individual will can easily be misunderstood as quietism, so she takes pains to allay this suspicion ("Mirror," chap. 29, 109f.). Yet for her there is not the slightest doubt: the annihilated souls are the real "nobly born,"[30] who are capable of true love of God. They know that the Nothing they have chosen is a rich Nothing, for it contains the richness of God, in which they find themselves in perfect peace and freedom.

Herein lies one reason why Marguerite has been of particular interest to women's studies. Scholars have thought to discover in her a woman who, with her special brand of mysticism, succeeded in breaking out of the social and ecclesiastical bonds by which the medieval woman felt herself constrained. At a time when women were associated with the body and a special capacity for suffering, this bid for freedom was necessarily an explosive force. It may be, as some have contended,[31] that Marguerite appealed to her contemporaries with the claim that she had attained perfect freedom. If her will is entirely subsumed in the will of God, and only God is active in her, then for her as a woman this means that she effectively attains a position "beyond all authority,"[32] including any kind of male authority. There is probably some truth in the idea that if a woman could be convinced that she has come as close as possible to the goal of perfection, this mysticism of freedom gave her more than adequate compensation for the denial of the office of priest.[33] Nevertheless, it is questionable whether Marguerite achieved through her text the "self-realization" that women were denied.[34] This concept, which goes back to Herder and Hegel, would certainly have meant nothing to her;[35] quite the contrary, she is willing to take the radical decision to "suspend her individuality" and put herself entirely in God's hands in loving devotion. There are, of course, ultimately no rational grounds for this complete relinquishment of the "I," not even the fear of God as a gift of the Holy Spirit,[36] for love knows neither why nor wherefore.[37]

The fundamental reason, however, why Marguerite brought the charge of heresy upon herself is that she enjoys "dumbfounding" her readers with startling, sometimes even outrageous, phrasing. Understandably, to become "dumbfounded" is a favorite expression of hers, and statements containing such provocation as sending the virtues packing were assessed entirely out of context. It is initially startling to read that the annihilated soul, liberated for devotion to God, grants to nature all that nature wants (*"Mirror,"* 99–101), but close scrutiny reveals that this is neither a call to libertinism nor a lapse into heresy. Rather, what is meant is that those who have committed themselves entirely to the will of God will do nothing natural that is not permissible, nothing contrary to the divine. This follows also from her quotation of the words of Augustine: "Love, and do as you will" (on 1 Jn 4:7–21)—a soul that loves God is simply not able to do anything contrary to the will of God. As if to confirm this, the soul explicitly emphasizes at another point: "Lady Nature, I take leave of you" (*"Mirror,"* 104). How very different, by contrast, is the real heretics' insistence on an imperative need to satisfy nature, in order to guard against disturbance of mind and spirit.[38] It may well be that misunderstandings were inevitable, given the extremes of expression that often occur in the *Mirouer.* Does Marguerite not contend that she can guarantee the salvation of mankind? Does she not stress that everything was created for her sake? God never loved anything without her? It is in her that God's bounty is revealed? What she really means becomes comprehensible only if one takes as starting point her confession of her own inordinate evil, made with unsurpassable humility ("I am the sum of all evils"). Thus she wants to "represent" all sinners, to make herself the voice of all, so that the pronouncements about her especial grace can be claimed by *every* annihilated soul. Because she is aware of her extreme badness, for this very reason she is singled out to experience God's greatest bounty, so that she does indeed represent redemption, and redemption is made manifest in her in a singularly radical manner. Yet Marguerite is not by any means a "mediator of creation and salvation" as a result of this.[39] Nothing was further from her intention than to attenuate the meaning of Christ's act of redemption. Moreover, we find in other female mystics, such as Gertrud and Julian, the certainty that Christ would have died for them alone (the famous "pro me"). Her ultimate provocation is that she will "unencumber herself" from God, but her explanation makes this comprehensible:

> Now work in us of yourself for our sakes without ourselves, as it pleases you, Lord. As for me, from now on, I am not afraid. I unencumber myself from you, and from myself, and from my neighbors, and I will tell you how. I release you, and myself, and all my neighbors; in the knowledge of your divine wisdom; in the outflowing of your divine power, in the governance of your divine goodness, for the sake of your divine will alone. And these divine things alone, annihilated, clear, and clarified by the divine majesty, says the Satisfied Soul, have given me freeness from all things without expecting any thing in return.... And when such nothingness is, then God sees Himself in such a creature, without any hindrance from His creature.[40]

The boldness of her theological statements results in language that soars to philosophical heights without negating its own sensual quality, which is sometimes intensified to reach a lyric-hymnic climax. The *Mirouer* is also a stylistically impressive masterpiece of intellectual prose, which structures abstract lines of thought concisely and persuasively,[41] and draws the reader into its exciting rhythms. The density of the text has been described with great sensitivity by Giovanna Fozzer,[42] who identified litotes as the most important figure of speech, an affirmation by negation of the contrary, as in the statement that God "is unfathomable, except for himself."[43]

Reception of the *Mirouer des simples âmes* through the Middle English Translation

Thirteen versions of Marguerite Porete's *Mirouer* have survived in four languages (Middle French, Middle English, Italian, Latin). The Middle English version is particularly significant since, as has recently been recognized, it can help to clarify definitively the underlying original text and yield important information about the first phase of reception; it was based on a French manuscript derived from the archetype,[44] and is therefore closer to the original text than any other manuscript.[45] It includes parts that do not occur in the extant French version or in the Latin translation. As has recently been shown, it sometimes has bolder wording than other versions. In his most recent research Lerner arrives at the astonishing conclusion: "If one really wants to come closest to what Marguerite wrote, not counting composition in the French language, one should consult the Middle English translation."[46] However, the English translation is largely confined to the work's main part, namely chapters 1–119, parts of 122 and 134, and 135 (whereas the relevant part of chap. 134 and chap. 135 are missing in the Middle French text), as well as the opening *Approbatio* provided by three theologians.[47]

Like the fourteenth-century Latin version, so also the Middle English version has no division into chapters (though it does have apparently very arbitrary Roman section numbers), which is an indication of the state of the original text. The translator, however, used a French copy. Since it was corrupt at some points, he did not always convey clearly the meaning of the original.[48] Marguerite's cumulative, dense language and style[49] was a problem for him, too, as he himself says, so that he was repeatedly obliged to translate the sense rather than the words. Yet it is wrong to maintain that the *Mirouer* is untranslatable.[50] And even if the English text at times descends into absurdity, its prose is a great stylistic achievement; its rhythm carries the reader forward. A further contributory factor is the frequent argumentative repetition, a familiar feature of other English texts as well. Often a word is used with a stem related to the French; occasionally a French term even remains untranslated ("Avant parlour," 314; "anyentised...souls," 298)[51], which indicates very clearly the assumption that the readers could understand French. On one occasion he introduces an effective English pun. The *Mirouer's* original idea that the soul possesses "a something" of God, or rather, something *more,* that comes from God, is heightened by M.N. to the superlative "most," and this yields a play with "most" = fermented drink;[52] the "something" of God inebriates the soul. The writer seeks to put into words the mystic *unio:*

> but þe mooste…makinge drunke wiþouten faile, is þe wyne of þe souerayn fauset, of þe whiche noon drinkeþ but þe Trinite. And it is of þis fauset, wiþouten whiche sche drinkeþ, soule nouȝted-drunken, soule fre-drunken, soule forȝeten-drunken; but riȝt drunken and more þan drunke of þat she neuer dranke ne neuer schal drinke.…And þe Uirgyne Marie dranke of þat aftir, and of þe mooste hiȝe drinke is þis noble lady drunke. After hem drinken þe brennynge seraphyns, wiþ þe whiche wynges þese fre soules fleen. (276.16–27)

> But the most…intoxicating is the wine from the tap at the top. This is the supreme beverage which none drinks except the Trinity. And from this beverage, without her drinking of it, the Annihilated Soul is inebriated, the intoxicated Unencumbered Soul, the drunken Forgotten Soul, very inebriated, more than inebriated from what she never drinks nor ever will drink.…And the Virgin Mary drinks at the one after and this noble lady is intoxicated by the most High. And after her, the ardent Seraphim drink, on the wings of whom these Free Souls fly.[53]

The image of the seraphim drinking for love is amazing! Among the text's powerful and unforgettable images, metaphorical phrases of flowing and streaming prevail (the soul swims in the sea of joy, 278; there are floods, waves, fluences of divine love, 294; she ships and sails and floats and swims, 315). This brings to mind another beguine of the thirteenth century, Mechthild of Magdeburg, with her *Flowing Light of the Godhead.* The metaphor of the soul united with God like a drop of water in the sea or in a vessel of wine deserves special attention, for it is favored not only by the beguines, but also by Bernard of Clairvaux,[54] Meister Eckhart, and Johannes Tauler.[55] Another daring idea is: "Throweth me in the middle of divine love…in which I am ydreint" (314). The translator M.N. lets himself be carried away by this, as it were, when he says of the soul at the fifth stage: "Sche is al molten in God" (313).[56] Yet the author also shows herself well versed in linguistic abstraction— as in the paradoxical reevaluation of the antithesis between "nought" and "ought," "nought" and "al," "noon" and "oon." This kind of dialectic is very familiar to readers of *The Cloud of Unknowing*. It is an overall merit of the English translation that it is not dominated by rhetorical "telling," but by a rhythmical flow that, at times truly incantatory, carries the reader over the incomprehensibility of certain passages.[57] At times it seems that the "enthusiasm" of the English translator is taking him in the direction of glossolalia, speaking in tongues.

There can be no doubt that the *Mirouer/Mirror* contains a certain subversive potential, although it is not directly connected with the Continental movement of the Free Spirit. Yet if the opinion prevails that in England insular spirituality and piety were very different and that the *Mirouer* did not exert a profound influence, it must be answered that a translation of the *Mirouer* did at least exist.[58] It can no longer be maintained that, since the *Mirror* manuscripts belonged to Carthusians,[59] the text's reception was mostly restricted to this order.[60] Watson's justified warning has been overlooked: "The fact that a work only survives in copies associated with Carthusians may testify to the high survival rate of their manuscripts, rather than being a sign that the work originated within the order and did not circulate outside; the short text of Julian's *Revelation* and *The Book of Margery Kempe* both survive entirely in Carthusian copies, but this does not imply that either was connected with the order."[61] Watson goes on to observe that "the translation of the *Mirouer* gave a strong impulse to medieval English mysticism with regard both to themes and to language and style, even if the translation is largely restricted to the first part of the work."[62]

The existence of the *Mirouer* translation attests English interest in new Continental ideas, as does the astonishing fact that some of the *Mirouer*'s "problematical" statements have been preserved not in the extant Middle French version, but *only* in the Middle English (and Latin) versions. This was observed by Lerner, who is surely correct in saying that "Marguerite's work also had a vigorous life in England."[63]

Moreover, it is of great significance that, in his own prologue to his Latin translation of *The Cloud of Unknowing*, Richard Methley deliberately opposes the "heresim begardorum," thus confirming indirectly the existence of support in England for the beghards—the male "variant" of the beguines—or, at least, familiarity with the beghard movement (MS Pembroke College Cambridge 221, f. 1v); and it is significant likewise that this manuscript also contains his Latin version of the *Mirouer*, which brings the *Mirror* into a relationship with the beghards. Marguerite asks at the end of her *Mirouer*: What will the beguines say? Beguines were thus among the first to whom the *Mirouer* was addressed.

What makes the *Mirror* still more intriguing is the fact that the translator M.N. glossed the text at various points. Hitherto the glosses have not
been adequately understood; it is not easy to evaluate them, and sometimes
their significance has been overestimated.[64] The insertion of glosses by the
anonymous M.N. is in fact less remarkable than it might seem, for the idea is
suggested by the *Mirouer* itself—in two different ways. First, the *Mirror* sometimes identifies a supplementary explanation of its own as a gloss requiring
attention (e.g., "Listen to the gloss," 238:26). Second, Porete may challenge
her readers to gloss a passage themselves ("Gloss these words if you want to
understand them," 270:19). It follows that the English translator is responding
to the challenge in his own way, and that his glosses cannot simply be interpreted as safeguarding the orthodoxy of the text. He may say in his preface
that he inserts them where they seem most needed (248:26); but sometimes,
just when he comes to theologically problematic passages, he enigmatically
passes up the chance to comment. Repeatedly he remains silent, prompting
the question: What has happened to the commentator M.N.? Did he not
want to do away with misunderstandings?[65] Furthermore, even when he did
insert a gloss, it was not always with full understanding. He does not seem
to be aware that he has before him a heretical text that needs to be brought
into line;[66] for in the prologue to his own translation he praises the work
as being "of lofty divine matters and of lofty spiritual feelings" (247:14). His
commentary reveals that the language of the text impresses and fascinates
him, and also that he is unable to withstand its influence.[67]

It is therefore wholly inappropriate to seek in the translator's fourteen
glosses, in whole or in part, the fifteen articles rejected as heretical in Paris in
1310, or to try to hear echoes of them.[68] Colledge and Guarnieri, however,
attempted to reconstruct eleven incriminating statements of the original
indictment,[69] and to prove the *Mirouer*'s heterodoxy. How such an idea
could arise is difficult to understand, if for no other reason than that M.N.'s
commentary does not pursue a consistent pattern. Only three of the original articles of the charges have survived, which match tenets condemned
in the trial of beghards and beguines at Vienne, and these are reflected in
the *Mirouer*,[70] namely the statements that a free soul bids farewell to the
virtues, that she no longer heeds the consolations and gifts of God, and that
she is willing to give to nature what nature desires.[71] Without any doubt,
the *Mirouer* cannot be "exonerated" from a certain heretical tendency; yet
that is precisely what makes it so interesting, indeed exciting,[72] and all the
more so because M.N., as already mentioned, is far from defusing all the
problematic passages. For the rest, he relies on the likelihood that the reader

will pick up the right meaning at a second or third reading—a reiterative mode of reading as suggested by the *Cloud* author. It is safe to assume that the translation of the *Mirouer* brought a powerful new impetus to medieval English mysticism.

The *Mirouer/Mirror* in Its Relation to Contemporary Court Culture and the Feminization of Discourse

In a way unnoticed by research so far, there seems to be a connection between *The Mirror of Simple Souls* and English court circles. The very form of the *Mirouer* was influenced by courtly literary tradition: it is written as a great polylogue, which is sometimes only implied, and at other times entirely suspended;[73] the speakers are a large number of allegorical figures or personifications, among them the soul, love, reason, pure nobility, the light of faith, truth, temptation, faith, hope, and charity, the gift of discernment, etc., most of whom are feminine. This formal arrangement cannot fully be explained by the *Speculum* tradition, as is usually maintained, but reflects above all the influence of the great literary innovation of thirteenth-century France, the *Roman de la rose*.[74] This most astonishing epic poem, which had introduced the complex system of allegorical figures discussing a central theme, became an enormously important model for the literature that followed,[75] and by its form the *Mirouer* impressively testifies to this tradition.[76] This formal analogy between the *Mirouer* and the *Roman de la rose* underlines the thematic analogies, and therefore we may conclude that in its own way the *Mirror* was drawn into the intellectual discussion in courtly circles.

The central theme of the *Roman de la rose,* begun by Guillaume de Lorris and continued by Jean de Meun, is courtly love as developed by the troubadours, its ideal and its causes of disappointment. It launched discussion—in France as well as in England—of the repositioning of women's social status in the relation between the sexes, and of the evaluation of eroticism. Two feuding camps arose of defenders and critics of the cultural representation of women and secular love. Even the French and English royal houses took sides in this literary feud.[77] The critics of the *Roman de la rose* included Christine de Pizan and also the famous theologian Jean Gerson, who preferred reading Bonaventura's *Itinerarium mentis in Deum,*[78] a major work of mysticism, to the *Roman de la rose.*

The English translator was surely aware that the *Mirror* has indeed something to do with the question of women's position in the court. We therefore may further surmise that he (indirectly and subtly) tried to establish a closer contact between this mystical text and the English court audience, as it is represented in the Prologue to Chaucer's great poem *The Legend of Good Women*.

In the Prologue to this poem Chaucer develops a courtly dream allegory in typically ironic manner and in allusion to the framing dream of the *Roman de la rose*. After the narrator-poet has announced that he loves a flower named daisy above all else, he has a dream, in which Alceste, as the ideal loving woman, appears to him clothed as a daisy flower with flower petals as well as a crown of pearls (= the second meaning of the word "marguerite"!) around her head. With this new creation of a mythological character, Chaucer makes an ambitious and yet playful attempt to counterpose a complex secular religion of love to the Christian religion of love (see figure 10). Alceste is the ideal loving courtly lady, who also possesses Christian values such as mercy. (The extent to which Alceste is intended to recall good Queen Anne who then died young, and the God of Love Richard II, is controversial, and need not delay us here.) She is accompanied by the love god Amor, who reproaches the poet for having caused great damage to Love by translating the heretical *Roman de la rose* and by his epic poem *Troilus and Criseyde* with Criseyde as a false woman. Alceste pities the poet and asks the love god to pardon him. He agrees, provided that he is willing to perform an act of penance. She then commands the poet to compose a series of legends of secular martyrs to Love betrayed, a profane version of Christian hagiography: the profane religion has its own women martyrs. They end tragically and cannot hope that their suffering will ever be rewarded.[79]

Despite this "tragic" theme, the Prologue charms us by its pervading playfulness, and yet Chaucer opens the entire Prologue by calling to mind that there would be an alternative to secular love: the love of God; the reader is reminded that true joy can only be found in heaven, although nobody, not even "Bernard the monk,"[80] who is very probably Bernard of Clairvaux, can properly describe it. Therefore Chaucer decides to choose earthly love as the subject of his poetic art.

I would now like to suggest that the author of the *Mirror* translation wanted to introduce Porete's *Mirouer* into the English court as a text in which this heavenly, mystical love is praised with the greatest intensity, and in which true and lasting joy is promised. He might well have wished to recommend a different path leading beyond the painful limitations of earthly love experiences. It seems to me that the translator knows perfectly well what he is doing when, in a context where the original *Mirouer* praises the precious soul as an invaluable pearl (marguerite), he on one occasion replaces the metaphor of "pearl" by the image of a daisy, curiously a "*precious* daies iȝe" (p. 294:4). Why is the soul denied the attribute of being a costly pearl,

Figure 10. Geoffrey Chaucer with a daisy. Miniature, late sixteenth century. British Library MS Add 5141, fol. 1. By permission of The British Library Board.

although the context suggests primarily a female being who is even worthy of being addressed as most nobly born? And elsewhere the free soul is frequently compared or identified with images of costliness (emerald, gem, star, etc.).[81] It now seems that, with his surprising decision to introduce the daisy into his translation, the anonymous translator apparently wanted to intensify the connection of his text with the English court, which is "headed" by the great Alceste/daisy.

The soul's "transformation" into the daisy signifies a female target audience. It intensifies the fact, well known in research, that in the *Mirouer* there is a preponderance of a feminine discourse. The love god Amor is transformed into lady love, and the impression is generated that the text has been composed for a female elite audience. Thus the translator of the *Mirouer,* suggesting that behind lady love there is ultimately God as pure love, has fully achieved his aim: to heighten the *fin'amor* of the troubadours through mystical love.

One may therefore also give some thought to the question of how the *Mirouer* will have reached the British Isles. It has been suggested that it may have been "imported" from Continental charterhouses after 1414, by the charterhouse founded by Henry V in Sheen in that year.[82] However, I think it very probable that this text, attractive especially for the aristocracy with its interweaving of "courtly" elements, reached England much earlier. It is interesting in this connection that Edward III's wife, Philippa, came from the province of Hainaut where Marguerite Porete lived and wrote.[83] "Philippa of Hainaut, who was born in Valenciennes and customarily resided there, was married by proxy to Edward III in Valenciennes before she crossed over to London for the formal marriage."[84] Her retinue included a certain Walter de Manny, from the same region, who subsequently joined with Michael Northburgh, bishop of London, in founding the London Charterhouse.[85] There is something to be said for the possibility suggested by Clare Kirchberger that the translator's and glossator's initials "M.N." stand for Michael Northburgh.[86] Among Philippa's servants was Chaucer's wife-to-be Philippa, daughter of Sir Paon de Roet, another of Queen Philippa's fellow countrymen. In Hainaut there will have been vivid memories of Marguerite Porete. Above all, there were adherents to the tenets of the Free Spirit movement in the region.[87] It has been recognized for a long time that there were lively contacts between French and English court circles. Furthermore, we know of Lollard interests on the part of individual knights at the court of Richard II, especially of Sir John Montague, third Earl of Salisbury, with whom Chaucer was acquainted and who was a friend of Christine de Pizan.[88] There must have been some admirers of the *Mirouer* in these "left-wing orthodox intellectual" circles, and it is remarkable that the translator chose to translate not the Latin but rather the "original" French text, in which the very language could spark off courtly associations. In conclusion, the contention that the *Mirouer* found in England an uncomprehending or watered-down reception, because of "specifically Insular religious language," is unfounded;[89] there is no reason to exaggerate the differences between Continental and English mystical interests.

CHAPTER 7

The Cloud of Unknowing and Related Tracts

To many readers the term "English mysticism in the Middle Ages" will immediately bring to mind the well-known and ever-popular *Cloud of Unknowing.* Some of them turn to it in the belief that it offers Christians a form of contemplation that can match Zen Buddhist spiritual experience. In Europe, and in America, it has opened up a possibility of fruitful dialogue with the spirituality of the Far East, and especially in Japan it has aroused great interest. Yet in the course of widespread leveling of the differences between Christian and Eastern traditions, there is now a risk that the Middle English work will be misunderstood and that its true intention will be completely ignored.[1] In recent years, scholarly interest in *The Cloud of Unknowing* and the texts related to it has decreased somewhat, owing to the current preference for the women mystics. It counts against the unknown author that he has been charged with a touch of misogyny and subliminal sexism, which is unfair, for in some ways the work converges with *The Mirror of Simple Souls,* written by a woman.

The Cloud of Unknowing is the bold endeavor of a late fourteenth-century author evidently still young; it continues the English apophatic tradition, and it is written in a refreshingly individual tone of voice. The promise of the subtitle ("in þe whiche a soule is onyd wiþ God") already imparts its mystagogic intent; yet this cannot of course be fulfilled by textual discourse. Concerned as it is with the impossibility of knowing God, *Cloud* takes its orientation from the great work of Pseudo-Dionysius Areopagita, who in turn followed on from Gregory of Nyssa (ca. 331/340–after 394). Both were influenced by Neoplatonic thought, and for both God is "over-bright darkness"[2]; the human being is blinded by the unearthly plenitude of light and therefore unable to see God's light. In his exegesis of the Exodus pericope relating Moses's encounter with God on Mount Sinai, Gregory already stressed that God can neither be known by man nor grasped in human categories: he remains ever hidden behind a cloud as the One who cannot be named, and has no name. This thesis was developed in philosophical depth by Dionysius in his most important work, *Mystical Theology*. There he outlines his apophatic theology, according to which it is possible only to say what God is *not;* he is neither life nor substance nor spirit, nor even light. Yet, as a Christian, Dionysius knows very well that many names for God are found in the Bible. "Dionysius does not simply reject these names, rather he interprets them as assistance provided by God, on which man is dependent because of his limitations."[3] He writes a further entire book devoted to the divine names, and the possibility of affirmative theology. Thus for Dionysius, too, there is a positive path toward knowledge of God through his revelation in the Bible, even if this path remains limited and provisional. And he does not entirely exclude definition of God by means of indicative analogies. God is "souereyn-substancialy" (p. 122.9–10)[4] above all living beings. The *Cloud* author's most impressive English translation preserves the original's unsurpassable paradox when it says that God dwells in "souereyn-schining derknes" (124.4). Although everything strives to return to God, yet, as Dionysius insists, he can never be reached; turning to him in thought and prayer is all that is possible. And only when thought ends is union in the sense of momentary ecstasy possible. If in this state "the boundaries of reason are crossed, this does not mean that the process is affective or emotional."[5]

The Canon of the *Cloud* Author's Works

The anonymous author chooses as his main work's title the image of the cloud of unknowing, a popular image in the negative theology tradition. With this concept the author wants to suggest to a young reader that in order to approach God, he must rid himself of all human notions and prepare himself for unconditional, loving devotion to God's "bare essence," following an act of liberation from all things earthly that was called *kenosis* in the Eastern Church tradition. This requires a second cloud, the cloud of forgetting; with its help, all notions other than the thought of God must be covered over.

The mystagogy of *Cloud* is deepened in a second extensive work, *The Book of Privy Counselling* (*BPC*). Here the author addresses an adept personally known to him, who is no longer a novice and who has turned to him with questions and criticism; he may be identical with the addressee of *Cloud*. Certain aspects of *Cloud* are explained to him more precisely and in more detail. Because of its greater philosophical and theological depth, this text may be regarded as prolegomenon to the remaining works, five shorter writings. All the texts of the *Cloud* group are linked by thematic and stylistic correspondences.

Through the self-referential mention of titles of some of his own works the author indicates a certain development (*BPC*, 87–88),[6] and the impression that *Cloud* is an early work is confirmed. It was presumably followed by the translation of *Mystica theologia,* which he also mentions;[7] the translation proves how deeply he was affected by this tradition.[8] *BPC* probably followed next. Another early work, perhaps even earlier than *Cloud,* is the *Pistle of Preier,* in which the Pseudo-Dionysian themes are not yet developed; nor do they occur in *A Pistle of Discrecioun of Stirings.* This title refers to the spiritual gift of discernment (*discretio*), which is of great importance for the English mystics, and especially for women (viz. Julian and Margery Kempe).[9] It is dealt with in a further tract (*A Tretis of Discrescyon of Spirites*), which has less mystical content than any of the other texts in the group,[10] but clearly tends toward mystagogy. Much had already been written on this theme; the text relies substantially on various excerpts incorporated from two sermons by Bernard of Clairvaux.[11] Another work in this circle of texts, the *Tretyse of þe Stodye of Wysdome þat Men Clepen Beniamyn,* is a free and very abbreviated paraphrase of the Scotsman Richard of St. Victor's *The Twelve Patriarchs* (or *Benjamin minor*).[12] There can be little doubt regarding the *Cloud* author's responsibility for this text,[13] even if not everything sounds familiar; yet an author cannot be expected to reproduce exactly the same statement in each new work; he must be allowed to "develop" his thoughts and realign his emphases.

The *Cloud* Group's Fundamental Line of Thought

The relationship of the mystically inclined human being to God is discussed in most detail in *Cloud* and in *BPC*. A prerequisite for the experience of God is clarification of the question of the essence of God and man (going beyond Pseudo-Dionysius). Before long, one finds the philosophical term *being* adopted in *Cloud,* but it is difficult to ascertain the ontological meaning of the term in this context, since the vernacular offers no possibility of distinguishing between *ens, esse, essentia,* and *existentia.*[14] Yet when the author alludes several times to the famous distinction drawn by Thomas Aquinas—everything depends on knowing *that* God is, not *what* he is—he most probably has in mind the medieval discussion of the relationship between *esse* and *essentia*. The existence of God must be stressed: "*Beyng* as verbal noun means the existential presence of a concrete being; it emphasizes the principle of being, *esse*, and signifies—in dependence on *esse*—the principle of being of *essentia* as signature of this being."[15] God, who can be spoken of only as pure being, also gives the soul her being (*BPC*, 75.31), but differs from her entirely. After all, JHWH communicated his name to Moses only as "I am"; all divine qualities are "hidden and contained in þis little word 'is'" (*BPC*, 80.38–39). Since man has his own being from God, it behooves him to feel this being, not to ask *what* he is, but to feel *þat* he is; for the "trewe knowyng & ... feling of þiself" (*Cloud*, 23.14) is at the same time the prerequisite for "a trewe knowyng & a felyng of God as he is, not as he is in hymself" (*Cloud*, 23.15–16). As so often in Christian mysticism, the soul is also defined as a mirror in which God is reflected, and which should be used for cognition of God. In order to ensure that it serves its cognitive purpose, the mirror must naturally be cleansed (as Bernard of Clairvaux and other Cistercians, Richard Rolle, and Walter Hilton also argue); this corresponds in part to the stage of *purgatio*. Implicit in this is the implementation of the fundamental Christian challenge, going back to Jesus himself, of vanquishing pride and arrogance by means of "self-denial" (*abnegatio*, Mt 16:24). For the *Cloud* author, it is precisely the nullifying of the self ("nouȝtnyng of itself," *BPC*, 84.26) that leads to the experience of the divine All ("þis hyȝe allyng of God," *BPC*, 84.27).[16] It is as an extension of this challenge that the desire for accurate knowledge of the state of the self should be understood; here we encounter once more the very important Socratic, and especially Bernardine, requirement for self-knowledge, the *gnothi seauton*.[17]

Familiar with the long mystical tradition of the "triplex via," the author introduces to his reader the important theological theme of spiritual ascent to God. Instead of falling back on the Latin terms *lectio, meditatio,* and *oratio,* he favors "reding," "thinkyng," and "preiing." Each higher stage presupposes the preceding one.[18] For the author, however, the three stages combined do not yet come close to the true contemplation that prepares human beings for the encounter with God. They are applicable to beginners (*incipientes*) and the more advanced (profiters, *proficientes*), as understood by Gregory the Great, but the perfect (perfite, *perfecti*) are not yet included. Strikingly, traditional meditation is not esteemed very highly; it does not constitute the decisive prerequisite for *contemplatio,* which is "poured in from above and not built up from below."[19] The author therefore displays "no great interest [in]...the classical three-stage prayer."[20] When he refers for more profound study to the work of another unnamed author, he probably has in mind the *Scala claustralium* of Guigo II, which he surely esteemed very highly; it had been translated into Middle English, and the style is very reminiscent of *Cloud*, as has been noted.[21] Nor can the existence of the *Pistle of Preier* disguise the fact that he does not devote undivided attention to prayer. Since *oratio* is not named as a constitutive part of *contemplatio* in so many words, the question arises: is prayer devalued in these texts? The young author offers the reader a definition that initially seems disappointingly unsophisticated: prayer is the request to God (who embraces all that is good) for what is good, and for delivery from sin (a collective term for all evil, *Cloud,* 42.32–33). Gradually it emerges that at bottom the *Cloud* author has a differentiated understanding of the term "prayer." The liturgical prayers of the church are not rejected, but for contemplation as such it is necessary to go beyond them.[22] For the mystic, the highest form of prayer is the yearning devotion to God that occurs in *contemplatio,* or the experience of his presence, for which reason Julian expressly observes in the short version of her *Revelation* that she does not pray; and Marguerite Porete takes the same view. For talk of the mystical experience of *unio,* the author has recourse to the traditional terms *raptus* ("rauisching," *Cloud,* 7.4) and *excessus* ("excesse," *BPC,* 85.23), of which more will be said below. Although the full title of *Cloud* announces that in this book the soul will "enter into union" with God, this is not fulfilled by the text itself. The supplicant remains at a distance, before a cloud understood as the dazzling glare of over-powerful divine light. At the same time he feels the heat emanating from it, and experiences an *apprehensio Dei* (*Cloud,* 34.31–40).[23] He also receives the promise that God "will...sumtyme...seend oute a beme of goostly liȝt...& schewe þee sum of his priuete" (*Cloud,* 34.31–33); "cleer siȝt schal neuer man haue here in þis liif; bot þe felyng mowe men haue þorow grace." (*Cloud,* 19.8–9).[24] To the terms *rauisching* and *excesse* is added the further term *felyng,* so characteristic of this author, which is explored more profoundly in *BPC* than in *Cloud.* The supplicant must persist in awareness of the *felyng* of his own self, until the despairing question arises, amid great sadness, as to why he was brought forth from his mother's womb (the question formulated by Job in his despair, and taken up by Richard Rolle). Then, however, the wish to exist no longer is transformed into gratitude for existence. Relinquishing the *felyng* of the self means becoming capable of experiencing the *felyng* of God (*BPC,* 89.7–13). It is clear that the concept comprises not so much an emotional component as an "awareness" focused lovingly on God.[25] Here the author differs significantly from Richard Rolle, who had described *contemplatio* as a gaze penetrating into heaven. For the *Cloud* author, too, *beholding* is part of contemplation, but this is a "blind" gaze, because it is always curtained in cloud and sees nothing of God.[26] In Julian of Norwich and Margery Kempe we shall encounter a very different mystical experience, whereas that of Walter Hilton is strikingly similar.

The *Cloud* author describes the process of contemplation in highly differentiated terms, often as mystical "work" and "trauayle," for everything familiar is to be plunged into a cloud of forgetting, including all "perception of creaturely objects," and "self-awareness and even the names of God and attributes of God."[27] Moreover, man is required to maintain desire for God, for a long time and undeviatingly, as "nakid entent vnto God" (*Cloud,* 9.31), and to persevere in "blinde beholdyng" (*Cloud,* 17.33) of divine being; in other words, man must learn to "dwell" in the cloud of unknowing. Here the author intensifies traditional metaphorical language.[28] He is fascinated by the Pseudo-Dionysian paradox: "þe moste goodly knowyng of God is þat, þe whiche is knowyn bi vnknowyng" (*Cloud,* 70.5–6). Yet he makes plain that in this contemplative "work" God is the "cheef worcher" (*BPC,* 83.35),[29] the *actor principalis* in scholastic terminology.

Such paradoxical talk of the decisive quality of "nothing" can be matched in modern physics. Scientists have realized that there is immense energy in nothingness. Looking at the tranquil surface of the sea can arouse the impression of nothingness, belying the variegated world below.

The *Cloud* Author's Theological "Anthropology"

A recent systematic investigation has sought to ascertain, from a theological standpoint, the psychological understanding on which the work of the *Cloud* author is based.[30] First of all, the young neophyte is reminded of his creatureliness, of how quickly a lifetime passes, and he is admonished not to enslave himself to the time he has received as a gift, but to handle it responsibly, constantly renewing his decision for Christ. Since the human being receives time as a gift from God, he is accountable to God for the use of every atom of time (*Cloud,* 11.18–29).[31]

The author's image of the human being is essentially Augustinian, but he does not differentiate between *imago* and *similitudo* (as was usual in the tradition) in terms of similarity by nature and by grace, for which reason he uses *ymage* and *liknes* almost as synonyms. Following Gn 1:27, the human being is said to be both God's *imago creata* and *imago trinitatis.*[32] The author endeavors to build up his mystical instruction "on a solid creation-theological basis."[33] Man's likeness to God,[34] subsisting in his body-soul, has been deformed by sin; he has let himself become perverted into a crooked person (the Augustinian *homo curvatus*), with crooked gait and "entent" (*Cloud,* 22.2), which

Ancrene Wisse already lamented.[35] Yet through the act of "reforming grace" the likeness can be restored, and the soul can enter into union with God. Indeed, this can even enable man to attain deification, enhancing further the worth that pertains to him through his likeness to the deity; but *theiosis* or *deificatio,* which is supported by the Bible, occurs with a paradoxical restriction, since it is bestowed by grace (*Cloud,* 67.19), and the human being remains beneath God, and does not merge with him.[36]

In the *trinitas creata* of the soul the three potentialities, *memoria, intelligentia* (*intellectus, ratio*), and *voluntas,* "correspond" to the Trinity. In Middle English spiritual texts the terms appear in diverse linguistic forms; the *Cloud* author speaks of *mynde, reson,* and *wille,* or *mynde, witte,* and *wille* or *affeccion.* (*Spirit* appears as hypernym, in the manner of a leitmotif, but is itself subject to differentiation.)[37] *Mynde* means significantly more than *memoria* and encompasses *mens* as well; it represents "the integrative center of human personality, in which, in a special manner, man's capacity for transcendence is located."[38] Most important is the "immediacy of God" offered by *mynde* as "personality center,"[39] where meditation, prayer, and contemplation occur. Yet for the *Cloud* author, the soul transcends *mynde* in ecstatic *unio.*

It must be conceded that ultimately it is impossible to draw a clear distinction between the terms the *Cloud* author uses for the total intellective potentiality of the soul. Thus *reson* corresponds on the one hand to Augustinian *ratio,* and as *ratio superior* it is the eye of the soul (*Cloud,* 13.42; 39.38); while at the same time, *reson* is the "basic intellective-cognitive faculty."[40] On the other hand, the term may be replaced by *beholding* or *understondyng.* *Witte* and *understondyng* may also surpass *reson,* because it does not cognize discursively and reflexively, but by gazing and contemplating; yet to translate *reson* regularly as "understanding" and *understondyng* as "reason," as Steinmetz suggests, is not appropriate, since the *Cloud* author himself does not differentiate clearly; for him, *understondyng* may simply mean "comprehension."[41]

Things are made even more complicated by the fact that the *Cloud* author, like Hilton, speaks of *goostly wittes,* but this does not refer to the inner, spiritual senses that have already been discussed several times, although these are included, as we shall see; rather, the *goostly wittes* represent "part of the basic intellective-cognitive faculty";[42] they are the *vnderstondable worchinges* (*BPC,* 120.11), while Hilton uses the term to denote the three major powers of the soul.[43] *Wille* (and *herte* or *affeccion*) as translation of *voluntas* (or *affectus*) refers to an organ "that produces an actual striving movement" occurring "within the field of human emotionality";[44] *entent* and *steryng* are terms for the act of striving toward God with the aim of "having" him; *felyng* and *affeccion* denote emotional qualities.[45]

The *Cloud* author profits from the tract *The Twelve Patriarchs* (*Benjamin minor*) by Richard of St. Victor, which introduces two subsidiary powers of the soul, namely *imaginatio* and *sensualitas,* on the basis of allegorization of the relationship between Rachel and Leah; the *Cloud* author adopts these as *ymaginacion* and *sensualite.* An interesting divergence from Richard of St. Victor has been noted several times: unlike in Richard, the subsidiary faculty of *ymaginacion,* conceived in terms of power to imagine, is almost always assessed negatively; it leads to vain imaginings that detract from man's spiritual calling, indeed to complete "scattering" of the spirit, which must dwell entirely in the "no3where" (*Cloud,* 67.35). Richard of St. Victor has a different reading because he recognizes in *imaginatio* the necessary *handmaid* of reason, even if she repeatedly distracts the adept from what is essential and conjures up seductive fantasies. For Richard *imaginatio* is also the power that enables the idea of the beauty of the celestial world to grow (*Stodye of Wysdome,* 135). Not so for the *Cloud* author. Intent on orthodoxy and conscious of tradition, he warns against imaginative, intellectual *curiositas;* contempt of theological erudition in mystical contexts is well known.[46] Likewise he dismisses the sectarians and enthusiasts in particular, who are not able to distinguish between the sensual and the spiritual, and who confuse the value of the two.[47] Because *ymaginacion* is almost always negatively defined by the *Cloud* author, there is a restrictive element in his texts, and one result of this is that the emotion of joy arises only in moderation, with far less intensity than in Richard Rolle or Julian, and, almost always, only as a preliminary to the joy of heaven. *Sensualite* is used as a collective term for the five senses, but does not denote, as it does in Julian, the sensual component of the soul in its entirety, and, like the *imaginatio* that leads along the path to *curiositas,* it is held in low esteem. In the reworking of Richard's *Benjamin minor,* by contrast, *sensualite* is still the *prerequisite* for the ability to feel (*Stodye of Wysdome,* 129.20).

The Influence of Thomas Gallus on the *Cloud* Texts

In order to grasp what is new and individual in the *Cloud* author's texts, it is helpful to take seriously his avowal that he was strongly influenced by Thomas Gallus, who was the first abbot of Vercelli (from 1219 until his death in 1246—therefore also called Vercellensis), and an Augustinian canon of St. Victor.[48] As the last great Victorine, Thomas Gallus stands firmly in the Augustinian and also in the Cistercian tradition.[49] In recent scholarly studies of mysticism this abbot of Vercelli is held in very high esteem. More than any other medieval theologian, he concerned himself with Pseudo-Dionysius. He helped to promote very successfully the influence of the Latin rendering of the *Corpus Dionysiacum* by Johannes Sarracenus, who strove to reconcile these works with orthodoxy.[50] His commentary on the *Mystica theologia* is recognized as a "fundamental event in the development of Christian spirituality";[51] this is for Thomas the most important Dionysian text. And the *Cloud* author followed Thomas Gallus. His mention of this, and of the great influence Thomas had on him, has for a long time been played down, which has to do with the fact that scholars have mistakenly tended to regard the *Cloud* author as a Carthusian.[52]

In the foreword to his translation of the *Mystica theologia,* in which he mentions Thomas, the anonymous *Cloud* author already provides an instance of his profound understanding of the great theologian. In translating the title as *Deonise* Hid [emphasis added] *Diuinite,* he demonstrates that he knows, as did Thomas,[53] that "'mystical' is derived from Greek *myo,* which means 'close' or 'learn/teach.'" Theology is said to be "closed" in "darkness" (*caligo*),[54] and therefore hidden. Accordingly, the *Cloud* author translates the adjective "mystica" as "hid"; it is a question of divinity hidden in darkness. This darkness is "mystical" because, as Thomas observes, "it closes [i.e., suspends] all cognitive powers." Ruh rightly clarifies that the intention is not to propagate an understanding of "mystical" as dark and mysterious, but rather that "the darkness is ours."[55] Thomas insists further:

> God locks himself away by concealing himself and binding all cognitive powers (*cognitiones cognitivae*) in the First Cause of all [being]. Through this darkness, free from himself and from All, that is to say, above all intellection (*superintellectualiter*), Moses is united with God, and is elevated in an entirely ineffable and unseeable manner to a state of inconceivability. It is the state of which Paul says: "It is no longer I who live, but it is Christ who lives in me" (Gal 2:20).[56]

As Ruh emphasizes, Thomas Gallus has a precise notion of the "mystical" in the *Mystica theologia*. Moses enters into darkness, as in Dionysius, but mystical cognition of God unfolds, quite differently, in the ecstasy of *loving union,* and this takes Thomas beyond Pseudo-Dionysius. He sets a new emphasis in the traditional psychology by venturing to describe the potentiality of the human will, *voluntas,* as the decisive power of the soul, *principalis affectio.*[57] He says that this potentiality makes possible the experience of God in *love,* beyond the important cognitive knowledge of God. Here the *Cloud* author follows with a quite similar strategy: he, too, declares the will to be the main effective power ("principal worching miȝt," *Cloud,* 10.33–34), and for his part equates *affectio* (or *affectus*) with love, which also recalls Aelred of Rievaulx.[58] While God cannot be comprehended by reason, for love he is "al comprehensible at þe fulle" (*Cloud*, 10.36–37) as a form of the will; which means that *Cloud* does indeed speak of the possibility of *knowledge* of God, but only through the "deed of love," which is at the same time a "deed of cognition."[59] Again he is in agreement with Thomas Gallus, who teaches that the human being comprehends "in union the *incomprehensibilitas* of God."[60]

Still following Thomas Gallus, *Cloud* goes on to provide more detail regarding the place and manner of the soul's union with God: the human being must make his way to "þe hiȝest & þe souereynest pointe of þe sp[i]rit" (*Cloud*, 41.12–13), which may also be called his deepest depth, since a *coincidentia oppositorum* occurs in the realm of the spirit—"þe depnes of spirit, þe whiche is þe heiȝt (for in goostlynes alle is one)," lines 24–25—as is said in anticipation of Nicholas of Cusa. This mystical paradox has also been referred to as ground of the soul.[61] The highest point of the spirit is the traditional *apex mentis* (or *acies mentis*, as in Rolle, for instance in his *Expositio super novem lectiones mortuorum*).[62] In Thomas and in *Cloud*, however, it is reinterpreted as *apex affectionis*.[63] In the *Mystica theologia* Thomas also introduces the term *scintilla synderesis*, the spark of the soul.[64] Here the author of *Cloud* simplifies,[65] and equates *scintilla* with the *apex mentis*, or he relinquishes it, or merely alludes to it—as when he describes love's devotion as "a sodeyn steryng...speedly springing unto God as sparcle fro þe cole" (*Cloud*, 12.23–24);[66] but it is of crucial importance that he leaves the basic concept intact.

The acme of the will's soul-power, once more, is love "in the form of ecstasy. It wrests man out of himself to God, and God to man."[67] Thomas Vercellensis calls ecstasy *excessus mentis*, a concept taken up by the *Cloud* author in his allegorical exegesis of Benjamin following Richard of St. Victor's *Benjamin minor*; Benjamin is said to represent all those "þat in *excesse of loue* [emphasis added] ben rauisc[h]id abouen mynde" (*BPC*, 85.20–21), whereby Richard's *mens* is rendered as "loue," entirely in Thomas's vein. It is well said that reason dies in love's ecstasy (*BPC*, 85.16). At the same time, the soul's yearning love is the *response* to God's love, which preceded it. Thus union occurs as complete concord between the human and the divine will. This was not pronounced so clearly by Richard of St. Victor; the *Cloud* author, therefore, even while following Richard's *Benjamin minor*, "strengthened the function of the will in the spirit of Thomas Gallus, especially in chapters 63–66 of the *Cloud*."[68] It has also been said with some justification that the unconditional loving devotion, the "nakid entent" of the *Cloud* author, occurred first in Thomas Gallus.[69]

The fact that Thomas locates decisive cognitive potentiality in love is especially reflected in his great interest in the Song of Songs, which prompted him to write important commentaries on the *Canticum canticorum*.[70] Furthermore, he made a revolutionary attempt to incorporate the perspective of the Song of Songs into his interpretation of Pseudo-Dionysius, as Kurt Ruh has pointed out:

> With affective capability Thomas Gallus introduces into Dionysian mysticism a "home" element from the theology and spirituality of the Victorines, and also of the great Cistercian theologians of the 12th century.... Elucidations of Dionysius and the Song of Songs mutually influence one another in his work, and those of the Song indeed become all-pervasive, and this unparalleled innovation gives the modest provincial abbot (with no higher academic title) a significance in the history of ideas that has been recognized only by a few specialists.[71]

A Daring Synthesis of Negative and Bernardine Mysticism

The *Cloud* author undertakes a comparable attempt to incorporate the mysticism of love into Dionysian mysticism of being, and likewise achieves in his texts a very remarkable individual quality, which as yet has not been described with sufficient precision. Careful reading of the English translation of the Gallus version of *Mystica theologia* reveals that this is announced in the text by the supplementary remark that it is important "to fele in *experience* [emphasis added] þe presence of hym þat is abouen alle þinges" (*Deonise Hid Diuinite,* 123.20–21).[72] Like Thomas, the *Cloud* author has recourse indirectly to Bernard of Clairvaux, who stresses the significance of individual *experience* in his sermons on the Song of Songs. He quotes the *Canticum canticorum* several times, which results in a surprising appearance of God as bridegroom of the soul (*Cloud,* 8.28), thus in the person of Jesus, and no longer the God who cannot be named. In Richard of St. Victor's *Benjamin minor* the lover was both Christ and Aeterna Sapientia, and therefore male as well as female. We read furthermore that the soul should let herself be drawn by God with a rope of love (*Cloud,* 8.7)—as demanded also by Thomas, who developed this image from biblical passages.[73] It may remind us, *Cloud* says, that God himself "drew" the soul through his grace to the contemplative form of life (*Cloud,* 8.14); therefore she should put forward the foot of her love on the path to consummate life.[74] And the impulse of the will directed toward God the unknowable is now shaped into the image of a sharp arrow of yearning love, which must pierce and penetrate the cloud of unknowing (*Cloud*, 14.29–30).

The more deeply one goes into these texts, the more one becomes aware of the extent to which the language of the *Cloud* author is "charged" with Cistercian sensuality.[75] The text speaks of Bernardine "swetnes" (*Cloud*, 52.15) and "swete felynges" (*Cloud*, 52.20), though the author rates these qualities merely as "accydentes" (*Cloud*, 51.24). There is an appeal to the inner senses (*Cloud*, 69), and the use of this concept has some influence on the texts' discourse.[76] Indeed, it may be said to continue a tradition established by *Ancrene Wisse* and Richard Rolle. Particularly reminiscent of *Ancrene Wisse* is the dominance of haptic metaphor: "To a striking degree the *Cloud* author puts the haptic senses of spiritual *tactus* and *gustus* in the foreground, and admits spiritual *visus* only in the sense of the super-intellective eye of love."[77] Such sensual experiences are neither rejected nor indispensable; it is important that they are not condemned, because this shows that the author silently accepts Richard Rolle's spiritual language of the senses, of which there are constant reminders.[78] Scholars have repeatedly judged, without sufficient reflection, that the *Cloud* author's criticism of intense sensual metaphor, expressed several times, is directed against Richard Rolle's mysticism, and especially against its reception by his supporters,[79] but this is not the case. In *Cloud* the impassioned fire of love, familiar to us especially from *Ancrene Wisse* and the works of Richard Rolle, is once more set alight. The soul ties the knot of burning love with Jesus (*Cloud*, 49.11–12)[80] and celebrates mystical marriage with him (*Pistle of Preier*, 106.15). Without question, this love is imbued with Bernardine extravagance and insatiability (*Cloud*, 44.16–24),[81] and takes us a fair distance from the "image-less" ideal of Pseudo-Dionysian mysticism. One recurrent theme is that of divine appropriation: it is fortunate for our author that in Middle English the morphological similarity between "good" and "God" means that the former is inscribed, as it were, in the latter. The apophatic approach is entirely suspended when the reader is advised to apply the words "good gracyous God" like a poultice in order to heal his sick soul (*BPC*, 77.27–28).[82] Whence such frivolous audacity? The image was evidently suggested by the Song of Songs, "Set me as a seal upon your heart, as a seal upon your arm!" (Sg 8:6). The thrust of Cistercian linguistic fantasy, already a powerful influence in shaping the work of Thomas Gallus, was of great intensity.

The author immerses us even further in the Bernardine tradition when he once more takes up the traditional motif, popular since the thirteenth century especially among women, of radical *imitatio* of the naked Christ—"nudus nudum Christum sequi"—and when he evaluates the choice of the anchoritic life as an *imitatio* of this sort, as *Ancrene Wisse* had done.[83] He goes so far as to present sacrifice undertaken by the human being, a devotional offering-up-of-oneself for God, as an echo of Christ's sacrifice,[84] whereby the person has the sense of being transformed into a cross, as seen in the lives of the *Ancrene Wisse* recluses.[85] For the *Cloud* author, love of God includes love of the crucified Christ. Like Bernard (and Hilton), he emphasizes, with reference to Jesus's words, that Christ is at once the doorkeeper and the door to the highest experience of God (*BPC*, 90–91, Jn 10:9; or the giver and the gift); the entrance is by way of *memoria* of Christ's Passion; yet he never dwells on it for long, since, in his view, its vital importance is above all for beginners in the life of faith (*BPC*, 90.11–92.2). Ultimately the adept must leave behind the thought of his humanity; for the author, the actual aim of knowledge of God is to advance by way of love of Jesus God-and-man to pure, spiritual love of God, *amor castus*; here he rejoins the Dionysian tradition. In the *Pistle of Preier* he comments in detail on this Bernardine "chast loue" (105). Spiritualized love-longing is linked—as in Thomas Gallus—with apophatic yearning for the *unimaginable* God, liberated from all concrete points of reference ("I wole... chese to my loue þat þing þat I cannot þink," *Cloud*, 14.21–22). The author is in total agreement with Bernard and Walter Hilton (*Scale of Perfection, Mixed Life*) when he says that it was therefore necessary for Jesus to leave behind the materiality of his physical existence and ascend into the pure world of spirit (*BPC*, 98.17–24);[86] there—alluding to the Athanasian Creed—he was united with God the Father "in onheed of persone" (*Cloud*, 63.9). The anonymous author affirms the incarnation of God, but for him it is enough that the incarnation was of limited duration. Here we have to do with a theological thesis that recurs from time to time, inevitably weakening the mystery of the incarnation. It was not propounded by the monk of Farne—and most decidedly not by Julian of Norwich, as will be demonstrated later. Pseudo-Dionysius himself, as a Christian, does not remain silent regarding the incarnation of the divine in Christ, but this theme is accorded a rather peripheral place in his mysticism; he had already transformed Christ-mysticism into God-mysticism.[87]

In what is probably his first major work, *The Cloud of Unknowing*, the anonymous author tries to give vivid expression to his experience of mysticism by means of exegetical treatment of the biblical lection of Mary and Martha; in other cases, too, he has a knack of offering telling interpretations of biblical texts. Most striking is his interpretation that Jesus does not wish his warning to Martha—she should not let herself be so busy that she forgets the one thing necessary—to be understood as serious criticism, but rather as loving admonishment. Following the tradition, for him Mary is the model of contemplation. She is absorbed in her love of Jesus, which is lauded as "sweet" (*Cloud,* 30.31), and responds to his much greater love. She was so "feruently occupied in sperit aboute þe loue of his Godheed" (lines 33–34) that she no longer heeded his bodily presence, his beauty, but abandoned herself in the darkness of *kenosis* only to his abstract, bodiless divinity, "sche *heng up* [emphasis added] hire loue & hir longing desire in þis cloude of unknowing" (line 25), at which point the author is alluding to a concise definition of mystical devotion in Richard of St. Victor and Guigo II: "elevatio mentis in Deum *suspensae* [emphasis added]."[88] Thus Mary represents for the *Cloud* author the highest level of contemplation of the mystery of being, distanced from everything concrete, even from the thought of the suffering of Christ and *compassio* with Christ on the cross, as altogether from *amor carnalis.*[89] But is there not something problematic in this exegesis? Does it not run in two directions at once? The author would like to invoke Mary as exemplum for the totally apophatic love of unknowable God, whereas she appears in the Gospel narratives as exemplifying the spiritual-sensual love of God made *man* as well, which he has included on other occasions with numerous references to the Bernardine mysticism of love, but which at this point he does not wish to animate in the narrative, even though he repeatedly contrasts the spiritual "coveting" of the one and only good with the worldly desire for material possessions already typical of his age ("concupiscence" as cause of original sin).

If Meister Eckhart had set eyes on this exegesis, he would have offered his own highly individual critique. He, namely, was entirely on Martha's side, and maintained, contrary to all authority of tradition, that there was something immature in Mary's love, since she was "so full of yearning: she longed for something, she did not know what; she wanted something, she did not know what. We suspect that she, dear Mary, sat there more for pleasure than for spiritual profit."[90] For Eckhart it is Martha, not Mary, who attains "inner freedom" and has recognized "the one thing necessary: God."[91] In his view, Martha has already reached unity of love of God and neighbor, which Mary will attain only at some future time, since her mystical experience is still "eroticism of the soul rather than active love."[92] It is not surprising that the *Cloud* author gives his primarily anchoritic reader(s) no more than a mild reminder of the need for neighborly love, since his all-embracing theme is the love of God. Yet he does speak of the necessity of neighborly love for God's sake (*Cloud,* 33.22–25), in accordance with tradition, especially the Bernardine tradition.

The more closely one studies the *Cloud* author's main texts, the more apparent it becomes that he is running into a dilemma. On the one hand, his "reversal" of the Dionysian approach through the mysticism of love leads him to present the object of love as person in the incarnate God-and-man. On the other hand, God for him is identical with "spirit," and this urgently needs to be expressed; here he feels supported by the evangelist's affirmation "God is spirit" (Jn 4:24), and by Paul's words, very popular among mystics, that he who adheres to God is of one and the same spirit (1 Cor 6:17, *Cloud*, 49.14–15; see also *Pistle of Preier*, 106.9–22), counsel that indeed becomes something of a topos in mysticism. At bottom the *Cloud* author's work is permeated by the call to "purity of *spirit*," a specifically Cistercian concept, whereby he does not hesitate to reinterpret one of Paul's statements to suit his own purpose, almost imperceptibly: it is no longer the *body* as in Paul (1 Cor 6:19), but the *soul* that is the temple of the divine spirit (*Cloud*, 71.2–3). Moreover, he draws selectively on "Pauline" statements,[93] and chooses not to mention his message that God is "manifest in the *flesh*" (manifestatum est in carne, 1 Tm 3:16). Later, Julian of Norwich will also interpret Paul selectively to suit her purpose, but her aim is quite the reverse, namely to "pinpoint" knowledge of God in his humanity.

The Devaluation of Corporeality—an Anthropological Dilemma

Without question, for the *Cloud* author the Christian definition of the human being as *personal unity* of body, soul, and spirit threatens to recede into the background. It is true that he does insist on one occasion that he by no means wishes to separate body and soul, which God has joined together, and that God must be served by both (*Cloud*, 50.14–15). It would therefore not be right to impute to him a dualistic concept. Yet the body must be subordinated entirely to the soul, for corporeality is regarded as a well of stinking sin (*BPC*, 92.7–8); the whole person is addressed as sinful "lump" (*Cloud*, 45.34–35), as *massa putredinis* along the lines of Innocent III's newly formulated *contemptus mundi* and of Richard Rolle. It is only the *incorporeal* powers that can contribute to union with God, as we have seen, for contemplation with the aim of *unitio* is a "work of the spirit" (*Cloud*, 15.33), as Thomas Gallus already insisted, who understood the union of the human spirit with the divine on New Testament lines (e.g. Rom 8:5; 1 Cor 2:10, 2:16; and Jn 16:13, 14:17). However, close scrutiny reveals that the *Cloud* author is less opposed to the body than at first seems; for the *Pistle of Preier* says that on earth both "substaunces," body and soul, may reach perfection, and the two may be joined in immortality (107.19–31). Thus, by incorporating incarnation theology the anonymous author went some way toward countering hostility toward the body, even if unintentionally rather than deliberately.

It is hardly surprising that he derives the necessary theological tools, albeit with modifications, from the letters of the apostle Paul, whom he mentions several times; from the time of Adam man has been enslaved to sin; Christ, as new Adam, has freed him from sin. He can be returned to his original state by grace ("refourmyd by grace," *Cloud,* 11.5). Now there is a chance of freedom for the children of God (*Discr. of Stirings,* 114.26–29), and this theme of freedom is, of course, of great importance to the author. But the children must remain true to the "vocatio" (1 Cor 7) they have received from God. With an arresting allusion to Pauline clothing metaphor, the author recommends that the reader should divest himself of his self—like a good lover—in an act of total "noughting," in order to be aware only of God, or to be able, in "concrete" terms, to put on Christ as his clothing (*BPC,* 89.14–22). Here the author employs a feature of Pauline Christology in order to renew the link to the Dionysian tradition. It is impressive to see on several occasions how he discovers such "interfaces" for linking the two mystical approaches. He does not hesitate to smooth over any contradiction that may remain, as when he describes God as mankind's "grounde" (*BPC,* 81.16), while in a different context he follows Paul, according to whom the faithful are all members of one *corpus mysticum* (*Cloud,* 33.34–35), of which Christ forms the head while he is also the ground (*fundamentum,* 1 Cor 3:11) of man. God and Jesus are for him, as for Walter Hilton, without regard to Trinitarian differentiations, "one and the same" (e.g., 116.28–29).

When the *Cloud* author, having taken his lead from Thomas Gallus, gives preference to love in answering the old question as to what makes possible the deepest form of cognition of God, this does not mean that he, or Thomas, should be described as anti-intellectual; he does not by any means demand that rational thought be excluded on the path to experience of God. This is attested by the intellectual conduct of discourse and by the emphatic insistence on God's spirit nature. His conviction that through the experience of loving union with God it is also possible to gain a form of transcendental cognition conforms to a long mystical tradition, as has rightly been observed.[94] Had not the great Cistercian William of St. Thierry already attested something similar with his famous "Amor ipse intellectus est"?[95] Had he not suggested that knowledge is possible through love, and *only* through love? And did not the *St. Trudpert Hohelied* already call itself a book of loving cognition of God? Therefore the *Cloud* author could sometimes use the words *knowing* and *lovyng* as synonyms, which is in line with Rolle's view.[96] Meister Eckhart, of course, would once more raise objections to this proclamation of loving knowledge of God: according to him, love does not enable ascent to God; this is the prerogative of the intellect, which is superior to love. Thought takes God naked,[97] for reason is nobler than the will:

The will takes [understands] God beneath the clothing of goodness, reason takes God naked, disrobed of goodness and being. Goodness is a garment beneath which God is hidden, and the will takes God beneath this robe of goodness. Were it not for God's goodness, my will would not want him at all.... I am not blessed because God is good, I am blessed because God is rational and I recognize this.[98]

For Eckhart, too, love plays an active part, but principally when God has made himself manifest to the soul: "And from this comes the teaching that man shall love God and . . . be intent on him (alone) with no reservation."[99] *Cloud* is not too far from Eckhart when it closes with the Augustinian reflection that a Christian's whole life consists of "holy desire" (74.27; very similarly expressed by Hilton). Even if the *Cloud* author cannot do more than proclaim that fulfillment can be experienced only as a brief foretaste, yet he is one with Eckhart ("wan als vil bist dû in gote, als vil dû bist in vride"; inasmuch as you are in God, you are in peace)[100] and with many other mystics in looking forward to blissful rest and consoling peace ("But eagerly loving and desiring to have God is great, utmost comfort, true ghostly peace, and foretaste of the endless rest," *Discr. of Stirings,* 118.13–14; modern English trans.).

Author and Public of the *Cloud* and Related Works

The author is equipped with a finely developed linguistic sensibility and mastery of language, which enable him to interest the reader in his complicated subject matter, and this is a key reason for the popularity of *The Cloud of Unknowing.* He is able to formulate impressive paradoxes and oxymora, which, according to Alois M. Haas, are an essential feature of mystical language in general.[101] He is also fascinated by the possibilities and limits of linguistic expressive capability, although he hardly expanded this capability through lasting additions to the vocabulary (unlike Eckhart and other German mystics), because the English language developed in different directions. He already had an awareness of the "materiality" of language; he asks the reader to consider that it is formed by the bodily organ of the tongue. He therefore warns against talking of the spiritual in spatial categories, and against using prepositions such as *in* and *up* (*Cloud,* pp. 52–53, 54, 60, 61, 62,

63, 67). Although he insists that God eludes all attempts at description, yet as an author he can take advantage of the analogous manner of speech that gives concrete sensual form to the spiritual.[102] As a further means of escaping the linguistic impasse of having to name the ineffable, he suggests using for the divine a word of one syllable as a kind of mantra; for a monosyllabic word like "God," spoken on a short in-breath, is most appropriate for the spirit, as also for human existence. Thus, when the human being finds himself in dire straits, he utters a one-syllable call for help (e.g., "Fire!"). Union with God, however, occurs beyond language, in complete silence.

For himself, the author has accepted that language must have recourse to bodily analogies when it expresses spiritual content, and that, like the Bible, it must draw on mythical discourse. Therefore, he often chooses images from everyday life, which contribute to a certain personal "aura." The graphic title "The Cloud of Unknowing" lay waiting, as it were, in the apophatic tradition; it is idle to ask who ultimately prompted it.[103]

At times the author "battles" with language, as does Walter Hilton. He warns against a false, exterior grasp of *feelings* (chaps. 48–52). But to maintain that he demythologizes theological talk of God in anticipation of Rudolf Bultmann is wide of the mark.[104] Quite the contrary, he sometimes clothes his mystagogic advice deliberately in childish language (*Cloud,* 48.34) and does not stop short of advising the reader to play a trick on God now and then, for there is something "ludic" in this love between totally unequal partners.[105] Origen takes a different approach, for in his writings it is God who sometimes has to trick the human being in order to reach his pedagogic goal.[106] The *Cloud* author, seeking to combine incarnation and negative theology, puts forward both concrete spiritual sensuality, at times with astonishing imagery, *and* complete abstraction from all concrete ideas in longing for God. Following on from the tradition of negative theology obliges the author to engage in vernacular philosophical-theological discourse, which he conducts very skillfully, even if he does not venture to overstep the bounds of theological thought. For instance, he does not adopt the Dionysian notion that God cannot be defined even as "being." His achievement consists not least in shrewd simplification, for instance with regard to the substitution of *apex mentis* for *scintilla synderesis.* The powerful influence exerted by Thomas Gallus on the shaping of *Cloud* in subject matter and linguistic style has become very clear. It is no exaggeration to say that to a certain degree the *Cloud* author took Thomas's *stilus communis* as his model;[107] he learned from him also by translating the *Mystica theologia.*[108] He knows how to establish a dialogue with his reader, by providing fictional reactions or questions, and he habitually rules out the possibility of misunderstandings by means of an

"I say not," which is then followed by a statement of his actual intention, "but I say..." Yet the question-and-answer technique is more than a mere rhetorical game;[109] it serves the mystagogic purpose of leading the reader toward inner experience. Moreover, he is very fond of arranging his thoughts and terms in "ring and string compositions," which remind Tixier of the circle of petals in a flower.[110]

One of the ways of achieving the rhythm so characteristic of mystical texts, here as elsewhere, is by frequent thematic repetitions. All this gives rise to the impression that an author with a distinct identity of his own—a dynamically engaged scholar, a member of an elite class—is turning quite personally to his reader with an appellative thrust. He combines all the merits of a spiritual English prose that has been maturing over a long period, and has indeed become an art form, having reached its most recent peak in Richard Rolle.

What more can we gather from the *Cloud of Unknowing* group of texts about the author? He is not only a very competent theologian, with roots in Augustinian theology; he also speaks from personal experience and from the conviction of his vocation as a well-versed practicing mystic,[111] and he may have been a priest. His competence in mystical matters is attested by the fire of his argumentation and the intensity of his language. Most probably he studied in Cambridge or Oxford, yet his great learning and unusual theological interests also point toward Paris, and make it likely that he had contacts with the canons of the Victorine foundation. Very probably he completed his studies with a master's degree. Like Walter Hilton, he insists on observance of ecclesiastical doctrine, and is very attentive to the difference between false and true Pauline freedom. With regard to ascetic practices, he pleads for moderation. He writes with great humility (calling himself "a wreche vnworþy to teche any creature," *Cloud*, 72.17), and speaks of his unbridled tongue ("my boystouse beestly tonge," *BPC*, 87.17); but he asserts his authority ("souereinte," *BPC*, 87.7) over the neophyte. He has to accept the addressee's criticism that his writings are too difficult to understand (*BPC*, 76.20–37); nonetheless, he is glad that through his teaching he can help his reader to experience grace.

In recent scholarship—for whatever reason—a consensus has arisen that the author was a Carthusian. A new edition of the entire group of texts was even brought out in the series Analecta Cartusiana. However, this theory is highly problematic, because the author clearly has contacts with the world, and he takes pains to achieve a precise distinction between *vita activa* and *vita contemplativa* (an Augustinian concern).[112] There are four forms of life, "Comoun, Special, Singuler, & Parfite" (*Cloud*, 7.31); in this life, no more than a beginning toward perfection can be achieved; the form chosen by the addressee is the highest possible ("singuler") contemplative form of life, the *singulare propositum,* encountered in depth in Rolle. Yet the *Cloud* author's spiritual experience allows him to review all the forms. He subdivides both the active and the contemplative life into two parts each; they are linked with one another, because the higher part of the active life also constitutes the lower part of the contemplative life (*Cloud,* 17.15–16). Those who are active are, theologically speaking, not "fully" active unless they practice contemplative devotion from time to time; conversely, the contemplatives must participate in Christian activity. Both "converge" in the higher part of the active and the lower part of the contemplative life; the lesser contemplative devotes himself to "meditacions" on his own nothingness and the Passion of Christ "wiþ pite & compassion" (line 28), and on the goodness of God, while the higher part, the *vita contemplativa* in its actual sense, consists in the longing of those within the cloud for the sheer being of God. Without setting out to do so, the author is speaking here of those people who have chosen the "mixed life," but he is not willing to acknowledge this as a distinct form of life that can be voluntarily chosen. He never considers discounting the anchorites' claim to uniqueness.[113] We remember that the hermits took as their motto Isaiah's "Secretum meum mihi." They were proud of the secret experience of their own inwardness. The author is assuredly alluding to this when he advises the adept to direct his *secret* love ("a priue loue put," *Cloud,* 19.1) toward the cloud of unknowing. It is important that this is seen as a reemergence of a first twelfth-century individualism.

Do we glean any more information about the *Cloud* author's readers? He wrote his texts in part in answer to questions put to him, for which reason the epistolary form of the shorter tracts should not be seen as mere fiction. A young man has written of important things to the author, and is encouraged to ask for further explanations if the need should arise (*Cloud,* chap. 74), and the same reader seems to have received such explanations in *BPC.*[114] The actual recipient of *The Cloud of Unknowing* is a twenty-four-year-old man, who has recently been prompted by an inner calling to decide on a life as neophyte in contemplative, hermit-like withdrawal ("solitari forme & maner of leuyng," *Cloud,* 8.15–16). The addressee seems to have been fairly highly educated; avoiding a "Latinate" style need not be taken as proof of his being "illiterate," because the author may have been catering to a more extended circle of readers, beyond the few "specyal freendes in God" (*Cloud,* chap. 47, p. 49.2). In *A Pistle of Discrecioun of Stirings,* for instance, he responds with mild irritation when asked how one can recognize the right proportions between life in solitude and life in community. He introduces an interesting qualification: it is not a matter of when the reader should be alone and when

FIGURE 11. The pilgrim of the *Pèlerinage de la vie humaine* by Guillaume de Deguileville, supported by the staff of hope; it corresponds to the staff of hope emphatically praised by the *Cloud* author. Bibliothèque de Genève, MS fr. 182, fol. 59v. By permission of Bibliothèque de Genève.

in community, for God is hidden *in between* (*Discr. of Stirings,* 114.38–115.13). We may conclude further that this readership consisted of a relatively small, and at the same time aristocratic, circle, patently the same circle for whom *Mirouer* was translated. We should definitely consider the possibility that the intended readership further included a (young) female public;[115] it would be a serious mistake to believe that the very demanding, abstract–intellectual discourse of this author was not intended also for women. To counter any such assumption we need only think of the female audience of Meister Eckhart's German sermons or in particular of *The Mirror of Simple Souls.* That the *Cloud* author's works were handed on to women interested in contemplation is suggested by "A ȝong man *or a womman* [emphasis added], newe set to þe scole of deuocion" (*Cloud,* 47.20–21). The specific interest of this small elite circle[116] is reinforced by allusions to the culture of the court, extending even to the courtly bearing of God himself.[117] The author is, however, at pains to prevent his *Cloud of Unknowing* from falling into the wrong hands.

A further interesting point may be added in conclusion. In *BPC* the human being's submission to the divine will is illustrated by reference to a soft leather glove, a luxury clothing accessory available only to the nobility (*BPC,* 96.20). In *A Pistle of Discrecioun of Stirings,* the French crown appears in allegorical guise, with particular reference "in close-up" to the lily, the heraldic fleur-de-lis (*Discr. of Stirings,* 111.26–33). Here we find ourselves in the vicinity of the great allegorical work by the Cistercian Guillaume de Deguileville, who not only wrote *Le Roman de la fleur de lys,* but above all the verse epic *Le pèlerinage de la vie humaine* (ca. 1355);[118] the image of human life as pilgrimage, *in via* to the divine *patria,* is crucial to the latter text with its aim of pastoral edification (figure 11). Part of the impressive overall structural allegory is the staff of hope, which serves the pilgrim as spiritual support. And this staff of hope is offered with great emphasis by the *Cloud* author in his *Pistle of Prayer* (102.15–103.2), as support in achieving the perfection desired. Thus, the structural image of the pilgrimage is also, as we have seen, a basic idea of the mystics; it confirms that medieval mystical texts should be looked at in their wider literary and theological context.

 CHAPTER 8

Walter Hilton

England's Mystic Theologian

Walter Hilton, with his "modern"-sounding name, is regarded as the actual theologian of English mysticism. Hans Urs von Balthasar has praised him as the author who gave English mysticism its "definitive...shape," and he recalls that Thomas More considered Hilton's *Scale of Perfection* to be the decisive theological work of instruction for the English people up to the time of the Reformation.[1] There is no precise evidence regarding the date of Hilton's birth, or his origins, but it is unlikely that he was born later than 1343. His intellectual and literary activity, like that of the *Cloud* author, belongs to the last quarter of the fourteenth century. This was a troubled and extremely turbulent time of change in several respects, which would surely have encouraged some people to flee from the world. A voracious striving for material gain had become widespread, especially in the merchant class; small enterprises proliferated, greedy for profit. Money and possessions were of paramount importance, and among the higher classes, luxury, honors, and accumulation of offices were considered highly desirable. Decadence became pervasive in various ways, and the church was not free of it. Everything could be, and was, misused for worldly purposes. Even the ideals of monasticism were questioned and contested. Among the mendicant orders, it was now especially the Franciscans who succumbed to material temptations, although they had upheld the ideal of poverty with great insistence. And what of the head of the church? In 1378, while Hilton was leading a fully active life, two popes were elected (Urban VI was declared pope in Rome, Clement VII in Avignon). Assuredly, this notorious schism led to religious uncertainty for many of the faithful—and for some, to a bid for freedom by means of retreat into individual spiritual interiority. Sectarians and enthusiasts appeared with their own particular offers of salvation. Even among the clergy, old certainties began to waver. Grave shortcomings in the church motivated John Wyclif's various "pre-Reformation" attempts at renewal, up to the time of his death in 1384.

In a situation of this sort there was no shortage of work for canon lawyers; Walter Hilton had followed a course of study in canon law, even if he did not complete it with a doctorate. He may have been persuaded to follow this course of study by his family, rather than choosing it himself,[2] for his actual interest was in theology. We know at any rate of a Walter Hilton, bachelor of civil law and canon law, who appeared as a witness in 1375 in an episcopal consistory lawsuit in Ely, not far from Cambridge. He may have been associated at that time with a group of theologians in Cambridge and Ely that supported Thomas Arundel, the contentious theological champion of political order, who sought to combat the beginnings of Lollardy as bishop of Ely. When Arundel became bishop of York in 1388, it seems that Hilton again supported him, this time in suppressing certain undermining tendencies attributed to the Free Spirit movement. After Hilton had served as a canon lawyer for some time, he evidently gave up this activity in order to devote himself to the duties of a secular priest.[3] There are other examples of such a move.

It is striking that Hilton never comments directly on the problematical situation of the church, and the need for reform; he never mentions the schism, and only once does he seem to criticize "the practice of appointment to English benefices by Rome."[4] His concern was evidently with individuals' state of mind and faith.[5]

However, in the early 1380s, a particularly tumultuous time, he must have experienced a conversion that caused him to alter his plan of life and become a hermit, taking up a long-established English tradition. We have a letter from Hilton written to a priest who had likewise studied canon law and was thinking of renouncing secular life (*Epistola ad quemdam seculo renunciare volentem*). Hilton recommends that the priest should follow his vocation and give up the allurements and aberrations of the world (striving for material gain, riches, voluptuousness, corruption, ambition—Augustine's specific *cupiditas*), as he himself has done.[6] Yet it was not long before Hilton abandoned the hermit life.[7]

Evidently he felt drawn once more to the university. There he probably pursued the theological interests that are reflected so impressively in
his works.[8] His commitment to theology was presumably strengthened by
contact with the Franciscan Luis de Fontibus from Aragon, who lectured
on Peter Lombard's Commentary on the Psalms in Cambridge in 1383. In
later years, Hilton translated part of the lost original of the Spaniard's work
as *Eight Chapters on Perfection;* it is an attractive text, related in certain ways
to Hilton's own main work; it has no specifically Franciscan characteristics. Hilton also knew the influential *De remediis contra temptationes* by the
Augustinian monk William Flete, who likewise did not complete his course
of studies, but left Cambridge with a bachelor's degree, began a new life as
a hermit in Lecceto, Italy, and later belonged to a group of advisers around
Catherine of Siena; whether Hilton was personally acquainted with him is
unknown.

Thus it is very likely that Walter Hilton initially sought theological training in Cambridge. This would explain the profound theological knowledge,
hardly attainable by means of private study, that gave him the expertise to
accomplish the novel and influential *Scale of Perfection.* In 1386 he entered
the Augustine priory of Thurgarton near Southwell (Nottinghamshire). This
move may have been motivated not only by his unwillingness to relinquish
secular tasks entirely by becoming a monk, as is frequently said, but also
because it corresponded most closely to the theological training I suspect he
received from the Augustinians of St. Victor. He died in Thurgarton on the
Vigil of the Annunciation in 1395.

There is as yet no ultimate certainty regarding the canon of his works.
The great, two-part *Scale of Perfection* is the major work that stands out above
all others. Beyond that, there are several shorter vernacular texts—*Of Angels'
Song* and particularly *Mixed Life*—in which the combination of *vita activa*
with *vita contemplativa* is to be understood as a new form of life; there are also
the *Eight Chapters on Perfection* already mentioned, translated from a book by
Luis de Fontibus; most probably, the commentary on Psalm 90 (*Qui habitat*)
is also his.[9] There is less reason to ascribe to him a further commentary, on
Psalm 91 (*Bonum est*), which is transmitted together with *Qui habitat* in some
manuscripts.[10] In my view there is no reason at all to believe that he produced
the translation of James of Milan's *Stimulus amoris,* known as *The Prickynge of
Love* or *The Goad of Love;* Hilton's language has very little in common with
the powerful sensual imagery of the Franciscan Passion meditation and its
frequently voiced desire to enter into Christ's wounds.[11] His Latin writings
are mostly letters, a genre favored also by Rolle and the *Cloud* author.

On Hilton's Latin Texts

Unlike Richard Rolle, Walter Hilton wrote his main texts in English, as did the *Cloud* author. He wanted to meet the need for spiritual direction of lay people and religious who were not conversant with Latin, which was still the language of theology.[12] Yet he also wrote some important Latin texts, on which a few remarks must suffice. A Latin letter addressed to an anchorite,[13] *De imagine peccati* (On the image of sin), is thought to be his earliest (surviving) text, written at a time when Hilton was himself a hermit. The recipient, still a young man, had evidently been a respected and wealthy merchant ("mercator"), a social class to which Hilton's pastoral activities seem to have been particularly addressed.[14] As the title suggests, Hilton is already concerned here with his favorite theological-anthropological and Cistercian theme, the corruption of the soul's divine *imago* and *similitudo* into an ugly "ydolum" or "simulacrum."[15] The perverted "amor informis" turns it into the opposite of the "forma formans" of divine love. At the same time, Hilton studiously avoids mentioning the fact that Paul explicitly locates the temple of God in human flesh; like the *Cloud* author, he is willing to grant such a privilege only to the soul.[16] Notwithstanding this alteration of a Pauline tenet, Hilton's work does adopt the specifically Pauline themes of "God in us"[17] and the promise of freedom of the spirit.[18] It has often been surmised, and is indeed thoroughly plausible, that he deliberately took Rolle as his model when he opted, for a time, for the anchoritic way of life.

Another important letter regarding the usefulness and merits of the religious (*Epistola de utilitate et prerogativis religionis*) is addressed to Adam Horsley, a "finance official" in royal service,[19] whose intention of entering a religious order Hilton wishes to encourage. He approves Horsley's preference for Carthusian community and makes persuasive reference to "heretics" who contest the value of monastic life.[20] Hilton puts forward some remarkable reasons for recommending life in a monastic community: monastic discipline is very useful in overcoming inordinate self-love; it also avoids the extremes of "praesumptio" (= "curiositas") and "desperacio." Did an inner crisis of his own lead to this insight? Did he discover for himself the justification of the old charge leveled against the anchorites, that they were egoistically concerned only with their own salvation, and does he therefore subscribe to the recommendation of the hermits' opponents—namely, that a life in holy orders is preferable? This seems very likely, yet any unease that he may have felt did not penetrate too deeply; for after renouncing the solitary life he went on to convey to others, in his major work, the anchorites' spiritual merits. Not long after this letter, Horsley entered the Beauvale Charterhouse.

Hilton, too, opted for life in a monastic community at around this time.[21] Although he had a high regard for the Carthusian solitaries, he decided in favor of the Augustinians, evidently because their *cura pastoralis* enabled them to maintain some contact with the outside world and respond in just measure to the objections regarding the social deficit of the anchoritic life. (The author of *Ancrene Wisse* was most probably also an Augustinian canon.) A further reason may well have been the Augustinian influence on Hilton's theological formation. In true Augustinian spirit, he sees the highest reward of the spiritual life in *enjoyment* of most intimate love (*in fruicione intimi amoris*).[22]

An anchorite and priest is the addressee of a letter on reading the Bible, the right inner attitude, prayer, meditation, and other matters (*Epistola de leccione, intencione, oracione, meditacione et aliis*). The recipient seems to have been well educated. Hilton is not entirely satisfied with the man's state of mind, and raises an unusual objection to it: he is too grandiloquent, eager for knowledge ("curiosus"), and indeed addicted to science ("sciencie multum auida");[23] he still clings too much to unbridled thought and therefore runs the risk of being dazzled by heterodox teaching, a threat noted also by the *Cloud* author. The young man reveals stirrings of criticism of the church and doubts about the unchanging liturgical practice with its "prayers of the hours," and wonders whether God would not be better served by contemplative devotion.[24] Hilton answers that this is not the right understanding of "freedom." Interestingly, what Hilton here fears is that the addressee may be seduced by the movement of the Free Spirit.[25] The letter, presumably written earlier than the *Scale of Perfection*,[26] has all the authority of a recognized spiritual counselor. In fact, his broadsides are aimed less at heretics (who need to be combated) than at superficial ecstatics and enthusiasts. The reader is reminded of the core of Christian belief, and perhaps Hilton indirectly includes himself in the admonishment to acknowledge the fundamental significance of the Bible as guiding principle.[27] Pauline Christology, especially, is brought to mind— belief in Christ crucified (1 Cor 2:2).[28] At all events, Hilton would like to guide the recipient of the letter, whose intellectual activities he follows with a degree of skepticism, to the recognition that God himself is the fire of love, who kindles the fire in him,[29] that God draws his *affectum* and *intellectum* to himself. The term *affectus* for "power of love" occurs very frequently and recalls Aelred and Bernard; the latter is tellingly placed above all other authorities,[30] which makes very good sense, since Hilton follows Bernard in stressing individual experience.[31] A special point of great interest is that Hilton alludes to Origen's theme of the birth of God in the soul— "Concepisti Christum" (you have conceived Christ); "Christus formetur et firmetur in te"),[32]—a theme that is rare in English mystics, though more frequent in German mysticism.[33] This will probably have been taken from the great sermon by Guerric of Igny already mentioned, or from Aelred, rather than from Rhenish mysticism.[34] On the other hand, it is feasible that Hilton's great intellectual agility did in fact enable him to put out feelers to the Continent, and that he first became acquainted there with this theme.

Finally, during his later years as an Augustinian canon, Hilton presumably also wrote a text of very considerable importance in the history of religion, concerning the religious cult of images and the iconographic controversy (*De adoracione ymaginum*).[35] It inquires into the extent to which religious images are admissible for the spiritual life, and whether they encourage sheer idolatry. The author's stance should be understood as a concrete reaction to the Wycliffite iconoclasts of the years 1385 to 1395.[36] Hilton defends portrayals of Christ, the saints, and Mary by arguing that such images do not have an end in themselves, and are not the thing itself (*res*), but only a sign of it (*signa*), and therefore a means to an end—a distinction drawn by Augustine's linguistic semantics in *De magistro*.[37] Their purpose lies in strengthening weak human nature; with them it is possible to teach and to touch, since they appeal to intellect and emotion.[38] Portrayals of the Passion or of the saints serve only as reminders; they intensify devotion.[39] The images are especially useful for beginners and for those who have made some progress in the faith, because these people, in Paul's words, cannot yet digest solid food, but only milk. Aelred had used very similar arguments in addressing his enclosed sister. But the more perfect the Christian is, the less need he has of the support of images. At this point it is only fair to observe that in his own work Hilton does not hesitate to make effective use of graphic imagery.

Mixed Life and *Of Angels' Song*

In *Mixed Life* Hilton recommends specifically a mixed ("medeled") life as practical compromise for lay people with social, professional, or personal obligations, as well as for people in religious orders engaging in pastoral care.[40] His tract is addressed to a wealthy lord of his acquaintance with a large household and tenants;[41] yet this may perhaps be merely a fictitious person. In commending this mixed form of life, Hilton extols Christ himself as the greatest exemplum. Once more, reading the Bible is expressly recommended; it helps to kindle love of God and longing for him. At the same time, Hilton advises the man, who has some inclination toward mysticism, not to strive for slavish imitation of monastic contemplation—that is, not to be too anxious to intensify his devotions, or to ascend (with Bernard) from contemplation of Christ's humanity to "knowynge or feelynge more goosteli of þe god-hede,"[42] because there is a danger of going astray.[43] Rather, he should be content with what is within his reach, remain open to the workings of grace, and do service to any neighbor in need.

Among Hilton's shorter vernacular texts, his tract on the music of the angels (*Of Angels' Song*) merits attention; here, too, he is concerned with the role of the human imagination's sensuality in communicating spiritual matters. Hilton's major work testifies to his great interest in angels—in which he differs, for instance, from Julian of Norwich. Although the astonishing choice of angel music as the subject of an entire tract may be attributed in part to Richard Rolle's extensive efforts to make his readers truly aware of it, the immediate prompting was a request from a person close to Hilton, who wanted to learn from him what angels' song and heavenly music actually were, and how they could be experienced. Beneath the surface there probably lay a desire for protection against the diabolic seduction that could ensue from sensory delusions.[44]

Here Hilton stresses that in her lower form, her sensuality, the soul can be made joyful in spirit by the experience of the inner senses. Thus she experiences the name of Jesus as in *Dulcis Iesu memoria* as "hony, and als sang,"[45] and reacts to this with psalms and songs of praise. Hilton does not actually mention the *iubilus* as musical-ecstatic self-expression here or, as far as I can see, anywhere else in his work; he merely circumscribes it. He comes up with the highly original notion that through her love for God the soul is ravished by "the presence of angels . . . oute of mynde of al erthli and fleschly thyngs into a hevenly ioy."[46] This statement recalls the motif of the singing angel as psychopomp, leading the dying man to heaven, which occurs in various forms in the Middle Ages,[47] particularly in the Cistercian Deguileville's *Pèlerinage de l'âme,* in which singing angels play a major part; they sing "inset songs" and guide souls to heaven amid great joy.[48] The actual experience of angel song is for Hilton, as for others, a gift of grace beyond mimesis, that cannot be described because it transcends anything that human beings can imagine.[49]

For a long time it was widely held that Hilton considered Rolle's imagery dangerously excessive, and wanted to warn people against it. But this assumption cannot be sustained. Much of what we read in Hilton's tract corresponds to Rolle's "musical mysticism." When Hilton warns against false, illusory celestial music, he surely does not mean the *melos* that constitutes the essence of Rolle's mystical experience (neither here, nor in *Scale of Perfection,* pt. 1, chap. 10);[50] for he, too, could speak in his *De imagine peccati* of the "heavenly melos" (*melos celicum*)[51] and extol the bliss of experiencing mystical music in the *Dulcis Iesu memoria* tradition, without seeing any need to dwell on the misunderstanding of this musical concept to which some of Rolle's successors succumbed. He takes to task the enthusiasts who make great efforts to overcome their sins and perceive heavenly things ("be violence"),[52] but only succeed in overtaxing their psychological and physical powers. He is convinced that this can result in harmful fantasies, leading to heresy. (*Ancrene Wisse* and *The Cloud of Unknowing* had already warned of this danger.) Assuredly, in his description of angels' song Hilton is not concerned to define or locate the experiencing of celestial music with theological precision. If he had wanted to act as a critic of Rolle's language, he would not have extolled the fire of mystical love with similar intensity, and he would not have shown such modesty as he does in this tract. He would have us know that in this matter he has no ultimate certainty, because he lacks the "felyng" of actual mystical experience; if another person comes through grace to a different understanding, he will be glad to retract his argument.[53]

Hilton's Vernacular Masterpiece: *The Scale of Perfection*

Hilton's major work, the vernacular *Scale of Perfection,* is an impressive spiritual guide, on which his timeless spiritual authority is grounded. Late-medieval appreciation of its two books is attested by its transmission in more than forty manuscripts, and by the translation into Latin by the Carmelite Thomas Fishlake, undertaken around 1400.[54] *Scale* probably dates from Hilton's years as an Augustinian canon (between 1386 and 1395). The first part was conceived primarily as a spiritual rule of life for a recluse, as is revealed in the text (*Scale* 1:32 and 79).[55] Manuscript evidence leads to the conclusion that initially only the first part, which was particularly popular, was in circulation, and that Hilton wrote the second part somewhat later.[56] The recluse was presumably a real person, since a few concrete remarks relate to her directly. She comes from a very well-placed background ("richesse" is spoken of, *Scale* 1:33), and still habitually thinks in material categories; she may have been a member of the aristocracy. She is not highly educated; Latin quotations are translated for her. However, she seems to have had a certain inclination toward individual theological thinking and questioning. Thus she is admonished to relinquish her own intellect, not to doubt ecclesiastical authorities, to adopt only the faith of the church, and not to throw in her lot with the heretics.

The title picks up the old image of the ladder ascending to the heavens; its Christian use goes back to the ladder seen by Jacob in his dream (Gn 28:12); it also recalls Guigo II's important *Scala claustralium.* The work does not fulfill systematically the expectation of a step-by-step ascent to perfection, as evoked by the image of the ladder. Within the tradition, Origen was the first to stress the ideal of perfection. Concrete models for the text can be found in the famous recluses' rules of life, Aelred's *Institutio inclusarum* (translated into English at least twice in the fourteenth century), *Ancrene Wisse* (and the *Meditationes vitae Christi*), as well as Rolle's *Form of Living*. The recipient is not addressed again as the text proceeds. Hilton takes the opportunity to include a wider readership, "A man or a woman" (e.g., *Scale* 1:123), as the *Cloud* author had done; but his starting point is repeatedly masculine. The situation is similar in the second part of the *Scale*. The initial addressee again seems to be a female recluse (perhaps the same one). Hilton warns against ingratitude for food that does not taste good; the *Ancrene Wisse* recluses were admonished to accept donations of food with gratitude, even if they did not like the taste. This time, however, Hilton is writing for a very mixed readership, or audience, no longer made up only of recluses or religious, but also of people with less education and with more, including in the latter case persons with some knowledge of Latin.

One point of interest is that in the first part of the *Scale* Hilton deals with the old charge brought against recluses, namely that they devote themselves only to their own self-perfection and pay no attention whatsoever to active works of charity. We already saw how, on this account, Meister Eckhart gave pride of place to Martha rather than Mary, and Hilton himself gave up the eremitic life, presumably for the same reason. He is still convinced of the great spiritual qualities of this form of life, but he reminds the reader of her obligation to love her neighbor (*Scale* 1:106–7). Aelred, too, demands neighborly love from his recluse, which must be undertaken for God. She also has a divine obligation to love her enemy, and may not condemn anyone. But he adds the admonishment familiar from *Ancrene Wisse* that she must not take her philanthropy too far; she seems to receive a disproportionate number of visitors. Nor should she leave her cell under any circumstances, whereby it may come as a surprise that she should have been able to do so at all. A recluse was not always enclosed permanently; occasionally she received permission to take part in a pilgrimage.[57] In Germany two cases are known in which a recluse was even handed a key of her own when she was enclosed.[58] The rules of life imposed on the recluse by Hilton's book are in fact very moderate: idleness is strictly to be avoided (as in *Benedict's Rule* and in Aelred); the guiding principle for the conduct of life overall, and especially for ascetic practice, is "discrecion," which alone makes possible a wholesome moderation—an instruction which is something of a topos in the English texts. Therefore, severe self-chastisement, and especially self-scourging (*Scale* 1:32) is rejected, as is customary in English mysticism.[59]

It is often asserted, mistakenly, that the two parts of the *Scale* differ greatly from one another in their themes. And there is a widely held view that in the first book Hilton tended toward a theocentric orientation, under the influence of *Cloud,* while in the second part he inclined toward Christocentric piety; in the second book, the name of Jesus frequently replaces the name of God.[60] However, without question, wherever God is mentioned in the first book, Jesus is also meant—in accordance with the theology of the entire work, and with that of the *Cloud* author. Without doubt, Hilton wanted the two parts to be understood as a coherent whole;[61] they are closely connected with one another and form a convincing entity. Ostensibly the second part was motivated by the desire of the reader of the first part to receive more detailed discussion of its subject matter (recalling the fact that *The Book of Privy Counselling* was presented as response to the recipient's request for deeper discussion of *The Cloud of Unknowing*). Whereas the first book circulated without a title, for the complete work Hilton chose the title *Scala perfectionis,* to which the second part alludes.[62]

Two distinctive characteristics immediately strike the reader of *The Scale of Perfection*. First, far more than most other English mystical texts, it is concerned with human *interiority*. Hilton never tires of stressing the decisive importance of withdrawing entirely into one's innermost self. Second, the impact of *Scale* as a unified whole is reinforced by deliberate recourse to Paul, a significant fact already encountered in *Ancrene Wisse,* Rolle, and the *Cloud* author. Hilton, like his medieval contemporaries, sees Paul as a mystic and gives a mystical interpretation to "we in Christ and Christ in us." Moreover, at the end of the first book Hilton quotes Paul's statement that he must look after his faithful until Christ is born in the soul (he had already alluded to this in his *Epistola de leccione*).[63] Hilton sees Paul as spiritual mother pro tempore, since he "baar me and thee and othere also with traveile, as a woman bereth a child, unto the tyme that Crist hath His ful schap in us and we in Hym" (*Scale* 2:132). Since Hilton repeatedly denies for his own part any experience of contemplative *unio,* he cannot be expected to focus specifically on *unio* as such, and it is significant that Paul's ecstasy is not mentioned, from which we may conclude that Hilton is content, in composing his major work, with a mystagogic and pastoral intention.

Theological Anthropology

Although Hilton is acclaimed as *the* theologian among the English mystics, Julian of Norwich surpasses him in individuality and profundity of thought, yet even she learned something from him. He is firmly rooted in the patristic tradition, but any attempt to isolate separate "building blocks" in his work leads only to a hazy overall impression, especially when an attempt is made to identify numerous names. We can exclude the imputed influence of Franciscan theology (Duns Scotus, Ockham) as inaccurate or insignificant.[64] It is much more useful to inquire into the main outlines of his theological structure. He mentions by name Gregory the Great, Anselm of Canterbury, Hugh and Richard of St. Victor, Thomas Aquinas; it is hardly necessary to emphasize that as an Augustinian canon he owes a great deal to Augustine.[65] In general, the early Cistercians (William, Gilbert of Hoyland)[66] were the inspiration behind the development of his spirituality. These influences came together, as we have seen, in the Augustinians of St. Victor, under whom Hilton may have studied. *One* Cistercian must be given especial mention, whom he praises above all others in one of his Latin texts: Bernard of Clairvaux (esp. the commentary on the Song of Songs and the tract *De diligendo Deo*).[67] Scholars have identified numerous Bernardine echoes, and it has rightly been said that "Bernard's influence is pervasive throughout Hilton's writings."[68] Yet it has often been deemed sufficient merely to identify isolated echoes, while neglecting the pervasive Bernardine "grounding." Finally, attention must be drawn to the affinity with the towering, still very recent, figure of the hermit Richard Rolle, whose language, full of spiritual sensuality, transmits the torch of incandescent love.

In the first part of *Scale* Hilton unfolds the doctrine of man as the image of God, which was very important to Augustine and especially to Cistercian theological anthropology. For Hilton the soul has two constituent parts, *sensualite* and *reason (Scale* 2:159); *reason,* the *anima rationalis,* is again made up of an upper and a lower part. Through the structure of the upper part, the *ratio superior,* with its soul-powers of *mind, reason,* and *will* as understood by Augustine, the soul is created as a trinity. The *Cloud* author had already argued along these lines, making it unnecessary for us to dwell again on this way of thinking. For Hilton, as for the author of *Cloud,* oneness with God is made possible by the upper part of the *anima rationalis* ("the ouere partie of resoun," *Scale* 1:159), or the *acies mentis* ("poynt of thi thought," e.g. *Scale* 1:57).[69] Woman, however, is equated with the lower part, the *ratio inferior,* because her part is to obey: "And the nethere is likned to a woman, for it schulde be buxum to the overe partie of resoun, as a woman is buxum to man" (*Scale* pt. 2, chap. 13, p. 159).

From the *imago Dei* theory is derived the call for self-scrutiny, essential also to Bernard and the *Cloud* author, since knowledge of the self is an important step toward knowledge of God. Self-knowledge also leads to humility, making man aware of the great distance he has put between himself and the primordial divine image. Here Hilton recalls Jesus's insistence that denial of the self must precede the decision for discipleship. Like Augustine and Gregory the Great, whom he mentions by name,[70] Hilton augments denial of the self, as does the *Cloud* author, even to the point of self-hatred and horror (*Scale* 2:174); this is then mitigated by his demand—prompted by the love of God and shared by Augustine and Bernard—for love of self, combined with love of all creatures (*Scale* 1:110–11), since God may be found in all his created beings. At the same time, Hilton insists on the continuing indestructible dignity of man, on account of his likeness to God (and as child of God)—a grand and long-neglected notion, rediscovered by modern theology in all its significance. Yet through sin man's upright (*rectus*) bearing, which should be rising heavenward, has become curved in the Augustinian sense (*curvatus*), as has already been seen in the *Cloud* author, and prior to that, in *Ancrene Wisse* (*Scale* 2:200).[71]

Hilton goes on to develop an astonishingly original interpretation of the *imago Dei* doctrine, which eloquently confirms his ability to think in images. He raises this doctrine to a new graphic sensuality and plastic three-dimensionality, giving his anthropology a compelling vividness. For Hilton, namely, the divine image in the soul has been contaminated and transformed into a graven image (*Scale* 1:126). The fleshly *simulacrum* whose parts are formed by sin, like the belly, has obscured the divine *imago,* blackened it, and indeed entirely covered it over. A person who is not baptized no longer has the primordial image; its place has been taken by the image of the devil.[72] As was customary in the Middle Ages, Hilton expresses the "diabolic" idolatrous perversion of this image by giving the face the features of Mohammed as the head of the inimical religion. Hilton's "two-image doctrine"[73] is completed by the notion that the idol is clad not with seemly clothing but only with a stinking cloth (*Scale* 1:90). Man's task is to work toward restoration of the image of Jesus, or God, in the soul through faith; only then can Christ's provision of outer vesture occur, as envisaged by Paul. Thus Hilton succeeds in giving original, vivid shape to a vital theological theme.[74]

The perversion of the divine image in the soul also causes her to be subjected to darkness. In demonstrating to his reader that this makes it very difficult for anyone to find the treasure concealed within, Hilton employs a hermeneutic process that shows him to be a master of combinatory Bible exegesis, as was Richard Rolle. Since the addressee of part 1 of the *Scale* has lost Jesus, she must dig deep into her soul. The starting point of his argumentation is Jesus's parable of the woman who watches over ten drachmas in her house, and is now urgently seeking one of the coins, which she has lost (Lk 15:8–10; *Scale* 1, chap. 48, pp. 86–87). Because of the darkness in her oriental house, she finds it only after lighting a lamp. When her search is successful she is beside herself with joy. While the drachma displays the portrait of the imperator, Hilton identifies the coin with Jesus, who can be found in the soul with the help of the lamp, interpreted as the word of God (alluding to the popular biblical verse, Ps 119:105), and especially as the reason of the *anima rationalis*. Through associative linking of text citations, Jesus, who has been lost, is identified not only with the coin, the "penni," but also with the *Deus absconditus* of Isaiah (Is 45:15; a motif favored by Meister Eckhart and Johannes Tauler),[75] and as the hidden treasure in the field for which man must dig. This is theologically absolutely correct, for in this parable (Mt 13:44) Jesus means the kingdom of heaven that dawned with him; but at the same time there is a mystical application of the Pauline "Christ in me," who for him is synonymous with God, but whose human figure is also duly acknowledged here. The process of association then leads to the tale of Jesus sleeping in the boat with his disciples during a storm on the Sea of Galilee. This is an impressive attempt to give exegesis a tropological turn, through which Hilton arrives at an interpretation of this story entirely different from that of Tauler. While Tauler uses the text to focus on the theme of "mystical dereliction,"[76] Hilton promises the reader hope of the joyful experience of God's proximity: "Jhesu slepeth in thyn herte gosteli" (*Scale* 1:88). Jesus sleeps, as it were, the archetypal sleep of innocent introversion in the boat of the soul, untouched by the tumult of the world; he need only be discovered and roused by the believer. At the same time, the believer is indirectly challenged to rival the sleeping son of God, and to practice trusting, sovereign tranquillity; which means that the theme of "releasement" ("Gelassenheit," mystical "gelazenheit"), so important in Rhenish mysticism,[77] is here coming to the fore in English mysticism, even if no separate term for it is available in English.

In his exegesis Hilton is remarkably successful at melding his biblical references into one, and at facilitating visualization of the central Pauline notion of Christ's reciprocal attachment to man, to an extent unprecedented in English mysticism. He sets out to show how the soul may experience anew her likeness to God, through the hard travail of scrutiny of conscience and *annihilatio* of the self, and above all through God's care.

Admittedly, Hilton cannot see his way to integrating man's corporeality—considered by some to be morally neutral—into the idea of the likeness of God, because his vision is always restricted to the corrupting quality of *sensualite* (as was that of the *Cloud* author). His "potentially flesh-hating statements" have rightly been deplored,[78] but it has also been observed that he was no Manichaean; likewise the *Cloud* author, and Aelred before him, had

refuted the suspicion of Manichaeism. The wholesome influence of Origen
has evidently been suspended here, as for the *Cloud* author; but the target
of his strictures is not the flesh as such, but rather the "faculties of the soul
directed towards created and fallen things opposed to God, and thus towards
sin."[79] With direct reference to Paul, he associates the two-image doctrine
with the two "laws" to which man is subject: in the soul, man complies with
God's law through his will and reason; with his sensuality, he fulfills the law of
sin.[80] Hilton is not committed to the devaluation of sensuality as such—the
future ennobling of the flesh through bodily resurrection is a truth of faith
for him as for others (*Scale* 2:141)[81]—but rather to the notion that man was
corrupted to a heavy lump of bodily corruption ("an hevy lompe of bodili
corrupcioun," *Scale* 2:245; similarly in *Cloud,* drawing on Augustine) when
his originally neutral *sensualite* lapsed into sin.[82] Therefore he does not punish
human sensuality with severe asceticism or chastisement.[83]

Yet Walter Hilton is an author capable of change, as a glance at the tract *Of
Angels' Song* makes clear. In this tract he seems to articulate a more advanced
insight when he asserts that the soul is transformed into the deity with abounding love, and this affects also the *lower* part, sensuality ("In this maner wyse a
saule es mad gastli in the sensualite be habundaunce of charite that es in the
substance of the saule");[84] especially in her sensuality, formerly responsible for
sin, the soul undergoes this new, joyful, spiritual experience. At the same time,
her eyes are opened to the fact that God alone is to be seen, heard, and felt in
all creatures,[85] a striking statement that also occurs in *Scale*. Behind it is Paul's
proclamation that in all things God is everything ("all in all"), which was
adopted by Augustine and Bernard. It will be taken up again, most impressively, by Julian of Norwich (see the further discussion in chaps. 9 and 11).

Furthermore, in Hilton's work, too, the soul is promised the *deificatio* articulated in *Cloud*. She joins the ranks of those referred to by Paul as sons of
God, or perceives herself as child of God. This experience of God through
Jesus the beloved is, of course, a gift of grace, which she does not control; it
can be felt only for brief moments, because he repeatedly withdraws, and
therefore the human being must accept an alternation of absence and presence (*Scale* 2:243)—a discourse in accord, once again, with the author of *The
Cloud of Unknowing.*

On Hilton's View of Contemplation, Prayer, and Meditation

Although the actual purpose of the rule of life in the first part of *Scale* is
to provide mystagogic instruction leading toward inner experience of God,
Hilton diverges from the usual terminological differentiation of the separate

steps into *lectio, meditatio, oratio,* and *contemplatio.* Since *lectio* is available to his addressee only to a limited degree, owing to her lack of formal education, he passes over this stage and begins, surprisingly, with *contemplatio* as a superordinate term, which is then subdivided three or four times. The lowest stage of contemplation is taken to be the merely knowledgeable, scholarly familiarity with the path to mystical experience through Bible study and patristic doctrine, still lacking in love. The second form of contemplation comprises two levels; the lower is a "tasting of the sweetness of God" received in faith (*Scale* 1:36), which may occur, unexpectedly, even in busily active people as a gift of grace (as Augustinian *gratia gratis data*), but cannot be willed to occur, and lasts only for a short time. The higher level of the second form of contemplation is the domain of religious who have rejected the world and who, "in great rest of body and soul" (*Scale* 1:37), aim to abandon themselves entirely to devotion, which may take the form of affective love, or of prayer and meditation. Whoever is at the second stage longs for the highest form of *contemplatio,* through which perfection is attained "by ravishing" (*Scale* 1:38) of the boundless love of God (*Scale* 1:56), in Bernard's sense, in oneness of knowing and loving, and conforming to the image of the Trinity in celestial joy. Nothing can be more pleasing to the soul than to experience the gracious presence of Jesus within, and to be nourished with the favor of his face not otherwise to be seen ("priveli perceivynge the gracious presence of Jhesu, feleabli feed with favour of His unseable blissid face," *Scale* 2:245).

Since prayer and meditation fulfill an important function in the second form of contemplation, Hilton likewise pays close attention to them. In fact, prayer—the subject of chapters 24–33 of the first part of the *Scale,* and chapter 42 of the second part—is indeed the most essential constituent of contemplation.[86] Here again he differentiates, and distinguishes between three forms of prayer. The first is verbal prayer, made up principally of liturgical texts, not least the psalms. The second form of prayer is practiced verbally, but without any preformulated text; this is for Hilton "the most intense stage."[87] The third form is a continuous prayer without language, in inner, incandescent loving devotion, a dynamic fire of love-longing for God (*Scale* 1:58).[88] As he goes on to explain in the second part, the soul is entirely transformed into the fire of love, and every word of secret prayer is like a spark leaping up from a fire, cleansing all the powers of the soul and turning them into love ("and therfore eche word that it priveli praieth is like unto a sparcle springynge out of a fierbrond, that clanseth alle the myghtes of the soule and turneth hem into love," *Scale* 2:247), and he adds the defining notion that prayer transports the devotee, as it were, into the presence of

Jesus.[89] With this discussion of the different forms of prayer, Hilton helps the reader to understand its form and function, and it is therefore not surprising that he was regarded for a long time as *the* English authority on the subject.[90] Admittedly, he confesses that he himself has not achieved all that he writes of in relation to prayer, but this should probably be read as an instance of the "modesty topos."

After dealing with prayer, Hilton turns to meditation as the next part of *contemplatio*. *Meditatio* often results from biblical *lectio*, but he passes over this traditional association, since reading the Bible is not an option for his addressee, as we have seen. Rather, *compunctio*, the God-given remorse for personal failure, and the ensuing tears, are a focus of *meditatio*, as is, most especially, the visualization of Christ's Passion, resulting in empathetic compassion with Christ's sufferings on the cross. Hilton says that God gives some tenderhearted women such capacity for devotion that they melt into tears at the mere mention of his precious Passion. This is why, later on, Margery Kempe makes direct mention of "Hilton's book."[91] Hilton continues the tradition, started by Anselm and taken to a high peak by Aelred, of attaching great importance to his addressee's direct participation in the events of the Passion, as one who is present. In this process, imagination has a positive function (unlike in *The Cloud of Unknowing*): it is through the reader's imagination and creative fantasy that the affective Cistercian *amor carnalis* of God incarnate is developed ("fleischli love of God, as Seynt Bernard callith it," *Scale* pt. 1, chap. 35, p. 68). Hilton does not describe in detail how this may come about, but like Bernard he stresses the need to overcome *amor carnalis* through *amor spiritualis* or *amor castus,* in order to experience entirely the love of the spiritual being of God (with which the *Cloud* author concurs).[92]

Of course, in *oratio* and *meditatio* there is also an intensification of the spiritual senses (e.g. drunkenness, *Scale* 1, chap. 44, pp. 81–82; the olfactory senses, e.g. *Scale* 2, chap. 42, which talks of the fragrance of prayer).[93] But particularly marked is Hilton's use, already touched upon, of the fire imagery so richly attested and grounded in the Bible; he takes it up with an intensity reminiscent of Bernard and several other theological writers, but above all of Richard Rolle and the *Cloud* author, when he says that the touch of the tiniest spark of divine light is more than can be endured, so that the human being bursts asunder through intensity of love (*Scale* 2:203). The term "metaphor" is inadequate for such an existentially shattering experience. The fire may not exist physically, but, as Jeremiah knew, its effect is *like* that of real fire, it is of comparable violence and can affect the body, or extend to it, as Hilton allows (*Scale* 1, chap. 31; *Scale* 1, chaps. 26, 28, 33; God as "consuming fire" [*ignis consumens*], p. 216). With his mystagogic work Hilton wants to contribute to the fulfillment of Jesus's purpose, so frequently cited (since *Ancrene Wisse*): "I am come to send fire on the earth; and what will I, if it be already kindled?" (Lk 12:49; also *Latin Writings,* 2:230).

The second part of the *Scale* often refers to prayer and meditation together. This part, namely, is essentially concerned to show how the higher form of contemplation that leads to perfection is constructed on the fundaments of faith and is open to all, not only to religious. Hilton discusses this with the famous and original terminological distinction that predominates in the second part: he differentiates between "reforming in faith" and "reforming in faith and feeling." For the ordinary Christian, "reforming in faith" is enough, *belief* in Christ's act of salvation and in the effectiveness of the sacraments of baptism and penance. This is stressed by allusion to Paul (Rom 5:1): "he that is maad rightful bi baptym or penaunce, he lyveth in feith, the whiche sufficeth to savacion and to heveneli pees, as Seynt Poul seith: *Iustificati ex fide, pacem habemus ad Deum*" (*Scale* 2:148).[94] Since the Christian must constantly strive to shape his will in harmony with the will of God, "reforming in faith" is the prerequisite also for the true path of the contemplative, who then, on account of his continuing liability to lapse into sin, is in need of a new *conversio* or *reformatio* beyond the stage of belief, not only in "faith" but also in "feeling," in order to ascend to the peak of contemplation. Even if "reforming in faith and feeling" may lead to *unio,* Hilton distinguishes this from "reforming in feeling," which consists in the soul's pure beholding of God, not yet possible on earth, whereby "reforming" then belongs to the past. He clarifies the threefold "reforming" by means of a telling comparison with varying perceptions of the sun: the first stage is comparable to a blind person who cannot yet see the sun, but has to believe in it; the second corresponds to gazing at the sun with eyes closed, partially perceptible through its warm rays; the third, direct view of the sun corresponds to the pure beholding of God.[95]

Knowing God through Loving God: An Old Theme Newly Interpreted

It is not at all easy to see what Hilton actually means by the term "feelyng," so important for English mysticism. We may start from the close association of feelyng with Pauline theology, especially Rom 12:2, where the apostle warns against conforming to the world ("conformari"), because everything depends on being reformed ("reformari") "in newed of felynge" (in novitate *sensus; Scale* 2, chap. 31). Thus for Hilton "feelyng" functions as translation for *sensus,* which is in turn a rendering of the weighty philosophical

Greek term *nous,* encompassing the fields of consciousness, rationality, and feeling, and thereby the core of personality;[96] it was a central concept of the twelfth-century mystics.[97] Hilton's range of meaning is equally extensive, and "feelyng" relates to the experience or knowledge of God. With the help of further citations from Paul he tries to make his notion of knowledge of God more precise, and it is indeed very remarkable to observe the extent to which his theology is based on Paul, as received by Bernard of Clairvaux and William of St. Thierry. The highest form of knowledge occurs in the reforming of *mens* in the soul center ("renovamini spiritu *mentis* vestrae"), as we learn through a further Pauline reference. Hilton equates *mens* with *ratio superior;* for him, the likeness of God in man is to be sought in "reson." But in addition to the comprehending intellect, the affective-voluntative capability participates in experience of God; this, too, is implicit in "feelynge," which can be used collectively for the inner, spiritual senses. A "perfight knowynge of God" (*Scale* 2:211) occurs in the highest consummation of the human being's *reformatio;* it is the "newe feelynge" (*Scale* 2:211)—the directing of the whole person's striving toward desire for God in love. In essence this had already been suggested in *Scale* 1 by a long quotation from Paul's "canticle of love" (1 Cor 13).

It would, however, be wrong to seek in Hilton's *Scale* a two-part, strictly differentiated experience of God, through knowing and loving,[98] even if this is a fundamental theme in the Late Middle Ages.[99] For he is never concerned with a need for separate intellectual, epistemological knowledge of God, but rather, continuously, with *loving* knowledge, although he may sometimes appear to see in knowledge the power to kindle love. The matter is resolved most clearly in chapter 34 of the second part. Although Hilton explains here that "love cometh oute of knowynge and not knowynge of love" (*Scale* 2:217), this sentence can only be understood correctly in context: by a typi-cally mystical paradox, the statement is then reversed, inasmuch as "love" is made the precondition for this "knowynge"—the prior "unformed" love of God. God bestows himself on man in love and grace through the divine spirit, being himself "both the giver and the gift," directly quoting William of St. Thierry.[100] Therefore Hilton recommends to his readers that they should desire only love ("thou schuldest oonli *coveiten* love," *Scale* 2:217, emphasis added). It is worth noting that, in a materialistic age gripped by avidity and craving, Hilton—like the *Cloud* author—uses the verb "coveiten," which is etymologically linked with *cupiditas:* one form of cupidity must be driven out by a different, higher one. The longed-for, anterior, divine love is the reason "whi this soule cometh to this knowynge and to this love that cometh of it" (*Scale* 2:218). Here Hilton is entirely in accord with the verse he quotes from the First Letter of John: "We love him, because he first loved us" (1 Jn 4:19).[101]

Therefore, when "understanding," "vision," "contemplation" are offered as translations of the term "feeling," they can be no more than approximations, covering only one of its multiple meanings at a time, from one perspective.[102] For the rest, Hilton adopts a very modest stance when it comes to *unio* itself. He refers to the requisite experience, which he himself has not gained in sufficient measure. It is also striking that although, as far as I can see, he does not refer to the mystical *raptus* of the apostle Paul, yet "ravishen" or "ravishing" are the words he favors for the process of mystical union through divine special grace (*gratia specialis*).[103] With regard to union itself, he is content to offer the future prospect of divine "presence."

Hilton's terminology does not enable him to define his theological position with total clarity, as is demonstrated by contradictory research outcomes. On account of a misunderstanding, even Minnis, in his profound and otherwise very useful essay, was drawn into a contradiction which turns the argument upside down. In his view, Hilton was writing for a less elite readership, indeed for "lesser mortals,"[104] than was the author of *The Cloud of Unknowing,* but nevertheless attached greater importance to knowledge of God through "intellection":

> However, it would seem that the intellect plays the dominant role. The view of Gallus and the *Cloud* author that the principal affection is a cognitive power, and the highest one possessed by the human soul, is not shared by Hilton, who believes rather that the supreme cognitive faculty is the intellect, which is, considered in relation to the other human faculties, superior to the will or *affectus.* In the mental ascent through the degrees of perfection the intellect leads the way, since affection follows intellection: "lufe comiþ oute of knowynge & not knowynge oute of luf."[105]

Yet why should Hilton, of all people, give preference to *intellectual* knowledge of God for his less intellectual readers? Here the emphatically affective character of Hilton's mysticism is overlooked, which leads him, appropriately enough, to recommend Bernard to the recipient of one of his epistles. Of course, he does not demand, as the *Cloud* author does, that God should be loved in spite of the impossibility of knowing him, for in order to love it is necessary to know why one should love; "loving" presupposes "understanding," as another Cistercian, the great William of St. Thierry, puts it in one of his *Meditations:* "for nothing is loved except by being understood, nor understood except by being loved, and when a man is found worthy to enjoy a thing he does not do so unless he also both loves and understands it."[106] By knowledge of God, Hilton does not mean a deep intellectual experience, which he could not expect of "lesser mortals" in any case, but rather a knowledge of God as revealed to man in holy scripture, and tailored according to his needs (chap. 40).

For Hilton this results in a close interweaving of knowing and loving, which is entirely in accord with the understanding of the *Cloud* author. Moreover, he is in agreement with the anonymous author of that work (and the apophatic tradition) in teaching the necessity of total congruence between the divine and the human will. Protracted study of Hilton's *Scale* does not dispel the impression that there are numerous highly interesting points of contact with the author of *Cloud*.[107] Hilton, too, touches on the limits of the linguistic potential for expressing transcendence; he knows that language must resort to images and therefore cannot be taken literally. Just like the *Cloud* author, he warns against a literal understanding of the spatial prepositions "above" and "within" (*Scale* 2:215.) Thus Hilton is carrying forward the apophatic tradition, even if scholars often overlook this fact; he speaks of the need for the human being intent on experiencing God to take upon himself the hard travail of loosening all ties, and entering into darkness, for which reason Hans Urs von Balthasar even gained the impression that he was anticipating St. John of the Cross's theology of the night.[108]

Hilton evokes this darkness with the help of a rightly famous allegory, based on the narrative of a journey to Jerusalem (*Scale* 2, chaps. 21–23).[109] Structurally it may be regarded as a pendant to the allegory of the lost drachma in the first book. Jerusalem, the city built aloft, whose name gave promise of the "vision of peace," was the prime goal of pilgrimage, and tropologically it meant the highest, perfect love of God. Hilton begins his allegoresis by pointing out that pilgrims on the path to the spiritual Jerusalem have an experience comparable to that of the traveler who approaches a city already veiled in *darkness,* and wants to spend the night there before proceeding on his travels next day. His experience of night results, in the first instance, from having bid farewell to all that he loves, including wife and child. Behind this lies *kenosis,* familiar to us from the *Cloud* author, the letting go of all worldly ties and desires, a renunciation to be understood as a nothingness, as naked exposure, also as a dying and simultaneously as an act of liberation from any stirring of individual will. All concrete notions of God must be relinquished, too. As in the case of the *Cloud* author, such humble submission comes from the recognition that one cannot know of God "what He is," nor can one know him "as He is"; at most one may recognize fundamental qualities ("an unchaungeable beynge, a sovereyn myght, sovereyn sothfastnesse,"

Scale 2, chap. 32, p. 212). Therefore the mystic pilgrim, who has freed himself of all desire by hard spiritual travail, while warding off various hazards of the journey, makes himself ready to "dwell" patiently in the darkness of inner solitude—as does the recipient of *Cloud.* In this way he prepares himself for mystical "feeling": he passes through the "gate of contemplacioun" (*Scale* 2:197), and he sees how the darkness seems for a moment illuminated, "bright as light." For just as the traveler approaching the city lying in darkness sees flashes of light (*Scale* 2, chap. 25, p. 189), so God will send a ray of his divine light into the pilgrim's inner night (*Scale* 2:198–99). This, too, we know from the *Cloud* texts.[110] It transforms the dark nothingness or night of the soul into a *"rich* nothing" ("riche nought," ibid.; the rhetorical figure of *adnominatio* in "this nought and this nyght," *Scale* 2:187, is worth noting; the whole of chap. 24 is especially important).

This encouraging allegory shows that Hilton, at the end of the second part of *Scale,* consciously sets out to create a framework that contains some apophatic features. This results in the numerous linguistic echoes of the *Cloud* texts, extending to direct links with certain chapters. The framework that he created in the second part of his *Scale* is supplemented by Christological themes. We recall the long tradition of attempts to integrate Christological material into apophatic mysticism; the *Cloud* author had already "amalgamated" it with his apophatic approach. For instance, he had required the reader to bare himself in order to put on the clothing of Christ, a request that occurs in just the same way in Hilton. The amalgamation is intensified by Hilton's consciously polysemic use of the words *mirk* and *mirkness.* This artistic "sleight of hand" has led some scholars to overlook the fact that there is no need to talk of Hilton's theology as different from that of *Cloud:* darkness prevails initially in the soul because of her remoteness from Jesus through sin. Yet if she is ready to recognize this, and to free herself in consequence from false inner strivings, as well as from worldly allurements, she will also take the further step, and "dwell" (the *Cloud* author uses the same word) in a darkness of not-yet-knowing and not-yet-seeing the divinity. Through grace she discovers in this darkness not God the unknowable, but Jesus, who, as she is told, is identical with God ("whanne I seie grace wirketh I meene love, Jhesu, and God: for al is oon," *Scale* 2:250). In consequence of this "finding," the soul now perceives herself also as the bride of Christ. Through her "reforming in feeling" she experiences his presence with her activated inner senses; she enjoys the encounter with Jesus, the "curtais daliaunce" (*Scale* 2:256) with his love, and the "homlinesse" (*Scale* 2:244) in the secret chamber of the heart, an especially important motif in English mysticism. The name of Jesus is the spiritually perceived "oleum effusum"

of the Song of Songs, interpreted so passionately by Richard Rolle. God lets
himself be tasted as the hidden spiritual manna, and he brings the brightly
burning heart to melting point. The motif of *mortifcatio,* spiritual death and
being dead to the world, is refreshingly overlaid, as it were, in the mystical darkness by the waking sleep of the bride in the Song of Songs ("Ego
dormio et cor meum vigilat"; the *Cloud* author speaks of this sleep as well).
The most important mode of experience in mystic "feeling" arises, however,
through opening of the inner eye, which beholds the beauty of God; this
is dealt with also in the psalm commentary *Qui habitat,* presumably by
Hilton.[111] By means of this eye, the soul also hopes to experience something
of the secret "privetees" (*Scale* 2:221) of the deity, which fascinated the
mystics time and again.

With this line of argument Hilton wanted to show that the person who
voluntarily enters into the lightsome darkness and private solitude of the
heart[112] can lead a life entirely in keeping with the old eremitic motto of
"Secretum meum mihi" (Is 24:16; Mi priveté to me, *Scale* 2:239). Christ
himself guides the soul into solitude, in the words of a popular quotation
from Hosea ("ducam eam in solitudinem," Hos 2:14), in order to speak
with her.

This is astonishing; for was Hilton not seeking in *Scale* 2 to *extend* the
possibility of contemplative experience? And now comes a return to eremitic
spirituality! This, and the striking accumulation of traditional biblical passages referring to mysticism, again put the primary addressee in a place apart.
In my view, the apparent contradiction is resolved by Hilton's evident choice
of Aelred as model, which leads him seemingly to the native origins of
Cistercian reclusion. This thought is prompted by Hilton's talk of the *friendship* between the soul and Jesus (*Scale* 2:252), specifically emphasized by
Aelred; and, just like Aelred, he traces it back to Jesus himself (Jn 15:15).
A further reminder of Aelred (as well as of Isaac of Stella) is Hilton's already
discussed exhortation to perceive lovingly the entire universe, since through
this, too, an experience of God becomes possible ("Bi this cité [Jerusalem] is
undirstonde the université of alle creatures... and in alle I seke him that my
soule loveth," *Scale* 2:257). In a similar vein, Aelred had unfolded the cosmic
aspect of love: "Since God can be spoken of as *amicitia* just as legitimately
as he can be named *caritas* or *amor,* then friendship is another name for the
power of uniting that is spread throughout the whole universe."[113] The most
marked correspondence between the Hilton of the *Scale* and Aelred lies in
their love for Jesus: Aelred and the late Hilton see in Jesus not God incarnate
merely *for a space of time,* but the incarnation of God as such. The human
being reformed by mystical "feeling" has gained the capability to behold

God, as it were, behind the human Jesus; he no longer needs to leave behind the love of the corporeal person, the *amor carnalis,* according to Bernard's instruction, but rather, he loves Jesus simultaneously as man and God. Thus for Hilton knowledge of God, in a nutshell, means recognition of the identity of humanity and deity in Jesus. Yet because of his dualistic image of man he has to "struggle" in order to make such a statement (2:62, "gostly siȝt of the Godhed in the manhede"). There is a certain satisfaction in seeing how even the late Hilton cannot resist stressing that Jesus is above all divine. Julian of Norwich will be the first to succeed in discovering the divinity in corporeality without reserve. With his emphasis on the incarnation of God, Hilton rendered a special service to his expanded readership in terms of "deproblematizing" affective loving devotion; he made God more accessible. In this line of argument he was well served by his skill in combining different passages of the Bible. Thus he contributed to the "homeliness," the genial *familiaritas,* between man and God that he extolled, and this even affected his prose style with its pleasant, catching rhythm, its measured and skillfully deployed rhetorical features, which puts Hilton among the great prose stylists of late-medieval England.

Toward the end of the *Scale* the "biblical" tendency, present from the beginning in Hilton's work, breaks fresh ground. Astonishingly, he even encourages his readers to read the Bible for themselves. With the utmost aplomb he flouts the well-known prohibitions, for the lay public, with regard to reading and understanding the Bible for themselves. He boldly maintains that the unlettered as well as the learned are capable of reading the Bible, or listening to it being read (*Scale* 2, chap. 43, pp. 250–54).[114] He unequivocally asserts that through Christ the soul is made wise enough to understand holy scripture in its entirety (*Scale* 2:251).[115] Hilton even seeks to give added weight to his recommendation of Bible reading by alluding to the lesson of the disciples on the way to Emmaus. Just as Christ himself opened their eyes to a right understanding of scripture, so also he reveals himself to the reader engrossed in the Bible today (*Scale* 2:254), for holy scripture should be understood as his love letters; with this metaphoric language, Hilton takes up an image familiar from *Ancrene Wisse* and related texts. A further image follows: holy scripture should be understood as Jesus's murmuring and whispering with the soul. Hilton's general recommendation of Bible reading was still possible because Archbishop Arundel only prohibited the English translation of *Sacra pagina* with his *Constitutions* of 1407–9.[116] It is also feasible that in this matter Hilton was able to benefit indirectly from being a member of the Arundel circle.[117] Moreover, it has been pointed out that the *Constitutions* were not always applied with maximum severity.[118] Whatever the case may be, it is astonishing to observe a certain pre-Reformation stance in this recommendation of Bible reading for all Christians. Hilton is picking up a specifically English trend, but at the same time his recommendation should be viewed in the context of diverse contemporary attempts (including those of the Lollards, especially the Wyclif Bible, but also of *The Cloud of Unknowing, Piers Plowman,* and *Dives and Pauper* as well as the *Book to a Mother*) to restore to the Bible its absolute authority.[119] Doubtless for safety's sake, he regularly bases his comments and explanations on the Latin text.[120]

The English Reformation has indeed been seen "as the evolution of a distinctively English religious culture,"[121] occurring in the religious changes taking place, especially in the diocese of York, between 1350 and 1450. There is a whole series of points of contact with the Lollards. The sacrament of the Eucharist, for instance, is rarely mentioned in Hilton (or in the other mystics). Scholarship is met with skepticism, or even rejection, and preference is given to biblical simplicity. This may explain why Wyclif, of all people, is sympathetic toward the hermits![122] At all events, it is clear that the mystics and Lollards concur in the intensity of their recourse to Paul. Of course, there is a certain risk now of ascribing to a Lollard way of thinking something that is basically biblical, and therefore doctrinally orthodox. For instance, we read, in an interpretation of *The Recluse* (a Lollard reworking of *Ancrene Wisse*) of the "Wycliffite conception of the equality of all real believers,"[123] yet this notion is by no means only Wycliffite, but rather, genuinely Pauline, and indeed, as we have seen, a central tenet of the Christian faith. "In Paul this has already become a formula, which he repeats several times: 'There is neither Jew nor Greek, there is neither bond nor free, there is neither male nor female: for ye are all one in Christ Jesus'"[124] (Gal 3:28; also 1 Cor 12:13 and Rom 10:12).[125]

The Reflection of the Movement of the Free Spirit in Hilton, the *Cloud* Author, and *The Mirror of Simple Souls*

Investigation of the reception of Marguerite Porete's *Mirouer des simples âmes* led to the conclusion that in England, as elsewhere, there must have been some who sympathized with the movement of the Free Spirit.[126] This is attested indirectly by the English translation of the *Mirouer,* even if the text is associated with the movement only in part. Recent research has shown that the movement did not involve a homogeneous group, but rather a loose association of like-minded individual mystics, both male and female. The warning given in a Latin rendering of *Cloud* against the heresy of the beghards (a term that is used quasi-synonymously for the adherents of the freedom movement) has also been noted.

Yet, are there any indications of a close affinity between the *Cloud* texts or Walter Hilton and this specific Free Spirit idea?[127] All the texts take particularly seriously Christ's demand for self-denial as prerequisite for his *imitatio;* they are spellbound by the dialectical recognition that individual nothingness enables experience of the divine All, and when Marguerite, contrary to all logic, heightens the demand for her own annihilation to the point of desiring to feel herself as *less* than nothing, the *Cloud* author follows her, even in this intensification, word for word. She extols this nothing as a "rich Nothing" (see chap. 7), and Hilton takes this up *verbatim.* All these texts speak of the necessary human experience of darkness, and the ensuing joyfulness brought by a ray of divine light. The *Cloud* texts and Hilton (*Cloud,* "liȝty derknes"; Hilton, "lighti merkenesse," *Scale* 2:236) yield close parallels to *Mirror. Unio* with God, the ultimately unknowable, is of brief duration, and can be experienced only as a pledge or foretaste of lasting union to come. However, the presence of God is indeed experienced, and the significance of prayer dwindles for the *Cloud* author as for Marguerite, its aim having been fulfilled. Yet this experience requires a prior "purité of spirit" (frequently in *Cloud;* Hilton, *Scale* 2:236; *Mirror,* chap. 24).

Marguerite and the adherents to the freedom movement, no less than a Meister Eckhart, find the freedom they long for by totally relinquishing any will of their own, in order to let God alone work within them. All of them are in accord with Augustinian voluntarism. Everything presupposes uncompromising dedication, *intentio,* as the *Cloud* author and Hilton unanimously agree.[128] When the *Cloud* author, and Hilton, like Marguerite Porete, speak of God as the actual initiator in the process of mystical contemplation, we are again in close proximity to *Mirror.* The anonymous author of *Cloud* embarks further on a bold tropological exegesis of the Old Testament Ark of the Covenant when he sees the mystical "work" of the soul prefigured in this artistically wrought "work" of the Ark (he is here influenced by *The Mystical Ark* of Richard of St. Victor): just as the Ark of the Covenant contained within itself the Mosaic tablets of the law, so also the mystical "work" contains within itself all virtues. Therefore, the author resolutely abbreviates discussion of the virtues in order to concentrate on humility and love, which comprise all the others.[129] Walter Hilton, too, stresses on one occasion that a soul intent on beholding God will no longer be intensely concerned with striving for virtues (*Scale* 2:225); but he, likewise, emphasizes humility and love. Even for Marguerite Porete, who had sent the virtues packing, these two represent the essence of all virtuousness. However, the *Cloud* group and Hilton stop short of any path toward quietism; instead, they take their orientation—as do many mystics—from Christ's assurance that "without me, ye can *do* nothing" (Jn 15:5; *Privy Counselling,* 92.39); that is, rather than relinquishing all actions of their own, they ensure that their deeds accord entirely with the divine will. But even Marguerite should not be charged overhastily with quietism, because she does not put the case for total inactivity; rather, she lets God be the sole effective initiator, as M.N. stresses in his gloss (*Mirror,* 258–59). Marguerite Porete and Meister Eckhart would agree with Dante's succinct and unsurpassable words: "E'n la sua volontade è nostra pace."[130]

However, there is a significant theological difference between Marguerite and the English texts, in *Mirror*'s conclusion that relinquishing every action attributable to the individual will also guarantee freedom from all sin, which means that there is therefore no need for the sacrament of confession, or indeed for any kind of religious practice—no need, even, for prayer. The *Cloud* author and Hilton disagree with this entirely; they recall the sacrament of penance and the necessity for discernment of spirits, going back ultimately to Paul. The conclusion that a human being can be free of sin, from the present moment on, is found neither in the *Cloud* group of texts nor in Hilton. Hilton emphatically rejects such indifference toward the sacrament of penance when he speaks of those deluded persons who deny the necessity of confession ("Thanne erreth he greteli that generali seith that confessioun of synne for to schewe to a prest is neither nedeful to a synnere ne bihoveful, and no man is bounden therto," *Scale* 2:146, 309–11).[131] Yet he also stresses that the person who has been cleansed by "reforming in faith and feeling" need no longer feel encumbered by sin. The *Cloud* author's relative lack of concern with confessional practice has caused some surprise in recent times. It has been suggested that he may have wished to distance himself from the spectacular penance of people such as Margery Kempe.[132] Yet it is far more probable that there was an inner affinity between this author and Marguerite's unequivocally contemplative stance.

This investigation of the relationship between *Mirror,* Hilton's *Scale,* and the texts of the *Cloud* group has uncovered a baffling ambivalence. On the one hand, their statements converge to a startling degree, so that we are entirely justified in speaking of a certain sympathy on the part of the English authors for the text "imported" from France, and a certain influence of the Free Spirit idea.[133] On the other hand, it seems that Hilton set great store by strict observation of orthodoxy, as is usually maintained without further qualification. It was indeed necessary to warn against ecstatics, enthusiasts, and quietists, as we see most clearly in the very important tract *The Chastising of God's Children.*[134] The English mystics writing after Richard Rolle were alert not only to the Lollards.[135] Julian is another mystic who made bold advances, and evoked a wide range of responses; whether she remained fully within the orthodox fold, or ventured into heterodoxy, is a tantalizing question, which will be considered in the next chapter.

CHAPTER 9

The Singular Vision of Julian of Norwich

Julian of Norwich is the most attractive and most original figure in medieval English mysticism. For many people she has become a spiritual authority through her unique revelations of the human love of a maternal God. Not only does her work move readers more deeply than any other English mystical text; it has also been described as the most significant theological achievement of late-medieval England.[1] Rowan Williams, archbishop of Canterbury from 2002 to 2012, goes so far as to surmise that her writings "may well be the most important work of Christian reflection in the English language."[2] It is therefore not surprising that her book, which, unlike those of the other English mystics, has never really been forgotten since the fifteenth century,[3] should have been "processed," quoted from, and adapted, in a wide range of publications. Today it is hardly an exaggeration to speak of a Julian industry. Her cell in Norwich, destroyed by German bombs in World War II, has been reconstructed and has become a tourist attraction. It is not difficult to understand the eagerness to shed light on her biography. The unresolved question as to how she lived before entering her cell has left the door wide open to speculation, giving rise to works of fiction and imagination. There is at least one stage play, and one film. Above all, T. S. Eliot's great *Four Quartets* deserve mention, written in London in 1943, while the city was the target of enemy bombs. In the final quartet, "Little Gidding," the poet integrated a few brief quotations from

Julian, notably the famous "All shall be well," to express a glimpse of hope and optimism, in dark times. In our own day, the musician Thomas Adès has taken up Julian's promise in his composition *Asyla,* looking at it through the skeptical awareness of a modern composer.

Evelyn Underhill drew attention to Julian in the early twentieth century, and called her "the first real English woman of letters,"[4] but scholarly interest developed rather slowly. Then, in the second half of the last century, scholars turned to her with great zeal, especially as feminist interests developed. Julian is indeed captivating for the originality of her theology, yet she needs to be assessed in the wider context of European female spirituality in the late Middle Ages, which has so far not received sufficient attention.[5]

Julian was born at the beginning of the year 1343 and was therefore a contemporary of the author of *The Cloud of Unknowing* and Walter Hilton, and of Geoffrey Chaucer as well as John Wyclif; she was still alive in 1416. She wrote her mystical work as a recluse, set apart from society, so that no reflection of particular contemporary issues or upheavals can be expected. However, she did not live in total isolation as an anchorite, but in the midst of bustling Norwich, and since people set great store by the counsel of this wise, self-assured woman, she received a fair number of visitors.[6] Thus her younger contemporary Margery Kempe gives an account of her own Norwich pilgrimage; on this occasion she sought Julian out, which shows that the great recluse must have been regarded as a spiritual authority beyond the limits of her city.

Julian gives no concrete details about her own person. We learn that at the age of thirty she survived a grave illness; at its crisis point, she experienced visions from which she gained deeper insights into the relationship between the human being and God. Margery Kempe refers to her as "Dame Ielyan," which is not itself very informative, since "Dame" simply translates the Latin honorific title "domina,"[7] with which anchoresses could be addressed; but certain characteristics in her work do make it very likely that she belonged to the aristocracy. Christ is frequently described as "courteous."[8] Mary is given the attribute "noble" (399),[9] and there are also several references to God's "nobility" (375, 521, 526, 545, 549). His frequent expressions of gratitude to her (found also in Mechthild of Magdeburg) can be explained as a feudal convention. It is very important to her that the soul by no means forfeits her dignity, notwithstanding her sin.[10] Finally, the courtly ceremonial that prevails in the celestial world as well as on earth is of crucial theological significance to her; she seeks to decode its semiotics in a great vision. All this, and the elevated style of her work overall, is indicative of an author who herself very likely comes from the aristocracy.

Given the lack of information about Julian of Norwich as a historical person, the question of her educational background is a particular problem. At all events, it is evident that she had a considerable knowledge of theology. The phenomenon of the *religiosae mulieres* will be discussed in connection with Margery Kempe; suffice it to say at this point that two types of devout women can be distinguished in the later Middle Ages: the highly educated and the unlettered. Leutgard of Tongeren, Christina Mirabilis, and Marie d'Oignies represent the "hagiographic type of the uneducated, unlettered woman, enabled by the grace of the Holy Spirit alone to understand the Latin text of Holy Scripture, discuss difficult theological problems, and gain the most lofty insights."[11] More significant, of course, were those women who had been carefully educated, and made high theological claims. Among them were Beatrix of Nazareth, and Juliana of Cornillon, who entered the lepers' house in the town and seems "to have received a thorough education in 'scriptura latina et gallica' which enables her to read texts by Augustine and Bernard, and even—on account of her astonishing memory—to retain verbatim more than twenty sermons on the Song of Songs by the famous Cistercian abbot."[12] Gertrud of Helfta wrote her works in Latin. Julian of Norwich, living in the late fourteenth and early fifteenth centuries, describes herself as a simple creature unlettered (285). Should this really be taken to mean that she was uneducated? Her level of reflection, her elevated theological, and indeed speculative, sophistication, her linguistic-stylistic individuality, and her knowledge of the Bible presuppose some knowledge of Latin, at least, and some theological training.[13] Did not *Ancrene Wisse* already speak of educated recluses, and warn them against being proud of their education? Mechthild of Magdeburg, who said that she had no knowledge of Latin, was another highly educated (aristocratic) woman.

Excursus: On the Textual Transmission of Julian's *A Revelation of Love*

The manuscript transmission of Julian's work is sparse.[14] There are two accounts of her visions, differing in extent and theological depth—the short version, *A Vision Showed…to a Devout Woman* (SV), and the long version, *A Revelation of Love* (LV). While the SV is contained in a miscellany compiled circa 1450, the manuscripts of the LV date from a time when the Middle Ages had long since passed, namely from the seventeenth century. The first readers of the LV were English Benedictines in two small nunneries in France, founded in Cambrai and Paris after the Catholics' expulsion from England. The SV is not a shortened version of LV, rather it precedes it.

However, it was not written immediately after Julian experienced her visions, as is widely assumed, but later, perhaps toward the end of the 1370s.[15] Before the SV was written down, Julian probably spent some time reflecting on what she had seen, since it is possible to discern the beginnings of trinitarian speculation and theological training, for instance when she comments on the "properte" of the divine persons (chap. 24). Here she puts into words the famous question as to whether she is prohibited from speaking of spiritual things merely on account of being a woman (p. 222.46–48). She points out that, after all, she is not concerned with preaching, which was forbidden to women, but communicates only what God, her inner teacher, has shown her.[16] In this way she avoids giving the impression of setting out to be a teacher of the church, which would have earned her a charge of heresy. Shrewdly cautious, she repeatedly stresses her conformity with ecclesiastical doctrine ("wilfully submyttes me to the techynge of haly kyrke," 244.49–50). On the other hand, she does not in any way doubt the rightness of her own interpretation of the visions she has seen,[17] and she is fully convinced that her visions serve the "profytte" (220.17) and "comforthe" (224.10) of her Christian neighbors (219.9), thereby fulfilling a parenetic function.

While the shorter text in all probability constitutes the original version of Julian's mystical opus, the longer version, which was written at the earliest in 1393, but perhaps later,[18] gives a more detailed account of her visionary experience. It bears the title, presumably her own, of *A Revelation of Love,* and sees the fifteen revelations she received as *one* great vision, supplemented in the following night by a closing revelation. Julian tells us that, prior to committing this experience to words, she spent fifteen years in frequent prayer, in order to grasp the deeper meaning of her visions; only after a further five years, in February 1393, did she gain the full clarity required to complete the definitive record of her revelations.[19]

We shall never know exactly why two very different versions of her revelations have been handed down, or how they relate to one another. Perhaps Julian wrote them for different purposes, or different groups of readers. *A Vision* refers several times to "contemplatives." Neither the SV nor (even less) *A Revelation of Love* gives cause to categorize her work as "autobiography," and only with reservations can they be classed as *vita* literature, since they recount only the one visionary experience, and not, as was usually the case with a nun's vita, "accounts of the vicissitudinous life of a prominent nun, her ascetic practice...her practice of prayer and temptations by the devil...[and] manifestations of divine grace."[20]

Julian's visions, on her own account, were received not as a sudden occurrence, but in fulfillment of detailed requests. As the short and long versions agree, she had requested three gifts from God—intense experience of the Passion of Christ, a bodily sickness, and finally the three wounds of *contritio, compassio,* and passionate longing for God. These three "manifestations of grace," as it is said later on, were, as divine *afflictions,* the prerequisites for ultimate elevation to heaven. She had already expressed the request for sickness in her youth, asking that it might befall her in her thirtieth year in a process of spiritual cleansing and strengthening, as did indeed occur.[21] In all she asks for *five* wounds, with which she strives for *imitatio Christi;* she wants to experience his five wounds at the age of thirty, at which age Jesus started out his path of suffering.[22] In this essentially Pauline sense, she sees her whole life as martyrdom, as being crucified and experiencing death with Christ (chap. 21), in accordance with the anchoritic self-understanding, specifically of the young women readers of *Ancrene Wisse.*

It is difficult to comprehend the lack, or paucity, of understanding that scholars have shown for these requests of Julian's. What can be said about a young woman's "timely" and urgent desire to be allowed to suffer a grave sickness at the age of thirty? The most recent, wholly ahistorical, attempt to relate the request for sickness to Julian's consciousness of her own femininity, from a gender perspective, lacks conviction, and does not warrant detailed discussion.[23] Suffice it to say that the desire for illness has nothing to do with Julian's awareness of the problems of female corporeality; as early as *Ancrene Wisse,* it is a man who longs in vain for a bodily sickness.[24] Yet why is sickness thought useful? One can understand the reasons by entering into the medieval way of thinking, although, as we shall see, it was not the only path. First, grave sickness increases the "chance" of dying earlier, and therefore of being with God sooner. Second, and this is the more interesting reason, bodily sickness is seen not only as an act of cleansing, but also as a strengthening, yielding the possibility of more intense *spiritual* experience. Now, for readers of the twentieth/twenty-first centuries, this notion should not seem entirely strange, comparable as it is to an understanding of artistic achievement expressed by Thomas Mann, which goes so far as to "equate sickness with human spirit and dignity."[25] Here, bodily infirmity is the consequence of overrefined artistic sensitivity.

The grave illness occurred in May 1373 and led her within a week to the brink of death. In accordance with ecclesiastical ritual, the priest came, with a boy carrying the crucifix. The priest instructed Julian to behold the crucified Christ. Soon she could no longer avert her gaze from the crucifix; it came to life, and she saw a light emanating from it. That the rest of the room fell into darkness, she interpreted as the simultaneous presence of evil, and she thought her last hour had come. Yet suddenly her pain vanished, and she felt herself restored to health, but still she longed to persist in her *compassio* with Christ on the cross. In the fifteen visions that last from four in the morning until midafternoon, Christ turns to her directly, and initiates her into profound theological mysteries. After the visions, she once more feels pain, accompanied by spiritual torments and aridity, but she is granted certainty that she does not yet have to die. In the following night she is torn from sleep by a nightmare; she thinks she is being strangled by the devil in the shape of a young man, while the whole room is filled with smoke and stench. Then she is suffused with great serenity and peace. After she has suffered a further brief illness, and overcome her doubts, Jesus appears to her with words of solace in a last great vision that draws everything together, and lasts until the early hours of the morning.

It is a very interesting phenomenon that Julian, who has so much to say theologically, sees her thoughts and conveys them to her readers in the form of visions. Recent research has paid particular attention to the vision as "genre." Julian differentiates between bodily, spiritual, and intellectual visions; in so doing, she adopts the Augustinian division into the basic forms of *visio corporalis, visio imaginativa,* and *visio intellectualis.*[26] It is possible that this distinction was familiar to her from the very detailed discussion in the anonymous *Chastising of God's Children.*[27] However, these terms do not adequately describe the phenomenon, because almost all medieval visions fall into the category of *spiritual* vision, and may be true or false.

Recently, Barbara Newman has set out a typology of visions; she differentiates between spontaneous paranormal visions in a waking state, visions experienced by religious in consequence of their spiritual meditation practice, aesthetic (i.e., above all poetic-fictitious), and finally supernatural visions, whereby the types may overlap.[28] For Julian, only the first two types are relevant: spontaneous waking visions, most likely to occur in close proximity to death, and creative visions based on meditative visualization practice, for which women are most likely to have a "visionary script."[29] This enables the inner eye to create a new vision.[30] An example of what Julian calls an imaginative vision is her sight of Mary as the person most afflicted by the events of the Passion; it is imaginative, because its spiritual "vision" sees "beyond" Mary's bodily appearance the wisdom, truth, and greatness of soul of this outwardly unremarkable, girl-like woman. An example of an intellectual vision is Julian's sight of God in one point (SV 226.1), and thence in all things. Finally, among the revelations she received there are verbal communications ("allocutions") or words of instruction, as well as words coming involuntarily to mind, but not spoken (666.3–4; SV 272.57–273.3).

It is reasonable to say that certain formal elements available to Julian helped her to generate the "scripts" of her visions. To begin with, they stem from her own practice of Passion meditation along the lines recommended by Aelred—even more than from the *Meditationes vitae Christi.* Evidently, *The Wooing of Our Lord* also made a lasting impression on her, as did contemporary artistic depictions of the Passion (especially East Anglian artifacts).[31] For all this, the crucifix in her cell is what actually prompted her bodily vision of Christ's suffering and death,[32] whereby she does not visualize *scenes* in a narrative continuum, but separate single pictures.[33] She is shown different "aspects" of the Passion, which follow one another in a consecutive sequence in the LV (unlike in the SV), but are interrupted intermittently by chapters with different themes. First of all, she sees Christ's crown of thorns in a kind of "close-up."[34] In a scene of unsurpassably vivid horror, very reminiscent of *The Wooing of Our Lord,* but even more intense, she observes the thorns piercing his head, the blood oozing out in heavy drops and gradually congealing into lumps, hair and flesh sticking to the thorns. The experience is re-created with a relentless realism that anticipates the depiction of Christ crucified in Grünewald's Isenheim altarpiece. Then she lowers her gaze a little, and only now does the whole face of Christ come "into the picture," and she gradually observes his entire scourged body, hanging limp on the cross, disfigured by the streams of blood flowing over it. This scene is reminiscent above all of Cistercian illuminations, which have formed part of her "script" (to continue with Newman's terminology).[35] The vision lingers on the bodily level of streaming blood, but leaves mimesis behind as medieval veneration of the blood sacrifice pursues its own course and is transformed into hyperbole: the blood flows into hell, spreads over the whole earth, penetrates the heavens, and pervades them eternally in token of victory (chap. 12). Before shrugging off such use of metaphor, one should note that this theological image is still present in the famous last monologue spoken by Christopher Marlowe's Renaissance figure Doctor Faustus, when he recognizes that this blood will help him no more, and he will be lost for ever. In uttermost despair he calls: "See, see, where Christ's blood *streams in the firmament* [emphasis added], / One drop would save my soul, half a drop."[36]

Only after Julian's "fragmented" visualization of Christ's Passion, which arouses in her the wish to die in *mortificatio* for him, is a further motif introduced—the wound in Christ's side. Jesus himself points it out, and lets her see in it his riven heart, a rare image in English mysticism, free here from any erotic association (chap. 24, p. 394–97),[37] and not connected with the late-medieval reifying cult of the Sacred Heart of Jesus. Much later on,

Julian takes it up again and places it in the entirely original context of her interpretation of God as mother: while an earthly mother lays her child tenderly to her breast, the Jesus mother takes the child into his breast through the wound in his side, and offers it a foretaste of his divinity and heavenly bliss (chap. 60). This transformation of the traditional motif of Christ's wound succinctly demonstrates Julian's singularity.[38]

Julian's position as "visionary" is a complex one. She is moved by the cruel realism of the Passion events, and this elicits her *compassio* with the suffering son of God; yet she also recognizes Christ's compassion for mankind stricken by sin. In striving to emulate Christ, she extends the term *compassio* to include sympathy for her neighbors, for any who feel compassion toward neighbors are in Christ (chap. 28). However, in apparent contrast, Julian remains a distanced onlooker at the Passion events, which a Margery Kempe could never be. While Margery needs to shout out her pain at the son of God's suffering and death, which she re-experiences as happening ever anew, Julian is at all times aware that he suffered gladly long ago, and that she therefore has good reason for triumphant and joyful serenity. Thus she perceives without *inner* dismay the realistic details of his suffering, and his body streaming with blood.[39] She sees how the crucified Christ suddenly alters his facial expression entirely and radiates happiness, and, most astonishingly, reaches the end of his Passion on the cross with joy, ready to undergo the experience anew for every loved person if required (e.g. SV, chap. 12). She does not describe the actual moment of Christ's death.

This reveals a definite stylistic tendency in Julian's *A Revelation of Love*: as the *visio passionalis* with focus on the "head of blood and wounds" ("Salve caput cruentatum")[40] gradually fades, a theological and intellectual vision without images develops,[41] and Julian moves from the bodily to the spiritual plane—an unfeminine move in medieval understanding.[42] For the most part, she "sees" only the auditions and "locutions" granted to her by God or Jesus, but she joins the insights granted to her by God with her own theological reflections, so that, as has been noted,[43] divine and human proclamation may merge with one another indistinguishably (e.g. chap. 48). Moreover, as the visionary-figurative quality diminishes, the striking exceptions—the parable to be discussed below of lord and servant, and the indwelling of God in the city of the soul—produce an even greater impact. One of the fascinating features of Julian's work is, undoubtedly, her intuitive grasp of the significance of sight as a fundamental form of human cognition, and of the human predisposition to think in concrete images, drawing on an inner archetypal treasury of images. Since she links thinking and seeing, she is even able to speak of gazing on nothing.[44]

On Julian's Theological Self-Assurance—A New "Apostola"

In a sense Julian harks back to earlier times, yet she is also a theological and prophetic visionary, without precedent in England. The more closely one looks, the more one is reminded of the great Continental visionary women, especially of those connected with the nunnery of Helfta. Compared to these, Julian is impressive for her individuality, and also for the enormous self-assurance that leaves her in no doubt but that she must communicate to her fellow Christians the revelations she has seen. Since a woman was not allowed to deliver theological teaching, it was customary for female visions or ecstatic experiences, or a vita, to be recorded only when prompted by a confessor's "instruction to write," in some cases citing the authority of a commission from God, which was also intended to guarantee the orthodoxy of what was being said.[45] Mechthild of Magdeburg explicitly mentions an instruction of this sort given by her confessor Heinrich of Halle,[46] but she also feels compelled to write by God. At the age of twelve she had received a definitive token of grace that moved her to flee the world. Adelheid Langmann, nun and scribe, "records her experiences of grace in her own hand... but in contact with, and with the knowledge of, a Dominican, who issues the 'instruction to write'"[47]—in what seems like an official process. There are significant relationships between Henry Suso and Elsbeth Stagel, between Henry of Nördlingen and Margarethe Ebner, and between Konrad of Füssen and Christine Ebner.[48] Sometimes a "spiritual confidante" takes over the confessor's role, as in the case of Juliana of Cornillon, who owed much to a Liège recluse, and who initiated the feast of Corpus Christi through her visions.[49] In the Cistercian nunnery of Helfta, to which the aging beguine Mechthild of Magdeburg retired, there arose an important "literature of Vita and revelation," to which Mechthild of Hackeborn's *Liber specialis gratiae* and Gertrud the Great's *Legatus divinae pietatis* belong.[50] It seems that in Helfta "the Vita texts arose in the sisters' circle, i.e. without the participation of the convent's confessors."[51] Of great interest is the joint work in Latin by the two Cistercian nuns of Helfta, Mechthild of Hackeborn and Gertrud of Helfta.[52] Mechthild (again commissioned by God) in all probability recorded part of her *Liber specialis gratiae* herself—in Latin; the bulk of the book was written likewise in Latin by Gertrud and another anonymous sister, commissioned by the nunnery, but ultimately at God's behest, for the benefit of others. The definitive voice of the abbess then pronounced the approbation. The anonymous sister also wrote the major part of Gertrud's *Legatus,* to which Gertrud herself contributed only Book 2.[53]

This comparison reveals something fundamentally new in Julian of Norwich: in her work there is no reference, of the kind usual in a Continental woman's vita, to a community of nuns. While certain parts of a Continental nun's vita might be written in the first person, the preference was for the more distant third person,[54] whereas Julian, without exception, speaks in the first person, because she herself vouches for the genuineness of the visions she has received; therefore she recounts what she saw without consulting a (critical) confessor. Evidently, no spiritual director instructed her to write down her visions. Such self-assurance presupposes a considerable level of education. She feels within herself the command of God, but she also longs to serve her neighbor by means of writing. This is new in the field of women's mysticism, although Richard Rolle had precisely this self-understanding, as we have seen. A priest visited Julian during her illness and was impressed; she notes that she was very glad to be taken seriously by him, but does not heed his encouraging comment, because she does not believe that she can tell her visions to any priest. Of course, she may nonetheless have consulted a cleric, but it is crucial for any assessment of her self-understanding that she makes no mention of any such consultation. The anonymous *Chastising of God's Children,* a tract she may have known and which takes a very critical view of women's visions, considers it important that in the event of such a vision a wise and knowledgeable man should be consulted.[55] One reason for Julian's unwillingness to confide in anyone was that she did not think it possible that she would be believed (chap. 21). Later, God confirms to her directly the correctness of the priest's observation that she was not delirious. Then God himself strongly urges her to write ("byddying me fulle myghtly," 652.21; SV 219, 222), entirely in accordance with her own firm conviction ("felyng," 511.11).

We can say with certainty that Julian wrote her work as a recluse. Felicity Riddy has rightly warned against too romantic a notion of the life of a medieval recluse; Julian lived in the middle of a city.[56] There are sound theological reasons to believe that she must have been a recluse in her youth, and that her lived anchoritic spirituality created the preconditions for her visions. For instance, had she not in her early years wished for a sickness in her thirtieth year that would intensify spiritual experience? With regard to her education, even without a monastic institution she could procure theological literature, and read it, or have it read to her. The notion of Julian as a woman who had at her disposal knowledge customarily restricted at the time to male clerics is by no means "in some way exhilarating."[57] We tend to take too narrow a view of what was possible in the Middle Ages. Julian differs markedly from Continental women visionaries or mystics by not giving any indication of having submitted her book to a cleric for assessment or sanction; nowhere can we discern a "masculine editorial voice."[58] In a Continental nun's vita, it is not unusual for a nun blessed by visionary gifts of grace to keep this to herself "for years on end,"[59] but then, unlike Julian, to turn to a confessor for advice, and for this to result in a cooperation between the two.[60] Instead of this, Julian relies entirely on the rightness of what she has seen. Nonetheless, it has been said: "It is inconceivable that she could publish a book in Norwich without official sanction."[61] In fact, there is no reason to suppose that she did publish her book; rather, a manuscript was prepared for a specific purpose (how, we do not know), presumably to meet the needs only of a small, elite readership, which also explains why we know nothing of any direct, late-medieval impact of Julian's work. Kathryn Kerby-Fulton has commented aptly on this problem in speaking of the special "manuscript culture" of the Middle Ages, which could mean "an enormously empowering mode of publication for the adventurous author."[62] Marguerite Porete, too, wrote for an elite readership. That Julian's text was not officially sanctioned can be surmised with a fair degree of certainty if we take a closer look at the more profound theological level of her work: she herself feels the need with striking frequency to assure the reader of her orthodoxy. She was aware that her visions cannot be reconciled at all points with the Bible and the doctrine of the church. Yet with characteristic self-assurance, new among lay people at that time, she has no doubt but that her visions come from God, and only from God. Moreover, this places her in a certain way on the same level as the apostles, especially Peter and John, of whom it is said in the Acts of the Apostles that they were uneducated people ("sine litteris"; Gk. "agrammatoi," Acts 4:13), yet they exerted definitive authority because they had personal experience of Jesus, and *saw* him.[63] Therefore, notwithstanding their lack of learning, they had no choice but to speak of what they had heard and seen (Acts 4:20).

With Paul it is rather different, because he did not see Jesus bodily, but "only" in a vision (Acts 9:3–9; 2 Cor 12:1–4, when he also heard him); and he had further visions (2 Cor 12:2–4, 7). Julian, too, encountered Jesus in a vision: "it was he himself I saw" (497.28). She will have been aware of this parallel, which must have affected her theological self-awareness, for she recognized that her situation was similar to that of the apostles; for her, too, although theologically a lay woman, it is impossible to remain silent about divine "mysteries" that she herself has seen and heard. This puts her on a par with the apostles, including Paul.

There are some interesting Continental precursors. Of Christina of Hane it was said that she rose in power like the sun for the salvation of

Christianity,[64] she was chosen by God from eternity as an instrument of grace. Margareta Contracta has the theologically audacious thought that the whole world will be revived by her heart.[65] There is a certain theological affinity between Julian and Gertrud of Helfta, who both claim to be prophetically inspired, and Gertrud is also a new Apostola, likewise familiar with biblical writing. She, of course, wrote in Latin and was described by her fellow nuns as "Theologa."[66] A further forerunner is the beguine Mechthild of Magdeburg, also in her last years a nun of Helfta. Like Julian, she feels herself expressly chosen by God as messenger, and endowed with immense authority in consequence.[67] Mechthild of Hackeborn unambiguously claims to mediate as the apostles did.[68] While Kurt Ruh suggests that this should be taken with a pinch of salt, the comparison with other visionary women shows that she means it very seriously. Several more points of contact between Julian and the nuns of Helfta will emerge as this chapter proceeds.[69]

With their sense of mission these women bridge the broad historical gap that separates them from Christ's life on earth, as did medieval painters in familiar ways. Yet while, in painting, medieval people are usually included in salvation events as distanced worshippers (often much reduced in size), the women mystics act in direct partnership with Christ and Mary. Through her visions, which mediate glimpses of God's mysteries intended to expand mankind's knowledge of his plan for salvation history, Julian becomes a mediator, a messenger, indeed a new Apostola. She is convinced that God's talking to human beings did not end with the prophet's visions in the book of Revelation, but is continued in the present. She is therefore fulfilling a thoroughly prophetic mission, for the benefit of many people ("for the profytte of many oder," SV 220.17–18). Of course, the church was vehemently opposed to women visionaries. Most radical was Jean Gerson, in the early fifteenth century, who dismissed all female visionaries as heretical, and, on apostolic authority, forbade them to teach publicly.[70] There were, however, exceptions. Recently attention has been drawn to Hugh of St. Cher, whose *De prophetia* evaluated learned statements by women as serious theological insights, if the women led a fittingly sober life and appeared as prophetesses; for the prophet's charisma "did enjoy great prestige owing to its biblical connotations.... By describing prophesy as a charisma, Hugh now related it to the charismatic qualities of Christian leaders in the New Testament, their gifts of grace for preaching and teaching or discerning the spirits" (1 Cor 12:4–11).[71] In church history, up to the present day, the fact has been overlooked (or passed over) that when Paul prohibited women from speaking in church he made one exception—namely, if a woman's words had a *prophetic* function.[72] Here, influences from classical antiquity will have played a part.

Since Julian follows Paul's widely known statement in 1 Cor 14:33–36 that women must keep silence in the assembly—which is in tension with 1 Cor 11—she cannot appear as a teacher, but she finds a clever way out of this dilemma. With striking frequency she emphasizes that God "taught" her this or that insight. By *reporting* this divine teaching, she herself functions indirectly as teacher, and prophet. It remains very astonishing that, unlike many other women visionaries,[73] she never doubts for a moment the authenticity of her visions, or, in consequence, the revelation of God's will, whereby, on one occasion, she disarmingly identifies God's will with her own volition (chap. 9). Hildegard of Bingen was another woman who never doubted the genuineness of her visions. It would not have occurred to Hildegard or Julian that they had received merely "private revelations." Julian affirms—not least as a shrewd precaution—that she will always judge her visions (expressed by the term "felyng," 511.11) in accordance with ecclesiastical doctrine; but she follows them in cases where they do in fact diverge from orthodox faith, even when she herself is not free from questions and doubts (417.2–3), for nothing can shake her conviction that her revelations come directly from God, who for her is also the highest ecclesiastical authority.[74] Fittingly, most chapters have an immediacy, even abruptness, in their opening, and seek to turn the reader's gaze to God, on whom she intends her work to be entirely founded.

Cistercian Coloring

Without question, Julian is rooted in tradition through Cistercian-Bernardine themes that still have power for her.[75] Such a theme is her definition of love as a gift. This is love of God for his own sake, a fundamental thought of Bernard's *De diligendo Deo,* self-love of the human being "in God," and love for everything living "for God" (727.14). Bernard and Julian converge in holding that love of God is the precondition for true love of one's neighbor; it is possible to love one's neighbor only in God and for God. However, while for Bernard self-knowledge or self-love is an important prerequisite for knowledge of God, Julian conversely places knowledge of God before self-knowledge (chap. 46)—though she does also state the opposite (chap. 56).[76] She does not follow Bernard's demand that the human being must leave behind love for God as man, in order to progress to pure knowledge of God; for her, knowledge of God is possible precisely because of his incarnation in Christ and through his presence in the created world. To this must be added her specifically Cistercian concept of God as mother, to which we shall turn later. It seems to me that this concept is crucial to our understanding of her theology with its "revolutionary" potential; it means that she also emphasizes Christ's teaching of man as child of God, entitled to address the father as Abba.

There is a further trace of Bernard's (and William of St. Thierry's) theology in the idea that God draws the soul toward himself (also an allusion to the Gospel of John), but she goes well beyond Bernard in the strong emphasis she attaches to the insatiable love-yearning of the divine beloved, the *Deus desiderans* (e.g., 656.20–24). His yearning does not diminish, although he constantly "drawyth and dryngkyth" (679.7; 418.14–20 and n.). Julian often articulates this motif, widespread in English mysticism, but more frequent in her work than elsewhere.[77] The Cistercian Gertrud of Helfta defines divine love-longing for the human being in comparable terms.[78] For Julian, God's yearning is reciprocated by the soul's love-longing for God ("oure kyndely wille is to haue god, and the good wylle of god is to haue vs," 308.57–58; "tyll we shal dye in longyng for loue," 481.49). Like Gertrud of Helfta and *The Mirror of Simple Souls,* Julian does not often describe Christ's relationship to the soul as that of a lover, friend, or bridegroom. Like many late-medieval women, she renounces the language of nuptial mysticism, and when she talks, on several occasions, of the soul penetrating God, her language scales back the sensual component. She is God's "darlyng" (395.16), but her lover is the Lord, as creator, father, and brother; she avoids unambiguous fixing of the partners' roles.

However, Bernard in his 25th sermon on the Song of Songs saw in beauty one of God's attributes, which generates an affective response. Likewise we encounter in the LV Julian's striking praise of the luminous *beauty* of God (723–25),[79] and in Christ's beautiful face she recognizes a link between heaven and earth (328–29). Since she sets great store by the corporeal side of human existence,[80] it is not surprising that she alone, among English mystics, is deeply impressed by the so-called *vera icon,* in St. Peter's Church in Rome, which was thought to represent the imprint of Christ's human face in Veronica's shroud. Copies were made for sale, and Chaucer's Pardoner had one of them sewn onto his cap. We should take seriously her saying that she *remembered* the Sudarium of Rome, because this and the manner in which she alludes to the reactions of the pilgrims seem to suggest that she saw it there. This assumption gains probability by the fact that there existed a special English pilgrims' guide, the "stacions of Rome" of 1370.[81] We have evidence from the Continent that even recluses were given permission to participate in a pilgrimage (see chap. 3). It was believed at that time that as *vera icon* the shroud attested God's incarnation, and around 1400 "Veronicas appear showing the face of Christ with the Crown of thorns."[82] For Julian, the shroud provides hermeneutic clarity for her second revelation: having

FIGURE 12.   Painting of St. Veronica with the Sudarium, by the unknown Master of St. Veronica (1480?). Munich Bayerische Staatsgemäldesammlungen—Alte Pinakothek. Inv.Nr. 11886. By permission of bpk /Bayerische Staatsgemäldesammlungen.

observed the crucifix in her cell, she saw the changing of color in Christ's face, while not knowing whether this was a vision or not; it was the remembrance of the Sudarium that assured her of the reality of her vision, because it presented a paradoxical effect: on the one hand its dark color suggested the Passion necessitated by the fallen state of man, and on the other hand it reflected the shining divine brightness of Christ's resurrection—a paradox that in my view is expressed very effectively in the painting by the Master of Saint Veronica (figure 12).

As far as Julian is concerned, it would, however, be wrong to see an aestheticizing tendency in her book;[83] rather, although she sees Christ's suffering and dying in terribly realistic concreteness, she is also aware of God's *impassibilitas* (his inability to die, 191.20?); he preserves his divine beauty, even in his Passion. Thus the way in which she integrates the shroud in her discussion testifies again to her profound theological thinking.[84]

The Role of Prayer in Julian's Theology

Julian's thoughts on *oratio* as the second stage on the path to *unio* are founded on profound perspicacity stemming from personal experience, although they were probably also influenced by Walter Hilton's doctrine of prayer.[85] For her, prayer includes an act of seeking, culminating in mutual enjoyment of God and the soul (SV 247–48), which echoes the Augustinian *fruitio*. In prayer the soul desires God himself,[86] which requires that God's freely granted grace first touch the person in prayer ("I am grounde [*causa*] of thy besekyng," 461.11 and SV 259.20–21);[87] that he bestows the prayer enabling communion with him is one of the mystics' basic convictions. When prayer occurs in this spirit,[88] the devotee commits himself to the divine will according to the Lord's Prayer petition ("Than shalle we nothyng wylle ne desyer but the wylle of oure lorde," 416.22–23).[89] This is familiar from the *Cloud* group and from Walter Hilton. Meister Eckhart and the *Mirouer des simples âmes* relinquish prayer; since the soul has freed herself from any will of her own and lets God take full effect within her, she no longer sees any reason to pray. "Reclusive purity cannot pray, for whoever prays, desires something from God. . . . But the heart that has withdrawn from the world desires nothing, and has nothing it would like to be rid of. Therefore it is untrammeled by prayer."[90] Julian, for whose spiritual life prayer is important, goes part of the way with Meister Eckhart and also Marguerite Porete when she affirms in the SV that the soul who is already in communion with God does not need to pray since she has everything: "for whate tyme that mannes saule es

hamelye with god, hym nedes nought to praye . . . when we see god we hafe
that we desyre, and than nedes vs nought to praye" (SV 261.54–262.65). Yet
in the LV she recommends prayer even in the absence of any inclination to
pray. Like Marguerite, she ventures further to great theological insights, for
instance with the thought that prayer "makes us like God in quality, as we
are by nature" (makyth vs lyke to hym selfe in condescion as we be in kynde,
464.40–41). Indeed, "God's love is so great that he considers us partners in
his good deed" (SV 260–61; "the luff of god es so mykille that he haldes vs
parcyners [partners] of his goode deede," SV 260.43–44). Her understanding of prayer also encompasses the possibility of its being at times equated
with a "beholding," a spiritual vision (Gk. *theoria*) of the immediate presence
of God;[91] thus prayer leads to the experience of simple being-with-God.[92]
Walter Hilton had spoken especially of this presence of God in connection
with his "theory" of prayer. Julian adds the familiar mystics' caveat that God
does not reveal himself here below in his essence; but the more he lets himself be known, the more intense human yearning becomes (478.30–480.44),
and it can only be fully appeased by beholding God in the world to come.
For her, sight is naturally the most important of the spiritual senses.[93] Finally,
prayers of thanksgiving have particular relevance for her, since God gives her
thanks in return for the suffering that she takes upon herself for his sake.

Julian's stance in prayer can also be looked at from the appealing perspective of a conversation with God as "nonpareil partner."[94] Like Mechthild of
Magdeburg, with whom there are so many points of contact, she not only
receives visions, but is also granted theological insights by God through language alone. This enables her to respond, and enter into dialogue with God.
It is of course an asymmetrical dialogue, for Julian's replies are usually brief.
Her responses, however rare, are a conversation with her inner teacher,[95] and
may arise from prayer. They are clearly linked to her thoughts and reflections. It may happen that she only needs to articulate a theological idea,
without addressing it directly to Christ, for God to deliver a prompt answer
(chap. 5). Here Julian extends prayer into literary discourse, contributing to
deeper knowledge. Mechthild of Magdeburg had already undertaken this on
a far larger scale. Interestingly, Julian receives the great vision of a lord and
his servant in answer to a theological problem she had raised, but God does
not always satisfy her theological curiosity.

On Trinity and Incarnation in the Work of Julian of Norwich

Brief mention has already been made of the significance, for Julian, of human corporeality, and that it plays a major part in her theology. In her view,

God did not assume human form for his work of salvation for a limited duration, as some people believed; rather, he became a human being, and *remained* one, as the monk of Farne explicitly asserts: "nevermore did he leave the flesh."[96] Julian is therefore prepared to conclude that since God himself chose incarnation, he enhanced the value of the human body, both male and female. A further consequence is that Julian does not accept that women should be granted less esteem on account of being equated with the body—any more than Mechthild of Magdeburg[97] or Gertrud of Helfta accepted this. It gradually becomes clear that, for Julian, human corporeality has a relevance to experience of God unprecedented among English mystics. Before pursuing this further, it is necessary to inquire into her definitions of God and the soul.

With her characteristic breadth of vision, she turns her attention particularly to the dogma of the Trinity, which is in any case much more strongly reflected in women mystics than in the male writers considered so far.[98] Julian reflects the fundamental notion of this dogma: the triune God creates, loves, and preserves; he combines within himself the "appropriations" of power (in Julian, truth), wisdom, goodness ("God" is "good"—cf. the *Cloud* author), and, above all, love. The efficacy of a single person of the Trinity would be incomplete without that of the two others.[99] Moreover, the action of one person of the Trinity flows into that of another; permanent movement therefore belongs to God's being. Greek Orthodox theology developed the term "perichoresis" for this exchange within the Trinity. Love that is the father leads to love of the son, and this love is expressed in a love that is the Holy Ghost.[100] Since Julian's theology is a theology of love, it is grounded in the eternally flowing love within the Trinity.[101]

For Julian, human "access" to the mystery of the Trinity is possible only through Christ; he represents and signifies the whole Trinity (295.15). This has rightly been described as one of Julian's most profound theological insights.[102] Walter Hilton and the *Cloud* author had occasionally spoken of Jesus and God as identical. Julian's entire theology needs to be interpreted on the basis of the "christocentricity of [her] trinitarian vision."[103] Even more important, in my view, is that uncreated love establishes a trinitarian ontology that relates the entire real world to the love within the Trinity.[104] The Trinity as personal three-in-one relates to itself, and is complete in itself, but it also encompasses humanity. Therefore, perichoresis extends beyond the Trinity into the human sphere, and love within the Trinity comes into its own only through love for mankind, for "God and humanity are one."[105] Julian and Mechthild of Magdeburg converge, again, in their belief that God needs the human being.[106]

The Human Being as a Personal Unity

Julian sees the human being sanctified by divine incarnation, in unity of soul and body.[107] This is an insight into the essence of being already formulated by Origen, and widely taken up again by women mystics in particular (especially by Mechthild of Magdeburg and Gertrud of Helfta). In the *Cloud* author and Hilton this notion of the person was at risk, for their dualism of spirit and corrupted body hindered the thought of *personal* unity. Since Hilton emphasized the corruption of the body, for him the doctrine of man being God's image and likeness and a *unity* of body and soul could not fully come into its own. In contrast to Hilton, Julian fully acknowledges this personal unity of man as God's *imago* and *similitudo* ("ymage and...lykenes," 329.49); she calls him a created trinity ("a made trynyte," 568.40), which brings us once more to the Augustinian concept of the soul as *trinitas creata,*[108] especially because in Julian the Augustinian potentialities of *memoria, ratio, voluntas* also determine the likeness to God.[109]

The unity of the human being was made up in scholastic thought, as we have seen, of "substance" and "sensuality."[110] Substance is divided into a higher (inner) part, the actual substance, and a lower (outer) part, sensuality—which is linked with substance, and is indeed a part of it. It is important to recognize that higher rationality is located in the higher substance, lower rationality in the lower. We encounter once more the differentiation between *ratio superior* and *ratio inferior* already found in *the Cloud* texts and Hilton. While the higher part of the soul strives upward toward God, the lower part concentrates on cognition of the world. Yet Julian departs from the earlier Augustinian doctrine, that higher rationality is exclusively the preserve of Adam, the man, and that Eve must be content with lower rationality, that is, with a subservient function. She does not explicitly assign to women the same *ratio* as to men, but this is implied by her theology. Moreover, the concept of the human being as personal unity, so vitally important to Julian, disposes of a differentiation between man and woman.[111] Therefore, the "sensuality" of mankind, linked with substance, refers not only to the senses, but to the entire human being, with soul and body, and mode of existing in the world.[112]

Julian's anthropology is supplemented by the important tenet that the substance of the soul not only designates the human being's "creaturely being,"[113] as for the *Cloud* author, but was also part, even before the beginning of life on earth, of the substance of God, of actual "being" (chap. 42). It is referred to several times as "ground" of the soul, "ground" being one of Julian's favorite terms. This has nothing to do with the ground of the soul in Rhenish mysticism, but harks back to Pauline Christology

("He is the grounde, he is þe substannce," 611.14; [1 Cor 3:11]), and we find a similar usage in the *Cloud* texts and Hilton. At the same time, Julian is able to say that the soul was created from nothing (558.41). For her, with her highly developed appreciation of antitheses, the idea of the soul's association with divine substance is not irreconcilable with creation from nothing. She recalls that we derive from a "double" act of substantial and sensual creation (585.39–40).[114] The human being was created by God, through love, as natural substance (563–64), part of God's nature, and is sustained by his love, charity, and grace, for which reason Christ can also be called substance, indeed natural father or mother of all souls (chap. 54).[115] Mechthild of Magdeburg takes a similar view, and God says to her in a vision: "Lady Soul, you are so made one with my nature that there can be nothing more between you and me."[116] For greater precision, Julian analogously uses the term "kind" to express the nature, or being, of God, which is "kind unmade." Important theological relationships are broached via the polysemy of "kind": God's essence is kindness, he is the father of his created kindred, who are of his kind (cf. on this *Wohunge* in chap. 2). Nevertheless, there are no pantheistic implications in the idea of kinship between mankind and God;[117] yet Julian no doubt shows some Plotinian influence.[118]

After recalling the doctrine that the soul partakes in God's substance, Julian proceeds to formulate the bold notion that there is no difference between God and our essential nature, or the higher part of the soul ("I sawe no dyfference betwen god and oure substance, but as it were all god," 562.17–18; "I am substancyallye aned [united] to hym," SV 213.19). Here she converges once again with *The Mirror of Simple Souls,* and with Meister Eckhart.[119] By adding that human substance is subject to creation (562–63), she escapes the possible charge that her assertion of the identity of God with the human soul is heterodox. Nonetheless, this is a very bold statement. A further consequence of the human being's participation in divine being is that, for her, God is *closer* to us than is our own soul, on account of his "superessentiality." This leads to a paradoxical outcome in her quest for knowledge of God: as we have already observed, she concludes, on the one hand, that one must seek first to know God, and then to know "oure selfe, what we ar by him in kinde and in grace" (665.54–56); on the other hand, she makes a contrary recommendation that self-knowledge should be acquired first, in order to proceed to knowledge of God.[120] For the soul reflects God's sun so brightly that the mirror becomes the sun, though without losing its ontological difference. There is no reason to see in this a direct parallel to Meister Eckhart's famous mirror metaphor[121]—God is the ground of the soul, inasmuch as he lets himself be reflected in the soul—since the mirror metaphor occurs in other mystics as well (Rolle, *Cloud* author, Hilton). What Julian wants to convey, above all, is that when human beings turn away from God, they depart from the ground of the self.[122]

Equally original is Julian's assertion that in each one of us there is a desire to avoid sin, and to be good, deriving from the substance's immanent "godly will." Much has been written about the precise meaning of this term; I myself contributed to the discussion many years ago.[123] Today I am of the opinion that, although Julian's "godly wylle" is similar in some respects to the moral and mystical concept of the Stoic *scintilla* and *synderesis* in medieval theology,[124] she did not develop it from this concept; she stresses that the "godly will" of the human being predestined for salvation is in essence one with Christ as ground of the soul.[125] The most apt circumlocution is "good will stemming from God, and efficacious in the human being," or "divine efficacy" ("this is the werkyng whych is wrought contynually in ech soule that shalle be savyd, whych is the godly wylle," 582.10–11). Gertrud of Helfta is granted by Jesus the gift of the good will; it reflects "the generosity of divine love."[126] By contrast, Julian also speaks of an animal will, inherent in "sensuality."[127] The warning suffices, that sensuality's will has an animal quality when it chooses remoteness from God, and, as captive of its own self, withdraws into itself.[128] Everything depends on the efficacy of "mercy and grace" (566.17); "mercy" strengthens spiritual growth, "grace" gives it fulfillment (585.30–33).

This cannot obscure what is impressively new in Julian's view of the human being. She draws a novel conclusion from divine incarnation: since God descended not only into human substance, but also into human sensuality, and even dwelt in it, sensuality, most remarkably, can no longer be considered the chief cause of sin.[129] This leads her to pay scant attention to sexuality and asceticism. It is no longer of any importance to her that sensuality be suppressed; rather she proclaims the need for its "completion and reunion with the higher part of the soul."[130] Here she is in agreement with Mechthild of Magdeburg,[131] and with Gertrud of Helfta, who had spoken of a bodily core of being (*carnis substancia*) in order to indicate that the flesh, the body, is an essential part of the human being.[132]

Embodying the Spirit

Initially it will have seemed strange, even shocking, to Julian's medieval readers that she takes human corporeality as the starting point for her mystical theology.[133] Was the body not frequently regarded as inimical, disgusting, and in need of chastisement? Did not the ultimately Gnostic view of the body prevail in patristic tradition—that it was despicable as the main cause of sin? For the *contemptus mundi* attitude, to which Richard Rolle conformed to the utmost, the equation prevailed on a lowly level: *homo = humus*.[134] The texts of the *Cloud* group and Walter Hilton also devalued the body, but at least they registered the ultimate revaluation of corporeality through the resurrection of the body.

Since "sensuality" is part of "substance," for Julian there is also a "sensual soul," although there is no clear dividing line between the two parts of the soul.[135] Such comments on our "sensuall soule" (564.28) and the fact that our soul passes into our body through "inspiration," giving us sensuality (566.16–17), are among the most fascinating aspects of her theology. Her very complex concept of sensuality indeed encompasses our entire psychological and physical makeup, our individual psychosomatic existence.[136] It also comes very close to the Pauline notion of the flesh (Gk. *sarx*).[137] There is no question of a new dualism, since both substance and sensuality are constituents of the soul.[138]

In Julian the notion of the soul's spiritual senses, so widespread in English mysticism, is impressively reactivated and intensified. The final experience of God in the unconstrained *visio beatifica* is related to all the senses, "and we are all hidden in God without end, seeing him truly and feeling him wholly, hearing him spiritually, and smelling him delectably, and swallowing him sweetly" (481.51–53).[139] Here she also alludes to the sacrament of the Eucharist. So why does she speak at one point of the human being's "wrecchyd" (SV 211.20), dying, and putrefying flesh? Because she is giving expression to the concrete thought of her own sick, weakened body, without asserting its *moral* reprehensibility.[140] The body, with its sensuality, is perverted only when it disengages from divine substance and withdraws into itself.

It has rightly been observed, time and again, that this gives Julian a much less biased approach to everything creaturely. Even the natural functions of the body direct her attention to God,[141] not excepting bodily evacuation, creaturely needs, and the process of metabolism, which she offers up for consideration without any trace of false shame. Furthermore, although God's incarnation took place in man, for Julian its efficacy spreads to the whole created universe. Therefore Christ's Passion caused suffering to the whole of creation, as she affirms with deep sorrow.[142] Then again, since God is in everything, as she teaches in harmony with Paul,[143] he can be seen joyfully in all things ("the fulhed of joy is to beholde god in alle," 433.13–14; "See I am in all thyngs," 340.52; "in man is god, and in god is alle," 322:16).

The Indwelling of God and the Soul

This overview of important aspects of Julian's theology provides the necessary preliminary to an evaluation of her mysticism, which is formulated most intensely in her last great vision. There she becomes aware of Jesus in her soul, which has expanded into an exceedingly large, noble city. He chooses the *sensual* soul, sensuality, as his dwelling. In it he is regally enthroned, and enclosed ("That wurschypfull cytte that oure lorde Jhesu syttyth in, it is oure sensualyte, in whych he is enclosyd," 572.23–24). Although he is the Pauline *kyrios,* he is not unapproachable; he can be experienced especially by the senses. Such enjoyment of God (*fruitio*) was already an essential notion for Augustine.[144] Through choosing Mary's corporeality as his dwelling, he entered into the sensuality of all believers, and *sanctified* it in so doing.[145] From this stems Julian's view that epistemological knowledge is strongly rooted in the corporeal, and indeed starts from the body, if not entirely, then to a considerable degree. It is the body that makes possible her intense *spiritual* experience:[146] "for her, the milieu of the Holy Spirit is precisely the world of sense—a marvellous concept."[147] The whole Trinity takes up residence in the soul, with all its qualities, and especially with love. Conversely, the soul resides in God ("oure soule syttyth in god in very rest," 571.14; "oure soule that is made dwellyth in god in substance, of whych substance by god we be that we be," 562.14–16). We experience God and know him by becoming *lovingly* aware of him; for we are enclosed in him, and he in us (307.43–44, 49). This indwelling is not specified as a brief experience of *unio,* but is a lasting oneness-of-being, as proclaimed also by Gertrud of Helfta.[148] Here Julian displays the two aspects of the apostle Paul's mystical theology, his dual statement of mankind in Christ and Christ in man, or, as the theologian Wikenhauser puts it: "Love, now as personified in Christ, is also the principle of Pauline mysticism, which . . . rests on two pillars: the identifying formula 'Christ in me' and the embracing formula 'in Christ,' which was made concrete ecclesiologically in the notion of the mystical body of Christ. Paul already reflected on his Damascus experience in his Christology, but did so even more in his mysticism."[149] Paul challenges his audience in concrete terms to "put on" Christ (Rom 13:14; Gal 3:27), and Julian is expressing the same idea when she says "He is our clothing" (SV 212.3–4). The *Cloud* author and Hilton had recourse to Paul's instruction to undress and put on Christ, but Julian's interpretation is decidedly more individual, especially the bold reversal in her assertion that we undress him when he yearningly visits the soul. Mechthild of Magdeburg expresses an astonishingly similar thought: "You clothe yourself with my soul, and you are its closest piece of clothing."

Likewise Gertrud, the other famous nun of Helfta, suggests figuratively that God lets the human being's love change his clothes.[150] All three women imply familiarity with the idea that God needs the human being, as the human being needs God.

This figurative language is surpassed by a climax, more intimate in nature, in chap. 67 of the LV: in the human being God feels "most homely," here he is most "at home" ("in vs is his homelyest home and his endlesse dwellyng," 641.16–17).[151] Again, this motif, which should not be taken as clumsy or childish familiarity, is not unknown in English mysticism. Julian will have been prompted to use these words by the theological motif of heaven as the Christian's home (Phil 3:20; Heb 13:14), which she now converts into the image of the soul as God's home.[152] The same metaphorical usage is again found in Mechthild of Magdeburg, who had also discovered God in human corporeality.[153]

It is important to note that although Julian recounts her sight of God residing as Trinity in her soul, she does not speak of a merging of the soul and God, and she is altogether reticent with regard to her own mystical experience—notwithstanding her great self-assurance. In this she once more resembles Mechthild of Magdeburg, who also hardly speaks of her own ecstasy; the experience is not a violent *raptus,* but rather a state of gentleness.[154] Nor does Julian wish to convey mystagogic guidance as such, but only her certainty of God's heartfelt love—for herself and for believers in general—and she therefore favors the pronoun "we," rather than "I" (524.129). Nevertheless, it must be noted that Julian's work does not begin with the information that she has received visions from God, which she now wishes to communicate to the reader. Rather, she derives general theological insights from her visions, in very powerful language; and one of them is the Pauline doctrine of the community of all believers in the one *corpus mysticum* of Christ.[155]

Pseudo-Dionysian Echoes in Julian's Theology

Julian's intellectual agility and her alertness to opposites explain why she is impressed, for a time, by the Pseudo-Dionysian tradition, although it can hardly be harmonized with her incarnation theology. Likewise, the *Cloud* author, Hilton, and Marguerite Porete (and Hadewych and Mechthild of Magdeburg) were not averse to incorporating into their works some elements of a mysticism entirely contrary to their own apophatic approach. Influenced by the Pseudo-Dionysian tradition, Julian experiences an intellectual vision in which she sees God in one point, and she becomes aware of the indivisible

FIGURE 13.   Christ holding the universe in his arms; in Aristotle, *Libri Naturales* (*Works on Natural Philosophy*). British Library, MS Harley 3487, fol. 65v. By permission of The British Library Board.

unity and infinity of God, almost as does Nicholas of Cusa through the *coincidentia oppositorum*.[156]

In a famous intellectual vision she sees in her hand a spherical object, as small as a hazelnut (chap. 5). This image reveals proximity to the Pseudo-Dionysian tradition, to which she now alludes by name (confusing Dionysius with France's patron saint). She sees in the nut something eminently real and elemental, namely, the created world, or God's relationship with it.[157] Recognizing, on the one hand, the smallness and nothingness of all created things, she gains the Pseudo-Dionysian insight that the soul must be "noughted," and must empty itself of all concrete thoughts and ties in *kenosis,* in order to be free for the love of God.[158] Yet, on the other hand, is she not convinced that God created the world, in which he himself became flesh, in sensual beauty? And does he not let himself be experienced in this world, which he loves? Alert as she is to stark contrasts, Julian feels the need to persist with this antinomy. Both perspectives make sense to her: the world is nothing, but at the same time it is a manifestation of God. Decisive for her is the dawning recognition that there is no foundation for fear that the tiny sphere will fall to pieces in its fragility and nothingness; through its very contingency it is preserved, because God, who created it from his being, lovingly holds it together (figure 13).[159] It is interesting that Gertrud of Helfta uses the image of the nut (*nux*) to describe the kernel of unsurpassable divine sweetness.[160]

The central point of Julian's theology may be summarized at this halfway point as follows: God is boundless, unconditional, and all-embracing love; he is bound to all creatures in love; indeed, he is in all creatures. She is certain that God created human beings in pure, immutable joy, in expression of his goodness. They in turn rejoice in him and "enjoy" him in all things; having him means having everything. Like a leitmotif, "enjoien" pervades her work; it is used in the Augustinian sense of *fruitio Dei.*[161] Like many other mystics, particularly Marguerite Porete, who sees the soul swim in a sea of joy, she wants to give expression to her discovery that Christians have reason to rejoice.[162] For her, love and joy are constantly linked to one another, while thoughts of suffering and human failure fade away.[163] There are vivid reminders of Richard Rolle and Marguerite Porete, but most astonishing is the relationship of her discourse to Gertrud of Helfta, especially to Gertrud's *Exercitia spiritualia.*[164]

The Revival of a Time-Honored Theological Idea: God as Mother

Her refined sensitivity to language alerts Julian of Norwich to the expressive qualities of individual words and terms; she reflects not only on their meaning, but also on their sound. She is moved by the "greatness" of this word "ever" (393.45). She comes to realize that God loved human beings before the beginning of time, and that he intends to guide them to bliss without end—unlike the librettist of J. S. Bach's cantata "O Ewigkeit, du Donnerwort, du Schwert, das durch die Seele bohrt" (O eternity, you word of thunder, O sword that bores through the soul), who is deeply affected by the threat of eternal damnation, an association of ideas that does not occur to Julian. "Child" is another word that moves her deeply. For reasons quite different from those of the Romantics, and without any trace of infantilism, she affirms that there is "none hygher stature in this lyfe than childehode" (617.42–43). She says this with reference to a New Testament theme that lay dormant for a long time in theology and had to be rediscovered in recent times: the notion of man as child of God, through which he is made especially worthy, because it makes him a brother of the "son of man."[165] Julian affirms this idea particularly strongly by combining it with the theological theme of divine motherhood. For her, God is not only father, but also mother—another term that resonates strongly for Julian; she thrills to the sound of the "feyer [fair] louely worde: Moder" (598.45). Evidently she had the good fortune to experience deep, tender motherly love—her own mother gave her support and comfort when she thought she was on the brink of death. Her talk of the love of God has great power, not least because she experiences him as mother.[166]

In this, Julian "revitalizes" a notion (only in the LV of *A Revelation,* chaps. 59–64) that had existed in the Christian tradition since biblical times, but had increasingly either been relegated to the background, ignored, or even forgotten. Yet the Cistercians, not least Aelred of Rievaulx in his *Institutio inclusarum,* had taken it up,[167] and this motif is one of the reasons why Julian's *A Revelation of Love* has aroused great interest in recent times.[168] She succeeds in bringing it to life in a most fascinating way, by filling it with a depth gained from long theological reflection, but also with a tenderness (for example p. 503.31–32) rarely found in English mysticism, and only exceptionally in theology (for example in Bernard of Clairvaux).[169] Julian declares Jesus to be "oure very moder" (589.9), who hangs on the cross, and the implication is that God as mother gives new birth to the human being.

The key to understanding this idea is that God, although traditionally thought of as male, yet has specifically maternal qualities.[170] The second appropriation of the Trinity, namely wisdom—after power, and before love—was attributed to Christ; the eternal wisdom of the Old Testament, also conceived of as mother, was associated with him (582.13; Ecclus 24: 24–26).[171] This offers the first prompting for the notion of God as mother, as has been seen in the case of Richard Rolle.

Nobody before Julian had thrown such profound light on the theme of Christ's motherhood, or interpreted divine incarnation as an act of divine motherhood with such intensity (chap. 59). *Ancrene Wisse* had introduced the idea that Jesus, during Mary's pregnancy, lived as a solitary in her womb. Divine mercy reminds Gertrud of Helfta of motherhood.[172] Yet Julian goes beyond this in her thinking and recognizes that every human mother bears her child ultimately for sorrow and death. To her subsequent inquiry into the meaning, or importance, of this recognition—"A, what is that?"—she herself provides the answer: God alone gives birth to the human being for the experience of joy, and to enter into life evermore (595.18–600.65).

Julian's Central Vision as a Parable Interpreted

Julian of Norwich has shown herself to be a very bold and courageous author. In the long period of at least twenty years between receiving her visions and recording them in the LV, she not only reflected at length on their meaning, but also gained considerable theological knowledge; she is particularly well acquainted with the New Testament.[173]

Her great vision of a lord and his servant helped her to clarify her individual theology. What she is shown is comparable to one of Jesus's parables,[174] a form of narrative theology, but she "decodes" it in two different ways. Center stage sits the lord in grave tranquillity, looking down "full louely and swetly and mekely" (514.12) on the servant standing before him, to whom he gives a commission. The servant, very eager to do his master's will, leaps up and runs off, but in his eagerness to serve he falls into a ditch, is seriously injured, and cannot get up alone. Since he perceives nothing around him, and cannot even behold his lord, he is totally disconsolate, although the lord is close by. Thus he foolishly remains in pain and isolation. Julian can see no reason why his situation should be interpreted as punishment for a misdeed, since he has displayed only good will and love-longing.

Very soon, however, she gains certainty that the lord and servant represent the story of God and Adam, and beyond Adam (following Paul) the human being as such, as man or woman. For her, it is Adam who commits the first misdeed, and, interestingly, Eve does not appear at all.[175] Adam wishes nothing more than to perform God's will for love, and runs off diligently; he does not infringe a divine prohibition deliberately, but only through negligence, human frailty, or "blindness."[176] There is no mention of the serpent's temptation, or of wanting to be like God. Julian also implies that eating the fruit does not mean that Adam accepts the insinuation of the devil (not even named) that he could equal God, but that it was simply a matter of Adam's blindness, which did not really call into question his willingness to obey. Yet through this very blindness he falls into a ditch—an uncommonly bold, certainly not orthodox reinterpretation of the fall. As if to avert any charge of heterodoxy, in another passage (chap. 29) Julian slips in the contrary thesis, that Adam's sin caused the gravest harm. Yet in this key parable

Julian directs attention, as has rightly been noted,[177] to Adam's state after the fall; he withdraws into himself in self-pity, and suffers great pain, so that his view of God as helper is obstructed. God, however, is full of immutable love and feels pity for Adam, who now has to suffer his own weakness as punishment. This implies that God allows human suffering because it arises from the world's contingency, but that he partakes in this suffering in order to overcome it.

The scene soon fades, but Julian is preoccupied with its theological meaning for a long time. Total understanding of the parable, and of her visions altogether, is deferred for almost twenty years. The parable is shown her a second time, albeit in altered form.[178] Medieval writers and thinkers often looked for the meaning of correspondences, and Julian discovers semiotic significance in external details, especially details of courtly bearing.[179] The lord would like to make good the rigors suffered by his servant, who served him with good will, for whom he feels constant love, and who is therefore to be honored even more than before his fall. In the second showing, the servant arouses a different impression. He stands at his lord's left side, and is clad in Adam's close-fitting gardener's smock—white, but old, worn out, and sweaty, which Julian considers unsuitable. Again he runs off very eagerly to do his lord's bidding, and ends with a fall. Gradually she becomes aware that, this time, the servant "signifies" not only Adam and mankind but also Christ, who sees himself as gardener of his church,[180] and who said of himself that he had come to serve (Mt 20:28). His willing, diligent trajectory ends with the "fall" into Mary's womb: Adam and Christ in one person—without doubt a bold way of seeing, but grounded in Paul's words that, as sin (and, through it, death) came into the world through man, so also it was vanquished through man (1 Cor 15:21).[181] Paul affirms at the same time "the unending grandeur" of Christ's act of salvation,[182] whereas Julian wants to affirm what Christ and Adam (i.e., man) have in common, and she obliterates the dividing line between them. For her, they are linked inseparably to one another; the second person of the Trinity "falls" with Adam, inasmuch as the death that Adam brought upon himself through his fall is accepted and overcome by Christ when he accepts human nature and sentence of death.[183] Therefore, through Christ's Passion, death, and resurrection the doomed human body is not only purified, but vested in unique beauty, and Adam, liberated from hell, is ennobled, and elevated to honor without end.

For Julian, Christ undertook his deed of atonement with a *joy* that pervades the entire Trinity. Indeed, he was "predestined" to do so, since he had the closest ties with human beings in substance and love, in preexistence, before they were created as living beings ("or that he made vs he louyd vs, and when we were made we louyd hym," 558.36–37).[184] Christ was with God as Eternal Wisdom, in Old Testament terms, and it was his love for mankind that drove him to descend (591–93). Human beings, who stem from Christ as their mother,[185] return with him to heaven,[186] where they attain the highest honor. In Julian—as in Mechthild of Magdeburg[187]—they were not created to replace the fallen angels, according to a doctrine widespread especially in lay circles, but simply out of unsullied divine love and goodness.[188] Nor does the triune God take counsel as to how mankind can be saved;[189] rather, God comes for love, fulfilling his own need. This is a theory contested by tradition, but paralleled remarkably once again in Mechthild of Magdeburg.[190]

The great parable of lord and servant, which is at the heart of Julian's theology, has a concrete social setting. On the one hand, it is governed by the principle of lordship in Julian's familiar feudal society. On the other hand, the lord in this narrative shows no trace of lordly, authoritarian bearing, and does not savor his immense sovereignty, which goes beyond the ideal of courtesy, or is indeed, in association with love, the highest form of courtesy. The servant acts in joyful obedience, and with natural humility.

Closer scrutiny reveals that the lord's bearing, too, is "humble," just as the Jesus of the Gospels defines himself in one of his own parables as destined to serve. The lord, who might be expected to embody the patriarchal power of the first person of the Trinity, shows himself to be a humble Christ, by no means primarily the *kyrios* of Pauline theology (according to the Protestant interpretation).[191]

This can only be explained in terms of Julian, the aristocrat, "defeudalizing" and "deconstructing" the lord-and-servant relationship, and taking away the elite element of the courtly setting she evokes. What remains is a father-son relationship, in part still patriarchal, but entirely loving, with some maternal features. The ambivalent parable also enables Julian to recognize the similarity between Adam and Christ as sons of God; Christ makes human beings his siblings before God. We remember that *The Wooing of Our Lord* had already emphasized Christ's *natural relationship* with human beings. For Julian, the central aspect of the Christian faith is a *personal* relationship between the human being and God-made-man, taking shape in a tender love conveyed through Julian's "feminine," person-orientated talk even more clearly than through the theological language of the apostle Paul. It has rightly been said that in the Middle Ages divine love was proclaimed nowhere more movingly than by Julian of Norwich.[192] She even surpasses Marguerite Porete's celebration of love in *The Mirror of Simple Souls.* In diverse ways, Mechthild of Magdeburg and Gertrud of Helfta were Julian's predecessors, with their "theology of love."[193]

The Problem of Sin in Julian's Soteriology

With her impressive ability to open up new approaches to theological problems, Julian also succeeded in reflecting in a most original way on the problem of human sinfulness. What does sin mean for her? An astonishingly modern feature is that she does not speak of sins, but only of the one "sin against God." In the SV, she addresses sin directly, and inquires into its being: "Ah, wretched sin! What are you? You are nothing" (p. 35; A wriched synne, whate ert thou? Thowe er nought, SV 271.26). For Julian, as for Gertrud, sin is not something with an actual existence ("I sawe noght synne," SV 245.65–66); it has no being, but is only an ontological lack of goodness—according to Augustine's famous definition, taken over by Thomas Aquinas, a *privatio boni*.[194] It signals a condition of alienation from God, and therefore yields "the opposite to union."[195] While the Christian, according to Paul, is destined for the freedom of the children of God, sin means lack of freedom; it is also "un-kind" in the sense of "un-natural."[196] The consequence of separation from God is life in exile, in the Augustinian-Bernardine *regio dissimilitudinis*.[197] Because sin leads to remoteness from God, it causes suffering to the human being in the here and now.[198] For Julian, as for most mystics, this remoteness from God is already hell (she sees "none harder helle than synne," 458.39–40); it actually causes more pain than hell (457–58), so that she, like most other mystics, gives no description of hell.

It is therefore consistent, though no less astounding, that in Julian's theology God does not reproach the human being for sin ("he blames not me for synne," SV 246.76–77). He knows that sin determines his relationship with the human being, who constantly sins in God's eyes because no action is possible without him. Julian also takes a very modern view of death, which for her is no longer Paul's "wages of sin," and is felt only briefly, since it is overcome by the joy of the eternal beholding of God (chap. 72, 659–661.22).

Instead of dwelling on negative contemplation of sin, Julian recognizes in it a "pedagogical" opportunity to support knowledge of the self and of God.[199] Her understanding of sin culminates in the famous description "Synne is behouely" (405.13), which recognizes it as an inevitable concomitant of human destiny.[200] She sees the moral failing of man as a necessary consequence of his *sensuality*.[201] Instead of reproaching or punishing man for his misdeeds, God counters sin with his healing love, as was already suggested in the great vision of lord and servant; sin is "behovely," and has an

"indispensable" purpose in the relationship of man to God.[202] It has rightly
been said that the motive force for Christ's suffering is love, not sin.[203] If
man with his failings returns God's love, and turns to him anew in love, his
worth is not diminished; rather, sin helps him in the end to gain honor.[204]
Here a courtly influence is discernible, which Julian then develops in her
own way. Chrétien de Troyes's great romance *Perceval* comes to mind, in
which the "hero" commits a sin (according to Julian's definition) but is
by no means less worthy on this account; rather, he gains further honor.
A connection of this sort has been revealed to Julian in David's culpability,
as in many other saint, so she does not hesitate to proclaim that "God also
showed me that sin is not shameful to man, but his glory" (p. 26); "syn is
na schame, bot wirschippe to mann" (SV 255.17)[205]—an extraordinarily
paradoxical statement.[206] Thus for Julian the "honor" of the human being is
indeed greater than if the fall had not occurred, a thought reminiscent of the
felix culpa as known, for instance, to Gertrud of Helfta,[207] but exceeding it by
far in its boldness.[208] *Felix culpa* understands guilt as leading to more sublime
revelation of the love of God,[209] whereas Julian takes from it a paradoxical
gain in human worth and honor. The power of sin is of course annulled
by God's "curtesy" only for the faithful,[210] for which reason *A Revelation
of Love* stresses the function of mercy and grace, divine attributes already
named in the Old Testament.

   It might be said that Julian makes things too easy for herself with regard
to the phenomenon of evil in the world, and David Aers has commented
shrewdly on this; he shows how she ignores the whole aspect of "social sin,"
of man's desire to destroy other people and himself.[211] She is convinced of
the fundamental goodness of the human being, linked with God from the
beginning through her natural substance, and she therefore says nothing of
the origin of the "beastly will" as opposed to the "godly will";[212] she only
affirms that their own resources do not enable human beings to do good.
Does it follow that evil is at bottom irrelevant to her? In fact, it scarcely
interests her, because it was not shown to her (she hears "lyttyle mencion
of evyille," 428.16).[213] But is she aware of the theological consequences of
her hypotheses? If God is in everything, and everything that happens is good
(340.48–49), if God, without whom the human being can do nothing, is also
the only doer (there exists "no doer but he," 340.42–43), is he not also in evil,
and even the cause of evil? Angela of Foligno took this very step: "'I recognize also that he is present in an evil spirit no less than in a good angel'...Here
God is understood very directly as *esse omnium* in all created beings."[214]
Julian, however, answers in true medieval spirit that "god is alle thyng that
is good" (318.15)—this being the appropriation of the third person of the

Trinity—and the evil in the world causes him suffering (434.22). Hence the reassuring question: "how shoulde any thing be a mysse?" (341.55–56).

Julian does face up to the great theological and philosophical problem of theodicy.[215] Like others, she is disturbed by the question of the cause of all the world's suffering, the source and meaning of "alle oure woo" (610.4), that Milton's great *Paradise Lost* will set out to recount (Book I, line 3). She seeks an answer to the human question posed ever anew, as to why God "sufferde synne to come" (407.41–42), and how this can be reconciled with his loving goodness. The answer she receives and conveys is essentially identical to a philosophical explanation offered by modern theology: God was able to create only an imperfect, contingent world, to which he is nonetheless entirely committed in loving devotion. "A perfect world would have become a second God. This would have led to the self-annullment of the divine."[216] Julian says: "The Holy Trinity would not have been completely satisfied with the creation of man's soul if he could have made it any better, any fairer, any nobler than he did create it." ("yf þe blessyd trynyte myght a made mannes soule ony better, ony feyerer, ony nobeler than it was made, he shulde nott a been full plesyd with makyng of mannys soule" (643–44). For her, the problem of the world and mankind's imperfection and proneness to suffering is overcome by her sight of the *healing* and redemption of the harmed and the wounded.[217] Here she recognized most intriguingly the therapeutic character of the Christian religion, again anticipating modern discoveries.[218]

Julian's Reception of St. Paul

Julian's remarkable originality leads us to inquire into the *sources* of her intellectual creativity. The fact that she writes in the vernacular has recently been taken as testimony of a "vernacular theology," and it is affirmed that she could have acquired her sophisticated ability to deal with key questions, such as the final reconciliation of the problem of sin and the definition of evil, from her great knowledge of "contemporary didactic and devotional vernacular literature."[219] This is a simplistic view that does not do justice to Julian's intellectual originality, for she had at her disposal, incontestably, a considerable knowledge of patristics and familiarity with the Bible. No doubt she is familiar with the traditional three-stage path of *lectio, oratio* or *meditatio, contemplatio.* Although she does not pay specific attention to the first stage, *lectio divina*, it emerges from her work beyond doubt that her theological thinking, and in part also her visions, were stimulated by a thorough knowledge of holy scripture, however this was acquired.[220]

It is difficult to understand how her roots in the biblical-patristic tradition could simply be ignored.[221] For a proper understanding of her theological achievement, the comparison with Gertrud of Helfta, with whom she has so much in common, is helpful. Gertrud still writes in Latin, but if her work had survived in Middle High German it would surely, though falsely, be cited as an instance of the new vernacular theology. So profound is Gertrud's knowledge of the Bible that a new edition of her *Exercitia spiritualia* records no fewer than five hundred quotations from holy scripture, or biblical allusions. Colledge and Walsh's edition may have registered too many instances of Julian's use of the Bible, but without doubt she had a comparable knowledge of this main source,[222] and, as has been shown, it was not necessary to be a Lollard in order to be convinced of the towering significance of the Bible, a significance already stressed by Origen and Augustine. Gertrud of Helfta was designated a "theologa" in the Middle Ages, and Julian of Norwich deserves the same appellation. Her originality is a direct result of the accomplished use she makes of her profound familiarity with the New Testament, and this can hardly be overstated; in her work, a new pre-Reformation approach to the biblical texts can be discerned. Julian no longer sees them simply as inspired divine testimonies; rather, she takes them as literary texts requiring interpretation, and she evidently also knows that a text's reception can be subject to change. Therefore she does not hesitate to apply a yardstick to the biblical text, and the yardstick is what Christ has shown her. Biblical statements, like others, must submit to this measure. Julian has a thoroughly modern theological understanding that Christian reception of the Bible must develop.

She had evidently been struck by numerous contradictory statements in the Bible, and by great discrepancies in Paul's writings, to which she reacted without bias.[223] Without doubt, she was aware of them. Several times she mentions the apostle by name. Her knowledge of Pauline theology is also indicated by the metaphor of Christ as human "clothing," which has already been noted. As will become apparent, Julian represents the high point of Pauline reception among English mystics (whether she knew Paul's writings in Latin or English is immaterial for our present purposes).

The recent "New Perspective on Paul" has directed particular attention to certain tensions and contradictions in Paul.[224] It has been recognized that he assesses Mosaic "law" very differently in different places. At one point, it is important to him that the law be fulfilled; at another point, this is not regarded as indispensable. The punishment deserved for noncompliance with the law is meted out not to the human being, but to Christ as his representative. Through faith in him, however, the human being can be "righteoused."[225] In arguing along these lines, Paul makes use in his letters to the

Galatians and Ephesians of thoroughly "forensic terminology."[226] Following Paul, the doctrine of righteousness by faith is central to Protestant theology.[227] Against this background, it is all the more astonishing that Julian pays no attention to the necessity of a life according to the law (by contrast, for instance, with the *Cloud* author and Walter Hilton); she looks at things from a quite different angle.

However much Julian may take essential themes and images from Paul, as was customary in the mystical tradition from *Ancrene Wisse* onward, especially in Walter Hilton, she clearly selects from among Paul's contradictory statements, and in so doing she indicates, implicitly at least, a certain uneasiness with some aspects of his theology.[228] To say this of a medieval lay authoress may seem bold, but since her partial reliance on Paul is beyond doubt, the occasions on which she diverges from him should not be obscured. It is my view that she noticed the discrepancies in Paul and sought to resolve them in an exciting way of her own. A modern scholar who has done much for a new understanding of Paul is of the opinion that the Pauline contradictions must be tolerated;[229] but Julian cannot accept this. Nor could the author of the Letter of James, who meant so much to the *Ancrene Wisse* author; he contradicted Paul by maintaining that righteousness by faith alone, without works, was unthinkable (whereby theologians believe that he misunderstood Paul). When central questions of human existence and destiny are at stake, Julian wants to offer clear, comprehensible answers, and she derives her right to do so from the visions she has received as theologian and prophet.

Attempting to Resolve Pauline Contradictions

The greatest inconsistency in the apostle Paul's theology lies in his interpretation of Christ and the relationship between God and mankind. On the one hand, Christ is born as man, and accepted by God as his son, in order that he may save mankind (the so-called adoptionist Christology);[230] on the other hand, he was always with God in divine form and is elevated once more as *kyrios* after his human life. Again, Paul considers on the one hand that God predestined man to sin, in order to be able to condemn and then finally to save him. On the other hand, he seems to articulate the opposite tenet, whereby God will save mankind when he comes again, without prior wrathful judgment; therefore nobody need live in fear of damnation. What Paul really thinks remains uncertain; he solves the problem by indicating that the solution is a divine mystery.[231] Paul is in favor of both views, contradictory as they are. Thus his statement on man's ultimate fate is, even for Eugen Biser, "ambivalent, or at least lacking in balance": "On the one hand, he considers that 'our life is a matter of faith, not of sight' (2 Cor 5:7) and after death we 'must appear before Christ' (5:10); on the other hand, he affirms that for those 'who are in Christ Jesus' there is nothing to be condemned (Rom 8:1), so that judgment can mean at most a purgatorial fire."[232] If, for Paul as for others, *love* is fulfillment of the law, then the loving person cannot harm another or accrue real guilt.[233]

Julian, for her part, accepts only Paul's last position, and quotes directly his reassurance that nothing can separate the human being from the love of God (355.19). For this reason, the Pauline doctrine of justification is not definitive, any more than it is for the other English mystics (except for Walter Hilton, who, however, also quotes the affirmation that "nothing can separate us from the love of God").[234] As a woman she is particularly moved by the concept of the human being as child of God (combined with divine motherhood; 564). Consequently she cannot reconcile this with an image of God as a father who subjects his children to a *judicial* system, and would have to curse them in the event of failure if his son did not take the curse upon himself. Her "preferred theology" withdraws the entire basis of juridical argumentation. If love is fulfillment of the law, it does not abrogate the law, as is often found, but rather embraces it, since a life in love will also fulfill the law's essential requirements.[235]

It is no less intriguing that Julian has also abandoned the idea of atonement, as if in prescience of modern reservations, inasmuch as she "liberates" herself from the notion of law and regards sin only as remoteness from God, and from his will. For her it is clear that God in his love *foresaw* the weakness and blindness of his creatures, and let his son accomplish the work of healing salvation through love. The deed of salvation is therefore free from any thought of cultic sacrifice as satisfaction for an angered father. Nevertheless, in order to meet the requirements of orthodoxy, she cannot avoid alluding to the idea of atonement (although she interestingly says in chap. 50 only that the human being has sinned since the time of the first man, which does not actually include the doctrine of original sin; 511.10–512.28). Julian may have realized that Paul "can make use of very different ideas in order to express the salvific meaning of the Cross,"[236] and that he may speak both of "atonement" (through cultic sacrifice) and of "reconciliation"; but for her it is only reconciliation that counts, as is also inherent in the original meaning of the term "atonement"—at-one-ment, the restoration of the unity between God and man destroyed by sin—so that she can proclaim with the utmost simplicity that God will "make vs all att one with hym" (656.23). This puts her at a great distance from the atonement theology of the Letter to the Hebrews, and it is remarkable that Gertrud, too, scarcely cites this letter.[237]

Like Gertrud before her, Julian also deliberately lets go of the Anselmian theory of satisfaction,[238] which was based on the feudal legal concept that a misdeed can only be atoned by a person of higher "social" standing (as at the beginning of Hilton's *Scale* 2).[239] Julian was well aware of Anselm's theory; she knows that he sees God's "honor" violated and stresses the need for "redemption" of this sin through atonement.[240] She, too, speaks of "gloriouse asethe [satisfaction]" (SV 247.10), but her theology cannot be reconciled with the doctrine that Christ's death brought about vicarious satisfaction for man's sin. Alluding directly to Anselm, she breathtakingly turns the idea of satisfaction upside down by talking of man's gain in "worship" through his very liability to sin, rather than of any diminution of God's honor. Christ does not direct to God the Father the question as to whether he is satisfied with the reparation of sin, but rather to the human being: "Arte thou well apayd that I sufferyd for thee?" (382.2–3). He then adds that if the soul is satisfied, then so is he.[241] Gertrud had expressed a similar view, but with a more concrete image: Christ has paid her dowry, which set her free, so for her, too, atonement is not of prime importance.[242] In sum, Julian develops an extremely bold and modern *theologia crucis*. Salvation comes about only when the human being returns God's love and is united with him anew—since he is love[243]—and through God's suffering and death, bestowed on man with compassion unto death, which admits him to the resurrection. One might say that in Julian a tendency to ward off fear of damnation, which runs through the major English mystical texts, reaches its climax.

Therefore, for Julian, unlike for Paul, the idea of God as judge at the end of the world occurs only as a very subordinate theme, if at all; she would like to take away people's terror at this prospect, as was also Gertrud of Helfta's aim.[244] It is worth recalling that however saintly their lives may have been, not even the mystics were free from fear of damnation, because they were mindful of Paul's admonishment that all must render their account before God on the Day of Judgment and none can be sure of salvation (SV 230.14–231.36). The most vivid example is perhaps that of the mighty Bernard of Clairvaux in his 16th sermon on the Song of Songs, where he speaks of himself as a man deserving the divine majesty's sentence of death.[245] The mystical texts affirm time and again that no one who loves God need be afraid;[246] nonetheless, timorous uncertainty may gain the upper hand for one or other of them. Richard Rolle frequently impresses upon his readers or listeners the horror of eternal damnation, and he himself is weighed down by the thought of the Last Judgment. This is not surprising when one considers that Jesus "did not abandon John the

Baptist's proclamation of judgment, [but . . .] intensified it," and that "many parables . . . [show] with dire threatening the dual outcome of judgment: the redemption of some for eternal salvation and the destruction of others with no hope, ever, of salvation."[247] Yet Julian does not accept that the direct encounter with God should take place amid "weeping and gnashing of teeth" (Mt 13:50), or prepared for "with fear and trembling" (Phil 2:12). She is supported by Jesus's words in St. Luke's version of the Sermon on the Mount, often overlooked, but to which Eugen Biser has drawn attention, that God is "kind to the ungrateful and the wicked" (Lk 6:35). For her, God always remains humanly "approachable," so that the notion of a wrathful God in judgment loses its terror.

It is no exaggeration to say that this courageous woman of Norwich ventures on a breathtaking, and indeed subversive, liberation from the familiar "theology of intimidation." Inspired by her enlightened spirit, she vehemently contradicts the image of a wrathful God and takes away the minatory quality of the Last Judgment.[248] She even looks forward to this day, as she rather provocatively affirms, for she expects neither reward nor punishment. With the great authority of her "sense of mission" she recognizes only the Pauline statement that there is nothing damnable in those who are in Christ.

The apostle Paul's contrary message, that God in his wrath may deny the sinner mercy and condemn him to eternal death, she passes over in silence, or she relegates it entirely to the background, and provides once more an astonishing justification, which she believes to be sanctioned by God himself: she did not *see* in her vision the wrath of God ("I saw no wrath," *A Revelation,* 500.6–7; in *A Vision* his anger is mentioned, but without comment). She asks herself why he should be angry with his own creation. For her, the notion that also occurs in Paul, that God caused humankind to sin, or let the fall happen, in order then to be able to save human beings, is unthinkable. Only her interpretation of sin as "behoveli" seems to have some support in Paul. The appropriations of God's being, his power, wisdom, and love, his kindness, loyalty, and peaceable nature, exclude the possibility of divine wrath (493). This arises, as she affirms with great psychological understanding, only from lack of sovereignty, and signals a deficiency in power, wisdom, or kindness, which is inconceivable in God (500). God's never-ending friendship with man takes away all possibility of lasting anger (505–6). Moreover, for Julian there is a further existential reason for the absence of God's anger: if he was angry, even if only for a short while, we could not exist (506.15–16). Therefore she asserts it to be "the most vnpossible" that God should be angry (505.8–9), for the divine Trinity is love.

This new theological approach in her reflection on Pauline texts is particularly bold because the notion of a wrathful God is anchored very firmly in the Bible and in the patristic tradition. *Ancrene Wisse,* probably very much appreciated by Julian, adamantly confronts readers who regard God as too "gentle" to punish sin retributively; this text impressively proves the opposite with a long list of "conclusive" biblical examples.[249] It is again most astonishing to see with what ease Julian sets herself apart from a firmly established theological tradition, even if she can cite Paul as saying on one occasion: "For God has destined us not for wrath" (1 Thes 5:9). Admittedly, her courageous indirect "objection" to God's intimidating wrath did not immediately resonate with others, for the time was not yet ripe for theological renewal of this sort.

Even today, such an attempt, though it may find approval, may also be met with weighty theological criticism. The objection is that a Christian image of God without his potential for wrath is incomplete, and simplistic; for his greatness comprises also his dark side, unfathomable for man.[250] This cannot be entirely refuted, when one considers that in the Old Testament God is already "ambivalent," not only wrathful, as is commonly believed, but also full of grace and mercy, forbearing, and "abounding in steadfast love and faithfulness" (Ex 34:6).[251] Nevertheless, the main objection to the thought of a wrathful God persists, namely the generation of fear and terror, that has caused so much suffering in the history of the church; for Christians have been "infected" or inflamed by the notion of a wrathful God time and again when it came to combating and punishing obdurate infidels with violence infused with anger. Herein lies one of the roots of intolerance in Christian history. With a theology such as that proclaimed by Julian of Norwich, there would have been neither injustice nor violence in the service of Christ. Origen was in some ways a "precursor"; for him fear was transmuted into reverential awe and ultimately overcome by love, as the First Letter of John had already suggested.[252]

Julian and Apocatastasis

Julian, like many late-medieval women, is troubled by a related theme that arises in this context, namely, how belief in the all-embracing love of God can be reconciled with predestination, purgatory, hell, and eternal damnation, whereby one part of humanity is predestined to be saved, and another, without especial culpability, to be eternally forsaken. Can the human being comprehend Paul's words: "So then he has mercy on whomsoever he chooses, and he hardens the heart of whomsoever he chooses" (Rom 9:18) and God's utterance "I will have mercy on whom I have mercy" (Rom 9:15)? If God's "will" is the final cause, is this anything more than arbitrary will? Paul had no explanation for predestination, and therefore curtailed any discussion: "But who indeed are you, a human being, to argue with God?" (Rom 9:20, alluding to the story of Jacob and Esau).[253] Augustine's later doctrine of mercy, in particular his interpretation of the Letter to the Romans, developed above all in *De diversis questionibus ad Simplicianum* 1/2, culminates in the question and rebuttal: "IS THERE INJUSTICE IN GOD? OUT OF THE QUESTION!"[254] His final argument is that we are confronted here with higher, divine (for us, incomprehensible) justice.[255] The solution Augustine offers is that predestination cannot be branded as arbitrary according to human criteria, but must be accepted as a superordinate principle, into which man has no insight.

For Julian, however, a divine arbitrary will is quite unthinkable, for she believes that human beings are guided in love by God's providence ("for[eseing] wysdom," 337.9; "forsyght," 728.7), emanating from his love and returning to his love (reminiscent of *The Mirror of Simple Souls*, another work by a woman). William of Ockham accepted the Augustinian line of argument when he proclaimed: "The cause of God's predestination of some for no reason and others for a reason is simply the *divine will* [emphasis added]."[256] Julian of Norwich cannot agree. She is convinced in her innermost being that all human beings have the same chance of eternal salvation. She is also far from any thought of divine predestination in the usual sense because she has been shown that the human soul-substance has a preexistence. To recapitulate: before the creation of man as soul and body, the soul-substance was united in love with the substance of God or Christ, was loved by God, and will return to God.

Julian's belief in the close "substantial" bond between human beings and God also prevents Augustine's doctrine of grace from resonating with her. However, she accepts the church's teaching (425.46) that there are people who freely choose to deny God, and that such people have to suffer the punishment of eternal damnation; she also conforms to the belief that the devil exerts his power in order to win souls for his kingdom, and, like others, she takes great pains to guard against him. Nevertheless, she seems uncertain, or uncomfortable, with regard to "hell" and "purgatory" in the articles of faith. After all, purgatory had only been institutionalized ecclesiastically some 170 years prior to her birth.[257] In her visions she is shown nothing of hell or purgatory, whereas Mechthild of Magdeburg, for example, is pleased when God takes vengeance on the wicked.[258] Julian allows us a glimpse of her conviction that no misdeed justifies eternal punishment, contrary as this may be to the final tenet of the Athanasian Creed, which promises eternal joy to the good and damns the wicked in eternity.

Julian gains from one of her visions the comforting certainty that God "shalle make althyng wele" (426.51); she holds fast to her famous affirmation that "alle shalle be wele, and alle shalle be wele, and alle maner of thynge shalle be wele" (405.13–14; SV 245.72–73). This theory of *apokatastasis panton,* restitution and salvation of all at the end of time, already suggested in Acts 3:21, was put forward notably by Origen, who was not unknown in Norwich in Julian's day.[259] However, he intended this *restitutio* to be understood only as "universal hope" and did not teach redemption of the devil. Ambrose, too, was persuaded by the concept of "universal salvation, though [likewise] not for the devil,"[260] and Gregory of Nyssa recognized the usefulness of apocatastasis since "eternal punishment would lead to the assumption of a vengeful God."[261] Augustine, as already mentioned, was guided by the notion of justice and even revenge, and was unable to let sin pass unpunished.

The idea of apocatastasis has fascinated people down the ages, and has found its way into major works of European culture, such as Friedrich Schiller's "Ode to Joy" ("All sinners shall be forgiven / And hell shall be no more" [eliminated by Beethoven]), the end of Part 2 of Goethe's *Faust,*[262] and Richard Wagner's music drama *Parsifal.*[263] It appealed particularly to women, who devoted themselves most diligently to prayer for souls in purgatory.[264] It was rigorously rejected by Walter Hilton, *Scale* 2, chap. 10. In taking up the idea, Julian is well aware that everything is by no means good, as long as a single soul remains unredeemed;[265] she believes that only when all people have been brought back to God, and are reintegrated in him, will divine creation be perfected.[266] It has also been observed that Julian expresses her ideas on this subject with shrewd caution by expressly referring the concept of salvation to all those who are saved by divine grace, leaving open the question of whether the promise "all shall be well" applies only to these recipients of grace or to all mankind ("all mankynd that shall be savyd," 399.15).[267] To a certain extent Julian can draw support from one eschatological variant put forward by the apostle Paul, which states that God takes pity on *all* (Rom 11:32), so that his love for all people will in the end take effect for all.[268] On the other hand, for Paul, as mentioned, God's plan of salvation for mankind remains his "secret mystery."[269] Julian foresees that God himself will initiate an act of reconciliation; early on, she is even promised that she will be allowed to witness this: "I shall make well all that is not well, and thou shalt see it" (284.39–40), but in spite of repeated allusions the promise is not kept, and we are reminded that God does not reveal his mysteries. Yet his assurance of salvation turns her hope into certainty that his goodness cannot but save human beings at the end of time,[270] because he loves them as their mother ("we be brought agayne by the moderhed of mercy and grace in to oure kyndly stede, where that we ware in," 594.3–6).[271] Evidently, of the four groups of people listed by Augustine,[272] she has in mind neither the entirely good nor the entirely bad, but the large number of those who are neither wholly good nor wholly bad.

Moving toward a Theology of the Future

The reader of Julian's *A Revelation of Love* will note her liking for antitheses, antinomies, paradoxes, and contrasts, and her simultaneous tendency to attenuate or reconcile them. Her proclamation of her visions flows into a beholding of God as endless light, and also as peace, since God for her is peace and serenity, a thought that permeates her entire work (and medieval mysticism in general; cf. also Rom 14:17). The thought of peace is all the more telling because she is writing during the turmoil of the Hundred Years' War. However, her expectations are not directed toward the second coming of Christ and the beginning of his world dominion in justice and peace; rather, her book ends with a specifically mystical openness, referring to itself as not yet performed (731.2–3).[273] She implies that ultimate *unio* can occur only as future beholding "in God" (734.27). Yet among the lasting impressions made by her work are the description of divine indwelling in the soul and the dramatic conclusion with its joyful praise of all-conquering love:

> I often desired to know what our Lord meant [by showing me these visions]. And fifteen years and more later I received an answer for my spiritual understanding with these words: "What, do you really want to know what your Lord meant in this matter? Be assured that love was what he meant. Who showed you this? Love. What did he show? Love. Why did he show it to you? For love." (I desyerde oftyntymes to witt in what was oure lords menyng. And xv yere after and mor, I was answeryd in gostly vnderstondyng, seyeng thus: What, woldest thou wytt thy lordes menyng in this thyng? Wytt it wele, loue was his menyng. Who shewyth it the? Loue. (What shewid he the? Love.) Wherfore shewith he it the? For loue. (LV 732.13–733.17)

God loved human beings before he created them, she adds, and loves them unceasingly, and in this love he cares for them without end. With unobtrusive rhetorical figures, including repetitions with minor variations, she achieves a unique, almost hymnic effect.

It is hardly surprising that Julian of Norwich appeals particularly to today's readers, since in many respects her theology is less medieval than "modern," inasmuch as she seeks with a new theological approach of our own time. In his New Theology, Eugen Biser attempts to develop further the interpretation of the Christian message, and to relegate to the background, dismiss, or reinterpret in a comprehensible manner the objections to Christianity raised in our post-Enlightenment and post-criticism-of-religion era, which have led to loss of faith for many people. As has been suggested, Julian evidently anticipated this to some degree and ventured to "think further" on the Christian message, and the theologian is called upon to "think further," as a Protestant scholar has recently affirmed.[274] Nicholas Watson has aptly observed that one of the boldest aspects of Julian's theology is her view that even God's truth as revealed to the church can claim no more than provisional validity.[275] This is the impression created by her great theological vision; its boldness looks far into the future. Notwithstanding occasional overexuberant wording that may tend toward heterodoxy, one can only marvel at the incredible self-assurance of Julian of Norwich, six hundred years ago, in undertaking a new interpretation of the Bible in the spirit of theological "thinking further."

Today it seems thoroughly surprising that she did not encounter conflict with the church for exceeding the bounds of orthodoxy.[276] There are definite echoes of *The Mirror of Simple Souls:* when she undertakes her own definition of the church, for instance; or provides a summa of the faithful; or picks up, as did Marguerite, the notion that the soul was with God before the beginning of time. Both agree, above all, in their magnificent praise of the uniqueness of divine love. The textual postscript (possibly attributable to the scribe) adds a notable recommendation, namely that statements in the text should not be regarded in isolation, but rather in their overall context. That she was left in peace despite Archbishop Arundel's attempt at censorship with his *Constitutions* probably resulted largely, as Kerby-Fulton convincingly argues, from the fact that the "manuscript culture" of the time made it possible for books to be produced for, and restricted to, a small circle of readers.[277]

In spite of the inadequacy of human language, in her case the English vernacular, Julian succeeds in conveying her profound theological insights with magisterial skill. Although she tends to think pictorially in the images of her visions, to a degree not surpassed by any other English theological text, she also has a marked leaning toward abstraction; her subtle thoughts are reflected in a large number of newly formed abstract nouns, not only scholastic loan-translations but also ad hoc neologisms.[278] This abstract tendency is counterbalanced by the simplicity and clarity of uncomplicated and memorable syntax. The tone of her prose ranges from that of the didactic sermon to the spontaneity of conversation. Finally, there is an attractive rhythm in her prose, which can create positively "musical" effects. Thus she carries forward the tradition of English religious prose with masterly skill.[279] Nevertheless, the reception of her work was, as has been said, confined to a small elite; a Julian cult emerged only in our day. The time was not yet ripe for her fascinating theological vision, similar in essential respects to that of the Helfta mystics.

Excursus: Unsolved Problems in Julian's Biography

Julian's intriguing originality leads us to return to the question of her personal identity. She must have been a highly sensitive and imaginative woman, but also endowed with great strength. She tells us that she lives as a pilgrim in (and from) the tension between "here" and "there," the here and not-yet. But what sort of life did she lead before and during the time of her visions? Was she a lay person, or perhaps a nun who then became a recluse? Or was she already a recluse from early youth? Some of the answers suggested prove very unsatisfactory. The argument that she was a lay person because she often speaks of her "fellow Christians" and therefore identifies herself with lay Christians, for whom she was writing,[280] lacks conviction, because the medieval "even-Christen" refers (as in Richard Rolle) simply to her readers, for whom she wrote in fulfillment of neighborly duty ("for the profytte of many oder").

There are ample grounds to surmise that Julian was already free of worldly ties when she received her revelations; for the world with its bustle, temptations, challenges, and pompous self-importance does not feature in her work, unlike in Margery Kempe (although she does once mention a person dear to her).[281] The concrete suggestion has been made that Julian was a nun in the Benedictine priory of Carrow, not far from her cell, and that she subsequently resolved on the anchoritic life.[282] This would be in keeping with the life pattern of other women dedicated to God.[283] After all, the change from the status of nun to that of recluse was a step toward greater spiritual perfection. Yet it is hardly conceivable that as a nun she would have kept her visions to herself, rather than discussing them with her fellow nuns. All the arguments adduced in support of the assumption that she was living as a nun in Carrow priory when she received her visions fall short of the mark.[284] Julian's singularity is what makes her so intriguing. Another theory has it that her visions were what caused her to renounce secular life and become a recluse, "the logical and accepted thing for a woman to do"[285]—rather too logical, perhaps, to be true. One important part of the picture is that she lived her life as an anchorite amid the bustle of Norwich and was held in high regard by the citizens who sought her spiritual counsel.

The numerous attempts to shed light on Julian's life have often involved too much speculation, in the absence of key facts. Less attention is paid to the text, which is, however, all that we have; and it is possible to discern more from it. Her impressive self-assurance and the text's high level of reflection suggest to me that her parents had great spiritual ambitions, and therefore destined her in childhood for the spiritual life. In this connection it is worth returning to a statement in *A Talkyng of þe Loue of God*. Here the recluse avows that as a child she promised herself to Jesus "at chirche dore" in a solemn act of betrothal.[286] Julian, too, may have been betrothed to Christ as a child, which would mean in concrete terms that her parents, like the parents of Mechthild of Hackeborn and Gertrud of Helfta, entrusted their daughter to a monastery as a child. Since Julian says that there is no higher state than childhood, it is likely that she had good reason to dedicate this state in particular to God. She would then have become a recluse in adulthood. Most probably, she followed the example of the aristocratic sisters of *Ancrene Wisse*, a work very popular in the fourteenth century, whose aristocratic-spiritual ambition led them to decide in early youth on an anchoritic life of "fiery love of God."[287] The instruction of a spiritual guide probably led her in early youth to a high level of spiritual experience.[288] S. Bhattacharji considers it very likely "that Julian gained much from the eremitic tradition as it was practised in England in her time."[289] At all events, it seems inconceivable that Julian's spirituality began "in the homeliness of her early life, the domestic world in which she was formed."[290] Such a view is far removed from the intensity of medieval experience.

The assumption that Julian was a recluse from early youth is strengthened most of all by the fact that it was in her youth, long before her revelations, that she asked God for certain gifts of grace. This means that her illness should be understood as crisis and consequence of her extreme form of life, and her visions as "fruit" of this particular spiritual life. As Ernst Benz has most perceptively put it: "This rapid sequence of sixteen visions makes it seem that the spiritual love accumulated through a life of complete withdrawal from the world in the enclosed cell of a recluse, the fruit of unceasingly practiced prayer and uninterrupted contemplation . . . this accumulated fuel of Julian's spiritual love was suddenly set alight by a spark from above, and flamed up in a mighty fire."[291] This is not contradicted by the fact that she received visits during her illness.[292] A cell could indeed provide space for visitors.[293] Moreover, the anonymous author of *Ancrene Wisse* mentions possible visits from family and friends—and Julian of Norwich conversed for many days with Margery Kempe, who came seeking her advice. More-over, the description of the recluse Wulfric of Haselbury's cell shows very clearly that the accommodation could be spacious enough to receive visitors. There was an anteroom where "his servant prepared his food. His scribe, when he employed one, worked, and his visitors sat and spoke with him at a window with an opening shutter.... He often gave hospitality of a frugal kind to those who came to see him."[294]

Julian's name poses another interesting problem, since we do not know whether it was her baptismal name. She may have received it at the beginning of her anchoritic life, from the patron saint of St. Julian's Church, alongside which her cell was built. But the name must have had symbolic meaning for her as well. As a recluse she saw herself as a pilgrim on the way to her eternal home. While pilgrims in the real world received nourishment on their long journey in the St. Julian inn, she received lasting spiritual nourishment through her "bonding" to the St. Julian Church. The sisters for whom *Ancrene Wisse* was written affirmed emphatically that they saw their own cell as a kind of "Julian inn."[295]

✒ CHAPTER 10

Margery Kempe

The Shocking "Fool in Christ"

We now turn to the second late-medieval Englishwoman whose work has come down to us. Margery Kempe does not reach Julian's intellectual or spiritual stature, and is altogether different in temperament; yet she provides a colorful addition to our picture of spirituality in England in the Late Middle Ages. Her well-known only work, *The Book of Margery Kempe,* is remarkable in many ways, and controversial; until the 1930s it was known only from contemplative excerpts printed by Wynkyn de Worde.[1] She has often been denied recognition as a genuine mystic, by myself as well as others. The bone of contention during her lifetime, and still for many people today, was the extreme form of her religious experience, which was expressed in violent weeping, frequently accompanied by loud cries, and was for the most part considered intolerable. It was enough to engender suspicion of heresy, or her behavior was regarded as female hysteria.

For a long time Kempe used to be admitted only to the second rank of mystics, yet there has been great progress in research; we have learned to judge her more impartially. The first major step in the right direction was taken by Hope Emily Allen, who drew on Continental mystical writings for comparison, especially on biographies of women mystics,[2] for it is possible to do Kempe justice only when she is integrated into the European context of late-medieval women's mysticism. That Allen nonetheless saw in Margery Kempe only a second-rate mystic is due to a lacking understanding of the theological underpinning of her spirituality. This chapter will try to contribute to such underpinning.

Kempe lived in an age already characterized by rampant materialism, but in which popular piety also flowered, especially in East Anglia. Lynn was a busy trading town, with a "modern" monetary economy. Hanseatic merchants had premises there, and Lynn traders were represented in Danzig. Flourishing trade links (especially export of fine cloth, wool, grain, and salt, and import of wine, herring, timber, pitch, tar, and furs)[3] make it very likely that there was also a degree of cultural transfer, that is, contact with Continental cultural trends resulting in the "importing" of texts of late-medieval Continental spiritual interest, even if the Carthusian order was largely responsible for mediating such texts. It is therefore hardly surprising that we find in this region a paradoxical juxtaposition of down-to-earth worldly materialism and desire for spiritual experience—a simultaneity not unknown in our own time.

This ambivalence applies particularly to Margery Kempe, a member of the prosperous merchant class who ultimately sought to open her life entirely to Christian spirituality. As daughter of the socially influential citizen John Brunham—Brunham was five times mayor of Lynn, held other public offices, and was even a member of Parliament[4]—she would have received some measure of schooling in early youth, and education in matters of mind and spirit.[5]

There has been much comment on the fact that, after the birth of her first child, Kempe suffered for some eight months from emotional disturbance and a grave illness, identifiable in terms of modern pathology as postpartum psychosis,[6] and that she tells how she was healed by a vision in which Christ appeared to her in a red silk robe[7] and asked her why she had turned away from him. Yet only when economic problems and conflicts in society begin to emerge does her definitive religious conversion occur, a pattern typical of many a saint's vita. One night, to the accompaniment of "mirth" and celestial melody, she was overwhelmed by mystical *raptus* ("drawt"),[8] which continued to recur, as she repeatedly affirms. This motif of celestial music recalls Richard Rolle's experience of *canor*.

Her new path was accompanied by severe penance and asceticism, which she later moderated, and above all by the desire for an end of conjugal sexual love. Sexuality predominates among her sins, and she never succeeded in integrating it into her overall personality in a way that could satisfy her natural instinct. Her confession that God would have preserved her virginity if she had been killed at the baptismal font, and that with her husband (her only earthly lover, as she protests, p. 235:3824–25) she enjoyed "inordinate loves" (332:6077–78), suggests that she did not enter marriage as a virgin (135:1618–24).

Nevertheless, it is an oversimplification to propose that she identified sin as such with sexuality.[9] Nor is Kempe the only mystically inclined medieval woman to have experienced sexuality with such intensity. In consequence of her *conversio* she wants to renounce sexuality entirely, but she goes through years of severe temptation, practices intensive penance, and punishes herself by wearing a *cilicium* (hair shirt); the desire for intimacy with her husband diminishes (although she bore him fourteen children). Temptation arises, however, in the form of a stranger who appears all the more seductive (chap. 4); apparently interested, he eventually rejects her. When she realizes with hindsight that she had wanted to sin, that theologically she had given her consent, she is close to despair, feels herself to be in hell, and believes she deserves no mercy.

Yet this profound crisis in mind and spirit finally seals her change of life. Jesus himself appears to her in a vision and assures her of his forgiveness, rendering the hair shirt superfluous, and this is the first of a long sequence of auditions and visions of grace that transpose her back to the Christian act of salvation; she bridges the wide historical gap to the Gospel events and experiences them in the here and now. At the same time she begins to meditate, following Jesus's instructions. In her meditations—harmonized with the commemorative days of the ecclesiastical calendar—she cultivates familiarity with Saints Anne, Mary, and Elizabeth, and participates directly in their activities. In contrast to Julian of Norwich, she had the authenticity of her visions and auditions confirmed several times by religious authorities; Christ himself instructs her to seek confirmation on one occasion. A Dominican recluse summarizes his response in the "sanctifying" image that she has been suckled at Christ's breast.[10] She also received definitive approval from the Carmelite theologian Alan of Lynn; and her parish priest and confessor, Robert Spryngolde, played a very important part.

Kempe resolved to lead a spiritual life in the secular world, and the narratives of her diverse journeys are of some interest; she embarked on travel, as she says, at Christ's command,[11] and she was accompanied for a time by her husband. Particularly well known is her description of the day before the summer solstice, 1413, when she concluded a remarkable contract with her husband: if he would agree to conjugal abstinence, she would help him pay his debts; in this way she bought her freedom from conjugal "debt." It also suggests that, after the personal forgiveness granted by Christ, she had gained a more relaxed attitude to sexuality and had been willing to resume intimate relations with her partner. Yet her actual goal is to uphold the oath

FIGURE 14. Jerusalem and its surroundings, from Konrad von Grünemberg, *Pilgerreise nach Jerusalem* (Pilgrimage to Jerusalem), 1486. Manuscript St. Peter pap. 32, Bl. 35v–36r. Badische Landesbibliothek Karlsruhe. By permission of the Badische Landesbibliothek Karlsruhe.

of chastity, in order to live entirely for God. For a time the couple stay together, until the malicious slander of society becomes intolerable. She is gratified by Christ's "instruction" that she should make the short journey to Norwich, to visit not only the vicar of St. Stephen's, Richard Caister, for confirmation of the genuineness of her visions, but also the famous recluse Julian. This encounter, as will become apparent, contributed greatly to her progress toward spiritual maturity.[12]

A few months after relinquishing conjugal intimacy, she resolved to embark on the longed-for pilgrimage to the Holy Land, which was highly unusual for a woman without male companion at the time,[13] being difficult and extremely dangerous; it required great courage.[14] *The Book of Margery Kempe* (BMK) gives a detailed account of her Jerusalem experiences (see figure 14). The sight of Golgotha first added to her tears and sighs the discoloring of her face and then, most notably, the shrieks and convulsions, combined with tottering gait, that her contemporaries diagnosed as attacks of falling sickness (epilepsy). The compulsion to shriek stayed with her for ten years, causing great annoyance to those around her.[15]

On her return journey from the Holy Land, Margery Kempe visited Assisi from Venice, with a companion to protect her. It is remarkable that although she mentions meeting a Franciscan, for her Assisi does not evoke recollections of Francis. Only in the Eternal City, where she arrives in late summer or autumn 1414, does she find understanding and sympathy for her violent tears; her tottering is interpreted as spiritual inebriation, resulting from her spiritual love-wound.[16]

Her definitive experience in Rome was the vision of her mystical marriage to God during a visit to the Church of the Apostles. That this church and this event are inscribed particularly clearly in her memory has thoroughly programmatic relevance, to which we shall return. Her tracing of Birgitta of Sweden's footsteps will be considered later.

Soon after her return to Lynn her resolve ripens—again on Christ's "instruction"—to undertake a new pilgrimage, this time to the famous Santiago de Compostela. However, her account of this is brief and restrained, suggesting that the pilgrimage did not measure up to her expectations. In fact, this particular pilgrimage generated a fair number of "accounts of disappointed pilgrims in the 15th century."[17] Thereafter, Margery's problems with society increase, especially with the clergy. She is adversely affected by the ecclesiastical anxiety caused by Lollard activities, and she is even accused of being a supporter of the Lollard knight Sir John Oldcastle, still at liberty at this point, who was charged with revolting against Henry V and eventually hanged and burnt.[18]

For Kempe a turbulent phase begins, with a characteristic pattern of contradictory tensions. This is discernible first in society's reactions to her. She was accused of religious hypocrisy and immorality, but her profound faith aroused respect. Yet it distressed her greatly that a popular Franciscan preacher, of all people, prohibited her from attending his sermons on account of her disturbing behavior. Furthermore, she was threatened with death at the stake, which heretics had to expect (as laid down in the tract *De haeretico comburendo*), but she was assessed as orthodox even by archbishops, including Arundel. As a mayor's daughter, and especially through her trust in God, she had sufficient self-assurance to reproach members of the clergy—charitably, but very frankly—with perverting their great divine mission.

In a sequel to book 1 of *BMK,* remarkably short, but strikingly full of life-world details, we hear of family happenings and of how Margery felt compelled by God some time later to accompany her daughter-in-law on a voyage to Prussia—without the knowledge of her scribe/confessor, whom she deceives in a manner hard to understand. Margery finds a male companion, who plays off his manly strength against her and wants to abandon her for the usual reason of her religious enthusiasm. She travels by land without male protection, with great difficulty and repeated disappointments. Back in England, she pays a visit to the new contemplative center of the Syon and Sheen monasteries, but her report of this is surprisingly brief.

We learn nothing of her last years. With caution, it is possible to adduce one detail from two contemporary documents: it seems that, in spite of her spiritual "extravagance," she regained her social standing late in life, since a "Margerie Kempe" is mentioned in 1438 in a document of the Holy Trinity merchant guild in Lynn, at the time when her biography was being composed.[19] The likelihood that this refers to "our" Margery Kempe is strengthened by the fact that her father had been a member, and alderman, of this very influential merchant guild. She probably did not live much beyond 1439.

The Emergence of a Life Pattern: *Imitatio Christi, Vita Apostolica*

The more detailed of *BMK*'s two prefaces (written by the second scribe, but surely in keeping thematically with Kempe's intentions) points the way toward a theologically sound understanding of her life: her purpose was to follow her redeemer, for this was "the way of high perfection" (pp. 41–42). Her decision to renounce the world and practice *imitatio Christi,* without the shelter of a monastery environment or protective cell, makes her an exceptional exemplum for her lay contemporaries. Yet she maintains close contact with hermits and recluses living in seclusion from the world, and is especially friendly with one of them; she travels to the next city to visit the recluse Julian.[20]

Kempe's ideal of *imitatio Christi* is attested throughout her book by echoes of the Gospels, especially of the "mystical" Gospel of John. Altogether, her popular piety has a distinctly biblical quality characteristic of English mysticism. She not only mentions the Gospel as foundation of her piety (101:993), but also derives from it the challenge to relinquish personal property, and all personal ties. She is comforted by the promise that the resolve to do God's will alone will lead, as for the great mystics, to the Pauline mutual indwelling of the human being and God.

She was in touch with numerous clerics, and with their help her life was "shaped by books."[21] She mentions Rolle's *Incendium amoris* and Hilton's book, which undoubtedly refers to his *Scale of Perfection,*[22] as well as the *Stimulus amoris* of Jacobus of Milan; later the scribe adds the biographies of Marie d'Oignies and Elizabeth of Hungary.

Kempe's theological knowledge and great thirst for education were seriously underestimated for a long time.[23] In view of the high social status of her family, the widely held assumption that she could read only a little, if at all, and could not write, is untenable. Moreover, God says to her in one of her auditions that he is pleased with her, whether she reads or is read to, which implies that she was at least *capable* of reading.[24] It has even been argued convincingly that her command of Latin, small as it was, enabled her to understand what she heard in Latin—that is, that she had some basic theological understanding.[25]

She does not exemplify the contrast between orality and literacy;[26] rather, both traditions are important to her as mediated by aurality, the reception of literature by oral communication. Attention has rightly been drawn to this in recent times.[27] Such communication was already practiced in antiquity, and continued in individual cases far beyond the Middle Ages and Renaissance.[28] Indeed, our own medium of the audiobook maintains the tradition.[29] A text communicated in this way may gain through the performative concretization provided by the actor as narrator. It seems likely that Margery Kempe preferred to let the "action" of a "performing" reader convey a text's full impact, for this enabled her to react with greater intensity, giving free rein to her emotions. Therefore it was a most welcome enrichment that for eight years a young priest *read* to her works of her own choosing as well as his; her literary competence was evidently sufficient to make such choices; she must even have been familiar with the book trade, for how else could she have suggested to the young priest what she wished to have read to her?[30]

Venturing on a Life of Poverty

More attention needs to be paid to the astonishing fact that, in referring to Marie d'Oignies and Elizabeth of Hungary, *BMK* takes us back to the late twelfth century and the start of the beguine movement, even if Kempe herself cannot be regarded as a genuine latter-day beguine, since we do not find in her any serious, intensive measure of social involvement. One of the original aims of these *mulieres religiosae,* under Cistercian influence, was to lead a life of complete poverty, following the naked Christ in their own nakedness (*nuda nudum Christum sequi*). Kempe would also like to lead a life of poverty for Christ—it is even broached in the introductory section of her work—but in her day it was particularly difficult to follow the religious ideal of poverty. As we have seen, she was a child of the flourishing late-medieval merchant class, and not free from social norms with regard to money and material possessions.[31] Jesus warned the rich against material goods (Mt 19:20–26), and this troubled her; in her opinion, it was easier for the rich to follow Christ's commandments (300).

For some time after her "conversion" she still had enough money to pay her husband's debts in exchange for his willingness to live in abstinence. Although having traveled with a maidservant to the Holy Land and to holy places in Italy, it was only in Rome that she was suddenly instructed by Christ to give all her money to the poor for love of him.[32] She would not have decided "voluntarily" on total destitution; the instruction was given as penance for some unstated reason.[33] It is questionable whether she fully grasped the sense of this sudden change in her circumstances; she not only rid herself of her own money, but also distributed to the poor the money borrowed from her traveling companion, for which she was justly rebuked by the damaged party.

Nevertheless, she thanks God for her experience of poverty in Rome, and for having felt solidarity with society's outcasts. Occasionally we hear of her charitable services, of support given to a poor old woman, to the sick and the dying, and even of kissing female lepers (in clear imitation of Elizabeth of Hungary).[34] At least she has the earnest will to supplement love of God with social *caritas,* in the spirit of the New Testament. For a long time after her return home she continues to live in poverty and is therefore repeatedly dependent on benefactors. However, a consistent life of poverty may involve begging, but not borrowing money and amassing large debts as Margery did (219:3461). By the time she decided to accompany her daughter-in-law to Pomerania, at the latest, she must once more have had funds, albeit inadequate, at her disposal (393:7642). She gets into material difficulties, but separates from a group of poor people whose company she cannot abide. In old age, her probable membership of the Holy Trinity merchants' guild suggests

that she was no longer classed among the despised poor. It therefore seems
that she did not see her true sacrifice for discipleship of Christ in terms of
her own personal poverty. It is more than problematic to talk of her glowing
espousement of poverty,[35] and there is no reason whatsoever to draw a parallel
between Margery Kempe and Francis's espousal with Donna Povertà. Indeed
no imitation of Francis can be discerned with Margery Kempe.

Margery Kempe's Marital Ambiguity

The *mulieres religiosae,* including Margery Kempe, feel themselves to be brides
of Christ. But a closer reading reveals that the *Lives* of these women tend to
avoid detailed bridal mysticism culminating in *unio* and the poetic love, for
instance, of the Song of Songs, and the same holds true for Kempe. These
women proceed in theologically impeccable fashion by grounding their
interpersonal relationship with the godhead initially in the dogma of the
Trinity; they grasp the sense of talking of a triune God, consisting of three
persons united in love. In the same way God communicates with Margery,
sometimes as Father, as Son, or as all three persons as "o substawns in God-
hede" (115.1251–61). And it is Christ himself who, repeating his Gospel
words that those who do his Father's will are mother, brother, and sister to
him, refutes the idea of a human, clearly defined love relationship with Margery; frequently she is addressed as his daughter. Yet she is "drawyn" to "ower
Lord" (50.154), who is both Father and Son. A comparable "drawing" can be
observed in Mechthild of Magdeburg. "Mechthild, like Mary or even Marguerite Porete, is the 'bride of the Holy Trinity,'" and there are "a number
of texts that present the unconditionally Trinitarian character of Mechthild's
notion of union, many of which do not have erotic content."[36] Despite
Christ's suspension of family relationships, he is Margery's beloved, who has
redeemed her through his love, and instructed her to acquire a ring engraved
with *Jesus est amor meus* (178:2543); yet she very rarely turns to Christ himself, and addresses only a few words of love to him; the dialogues consist
largely of Christ's words to her. What we find after the marriage scene is a
reinterpretation of the bridal fire of love as the sin-consuming flame of the
Holy Ghost, so that the *third* person of the Trinity comes into play. And only
when the joining of the "matrimonial couple" has been defined in terms
of love of the *Holy Ghost,* does Jesus encourage Margery to let her soul
embrace him and kiss him on mouth, head, and feet. It is therefore not possible to read what happens here merely as a love relationship based on erotic
desire (192–96).[37] The language used to describe her intimacy in the bed is
far removed, for instance, from the sensual and erotic imagery that occurs in

other women mystics,[38] of which we see only a trace in the adornment of the chamber of the heart with flowers and spices, alluding to the *lectulus floridus* of the Song of Songs (373:7089–107). Kempe is at pains to maintain a distance between the erotically sexual and the spiritual, and one reason for this probably lies in her recalling the words with which Jesus radically suspends family relationships for those living in the kingdom of God, and which had gained great importance in the Wooing Group: "For whoever does the will of my Father in heaven is my brother and sister and mother" (Mt 12:50). Margery Kempe, thoroughly familiar with the Gospels, is not only Christ's wife, but also his daughter and indeed—in a perfectly biblical sense—his mother (196:2944–79).[39]

The Middle Ages loved paradoxes. The opening of canto 33 in Dante's *Paradiso* addresses Mary as "Vergine madre, figlia del tuo figlio," a form of words made comprehensible only by the long-neglected theological theme of the human being as child of God.[40] Margery Kempe, otherwise so conscious of the body, imposes the utmost restraint on herself when it comes to bodily contact with Jesus, and the cult of wounds, much cherished in popular piety.[41] How different is her reaction from the widely practiced visualization of Christ's bloody open wounds that enabled the believer to penetrate wholly and "really" into his body, and to become entirely one with him, heart for heart, or at least find refuge and protection there. Thus Aelred's rule of life requires the meditating reader to "creep into his holy side, where blood and water oozed out, and hide there like a dove in the rock, and enjoy the drops of his blood, until your lips are covered in scarlet." There are echoes of such biblical-theological phraseology in *BMK,* and she is perhaps reminded of Rolle's *Meditations on the Passion* (Version B),[42] as she weeps to see Christ's body so mutilated by wounds, *but she has no wish to touch the bleeding gashes,* let alone to penetrate them. Unlike, for instance, the Franciscan *Stimulus amoris,* where penetration of the son of God's bleeding wounds is a recurrent theme, *BMK* relinquishes direct bodily contact, in humble awe.[43]

Nevertheless, powerful tendencies of the time caused a certain inner split that requires precise differentiation. Strong emotions generated by the mystery of the incarnation coalesce with contemporary materialization of the spiritual, leading, in women, to concentration on the childhood of Jesus. Kempe knows that for her spiritual life it is important to understand the bodily as metaphor for the spiritual; she is familiar with the concept of the spiritual senses, but she is aware that there is always a danger of bodily experience becoming in a sense absolute, and taking on an inappropriate, singular relevance, for instance in her maternal care of the child Jesus, where there are resonances of her own bodily experience of motherhood.[44]

The Theological Significance of Margery Kempe's Tears

Margery's devotion probably finds its most characteristic release in her excessive tears. Weeping, like laughter, expressing emotion, and sometimes accompanied by other modes of expression, should, however, not be construed simply as concretization of "female piety," as is often the case nowadays. In earlier times men, too, were much more willing than they are today to abandon themselves to tears. Tears are frequently mentioned in the Bible. For example, they are shed in the Psalms over abandonment by God, and persecution, and in Jeremiah's lamentations over Israel's Babylonian captivity ("Let tears stream down like a torrent," Lam 2:18). Tears may take on figurative abundance, as in the prophet Malachi: "You cover the Lord's altar with tears" (Mal 2:13). Peter weeps bitterly after denying his Lord. Jesus himself weeps for Jerusalem, and instructs the daughters of Jerusalem to weep for themselves (Lk 23:28), while Kempe weeps over the weeping Jesus (279:4803). Shrieking combined with weeping is also attested in the Bible. For instance, the Letter to the Hebrews speaks of prayers with "loud cries and tears" (Heb 5:7). Above all, Kempe will have been reenacting the cry with which Christ's Passion ended, immediately before his death.

For many people, men as well as women—not least for Margery Kempe—Mary Magdalen, "patron saint of those who weep,"[45] could serve as a model for a Christian life intent on penance. In the religious drama *Christ's Resurrection* (editorial title; Oxford, Bodleian Library, MS E Museo 160), Peter is brought into the resurrection events. He weeps violently and bitterly over his denial of the Lord, and falls to the ground; Andrew consoles him by referring to the frailty of man,[46] that is, of the human being, but here primarily man, whereas such frailty was customarily ascribed to women (cf. "frailty, thy name is woman," *Hamlet* 1.2.146).

The wider context makes it possible to show that Margery Kempe's tears have a theological raison d'être. The opening of *BMK* tells how her tears came daily as a gift of grace sent by God, leading some people to maintain in scorn that she could make them flow at will (43:42–43); but in an audition Christ himself claims to be master of them. Because they are a gift of grace Kempe has to contradict the apostles when they require her to end her weeping, which increases in frequency and duration and may finally last for many hours, so that she loses all sense of time. Whenever she is reminded of Jesus's Passion by optical impressions, such as a crucifix or the Pietà popular in her time (*imago pietatis*),[47] or a suffering creature (286:4957), her tears begin to flow;[48] in her innermost self she experiences Christ's crucifixion anew as a shattering event in the here and now.

It has been shown that Kempe continues a long-established patristic focus on the significance of tears in Christian life that began with Cassian.[49] Particularly relevant were tears of remorse (*compunctio*) for personal guilt that caused the suffering and death of Christ on the cross.[50] The ability to weep tears of "contrition, compassion, devotion" was regarded as the greatest gift of grace bestowed by the Holy Spirit;[51] Margery Kempe is aware of this.[52] She cites Jerome's authority for sanctioning her tears. He even appears to her when she visits his grave in Rome and praises her for her tears, through which many will be saved (210:3261–75). Later, in conversation with Christ, she longs to be able to weep such tears as will force him to suspend his vengeance on grave sinners (277:4750–55). Her tears are a visible part of her atonement mission, which distinguishes them clearly from the numerous other examples of abundant weeping in the lives of female mystics.[53]

Yet to understand Kempe's tears only as tears of penance and vicarious atonement would not account fully for their significance. When she cannot weep she is dry ("bareyn," 359:6717); only when her tears flow once more can she talk of the sweetness of weeping over God's love (379:7264). This intensity brings a new feeling to her weeping. She wishes no other consolation on earth, no other joy than these tears of devotion and yearning for heaven, which are also her necessary response to God's unfathomable love for mankind.[54] Yet her joy cannot be compared with that felt, for instance, by Julian of Norwich, for Kempe lacks the important sense of being set free that gives rise to unbridled jubilation. When she experiences a feeling of intense joy, especially during the Eucharist, she may also think herself on the brink of death. C. Benke makes these connections very clear: "Drawn into the nexus of Trinitarian love... Margery Kempe alternates between the extremes of gratitude on the one hand and, on the other, the need to die of this love, embodied through strange gestures and facial expressions, or through her 'abundance of tears.' She shrieks out her inadequacy in the face of this 'excess of love,' and her feeling that she is about to burst."[55] Shrieking and sobbing are nonverbal, rather than hysterical, expressions of "a creature oppressed by love." From a certain moment on, Margery is no longer able to withstand the "offensive action" of this divine love and the associated tension. Her cries are an escape valve in a particular kind of stress release.[56] "Her tears (crying, weeping, sobbing, etc.) are an emotional response to meditation primarily on the Passion of Christ, an embodiment of the 'flood of love' that fills her."[57]

At the same time her tears of *compassio* with the suffering Christ also take on a "histrionic element,"[58] a certain theatricality, although the performative component in Margery Kempe should not be overemphasized. Exceptional as she is, she is not simply an individual seeking to realize her subjectivity in anticipation of Renaissance tendencies toward self-fashioning.[59] Such an interpretation neglects the threat to her very existence so crucial to the understanding of Margery's personality, which culminates in "I dey! I dey!" (276:4711) when she is confronted with the Passion of Christ, and in the confession of her inability to suffer any longer either the experience of pain or the superabundance of love and grace.[60] She yields to this experience, knowing full well that it can lead her to the brink of death ("[t]he Passyon of Crist sleth me!" 209:3247).

There is evidently some connection between the shattering effect of this experience and an ancient theory according to which Christ's suffering has not ended.[61] Mechthild of Magdeburg held that Christ's Passion will continue until the Day of Judgment,[62] and Blaise Pascal follows the Letter to the Colossians in affirming that "the agony of Jesus will last until the end of the world."[63] Yet in the Middle Ages such associations had already faded somewhat into oblivion; had that not been the case, the Franciscan preacher would not have been able to pronounce such an exclusively negative verdict on Margery Kempe, and people would not have tried to comfort her by observing that Christ died long ago.

Kempe's devotional practice is commonly described as Franciscan;[64] but such a classification is rendered doubtful by the absence of the cult of wounds in her work. Nor can it simply be asserted that she was influenced by the *Meditationes vitae Christi,* widely known from the translation, with modifications, by Nicholas Love (*The Mirror of the Blessed Life of Jesus Christ*).[65] This Franciscan text was not the first to offer a concrete presentation of the central stages of the act of salvation.[66] This had already been accomplished most excellently, as we have seen, in Aelred's great meditations, particularly those on the Passion, in his *De institutione inclusarum,* available in English translations in Margery Kempe's day. The link between Margery Kempe and Aelred was recognized by Clarissa Atkinson many years ago.[67] In the text by Aelred, a male author, there is even more differentiation of the role of tears, and it is very likely that Kempe is carrying forward this English tradition with her biblical meditations and immersion in the suffering of Christ. She clearly continues the central practice recommended by the abbot of Rievaulx, of enacting *compassio* through direct participation in the events of the Passion.

A final reason for Margery Kempe's violent experience of suffering has to be her evidently depressive disposition, exacerbated by the age in which she lived. She is in this respect typical of the Late Middle Ages, which, as Huizinga has demonstrated, were equally fascinated and dejected by the phenomenon of death and the evidence of human decay.[68] It was the heyday of the Dance of Death in multifarious iconography and drama. When a priest, as Kempe recounts, takes as text for his sermon "Jesus is dead" (313:5619), he accurately reflects a contemporary perception. Yet theologically the statement is highly questionable, since it ignores the defining moment of the resurrection, without which, according to Paul, our faith is dead (1 Cor 15:14).

Tracing Great Female Precursors

Living while the Middle Ages were declining, Margery still shows astonishingly strong links with the spirituality of the beguines. As is well known, the scribe of *BMK* is reminded of Marie d'Oignies particularly by Margery's violent tears; the extent of the correspondences between Margery Kempe and Marie, born some two hundred years earlier, goes, however, far beyond their intense affectivity. Marie d'Oignies was married at the age of fourteen but persuaded her husband to agree to a Josephite marriage: "The couple gave themselves to service of the outcasts of society, the lepers...for the Lord's sake."[69] We owe her biography to Jacques de Vitry, whose enthusiasm for her spirituality still shines forth from his text; it was later supplemented by the Dominican Thomas of Cantimpré.[70] Jacques famously praised the *sanctae modernae* in whom God is active in the present time.[71] What Jacques found so fascinating in Marie was, in brief, the brightly burning fire of mystical loving devotion, expressed in uninhibited, sensually intense language, influenced by the Cistercians.

The gift of prophecy is another spiritual form of expression linking Margery Kempe to the beguines. Both Marie and Margery warn against imminent dangers; both recognize the errors of certain clerics, and take them to task. Kempe's criticism of female luxury and vanity, and her dedication to accompaniment of the dying, also remind us of Marie. Marie, like pious women of her time in general, has a strong urge to go on pilgrimage to Jerusalem. For a long time—like Kempe—she gives up eating meat. She wears a white woolen tunic and a white cloak, and Kempe, too, has to wear white clothing according to the will of Christ. The two women share the wish for frequent confession, and the certainty that they will be spared purgatory. Both women's activities are guided by the Holy Spirit. Above all, there is the wish to receive frequent communion. Reverence for the Eucharist "is the most telling devotional motif of the mystical religious and semi-religious movement of the 12th and 13th centuries. Women's yearning for the host could be so powerful that they would use any means at their disposal to find a priest who would offer them communion."[72] Margery Kempe is driven by this same intense longing.

The reader hears in detail how Marie and Margery were transported in their meditations to the childhood of Jesus. For both, mystical ecstasy occurs daily—with far greater frequency than is customary in the history of mysticism—and may last for a long time. Marie sometimes sleeps before the altar in church, with a book, and Margery, too, is found lying with a book in front of the altar, and, often, sleeping (see also figure 15). They love contemplative silence, rather than recitation of numerous prayers. Society inevitably regards both women as fools. Affliction in the form of sickness is a pleasure to both, because they believe it brings them closer to their true, eternal home.

A further instance of correspondence, hardly noted hitherto, merits particular attention. This is the powerful longing that Marie and Margery share for the sermon. The incipient beguine movement needs to be viewed in conjunction with the twelfth-century reevaluation of the sermon.[73] Bernard's sermons on the Song of Songs not only upgraded the sermon as a genre in the context of Cistercian spirituality, but also shaped it into a performative speech-act.[74] Through the sermon, the presumably illiterate Marie gained a profound knowledge of holy scripture;[75] Margery Kempe likewise affirms that "she learnt by sermons" (98:942). The importance attached to the sermon is implicit also in Marie's sorrow that as a woman she was not allowed to preach, although it is possible that she may actually have made a name for herself as a preacher.[76] Hildegard of Bingen manifestly succeeded in preaching.[77] At all events, Marie finds clever means of compensating for her frustration: she passes on to further listeners parts of a sermon she has heard; or she shapes Gospel narratives into a chant, interpreting them spontaneously, even in rhyming verse (179). Yet she ardently prays God to send her a preacher. We are familiar with this request from Margery Kempe; Jesus promises to preach to her himself if none appears. When Marie meets Jacques, she is convinced that he is God's answer to her request: "Jacques submits to divine authority and Marie's wish."[78] Astonishingly, Jacques de Vitry freely admits his indebtedness to Marie, indeed he attributes to her "all the credit for his homiletic skill,"[79] which will subsequently move the pope to appoint him to preach the Crusade. He says that she knew how to encourage his preaching, after his initial trepidation. Evidently there is an "exchange between the two in a dynamic, lively process...actively and equally defined by both."[80] In all probability, Kempe was able to learn from Marie how to participate in preaching, even if indirectly, by means of encouragement: the young priest who read to her for several years learned much (as she points out) from her suggestions for their shared reading, and this "further education" will have benefited his sermons as well.[81] Seen in this light, Margery Kempe made her own contribution to preaching, or, to be more precise, to the training of a preacher, which was immensely important to her. Benke helps to fill in the picture with his suggestion that she viewed her superabundance of tears in itself as a form of preaching. Yet as time passed she had to acknowledge that, far from having the function of a sermon, her tears could have an unwanted negative effect, for which reason she withdrew ever further from society.

Jacques de Vitry's enthusiasm for the passionately loving Marie motivated him to write her biography. In quite similar vein, though very much later, Kempe was inspired by Marie. It is difficult to understand why this has so seldom been appreciated in Anglophone research on mysticism.[82] The numerous correspondences between the two women attest very clearly that Margery Kempe could, and did, see herself as a new *mulier religiosa*. As has already been suggested, she evidently knew Marie's biography well, long before her scribe was alerted to it.[83] So why did she not simply cite the authority of Marie? Is it possible that Kempe herself was not the one who alerted the scribe to Marie's biography? Since he could hardly admit this himself, a less direct form of words was required. It cannot be the case that he hoped to become an English Jacques de Vitry, for there is no trace in his attitude toward Kempe of the theological veneration felt by Jacques for Marie.[84] Yet, whatever the explanation, there are striking correspondences between Marie's vita and *BMK*. It therefore makes little sense to look to any other woman mystic for *exclusive* influence on Margery Kempe's spiritual formation; several of the *Lives* of later female mystics were modeled on this most famous early *mulier religiosa*.

Kempe was aware of one painful and essential difference between Marie d'Oignies and herself: she was a sexually experienced woman. For a long time her attitude toward bodily sensuality was ambivalent, as has frequently been noted.[85] Attempts to overcome or sublimate sexuality are therefore much more pronounced in Kempe than in Marie d'Oignies. The beguine from Brabant won her battle against sensuality without too many difficulties. Kempe, by contrast, received Christ's assurance that he regarded her as his virgin bride in spite of her sexual experience (138:1682). Nonetheless she was also interested in other women's *Lives*—especially in those of married women, namely Elizabeth of Hungary/Thuringia and Birgitta of Sweden, perhaps also Dorothy of Montau. These women are "related" to one another spiritually by their commitment to a new ideal of womanhood encountered first among the beguines, especially Marie.

Margery Kempe and Elizabeth of Hungary

Elizabeth of Hungary (1207–31) is mentioned by name in *BMK* as an exemplary woman. Doubtless, comparison with this revered aristocratic saint was

FIGURE 15. St. Elizabeth of Hungary prostrate before an altar in humble devotion. From a Freiburg Elisabeth ms. (1481), with paintings by Sibilla von Bondorf. By permission of Professor Werner Heiland-Justi.

intended to add "weight" to Kempe's own vita. For her contemporaries, Elizabeth as a new *paupercula* recalled Marie d'Oignies.[86] She devoted herself entirely to the poor in utmost self-denial and, like Kempe, was derided as a fool. After the death of her husband while on Crusade, she had to leave the court of Thuringia, and eventually settled in Marburg, where she founded a hospital and devoted herself entirely, unconditionally, and in total poverty, to care of the sick as *soror in saeculo*. She lived this ideal of poverty under the direct influence of early (Cistercian) beguine spirituality rather than as a follower of Francis. She was never a Franciscan tertiary, as recent research has shown. Like Marie d'Oignies and Margery Kempe, Elizabeth was most profoundly moved by the Passion and death of Jesus, and wept copiously. Because of their conjugal abstinence Elizabeth and Margery Kempe were regarded as chaste, indeed virginal, brides of Christ, and both were endowed with the gift of prophecy.

Of course such a comparison, to which further details could be added, also reveals considerable differences in the personalities of the two women. Elizabeth seems less remote from our own age, and is more reconciled to the vagaries of human instinct. She is characterized by serenity and an inner feeling of great joy, rather than inner tension, and this contributes to her greatness.

There is no scholarly consensus as to how Kempe learned of Elizabeth, or what is meant by the "tretys" she mentions (296:5174). However, the impressive balance of research made available in Elizabeth's jubilee year, 2007, provides a possible answer. Largely responsible for making the saint known in the Late Middle Ages was Dietrich of Apolda, an Erfurt Dominican, who is scarcely mentioned in Anglophone research on Margery Kempe. His biography, written circa 1289–97, is marked by a thoroughly "modern" search for truth. The sources available to him were the *Summa vitae* by Elizabeth's confessor Conrad of Marburg, the *Libellus*, a summary of the statements provided by four of her female companions in support of her canonization, and the short vita written after her canonization by the Rhineland Cistercian Caesarius of Heisterbach, as well as the legend contained in the enormously widespread *Legenda aurea* (ca. 1270) of the Dominican James of Varazze (Jacobus de Voragine).[87]

What makes Dietrich's biography particularly interesting in the present context is that he "clothes the saint in the garb of a mystic." She speaks with God, "who desires to be with her"; there is even a description of her mystical ecstasy. Elizabeth receives *angelicas visitaciones, visiones et allocuciones multasque revelaciones,* during which "she sees Jesus *facie ad faciem*."[88] Dietrich wanted to impart deep understanding of her, especially to the Cistercian nuns for whom he was initially writing.[89] His additional information, that her *raptus* occurred frequently and lasted a long time, establishes the connection with the *mulieres religiosae,* for whom, as for Margery, this was a distinctive characteristic.

This "mystic making" is all the more significant because there was a widely known text titled *Revelations of St. Elizabeth of Hungary* (*Revelationes B. Elisabeth*) that Kempe knew and quoted. It has parallels with *BMK,* and two Middle English translations of the text have survived.[90] It claims that Elizabeth had thirteen auditions, or dialogues, with Mary or Christ, again attributing mystical qualities to her. In *The Middle English Mystics,* not as yet familiar with Dietrich of Apolda's biography, I suggested (and was followed by Barratt and McNamer)[91] that the tract had been mistakenly attributed to St. Elizabeth and should be ascribed to a different Elizabeth of Hungary, namely Elizabeth of Töss, daughter of Andreas III, the last king of the Arpad dynasty and nephew of St. Elizabeth. In the meantime it has become apparent that this is not convincing. Nor is there any reason to deny St. Elizabeth's authorship on the grounds that she is referred to in the *Revelationes* as "virgin"; after the death of her husband she promised to follow the ideal of chastity, which meant a great deal to her, and made it possible for her to be classed as virgin once again, as previously mentioned.[92] The dominant role given to Mary in the *Revelationes* is in no way surprising, since profound veneration of Mary was part of Elizabeth's early Cistercian upbringing and education.

It therefore seems that the *Revelationes* should be attributed to Elizabeth of Hungary/Thuringia, and Dietrich of Apolda provides the reasons.[93] Yet whether she personally both experienced and recorded these revelations cannot be established with certainty. The most recent research suggests that Franciscan circles in Italy were responsible for the surviving text of the *Revelationes* and for the naming of Elizabeth as author.[94] We can be sure that Dietrich of Apolda's biography was widely known, and it most probably also reached England, thus enabling Margery Kempe to gain a picture of Elizabeth as mystic, which may even be true enough.

One point still needs to be clarified in this connection. Sheila Delany's conclusion has been widely accepted, that Kempe's "tretys" refers to the Elizabeth legend as added by Osbern Bokenham to his vernacular collection of legends of women saints.[95] This legend does indeed include relevant details from the biographical tradition, and it tells how the saint abandoned herself to contemplation, saw the heavens opening, and beheld Jesus, who spoke words of solace to her. Yet only through Dietrich of Apolda's biography do we learn how the *mystic* Elizabeth experienced mystical revelations, and even mystical *raptus.*

Further Lights on Margery Kempe's Mystic Path

The more one studies Margery Kempe, the stronger the impression becomes that she is repeatedly trying to obtain additional validation of her own spiritual life from the paths chosen by other female mystics. Since in her day, the great manifestations of late-medieval mysticism already belonged to the past, a kind of "collective fund"[96] of mystical experiences was available to her, and it was not difficult to borrow "movable pieces"[97] from individual biographies and adapt them as needed. It renders highly problematic any attempt to argue, as Ute Stargardt does,[98] following H. E. Allen, for the influence of any one particular mystic, such as Dorothy of Montau, whom Margery does not mention by name. Dorothy is certainly a very interesting woman; in Prussia, as the famous novelist Günter Grass tells us in his *Der Butt,* she was "the first woman to revolt against the paternal enforcement of medieval marriage."[99] Through Hanseatic trade links between Danzig and Lynn, Margery may have known Dorothy's vita, but Dorothy, for her part, was striving for a certain *imitatio* of Continental female mysticism.[100]

It is interesting to compare Margherita of Cortona and Angela of Foligno with Margery Kempe inasmuch as they, too, were sexually active for a long time,[101] and then, following conversion, went their own individual ways. Margherita was lured into extramarital sexuality, lived for a long time in an illicit relationship, and bore a son. After her conversion she became a Franciscan tertiary, dedicated herself to care of the sick, built a hospital, and moved into a cell.[102] She has a strong awareness of sin; nevertheless, she is in constant "auditive contact" with Christ,[103] who promises her a privileged place in heaven. She, too, experiences the Passion so violently that she emits shrieks of pain. For all her ardent love of Christ, there is no bridal mysticism; rather, like Margery, Margherita is usually Christ's daughter, sister, or brother, and she remains at a reverential distance. Angela also becomes a tertiary; she has read a great deal and acquired much learning through discussion,[104] again like Margery. Yet in her willingness to suffer she surpasses Margery: she feels the presence of Christ's cross within her, and she experiences a genuinely Franciscan *unio passionalis,*[105] which replaces nuptial eroticism, as recounted in her *Memoriale.*[106] She does not hesitate to discard all her clothing for Christ. Kempe, too, tells us that she wanted to offer herself naked for Christ, publicly displayed on a cart, in order to suffer shame and humiliation for his sake. Even more powerfully than Angela, Elizabeth of Spalbeek and Christina Mirabilis represent the radical type of Continental female mystic, unparalleled in England, yet their vitae were translated into English.[107] It is also important to recall St. Catherine of Siena, whose spiritual biography was written between 1383 and 1395 by her confessor Raimondo da Capua in his *Legenda major.* Attention has been drawn several times to similarities with Margery Kempe.[108]

Scholars looking for Continental parallels to Margery Kempe have paid surprisingly little attention to Mechthild of Hackeborn (1241–91); she is the third of the great women of the Helfta convent, after Mechthild of Magdeburg and Gertrud the Great. Her visions reflect the spirit of Bernard of Clairvaux very strongly and are contained in the *Liber specialis gratiae* (*The Booke of Gostlye Grace*), which was one of the most successful and widely read late-medieval books in the field of female spirituality. Its widespread vernacular reception began in the early fifteenth century.[109]

Mechthild of Hackeborn tends to linger on a received vision, as if she were describing a scenic tableau, with great love of detail. Mystical ecstasy has become a familiar daily occurrence for her. Ruh draws attention to the great difference between this daily occurrence and the mystical experience of the major female visionaries whom ecstasy overwhelms "like a life-threatening storm."[110] It comes as something of a shock that Christ functions as Mechthild's servant, "always at her beck and call."[111] It seems that this was the model for Kempe's equally startling statement that Christ is obedient to her will (100:983); he fulfills her every wish. However, nuptial union remains very rare for Mechthild, as for Gertrud of Helfta.[112] And in references to the Song of Songs the erotic lyric element is deliberately subdued, as in Margery Kempe.[113]

Birgitta of Sweden as the Predominant Model?

Against this background, what is to be made of the prevalent scholarly view that Kempe drew her most vital support from St. Birgitta of Sweden?[114] I think that, as there was a great English reverence for Birgitta, she was one of Margery's models, but at no point, when Kempe is speaking of the Swedish saint, do I note exceptional enthusiasm.[115] It is true, she knows St. Birgitta's *Book,* and God assures her that "rygth as I spak to Seynt Bryde, ryte so I speke to the, dowtyr, and . . . it is trewe every word that is wretyn in Brides boke" (*BMK,* 129.1529–130.1531); yet I cannot attribute too much weight to this too isolated statement of her alleged singular devotion to the spirituality of this saint, which does not justify the conclusion that "the model provided by S. Birgitta was a particularly powerful one, despite some evident dissimilarities."[116] As has repeatedly been pointed out, she follows in Birgitta's footsteps in Rome, but her account of this is extremely brief. She visits her death chamber, listens to a priest preach about her, kneels before the stone where Christ is said to have appeared to her—but all this does not prove unique interest in this saint, whose political and ecclesiastical influence was enormous, far in excess of anything we find in *BMK.* And there is no mention of the preparations for Birgitta's canonization that were being undertaken when Kempe visited Rome.

Therefore the chapters from Birgitta's *Revelations* printed by Lynn Staley in her edition of *BMK* do not contain anything of specific relevance. Most aspects of the saint's life that may have been exemplary for Kempe occur also in other women's vitae, such as distancing from the family, the decision for Christ, the resolve to lead an evangelical life, the contempt of society and persecution as a fool,[117] the suffering prompted by Christ's Passion, the fascination exerted by the dogma of the Trinity,[118] the gift of prophecy,[119] and finally the doubt over the authenticity of spiritual experience.[120] Birgitta, too, is rooted in the tradition of the *mulieres religiosae*. She took her orientation in part from the great Elizabeth, who in turn was influenced by Marie d'Oignies. Birgitta evidently believed that Elizabeth lapsed into poverty, and found greater "comforth" in it than in her previously elevated position.[121] She saw the pilgrimage to the Holy Land, which she felt encouraged to undertake by Christ himself,[122] as the pinnacle of her spiritual life.[123] The description of her experience of Christ's Passion has become famous. Yet not even this can be regarded as the definitive spur for the mayor's daughter from Lynn. Kempe surely did not need to know about Birgitta's spiritual experience in the Holy Land in order to feel motivated to travel to Jerusalem. Very probably, she did learn with great interest of Birgitta's anxieties, similar to her own, on account of the moral wrongdoings of her son Karl, who died "in good time," before committing himself to mortal sin.[124]

The differences between the two are, however, very great. Kempe's visions are restricted to a narrow range (with great biblical themes) and to the purely private sphere. Unlike those, for instance, of Mechthild of Hackeborn, they are often projections or fulfillment of private wishes. Regarding the wish to preach, Birgitta seeks a compromise, as Marie d'Oignies had done.[125] She becomes active in church politics, where her great rhetorical gifts are effectively deployed. She demands of the popes in Avignon that they return to Rome. This can hardly be compared with the much narrower viewpoint from which Kempe criticizes ecclesiastical and clerical abuse. While Birgitta advances to become Christ's spouse, Kempe mostly remains his daughter.[126] And she can, of course, offer nothing to compare with Birgitta's greatest achievement, the foundation of her new Bridgettine order.

All this shows very clearly that Birgitta should not be regarded in isolation as Kempe's model beyond all other *mulieres sanctae*;[127] nor can there be any question of an ambition on Kempe's part to appear as "devoted follower and imitator of Birgitta."[128] Given the gap between the two, it is not surprising that Birgitta is not mentioned at all in the second part of *BMK*. Thus, Kempe refers to the monastery of the Bridgettine order that lay on her way on her return journey by the name only of the neighboring Carthusian monastery at Sheen, where she obtains an indulgence. St. Bridget is not even mentioned once! She notes her surprise at meeting again with the hermit who had accompanied her for a while at the beginning of her journey, and reports a conversation with a young man wishing to join the Carthusian order. Does this narration reflect Margery's alleged singular veneration of St. Bridget? I think not. There is in fact no mention in the second part of *BMK* of any individual saint or mystic in relation to her (the only exception is the occasional mention of saints of the ecclesiastical calendar). This suggests not only that her veneration of Birgitta and other saints lessened in intensity, but also that toward the end of her life these great names had lost their exemplary quality, and only the *imitatio Christi* was really meaningful to her: she has left the world and is drawn to and united with him (385, 389). It is possible that Kempe, consciously or involuntarily, recognized the fascination previously exerted on her by too many *exempla,* and reacted accordingly. Perhaps she also arrived at a more profound understanding of the *imitatio Christi* and realized that it meant not only imitation of his suffering through "fasting, self-flagellation, and self-defilement,"[129] but also a renewal of life to proclaim God's sovereignty. It seems to have become clear to her that she no longer needed the earlier models, because she had found peace, and the *certainty* so long desired.

Revisiting Autobiographical Questions

As has been frequently pointed out, *BMK* often recalls the hagiographic tradition.[130] Margery has the gift of prophecy,[131] and miracles are ascribed to her; she "heals" a woman suffering from postpartum psychosis, drawing on her own similar experience. She is "a would-be saint,"[132] related in this respect to Richard Rolle, even if her humility is more convincing than his. Indisputably, she speaks of sainthood, and does not contradict a man who asks her to pray for him when she is a saint in heaven; rather, she wishes him sainthood as well (259:4347–50). On one occasion she even voices the hagiographically motivated desire to be beheaded for the salvation of mankind. The reader is pointedly reminded of her closeness to Mary Magdalen and St. Margaret. How such attempts to embellish her with a halo originated is no longer ascertainable.

There is a suggestion of hagiography when she describes the rapture caused by "mystical" birdsong. This does not exemplify the excessive "enthusiasm" that Walter Hilton is allegedly combating in *Of Angels' Song,* but the senses' perception of the spiritual and transcendent, inspired by birdsong down the ages. That Kempe cites this a second time toward the end of book 1 could be interpreted as a deliberate analogy to Elizabeth of Thuringia's last moments (reported in the *Legenda aurea*). In such music Elizabeth encountered the next world shortly before her death—and Kempe presumably wanted to achieve a similar conclusion to the *first part* of her biography.

Yet recent attempts to transform the hagiographic elements into the book's decisive literary or theological framework, and to interpret Kempe's entire spiritual life as imitation of one female saint in particular,[133] are not convincing, because the substantially shorter second part cannot be reconciled with such a view. Something has changed in the later text, and things are no longer as they were; neither is Margery Kempe's spiritual life the same it once was. For instance, she tells us that her compulsive cries have lessened. What we do hear, as before, is that she tries to live entirely according to the will of Christ, who continues to give her instructions, and that this gives her a sense of security, since he promises to take care of her and assures her of a safe return from her long journey. Nevertheless, her perilous adventure causes her great troubles; but she accepts them, and in particular the recurring slander and hostility, for the sake of Christ, whose suffering continues to cause her the utmost pain. Yet, as mentioned before, a spiritual development has taken place within her, and especially in these last years she no longer desires or requires individual saints as stabilizing models for her religious practice; instead she concentrates entirely on the core of the Christian way of life, the evangelical path of the *mulieres religiosae,* trying to live in perfect *imitatio Christi.*[134]

Altogether *BMK* is far more diverse than a saint's vita; it is rooted strongly in contemporary realism. Its contemporaneity makes it more like an autobiography, even if it begins only with Margery's conversion.[135] In evaluating her narrative it is important to remember that she had at her disposal samples of autobiography, and could look back on a long tradition of mystical autobiography (even if this was coming to an end in the late fourteenth century), whose major function was "merely to present by way of an exemplum the path to God of an 'unworthy sinner.'"[136] Holdenried describes the typical structure: "The structure of an exemplary vita is strictly schematic: conversion follows on a period of worldly sinfulness, usually dealt with in brief, and is followed by breakthrough and chastisement, as well as by accounts of temptation, slander, and persecution. The life story exemplifies a devotional pattern, and is a work of edification intended to encourage imitation."[137] *BMK* maintains this structure; we hear of Kempe's penance, slander, and persecution, but also that she was chosen. For her conversion, the phraseology current since Augustine's *Confessiones* of the experience of God as "drawing" is invoked.[138] In genre-historical terms, *BMK* is still a "spiritual autobiography" in the medieval sense; the typical elements are surprisingly clearly discernible, even if her initially sinful life is mentioned only briefly, and chastisement is dispensed with.

In spite of the medieval spiritual intensity that unfolds in book 1, it is also possible to trace in *BMK* an interesting trend toward *modern* autobiography, which owes much to the "ego-centredness" of mysticism and above all to the practical and professional requirements of the merchant world, such as descriptions of travel. The two are very interestingly combined in the two books of *BMK*.[139] The first book was written at a time when the vita of the medieval woman had already passed its peak. Nevertheless, Kempe composed a work of mystic introspection, looking back intently to the earlier texts in order to provide her own with theological legitimacy. Then her narrative in the second part offers a considerable measure of "modern," outward-looking description of the world as it really was, far beyond what was customary in a medieval vita. "Things of the world" prevail in the concluding part of her work; indeed, they almost completely fill it.[140] One might even say that in the second part we can trace an important aspect of the transition from medieval to modern autobiographical writing.

Margery Kempe's *Book*—the Result of Collaboration?

The story of how *BMK* came to be written down is unusual, and has aroused much comment. The first scribe's attempt does not get off the ground. A second scribe, a priest, has trouble completing the book because of the illegibility of the handwriting; his attempts, over a long period of time, to decipher the first text are eventually successful, whereupon he completes the first part, and adds the short second part two years later. He also composes a lengthy preface (an earlier one already existed), as well as chapter 24 and parts of chapters 25 and 62 (perhaps also chapters 82 and 83).[141]

This raises the pressing question of the scribe's contribution to the composition of *BMK*. What was the extent of his involvement? He was paid for his work, but it is hardly likely that he undertook the task purely for money; his pastoral and personal commitment is clearly discernible; he is moved by Kempe's story, and sheds tears. Since she could evidently read, but could not write well, she worked on her text with the help of this scribe who was also a theologian, but it is not likely that she dictated it to him, as Watson believes.[142] The scribe usually transposed the first-person accounts of her experiences into the third person.

The unusual genesis of the text necessarily affected its overall style. The fact that Kempe reported her experiences directly and *orally* to the scribe contributed to the work's style.[143] There is copious direct speech from her own mouth. Oral influence is also indicated by the frequency of sentences beginning with "And," "Than," "And than," "She," etc.

Assuredly, Kempe and her scribe would often have discussed wording before the text was written down; the exchange of questions and answers was exhausting, and took a toll on her bodily strength (383:7378–79). The scribe had a certain editorial function; he was equipped with literary skills, well informed about the stylistic and theological requirements of such a text, and ready to shape it accordingly. Recent scholarship tends to regard the text as a "coproduction" by Kempe and her scribe.[144] It is frankly impossible to determine exactly what comes from whom. On the other hand, it has been maintained that Kempe herself was responsible for "structure, arguments and most of its language."[145] I, too, am of the opinion that the text is largely her own work, constructed with her own language skills (honed by her familiarity with the many books read to her) and her considerable theological knowledge, hitherto unjustly neglected.

We hear in other cases of a completed biography being submitted to a theologian, or to several clerical authorities, for appraisal; Kempe tells us that theologians urged her to publish her experiences. Comparative references to the vitae of Marie d'Oignies, Elizabeth of Hungary, Birgitta of Sweden, and to other great mystical examples, help to guarantee irreproachable orthodoxy. Kempe frequently endeavored to assure herself of the authenticity of her mystical experiences by appealing to theological authorities, even bishops and archbishops. She also appreciated the great value of having her text sanctioned by a cleric-scribe,[146] something that Julian was obviously able to dispense with entirely.

Chapter 4 of *BMK* contains an interesting contribution by the amanuensis. Following several sentences that begin anaphorically with "Sche" and tell of Margery, the scribe identifies himself as "I," summarizes the narrative, and adds a biblical-pastoral admonition for the reader's benefit:

> Our merciful Lord Christ Jesus, seeing this creature's presumption, sent her, as it is written before, three years of great temptation, of which one of the hardest I purpose to write for an example for those who come after, so that they should not trust in their own selves, nor have joy in themselves as this creature had, for without doubt, our ghostly enemy sleeps not, but he full busily searches our complexions and our disposition, and wherever he finds us most frail, there, by our Lord's sufferance, he lays his snare [cf., for example, 1 Pt 5:8], which may no man escape by his own power.[147]

Since this chapter has to do with the sexual desire that caused Kempe much trouble, scholars have been inclined to hear her own voice in it.[148] However, the crucial point is that it is used for pastoral edification, and a theological reason is given for why human beings succumb to sexual temptation: God permits it ("be owyr Lordys sufferawns"). The detailed recapitulation of Kempe's delight in sensuality and her attempted adultery suggests that the scribe cleverly located the theme in this early chapter 4 in order to arouse the reader's interest. We can fairly confidently regard this as typical of the kind of structural intervention he undertook.[149]

He also underlines the literary qualities of the work in his long, rhetorically worded preface; Kempe undoubtedly provided the contents, but the style bears the mark of the "editor" scribe; it is larded with synonyms and doublets, and is intent on achieving a didactically effective climax (41:12–50); it stresses the textuality of *BMK*.[150]

There is no justification for regarding the work as "The *Book of Robert Spryngolde* about Margery Kempe."[151] For the more carefully one analyzes it, and compares it with other biographies of women mystics, the more likely it seems that the theological and editorial interventions of the rather timid scribe were actually quite limited.[152] He assuredly does not venture to make great changes to the words of Christ, or to the great visions. We should believe Kempe when she refers insistently to herself as having experienced and performed her book ("hirselfe that had al this tretys in felyng and werkyng," 384:7421). Overall, she deserves to be credited with literary skill, as is also proven, in my view, by the fact that the book ends with her collected prayers, which function as a kind of epilogue, and as a counterbalance to the introductory prologue. *BMK* is ultimately her work, even if not every word is hers, inasmuch as it was transformed into a "text" with vital help from her theologian scribe.

The Fruits of Julian's Theological Instruction

For Margery Kempe's gaining of theological maturity it is important to pay close attention to the account of her meeting with Julian. Kempe's visit to Julian is much more than the mere "interview" that has been suggested.[153] Two women of very different temperament and intellect encounter one another, their intense conversations spread over "many days," and touch on numerous problems, from woman to woman. The theological aspects of her book are likely to go back essentially to Julian rather than to additions by the priest-scribe.

On the occasion of Kempe's visit, Julian would have spoken at length of the central New Testament theme that God is love. Kempe, for her part, could assure Julian that she, too, was moved only by the thought of the loving bonds between God and the human being, by love of God, her neighbors, and her enemies; she was familiar with the Bernardine theme of loving all people in God and for God's sake; she was even bound in "charite" to the mayor who was not kindly disposed toward her—and to all people (237:3869). Indeed, she never has a slanderous word for others.[154] It could be said that her own book is filled with one great theme: the love of God for man as exemplified by his love for Margery Kempe, and her response to this love, treading in the path of God incarnate, attesting as she does so the experience of his grace.[155] *BMK* could well be titled *A Revelation of Love*.[156] When she experiences love as fire, there is no clear demarcation between "sensual" and "spiritual"; she indicates this through the image of the finger in the fire, recalling Richard Rolle (194:2897–98). There are several declarations of mutual love between Margery and her divine partner (301:5287–301). She is wounded by love (209:3245), she dies of longing; like Julian or Marguerite Porete, she is convinced that Christ would have died for her alone (99:958–61).

The two would have discussed in some detail the dogma of the Trinity, of astonishing interest to female mystics, and such discussion may well have influenced Kempe's brief speculation on the Trinity, which also demonstrates, however, her limited ability to follow the flight of Julian's lofty theological thinking. Kempe restricts herself to dogmatic details deriving from the Athanasian Creed, whereby her familiarity with this *Symbolum Quicumque,* the most detailed of the three, is remarkable. Each of the three persons of the Trinity, as she recounts, borrows the quality of the others, but the Holy Ghost, who "proceeds" from the other two (quoting from the *Symbolum Quicumque*), also has their appropriations ("propirteys"). Three different persons, united in potentiality, knowledge, and will, are in substance one God (374:7115–7119).[157] However, Kempe is more at home with the popular notion of the Trinity favored in women's mysticism; she experiences the appearance of God or the Trinity without fear and trembling, since God appears to her in familiar human form.[158]

Kempe is no more willing than Julian to speak of any actual experience of *unio. BMK*'s terms for this, such as "feelings," "homeliness," and "dalliance" (also "meditation" and "contemplation"), are familiar to us. Like Julian, she speaks of beholding God's "privity" and his "privy counsel" in her visions, but, by contrast with Julian, few of her "revelations" suggest actual seeing (but cf. 71–72); rather than claiming to have seen God, she moves at once to audition. She rarely uses "ravishing," Hilton's preferred term for the ecstasy of *raptus*. She understands "meditation" to mean mental prayer guided by God. He sends her "trance-visions" as she lies in the church and falls into a manner of sleep (370). She is granted such visions prior to her pilgrimage to Jerusalem.[159]

The two women surely also discussed the themes of predestination, Day of Judgment, and eternal damnation, as well as the problem of theodicy, of prime interest to women. Kempe's manner of alluding in her book to the theme of universalism, the "bringing back of all," also recalls Julian, although Kempe is entirely devoid of Julian's systematic and radical way of thinking. She would like to move God to redeem all human beings in the end. When she first voices this wish to Christ, she receives no answer.[160] She would like to banish the thought that God could ever damn irrevocably, whereupon Christ replies that she must accept his privy counsels (281:4846) as shown to her.

Then comes something very surprising: Kempe is thoroughly perplexed by the theodicy problem,[161] and everything in her rebels against the belief that eternal damnation could be included in God's plan, so she considers this vision to be a delusion of the devil. The temporary rebellion against God plunges her into a grave crisis that lasts for twelve days and takes her to the brink of despair—a moving occurrence, again revealing a very human side to her. The shattering experience tempts her several times to defy God by sinning deliberately, making random sexual advances,[162] but this is immediately followed by compulsive obsessions and fear of prostitution (282:4869–77). With the help of an angel as intermediary she is finally able, as she says, to overcome the temptation.

Yet after a time the problem of human damnation unsettles her again, with increased urgency: in an audition she asks Christ for clemency and grace for all people, since he does not desire the death of a sinner,[163] but rather that the sinner should reform and be saved. Julian had put forward the same argument. Margery repeats to him the words she has drawn from the Bible. Christ's answer—following a chapter division, for which there is no apparent reason—disregards the problem generated by his "arbitrary" selection via predestination of human free will ("I will be gracious, to whom I will be gracious," Ex 33:19, and esp. Rom 9:15–18), or rather, the problem is blunted by the argument that he damns only those who have deserved it, which is a bold defusing of the doctrine of predestination, even if quite common in the Middle Ages (chap. 65, p. 303; cf. the medieval reception of Job). Julian had avoided bringing in this argument as justification for predestination. Margery, praised by Christ for her "love" (302:5326),[164] declares herself satisfied by the argument—just as Julian finally accepts what the church teaches her to believe—even if she suggests at times that she finds it difficult to reconcile with the thought of God's all-embracing love; for she reminds her Lord that, as he well knows, he has no desire for revenge (302:5339). Kempe's love of her neighbor extends so far that she would not only like to free all the souls from hell, for there are enough there already (365:6894), but would let herself be chopped in pieces if she could save human beings from eternal damnation by such means (365:6891–92). She is a stranger to rigorous theological thought, and, all in all, does not maintain a consistent attitude. She can hardly bear the thought of eternal rebuttal, yet, in keeping with tradition, she is aware not only of a loving God, but also at times of a God who punishes. Contrary to Julian, she does not have the courage to consider the notion of universalism.[165] She is calmed by God's special assurance that he will not be angry with her (99:366), but she remains unsure.

Kempe is particularly anxious to receive from Julian confirmation of the authenticity of her spiritual experiences, which have made her a persona non grata in society, and exposed her frequently to open hostility. It must have been liberating for Kempe that Julian took her seriously and explained to her that she should accept as signs of God's goodness the various forms of divine "visitation" that she experienced.

When the conversation turns to Kempe's prime concern over her compulsion to weep, her excess of tears and related sobbing (often combined with cries), which she is unable to control, Julian remarkably regards this grieving over personal inadequacy, this genuine remorse, as spiritually valuable; and she makes a very important theological connection with a statement of the apostle Paul whom she knows so well, which runs: "Likewise the Spirit helps us in our weakness; for we do not know how to pray as we ought, but that very Spirit intercedes with sighs too deep for words" (Rom 8:26); Margery reports Julian's allusion to Paul in her narration of the discussions she had with her (*BMK,* 121.1359–122.1367). This Pauline statement is so highly favored by the mystics, especially in England, that it even occurs in the *Officium et miracula* compiled in support of Rolle's canonization.[166] It helps to attribute the involuntary sighs, and indeed the sobbing over which Kempe has no control, to the Holy Spirit, as a substitute for language. An interdisciplinary glance may help us to grasp the paramount importance of these words of the apostle: J. S. Bach, who had a profound knowledge of theology, and some knowledge, at least, of mysticism (as his library attests), selected this verse for his wonderful motet "Der Geist hilft unsrer Schwachheit auf" (The spirit strengthens our weakness). Much more could be said about the great theological significance of this assurance. What is important here is to stress the intensity of faith that these two women, and, much later, J. S. Bach, gained from Paul's assurance: what the human being cannot accomplish will be accomplished by the Holy Spirit. With the same conviction, Margery

Kempe assigns an essential role to the third person of the Trinity throughout *BMK* (from the very beginning, pp. 41:46, 118, prior to her visit to Julian; further, pp. 121, 194, 197); and therefore her concluding prayer appropriately begins with the hymn "Veni creator spiritus." She was strengthened in her belief that her mystical experiences were inspired by the spirit of God; she, too, relies on this divine authority.

Kempe would strongly refute the modern feminist line of argument that she perceived herself merely as body and was judged entirely on the basis of her bodily experience, in keeping with the medieval definition of women, and that she could therefore claim no mystical authority. To define women in terms of the "problematic nature of woman's position as flesh in medieval culture"[167] falls short of the mark. Nor is Kempe's spiritual position by any means marginal, as Lochrie, for instance, believes.[168] It is not possible to conduct precise and ideologically impartial research exclusively on the basis of gender criteria, which postdate, and are therefore not centrally relevant to, the field of medieval mysticism.

Conclusion

It has emerged very clearly that Margery Kempe needs to be understood without prejudice, on the basis of her Christian belief and the theology immanent in her work. She possessed a high measure of empathy, and deserves empathy from others.[169] The Carthusians of Mount Grace set an example in the Late Middle Ages; they saw in *BMK* a valuable testimony of mystical spirituality.[170] In true Christian humility she stands as "creature"— in the nonpejorative New Testament meaning of the word—before her Creator, whom she addresses at the beginning of her great prayer. Tragically, or at least uncomfortably, for her, she lived in what for her was a perilous time; the spiritual climate made it possible for her spiritual path to be totally misunderstood. She takes her orientation in large measure from the "textualized" vitae of women with spiritual-visionary experience, often dating from a very different time—Marie d'Oignies, Elizabeth of Hungary, Birgitta of Sweden (the latter a near-contemporary)—who sought to live out their piety in the secular world, but with far more concrete devotion to those who needed their help. Kempe encounters the greatest difficulties on her chosen path, which is more performance-oriented than the paths of her predecessors.

Kempe incurs suspicion of heresy because she communicates directly with God, although many others before her, such as the female mystics influenced by the beguines, had done the same. Like Julian, she refutes all ecclesiastical suspicion and stresses her adherence to the teaching of the holy church and her desire to please God (246:4068–69).[171] The Eucharist is of great significance to her. On the other hand, Christ tells Margery that he stands "above al Holy Cherch" (171:2366), and all mystics (male and female) accept this. He must be the measure for all, not least for her confessors.[172] Kempe's bold criticism of individual clerics is likewise a familiar component of mystical women's vitae. Like her, Mechthild of Magdeburg is moved to ask whether the transubstantiation wrought by a sinfully perverted priest is truly effective, and the question is answered in the affirmative. The exemplary story that Kempe recounts before the archbishop of York is not aimed, as Lollard criticism is, at the dogma of transubstantiation,[173] for this would never have occurred to her; rather, the drift of the narrative is directed against the worldliness of the cleric. She never attacks the theological establishment as such, but merely the perverted representative;[174] for her, the church retains undoubted spiritual authority.

Since Kempe had a great hunger for biblical knowledge, she longed to hear sermons every day—a legitimate desire. When she does not succeed in hearing a sermon, Christ himself promises to preach for her (208:3237).[175] Impressively, on her pilgrimage, she recites a Bible text she had learned by heart (158:2137–38). Citing the Bible as her authority, the mayor's daughter condemns the mayor of Leicester with great self-assurance. Her urge for biblical and theological knowledge cannot be attributed especially or exclusively to Lollard influence. Nor is it possible to agree unreservedly with the assertion that her knowledge of holy scripture "points to an area where Margery's learning is troublesome."[176] What area is meant? She wants to live according to the Gospel—which is the right, and indeed the duty, of the laity. Is it not said in Dante's *Commedia* that the Christian needs nothing more than the Old Testament and the New, and a spiritual guide (*Paradiso*, canto 5:76–78)? The only "danger" lies in the fundamental critical courage to pursue an independent line of thought—a courage demonstrated in Kempe's discussion of theodicy. Her trust in her own judgment might indeed have led her to oppose some aspects of ecclesiastical doctrine— she stops not far short of open opposition—but she remained loyal to the authority of her spiritual mother throughout her life. It is possible that her confessor encouraged her to keep her distance from the Lollards. That would amount to a further parallel with Marie d'Oignies, who was urged by Jacques de Vitry to oppose the doctrine of the Cathars vigorously, even if she agreed with them on some points.[177] It is evident time and again that Margery Kempe needs to be judged and understood not only synchronically, but also diachronically.

Above all, Kempe lived in an era when Christianity was still anchored in mankind with great vitality,[178] but theology was tending to flatten out, prior to a renewal set in motion by the Reform movement, from which Catholicism also benefited. There were various kinds of attenuation. One example is the suspicion of heresy that arose whenever anyone condemned swearing, although it was prohibited by Jesus himself, who, in turn, swears an oath to Margery. (Even the *Speculum Christiani* warns against swearing, on the authority of the Letter of James.)[179] It is bewildering to hear that Archbishop Arundel wants to take away the Lollard William Thorpe's Psalter because he fears that Thorpe could derive attacks on him from the Psalter.[180]

The confusion that arose in clerical circles over Kempe's wearing of a white garment (following the "will" of Christ) is also interesting. York's Archbishop Bowet accuses her of wanting to simulate virginity. He evidently does not know that, theologically, clothing of this color should not be decoded just as a claim to virginity; indeed, "this is the *only* moment in the *Book* which explicitly links the white clothes with virginity."[181] Kempe travels through late-medieval England and part of Prussia as a fool in Christ.[182] As we have seen, Marie d'Oignies, Elizabeth of Hungary, and Birgitta of Sweden were also considered fools. Yet Kempe gains great spiritual assurance from such hostility, for it marks the beginning of her *vita apostolica,* as is emphasized in great symbols on the occasion of her mystical marriage to God in the Church of the Apostles in Rome. She herself becomes a strengthening model for the faith of Christians who see themselves in her life as in a "mirror,"[183] or are able to see in her an example of a valid Christian life, although—or perhaps because—she repeatedly suffers from self-doubt and theological uncertainty.

Margery Kempe attains the highly significant role of Christ's representative on earth. Whoever hears her voice hears Christ's voice; whoever is against her is his enemy.[184] She participates in women's new theological self-image, manifested especially in late-medieval mysticism. But as a preponderantly strong woman she needed, or indeed invited, conflict, like Elizabeth of Hungary—the *mulier fortis* (Prv 31:10) of the High Middle Ages.[185] It is hard to appreciate all the nuances of this new self-awareness. Mechthild of Hackeborn lays claim to apostolic mediation, and Mechthild of Magdeburg has no less a companion than Paul on her flight to the third heaven. Margery Kempe belongs in this tradition, ready on the one hand to contradict even the apostles when necessary, while, on the other hand, garnering support from Paul,[186] who has to suffer her complaint that his prohibition of preaching caused her great trouble. Julian of Norwich became an Apostola of her Lord; to a certain extent this recurs, under her instruction, in Margery Kempe, who hears and sees the Lord in her visions, and Salih would see in her an "apostoless," too.[187] However, whereas Julian's task was to communicate new theological insights, Kempe's lot is to bear witness to her God through her conflictual life and her tears.

For Margery Kempe, medieval reception of the apostle Paul's teaching constituted the core of Christian faith, namely the proclamation of the oneness of God and man in the depths of the soul: Christ in you, you in Christ (2 Cor 5:17, Gal 2:20). She communicates this in manifold ways, through word and image. Christ may be "hid" but is by no means a *Deus absconditus;* rather, he wants to be found within the human being, as Walter Hilton had taught with the parable of the lost drachma. Not without reason does her prayer cite Paul and Augustine as her theological authorities (427:8510–11). Her numerous auditions need to be understood as variations on an old experience to which Augustine first applied the term "inner teacher" (*magister interior*), taking further the teaching of the New Testament.[188]

In this connection it is worth recalling Jesus's words, especially important for women's mysticism: "Apart from me, you can do nothing" (Jn 15:5). Herein lies the theological reason for Christ's imparting to Margery Kempe (and to many other women) numerous instructions, which make him the initiator of each of these women's own deeds, as has already been noted. Their wishes are reinterpreted as commands given to them by Christ, so that Margery and other women regard themselves merely as Christ's "executives" when they endeavor to translate their individual intentions into action. Margherita of Cortona (1247–97) lives in "constant contact with the lord,"[189] as does Mechthild of Hackeborn, to mention only two Continental examples. Such theologically motivated non-agency is particularly evident in Margery Kempe; for her, life was profoundly shaped by communication with Christ in allocutions that very often consist of his instructions to her. This continues to the last. Since for her, as for many mystics, the instructions of Christ as true head of the church have greater validity than any clerical authority, conflicts with the church are inevitable. Such conflicts must be borne with consolation drawn from the Gospels (Mk 13:11; Lk 12:11–12); and, in the end, "We must obey God, rather than any human authority" (Acts 5:29; Peter appealed to the authority of the Holy Ghost in resisting the prohibition of teaching).

On the basis of such insights and experiences, Margery Kempe is also convinced that she was commissioned directly by God to write her book (47:87). As she sees it, the time required is particularly well spent, even if her meditations and contemplations are shortened in consequence, because it will convert many readers (379:7287). At bottom, Kempe sees the book, the product of her labors and of the "craft" of her scribe, as Christ's own work, authorized by him.[190] Similarly for Julian, Gertrud the Great, and Mechthild of Magdeburg,[191] their own books were a medium of kerygmatic proclamation. Kempe's life and her book are not aimed at gaining "power,"[192] as is lightly argued nowadays, following Foucault; before God she remains entirely committed to Christian humility, and she desires above all to be a medium for the visible realization of the grace of God.[193] Therefore, for her, the book represents the highest form of love for her neighbor; and this enables her to overcome the problem of her violent weeping, which has troubled her so much. For even if many people have been unimpressed by this manifestation of her love, and repelled rather than converted in their inner selves, in her book she can proclaim with great intensity her love and compassion for all creatures, and God's love for human beings.

My own overall view of Margery Kempe is therefore very different from my earlier view. Previously, I was investigating only the language and imagery of the mystics, and I accepted the prevailing weight of opinion that Margery was neurotic and sick,[194] although I did include her among the English mystics because of Julian's very positive judgment of her.[195] Through the insights of more recent scholarship, and through looking at her not in isolation but from a European perspective, I have come to recognize her importance. Hardly anything exceptionable remains, apart from the intensity and frequency of her tears, whereas a few decades ago it was still possible to say: "There is nothing about Margery which is not sensational."[196]

Yet Margery Kempe seems to have only faint traces of one quality characteristic of other women mystics, namely the experience of inner joy. I do not understand how her book can be seen as "a theology and hermeneutic of mirth,"[197] for it has little of the inner joyfulness encountered in the work of Gertrud of Helfta, Marie d'Oignies, or Richard Rolle.[198] Although she admits having good cause for laughter, she is rarely moved to give verbal expression to her joy, in which respect she differs greatly from Julian, although she was strongly influenced by her. Nor does she actually feel moved to extol God. She stresses that her biography was written to praise God and magnify his name, but her text is entirely lacking in any hymnic ingredient, and she therefore has remarkably little use for the Psalms, unlike other mystical women, for whom the Psalter is an essential expressive element of spirituality. It is the only book of the Bible that the laity were permitted (at least on the Continent) to read.

Margery Kempe should be judged as a woman who sought to lead as intense and authentic a life as possible, grounded in the faith and mentality of her day. Her "personal consummation of faith"[199] was bound to show the influence of the times. Nor was she free from early capitalist consumerism and calculation of profit. As a onetime trader and later member of a merchant guild, she never doubted the possibility of quantifying immaterial goods and values: a certain quantity of tears could redeem a concrete number of souls from purgatory—a mercantile reckoning.[200] Nevertheless, she impressively carries forward the flow of English mysticism, and also anticipates a late-medieval piety that was about to be shaped on the Continent into the great movement of Devotio Moderna, given momentum by Thomas à Kempis's famous *Imitatio Christi* only a decade or so after the composition of her book.[201]

❧ CHAPTER 11

Some Aspects of Popularizing Mysticism in Late Medieval England

Beginning with the later fourteenth century, the growth of a new critical self-awareness among the laity can be discerned. The wish for a return to the sources, for New Testament piety, was voiced ever more strongly, as was evident in the case of Margery Kempe. Considerable numbers of people became unwilling to pursue experience of God solely under the auspices of the church; ecclesiastical authority was frequently called into question. New trends toward reform and religious movements developed, such as Devotio Moderna. However, such Continental groupings and "mass movements" did not gain a firm footing in England. It is important to realize that this new religious awareness was not an entirely new phenomenon; what was new was that it spread over to a widening and increasingly "bourgeois" public; its democratizing impulse has been adequately recognized. This age has rightly been called an age of translation; since there was a mass demand for new literature of contemplative content, it had to be met to a great extent by translations of existing texts, many being taken from the Continent.

A new genre of religious texts, the "compilation," gained wide popularity; it was seen as a very useful medium because parts of important works could be integrated into new contexts. Compilations proved thus particularly fruitful for the spiritual life. At first they consisted largely of extracts from Latin texts and circulated in monastic circles. Then collections of excerpts were made in English, and widely used. For example, the great popularity of Rolle's very extensive works meant that his texts were frequently integrated into compilations. Compilers had recourse to his works especially in connection with the cult of the Name of Jesus that originated among the Cistercians, and use was made above all of his commentary on the opening verses of the Song of Songs. This so-called *Encomium nominis Iesu* was detached from its context and integrated into a new compilation, the *Oleum effusum*.[1]

A keen interest in spiritual literature and in new texts, primarily in the vernacular, can be seen even on the part of monks, and especially nuns, who had no longer a sufficient command of Latin. Sometimes the religious orders' demand for new reading material was met by texts composed with the laity in mind, even by ones originally composed for recluses, and written in the vernacular. This explains, for instance, *Ancrene Wisse*'s great wave of popularity in the later fourteenth century and then in the fifteenth century, and two surviving Middle English translations of Aelred's *Institutio inclusarum*. The first one was included in the famous Vernon manuscript; it seems to have been compiled for a nunnery or for some other religious community,[2] and contains, in addition to *Ancrene Wisse* and *The Scale of Perfection*, dozens of mystical and devotional texts, including various letters by Richard Rolle and *A Talkyng of þe Loue of God,* the extensive pastoral-didactic *Cursor mundi,* Edmund of Abingdon's *Speculum ecclesiae,* and the great didactic poem *The Prick of Conscience,* as well as the "epic" *Piers Plowman.*

Important information about late-medieval readers of spiritual literature, including their social standing, can be gleaned from manuscript ownership, wills, bequests, and sometimes from dedications.[3] Scholars have shown that women made up an important segment of this reading public. A considerable proportion of them still belonged, like the often mentioned Margaret Beaufort, to the aristocracy.[4] As we have seen, aristocratic religious in earlier centuries were intent on matching their social standing with spiritual elitism, and the same intention is clearly discernible among late-medieval aristocratic readers or those from the gentry.[5]

Among the mystics, Walter Hilton was the one who, as we have seen, articulated this problem most clearly in his tract *Mixed Life.* Lady Margaret Beaufort had it added to Wynkyn de Worde's edition of *The Scale of Perfection* that she had commissioned,[6] evidently recognizing Hilton's attempt in this short tract to adapt the *Scale*'s mystagogic guidance for readers leading an active life. The fact that Hilton's *Scale* and *Mixed Life* occur together in three manuscript compilations made for lay people (the Vernon, Simeon, and Thornton manuscripts) demonstrates that this was a common lay perception.[7]

While Richard Rolle and the *Cloud* author had already tried to identify within *contemplatio* a domain accessible also to the normal Christian,[8]
Hilton, as we have seen, aims specifically for a mixed ("medeled") life[9] as
practical compromise for lay people with social, professional, or personal
obligations.[10] His tract is addressed to a wealthy lord with a large household and tenants.[11] In commending this mixed form of life to a wealthy
lord, Hilton advises the man not to strive for slavish imitation of monastic
contemplation—that is, not to be too anxious to intensify his devotions,
because there is a danger of going astray.[12] Rather, he should be content
with what is within his reach, and remain open to the workings of grace.
Given that the prosperous merchant class and the lesser nobility made up
a further important segment of the readership of spiritual literature, and a
pronounced "materialistic" trend had spread throughout society, it is, however, significant that Hilton takes up a theme of special relevance to the
laity already emphasized in his *Scale of Perfection,* namely greed for material
goods. He counters this trend with the rather astonishing exhortation: "be
þou couetous of þe ioies of heuene, and þou schalt / haue worschipes and
richesses þat euere schal laste."[13]

The Abbey of the Holy Ghost

We now turn our attention to a very popular type of allegorical prose, which
discusses an abstract theme through the interaction of a "system" of allegorical personifications who behave like human beings.

One such text is the attractive allegory *The Abbey of the Holy Ghost.*[14] In an
age familiar with thinking in pictures, it is no surprise that lay readers who
wanted to lead a mixed life and to turn temporarily to contemplation should
be offered a cloister of the heart (*claustrum animae*).[15] This monastery in the
bosom of the faithful, which enjoyed great popularity, can be traced back
to Pauline statements of the human being as temple of God, and of divine
indwelling in the house of the soul. The *Abbey* was translated from a popular
French text with significant alterations,[16] and was later supplemented by the
companion piece titled *The Charter of the Abbey of the Holy Ghost,* which we
do not have space to discuss.

The reader of the *Abbey* learns that fulfilling the basic requirements of the
Christian faith may grant access to a private interior cloister, which has been
erected on the foundation of "conscience," used in the sense of moral consciousness (thus translating *syneidesis* [*consciencia*], which occurs also in Paul
[Rom 2:14–15]).[17] And it has been shown that, interestingly, like so many
texts, *The Abbey of the Holy Ghost,* with this theme of practicing self-discipline

and doing penance, has recourse to *Ancrene Wisse*[18] as a text that could be used as a new "rule of life" for the contemplative laity. We read, moreover, that the abbey church is situated on a river fed by tears of contrition, which might be indicative of Cistercian associations, since the preferred site for Cistercian monasteries was by streams or rivers. Lady Charity functions as abbess and guarantees that contemplative life of the individual "solitary" soul is regulated. All the virtues as officeholders in the abbey are female, too, but this does not have to mean that the text was originally composed for women, as Blake surmises;[19] it may result simply from the fact that in the Roman-Latin tradition the virtues were of feminine gender. Nevertheless, as in *The Mirror of Simple Souls,* there is an unmistakable female "preponderance," likely to appeal particularly to women readers, although the *Abbey* is addressed to both men and women. The work's theological and, on occasion, mystical themes can be traced back to words of Jesus. The high regard in which allegories were held in the late Middle Ages means that the text should not be classified simply as didactic and functional, and belittled as such; rather, it should be understood as impressive evidence of a thinking-in-pictures typical of the time. This is exemplified magnificently in *Piers Plowman,* of which more will be said below. Nor should we forget *The Book to a Mother,* composed by a priest for his widowed mother. In it, we encounter once more the lay need to enhance piety until it becomes *contemplatio* that can be experienced in the inner cloister of the soul, where it may even happen that God is born. She experiences Jesus with the greatest immediacy, as if she were present at his Passion, and the whole work is permeated with quotations from the Bible, anticipating Wycliffite practice.[20]

It is of some interest that the popularity of a temporary contemplative "retreat" into one's own private inner self, in order to attain mystical cognition of God by way of self-knowledge, seems in the late Middle Ages to have been the reason for an almost total neglect of a further path to knowing God, namely the reverent study of God's creation of nature in universal harmony. Cognition of God through an intense devotion to nature was part of early scholastic theological teaching. In the twelfth century, the superb Cistercian theologian and philosopher Alain of Lille performed his great artistic achievement of presenting in his *Complaint of Nature* a most impressive personified Nature who appears "as an expansive character conducting an extended dialogue with a figure of *humana natura* iself."[21] Natura wants to make the human being aware of the elevating value of a study of everything created, which can serve as a book, a painting or a mirror reflecting the unique greatness of God. This insight was also proclaimed by Isaac of Étoile (Stella), another Cistercian of the twelfth century, whose real importance is only now being discovered.[22] He explains that whatever is in creation exists because it has received its being from God who alone is his own being. Therefore, by contemplating any creature in the created universe, we may be inspired to cognitive contemplation of God. What unites all created beings and holds them together in a single whole is the Creator's love, because he formed nature out of love. Research has shown that such a view is a manifestation of the Cistercian *Carta caritatis prior,* established, as we have seen, by Stephen Harding, which has love at its center. However, it appears that the adherents of the mixed life, motivated by "spiritual ambition" as they were,[23] did obviously not avail themselves of the possible enjoyment of a brief "foretaste of eternity" in contemplating nature.[24] Could it be that in the fourteenth and fifteenth centuries these early members of a capitalist society were already debarred from an immediate, spiritual view of nature? Be that as it may, the Cistercian doctrine that man may read God's greatness in the traces he left in his creation was a theological insight on which later Franciscan mystics could build (cf. also chap. 8).

The *Meditationes vitae Christi* and Nicholas Love's *Mirror of the Blessed Life of Jesus Christ*

Before we enter on the genre of religious drama, with the allegorical morality plays as its spiritual climax, a few words should be said on the famous and very popular Franciscan *Meditationes vitae Christi* and in particular on their English reception by Nicholas Love.[25] They have long been considered the work of Bonaventure, but in fact they were written by the early fourteenth-century Johannes de Caulibus; yet here we are again confronted with a Franciscan *development* of a preceding Cistercian mystical affectivity. The text frequently cites Bernard of Clairvaux (although the references are often to pseudo-Bernardine writings). It was, as we have seen, Aelred of Rievaulx who (following Anselm of Canterbury) provided the definitive model for this genre in the magnificent Passion meditation written for his sister, and on this the *Meditationes* could build.

What Aelred introduced into the Passion meditation, namely present visualization of Christ's suffering and death, and involvement of the meditating participants, was taken up and developed further. The meditating woman is addressed, and asked what she now wishes to do. Aelred had already challenged the reader of his *Institutio:* "And you...what now...you without tears?"[26]

It need hardly be stressed that these *Meditationes* exerted a great influence on late-medieval spiritual literature in England; a considerable number of

English texts derive from them. They fed particularly into the mystery plays, in which the dramatizing of salvation history consistently extends the performative character of the *Meditationes.* This is especially true of their excellent adaptation titled *The Mirror of the Blessed Life of Jesus Christ* by Nicholas Love,[27] one of the early priors of Mount Grace Charterhouse in Yorkshire, founded in 1398. This was a much-shortened version, with central focus on the Passion. Like the Latin *Meditationes* from which it was derived, the very popular text (extant in close to sixty manuscripts) served throughout the country as source and inspiration for affective contemplation of the mystery of the incarnation.[28]

In his *Mirror of the Blessed Life of Jesus Christ* Nicholas Love maintains that the *Meditationes* were written originally for a "religiouse woman,"[29] a nun. Likewise, he is undertaking his translation in the first instance for religious, who have renounced the world, but then also for lay readers. He has a deep sense of English mysticism and makes positive mention of Walter Hilton. Touchingly he speaks of the mystical love between Christ and John, the latter reclining on Christ's breast,[30] a motif especially favored in the Cistercian tradition, as we have seen. Yet he sees his readers as "symple soule[s]," for whom meditation on Christ's life on earth is much more appropriate than "hiȝe contemplacion of the godhed," and safer.[31] Thus he excludes the possibility of Bernard's *amor castus,* which seeks to ascend via the highest stage of contemplation, Christ's humanity (*amor carnalis*), to purely spiritual love of God. Yet the text's contemplative stance is still in the tradition of Bernard and Aelred, for it aims to kindle the most powerful fire of love.[32] Furthermore, Nicholas Love seems to be well acquainted with *Ancrene Wisse,* alluding to it directly when he adopts the notion that Jesus himself experienced the life of a recluse through his gestation in Mary's womb.[33] The affective presentation of the Passion is intensified further, and to this extent the text may be described as characteristically Franciscan. As far as I can see, apart from John of Howden's Latin *Philomena* poem and *Piers Plowman,* this is the only text to make explicit mention of "Seynt Francese" in the entire history of English mysticism. Nicholas Love is very concerned to guard against any form of heterodoxy. As "simple souls," his women readers must be protected against the errors with which *The Mirror of Simple Souls,* in his view, seeks to capture readers; perhaps it is with this in mind that Love also calls his *Meditationes* "Mirror." The Lollards are a further target: the author adds a strictly orthodox tract on the Eucharist—which, with the exception of Margery Kempe, is only occasionally mentioned by the English mystics—in order to guard against their teaching on this sacrament. Suso's *Horologium sapientiae,* available to him in English translation, was his inspiration.[34] The sacrament's power to intensify the mystical fire of love was clearly very important to him; yet his goal was to strengthen faith through testifying to the experience of sacramental grace.[35]

Love's style has often been praised, and described as elegant, lucid, and precise.[36] He constructs well-balanced sentences, and very skillfully employs "parallelism and repetition and accumulation of phrases and clauses" in shaping emotional climaxes;[37] with considerable sophistication he carries forward the tradition of devotional prose schooled on Latin models.[38]

Mystic Themes in English Religious Drama

The great cycles of religious plays are of some interest to a history of English mysticism and spirituality. Scholars have already shown that the affective animation and visualization of Jesus's life and sufferings in the *Meditationes vitae Christi* and Nicholas Love's *Mirror,* together with related vernacular texts such as the *Northern Passion,* offered important stimuli for these plays.[39]

First, a brief glance at the Chester plays: in the scene of the Last Supper, a stage direction requires that John be sleeping in Christ's lap ("tunc occumbit Jesus ac Johannes in suo gremio dormiet").[40] Only this cycle dramatizes the bodily proximity of master and disciple; there is no further indication of mystic *unio,* but it will be understood by those with sufficient knowledge and mystical experience. In the Day of Judgment scene, John recalls the motif briefly but perceptively: "I lay in great longinge / upon my maisters barme [bosom] slepinge / My ghost was ravished to heven."[41]

For traces of mysticism, the N-Town plays are worth considering. The clerkly author makes no secret of his profound learning; he incorporates into his text metapoetic allusions to grammar, prosody, and rhetorical *cursus,* drawing attention to the text's exquisite form and structure, which cannot be investigated further in the present work. At the same time he acknowledges the audience's legitimate expectation to be entertained—and he deliberately assigns his commentary to a figure called "Contemplatio." This striking figure was inspired by Nicholas Love's *Mirror,*[42] in which, as mentioned above, a marginal "Contemplatio" points the reader toward a meditative level. In the play, Contemplatio's appearances coincide with Mary's, highlighting her importance. The audience is drawn into events especially through identification with Mary's compassion (above all in the crucifixion scene). Mary first faints, then wishes to hang with her son on the cross, as the speaker in the *Wohunge of Ure Lauerd* had demanded: "hang me up here on þis tre... For þer he is, þer wold I be."[43] The ensuing stage direction "*Here þei xal take oure Lady from þe crosse*" could be taken to mean her "deposition" from the cross, attesting most powerfully that this is a living tradition. In the same way the reader of *Wohunge* identified with the narrator, whose heartfelt wish was to hang with Christ on the cross.

The loving and detailed dramatization of Mary's death and Assumption is in keeping with late-medieval popular piety, and vividly reminiscent of Margery Kempe. The Marian legend dates from the late fourth century and became widely known, especially after it was incorporated into the *Legenda aurea,* as "Transitus beatae Mariae virginis." Christ (Sapientia) commissions an Annunciation angel for the second time; on this second occasion he is to tell Mary that she will soon be taken up into heaven. The angel appears to Mary, accompanied by celestial music ("Hic descendet Angelus ludentibus citharis").[44] This scene, interesting to us because of Rolle's affective devotion to celestial *melos,* has many analogues in medieval iconography, where the visual arts show angels with musical instruments in this scene. In the early and High Middle Ages this should not be interpreted as vocal ensemble accompanied by instruments,[45] since celestial music was thought of as exclusively vocal, but the N-Town plays date from a time when instrumental music had been admitted to depictions of heaven. After Mary's death her soul passes to God's bosom, accompanied by the choir of the celestial court ("Hic cantabit omnis celestis curia").[46] When the soul of the mother of God has returned to her body, God ascends with the "bodily" Mary to heaven, and (for the second time) divine two-part organum songs resound, which Rolle had imitated with such virtuosity in *Melos amoris* ("Et hic assendent in celum cantantibus organis").[47] This climax exemplifies very well the function of angel music in the religious plays. Music in a dramatic performance is used to generate or intensify audience emotions, as is the case today in the secular field, especially in film and television. Rosemary Woolf rightly pointed out that this great Marian scene can be experienced to full effect only when it is read as a kind of libretto, with full realization of the musical component.[48] Altogether, the specific skills and enormous practical-theatrical competence of the N-Town plays have not as yet received sufficient attention from scholars.

With regard to activation of audience emotion, however, the N-Town plays are surpassed by the Towneley plays, starting with Jacob's appealing report: "I haue seyn [seen] in this place, / god of heuen face to face."[49] As in Old Testament theology, the vision of God occurs here on earth. The last words spoken by Jesus to his disciples at the Passover meal express the core of mysticism: "I in you, and ye in me."[50] We witness Mary's moving lament, as Jesus is shown streaming with blood, according to ancient Cistercian tradition.[51] From the cross he looks down on his wounds; that he bled for love is stressed by means of anaphor.[52] Longing to be loved in return, he spreads out his arms in an *amplexus* gesture. In the manner of the famous "Improperia," he asks how man has thanked him.[53] Thomas, representing all who see, weeps over the streams of blood (cf. Bernard's 22nd sermon on the Song of Songs).[54] The consequences of the Passion events, Christ's act of redemption undertaken for love of the human being, are presented here in a manner that recalls the affective *Meditations on the Passion* attributed to Rolle and his lyric poetry, especially the extensive poem "Ihesu swet, nowe wil I synge";[55] it also recalls Margery Kempe's intensity of experience. The great spiritual affectivity of the N-Town plays and the Towneley plays suggests that there may be some significance in the fact that they come from East Anglia, where Julian of Norwich and Margery Kempe lived. In this connection, it does not matter very much whether there is a close link between the N-Town plays and Norwich, or whether they come from the busy spiritual center of Bury St. Edmunds, or Thetford.[56]

The Towneley plays contain a further surprise: it is very remarkable that this cycle, imbued with profound piety and high drama, gives a not very creditable part to the apostle Paul. He refuses to hear "what's new" from women, and heaps up prejudices against them—Paul the misogynist. The author, by contrast, has Mary Magdalen appear not with rumors or lies, but with the joyful news of Christ's resurrection, belying the prejudice that women cannot be believed. She gives Paul a reproachful answer, saying that his view of her is wrong.[57] Paul is "convicted" of the falseness of his antifeminine position. This may call to mind Margery Kempe, who did not hesitate to complain to Paul that he had caused her a lot of suffering, for which he apologized to her, and it may remind us also of Julian's indirect opposition to the ecclesiastical decree, derived from Paul, that women must remain silent.

Thematic Parallels in the Morality Plays

Our attention is drawn once more to the power of allegory in shaping spiritual subject matter. Here, abstract terms used to describe the process of mystical experience even become dramatic characters. The need to "see" and to "show" spiritual processes in visible form grows ever stronger. A morality play of great interest for our context, titled *Wisdom Who Is Christ,* or *Mind, Will and Understanding,* was compiled in East Anglia, evidently in Bury St. Edmunds; it is one of the three so-called Macro plays.[58] It relates in a special way to the mystical texts, in particular to the *Cloud* group and to Walter Hilton's works, because it is very much concerned with the soul, and, following Augustine, with the soul's likeness to God. The soul comprises two parts, *sensualite* and *ratio* (*inferior* and *superior*). As in Hilton, the soul's *memoria* ("mind") is sometimes the faculty of remembering, but at other times it is used in the sense of *mens*. The text opts for a voluntaristic line: the will has to be taken for the deed; in addition, as for the mystics, the human being can do nothing without God. The play makes skillful use of an English translation of Suso's *Horologium sapientiae*. Suso follows an ancient tradition in presenting Christ as Wisdom—a Christian interpretation of Old Testament *Sapientia*—and the play evidently relies on Suso's tract in presenting Christ likewise as Wisdom. He turns to Anima, the human soul, and alludes to the Song of Songs in explaining to her how she is made, what significance her three traditional powers of Mind, Will, and Understanding have, and how she has at her disposal not only outer senses but also an equivalent number of inner senses, which then appear in a dumb show. The essential concept of the inner senses, derived from Origen and so important for English spirituality, is very effectively made concrete. Yet how the inner senses relate to the three powers of the soul is not clarified, any more than in the *Cloud* author or Hilton; on one occasion they are compared to the wise virgins. This morality play again raises the question of knowledge of God, and again the answer follows the tradition of Augustine and Bernard of Clairvaux: the ascent to knowledge of God depends on knowledge of the self.

Yet the harmony of the three powers of the soul is disturbed by the appearance of Lucifer, who tries to prove that a *vita contemplativa* is not what God intends. He produces arguments that are indeed diabolical, in that they have a certain undeniable Christian validity: for instance, Jesus's life was contemplative during his forty days in the desert, but thoroughly active in his mission, thus proving that the *vita mixta* is the perfect Christian form of life. This way of arguing appears all the more "diabolical" by the fact that no less a man than Walter Hilton defined Christ's life as a "mixed life."[59] It cannot be maintained that the playwright wanted to discredit or negate the *vita mixta,* simply because he lets the devil himself defend it. Rather, he makes his tempter especially diabolical by having him articulate forceful arguments to ensnare the listener—like Goethe with his Mephisto in *Faust*. His persuasive skill is highly refined; he uses his "orthodox" defense of the *vita mixta* only as a starting point for his actual purpose of imperceptibly insinuating the worldly, sensual life as the only attractive one, while any thought of contemplation fades ever further. All three powers of the soul are thoroughly perverted, allowing themselves to be tempted and lured to sensual pleasures, so that "Wille" can only cry: "A woman me semeth an hevynly sight!" (*Wisdom,* in *Macro Plays*, p. 134).[60] The play is not designed for reading and meditation; it was indeed performed, and carries conviction through its lively, often humorous, dialogue, and because it is able to give concrete embodiment onstage to abstract themes such as the structure of the soul, responding in full measure to the needs of the time.

However, a question mark remains over the originally intended audience. The play's starting point is the *vita contemplativa,* and the merit of such a life is reaffirmed at the end. This is a strong indication of monastic provenance and led to the assumption, long ago, that the play was performed for monks.[61] This was strengthened further by the discovery that the scribe and first owner of the Macro manuscript was a monk of Bury St. Edmunds.[62] Other suggestions, that the work was performed in the London Inns of Court, or even by a professional theater group,[63] are less plausible. Nevertheless, it may well be that the audience at a performance of *Wisdom Who Is Christ* could have included lay persons, since they, too, would have appreciated its criticism of the sinful life of the world and would have felt themselves supported in their faith. A mixed audience of this sort would provide a further instance of the late-medieval tendency to popularize mystical texts originally intended for a restricted circle.

The Castle of Perseverance

The Castle of Perseverance (again from the Bury St. Edmunds region of East Anglia) is very probably the earliest morality play, and particularly representative of late-medieval English piety.[64] In this play the whole structure is shaped by allegory—as in the famous *Everyman.* The bare outline of the plot is as follows: Humanum Genus, representing all humanity and therefore also the audience, is fought over by angels and devils, and especially by the three traditional enemies, the world, the flesh, and the devil; finding himself exposed to the seductions of Covetousness, Humanum Genus is held back by Penitence and Confession, and finally commits himself to the protection of the Castle of Perseverance, which is surrounded by a moat filled with water; the evil powers attacking the castle are repelled by the virtues, but Covetousness urges Humanum Genus to abandon the protection of the castle; Death appears, the protagonist's possessions are seized, and the soul goes to hell; in the ensuing debate between God and his four daughters over the precedence of justice or mercy, mercy wins, and in consequence the soul of Humanum Genus is liberated from hell.

The Castle of Perseverance has long aroused great interest for a particular reason: the manuscript includes a diagram that at first glance seems to provide important information about performance practice, but then gives rise to further speculation (see figure 16). R. W. Southern took the sketch to indicate a theater in the round, or amphitheater, surrounded by an outer ditch. According to this interpretation, the peripatetic acting company would have needed to create the stage anew for each change of location, which would have meant digging a new ditch every time. The earth turned up would have served to provide raised seating for the audience beyond the ditch.[65] The technical and practical difficulties make this interpretation hardly plausible.

The diagram has never been seen for what it really is, namely a graphic representation of the detailed allegory contained in the text, and thus the optical realization of the play's spiritual essence. Only N. Crohn Schmitt has come close to the true interpretation;[66] she raised doubts regarding the substance of R. W. Southern's theory, and related the diagram and the ditch to popular late-medieval castle allegories. She rightly observes that the moat has *symbolic* meaning, and refers particularly to *The Castle of Love,* the English version of Robert Grosseteste's *Château d'amour.*[67] In the English rhymed poem, however, the castle symbolizes Mary, a fountain of grace, without which, as the narrator goes on to say, he is lost "unless a stream of thy grace comes to me soon."[68] Crohn Schmitt draws on further allegories to suggest that "the river, and, by association, the water in the ditch, were important not merely as fortification for the castle, but in their own right"; crossing the water with its cleansing power brings about a "transformation of the soul."[69] Crohn Schmitt starts out on the right path, but her conclusion is not fully convincing; for the water in the Castle of Perseverance moat is not, as she concludes, the flood of Mary's tears—the Mother of God plays no central part in this allegory.

The crucial fact is that the moat is to be filled with Humankind's own tears of contrition, which he must shed if he wants to be saved. We have seen that the Abbey of the Holy Ghost, too, lies beside a tears-of-contrition stream that cleanses the soul in order for her to become the seat of God.[70] As has been shown in a different context, this notion is based on a great theological tradition. Seen in this light, tears of contrition are a work of grace; in *The Castle of Perseverance,* the slothful deadly sin Accidia tries to ensure that the ditch runs dry in order to prevent grace from taking effect.[71]

Hitherto the fact has been entirely overlooked that the central allegory of *The Castle of Perseverance* is precisely delineated in *Ancrene Wisse,* so important for its theology. This provides further powerful evidence of late-medieval reception of *Ancrene Wisse,*[72] whose readers were told that they live in a well-defended castle—an allegory of the soul with a rich tradition going back to Luke, chapter 10 (also a central metaphor in *Sawles Warde*). The castle provides defense against the devil, and *Ancrene Wisse* goes on to say that around it runs a moat filled with water (a symbol of humility), providing further

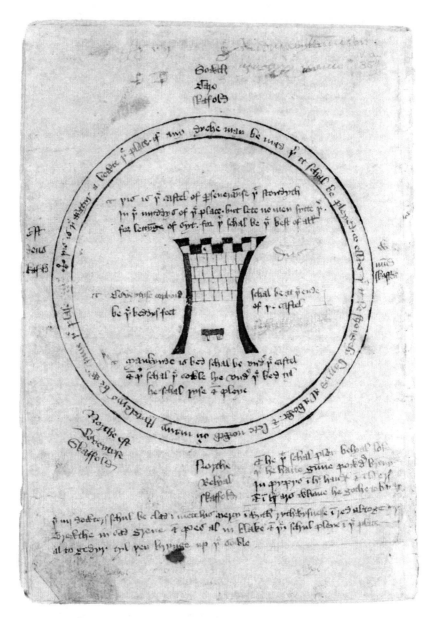

FIGURE 16. Stage diagram for the morality play *The Castle of Perseverance*. Folger Shakespeare Library, MS V.a.354, fol. 191v. By permission of the Folger Shakespeare Library.

protection against the devil's assaults. The water is nothing other than their own *tears of contrition*. The biblical model is Jeremiah, who wants to summon wailing women "so that our eyes may run down with tears, and our eyelids flow with water" (Jer 9:18) to mourn the people's estrangement from God.

This conveys to the *Ancrene Wisse* recluses the enormous significance of tears that accompany prayer as a gift of grace:

> Whoever can have God's gift of tears in prayer may do with God all that she wants. For so we read: *Oratio lenit, lacrima cogit; hec ungit, illa pungit*—"Happy prayers soften and please our Lord, but tears take him by storm."... When a castle or town is assailed, those within pour scalding water out, and so guard the walls. And you should do just the same as often as the enemy assails your castle, and the city of the soul: with heartfelt prayers, pour out scalding tears over him... where this water is, the enemy surely flees lest he be scalded. *And another illustration: if a castle has a moat around it, and there is water in the moat, that castle is unafraid of its enemies. Every good person against whom the devil makes war is a castle. But if you have the deep moat of deep humility and wet tears around it, you are a strong castle, the warrior of hell may long assail you and waste his time... a great temptation, which is the enemy's blast, is stilled with the soft rain of a few tearful words.*[73] (original italics)

Thus the core of *The Castle of Perseverance*'s central allegory is set out clearly and in great detail in *Ancrene Wisse*. As in this guide for the spiritual life, Humanum Genus must weep floods of tears of contrition for his sins, and with his tears he must fill the castle moat, for protection and cleansing. We have every reason to suppose that *Ancrene Wisse* was an important stimulus for one of the greatest English morality plays.

These comments will have brought to mind Margery Kempe, the "specialist," as it were, in the flow of tears of contrition, whose entire life bears witness to the meaning of tears for the medieval understanding of faith. She lived in Lynn, not very far from Bury St. Edmunds, where *The Castle of Perseverance* probably originated. She might have followed a performance of the play with particular attention. Interestingly, Julian of Norwich recommended especially the virtue of "Perseverance" when Margery Kempe came asking for advice; and Margery practiced this virtue very thoroughly in her life; she also accords it an appropriate place in her book, which ends very meaningfully with her prayer's evocation of "perseverawns."[74]

We cannot end our survey without a brief look at *The Vision of William concerning Piers the Plowman* (extant in three different versions: A-Text, ca. 1370; B-Text, ca. 1377–79; C-Text, after 1390). This dream vision, with a few further texts, picks up the formal characteristics of Old English alliterative verse, and the fourteenth-century "alliterative revival" is a most interesting literary-historical phenomenon. Langland, second only to Chaucer among Middle English poets, was a farmer's son and received a theological education in the Benedictine monastery of Great Malvern (Worcestershire).

What the poem actually sets out to say is not entirely clear; the author himself struggled to convey his purpose in successive versions. So much is certain: the work is concerned with the question of religious truth, and the possibility of a righteous Christian life under the guidance of Peter the Plowman, in an unjust world corrupted by material greed, where even the church gives cause for caustic criticism. Detailed interpretation involves particular difficulties, and the present study can do no more than offer a few brief observations. The narrator with the allegorically ambivalent name of Will, combining intellect with will, is sent by the personification of Holy Church on an inner journey, to find a path to the perfection that the mystics also desired. This is fundamentally a quest, which is also, of course, the basis of the Grail literature. It proceeds through several stages, called Do Wel, Do Bet (= Do Better), Do Best, but it is extremely difficult to elucidate their precise meaning because the quest is redefined several times. It is at least clear that the most important prerequisites for perfection are humility and love, which are also the cardinal virtues to which most importance is attached in the *Cloud* texts, Walter Hilton's work, and *The Mirror of Simple Souls*. The voice of Devotio Moderna is also heard in the distance, although this Continental movement never gained a firm footing in England.

Inasmuch as love is a basic motif throughout, at least in the B-Text, Langland shares one important feature with the English mystics. Unlike the mystics, however, he does not make specific *knowledge* of God an important theme. Looking at *Piers Plowman* in the context of late-medieval spiritual literature shows very clearly how Langland departs from the central messages of Rolle (whose writings he evidently knew),[75] the *Cloud* author, and Hilton on the question of mystical *unio*. In spite of his sympathy for the life of the religious, his thoughts are focused on his neighbor; he is very concerned for the well-being of his *fellow humans,* and loving attention to them is recognized as a task of paramount importance.

In *Piers Plowman* Bernard of Clairvaux is once more given exceptional authority—in the context of his emphatic call to love God, one's neighbors, one's enemies, and oneself. Particular importance is attached to self-knowledge, seen by Bernard as essential; it frequently occurs in conjunction with Conscience, used primarily to mean "consciousness," as in *The Abbey of the Holy Ghost*. Furthermore, as for Bernard and for the Cistercians in general, reading the Bible is important; the frequent quotations from the Bible incorporated into the running text are not taken from pastoral handbooks, but are indicative of Langland's direct knowledge of the Bible. Scholars have

recognized the closeness of *Piers Plowman* to *Ancrene Wisse,* and have attributed it to the popularity of allegory.[76] Yet there are further obvious reasons.
I would like to draw attention particularly to the emphasis given in *Ancrene
Wisse* to Christ as chivalric hero who has saved the soul from great danger;[77]
with this allegory, the prose text matches the alliterative poem in content
as well as form. Like Julian of Norwich, Langland puzzles over predestination, and there is a reminder of "reform" thinking in the admonition not
to rely on the law, but to follow only the law of love.[78] The recurrent call to
love is accompanied by the demand for a life of poverty. This has led to the
assumption of Franciscan influence on *Piers Plowman,* which is, however,
unfounded. It should be remembered that the demand for a life of poverty
was by no means a new discovery on the part of the Franciscans; such a life
had already been extolled, and lived, by the Cistercians. Interestingly, on
this subject Langland calls to mind four fathers: Dominic, Francis, Benedict,
and Bernard.[79] *Piers Plowman* is an entire theological universe, still awaiting
precise interpretation.

✠ CONCLUSION

The present study has tried to take a fresh look at medieval English mysticism, based on the underlying theological tradition and the wider European perspective. We have seen that more attention needs to be paid to the vivid exchange of ideas, which reflects an astounding medieval mobility in spite of the great difficulties of travel. Richard Rolle, for one, can be viewed and evaluated more fully in the light of this mobility, and his highly developed sensibility facilitates an exceptionally sensuous and richly differentiated, almost "feminine" language, which has rightly been compared with that of Henry Suso. Both were strongly influenced by Bernard of Clairvaux, even if the writings of Suso, as a pupil of Eckhart, are rooted in Dominican theology. It has been pointed out by B. McGinn that Rolle and Suso are among the first male mystics to describe celestial sweetness, divine fragrance, heavenly song, and mystical dance. And both are characterized by the IHS monogram of Jesus, inscribed on their breasts in manuscript illuminations. Rolle's huge Latin vocabulary and his virtuoso mastery of theological Latin support the tradition that he was a student at the Sorbonne. What reason could there be for satisfaction if this were not the case? It seems that denial of this tradition is rooted in a national pride that is no longer justified. We should also acknowledge that the author of *Ancrene Wisse,* and very probably Walter Hilton (according to the testimony of three *Scale of Perfection* manuscripts), may have studied in Paris. What is required today is a European perspective, for which the "interrelation" of the *Ancrene Wisse* and the *St. Trudpert Hohelied* is an instance in point.

As the marked preference for the solitary life in medieval England is concerned, we have to be on our guard against defining this too readily as a specific element of English spirituality. When Richard Rolle insists on retreating into the interiority of his own self, in order to enjoy the *secretum meum mihi*, there is no justification for arguing that this is an anchoritic ploy with which he seeks to cherish his own individuality; he is merely taking up the twelfth-century European eremitical ideal discussed at the beginning of the present study. Nor does it come as a surprise that this ideal recurs later on in Walter Hilton's writing; he had lived as an anchorite for some time before deciding to join the Augustinian canons, and he remains true to the same ideal when, toward the end of his *Scale of Perfection,* he desires to have the *secretum* reserved for himself. And was not the form of life of the early *Ancrene Wisse* intended to "replicate" the example of the desert fathers and mothers? Even if the "interiority" of medieval English mysticism has now become a main focus of interest, the very important beginnings, inspired by the Cistercians, must not be neglected, and the contribution of the Carthusians must not be exaggerated. There is less cause to believe that late medieval English Catholicism was qualified by a specific, original interiority than there is to observe the developing and unfolding of an anchoritic subjectivism that had emerged in England for the first time in the *Ancrene Wisse* and manifested itself again much later in the famous and lavishly illuminated fifteenth-century Carthusian manuscript BL MS Add. 37049, to which new attention has recently been drawn by J. Brantley. This subjectivism enabled the Carthusian monks to "live" and perform the *secretum meum mihi,* much as the three sisters of *Ancrene Wisse* had already done in their liturgical performances.

The decisive impulse for the hermits and anchorites to retreat from contemporary society is that they desired spiritual freedom. They took their lead from Paul, in anticipation, as it were, of Martin Luther's *Liberty of a Christian,* and their mystical teaching was based throughout on the theology of St. Paul. Unlike Luther, the author of *Ancrene Wisse* greatly appreciated the Letter of James, which may also have to do with the fact that in its implied criticism of Pauline teaching, the letter points to the necessity of proving faith by performing good deeds, and in particular of loving one's neighbor, which the anchorites are obliged to do like any Christian.

In conclusion, it is important to note that the reason why the English mystics, and in particular Walter Hilton, discuss the favorite Cistercian theme of the human soul's likeness to God is that they are preoccupied with human *dignity,* a theme already encountered in *Ancrene Wisse,* which was to become a hermeneutic subject for numerous women, such as Mechthild of Magdeburg, Gertrud of Helfta, Marguerite Porete, Hadewych, and Julian of Norwich. If it is true, as has been said, that the mystics contributed greatly to the figurative use of "nobility," then in England Julian of Norwich is one of the main propagators of a spiritual nobility that she defined in her own individual and daring way. In our own age, which increasingly entertains the gross error that the Enlightenment discovered and disseminated the idea of dignity as a late, post-Christian, "modern" value, it is vital to be aware that this great discovery is actually attributable to the early Jewish-Christian tradition.

Emphasis on the dignity of the individual human being implies, of course, a strong affirmation of corporeality as such. All the mystics we have considered finally succeed in giving up a dualistic mode of thought; understandably, the male writers have more difficulty with this than the female ones. Belief in the incarnation of God and the resurrection of the flesh helps the mystics to dismiss the traditional devaluation of the body; indeed they promise that the resurrected body will be granted perfection and splendor. Yet only very few of the English mystics, among whom Julian is the most remarkable, go so far as to acknowledge in the created, earthly body an appropriate medium for experience of the divine.

Origen's new and positive view of the body, no longer darkened by the Platonic tradition, attached real importance to the bodily senses for spiritual cognitive experience, and went so far as to assert the existence of analogous spiritual senses. As we have seen, they became an important ingredient of the English mystics' experiential reality. We have become used to this mystical paradox; yet in looking afresh at the concept of the spiritual senses we notice with astonishment that it anticipates an insight of recent research into neurological processes. As modern science has shown, the act of rational thinking cannot be entirely separated from bodily, instinctive, emotional processes; this may prevent the intellective faculty from gaining absolute autonomy. Thus the idea of a spiritual-sensual cooperative activity, which for the mystics is part of their unique experience, may gain plausibility even for the modern skeptic.

Since in the "Aristotelian" Middle Ages female existence was usually equated with the body and seen as lacking reason, Origen was greatly esteemed by some medieval women. Juliana of Cornillon, the inventor of the Corpus Christi feast, is an instance in point. However, as Origen's theology sometimes aroused suspicion of heresy, Elizabeth of Schönau, another female admirer, asked Mary in one of her visions whether he would be damned for all eternity. Mary's significant answer was that, since he worked and wrote for love, God would certainly judge him leniently.[1] Especially in Norwich, where the greatest number of heresy trials took place, there must have been some interest in daring theological thinking, and therefore also in the work of Origen. It is certain that Julian, for one, was especially open to the influence of Origen's theology.

It may well be that a major reason why Julian could venture on her daring theology was Adam Easton, who taught in Norwich in her youth and who became cardinal in 1381. His titular church was Santa Cecilia in Trastevere, where he was buried in 1397.[2] Easton was a most learned man and owned a comprehensive library, which contained some of Origen's writings, as we are told by the church historian W. A. Pantin. Easton may well have helped to establish a "left-orthodox" climate in Norwich. He knew and supported Birgitta of Sweden and Caterina of Siena, he promoted Birgitta's canonization, published in Norwich his *Defensorium Sanctae Birgittae,* and spoke generally in favor of women's theological visionary writings. However, I would not go so far as to consider him as a patron for Julian, as A. M. Reynolds and J. Bolton Holloway did in their Julian edition; Easton himself later got into great troubles with papal authority.

Some Continental women who took a positive view of corporeality belonged to the beguine movement, nourished in part by Cistercian theological thinking and meditative practice. Julian has enough in common with these women for us to speak of a spiritual affinity. And it has become evident that there are certain correspondences between her and the beguine Marguerite Porete. The two women have a distinctively optimistic stance, extolling the supreme intensity of divine love that enables them to contemplate the problem of sin with breathtaking nonchalance. There were no beguines proper in England, it is true, yet why does a manuscript exist with English translations of Continental beguine biographies? And what explanation can there be for the famous English Amherst Manuscript, which "joins" Marguerite Porete's *Mirror of Simple Souls* and Julian's early version of *A Revelation of Love?* It is interesting to note that evidence has been found that in Norwich, from 1427, there existed a group of women leading a communal life modeled on a *béguinage;* a second group is documented as existing circa 1443. These women must have felt themselves to be specially chosen, and they cultivated close contacts with Continental beguine communities, which may well have led to familiarity with major beguine texts as well. And it fits into this picture that Margery Kempe formed her own life pattern to a considerable extent on a beguine model. Julian did not live long beyond 1416, but such contacts will have existed prior to the date of the surviving documents. Once more, it is apparent that any notion of a specifically English piety is an ideal construct that does not entirely fit the facts.

Whereas it is impossible to define precisely what "singular" English piety might consist of, and whereas in England, as on the Continent, we find examples of passionate language and ecstatic rapture, there is good reason to point to one specific quality that does recur most strikingly in English mystical texts. This is the element of sweetness (*dulcedo*), which provides a link to the Cistercian "foundation," and is most impressively reflected in the notion of the tenderness of God as mother. In England joyful sweetness may also find artistic expression in medieval music and the visual arts; the consonance of thirds first heard in English cathedral music serves to arouse a pleasurable and satisfying feeling, as do the thirteenth-century sculptures in the cathedrals of Wells and Salisbury, and in Westminster Abbey, where, as has been shown by art-historical research, an attempt was made to preserve this distinctive English characteristic despite French influence. There is a feeling of joy in the work of the English mystics; even Margery Kempe laughs occasionally, and Julian of Norwich enjoys.

❧ Abbreviations

AC	Analecta Cartusiana
AW	*Ancrene Wisse*
AW CC	*Ancrene Wisse: A Corrected Edition of the Text in Cambridge, Corpus Christi College*
BMK	*The Book of Margery Kempe*
BPC	*The Book of Privy Counselling*
CAM	*Contra amatores mundi*
CCCM	Corpus Christianorum. Continuatio Medievalis. Turnhout, 1971–.
DR	*Downside Review*
DS	*Dictionnaire de spiritualité ascétique et mystique, doctrine et histoire.* Edited by M. Viller et al. Paris, 1937–94.
EETS	Early English Text Society: o.s. (original series); e.s. (extra series); s.s. (supplementary series). London: Oxford University Press.
EIC	*Essays in Criticism*
ELH	*English Literary History*
E P	English Psalter
ES	*English Studies*
EV	*Emendatio vitae*
FCEMN	*Fourteenth Century English Mystics Newsletter*
FL	*The Form of Living*
IA	*Incendium amoris*
L P	Latin Psalter
MA	*Melos amoris*
MAE	*Medium Aevum*
MGG	*Musik in Geschichte und Gegenwart: Allgemeine Enzyklopädie der Musik.* Edited by Friedrich Blume. 17 vols. Munich: dtv, 1989.
MLQ	*Modern Language Quarterly*
MLR	*Modern Language Review*
MMTE	Glasscoe, Marion, ed. *The Medieval Mystical Tradition in England.* The Exeter Symposium Series. Vol. 1., Exeter: University of Exeter, 1980; vol. 2, 1982; vol. 3, Cambridge: D. S. Brewer, 1984; and vol. 4, 1987; vol. 5, 1992; vol. 6, 1999 [enlarged title in 1999: *The Medieval Mystical Tradition in England, Ireland and Wales*]; vol. 7, ed. E. A. Jones, 2004.
MQ	*Mystics Quarterly*
MS	*Medieval Studies*
NL	*Expositio super novem lectiones mortuorum*
NM	*Neuphilologische Mitteilungen*

PL	*Patrologiae cursus completus, Series latina.* Edited by Jacques-Paul Migne. Paris, 1844–64.
PMLA	*Publications of the Modern Language Association of America*
RES	*Review of English Studies*
SM	*Studia Mystica*
SCC	*Commentary on the Song of Songs*
TH	*St. Trudpert Hohelied*

NOTES

Preface

1. Ruh, *Geschichte*, 4 vols.

2. McGinn, *Presence of God*, 4 vols. Quotations in the ensuing paragraphs are from vol. 1, *The Foundations of Mysticism*, xiii–xx.

3. Watson, "Middle English Mystics," 544, 551.

4. Mystical elements in major poetic works have had to be excluded.

5. Ruh, *Geschichte*, 1:17.

6. Of course, there are on occasion striking differences in emphasis between Latin and vernacular texts. For example, the prospect of the salvation of all human beings at the end of time (the so-called "apocatastasis")—a specifically female concern—is hardly touched on in the Latin but receives attention in vernacular works (see Watson, "Visions of Inclusion," 145–87).

7. Recent years have seen scholars apply methods besides the literary and the theological to the study of medieval mysticism—notably those of cultural theory, such as the postmodern readings of Derrida, which cannot be considered here. See Nelstrop, with Magill and Onishi, *Christian Mysticism*, 225–40.

1. The Development of Eremitical Mysticism in the British Isles

1. See for instance Southern, *Making of the Middle Ages,* and Constable, *Reformation of the Twelfth Century.*

2. See esp. Ullmann, *Individual and Society in the Middle Ages;* and Bynum, "Did the Twelfth Century Discover the Individual?" in Bynum, *Jesus as Mother,* 82–109; and Morris, *Discovery of the Individual.*

3. Jaeger, *Ennobling Love,* 157.

4. Ibid., 183.

5. Duby, *Age of the Cathedrals,* 124.

6. Langer, *Christliche Mystik im Mittelalter,* 88. See also Astell, *Song of Songs,* and Matter, *Voice of My Beloved,* 1990.

7. McGinn, *Presence of God*, vol. 1, *Foundations,* 118. See also the essential textual anthology: *Origen: Spirit and Fire.* There were works by Origen in Cistercian libraries; cf. Bell, *Index of Authors and Works.*

8. William of St. Thierry, *Nature and Dignity of Love.*

9. Ibid., 47–53.

10. Malcolm Moyes has demonstrated the importance of the Cistercians in Richard Rolle's commentary on Job; see *Richard Rolle's "Expositio,"* 1:55–58.

11. Leyser, *Hermits and the New Monasticism,* and Licence, *Hermits and Recluses.*

12. See Anson, *Call of the Desert*.

13. This section owes much to Gudrun Gleba, *Klosterleben im Mittelalter*, 18–29.

14. Dee Dyas ("Wildernesse Is Anlich Lif of Ancre Wununge") gives a useful, albeit rather too succinct, survey.

15. Antony was most likely not the first Christian hermit. St. Jerome contended that Paul the Hermit (230–341) was the first.

16. Athanasius, *Life of Antony*, 54ff. The standard English translation can be found in Athanasius, *Life of Antony and the Letter to Marcellinus*, trans. Gregg.

17. Leyser, *Hermits and the New Monasticism*, 10–12; Knowles, *Monastic Order in England*.

18. On the Christianization of Ireland, see Bitel, *Isle of the Saints*.

19. Colgrave, *Two Lives of Saint Cuthbert*.

20. See Mayr-Harting, *Coming of Christianity*, 237–39.

21. Leyser, *Hermits and the New Monasticism*, 12. See also McAvoy, *Anchoritic Traditions of Medieval Europe*, with essays on the Low Countries, the German-speaking regions, the Italian and Spanish traditions, medieval France, England, Ireland, Scotland, and Wales.

22. Peter Damian, *Liber de Dominus vobiscum*, 19, trans. Patricia McNulty, in *St. Peter Damian: Selected Writings on the Spiritual Life* (New York: Harper & Brothers, 1959).

23. Küsters, *Der verschlossene Garten*, 37.

24. Ibid., 254.

25. John of Forde, *The Life of Wulfric of Haselbury, Anchorite*, trans. Pauline Matarasso (Kalamazoo, MI: Cistercian Publications, 2011).

26. As with Wulfric, our information about Godric comes entirely from his biographer (and confessor) Reginald. See Reginald of Durham, "Life of St. Godric," in *Social Life in Britain from the Conquest to the Reformation*, ed. G. G. Coulton (Cambridge: Cambridge University Press, 1918), 415–20. My description owes much to Charles H. Talbot, "Godric of Finchale and Christina of Markyate," in Walsh, *Pre-Reformation English Spirituality*, 39–55.

27. Peter Dinzelbacher, "The Beginnings of Mysticism Experienced in Twelfth-Century England," *MMTE* 4 (1987), 111–31, 123.

28. Quoted from J. W. Rankin, "The Hymns of Saint Godric," *PMLA* 38 (1923): 699–711; and R. T. Davies, "St Godric, a Cry to Mary," in *Medieval English Lyrics* (London: Faber and Faber, 1963), 51; the translation follows Davies's suggestions. All translations of quotations in this book are, unless otherwise noted, by Charity Scott-Stokes.

29. See Victoria Tudor, "Reginald of Durham and St Godric of Finchale: A Study of a Twelfth-Century Hagiographer and his Major Subject" (PhD diss., Reading University, 1979); Colgrave, *Two Lives of Saint Cuthbert*; Ward, *Miracles and the Medieval Mind*, 76ff.

30. See esp. Bynum, *Jesus as Mother*, 110–69.

31. Küsters, *Der verschlossene Garten*, 46.

32. See Elkins, *Holy Women of Twelfth-Century England*; Kerr, *Religious Life for Women*; Wogan-Browne, *Saints' Lives*.

33. See, for instance, Sally Thompson, "Why English Nunneries Had No History: A Study of the Problems of the English Nunneries Founded after the Conquest," in *Medieval Religious Women*, vol. 1, *Distant Echoes*, ed. John A. Nichols and Lillian Thomas Shank (Kalamazoo, MI: Cistercian Publications, 1984), 131–49.

34. Doerr, *Das Institut der Inclusen*, 30.

35. As previously mentioned, Jerome and Cassian regarded this as the actual goal of monasticism. See also Warren, *Anchorites and Their Patrons*.

36. Küsters, *Der verschlossene Garten*, 137.

37. Küsters, *Der verschlossene Garten*, 134. Anneke Mulder-Bakker, in *Lives of the Anchoresses*, argues that the female urban recluses of the twelfth and thirteenth centuries lived without any definite rule and had not retired entirely from society.

38. Rosof, "Anchoress in the Twelfth and Thirteenth Centuries," 124, 127.

39. In Mulder-Bakker's view there were no female hermits, but Christina of Markyate would prove the contrary.

40. See esp. Küsters, *Der verschlossene Garten*, 140–41; Meyer, *Das "St. Katharinenthaler Schwesternbuch,"* 201–2; see Langland's critique of hermits in *Piers Plowman*, commented on by Jones, "Langland and the Hermits."

41. C. H. Talbot, ed., *"Liber confortatorius" of Goscelin of St Bertin. Analecta monastica*, ser. 3, *Studia Anselmiana* 37 (Rome, 1955), 1–117.

42. See Talbot, "Godric of Finchale and Christina of Markyate," 46–47.

43. Doerr, *Das Institut der Inclusen*, 12–14.

44. Ibid., 14–15.

45. *Life of Christina of Markyate*, ed. and trans. Talbot.

46. Ibid., 3.

47. Thomas Head, "The Marriages of Christina of Markyate," in Fanous and Leyser, *Christina of Markyate*, 119: "Autti and Beatrix…sought to form a bond between their daughter and a saint whose relics rested in their region." But Christina had promised herself to Christ alone.

48. This promise of fidelity suggests a famous worldly parallel with a much later work, Chaucer's *Canterbury Tales*—the famous Wife of Bath, who was united "at chirche dore" with each of her five husbands in succession (see chap. 4 below).

49. Leyser does not pay special attention to the parents' relationship to the prophecy made before the birth of their daughter; she assumes a certain "pretentiousness" in the choice of the name Theodora, but does not mention the religious associations (Fanous and Leyser, *Christina of Markyate*, introduction, 3).

50. Jaeger, *Ennobling Love*, 183.

51. See D. Gray, "Christina of Markyate: The Literary Background," in Fanous and Leyser, *Christina of Markyate*, 20; see also C. J. Holdsworth, "Christina of Markyate," in Baker, *Medieval Women*, 185–204.

52. See chap. 2 below.

53. Notwithstanding Kurt Ruh's contrary view, *Geschichte*, 2:114.

54. Leyser has made important comments on the intensity of Christina's visions. She rightly refutes the earlier scholarly view that in England, unlike on the Continent, female visions and heretical tendencies were unknown at this time (Fanous and Leyser, *Christina of Markyate*, 8).

55. See also Ruh, *Geschichte*, 2:113.

2. Early Cistercian Theology in England

1. For general treatments of the Cistercians in England see Knowles, *Monastic Order in England*, 346–62, and Burton, *Monastic and Religious Orders in Britain*, 63–85. For broader contributions of the Cistercians see Bruun, *Cambridge Companion to the*

Cistercian Order, Burton and Kerr, *Cistercians in the Middle Ages,* and Leclercq, *Love of Learning and the Desire for God,* esp. 191–235.

2. Stephen's profound achievement is the idea that the organization of the order should be established by love. See Burton and Kerr, *Cistercians of the Middle Ages,* 29ff. Stephen is entirely overlooked by Constance Hoffman Berman in *The Cistercian Evolution,* where she attempts to expose the early history of the order as a deliberate myth, based in part on forged documents, and to shift the order's actual development to the last quarter of the twelfth century. Her book has drawn strong criticism, e.g., by Chrysogonus Waddell, "Myth of Cistercian Origins."

3. Zaluska, *L'enluminure et le scriptorium de Cîteaux au XIIe siècle.* It contains Stephen's *Monitum.*

4. Bernard of Clairvaux, "Sermon on Conversion to the Clergy," II.3, in *Sermons on Conversion,* trans. Saïd. Geoffrey of Auxerre gives an account of Bernard's sermon in his *Vita prima* IV.11.10.

5. Bernard of Clairvaux, "Sermon on Conversion to the Clergy," xii: 24–xiii: 25.

6. Ruh, *Geschichte,* 1:250–51.

7. A translation of Bernard's sermons can be found in Bernard of Clairvaux, *Sermons on the Song of Songs,* trans. Walsh and Edmonds.

8. M. Ernst, "Die Identitätssicherung einer Paulusgemeinde durch den ʻPaulus' der Pastoralbriefe: Das Selbstverständnis der ersten Cistercienser und der hl. Bernhard als ʻzweiter Paulus,'" *Analecta Cisterciensia* 59 (2009): 288–309.

9. See McGuire, *Difficult Saint,* 189–225; Bynum, *Jesus as Mother,* 132–33.

10. Gilbert of Hoyland, *Sermons on the Song of Songs;* John of Forde, *Sermons on the Final Verses of the Song of Songs.*

11. See, for example, McGuire, *Difficult Saint.*

12. Guerric of Igny, "Second Sermon for the Annunciation," in McGinn, *Essential Writings of Christian Mysticism,* 406.

13. Quoted in Matarasso, *Cistercian World,* 133.

14. On the Victorines, see Knowles, *Evolution of Medieval Thought,* 141–49.

15. On Aelred see McGuire, *Brother and Lover,* and Squire, *Aelred of Rievaulx.* See also Marsha L. Dutton's introduction to Aelred of Rievaulx, *Spiritual Friendship,* trans. Braceland.

16. Aelred of Rievaulx, *Spiritual Friendship,* trans. Braceland, III: 133.

17. Jaeger, *Ennobling Love,* 110–14.

18. It would be wrong to suggest that all Aelred's monks were well disposed toward him; he was inclined to give preference to some, incautiously, and this could lead others to oppose him. See McGuire, *Brother and Lover,* 95.

19. Aelred of Rievaulx, *De speculo caritatis.* Quotations are taken mostly from *Mirror of Charity,* Webb and Walker, trans.

20. See Grabes, *Mutable Glass.*

21. Augustine interprets the title of Psalm 91, "A psalm for the Sabbath day," as the peace of one who has a clear conscience, who may hope for peace in the Lord (*Enarratio in Psalmos,* cited from Aurelius Augustinus, *Über die Psalmen,* selected and trans. into German by Hans Urs von Balthasar, Christliche Meister 20, 3rd ed. [Einsiedeln: Johannes Verlag, 1996], 191).

22. Millett draws attention to the possible influence of Plotinus's reception of Plato, referring to Pierre Courcelle, among others, who named Origen and Gregory of Nyssa as intermediaries (Millett, *Hali Meiþhad*, 32, n. 6/15–16); see also Hallier, *Monastic Theology of Aelred of Rievaulx*, 12.

23. McGinn, "Aelred of Rievaulx," in *Growth of Mysticism*, 309–23.

24. Hallier, *Monastic Theology of Aelred of Rievaulx*, 30.

25. See also Buchmüller, *Askese der Liebe*, 32. Augustine already reflected on affect in the illusory world of the theater (*Confessions*, III. 2, 76).

26. See Marsha L. Dutton's introduction to Aelred of Rievaulx, *Spiritual Friendship*, 23. All quotations from *Spiritual Friendship* are taken from Lawrence C. Braceland's translation.

27. Cicero, *De senectute, De amicitia, De divinatione*, ed., trans. W. A. Falconer (Cambridge, MA: Harvard University Press, 1964), 188.

28. McGinn, *Growth of Mysticism*, 319.

29. Because Aelred does not entirely exclude physical sensations, some have imputed a homoeroticism to him, albeit without real proof. See Russell, "Gay Abbot of Rievaulx"; also McGuire, *Brother and Lover;* Jaeger, *Ennobling Love*, 110–14.

30. The notion of the sweetness of God is specifically Cistercian only inasmuch as it frequently shapes their discourse; it is based on the Bible, e.g., on "Gustate et videte quam suavis est Dominus" (Ps 34:8). The fathers discussed it from Origen onward; see, e.g., *Origen: Spirit and Fire*, 267; see also Rosemary Hale, "'Taste and See, for God Is Sweet': Sensory Perception and Memory in Medieval Christian Mystical Experience," in Bartlett et al., *Vox Mystica*, 10.

31. Although Aelred addresses his sister directly, it is likely that he intended the *Rule* for more general usage. *De institutione inclusarum* circulated widely and would serve as the basis for numerous rules to follow, including *Ancrene Wisse*.

32. Aelred of Rievaulx, *Rule of Life for a Recluse*, trans. Macpherson, 41–102. All subsequent quotations are identified by paragraph numbers as found in the critical editions.

33. The originality, beauty, and linguistic sensuality of Aelred's meditations have often been praised, but without thorough investigation. Georgianna does not penetrate beneath the surface (*Solitary Self*, 46–49). Squire considers Aelred "the independent master of a technique which perhaps no one before had grasped so boldly and taught so vividly and clearly" (*Aelred of Rievaulx*, 69).

34. Ruh, *Geschichte*, 1:331–34; Ruh acutely observes the ways in which Aelred's narrative technique is employed for the sake of *memoria*. For instance, the soul is addressed as meditating subject and exhorted to consider what it sees—a "stylistic principle of intensification and emotionalization, that was to play a key part in the field of so-called affective mysticism." See also *DS* 10, cols. 908–9, s.v. "Méditation," and *DS* 2:2, cols. 1937–38, s.v. "Contemplation."

35. Ruh, *Geschichte*, 1:333. Buchmüller, too, mentions that Aelred addresses his sister with interjections, as if they were both participants in a sacred drama (Buchmüller, *Askese der Liebe*, 134).

36. See Ruth Smith, "Cistercian and Victorine Approaches to Contemplation: Understandings of Self in *A Rule of Life for a Recluse* and *The Twelve Patriarchs*," *MMTE* 6 (1999), 47–65.

37. John of Caulibus, *Meditations on the Life of Christ,* trans. Francis X. Taney Sr., Anne Miller, and C. Mary Stallings-Taney (Asheville, NC: Pegasus Press, 2000). On the dating of *Meditationes* see McNamer, "Origins of *Meditationes vitae Christ.*"

38. Buchmüller, following Hoste, sees in Aelred an anticipation of Franciscan adoration of the cross (Buchmüller, *Askese der Liebe,* 244). Dutton has also shown that Bonaventure, in his *Lignum vitae,* made intensive use of Aelred's first meditation on the life of Jesus ("The Cistercian Source: Aelred, Bonaventure, and Ignatius," in Elder, *Goad and Nail*).

39. Georgianna misunderstands these meditations when she endeavors to see in them "a sensual love of Christ" (*Solitary Self,* 49).

40. As the second person of the Trinity, Christ was often equated with *aeterna sapientia* and therefore "feminized." See Bynum, *Jesus as Mother;* M. L. Dutton, "Christ our Mother: Aelred's Iconography for Contemplative Union," in Elder, *Goad and Nail,* 21–45; see also chap. 5.

41. On the Christ-and-John groups see Lang, *Die Mystik mittelalterlicher Christus-Johannes-Gruppen.* Anselm of Canterbury in one of his meditations had already addressed the contemplating John with "pious affectivity"; yet he cannot simply identify with John's fervent union with Christ, but, typically, recalls his own grievous sins, is afraid of the terror of the Last Judgment, and therefore asks John to be his intercessor before God. "Oratio ad Sanctum Iohannem Evangelistam hominis timentis damnari," in *S. Anselmi Cantuariensis archiepiscopi opera omnia,* ed. Schmitt, 2:42–45.

42. The hymn has been edited twice: André Wilmart, ed., *Le "Jubilus" dit de Saint Bernard: Étude avec textes,* Storia e Letteratura 2 (Rome, 1944); Heinrich Lausberg, ed., *Hymnologische und hagiographische Studien I. Der Hymnus "Iesu dulcis memoria"* (Munich: Hueber, 1967), from which quotations are taken here.

43. See C. Dumont, "L'hymne 'Dulcis Iesu memoria': Le jubilus serait-t-il d'Aelred de Rievaulx?" *Collectanea cisterciensia* 55 (1993), 235. To the best of my knowledge, A. Wilmart was the first to suggest Aelred's authorship, but he then rejected the idea and simply considered it very probable that the poem was written by an English Cistercian ("Le 'Jubilus,'" 226–27); Moyes locates the origin of the hymn in one of the Cistercian houses in Yorkshire (*Richard Rolle's "Expositio,"* 1:34–37), and Buchmüller, not very convincingly, tried to prove once again that Aelred did write the hymn (*Askese der Liebe,* 139–42).

44. The text takes up and elaborates something of the language and spirit of Anselm of Canterbury's meditations (see *S. Anselmi Cantuariensis archiepiscopi opera omnia,* ed. Schmitt, 2:42), "IESU, IESU . . . Nomen dulce, nomen delectabile, nomen confortans peccatorem" (Meditatio I, 79, and also Meditatio X).

45. Eng. trans. by Edward Caswall, from *Lyra Catholica: Containing All the Hymns of the Roman Breviary and Missal, with Others from Various Sources,* trans. Caswall (London: James Burns, 1849).

46. Lausberg offers a detailed analysis. See Heinrich Lausberg, ed., *Hymnologische und hagiographische Studien I. Der Hymnus "Iesu dulcis memoria"* (Munich: Hueber, 1967).

47. *Carmina Burana: Die Lieder der Benediktbeurer Handschrift.* Dual-language Lat.-Ger. edition by Alfons Hilka and O. Schumann, based on Bernhard Bischoff's critical edition of the Latin text (Munich: dtv, 1979), 534.

48. *Sancti Bernardi opera,* 1:5, 15. Yet, the highly sensual intensity with which *Dulcis Iesu memoria* is meant to be "sung" makes it improbable that Aelred, who otherwise emphasizes *friendship* with God, should be regarded as its author. The passionate language of this hymn is more suggestive of a successor to Bernard, or indeed of Bernard himself.

49. Bauer, *Claustrum Animae,* 60.

50. *Origen: Spirit and Fire,* ed. von Balthasar, 46.

51. Brown, *Body and Society,* 172–73.

52. Cf. e.g. Gilson, *Mystical Theology of Saint Bernard,* 108–9.

53. See esp. Denis Renevey, "Anglo-Norman and Middle-English Translations and Adaptations of the Hymn *Dulcis Iesu memoria,*" in Ellis and Tixier, *Medieval Translator* 5, 264–83.

54. For John of Howden's Latin *Philomena* see Blume, *Hymnologische Beiträge,* vol. 4. André Wilmart demonstrated the influence of *Dulcis Iesu memoria* in "Le 'Jubilus,'" 90–93. When considering English reception of Cistercian spirituality, one should not concentrate too much on *Philomena,* which has an overly theatrical style that distinguishes it from *Dulcis Iesu memoria.* I also cannot agree with those who argue that Richard Rolle was especially influenced by *Philomena.* To my mind, any parallels can be explained by both Rolle and *Philomena* having recourse to the paradigmatic *Dulcis Iesu memoria.*

55. A further small group of related texts, the so-called Katherine Group, can be mentioned here only in passing. Their themes complement the Wooing Group and *Ancrene Wisse,* evidently for the same readership; they extol the great spiritual value of virginity and martyrdom.

56. *Wohunge,* ed. Thompson, lines 574–75.

57. See also Sarah McNamer, "Feeling," in Strohm, *Middle English,* esp. 249–50.

58. This link was already made by Augustine in sermon 218 (*PL* 38, col. 1087).

59. Rahner, "Die Gottesgeburt," 333–418.

60. Savage and Watson find the Passion meditation in this text "comparatively restrained" (*Anchoritic Spirituality,* 421).

61. *Benedict's Rule: A Translation and Commentary,* ed. Terrence G. Kardong (Collegeville, MN: Liturgical Press, 1996), 135.

62. *Wohunge,* ed. Thompson, xxi.

63. Ibid., xxvi.

64. Thompson sees the text in the tradition of rhythmic, alliterative prose reaching back until "the late Old English prose of such works as Aelfric's *Lives* and Wulfstan's homilies" (*Wohunge,* xxvi). It would be going too far to postulate, as some have, a Franciscan context or even an early German influence for *Wohunge.* See, e.g., Catherine Innes-Parker, "*Þe Wohunge of Ure Lauerd* and the Tradition of Affective Devotion: Rethinking Text and Audience," in Chewning, *Milieu and Context of the Wooing Group,* 96–122, 108.

65. *Anchoritic Spirituality,* ed. Savage and Watson, 14–15, rightly talks of "an ambitious spiritual and literary movement, all within a tiny area of the west of England, and involving, at the outside, a hundred people." See also E. Robertson, "Savoring 'Scientia,'" in Wada, *Companion,* 132.

66. This hypothesis was put forward in the late nineteenth century, when people began to take an interest in these texts, and it has recently been reasserted. See

E. Einenkel, "Eine englische schriftstellerin aus dem anfange des 12. jahrhunderts," *Anglia* 5 (1882): 265–82; Catherine Innes-Parker, "*Ancrene Wisse* and *Þe Wohunge of Ure Lauerd*," in Smith and Taylor, *Women, the Book and the Godly,* 137–47, 138. Thompson believes that the text was "written for (and perhaps, in some cases, by) devout women" (*Wohunge,* xv).

67. See Millett, "Women in No Man's Land," 86–103, esp. 98.

3. Ancrene Wisse

1. *Ancrene Wisse* is related to the Katherine Group and Wooing Group. See Dobson, *Origins of "Ancrene Wisse,"* 253–59.

2. Day, *English Text of the Ancrene Riwle,* 85. Unless otherwise noted, quotations from *AW* are taken from the English translation by Anne Savage and Nicholas Watson, in *Anchoritic Spirituality: Ancrene Wisse and Associated Works,* and are cited parenthetically in the text by page number.

3. *Ancrene Wisse: A Corrected Edition of the Text in Cambridge, Corpus Christi College, MS 402, with Variants from Other Manuscripts,* ed. Millett, 1:96.1076–97.1101. (Quotations from this edition are indicated by *AW CC*).

4. Ibid., 1091. There is, however, no reason to share Watson's view of a tendency toward adaptation of the text to suit the laity ("*Ancrene Wisse,* Religious Reform and the Late Middle Ages," in Wada, *Companion,* 203).

5. This is reminiscent of what is happening at the same time on the Continent, especially in southern Germany, where occasionally we see recluses' institutions converting into nunneries. See Küsters, *Der verschlossene Garten,* 141, and Burton, *Monastic and Religious Orders in Britain,* 63ff. I can see no justification for Millett's warning against such an assumption ("*Ancrene Wisse* and the Life of Perfection," *Leeds Studies in English* 33 [2002]: 54, 57–58).

6. It is true that multiple *AW* manuscripts with, at times, variant readings makes it impossible to talk of one authentic text. Still, I think we are justified to infer a central message, which I find more productive than focusing on marginal issues, which seems to be the current scholarly tendency.

7. E.g. "Inebriabuntur ab ubertate domus tuae" (Ps 36:8); "Comedite, amici, et bibite; Et inebriamini, carissimi" (Sg 5:1); on Bernard's theme of mystical drunkenness cf. Ruh, *Geschichte,* 1:262.

8. Cf. Robertson, "Savoring 'Scientia,'" in Wada, *Companion,* 129. On prayers of the hours see Millett, "*Ancrene Wisse* and the Book of Hours," in Renevey and Whitehead, *Writing Religious Women,* 21–40; see also Scott-Stokes, *Women's Books of Hours.* On liturgical "performance" see esp. Largier, *Die Kunst des Begehrens,* 51.

9. Gleba, *Klosterleben,* 22.

10. E.g. Gunn, *"Ancrene Wisse,"* 52; also vol. 2 (commentary) of *Ancrene Wisse: A Corrected Edition,* ed Millett; for recent essays, see further McAvoy, *Rhetoric and the Anchorhold.*

11. See D. Lomax, "Englische Pilger nach Santiago," and S. Moralejo, "Der Heilige Jakobus und die Wege seiner Ikonographie," both in Caucci von Saucken, *Santiago.* Recent theological research admits the possibility that the brother of Jesus was the author of the Letter of James: *Das Neue Testament,* ed. Berger and Nord, 73.

12. *Das Neue Testament,* ed. Berger and Nord, 73.

13. Gerd Theissen, "Nächstenliebe und Egalität. Jak 2,1–13 als Höhepunkt urchristlicher Ethik," in Gemünden, Konradt, and Theissen, *Der Jakobusbrief,* 135.

14. Human dignity is an important theme in the Middle Ages; see, e.g., William of St. Thierry, *De natura et dignitate amoris,* and *St. Trudperter Hohelied,* ed. Ohly, 416, n. 52.

15. *Das Neue Testament,* ed. and trans. Wilckens, 812.

16. Cf. von Gemünden, "Einsicht, Affekt und Verhalten," in Gemünden, Theissen, and Konradt, *Der Jakobusbrief,* 83–96.

17. *Das Neue Testament,* ed. and trans. Wilckens, 820.

18. Petra von Gemünden, "Die Wertung des Zorns im Jakobusbrief auf dem Hintergrund des antiken Kontexts und seine Einordnung," in Gemünden, Theissen, and Konradt, *Der Jakobusbrief,* 114–19.

19. Matthias Konradt, "Der Jakobusbrief als Brief des Jakobus," in Gemünden, Theissen, and Konradt, *Der Jakobusbrief,* 17.

20. Herein lies a serious misunderstanding on the part of feminist research; cf. chap. 1.

21. Cf. the commentary by Berger and Nord in their edition of William of St. Thierry, *Meditationen und Gebete,* on Meditation 8, 192.

22. *Das Neue Testament,* ed. and trans. Wilckens, 814.

23. Cf. Chenu, *L'éveil de la conscience.*

24. *St. Trudperter Hohelied,* ed. Ohly, 405.

25. This has been overlooked by Georgianna (*Solitary Self,* e.g. 75).

26. Pointed out by Largier, taking the famous hermit-saint Antony as example (*Kunst des Begehrens,* 98).

27. Cf. chap. 1, above.

28. *AW* 174. Although Shepherd (ed., *Ancrene Wisse,* xxiii) recognized that the spiritual interests of the *AW* author point toward the twelfth rather than the thirteenth century, and was not unduly impressed by an institutional decree of the Lateran Council of 1215, Dobson continued to insist on a later date without further justification in "The Date and Composition of *Ancrene Wisse,*" as did T. P. Dolan, "The Date of *Ancrene Wisse:* A Corroborative Note," *Notes and Queries* 219 (1974): 322–23. For a different view see Millett, "*Ancrene Wisse* and the Conditions of Confession" *ES* 80 (1999): 193–215.

29. For the New Testament topos of shared rule, see Angenendt, *Geschichte der Religiosität,* 725. Mechthild of Magdeburg is one of the female mystics who proffered a "self-assured gesture as judge" (*Mechthhild von Magdeburg,* ed. Vollmann-Profe, 761).

30. Theissen, "Ethos und Gemeinde im Jakobusbrief: Überlegungen zu seinem 'Sitz im Leben,'" in Gemünden, Theissen, and Konradt, *Der Jakobusbrief,* 163.

31. Theissen, "Nächstenliebe," ibid., 120.

32. This has been overlooked, e.g., by Nicholas Perkins in "Reading the Bible in *Sawles Warde* and *Ancrene Wisse,*" *MAE* 72 (2003): 207–37; see also the "classical" study by Beryl Smalley, *The Study of the Bible in the Middle Ages* (Oxford: Blackwell, 1952).

33. *Origen: Spirit and Fire,* ed. von Balthasar, 93.

34. Ibid., 95.

35. A Lollard redaction of *AW* (ed. J. Påhlsson [Lund, 1911; new ed. with notes, 1918]) accords the Letter of James equal value with the Gospels; see E. Colledge, "*The Recluse:* A Lollard Interpolated Version of the *Ancren Riwle*," *RES* 15 (1939): 12.

36. Of fundamental importance is F. Ohly's *Hohelied-Studien;* it is especially from this work that we know the high point reached by twelfth-century exegesis of the Song of Songs. Cf. also Matter, *Voice of My Beloved;* Astell, *Song of Songs in the Middle Ages;* and Turner, *Eros and Allegory.*

37. *Ancrene Wisse: A Corrected Edition,* ed. Millett, 2:xxix.

38. See P. Schindele, "Rectitudo und Puritas," in Kasper and Schreiner, *Zisterziensische Spiritualität,* 53–72.

39. *Sancti Bernardi opera* 1:153–62; see *St. Trudperter Hohelied,* ed. Ohly, 465; for a very good outline of this discussion prior to Bernard, see Ohly, ibid., 628–30.

40. Ruh, *Geschichte,* 1:229, 260.

41. Meyer, *Katharinenthaler Schwesternbuch,* 319; see also Langer, *Christliche Mystik,* 168–71.

42. "Throughout part VII love is thought of as a humble, creaturely communion with God, the outcome of the fulfilment of duty and obligations... [the author] does not exalt the life of pure contemplation" (*AW,* ed. Shepherd, lvii–lviii).

43. *St. Trudperter Hohelied,* ed. Ohly, 745; cf. Berger's and Nord's commentary in *Meditationen und Gebete,* 151–52.

44. Cf. *Ancrene Wisse,* ed. Shepherd, 23/4–8, and Shepherd's note, p. 59. Metaphors of the wounds are common, especially following the *Stimulus amoris* of James of Milan. The allegorization of Song of Songs 2:14 with reference to the wounds of Christ occurs as early as Gregory the Great, *In cantica* (*PL* 79, col. 499). Savage and Watson observe: "The motif recurs in Part VII... and again in *Wooing*" (*Anchoritic Spirituality,* 385). Interestingly, the wound motif is formulated with greater intensity in *AW* than in *Wohunge,* where the wound to Christ's side simply renders visible the "love letters," also mentioned in *AW.*

45. Kristen McQuinn: "'Crepe into That Blessed Syde': Enclosure Imagery in Aelred of Rievaulx's *De institutione inclusarum*," in McAvoy and Hughes-Edwards, *Anchorites, Wombs, and Tombs,* 95.

46. *Origen: Spirit and Fire,* ed. von Balthasar, 130; Berger and Nord in *Meditationen und Gebete,* 150–52.

47. Augustine talks of the formation of the church's sacraments from the blood and water of Christ's major wound (*Sermon* on John 19:34, *PL* 38, col. 1087).

48. *Ancrene Wisse: A Corrected Edition,* ed. Millett, 2:xliv.

49. *Anchoritic Spirituality,* ed. Savage and Watson, 16.

50. See *Origen: Spirit and Fire,* ed. von Balthasar, 249–54; see also K. Rahner, "Die Lehre von den 'geistlichen Sinnen' im Mittelalter, 137–72. On sense experiences see the essay by Price, "'Inner' and 'Outer,'" 193–208.

51. Angenendt, *Geschichte der Religiosität,* 258. On the subject of love, both bodily-erotic and spiritual-theological, as harmony between body and soul, see *St. Trudperter Hohelied,* ed. Ohly, 452; he mentions Bernard's view of the human being as an outstanding creation, bodily and in other ways (453, 491).

52. Fire takes away the rust of sin, but this does not refer to the stage of *purgatio;* see Ruh, *Geschichte,* 1:269.

53. *Origen: Spirit and Fire,* ed. von Balthasar, 325–30.

54. God speaks of himself as a devouring fire (Dt 4:24). For a fascinating description of God as fire and of mystic fire, see *The Homilies of Saint Gregory the Great,* Homily 8, 89ff. Fire issues forth from JHWH; to Moses he appears as fire in the burning bush, burning and not burning (*Wilhelm von Saint-Thierry. Meditationen und Gebete,* Meditation 4:15, 118–19; not contained in the edition of Sister Penelope). On fire as metaphor see also *St. Trudperter Hohelied,* ed. Ohly, 400.

55. J. R. Partington, *A History of Greek Fire and Gunpowder* (Baltimore: Johns Hopkins University Press, 1999), esp. 21–22. I. Bishop has shown that the *AW* author's use of Greek fire goes beyond what he found in his sources: see "'Greek Fire' in *Ancrene Wisse* and Contemporary Texts," *Notes and Queries* 224 (1979): 170–99. See also R. Hasenfratz, ed., *Ancrene Wisse,* 473–74, 223n.

56. Ruh, *Geschichte,* 1:231.

57. In Bernard's 83rd sermon on the Song of Songs, *Sancti Bernardi opera,* 2:302.

58. See Ruh, *Geschichte,* 1:307 (*De natura et dignitate amoris,* chap. 16ff.).

59. *St. Trudperter Hohelied,* ed. Ohly, 1171–72, 582.

60. E.g., "The anchoritic life is presented as essentially penitential, rewarded by union with God in the next world rather than this" (Millett, "The *Ancrene Wisse* Group," in Edwards, *Companion to Middle English Prose,* 2).

61. Gunn, *"Ancrene Wisse,"* 208.

62. See esp. Millett, "Women in No Man's Land," 86–103, esp. 93ff.; Gunn, *"Ancrene Wisse,"* 6; see also the earlier but still important study by Herbert Grundmann, "Litteratus-illitteratus: Der Wandel einer Bildungsnorm vom Altertum zum Mittelalter," *Archiv für Kulturgeschichte* 40 (1958): 1–65; more recently, esp. Robertson, "Savoring 'Scientia,'" in Wada, *Companion,* 126; also, Roy, "'Sharpen Your Mind with the Whetstone of Books,'" in Smith and Taylor, *Women, the Book and the Godly,* 113–22.

63. The three sisters, too, understand the gist of the Latin texts of the liturgy, which are sometimes quoted amply and without translation. Quotations from the Vulgate are translated, as was common practice at the time, but not always in their entirety, and at the end not at all, where one Latin sentence is used to explain another. The pressing question arises: Would their spiritual guide have to deny them their wish to preach if they had nothing to say? (*Ancrene Wisse: A Corrected Edition,* ed. Millett, 1:29.368). Relevant to this wish, incidentally, is the reevaluation of the sermon in the late twelfth and early thirteenth centuries.

64. See Riehle, *Middle English Mystics,* 33.

65. I have to withdraw my own earlier assertion (*Middle English Mystics,* 20).

66. Dobson already pursued this line of thought.

67. Dobson, *Origins,* 146.

68. Ibid., 142ff.; one characteristic text is Hugh of St. Victor's *De laude caritatis.* Bernard was in touch with William of Champeaux, founder of St. Victor, and a friend of Hugh of St. Victor (Dinzelbacher, *Bernhard von Clairvaux,* 33 and 189).

69. E.g., Dobson, *Origins,* 34ff., 38–39.

70. Ibid., 53 and 46. Derek Brewer was the first to point out the Augustinian connection and postulated a link with Wigmore (*Notes and Queries* n.s. 3 [1956]: 233); as Millett put it, "The relative austerity of his teaching and his debt to Bernard and his followers might suggest that he belonged to one of the independent Augustinian congregations, perhaps the Victorines" (Millett, *Hali Meiþhad,* xvii).

As previously mentioned, the most recent attempts (by Millett above all) to trace Dominican provenance for *AW* are not convincing. The development of a Dominican *cura monialium* made very slow progress; in 1259 a rule for female Dominicans was produced (see P. Marx, "Die Zeit der Orden: Einführung in die Ausstellung," in *Krone und Schleier*, 343). Women initially turned in larger numbers to the Cistercians, who, however, were unwelcoming because they did not feel able to respond to the need; the Dominicans, too, remained unresponsive (see K. Schreiner, "Seelsorge in Frauenklöstern—Sakramentale Dienste, geistliche Erbauung, ethische Disziplinierung," in *Krone und Schleier*, 56). I see no justification for Wada's belief that *AW*'s preaching style can be characterized as Dominican ("What Is *Ancrene Wisse*?" in Wada, *Companion*, 19). The theme of the Passion is not taken up so early by the Dominicans, nor can the recommendation to devote more time to *lectio* than to prayer be labeled simply as Dominican (Wada, *Companion*, 23), for it ultimately goes back to Jesus's words ("When you are praying, do not heap up empty phrases as the Gentiles do," Mt 6:7). Unfortunately, Wada does not find a satisfactory answer to her question, "What is *Ancrene Wisse*?"

71. On the Augustinian initiative, see Klaus Schreiner, "Ein Herz und eine Seele: Eine urchristliche Lebensform und ihre Institutionalisierung im augustinisch geprägten Mönchtum des hohen und späten Mittelalters," in Melville and Müller, *Regula sancti Augustini*, 1–48.

72. Herbers, *Jakobsweg*, 190.

73. Doerr, *Das Institut der Inclusen*, 101, 49; further, Gabriela Signori, "Anchorites in German-Speaking Regions," in McAvoy, *Anchoritic Traditions*, 43–61.

74. Theodosia Gray, *The Homilies of Saint Gregory the Great on the Book of the Prophet Ezekiel in English Translation*, ed. P. J. Cownie (Etna, CA: Center for Traditionalist Orthodox Studies, 1990), Homily 4, 40ff. (esp. 1.2.4).

75. See McGinn, *Presence of God*, vol. 1, *Foundations*, 115–16, for the combination of this ascent with Christocentrism. For the spiritual significance of the color green in *Sir Gawain and the Green Knight*, see McNamer's discussion in "Feeling," in Strohm, *Middle English*, 251–56.

76. *Origen: Spirit and Fire*, ed. von Balthasar, 91. For Origen's "threefold mode of understanding in the holy scripture" as historical—moral—mystical, see ibid., 103. Millett traces such metaphors of the bird in flight, symbolizing a cross, to Tertullian's *De oratione* (*Ancrene Wisse: A Corrected Edition*, ed. Millett, 2:111).

77. *Ancrene Wisse: A Corrected Edition*, ed. Millett, 2:xxxvi.

78. Millett asserts that no traces of the Benedictine Rule are to be found in *AW* (ibid., xxxiv).

79. See Dinzelbacher, *Bernhard von Clairvaux*, 116.

80. On this further, see Innes-Parker, "The Legacy of *Ancrene Wisse*," in Wade, *Companion*, 156–57.

81. H. E. Allen thought *AW* might have been written for the three sisters to whom the hermitage of Kilburn was granted around 1130 by the abbot and court of Westminster ("On the Origin of the *Ancrene Riwle*," *PMLA* 33 [1918]: 474–546); however, such an early date is implausible.

82. See *Ancrene Wisse*, ed. Shepherd, xxv–xxx.

83. See esp. Dobson, "Date and Composition of *Ancrene Wisse*."

84. Gunn, *"Ancrene Wisse,"* 19.

85. Ruh, *Geschichte,* 2:63.

86. *St. Trudperter Hohelied,* ed. Ohly, 328.

87. Ibid., 932 (notes; text: 160–61). Shepherd observed that the abbot Gottfried of Admont, "an effective and eclectic monastic preacher" in the years 1137 to 1165, interpreted and etymologized the three Marys in just the same way as *AW* (ed., *Ancrene Wisse,* 46–47); Gottfried's *Homiliae dominicales* may be found in *PL* 174 (21, col. 386–632); see U. Faust, "Gottfried von Admont: Ein monastischer Autor des 12. Jahrhunderts," *Studien und Mitteilungen zur Geschichte des Benediktinerordens und seiner Zweige* 75 (1964): 271–358.

88. Ruh, *Geschichte,* 2:62.

89. *Origen: Spirit and Fire,* ed. von Balthasar, 243; cf. also William of St. Thierry's "amor ipse intellectus est" (*St. Trudperter Hohelied,* ed. Ohly, 69).

90. Gunn correctly sees this connection, *"Ancrene Wisse,"* 171.

91. *St. Trudperter Hohelied,* ed. Ohly, 565.

92. The Katherine Group challenges the reader intellectually, with elegant prose style and sophisticated alliterating and rhythmical structure. See Millett, "Audience of the Saints' Lives," 128.

93. References to the *Wohunge* in *AW* include, e.g., *Ancrene Wisse: A Corrected Edition,* ed. Millett, 1:147. 95–96.

94. "Lo þus ure Lauerd woheþ" (*Ancrene Wisse: A Corrected Edition,* ed. Millett, 1:150.225; for the same motif, see *St. Trudperter Hohelied,* ed. Ohly, 434.

95. Cecily Clark, "Early Middle English Prose: Three Essays in Stylistics," *EIC* 18 (1968): 361–82, 364.

96. Ibid., 373 and 374. See also Millett, "Audience of the Saints' Lives," 138. Millett agrees that all of these texts belong together.

4. "Female" versus "Male" Spirituality?

1. *Love Rune* is a poem of 210 lines. The single surviving copy is found in an early Franciscan miscellany: Oxford, Jesus College MS 29, Part 2, fols. 187a–188b. Ca. 1270. For an edition, see Susanna Greer Fein, ed., *Moral Love Songs and Laments,* TEAMS Middle English Texts Series (Kalamazoo, MI: Medieval Institute Publications, 1998); for a recent more detailed interpretation see Denis Renevey, "1215–1349: Texts," in Fanous and Gillespie, *Cambridge Companion to Medieval English Mysticism,* 99–103, esp. 100.

2. "Incipit quidam cantus quem composuit frater Thomas de Hales de ordine fratrum Minorum ad instanciam cuiusdam puelle Deo dicate."

3. See, for instance, John V. Fleming, "The Friars and Medieval English Literature," in Wallace, *Cambridge History of Medieval English Literature,* 362–65; Douglas Gray, "Medieval English Mystical Lyrics," in Pollard and Boenig, *Mysticism and Spirituality in Medieval England,* 203–18; more recently, Gillespie, "Moral and Penitential Lyrics," in Duncan, *Companion to the Middle English Lyric,* 79–80.

4. See the online exhibition "The Vernon Manuscript: A Literary Hoard from Medieval England": http://www.bodleian.ox.ac.uk/about/exhibitions/online/vernon. See also Norman F. Blake, "Vernon Manuscript: Contents and Organization," in Pearsall, *Studies in the Vernon Manuscript,* 58.

5. *Talkyng*, ed. Westra, xxxi. This edition is a considerable improvement on the first edition by Horstmann (*Yorkshire Writers*, 2:345–66) but is still flawed. A copy of *Talking* is also included (though in fragmentary form) in the Simeon MS.

6. *Talkyng*, ed. Westra, xvi. Westra is confident about the date because of the "many late French words" it contains, but this is not totally convincing, because the words could well have been introduced by the scribe of the Vernon MS, who undertook some modifications of the texts.

7. M. Konrath describes the style of *Talking* as *pastiche*, "Eine übersehene Fassung der *Ureisen of Oure Louerde* und der *Wohunge of Ure Lauerd*." *Anglia* 41 (1918): 85–98.

8. The sources were discovered independently (as has been shown) by H. E. Allen and Konradt (see *Talkyng*, xvii).

9. *Talkyng*, ed. Westra, 10.13–26.13. Subsequent page and line references to *Talkyng* are given in parentheses in the text.

10. Denis Renevey reduces the noteworthiness of the text too much to its compilation technique ("Choices of the Compiler," 232–53).

11. I found a similar use of it by Elsbeth Hainburg of Villingen (Riehle, *Middle English Mystics*, 71 n. 41).

12. In Aelred's *Institutio inclusarum* and in *Þe Wohunge of Ure Lauerd*, sexual analogies were avoided when (Song of Songs) metaphors were used, nor was there any talk of *unio passionalis*. M. M. Sauer argues from a late twentieth-century feminist standpoint ("Cross-Dressing Souls: Same-Sex Desire and the Mystic Tradition in *A Talkyng of the Loue of God*," in Chewning, *Intersections of Sexuality and the Divine in Medieval Culture*, 157–81).

13. *Talkyng*, ed. Westra, xxii.

14. Ibid., 69.

15. It was customary for medieval writers to begin with a prefatory section in which they give a brief summary of what is to come. A number of standard themes would be covered, including *materia* (topics), *intentio* (goal or intention), and *modus tractandi* (mode of treatment). In the Benedictine tradition, *lectio divina* (divine reading) refers to the practice of scriptural reading, which leads one to prayer (*oratio*) and meditation (*meditatio*).

16. The seminal work on punctuation is M. B. Parkes, *Pause and Effect: An Introduction to the History of Punctuation in the West* (Berkeley: University of California Press, 1993).

17. Here I follow Morgan's argument in "Treatise in Cadence," 156–64.

18. M. M. Morgan, "*A Talkyng of the Love of God* and the Continuity of Stylistic Tradition in Middle English Prose Meditations," *RES* n.s. 3 (1952): 97–116; and Morgan, "Treatise in Cadence"; see also L. K. Smedick, "Cursus in Middle English: *A Talkyng of the Loue of God* Reconsidered," *MS* 37 (1975): 387–406; F. Quadlbauer, in *Lexikon des Mittelalters* (Stuttgart: Metzler, 1999), III, col. 389–93 s.v. "cursus."

19. Smedick, "Cursus in Middle English," 406.

20. Morgan, "Treatise in Cadence," 164. Sargent's attribution of the particular form of this work to Isidorian style is not convincing ("What Kind of Writing Is *A Talkyng of þe Love of God*?" in *The Milieu and Context of the Wooing Group*, ed. Susannah M. Chewning [Cardiff: University of Wales Press, 2010], 183–93).

21. This is assumed by Westra in *Talkyng,* xxxi, and by Innes-Parker, "Legacy of *Ancrene Wisse,*" 157.

22. Both surviving sources for *Talking,* the Vernon MS and the Simeon MS, are associated with female readership.

23. "From the tenth century until the sixteenth, marriage was a two-part ceremony. The legally binding pledge took place at the church door... and was followed by a nuptial Mass in the church" (*The Riverside Chaucer,* General Prologue 460 and p. 818n.); Christopher Brooke, *The Medieval Idea of Marriage* (Oxford: Oxford University Press, 1989); David D'Avray, *Medieval Marriage: Symbolism and Society* (Oxford: Oxford University Press, 2005).

24. Ruh, *Geschichte,* 2:299.

25. Head, "The Marriages of Christina of Markyate," in Fanous and Leyser, *Christina of Markyate,* 120.

26. *Mechthild von Magdeburg,* ed. Vollmann-Profe, 326 and 765; also, for instance, Gertrud of Helfta: "love... has, as it were, ... —if I may dare to speak thus— inebriated you even to madness in that you should join yourself with one so unlike you." *Herald of Divine Love,* II, 106.

27. *Talkyng,* ed. Westra, quoting Horstmann, who speaks of "imitation of Rolle's manner" (xxvi).

28. *Meditation B,* in *Richard Rolle,* ed. Ogilvie-Thomson, 82, 543.

29. Renevey's contention that this reflects an Anselmian piety is too imprecise ("Choices of the Compiler").

30. See also Innes-Parker: *"Talkyng*... incorporates the figure of the Lover-Knight into a passion sequence. The text thus serves as a link between the more conservative *Ancrene Wisse* and the fully developed affective mysticism of the fourteenth-century mystics" ("Legacy of *Ancrene Wisse,*" 157); yet, as has been shown, there is no reason to regard *AW* as more "conservative," and therefore more reserved.

31. See, above all, Farmer, "Meditations of the Monk of Farne," 142–245 (page citations in text are from this source).

32. Catto, "1349–1412: Culture and History," in Fanous and Gillespie, *Cambridge Companion to Medieval English Mysticism,* 122.

33. Pantin, "Monk-Solitary of Farne, 162; cf. also Pantin's *English Church in the Fourteenth Century,* 245–46. The manuscript dates from the middle of the fourteenth century (Pantin, "Monk-Solitary," 163).

34. So also *Meditations of a Fourteenth Century Monk,* ed. Farmer, 147–48 and frequently in the text.

35. "Your great love for God and continual contemplation of him eventually took such possession of your heart, that you fled the companionship of other men, and rejoicing to be deprived of human intercourse, went to Farne, and remained there for nine years alone." *Meditations of a Fourteenth Century Monk,* ed. Farmer, 153–54.

36. Ibid., 149; Farmer, "Meditations," 234.

37. According to Pantin ("Monk-Solitary," 175), Wilmart is inclined to ascribe it to a student of Bernard.

38. *Meditations of a Fourteenth Century Monk,* ed. Farmer, 47; Farmer, "Meditations," 170.

39. *Meditations of a Fourteenth Century Monk,* ed. Farmer, 64; Farmer, "Meditations," 182.

40. "It remains for us to seek another interpretation of this sign, for fear we too might gain no profit from it. Allegorically... I might take Christ's outstretched arms and hands to stand for the law and the prophets" (*Meditations of a Fourteenth Century Monk,* ed. Farmer, 66).

41. Ibid., 76; Farmer, "Meditations," 191.

42. *Meditations of a Fourteenth Century Monk,* ed. Farmer, 85; Farmer, "Meditations," 198.

43. Unlike Nicholas Watson, I do not regard it as any kind of shortcoming that the monk of Farne was allegedly unaware "of how affective theology was developing elsewhere in Europe" (Watson, "Melting into God the English Way," 45).

5. Richard Rolle of Hampole

1. Allen, *Writings,* 442–43.

2. See E. J. F. Arnould, "On Richard Rolle's Patrons: A New Reading," *MAE* 6 (1937): 122–24; also Hughes, *Pastors and Visionaries;* still useful for Rolle's biography is Comper, *Life of Richard Rolle.*

3. However, the "parallels" to the conversion of St. Francis of Assisi are less clear than Watson maintains (*Richard Rolle and the Invention of Authority* [hereafter *Invention*], 40–41).

4. Comper concludes from her investigations, e.g., of the 1375 library catalog of Oriel College, "Very little pains [*sic*] seems to have been taken to acquire any real mastery of Latin" (*Life of Richard Rolle,* 34ff.).

5. This is evident from the English Psalter and from *Melos amoris.* However, Comper found "no Greek work" (ibid., 36) and "no Greek fathers" (37) in the Oriel College library catalog.

6. M. Noetinger first sought to justify this assumption ("The biography of Richard Rolle," *Month* 147 [1926]: 22–30); also Allen, *Writings,* 490–500.

7. There is no reason to dismiss out of hand the statement regarding Rolle, "Vixit in Sorbona in 1326," found in a manuscript of the Bibliothèque de l'Arsenal, Paris, even if it dates from the seventeenth century. It is not possible here to reopen the question of how this record came to be made, but it is indisputable that Rolle's name strikingly occurs here in the context of the Sorbonne, and the evidence needs to be taken seriously (Riehle, *Middle English Mystics,* 7 and 171 n. 31). Arnould's attempt to dismiss it as meaningless is not convincing (Arnould, "Richard Rolle and the Sorbonne," *Bulletin of the John Rylands Library* 21 [1937]: 55–58; also in *Melos amoris,* ed. Arnould, 210–38; nor can Sargent, who supports Arnould's attempt, disprove the evidence, or do more than put forward his own opinion ("Richard Rolle, Sorbonnard?" *MAE* 57 [1988]: 284–90).

8. "Rolle's works do not display any remarkable erudition" (Sargent, "Richard Rolle, Sorbonnard?" 289).

9. *Psalter or Psalms of David,* ed. Bramley, 432.

10. *Incendium amoris,* ed. Deanesly, 240; in *MA,* scholastic terms such as *sophismata* (59) and *cathegorizare* (144) occur.

11. Ruh, *Geschichte,* 3:268.

12. Ibid., 269.

13. Ibid., 345.

14. *Incendium amoris*, ed. Deanesly, 161.

15. "pro uanitate" (ibid., 160).

16. Later he will use his commentary on Jeremiah's *Lamentationes* as springboard for a commentary on his own times, in which "doctores ecclesiae" pervert their office to such an extent that they become incapable of any spiritual *cura* (*D. Richardi pampolitani eremitae in threnos, sive lamentationes Ieremiae, compendiosa iuxta ac erudita enarratio* [Cologne, 1536], fol. 127).

17. *Melos amoris*, ed Arnould, 19; this criticism occurs also in *Incendium amoris*, 173.

18. "*Officium et miracula*," ed. Woolley, 23; the early commentary on the Song of Songs, *Super canticum canticorum*, warns that the end of the world is nigh (*Comment on the Canticles*, ed. Murray, 73).

19. Allen, *Writings*, 459.

20. The details of the circumstances leading to the break with his benefactor will remain forever obscure. Allen surmised that Dalton was angered by Rolle's condemnation of the wealth Dalton had amassed, and she thought that Dalton's interest in Rolle decreased when the latter withdrew entirely into contemplation; Dalton had intended to bind him to himself as preacher (*Writings*, 459, 463).

21. Ibid., 129.

22. *Comment on the Canticles*, ed. Murray, 48; Allen, *Writings*, 466–70.

23. "in principio conversionis meae," in *Comment on the Canticles*, ed. Murray, 48 (mentioned also in "*Officium et miracula*," ed. Woolley, 36).

24. See Volker Mertens, *Der Gral: Mythos und Literatur* (Stuttgart: Reclam, 2003), 113ff.

25. S. de Ford, for instance, speaks of "the beauty of women in general" as a great temptation for Rolle ("Mystical Union," 177).

26. "*Expositio*," ed. Moyes, 2:241.1–18.

27. *Melos amoris*, ed. Arnould, 113.10.

28. *Incendium amoris*, ed. Deanesly, 266.

29. *Melos amoris*, ed. Arnould, 76.

30. *The Letters of Abelard and Heloise*, trans. B. Radice (Harmondsworth, UK: Penguin, 1974), 99.

31. Toward the end of the fourteenth century the author of *The Cloud of Unknowing* still felt a need to warn against self-castration as being unhelpful (chap. 12).

32. *Emendatio vitae*, ed. Watson, 7.

33. "Letatur enim heremus a pauperibus Christi visitari" (*Judica me*, ed. Daly, 15); see also Küsters, *Der verschlossene Garten*, 136.

34. Ogilvie-Thomson also mentioned this possibility in her edition, *Rolle: Prose and Verse*, lxvii.

35. Glasscoe, *English Medieval Mystics*, 68–69.

36. He is presumably referring to this in his *Expositio* when he cites *Libellus de vita heremitarum* (2:196); see Watson, *Invention*, 44. On the authorship of the *Regula heremitarum* see ibid., 305, n. 21. The text of this *Regula* was edited by L. Oliger, "Regulae tres reclusorum et eremitarum Angliae saec. XIII–XIV," *Antonianum* 3 (1928): 151–90 and 299–320; see also Watson, "Richard Rolle as Elitist and Populist," 128.

37. Walter Hübner, "The Desert of Religion," *Archiv für das Studium der Neueren Sprachen und Literaturen* 126 (1911): 58–74 and 360–64, and the addendum by Allen, *Archiv für das Studium der Neueren Sprachen und Literaturen* 127 (1911): 388–90; further, James Hogg, *An Illustrated Yorkshire Carthusian Miscellany: British Library London, Additional MS 37049*, vol. 3, *The Illustrations*, AC 95.3 (Salzburg: Institut für Anglistik und Amerikanistik, 1981); and esp. Brantley, *Reading in the Wilderness*, 138–42.

38. Ruh's view is that the *Collationes* and the *Vitae patrum* that build upon them "proclaim the anchoritic and cenobitic ideal of the Egyptian desert fathers"; they helped to shape "spiritual life leading to mysticism, or including it, up to the High and Late Middle Ages" (Ruh, *Geschichte*, 1:119). Ruh also points out that Meister Eckhart had a low opinion of the hermits; for him, everything depended on the "inner desert of solitude" (ibid., 3:264).

39. Ibid., 451.

40. Watson, *Invention*, 42 (e.g., in the case of Christina of Markyate, Wulfric of Haselbury, and Robert of Knaresborough).

41. *Comment on the Canticles*, ed. Murray, 25–29; and *Melos amoris*, ed. Arnould, 147.

42. Quoted from Allen, *Writings*, 317; likewise, *Ancrene Wisse* talks of Jesus as prior.

43. Allen, *Writings*, 327; Rolle affirms that God must be obeyed rather than man (*Comment on the Canticles*, ed. Murray, 27).

44. See Küsters, *Der verschlossene Garten*, 108.

45. *Benedict's Rule*, ed. Kardong, 40; this is also pointed out by Watson, who rightly speaks of a "long tradition of satire against wandering hermits" (*Invention*, 45).

46. In her monograph Allen attempted at great length to throw light on a feud between Rolle and the Cistercian monks of Rievaulx or Byland (*Writings*, esp. 478–88). She argues that the spiritual fire of the founding age of the Cistercian order had long vanished, the monks had to contend with problems of hard reality, and they therefore harbored feelings of envy toward Richard, who put into practice that very spirituality to which they themselves should have been committed, according to the founder of their order. But does this exclude the possibility that Rolle wrote especially for the Cistercian monks, in order to elevate them to a higher spiritual level?

47. Watson, *Invention*, 43.

48. See Alford, "Biblical *Imitatio*," 10; also Watson, *Invention*, 39; Watson even considers, not without reason, that Rolle saw himself "as a latter-day martyr" (*Invention*, 51).

49. "nondum in publico predicando cogor dicere," *Judica me*, ed. Daly, 18. This may also mean that Rolle preferred writing to oral preaching (as also in *Judica me*, 117). Allen is of the opinion that he did not yet have a license to preach (*Writings*, 108): "proprie non possum predicare" (*Melos amoris*, ed. Arnould, 142). Watson believes that "he awaits an inner compulsion to preach" (*Invention*, 309). This interpretation, however, is at odds with Rolle's understanding of preaching; not long after his flight from Oxford he had already preached spontaneously at the vigil of the feast of the Assumption.

50. In the Middle Ages it was not unusual for sermon and tract to overlap (see Spencer, *English Preaching*, 34); this is clearly reflected in Rolle's texts.

51. In his *Expositio super novem lectiones*, he says of himself "predico" (ed. Moyes, 2:196).

52. Thus Rolle's preaching voice is a counterpart to the central significance that the sermon gained in German Dominican mysticism. Ruh points out that Western mysticism in its heyday attains its specific actuality through the sermon (*Geschichte*, 1:250), a statement that applies especially to Rhenish mysticism.

53. *Incendium amoris*, ed. Deanesly, 188; also quoted in the *Officium et miracula*.

54. Allen, *Writings*, 109.

55. *Regula Solitariorum, PL* 103, cols. 600–601.

56. "scientia Scripturarum valde solitario necessaria est," ibid., col. 599. There was also another rule by Peter Damian, *De institutis eremitarum, PL* 145, 335–64.

57. This is also pointed out by Alford, "Biblical *Imitatio*," 1ff.; and Watson, *Invention*, e.g. 123.

58. For Augustine's mastery of this technique, see especially his *De doctrina christiana*, e.g. IX:14.31 (*De doctrina christiana*, ed. Green, 70).

59. Bonaventura, *Breviloquium*. Christliche Meister 52 (Einsiedeln-Freiburg: Johannes Verlag, 2002), 36–39.

60. E.g., The *Glossa ordinaria*, Hugh of Strasbourg's *Compendium theologicae veritatis*, Peter Lombard's Catena on the Psalms. In the *Officium et miracula* it is said: "Desiderauit plenius et profundius imbui theologicis sacre scripture doctrinis quam phisicis aut secularis sciencie disciplinis" (23), also cited by Watson.

61. Allen, *Writings*, 149.

62. *Melos amoris*, ed. Arnould, 54. To assign Rolle's legitimation and self-understanding as author entirely to his mystical experience, as Watson does in his book, is therefore unsatisfactory. Of course Rolle is also aware that he must reckon with a certain amount of envy from those who are not willing to concede that he, as a mere beginner ("modernus," "*Expositio*," ed. Moyes, 2:195), can interpret holy scripture aptly ("congruenter").

63. Langer, *Christliche Mystik*, 178.

64. Ibid.

65. Ibid., 182; cf. also J. van Engen, *Rupert of Deutz* (Berkeley: University of California Press, 1983).

66. "*Expositio*," ed. Moyes, 1:18; cf. Thomas Aquinas, "Theologia quae sacra Scriptura dicitur," *Commentary on "De Trinitate" of Boethius*, quaestio 5 articulus 4; quoted from Bauer, *Claustrum Animae*, 32.

67. "Quid arguis, o impie, quem approbat Auctor?" (*Melos amoris*, ed. Arnould, 117.24).

68. Ibid., 54.

69. Bynum, "Formen weiblicher Frömmigkeit im späten Mittelalter," *Krone und Schleier*, 121.

70. For fundamentals of the medieval understanding of authorship, see Alastair Minnis, *Medieval Theory of Authorship: Scholastic Literary Attitudes in the Later Middle Ages* (London: Scolar Press, 1984).

71. See Grundmann, *Religiöse Bewegungen*, 79ff.

72. E.g., in chap. 5, *Contra amatores mundi*, ed. Theiner.

73. Cf. K. Stierle, *Francesco Petrarca: Ein Intellektueller im Europa des 14. Jahrhunderts* (Munich: Hanser, 2003).

74. See J. Hamburger, "Medieval Self-Fashioning: Authorship, Authority, and Autobiography in Seuse's *Exemplar*," in *Christ among the Medieval Dominicans*, ed.

K. Emery Jr. and J. P. Wawrykow (Notre Dame, IN: University of Notre Dame Press, 1998); Riehle, *Middle English Mystics*, 32.

75. See, for instance, Kurt Flasch, *Meister Eckhart: Die Geburt der 'Deutschen Mystik' aus dem Geist der arabischen Philosophie* (Munich: C. H. Beck, 2006), 16–19.

76. Very useful is Renevey's "Richard Rolle," in Dyas, Edden, and Ellis, *Approaching Medieval English Anchoritic and Mystical Texts*, 63–74.

77. So also Watson, *Invention*, 222. Recently, however, it has been pointed out in connection with German mysticism that no less a figure than Meister Eckhart also attained significant heights in the traditional Latin medium (Flasch, *Meister Eckhart*, 32).

78. See Denise Baker, "Active and Contemplative Lives," 85–102; also G. Constable, "The Interpretation of Mary and Martha," in *Three Studies in Medieval Religious and Social Thought* (Cambridge: Cambridge University Press, 1995), 3–141; John P. H. Clark, "Action and Contemplation in Walter Hilton," *DR* 97 (1979), 258–74; there are further useful observations in S. S. Hussey, "Walter Hilton: Traditionalist?" *MMTE* 1 (1980), 1–16.

79. Watson, *Invention*, 208–56. As Baker points out, "He... replaces his dyadic model with a triadic scheme and, it might be assumed, moves from the oppositional to the alternating or mixed model" ("Active and Contemplative Lives," 92); but it is important to remember that he still writes primarily for religious. Baker (ibid.) also puts forward contradictory arguments, conceding that, despite his respect for the active life, Rolle still upholds the opposition between *vita activa* and *vita contemplativa*.

80. *Emendatio vitae*, ed. Watson, 66, 130.

81. *Comment on the Canticles*, ed. Murray, 31; see also *Psalter or Psalms of David*, ed. Bramley, 484; cf. Hugh of St. Victor, *De institutione novitiorum*, PL 176, cols. 928–52.

82. So also in *Emendatio vitae* and *Ancrene Wisse*. Ogilvie-Thomson seems not to recognize this connection, since she talks with regard to Rolle's *Commandment* of an "odd emphasis on sitting" (*Rolle: Prose and Verse*, lxxiii).

83. E.g., *Melos amoris*, ed. Arnould, 5.20.

84. E.g., "In quibusdam fidelium plus sedet Deus," *Super apocalypsim*, in *Richard Rolle de Hampole*, ed. Marzac, 156. A good Continental example occurs in an illumination in Suso's *Büchlein der Ewigen Weisheit*; see K. Bihlmeyer, ed., *Heinrich Seuse: Deutsche Schriften* (Stuttgart: Kohlhammer, 1907), 255.

85. Watson, *Invention*, 185; Baker, "Active and Contemplative Lives," 88. Rolle greatly regrets this interruption.

86. E.g. in *"Expositio,"* ed. Moyes, 2:226. In Cassian's doctrine of contemplation and in Bonaventure's *triplex via*, prayer is also assigned to the second stage, *illuminatio* (Ruh, *Geschichte*, 1:114).

87. So also Watson, *Invention*, 65.

88. Glasscoe, *English Medieval Mystics*, 86.

89. *Emendatio vitae*, ed. Watson, 62.

90. Ibid., 63.

91. See Ruh, *Geschichte*, 1:332; "Méditation," in *DS* X, cols. 908–9; and "Contemplation" in *DS* 2/2, cols. 1937–38.

92. *Emendatio vitae*, ed. Watson, 52; see also Glasscoe, *English Medieval Mystics*, 88.

93. Also noted by Watson, *Invention*, 55.

94. Glasscoe, *English Medieval Mystics*, 88.

95. He discusses this point in great detail in *Super psalmum vicesimum,* ed. Dolan, 11, as also in *Contra amatores mundi,* ed. Theiner: "Est autem hec enigmatica visio et speculativa, non clara et perspicua," 88.194–95); "Paulus...non dixit quod vidit deum facie ad faciem, aut cives celestes, sed quod audivit archana dei....Unde audeo dicere quod nullis sanctorum conceditur in hac vita perfecta visio eterno-rum" (90.247–55).

96. *Emendatio vitae,* ed. Watson, 63. All page and line citations of *EV* are from this edition.

97. See, for instance, Comper, *Life of Richard Rolle,* 105.

98. In Aelred, too, we find two sorts of *contemplatio,* of the celestial and of God himself (see Buchmüller, *Askese der Liebe,* 304–32).

99. *Comment on the Canticles,* ed. Murray, 26.

100. On the other hand, on one occasion he concedes unabashed that he has never experienced direct vision of God ("id non expertus sum"; *Contra amatores mundi,* ed. Theiner, 90.245–46).

101. This was rightly observed by Lehmann; he quotes *Emendatio vitae:* "O bone Jesu, quis mihi det, ut sentiam te in me, qui nunc sentiri et non videri potes" (*Untersuchungen,* 10). Renevey made the same observation (*Language, Self and Love,* 115).

102. *Comment on the Canticles,* ed. Murray, 51; see also Bernard of Clairvaux, *On Loving God,* 6.16, 19; also Bernard's 79th sermon on the Song of Songs, *Sancti Bernardi opera,* 2:272–76.

103. Lehmann, *Untersuchungen,* 63.

104. Ibid., 65.

105. Ibid.; see also Jennings, "Richard Rolle," 193–200; and further Clark, "Theological Re-Assessment," and "Biblical Commentator."

106. Jennings, "Richard Rolle," 194; and *Emendatio vitae,* ed. Watson.

107. For a detailed description of the differences, see *Ego dormio* in *Rolle: Prose and Verse,* ed. Ogilvie-Thomson, 27.68–75; cf. also R. Allen, "'Singuler Lufe': Richard Rolle and the Grammar of Spiritual Ascent," in *MMTE* 3 (1984), 28–54.

108. Baker assigns it to religious ("Active and Contemplative Lives," 92).

109. From the time of Allen (*Writings,* 201–2) onward.

110. *PL* 196, 1213.

111. *De quattuor gradibus violentae caritatis, PL* 196, 1212.

112. Watson, *Invention,* 319.

113. Jennings, "Richard Rolle," 198–99.

114. E.g., 35.66–70.

115. *Contra amatores mundi,* ed. Theiner, 108.253.

116. Ibid., line 274.

117. This was entirely overlooked by Jennings; cf. also the monk of Farne, "Meditations" (1957), esp. 195–212, where he distinguishes between nine grades of love.

118. Cf. also Hugh of St. Victor's *De laude caritatis,* where we read that Caritas is so strong that she was able to draw God from heaven to earth with incomparably strong fetters (*PL* 176, col. 974); Watson also recognizes the influence of Hugh and Richard of St. Victor, and of Bernard *(Invention, e.g. 169);* further examples occur in Gregory the Great, e.g. *Hom. in Ez.,* 3.

119. E.g., *Incendium amoris,* ed. Deanesly, 210.

120. "*Expositio,*" ed. Moyes, 2:130.

121. See William Pollard, "Richard Rolle and the 'Eye of the Heart,'" in Pollard and Boenig, *Mysticism and Spirituality*, 85–106.

122. Thus in *Emendatio vitae* (ed. Watson), "Deum uere cognoscere, perfecte diligere," 68.176–177.

123. *De natura et dignitate amoris*, chap. 25.

124. See Ruh, *Geschichte*, 1:232, 254, 271.

125. *Incendium amoris*, ed. Deanesly, 254–55.

126. Its significance is unfortunately not sufficiently acknowledged by Watson (*Invention*, 55–56); see also *Emendatio vitae*, ed. Watson.

127. So also Bernard of Clairvaux; see Ruh, *Geschichte*, 1:269; also *"Officium et Miracula,"* ed. Woolley, 31.51.

128. Watson, *Invention*, 215; Watson also speaks of Rolle's "highly positive and anti-ascetic account of the contemplative life" (50).

129. Ruh, *Geschichte*, 1:166; Rolle speaks of his vision as "non...nisi raro...et non nisi raptim et momentanee" (*Comment on the Canticles*, ed. Murray, 69, 71).

130. See Watson, *Invention*, 63.

131. "hoc est contra quosdam qui breviter dicebant dulcedinem durare" (*Melos amoris*, ed. Arnould, 16.16–17).

132. As expressed in "multo spirituali exercitatus labore" (*Contra amatores mundi*, ed. Theiner, 87.157–58).

133. Knowles, *English Mystical Tradition;* Comper speaks of Rolle's "untidy mind," not in a negative sense, but in order to convey his inability to give a precise account of his mystical experience, or to differentiate between separate stages (*Life of Richard Rolle*, 85).

134. Bernard McGinn, "The English Mystics," in *Christian Spirituality*, vol. 2, *High Middle Ages and Reformation*, ed. Jill Raitt (New York: Crossroad, 1989), 197; Thomas Merton, "The English Mystics," in *Mystics and Zen Masters* (New York: Farrar, Straus and Giroux, 1967), 128–53.

135. M. Sargent describes Allen's attempt at establishing a canon as definitive and "indiscutable," but this is not entirely the case ("Richard Rolle de Hampole," *DS* 13, col. 577).

136. Wolfgang Riehle, "The Authorhsip of the *Prick of Conscience* Reconsidered," *Anglia* 111 (1993): 1–18.

137. It also happens that the Gospel reading for this feast day is Jesus's visit to Martha and Mary (Lk 10:38–42), where Jesus gives precedence to Mary in her contemplative love rather than to the busy Martha. Mystics frequently refer to this passage.

138. Astell, "Feminine *Figurae*," 121.

139. Gabriel M. Liegey, ed., "The 'Canticum Amoris' of Richard Rolle," *Traditio* 12 (1956): 369–91.

140. So also Allen, *English Writings*, xvii; see also Astell, "Feminine *Figurae*," 121. There are two editions of the poem, because the editor G. M. Liegey ("The 'Canticum amoris' of Richard Rolle," *Traditio* 12 [1956]: 369–91) was not aware of A. Wilmart's detailed commentary and edition ("'Le Cantique d'amour' de Richard Rolle," *Revue d'ascétique et de mystique* 82 [1940]: 131–48).

141. This is confirmed in his *Melos amoris*. Watson sees this as authorial "restraint" (*Invention*, 108), whereas Allen came to a diametrically opposed conclu-

sion; she misunderstood the basic character of the work and described its overall style as "crude and extravagant" (*Writings,* 90) and "offensively fantastic" (*English Writings,* xvii).

142. See K. Boklund-Lagopoulou, "*Yate of Heven:* Conceptions of the Female Body in the Religious Lyrics," in Renevey and Whitehead, *Writing Religious Women,* 133–54, esp. 139. She demonstrates how many poems to Mary use the language of courtly love but do not engage in praise of the physical beauty of the mother of God. If details are mentioned, these are usually of her eyes that look mercifully upon the faithful, and, above all, of her nurturing breasts or the womb that bore Christ, and the tears that she shed for him.

143. Watson already recognized that Rolle here applies to Mary many of the images and themes that he associates with Christ. Watson sees his purpose as praise (*Invention,* 107), but Rolle's aim is *unio* with Mary.

144. See Allen, *Writings,* 93.

145. Cf. Bernard of Clairvaux, "Plena es gratiarum, plena rore caelesti, innixa super dilectum," *Dominica infra octavam Assumptionis, Sancti Bernardi opera* 5: *Sermones* (1968), ed. Leclercq, Talbot, and Rochais, 274.

146. André Wilmart oversimplifies with his assertion that one must take the poem merely as the song of Rolle's enraptured soul ("Les idées comptent peu"); but he does give some examples of the great influence of the Song of Songs ("Le Cantique d'amour de Richard Rolle," *Revue d'ascétique et de mystique* 21 [1940]: 131–48).

147. Allen, *Writings,* 92. Astell attempts a psychological interpretation; she maintains that in the early *Canticum amoris* Rolle identified with Mary to the extent of total transformation into Mary, his feminine self, "reconciling him to his own feminine otherness. The integrated *anima* has completed and perfected his masculine self" ("Feminine *Figurae,*" 123).

148. Allen, *Writings,* 153; *Richard Rolle de Hampole,* ed. Marzac.

149. With the book of Revelation he was allowed to gaze upon the "mysteries" of God, to which the mystics return time and again; and it is worth noting that Paul already speaks of God's mysteries (e.g. 1 Cor 4:1).

150. *Richard Rolle de Hampole,* ed. Marzac, 118, and again in *Emendatio vitae,* ed. Watson, chap. 12. It is of secondary importance that Rolle also draws on the commentary of Pseudo-Anselm of Laon as source; Rolle's own "tone" is discernible in spite of the source. Watson draws on this passage for his theory of Rolle's authorial self-invention (*Invention,* 97–98).

151. Interestingly, the Revelation of John is also the model for Hildegard's visions (Ruh, *Geschichte,* 2:67).

152. See A. Weiser, *Theologie des Neuen Testaments: Die Theologie der Evangelien.* Kohlhammer Studienbücher Theologie 8 (Stuttgart: Kohlhammer, 1993), 2:214.

153. *Richard Rolle de Hampole,* ed. Marzac, 156.

154. For Paul, too, beholding the third heaven results from *raptus.* Dinzelbacher points out that, according to the charismatics' testimony, the mystical experience of union with God takes place within the soul, without images or words, while the visionary experience takes place outside the soul and can be expressed in images and words (*Vision und Visionsliteratur,* 56). Yet ultimately, and paradoxically, the visionary experience also occurs within the soul.

155. On this see the recent essay by Michael Sargent, "What Kind of Writing Is *A Talkyng of þe Love of God?*"

156. E.g., in Rolle's commentary on the Song of Songs: "cum... ad sola interna— scilicet divina—querenda, sapienda, contemplanda, celitus sublevamur," *Comment on the Canticles*, ed. Murray, 5.

157. Likewise Clark surmised: "It would seem that continuing reflection on these texts gave Rolle material with which to clothe his contemplative experience" ("Biblical Commentator," 193). Is there not a model for Rolle's warning against sensual women in the harlot Jezebel, whom he did not yet recognize as personifica- tion of Babylon? In any case, she represents for him all sensually appealing women ("omnes molles"), who arouse the "flamma libidinis" (*Super apocalypsim*, in *Richard Rolle de Hampole*, ed. Marzac, 144).

158. *Das Neue Testament*, ed. Wilckens, 919–28.

159. See Watson, *Invention*, 98.

160. *Judica me*, ed. Daly. It is not possible here to examine the rather complicated textual history of this work, which has survived in numerous manuscripts. Rolle extracts large excerpts from the *Oculus sacerdotis* by his contemporary and fellow- countryman William of Pagula, but makes his own characteristic selection of pas- sages, with the intention of compiling a composite preacher's handbook (Watson, *Invention*, 87). He creates an "independent and unusual structure" (Watson, *Invention*, 76) in four books.

161. *Judica me*, ed. Daly, liii.

162. Ibid., xi.

163. Watson, *Invention*, 277. It is interesting that Rolle especially recalls the anchorite Cuthbert, who played an important part in shaping the English eremitical tradition (*Incendium amoris*, ed. Deanesly, 181).

164. *Incendium amoris*, ed. Deanesly, 209.

165. "*Expositio*," ed. Moyes, 1:55–58.

166. Lehmann, *Untersuchungen*, 35.

167. Ibid., 39.

168. Ibid., 42.

169. Ibid., 48.

170. Ibid., 51.

171. Ibid., 56. Clark also makes the general observation that "as the *Incendium* makes plain, there is a certain interdependence between *fervor, canor* and *dulcor* in their various aspects and phases" ("Theological Re-Assessment," 112).

172. Watson observed that *canor* and *dulcor* occur not infrequently in *Incendium amoris*, but only as "offshoots" of *calor* (*Invention*, 121). This does not give sufficient recognition to the simultaneous presence of all three.

173. Ruh, *Geschichte*, 2:268–75.

174. Ibid., 282.

175. Ibid., 281.

176. *Comment on the Canticles*, ed. Murray, 80.

177. "Defensorium contra oblectratores [*sic*] eiusdem Ricardi, quod compo- suit Thomas Basseth sancte memorie." Basset's defense was edited by Allen (*Writ- ings*, 529–37) and by M. Sargent ("Contemporary Criticism of Richard Rolle," 160–87; Appendix: "A Diplomatic Transcript of Thomas Basset's *Defense* of Richard

Rolle," 188–205). Allen interprets the nonsense word "oblectratores" as scribal error for "oblatratores," which, however, involves unlikely word formation and meaning ("barker"); it seems more likely that the mysterious "oblectratores" is a corruption of "obiectatores" (opponents, critics). Hilton's "interpretation aids" for distinguishing genuine from illusory angels' music, in his text *Of Angels' Song,* are composed entirely in Rolle's spirit. They can hardly be understood as criticism of Rolle's mystical imagery; Rolle remains "orthodox" in his comments and offers no actual basis for misinterpretation at this point (cf. Watson, *Invention,* 261).

178. Further examples from *Melos amoris* include "mellifluum hominem," 174; "melosque dulcifluam," 181; "mellifluum melos," 185; "mellifluum nomen," 192; "feruor mellifluus," 205; "dulcifluam deuocionem," 241; "melliflua ... abundancia ardoris," 241; "mellifluas ... mentes nostras," 271; "mellicum mansionem," 244; "mellita Iesu memoria," 246; "in melliphona meditacione," 159. The Cistercian sensuality of Rolle's language, which matches the "eloquii suavitas," the sweet language of Bernard in his first sermon on the Song of Songs, is made very clear in the *Officium et miracula,* with the popular bee-and-honey comparison: "Labor dulcissimus apis eligitur. / instructor optimus mellita [loquitur, / docet, editorial add.] dulcissima fauus exprimitur" (*"Officium et Miracula,"* ed. Woolley, 13); see also, e.g., R. Fulton, "'Taste and See That the Lord Is Sweet' (Ps 33:9): The Flavour of God in the Monastic West," *Journal of Religion* 86 (2006): 169–204. Moyes calls Rolle "a Bernardine writer" (*"Expositio,"* 1:64).

179. Watson, *Invention,* 122.

180. It occurs esp. in *Super apocalypsim, Super psalmum vicesimum,* L P, E P. This is another reminder of Bernard of Clairvaux (see D. Sabersky, "'Nam iteratio, affectionis expressio est': Zum Stil Bernhards von Clairvaux," *Cîteaux* 36 [1985]: 5–20).

181. See Olmes, *Sprache und Stil,* for examples of repetition, comparison, alliteration, rhyme, rhythm, isocolon, parallelism, antithesis, anaphora, play on words, etc. (48–66). Olmes further demonstrates Rolle's competence in the use of the *cursus* (*planus, trispondaicus, velox, tardus,* and clause structure, 74–85). Watson (*Invention*) also gives numerous examples of Rolle's rhetorical skill; and see also *Contra amatores mundi,* ed. Theiner, 30–38.

182. Watson even claims that in *IA* Rolle "has declared a doctrine of *canor* to be the fundamental tenet of mystical theology" (*Invention,* 139).

183. E.g., *"Expositio,"* ed. Moyes, 1:88–89; frequently also in Watson, e.g., *Invention,* 20, where he even describes Rolle's "mystical experience of spiritual song" as "rhapsodic."

184. Watson also pointed out that the division into chapters was not made by Rolle (*Invention,* 118).

185. Ibid., 122.

186. *"Expositio,"* ed. Moyes, 1:53.

187. Ruh, *Geschichte,* 2:314.

188. Watson's view that this work is characterized especially by *dulcor* is therefore not justified (*Invention,* 148).

189. Allen speaks of a "diffuse and rambling exposition" (*Writings,* 62); Watson considers "the work for the most part ... has no organized evolution of ideas" (*Invention,* 148).

190. See *Comment on the Canticles,* ed. Murray, 5–6.

191. Watson, *Invention*, 148.

192. *Love of Learning*, 71–88; see also Ruh, *Geschichte*, 1:222–24 (on Guigo II ruminating in *contemplatio*). This combinatory and specifically Bernardine exegesis also occurs in a great work of female mysticism, Gertrud of Helfta's *Exercitia spiritualia;* see H. Keul and S. Ringler, "In der Freiheit des lebendigen Geistes: Helfta als geohistorischer Ort der deutschen Mystik," in *Aufbruch zu neuer Gottesrede: Die Mystik der Gertrud von Helfta,* ed. S. Ringler (Ostfildern: Schwabenverlag, 2007), 35.

193. *Comment on the Canticles,* ed. Murray, 59–80. See also Renevey's interpretation of this text and further biblical commentaries by Rolle, in *Language, Self and Love,* esp. 85ff.; and see further his article "Encoding and Decoding: Metaphorical Discourse of Love in Richard Rolle's Commentary on the First Verses of the Song of Songs," in Ellis and Tixier, *Medieval Translator* 5, 264–83.

194. *Encomium nominis Iesu* was printed in Horstmann, *Yorkshire Writers,* 1:186–91.

195. See Allen, *Writings,* 78–79; and *Comment on the Canticles,* ed. Murray, lxxxiv.

196. Wilmart includes the "Oleum effusum" in his "Le 'Jubilus,'" 275–80.

197. *Comment on the Canticles,* ed. Murray, 39–40. Cf. also Allen, *Writings,* 73–83; and *Comment on the Canticles,* ed. Murray, lix.

198. See also Renevey, "'The Name Poured Out,'" 127–47, and "Name above Names," 103–13, important also for further research references; unfortunately he repeats the unfounded opinion that "Walter Hilton was certainly cautious about some aspects of Richard Rolle's spirituality" ("Name above Names," 113).

199. See Robert Boenig, "The God-as-Mother Theme in Richard Rolle's Biblical Commentaries," *MQ* 10 (1984): 171–79.

200. *Comment on the Canticles,* ed. Murray, 22. Play on the dual gender of Christ occurs also in Suso (see McGinn, *Presence of God,* vol. 4, *Harvest,* 206–8).

201. Allen already noted this (*Writings,* 92).

202. *Contra amatores mundi,* ed. Theiner, 22. Parenthetical page/line citations in text are taken from this work.

203. On what follows, see the excellent commentary in Moyes, ed., *"Expositio."*

204. *"Expositio,"* ed. Moyes, 2:262. All *NL* quotations are from this source.

205. Ibid., 2:169.4–5.

206. It was recently pointed out that in *Ancrene Wisse* there are no fewer than fifteen quotations from Job; see Renevey, "Rolle, Anchoritic Culture, and the Office of the Dead," in Caie and Renevey, *Medieval Texts in Context,* 199.

207. Moyes makes important comments on this (*"Expositio,"* 1: esp. 87–88).

208. Lotario di Segni (Pope Innocent III), *De miseria condicionis humane,* ed. Robert E. Lewis (Athens: University of Georgia Press, 1978), 95.23. The Middle Ages liked to make an etymological connection between *homo* and *humus* (e.g., *"Expositio,"* ed. Moyes, 2:130), and this occurs, for instance, in Meister Eckhart, but not, as far as I can see, in Innocent III. For him, following the Bible, man consists of *terra, pulvis, lutum,* etc., and he decays to *cinis* (*De miseria,* 95ff.). Rolle's high regard for this work is attested in verbal echoes. Likewise significant in this context are the pseudo-Bernardine *Meditationes piissimae* (PL 184). The great model for medieval exegesis of the book of Job is, of course, Gregory the Great's famous work (M. Adriaen, ed., *Gregorii Magni moralia in Iob,* CC lat. 143 [Turnhout: Brepols, 1979]).

209. These introductory remarks on the book of Job follow Ludger Schwien-horst-Schönberger, "Das Buch Ijob," in *Stuttgarter Altes Testament: Einheitsüber-setzung mit Kommentar und Lexikon,* 3rd ed., ed. Erich Zenger (Stuttgart: Stuttgarter Bibelanstalt, 2005).

210. Ibid., 1033.

211. Ibid., 1035 (with reference to Augustine's *De magistro*). Cf. Augustine, *"Against the Academicians."*

212. Schwienhorst-Schönberger, 1036.

213. On the readership question see Renevey, "Looking for a Context," 201ff.

214. When he speaks at one point of a "libello de uita heremitarum" and a "libro de perfeccione & gloria sanctorum" (*"Expositio,"* ed. Moyes, 2:196.19–20), these titles do not identify books of his; they can therefore not be used for dating *Expositio*. (For the text's transmission history, see M. Moyes, "The Manuscripts and Early Printed Editions of Richard Rolle's *Expositio super novem lectiones mortuorum,"* *MMTE* 3 [1984], 81–103; and *"Expositio,"* ed. Moyes, vol. 2.)

215. Moyes comes to a similar conclusion: *"Expositio,"* 1:102.

216. Moyes rightly speaks of "some of Rolle's finest Latin prose," *"Expositio,"* 1:102; Watson also praises it in *Invention*.

217. So also Allen, *Writings,* 178.

218. Mary Louise Potter, ed., "Rolle's Latin Commentary on the Psalms" (PhD diss., Cornell University, 1929).

219. Allen, *Writings,* 185.

220. "Rolle's Latin Commentary on the Psalms," ed. Porter, esp. 239, 173.

221. The first modern edition was presented by James C. Dolan with his own translation: *The "Tractatus Super psalmum vicesimum" of Richard Rolle of Hampole,* Texts and Studies in Religion 57 (Lewiston, NY: E. Mellen Press, 1991).

222. "The Scotch wars brought king, court, and parliament as well as army to Yorkshire during these years, whence it [York] has been called the capital of England" (Allen, *Writings,* 128).

223. This was surmised by Allen: *Writings,* 186.

224. *"Tractatus,"* ed. Dolan, 3–4.

225. Allen, *Writings,* 245.

226. *Emendatio vitae,* ed. Watson, 36.90. For the first historical-critical edition of a Rolle text see, more recently, *De emendatione vitae: Eine kritische Ausgabe des latein-ischen Textes von Richard Rolle,* ed. Spahl.

227. Watson notes that "there is little overt autobiography" (*EV,* 21). However, he also comments that "There is . . . a surprising amount of autobiographical material to be found between the lines of the work. . . . But this hidden self-referentiality is developed into a picture of the spiritual life which has been abstracted and general-ized for non-eremitic readers more fully than in any of Rolle's other works" (*Inven-tion,* 209).

228. *Emendatio vitae,* ed. Watson, 64.68.

229. Of course, this implies a life of complete asceticism, which Rolle does not discuss *in extenso*. Watson mistakenly maintains that Rolle was "indifferent to asceti-cism, consistently commending the virtues of adequate food, comfort, and sleep, and in almost all his writings he even regards penitence . . . as important mainly to spiritual beginners" (*EV,* 12).

230. Clark speaks with reference to *EV* (and also to the early English tracts) of "Rolle's own corrective to the ebullient 'enthusiasm' of his earlier writing" ("Theological Re-Assessment," 129).

231. Clark, too, considers *EV* to be "carefully ordered and systematic" (ibid., 121).

232. *Emendatio vitae,* ed. Watson, 20.

233. So also Clark, "Theological Re-Assessment," 121.

234. Lk 22:30; see *Stuttgarter Neues Testament. Einheitsübersetzung mit Kommentar und Erklärungen* (Stuttgart, 2000), 169.

235. See Watson, "Middle English Mystics," 539–65; the work was then translated by Richard Misyn especially for those with no knowledge of Latin.

236. *Psalter or Psalms of David,* ed. Bramley, 1.

237. On this aspect cf. esp. Kuczynski, *Prophetic Song;* Kuczynski rightly points out that a former comparison between the English Psalter and the Lollard Psalter had unfairly characterized Rolle's translation as heretic in part. Kevin Gustavson argues for a Lollard quality in Rolle's EP: "Richard Rolle's *English Psalter* and the Making of a Lollard Text," *Viator* 33 (2002): 294–309.

238. Parts of Rolle's English Psalter have been edited in Fordham University dissertations; see Lagorio and Sargent (with R. Bradley), "English Mystical Writings," in Hartung and Burke Severs, *Manual of the Writings in Middle English* 9, chap. 23.

239. *The Psalter or Psalms of David,* ed. Bramley, 4.

240. E. Zenger, "Die Psalmen," in Zenger, *Stuttgarter Altes Testament,* 1036–1219; see also Zenger, "Das Buch der Psalmen," in Zenger et al., *Einleitung in das Alte Testament,* 4th ed. (Stuttgart: Kohlhammer, 2001), 309–26.

241. W. Irtenkauf, "The psalms are the framework and foundation of the entire Office [of the Hours]," *MGG,* 9:1909.

242. See Gillespie, "Mystic's Foot," 228, n. 42. Gillespie also cites Christina of Markyate's attested use of the Psalter in the eremitical life.

243. Zenger, "Die Psalmen," 1037; on repetition in Rolle, see the detailed article by Smedick, "Parallelism and Pointing," 404–67.

244. See Watson, *Invention,* 244; and Kuczynski, *Prophetic Song,* 14; this follows on from Minnis and Scott, *Medieval Literary Theory,* 19.28, 40ff.

245. Zenger, "Die Psalmen," 1039.

246. H. Volz, ed., *D. Martin Luther: Biblia: Das ist die ganzte Heilige Schrifft: Deudsch aufs new zugericht.* Wittenberg, 1545 (Munich: dtv 1974), 2:964.

247. Zenger, "Buch der Psalmen," 317.

248. Ibid., 326.

249. See the succinct comments by Clark, "Biblical Commentator," 176.

250. Ibid., 186: "Praise of the Holy Name begins by recalling Phil 2:10 ... while *Oleum effusum* points to Ps 44:7."

251. On Rolle's translation technique, see Roger Ellis, "The Choices of the Translator in the Late Middle English Period," *MMTE* 2 (1982), 18–48.

252. Ruh, *Geschichte,* 1:81.

253. Ibid., 81–82.

254. For Origen's early attempt at this in his fragmentary commentary on the Psalms, see J. W. Trigg, *Origen* (London: Routledge, 1998), 69.

255. Rolle's dependence on Peter Lombard was investigated by H. Middendorf (*Untersuchungen zu Richard Rolle von Hampole* [Magdeburg: Fock, 1888]), who greatly exaggerated this dependence, as Watson rightly observes (*Invention,* 329).

256. Watson in J. Wogan-Browne et al., *Idea of the Vernacular,* 244.

257. *Invention,* 245. Watson sees an increase in Rolle's dependence on Peter Lombard after a few dozen psalms.

258. *Enarratio in Psalmos, PL* 36; *Über die Psalmen,* selected and trans. Hans Urs von Balthasar (Einsiedeln: Johannes Verlag, 1996), 17.

259. Watson also saw this clearly (*Invention,* 246).

260. Gillespie pointed out that, in both commentaries on the Psalms, Rolle hardly misses an opportunity to provide the foot image with an affective quality, thereby reinforcing the love motif, and that in so doing he proceeds far more systematically than the *Glossa ordinaria* or Peter Lombard ("Mystic's Foot," 204).

261. Zenger, "Die Psalmen," 1086.

262. Watson, *Invention,* 244.

263. On the *iubilus,* see Sam Jones Womack Jr., "The *Jubilus* Theme in the Later Writings of Richard Rolle" (PhD diss., Duke University, 1961).

264. For the canon of these works, see *Rolle: Prose and Verse,* ed. Ogilvie-Thomson; see also Watson, *Invention,* chap. 9, 222–56. See also Frances Beer, "Richard Rolle and the Yorkshire Nuns," in *Women and Mystical Experience in the Middle Age*s (Cambridge: D. S. Brewer, 1992).

265. Watson, *Invention,* 275.

266. See Ellis, "Literary Approach to the Middle English Mystics," 99–119.

267. *Richard Rolle, Prose and Verse,* ed. Ogilvie-Thomson, 14. All English texts are quoted from this edition.

268. Quoted from *Rolle: Prose and Verse,* ed. Ogilvie-Thomson, 3.

269. McIlroy, *English Prose Treatises,* 141. For very useful observations on form, see Rygiel, "Structures and Style," 6–15. The biblical basis is perceptively examined by Annie Sutherland, "Biblical Text and Spiritual Experience in the English Epistles of Richard Rolle," *RES* 45 (2005): 695–711.

270. Riehle, *Middle English Mystics,* 120; see also Copeland, "Richard Rolle," 71.

271. It is useful to recall *The Interpretation of Dreams* by Artemidorus of Daldis, the *Somnium Scipionis,* and the significance of the dream in Chaucer; see S. F. Kruger, *Dreaming in the Middle Ages,* Cambridge Studies in Medieval Literature 14 (Cambridge: Cambridge University Press, 1992); Peter Brown, ed., *Reading Dreams: The Interpretation of Dreams from Chaucer to Shakespeare* (Oxford: Oxford University Press, 1999); on dreams and sleep in female mysticism, cf. Haas, *Gottleiden? Gottlieben,* 115–20.

272. Caldwell has shown how "form mirrors meaning": Rolle's use of rhetorical devices creates "syntactic symbolism," with skilful sound-and-rhythm effects ("Rhetorics of Enthusiasm and of Restraint," 9–16); see also Glasscoe, *English Medieval Mystics,* 81.

273. This is pointed out also by Copeland in her stimulating essay, "Richard Rolle," 71; see also Gunnel Cleve, "Some Remarks on Richard Rolle's Prose Style," *NM* 85 (1984): 115–21.

274. Copeland, "Richard Rolle," 71; Gillespie, "Mystic's Foot," 211.

275. *Rolle: Prose and Verse,* ed. Ogilvie-Thomson, lxvi.

276. Ibid.

277. McIlroy also rejects any comparison with Pandarus (*English Prose Treatises,* 68); Watson does not (*Invention,* 230).

278. *Rolle: Prose and Verse,* ed. Ogilvie-Thomson, 30–31, and notes, 205.

279. Ibid., 32.

280. Gillespie, "Mystic's Foot," 217.

281. Hanna considers that Rolle sometimes writes "in rhythmic cadences hanging rather ambiguously between prose and verse" ("Rolle and Related Works," 27); cf. also Smedick, "Parallelism and Pointing," 404–67. This style rather obscures the fact that the tendency toward classification commonly found in monastic literature also occurs in Rolle; this was overlooked even by the great Rolle scholar H. E. Allen, who therefore said there was no such organizing principle in his work (*Writings*, 275). There is, however, no justification for Watson's assertion that the second half of *The Form of Living* is "Rolle's last and greatest attempt to create a verbal equivalent of *canor* in English," which he sees as emerging from Smedick's "Parallelism and Pointing" (*Invention*, 252).

282. "The whole is plotted and controlled," the work proceeds with "repetition of detail"; everything is "carefully balanced" (Hanna, "Rolle and Related Works," 27).

283. Glasscoe, *English Medieval Mystics*, 100.

284. Gillespie, "Mystic's Foot."

285. See *Rolle: Prose and Verse*, ed. Ogilvie-Thomson, lxxxi–xci, 42–63.

286. They are included in *Rolle: Prose and Verse*, ed. Ogilvie-Thomson (64–83); see also the seminal study by M. F. Madigan, *The "Passio Domini" Theme in the Works of Richard Rolle;* see also the still useful essay by M. M. Morgan, "Versions of the Meditations on the Passion Ascribed to Richard Rolle," *MAE* 22 (1953): 93–103.

287. *Rolle: Prose and Verse*, ed. Ogilvie-Thomson, 50.

288. E.g., *Melos amoris*, ed. Arnould, 96–97.

289. "ut carnem nostram contagiosam castigemus" (*Melos amoris*, ed. Arnould, 85.17–18); "Corpus meum castigo et in servitutem redigo, ne aliis predicans reprobus efficiar" (ibid., 184.27–28).

290. See Madigan, *"Passio Domini" Theme in the Works of Richard Rolle.*

291. Glasscoe, *English Medieval Mystics*, 99.

292. *Rolle: Prose and Verse*, ed. Ogilvie-Thomson, 76.288–91.

293. W. F. Hodapp has drawn attention to the performative and transformative aspects of *Meditation B* and has rightly emphasized the importance of seeing how "the meditator becomes 'one of them' present with Christ on Calvary," as in vernacular drama ("Richard Rolle's Passion Meditations," 96–104); cf. also W. F. Hodapp, "Ritual and Performance in Richard Rolle's Passion Meditation B," in Suydam and Ziegler, *Performance and Transformation*, 241–72; see also Gillespie, "Strange Images of Death," 111–59.

294. In the monk of Farne's "Meditation Addressed to Christ Crucified," Christ hanging on the cross is also seen as a book opened for perusal (Farmer, *Meditations of a Fourteenth Century Monk*, chap. 53, 76).

295. Allen wants to see it as an early work (*Writings*, 120), Watson ascribes it to Rolle's middle period (*Invention*, 278), though without compelling evidence; the "internal evidence" of the texts' thematic dependence on one another is not conclusive.

296. *Melos amoris*, ed. Arnould, 9.34.

297. Watson has listed the parallels to the Song of Songs, and a few of those to *Contra amatores mundi* (*Invention*, 286–93).

298. It was attempted by Gabriel Liegey, "The Rhetorical Aspects of Richard Rolle's *Melos Contemplativorum*" (PhD diss., Columbia University, 1954); Arnould offers a more profound introduction in his *Melos amoris* edition, xvii–lxxi See also

F. Vandenbrouke's very good introduction to the French translation in *Le chant d'amour (Melos amoris)*, ed. et trad. par les moniales de Wisques, SC (Paris: Éditions de Cerf, 1971), 2 vols. See also de Ford, "Mystical Union"; Watson, *Invention*, 171–91; and Riehle, *Middle English Mystics*, 119–22.

299. Ruh, *Geschichte*, 1:258.

300. Ibid.

301. See also Astell, *Song of Songs in the Middle Ages*, 107, and P. P. Fite, "To 'Sytt and Syng of Luf Langyng.'"

302. Ruh, *Geschichte*, 1:259.

303. Cf. a central characterization of Amor in Ovid, "amor audacem facit animum" (*Metamorphoses* 4.96). See also Newman, *God and the Goddesses;* she speaks of the opposition between two parties, the Ovidians and the Augustinians, and of a "clash between secular and monastic theorists" (141).

304. Watson's interpretation, e.g. in *Invention*, and "Translation and Self-Canonization," differs from the interpretation offered here. For an interesting approach, see Gillespie, "Postcards from the Edge," 137–65.

305. Watson, "Melting into God the English Way," 45, n.

306. Riehle, *Middle English Mystics*, 75; Fyte, "To 'Sytt and Syng of Luf Langyng,'" 19–20.

307. Paul is praised as "perfectissimus predicator" (*Melos amoris*, ed. Arnould, 165).

308. He talks, for instance, of the houses of eternity (15), and entering their "atria" (35), of celestial palaces (76), of "Pascua paradisi" (47), of the "paradisica poma" (57), between which he may take his seat (74). For recent work on heaven see, e.g., Carolyn Muessig and A. Putter, eds., *Envisaging Heaven in the Middle Ages* (London: Routledge, 2006).

309. This was already recognized by F. Schulte, "Das musikalische Element," 37.

310. Augustine, *Conf.* IX:9. I am greatly indebted to my colleague in Graz, Rudolf Flotzinger, for important information relevant to the following section.

311. See, for instance, H. Hüschen, "Musik," in *MGG*, 9, cols. 975–90 (I use the first edition).

312. Aurelius Augustinus, *De musica, Bücher I und VI: Vom ästhetischen Urteil zur metaphysischen Erkenntnis*, with introduction and trans. by F. Hentschel (Hamburg, 2002), 6; *PL* 221.

313. Hammerstein, *Musik der Engel*, 132.

314. Roger Bragard, ed., *Jacobus von Lüttich:* Speculum Musicae. Corpus Scriptorum de Musica III (Rome, 1955), 22; cited from Hammerstein, *Musik der Engel*, 132.

315. Ibid.

316. Ibid., 133.

317. Schulte, "Das musikalische Element," 58.

318. Hammerstein, *Musik der Engel*, 129.

319. His first experience of *canor* after his conversion is described in this way (*Incendium amoris*, ed. Deanesly, 189).

320. *The Etymologies of Isidore of Seville*, trans. with introduction and notes by S. A. Barney et al. (Cambridge: Cambridge University Press, 2006), 3:xix, 4, 96.

321. Augustine mentions the effect of music on the emotions, *Enarrationes in Psalmos* 99.4 (cited in Wolfgang Buchmüller, "'Dulcis Iesu memoria': Poetische

Christusmystik bei Aelred von Rievaulx," in *Die Mystik des Gregorianischen Chorals,* ed. Simeon Wester et al., [Aachen: Bernardus-Verlag, 2007], 111).

322. See Bernhard Morbach, *Die Musikwelt des Mittelalters,* 2nd ed. (Kassel: Bärenreiter, 2005), esp. 194.

323. Watson, *Invention,* 178. Rolle's understanding of *canor* is assuredly also influenced by Augustine, *Enarratio in Psalmos:* Ps 42.

324. These comments, in particular, owe much to the advice of Rudolf Flotzinger; he also drew my attention to the fundamental study by Hammerstein.

325. *MGG* 10, "Organum," col. 222 (e.g., "et neupmata...amicabiliter organizent," *Melos amoris,* ed. Arnould, 34.9–11). In *Analecta Hymnica, neuma* and *organum* are assigned to different groups of singers who join together to "perform the melismata." A connection is also made with the "enigmatic" paraphonist choristers, who are themselves mentioned in *Melos amoris* (14.1); "paraphronistis" is evidently a misreading in Arnould's *Melos amoris* edition. At the same time, the "palinodiae" of *Analecta Hymnica* are mentioned; the meaning is equally unclear (*MGG* 10, "Organum," col. 225 [Hieronim Feicht]).

326. Hammerstein, *Musik der Engel,* 115.

327. It is not necessary to refer especially to Bernard or Hugh of Strasbourg (cf. Watson, *Invention,* 308), since the seraphim were regarded in the Middle Ages as the angel choir whose fire of love burned most brightly.

328. See also de Ford, "Mystical Union," 188.

329. Watson, *Invention,* 180.

330. Ibid., 178. Throughout Watson's book, misinterpretations of *canor* occur; e.g. in the statement that "proclamation of *canor*" is "an act of evangelism" (188). Further assessments of the function of excessive alliteration are found, esp. in "Translation and Self-Canonization": "The status of his writing is equivalent to the status of heavenly song itself" (174); "The gap between earthly and heavenly language is, for the holy man, so slight as to be insignificant" (179); *Melos amoris* is "a written version of his experience of *canor*" (179). Gillespie likewise sees an imitative approximation to *canor* ("Mystic's Foot," 211). He is closer to the mark when he stresses that Rolle's description of *canor* is intended as an "affective trigger" for those who long for it ("Postcards from the Edge," 216). He also speaks very aptly of "the timeless mellifluousness of the sweeping alliteration" (156).

331. It is worth considering the possibility that Rolle, with his superabundant style, also wanted to recall Aldhelm (ca. 700), an author with whom he has some features in common; Aldhelm made similarly abundant use of alliteration and inclined toward "a very individual, even eccentric, style with rare words, Grecisms, and self-coined words" (Aldhelm's *Epistola V ad Ehfridum,* in *Lateinische Prosa des Mittelalters,* lateinisch /deutsch, ed. and trans. Dorothea Walz [Stuttgart: Reclam, 1995], 94–98).

332. Argued by de Ford in "Mystical Union" and "Use and Function of Alliteration."

333. Gabriel M. Liegey, ed. "Richard Rolle's Carmen Prosaicum: An Edition and Commentary," *MS* 19 (1957): 15–36.

334. Ibid., 16.

335. Ruh, *Geschichte,* 2:500; tradition has it that a sweet sound from Elisabeth's throat was heard just before her death.

336. Hammerstein, *Musik der Engel,* 41. An important passage for the understanding of Rolle's response to *canor* is *MA,* 138.12–140.33.

337. Quoted from Hammerstein, *Musik der Engel,* 41.

338. Ibid., 39.

339. A work on the "Hymnos trishagios" is attributed to John of Damascus, according to M. Stöhr in *MGG,* "Hymnus." Repeated references to John of Howden's *Philomena* are long outdated.

340. "*Officium et Miracula,*" ed. Woolley, 77–80.

341. Schulte, "Das musikalische Element," 66.

342. Hammerstein, *Musik der Engel,* 177.

343. Thomas Aquinas, *Summa theologica,* quaestio 45, art. 4: "Claritas vestimentorum ejus designat futuram claritatem sanctorum quae superabitur a claritate Christi."

344. Rolle focuses also on the foreshortening of time ("Hic loquitur [Scriptura] in preterito," 189). On the phenomenon of foreshortening of time, see Alois M. Haas, "Mystische Eschatologie: Ein Durchblick," in *Ende und Vollendung: Eschatologische Perspektiven im Mittelalter,* ed. J. A. Aertsen and M. Pickavé, Miscellanea Mediaevalia 29 (Berlin: De Gruyter, 2002), 95–114.

345. Comper, *Life of Richard Rolle,* 85; Arnould calls the structure "prolix and orderless" (*Melos amoris,* xvii).

346. *Melos amoris,* ed. Arnould, xvii.

347. See, for instance, de Ford, "Mystical Union," esp. 180–81.

348. See *Melos amoris,* ed. Arnould, xvii.

349. Clark, "Biblical Commentator," 174.

350. F. Vandenbroucke, introduction to French translation of the *Melos amoris: Le chant d'amour,* 1:16.

351. Ibid., 53.

352. Dinzelbacher, *Bernhard von Clairvaux,* 59. Cf. also Anneke Mulder-Bakker, *The Invention of Saintliness,* Routledge Studies in Medieval Religion and Culture (London: Routledge, 2002).

353. He speaks of himself as "glorifice grandescens" (*MA,* 52), "granditer gradiens" (*MA,* 58 and 74). Specifically on this phenomenon, see Watson, *Invention,* and "Translation and Self-Canonization."

354. Cf. Alford, "Biblical *imitatio.*"

355. M. de La Bigne, *Magna bibliotheca veterum patrum* (Cologne, 1622), 836.

356. See esp. Copeland, "Richard Rolle," 55–80.

357. Augustine already demanded this in *De doctrina christiana,* bk. 4, esp. XVI:33.90ff., p. 236ff. John Philip Schneider was the first to investigate Rolle's style in detail, in *The Prose Style of Richard Rolle of Hampole, with Especial Reference to Its Euphuistic Tendencies* (Baltimore: J. H. Furst Co., 1906). See Olmes, *Sprache und Stil.* Theiner gives numerous examples of Rolle's rhetorical skill (ed., *Contra amatores mundi,* 30–38), and see also Watson, *Invention.*

358. See Lois Smedick, "Parallelism and Pointing," 404–67.

359. Watson, *Invention,* 260.

6. Marguerite Porete's *The Mirror of Simple Souls* and Its Reception in England

1. See, e.g., Lerner, "New Light," 112; also E. Colledge and J. C. Marler, "'Poverty of the Will': Ruusbroec, Eckhart and *The Mirror of Simple Souls,*" in *Jan van Ruusbroec: The Sources, Content, and Sequels of His Mysticism,* ed. P. Mommaers and

N. de Paepe, *Mediaevalia Lovaniensia* 1/12 (Louvain: Leuven University Press, 1984), 40; Hollywood, *Soul as Virgin Wife,* 173–76; McGinn, *Mystical Thought of Meister Eckhart,* 9.

2. E. Underhill was the first to draw attention to the text in modern times, in "The Mirror of Simple Souls," *Fortnightly Review* 95, n.s. 89 (1911): 345–55. The first edition was by Clare Kirchberger, *"The Mirror of Simple Souls" by an Unknown French Mystic of the Thirteenth Century: Translated into English by M.N.,* Orchard Books 15 (New York: Benziger Brothers, 1927). For more recent studies see especially the profound theological work by Irene Leicht, *Marguerite Porete.* Further studies include: Ruh, "'Le miroir des simples âmes' der Marguerite Porete," in *Verbum et Signum: Festschrift für Friedrich Ohly,* ed. Hans Fromm et al. (Munich: Fink, 1975), 2:365–87; Ruh, "Beginenmystik: Hadewijch, Mechthild von Magdeburg, Marguerite Porete," *Zeitschrift für deutsches Altertum und deutsche Literatur* 106 (1977): 265–77; Ruh, *Geschichte,* 2:338–71; Ulrich Heid, "Studien zu Marguerite Porete und ihrem 'Miroir des simples âmes,'" in Dinzelbacher and Bauer, *Religiöse Frauenbewegung,* 185–214; McGinn, *Meister Eckhart and the Beguine Mystics;* Stölting, *Christliche Frauenmystik.*

3. Lerner, "New Light," 93.

4. See Ruh, *Geschichte,* 2:338.

5. Leicht, *Marguerite Porete,* 87.

6. Modern English translations of the *Mirouer* are taken from *Marguerite Porete: "Mirror,"* ed. and trans. Babinsky (here chap. 69, 143–44); quotations of the Middle English *Mirror* are from *Margaret Porete,* ed. Doiron; the French *Mirouer* is quoted from *Le mirouer,* ed. Guarnieri.

7. See Leicht, *Marguerite Porete,* 38–42.

8. Ruh, *Geschichte,* 2:351.

9. Stölting, *Christliche Frauenmystik,* 404; on this see further Ruh, *Geschichte,* 2:356–57.

10. *Marguerite Porete: "Mirror,"* trans. Babinsky, chap. 115, p. 185; for the Middle English translation see *Margaret Porete,* ed. Doiron, 323–38, esp. 335; see also Leicht, *Marguerite Porete,* 218.

11. *Marguerite Porete: "Mirror,"* trans. Babinsky, chap. 21, p. 104. Sells talks of a gender balance in the Trinity (*Mystical Languages,* 136).

12. Ruh, *Geschichte,* 2:351–71.

13. Ibid., 355.

14. Stölting, *Christliche Frauenmystik,* 350; Ruh, *Geschichte,* 2:343.

15. Richard of St. Victor, *Twelve Patriarchs,* 73; cf. *Marguerite Porete: "Mirror,"* trans. Babinsky, 228, n. 74. "God is who Is" (Stölting, *Christliche Frauenmystik,* 375).

16. *Marguerite Porete: "Mirror,"* trans. Babinsky, 135; Stölting, *Christliche Frauenmystik,* 356.

17. Ibid.

18. Ibid., 379; Ruh, *Geschichte,* 2:362.

19. Watson, "Melting into God," 19–50.

20. See Leicht, *Marguerite Porete,* 177ff. This Cistercian influence has been noted several times, e.g. by Babinsky: "Christological Transformation in *The Mirror of Simple Souls* by Marguerite Porete," *Theology Today* 60 (2003): 34–48.

21. Notwithstanding what Watson says ("Melting into God"), there is a high degree of similarity.

22. Stölting, *Christliche Frauenmystik,* 369.

23. Ibid., 361–63; Ruh, *Geschichte,* 2:349.

24. Ibid., 348–49.

25. Robinson, *Nobility and Annihilation,* 37.

26. Ibid., 37–38.

27. Cf. Sells: the soul "no longer wishes not to have sinned," *Mystical Languages,* 121.

28. See esp. McGinn and his school: McGinn, *Meister Eckhart and the Beguine Mystics.*

29. See Leicht, *Marguerite Porete,* 192ff.; Stölting, *Christliche Frauenmystik,* 378; Ruh, *Geschichte,* 2:351.

30. *Marguerite Porete: "Mirror,"* trans. Babinsky, 127–28.

31. Stölting, *Christliche Frauenmystik,* 363–67.

32. Ibid., 363.

33. Lerner, *Heresy,* 230.

34. Stölting, *Christliche Frauenmystik,* 361.

35. Marguerite did not by any means intend, as Stölting speculates, to overcome the link between woman and the body with her recommendation that nature be given what nature requires (Stölting, *Christliche Frauenmystik,* 381).

36. Ibid., 367.

37. *Marguerite Porete: "Mirror,"* trans. Babinsky, 157.

38. Lerner, *Heresy,* 189.

39. Stölting, *Christliche Frauenmystik,* 337.

40. *Marguerite Porete: "Mirror,"* trans. Babinsky, chap. 92, p. 168.

41. Ruh, *Geschichte,* 2:344.

42. G. Fozzer, "Saggio estetico-letterario," in *Margherita Porete: Lo specchio delle anime simplici,* ed. Fozzer (Milano: Edizioni San Paolo, 1994), 68–71.

43. Quoted from Leicht, *Marguerite Porete,* 140.

44. Lerner, "New Light," 97.

45. Ibid., 100ff. Lerner draws attention to G. Hasenohr's important discovery, often overlooked, of two chapters from the original or its first copy, "La tradition du *Miroir des simples âmes* au XVe siècle: De Marguerite Porète (d. 1310) à Marguerite de Navarre," *Comptes rendus des séances de l'Académie des inscriptions et belles-lettres,* L'année 1999, janvier-mars (Paris, 1999), 1347–66; cf. also Watson, "Melting into God," 27, n. 21.

46. Lerner, "New Light," 114.

47. Stölting, *Christliche Frauenmystik,* 337.

48. Watson's assessment, however, is too negative ("Melting into God," 42).

49. L. Gnädinger, trans., Margareta Porete. *Der Spiegel der einfachen Seelen. Mystik der Freiheit* (Kevelaer: Topos plus, 2010), 268; according to Gnädinger, talking changes into a song of the soul produced by rhythmical, often rhymed and hymnically elevated prose (226); see also Stölting, *Christliche Frauenmystik,* 351–55.

50. See Watson, "Misrepresenting the Untranslatable."

51. The following quotations of the Middle English *Mirror* are from *Margaret Porete,* ed. Doiron.

52. This was first noted by Kirchberger in her edition, as indicated by *Margaret Porete,* ed. Doiron, 276.

53. *Marguerite Porete: "Mirror,"* trans. Babinsky, 106.

54. The water-in-wine image occurs first in Maximus Confessor (d. 622), then also in Bernard of Clairvaux (*Sancti Bernardi opera* III:X.28, 143), *On Loving God*, p. 30.

55. Lerner, *Heresy,* 63, 188.

56. See Watson, "Melting into God," 19–50.

57. Watson speaks of a rhetoric of ecstasy (ibid., 46); of the rhapsodic, essentially talkative kind (ibid., 47).

58. Watson, "Melting into God," 30.

59. E.g., Sargent, "*Le Mirouer des simples âmes,*" 443–65.

60. Cré, "Women in the Charterhouse?" 43–62.

61. Watson, "Melting into God," 32.

62. Chaps. 1–119; however, six leaves remained untranslated. See *Margaret Porete,* ed. Doiron, 345; but there is part of chap. 122, and also chaps. 134–36.

63. Lerner, "New Light," 71.

64. Typical of such misunderstanding is Kerby-Fulton's erroneous view that in England *Mirror* was "safeguarded by M.N.'s glosses" (*Books under Suspicion,* 277).

65. See Colledge and Guarnieri, "Glosses by 'M.N.,'" appendix to *Margaret Porete,* ed. Doiron, 358. Kerby-Fulton already notes that he sometimes dispenses with a gloss "where we would expect him to have panicked" (*Books under Suspicion,* 289).

66. Watson, "Melting into God," 37–38.

67. Noted by Watson, ibid., 35.

68. Stölting, *Christliche Frauenmystik,* 335; for detailed analysis, see Sargent, "*Le Mirouer des simples âmes,*" 361–68. It seems to me out of the question that the translator had a list of the condemned statements, as Leicht surmises (*Marguerite Porete,* 367), let alone that the glosses make it possible to "reconstruct a potentially condemned article" (ibid., 366).

69. *Margaret Porete,* ed. Doiron, 372. In his own Latin translation Richard Methley does not hesitate to interpret a statement *contra litteram* as orthodox (Colledge and Guarnieri, "Glosses by 'M.N.,'" 376–77).

70. Stölting, *Christliche Frauenmystik,* 339.

71. See Colledge and Guarnieri, "Glosses by 'M.N.,'" 358–82; for them, the glosses indicate heresy.

72. Ibid., 382. However, Colledge and Guarnieri are convinced that M.N. knew *The Cloud,* and they trace relationships between the texts (373). Furthermore, they look into Richard Methley's use of, and occasional comments on, the English *Mirror* for his Latin version. Sargent avoids an unambiguous stance on the question of heresy in the *Mirror,* and regrettably does not make a close connection between the *Mirror* and the English mystical tradition, notwithstanding his title "*Le Mirouer des simples âmes* and the English Mystical Tradition"; Doiron, editor of the Middle English text, tries to defend its orthodoxy, as does Orcibal, "'Le Miroir des simples âmes' et la 'secte' du Libre Esprit," *Revue de l'histoire des religions* 175 (1969): 35–60.

73. See Sells, *Mystical Languages,* 119.

74. Leicht, *Marguerite Porete;* Robinson, *Nobility and Annihilation,* 16–20, 103–4.

75. Ott, *Der Rosenroman,* 46.

76. Ibid., 27.

77. Ibid., 34.

78. Ibid., 38. Among the many sources used by Jean de Meun for his continuation of the *Roman de la rose* is the tract, also translated by him, *De spirituali amicitia* by Aelred of Rievaulx (Ott, *Rosenroman,* 119). Newman speaks of 'la mystique cortoise,' *From Virile Woman to WomanChrist,* chap. 5.

79. Julia Boffey and A. S. G. Edwards, "The Legend of Good Women," in *The Cambridge Companion to Chaucer,* 2nd ed., ed. Piero Boitani and Jill Mann (Cambridge: Cambridge University Press, 2003), 125; Robert Worth Frank Jr., *Chaucer and "The Legend of Good Women"* (Cambridge MA: Harvard University Press, 1972).

80. The reference is to Bernard of Clairvaux, in *Riverside Chaucer,* F 16, 1061.

81. See also Leicht, *Marguerite Porete,* 115 and 116n. It should be mentioned here that there was a French tradition of composing courtly poetry on the marguerite, which in French also meant daisy. Yet it does not make sense to argue that with his translation the translator wanted to connect the French *Mirouer* text with other contemporary French texts.

82. Lerner, *Heresy,* 74.

83. Long ago, C. Kirchberger, who was not aware of Marguerite's authorship, surmised that the work could have been written by Michael of Northburgh, bishop of London and cofounder of the London Charterhouse (*Margaret Porete,* ed. Doiron, 245). Northburgh was in the service of Edward III and oversaw the arrangements for his marriage to Philippa of Hainaut. The translator M.N. himself points out that the text was already in circulation and in some respects was misunderstood, for which reason he was adding his own glosses at this later date. For a more detailed discussion of Northburgh see Sargent, *"Le Mirouer des simples âmes,"* 444. In France there were numerous translators for the king (Ott, *Der Rosenroman,* 17).

84. Lerner, "New Light," 104.

85. Ibid., 103-4.

86. Ibid., 105: "No doubt exists that the three surviving Middle English manuscripts of the *Mirror,* all dating from the fifteenth century, are of Carthusian provenance." See also Thompson, *Carthusian Order in England,* 167-73.

87. *Margaret Porete,* ed. Doiron, 245; McFarlane, *Lancastrian Kings and Lollard Knights;* Tuck, "Carthusian Monks and Lollard Knights"; Paul Strohm and Thomas J. Heffernan, eds., *Reconstructing Chaucer* (Knoxville: University of Tennessee Press, 1985), 149-61.

88. On this see, e.g., McFarlane, *Lancastrian Kings and Lollard Knights,* 181; Tuck, "Carthusian Monks and Lollard Knights," 149-61; cf. also Ellis and Fanous: "Gaunt's interest in Wyclif, dating from soon after 1376, lasted at least until the Blackfriars Council of 1382," in *Cambridge Companion to Medieval English Mysticism,* 150; K. B. McFarlane, *John Wycliffe and the Beginnings of English Non-Conformity* (London: English Universities Press, 1966), 117-19, 125.

89. Watson, "Melting into God," 35.

7. *The Cloud of Unknowing* and Related Tracts

1. Today Maika W. Fowler would have even more cause to regret that an increasing number of critics and scholars claim an astonishing similarity between *The Cloud of Unknowing* and Buddhism; she offers a very useful assessment of the

differences ("Zen Buddhist Meditation and the *Cloud* Author's Prayer of Love," *DR* 113 [1995]: 289–308).

2. P. Chevallier, ed., *Dionysiaca* 1–2 (Paris: Desclée de Brouwer, 1937–49).

3. Volker Leppin, *Die christliche Mystik* (Munich: C. H. Beck, 2007), 29; on Pseudo-Dionysius, see esp. Ruh, *Geschichte*, 1, chap. 1; and McGinn, *Presence of God*, vol. 1, *Foundations:* "Anagogy and Apophaticism: The Mysticism of Dionysius," 157–82.

4. Quotations are taken from Hodgson's more recent edition of all the *Cloud* author's writings (*Cloud of Unknowing* [1982]).

5. Leppin, *Christliche Mystik*, 33.

6. Citations are from *The Cloud of Unknowing*, ed. Hodgson (1982). The sequence of titles named in *BPC* evidently reflects the chronology of their composition: see Clark, *"Cloud of Unknowing,"* 1:5; and Annie Sutherland, "The Dating and Authorship of the *Cloud* Corpus: A Reassessment of the Evidence," *MAE* 71 (2002): 82–100.

7. Thus also Hodgson in her first *Cloud* edition: *Cloud of Unknowing* (1958), lxxviii.

8. Cf. Kent Emery, *"The Cloud of Unknowing and Mystica Theologia,"* in Elder, *Roots of the Modern Christian Tradition*, vol. 2, *Spirituality of Western Christendom*, 46–70; and the more recent article by Cheryl Taylor, "The *Cloud*-Author's Remaking of the Pseudo-Dionysius's *Mystical Theology,"* *MAE* 75 (2006): 202–18; also Steinmetz, *Mystische Erfahrung:* "This Vercelli-Dionysian theology seems to have been important to the author not only for 'Hid Divinite' but also for his mystical teaching as a whole" (197–98).

9. See also Voaden, *God's Words, Women's Voices;* Nancy Caciola, *Discerning Spirits: Divine and Demonic Possession in the Middle Ages* (Ithaca, NY: Cornell University Press, 2003); and Steinmetz, *Mystische Erfahrung*.

10. *Cloud of Unknowing*, ed. Hodgson (1982), xiv.

11. From *Sermones de Diversis, PL* 183, cols. 600–5; see *Cloud of Unknowing*, ed. Hodgson (1982), 200.

12. Richard of St. Victor, *Twelve Patriarchs*.

13. Steinmetz gives a good survey of research on this problem, stressing the work's close relationship with the *Cloud*-group texts, but leaving open the question of authorship (*Mystische Erfahrung*, 97).

14. Ibid., 34; Steinmetz bases his discussion on R. Myles, "'This Litil Worde "Is"': The Existential Metaphysics of the *Cloud* Author," *Florilegium* 8 (1986): 140–68.

15. Steinmetz, *Mystische Erfahrung*, 34.

16. For discussion of this thesis and the freedom resulting from it, see N. D. O'Donoghue, "'This Noble Noughting and This High Alling': Self-Relinquishment in *The Cloud of Unknowing* and *The Epistle of Privy Counsel,"* *Journal of Studies in Mysticism* 2 (1979): 1–15.

17. See, for instance, Alois M. Haas, "Christliche Aspekte des 'Gnothi seauton': Selbsterkenntnis und Mystik," *Zeitschrift für deutsches Altertum und deutsche Literatur* 110 (1981): 71–96.

18. This theme is very well addressed by Steinmetz, *Mystische Erfahrung*, 151–70; see also the recent essay by K. Baier, "Meditation and Contemplation in High to Late Medi-

eval Europe," in *Yogic Perception, Meditation and Altered States of Consciousness*, ed. Eli Franco (Vienna: Verlag der Österreichischen Akademie der Wissenschaften, 2009), 325–49.

19. Steinmetz, *Mystische Erfahrung*, 156.

20. Ibid.

21. See P. Hodgson, "A Ladder of Foure Ronges by the Whiche Men Mowe Wele Clyme to Heven: A Study of the Prose Style of a Middle English Translation," *MLR* 44 (1949): 465–75; the original Latin text was edited by Edmund Colledge and James Walsh: *Guigues II le Chartreux: Lettre sur la vie contemplative (L'échelle des moines)*, SC 163 (Paris: Institut des Sources Chrétiennes, 1970), 45–52.

22. Cf. Steinmetz, *Mystische Erfahrung*, 157; and P. Rissanen, "The Prayer of Being in *The Cloud of Unknowing*," *MQ* 13 (1987): 140–45.

23. Steinmetz, *Mystische Erfahrung*, 207.

24. Forman, "Mystical Experience," 189.

25. Rightly interpreted in this way, e.g. by Tugwell, *Ways of Imperfection*, 179.

26. Cf. Steinmetz, *Mystische Erfahrung*, 175.

27. Ibid., 204.

28. Forman, "Mystical Experience," 186; also Tixier, "'Þis Louely Blinde Werk,'" in Pollard and Boenig, *Mysticism and Spirituality*, 122–37.

29. Cf. Steinmetz, *Mystische Erfahrung*, 94–96.

30. Ibid., esp. 195–211.

31. Important comments on this point in Steinmetz, *Mystische Erfahrung*; he relates the author's apparently original discussion of time to contemporary notions of physics (225).

32. Ibid., 40–54; Clark, *"Cloud of Unknowing,"* 160–61; Riehle, *Middle English Mystics*, 142–48. On this theme in general, see L. Scheffczyk, ed., *Der Mensch als Bild Gottes* (Darmstadt: Wissenschaftliche Buchgesellschaft, 1969).

33. Steinmetz, *Mystische Erfahrung*, 41.

34. Scheffczyk, *Mensch als Bild Gottes*.

35. Steinmetz, *Mystische Erfahrung*, 56–59.

36. On *deificatio* in English mysticism, cf. Riehle, *Middle English Mystics*, 150–52.

37. Steinmetz, *Mystische Erfahrung*, 40–50.

38. Ibid., 44.

39. Ibid., 45; Steinmetz also notes the manifold commentaries on these themes in the patristic tradition.

40. Ibid., 46.

41. Ibid., 47.

42. Ibid.

43. Ibid.

44. Ibid., 49.

45. Ibid., 51. A very good essay, with useful references, is Minnis, "Affection and Imagination," 323–66; see also the substantial contribution by J. A. Burrow, "Fantasy and Language in 'The Cloud of Unknowing,'" *EIC* 27 (1977): 283–98; Burrow deals with the phenomenon of "spiritual-sensual" language.

46. The ultimate foundation for this lies in Paul's words, frequently cited in mysticism, about puffed-up knowledge (1 Cor 8:1); *curiositas* is discussed in great detail in Steinmetz, *Mystische Erfahrung*, 63–87. This is also a favorite Cistercian theme.

47. Steinmetz, *Mystische Erfahrung,* 68. See also the interesting comment by Grace Jantzen: "'Cry Out and Write': Mysticism and the Struggle for Authority," in Lesley and Taylor, *Women, the Book and the Godly,* 67–76. Jantzen is absolutely right in affirming that the critical attitude toward people who are different was a basis for persecution of witches in later times (see the *Malleus maleficarum*), for which, however, the *Cloud* author cannot be held in any way responsible. In this connection, R. W. Englert's study, *Scattering and Oneing: A Study of Conflict in "The Cloud of Unknowing,"* AC 105 (Salzburg: Institut für Anglistik und Amerikanistik, 1983), is also interesting; as is Tony Chartrand-Burke, "Against the Proud Scholars of the Devil: Anti-Intellectual Rhetoric in *The Cloud of Unknowing,*" MQ 23 (1997): 115–30.

48. The fact that he was an Augustinian canon of St. Victor is important in this context; the Victorines gained great significance for English spirituality and mysticism, as the investigation of *Ancrene Wisse* has already shown. Thomas Gallus also had close personal connections with England, since he was very friendly with the Franciscan Adam Marsh and the bishop of Lincoln, Robert Grosseteste: see James Walsh, "'Sapientia Christianorum': The Doctrine of Thomas Gallus Abbot of Vercelli on Contemplation" (PhD diss., Pontifica Università, Rome, 1957), iii–iv.

49. Cf. Ruh, *Geschichte,* 3:59–81.

50. See ibid., 60, for detailed bibliographical references on Thomas Gallus; cf. also the very good more recent study by Lees, *Negative Language,* 2:181.

51. A. Combes, quoted from Ruh, *Geschichte,* 3:59.

52. E.g. Steinmetz in his book *Mystische Erfahrung.* This influence is confirmed, e.g., by Hodgson, ed., in *"Deonise Hid Diuinite,"* xxxix–xl, xlii, 119–29; A. J. Minnis, "The Sources of *The Cloud of Unknowing:* A Reconsideration," *MMTE* 2 (1982), 63–75; and Glasscoe, *English Medieval Mystics,* 174. Hodgson provides evidence that for his translation of the *Mystica theologia* the *Cloud* author used Gallus's *Extractio* and probably also his *Glossa* and/or the *explanatio* of *Mystica theologia.* Cf. also the very substantial article by Clark, "Sources and Theology." Clark, too, concedes a certain influence of Thomas Gallus on *Cloud* (ibid., 100), as also in his useful two-volume *"The Cloud of Unknowing": An Introduction,* thus confirming the present author's line of argument. However, Clark is heavily committed to the outdated principle of "source hunting" and does not reflect on what benefit there may be in ascertaining the sources of an author's ideas. The fact that there are sources is less interesting than the manner in which the author integrates them into his work, or uses them to shape something individual and new.

53. Following Johannes Sarracenus in his dedication to John of Salisbury (Ruh, *Geschichte* 3:73).

54. Ibid.

55. Ibid.

56. Thomas Gallus, quoted from Ruh, *Geschichte,* 3:75.

57. Ibid., 66; this theme is very well traced by Minnis, "Affection and Imagination," 65.

58. Minnis, "Affection and Imagination," 65.

59. Ibid.; see also Steinmetz, *Mystische Erfahrung,* e.g. 241.

60. Ruh, *Geschichte,* 3:76.

61. See also Riehle, *Middle English Mystics,* 152–64.

62. See Lees, *Negative Language,* 2:270ff.; Riehle, *Middle English Mystics,* 160; cf. more recently McGinn, *Presence of God,* vol. 4, *Harvest:* "The Mysticism of the Ground," 83–93, and "Meister Eckhart: Mystical Teacher and Preacher," 94–194.

63. See also Steinmetz, *Mystische Erfahrung,* 190; he cites the *apex affectualis* as synonym for *apex affectionis.*

64. Lees, *Negative Language,* 2:286; Ivánka understands it as a Stoic term: *Plato Christianus,* 2nd ed. (1990), esp. 342.

65. Bonaventure had also simplified Thomas (Ruh, *Geschichte,* 3:68).

66. Minnis, "Affection and Imagination," 64. Clark's assertion that "'scintilla' has become a common term in the Dionysian tradition" (*"Cloud of Unknowing,"* 2:48) goes too far; cf. also Riehle, *Middle English Mystics,* 152–64; further, Lees, *Negative Language,* 2:332–34; Tugwell, "Cloud of Unknowing," in Tugwell, *Ways of Imperfection,* 170–86; and Forman, "Mystical Experience," 49–61.

67. Ruh, *Geschichte,* 3:68; also 67.

68. Minnis rightly observes that the *Cloud* author gained much more than a mere "characteristic flavour" from Thomas ("Affection and Imagination," 67). At the same time he attached less value to *sensualite,* as compared with Richard: "Richard's link between will and sensualite is broken. As the faculty by which we choose good after it has been approved by the reason, and the power by which we are united with God, will is placed unequivocally above reason," which shows the influence of Gallus ("Affection and Imagination," 68). That the *Cloud* author differs from Richard of St. Victor in finding no positive aspects in imagination likewise points indirectly to the influence of Thomas Gallus ("Affection and Imagination," 69–70); nevertheless, the *Cloud* author translated Richard's *Benjamin minor* (cf. also Walsh, "The Cloud of Unknowing," in Walsh, *Pre-Reformation English Spirituality,* 170–81; and Steinmetz, *Mystische Erfahrung,* 48–54).

69. Patrick J. Gallacher, ed., *The Cloud of Unknowing* (Kalamazoo, MI: Medieval Institute Publications, 1997), introduction.

70. They were edited by J. Barbet, *Thomas Gallus: Commentaires du Cantique des cantiques* (Paris, 1967; Turnhout: Brepols, 2005).

71. Ruh, *Geschichte,* 3:76.

72. Page and line quotations from *Cloud of Unknowing,* ed. Hodgson (1982).

73. Ibid., 79; thus also in Bernard of Clairvaux, Hugh of St. Victor, and Richard of St. Victor; cf. also Steinmetz, *Mystische Erfahrung,* 182.

74. See Gillespie, "Mystic's Foot," in *MMTE* 2 (1982), 199–203; Steinmetz, *Mystische Erfahrung,* 180.

75. It is therefore difficult to understand why Minnis, in his valuable investigation of affection and imagination in the *Cloud* author and Hilton, makes no mention at all of Bernard of Clairvaux.

76. See Steinmetz, *Mystische Erfahrung,* 247–54.

77. Ibid., 247–50, 249.

78. Rolle knows *amor rationalis,* as we have seen, but he, too, puts the case for the exclusivity of love.

79. See Steinmetz, *Mystische Erfahrung,* 251–54.

80. Cf. also Riehle, *Middle English Mystics,* 51.

81. Although we repeatedly encounter Bernard's influence on the *Cloud* author, he is hardly mentioned in Hodgson's discussion of sources and influences in her

edition of 1982. Clark, however, traces the reception of Bernard and William ("Sources and Theology," 101–9). Steinmetz, *Mystische Erfahrung,* also makes useful observations on the influence of Bernard and Thomas Gallus.

82. It is important to note how the goodness of God, described by Pseudo-Dionysius as intrinsic (Ruh, *Geschichte,* 1:47), here flows from the author's pen.

83. Steinmetz, *Mystische Erfahrung,* 216.

84. Ibid., 191.

85. Ibid., 218; see also Karl-Heinz Steinmetz, "'Thiself a Cros to Thiself': Christ as *Signum Impressum* in the *Cloud*-Texts against the Background of Expressionistic Christology in Late Medieval Devotional Theology," *MMTE* 7 (2004), 132–47.

86. See also Steinmetz, *Mystische Erfahrung,* 219.

87. Ruh, *Geschichte,* 1:67.

88. Quoted from Steinmetz, *Mystische Erfahrung,* 183.

89. It is of interest that this demand of the "one thing needful" was also interpreted by Aelred as a freeing of the self from all that is contingent (Buchmüller, *Askese der Liebe,* 113).

90. Meister Eckhart, *Einheit mit Gott: Die bedeutendsten Schriften zur Mystik,* ed. Dietmar Mieth (Düsseldorf: Patmos, 2008).

91. Ibid., 165.

92. Ibid., 61.

93. Of course, he could not know that the letters of Timothy were penned by a different author, who followed Paul.

94. McGinn, "English Mystics," in Raitt, *Christian Spirituality* 2:202.

95. Ruh, *Geschichte,* 3:68. David N. Bell points out further that William's "Amor ipse notitia est" is already found in Gregory the Great, and that similar statements could be found in a dozen more authors, including Bernard, Aelred, Gilbert of Hoyland, Baldwin of Ford, Philip of Harvengt, Hugh of St. Victor, and Adam Scotus (*The Image and Likeness: The Augustinian Spirituality of William of St. Thierry* [Kalamazoo, MI: Cistercian Publications, 1984], 232).

96. This is pointed out by P. F. O'Mara, "The Light behind the Cloud of Unknowing," *SM* 19 (1998): 45–55; according to O'Mara, to call the mysticism of the *Cloud* author "non-cognitive" and that of Hilton "cognitive" probably makes too strict a distinction (52). Tixier had observed that in some authors "the teaching of Pseudo-Dionysius is given a warmer and more affective bent" ("'Þis Louely Blinde Werk,'" in Pollard and Boenig, *Mysticism and Spirituality,* 112).

97. Mieth, *Meister Eckhart,* 131–32.

98. Quoted from Ruh, *Geschichte,* 3:279.

99. Ibid., 352 ("*Castellum* sermon," text from Lk 10:38).

100. Ibid., 353.

101. See also T.-J. Morris, "Rhetorical Stance: An Approach to *The Cloud of Unknowing,*" *MQ* 15 (1989): 13–20. Hodgson rightly emphasizes the author's irony (*"Deonise Hid Diuinite,"* liii).

102. Denis Renevey, "'See by Ensaumple': Images and Imagination in the Writings of the Author of 'The Cloud of Unknowing,'" *Micrologus* 6 (1998): 225–43.

103. Yet the author has "taken the theologumenon of the 'cloud of unknowing' out of the Moses-on-Sinai exegesis and extended it into a broad *caligo* mysticism. In Richard of St. Victor, Bonaventure, Thomas Gallus Vercellensis, and Hugh of Balma,

caligo is a clearly delimited stage in the contemplative ascent, but for the *Cloud* author almost the entire contemplative path is 'overhung with clouds.' The anonymous author is therefore one of the most important representatives of an avowed mysticism of the night prior to St. John of the Cross" (Steinmetz, *Mystische Erfahrung*, 201).

104. P. R. Rovang, "Demythologizing Metaphor in the *Cloud of Unknowing*," *MQ* 18 (1992): 131–37; cf. also A. C. Spearing, "Language and Its Limits: *The Cloud of Unknowing* and *Pearl*," in Dyas, Edden, and Ellis, *Approaching Medieval English Anchoritic and Mystical Texts*, 75–86. Nike Kocijančič-Pokorn offers a not entirely convincing modern theory approach to the language of *Cloud* in "The Language and Discourse of *The Cloud of Unknowing*," *Literature and Theology* 11 (1997): 408–21.

105. See René Tixier, "'Good Gamesumli Pley': Games of Love in *The Cloud of Unknowing*," *DR* 108 (1990): 235–53.

106. *Origen: Spirit and Fire*, ed. von Balthasar, 345–48.

107. Ruh, *Geschichte*, 3:63.

108. Up to now the view has prevailed that Thomas Gallus's works appeared in the vernacular only in quotations in *Die siben strassen zu got* by the Franciscan Rudolf of Biberach (Lees, *Negative Language*, 2:313 n. and appendix 2). Yet the fruitful influence of Gallus's style on a vernacular language actually took full effect in *The Cloud of Unknowing*. Lees already suspected an influence of this sort: "It seems... entirely probable that the English author absorbed something of the fluency and flexibility of Gallus's style through his extensive reading in Gallus's works" (*Negative Language*, 2:369). For his translation of the *Mystica theologia* the *Cloud* author had used the Sarracenus version and, especially for the last chapters, the Gallus Vercellensis version. The translation is sometimes exact, while at other times it expands or simplifies and clarifies the Latin text; it is analyzed in detail by Hodgson (*"Deonise Hid Diuinite,"* xli–xliii, 118–29). According to Steinmetz, the *Cloud* author may be regarded "as one of the most skillful and creative translators into the vernacular of Gallus's motto 'Deus incomprehensibilis intellectu sed apprehensibilis affectu' and of many other terms" (*Mystische Erfahrung*, 199).

109. See Robert Englert, "'Of Another Mind': Ludic Imagery and Spiritual Doctrine in *The Cloud of Unknowing*," *SM* 8 (1985): 3–12.

110. "'Þis Louely Blinde Werk,'" in Pollard and Boenig, *Mysticism and Spirituality*, 135; cf. also René Tixier, "Mystique et pédagogie dans *The Cloud of Unknowing*" (PhD diss., Université de Nancy, 1988).

111. *Cloud of Unknowing*, ed. Hodgson (1944), lxxxiii; *Cloud of Unknowing*, ed. Hodgson (1982), x; Clark is of the opinion that "the author, like the recipient of the book, is a vowed contemplative" (*"Cloud of Unknowing,"* 2:224).

112. McGinn maintains without compelling evidence that the author lives "under monastic obedience" ("English Mystics," in Raitt, *Christian Spirituality*, 2:455; also Clark, *"Cloud of Unknowing,"* 1:20). It is true that two Latin translations of *Cloud* were made by Carthusians (ca. 1450 and 1491) and circulated by this order on the Continent. Yet this does not provide evidence of authorship; it simply confirms the well-known fact that the Carthusians did a great deal for the transmission and *circulation* of mystical texts, which was their great strength, and that they had wide contemplative interests. These interests did not lie in a particular theological-mystical "direction." The fact that the only surviving manuscript of *The Book of Margery Kempe*

comes from the Mount Grace Charterhouse, and a monk of this priory annotated the text, does not mean that the book was written there. Richard Methley, a Mount Grace Carthusian who translated *Cloud* into Latin about one hundred years after it was written, associated the term "status singularis" with hermits, and especially with Carthusians, but Clark is mistaken in seeing this as compelling proof (*"Cloud of Unknowing,"* 1:21, n. 11). And there is no justification for the postulate that the anonymous author belonged to the Beauvale Charterhouse (Clark, "Late Fourteenth-Century Cambridge Theology," 12; and Clark, *"Cloud of Unknowing,"* 1:17).

Things are more complicated when it comes to the allegedly numerous thematic links between the *Cloud* author and the Carthusian Hugh of Balma's *Viae Sion lugent.* Vigorous attempts have been made to suggest or prove *Cloud's* Carthusian origin on the basis of numerous comparisons with passages from Hugh's work (*Cloud of Unknowing,* ed. Hodgson (1982), xi; Clark, "Late Fourteenth-Century Cambridge Theology," 11; and Clark, *"Cloud of Unknowing,"* vol. 1). But it is necessary to exercise great caution because Hugh—like the *Cloud* author—was influenced by Thomas Gallus, so that Thomas may be the common source of both. Therefore, more or less clear parallels between *Cloud* and Hugh of Balma are not very informative. Minnis has demonstrated the extent of agreement between Hugh of Balma and Thomas Gallus, and makes the interesting observation that there is no parallel in the *Cloud* author for the most individual feature of Hugh's *Viae Sion lugent,* namely "its division of the contemplative way into the purgative, illuminative and unitive stages" ("Affection and Imagination," 72). Even if Hugh's tract did in fact provide the *Cloud* author with certain stimuli, this does not in any way support the hypothesis that the author of *Cloud,* and the writings related to it, was a Carthusian (notwithstanding Clark's contrary opinion). Moreover, Ruh has pointed out that although Hugh's origins were in Carthusian spirituality—for a time he was a charterhouse prior—far more significantly, his theology was Franciscan in orientation (*Geschichte,* 3:101). Clark has contributed greatly to the discovery of *Cloud's* sources, but his analysis is often distorted by the assumption of Carthusian affiliation. On the Carthusians in England, see, for instance, Steinmetz, *Mystische Erfahrung,* 140, nn. 1 and 2.

113. See Baker, "Active and Contemplative Lives," 94. Gregory the Great had already praised the *vita mixta,* which was lived consummately by Jesus (see *Cloud of Unknowing,* ed. Hodgson (1982), 156, nn. 2/7–13).

114. This is pointed out also by Clark, *"Cloud of Unknowing,"* 1:3.

115. Lees points this out (*Negative Language,* 2:457ff.). She criticizes—mistakenly, in my view—my association of these texts with a "lay movement of female piety" (Lees, *Negative Language,* 2:462), because she wishes to establish a Carthusian connection (2:463).

116. Doyle supports this view, on the evidence provided by the manuscripts, although such evidence is necessarily incomplete ("Survey"); cf. also the very useful supplementary discussion of these problems in Lees, *Negative Language,* 2:396ff.

117. Cf. also Riehle, *Middle English Mystics,* 53.

118. See, for instance, V. Honemann, "Das Leben als Pilgerfahrt zum Himmlischen Jerusalem in der *Pèlerinage de la vie humaine* des Guillaume de Deguileville," in *Himmel auf Erden / Heaven on Earth,* ed. Rudolf Suntrup and J. R. Veenstra, Medieval to Early Modern Culture / Kultureller Wandel vom Mittelalter zur Frühen Neuzeit 12 (Frankfurt am Main: Peter Lang, 2009), 107–22.

8. Walter Hilton

1. von Balthasar, *Walter Hilton: Glaube und Erfahrung.*
2. This is surmised by Kennedy, *Incarnational Element.*
3. David Knowles and Joy Russell-Smith, "Hilton (Walter)," *DS,* col. 526; see also Russell-Smith's important article, "Walter Hilton," *Month,* n.s. 22 (1959): 133–48; repr. in Walsh, *Pre-Reformation English Spirituality,* 182–97; see also Russell-Smith, "Walter Hilton and a Tract in the Defence of the Veneration of Images," *Dominican Studies* 7 (1954): 180–214; for Hilton's biography, see further the good account in *Scale of Perfection,* ed. Clark and Dorward, 13–53. A concise overview is given by Bestul, "Walter Hilton," in Dyas, Edden, and Ellis, *Approaching Medieval English Anchoritic and Mystical Texts,* 87–10. Once again, it is apparent that a full appreciation of the texts' literary and theological qualities would require a more thorough investigation. The most recent study is that by Margarete Hopf, *Der Weg zu christlicher Vollkommenheit:* see esp. p. 73.
4. Hopf, *Der Weg,* 73.
5. Also emphasized by Hopf, *Der Weg.*
6. MS BL Harley 2397 also attests that he is a hermit.
7. Helen Gardner already argued that Hilton had probably been inspired by Rolle to embark on the eremitic life but had come to feel it to be unsuitable ("Walter Hilton and the Mystical Tradition in England," 113). Gardner drew especially on Hilton's *De imagine peccati.*
8. Cf. Kennedy: "It is difficult to believe that in 1384 Hilton was at Cambridge to pursue legal studies, in view of what had apparently been the course of his life up to that date" (*Incarnational Element,* 34); S. S. Hussey assumed that Hilton undertook theological studies in Cambridge ca. 1383–84 ("Latin and English in *The Scale of Perfection,*" 457); see also Clark, "Late Fourteenth-Century Cambridge Theology," 1–16.
9. This is the view of Clark, "Walter Hilton and the Psalm Commentary *Qui Habitat,*" 235–62.
10. *Qui Habitat* and *Bonum Est* "have links with the style and even the theology of the *Cloud* as well as with Hilton" (Clark, "'Lightsome Darkness,'" 96); see also Clark, "The Problem of Walter Hilton's Authorship: *Bonum est, Benedictus,* and *Of Angels' Song,*" *DR* 101 (1983): 15–29. The *Benedictus* commentary is sometimes ascribed to Hilton but contains no compelling indication of his authorship.
11. *The Prickynge of Love,* ed. H. Kane; the modern English edition (C. Kirchberger, ed., *The Goad of Love* [London: Faber and Faber, 1952]) has a very good introduction; see also Clark, "Walter Hilton and the *Stimulus amoris,*" *DR* 102 (1984): 79–118; Clark regards Hilton as the probable author of the *Prickynge of Love.* For further details on the *Stimulus amoris,* see McGinn, *Presence of God,* vol. 3, *Flowering,* 118. McGinn does not question Hilton's responsibility for the rendering of this work into Middle English.
12. For this reason, *The Scale of Perfection* had been translated into Latin, and subsequently this translation was also read in Continental monasteries (see, for instance, Putter, "Walter Hilton's *Scale of Perfection,*" 34).
13. "cuidam Recluso" (*Walter Hilton's Latin Writings,* ed. Clark and Taylor, 1:73).
14. Ibid., 1:97; on these texts, see esp. the introductions by Clark and Taylor in *Walter Hilton's Latin Writings;* and by Clark and Dorward in their edition, *Walter Hilton: The Scale of Perfection.*

15. *Walter Hilton's Latin Writings,* 1:99.

16. Ibid., 98.

17. "Nichil Deo presencius nobis est... Tange eum digito [!] et desiderio cordis tui, vt totus conuertaris in illum. Ipse enim esse tuum est, vita tua est, sensus et racio tua est" (*Walter Hilton's Latin Writings,* 1:96).

18. Ibid.

19. See Clark, "Walter Hilton in Defence of the Religious Life," *DR* 103 (1985).

20. *Epistola de utilitate et prerogativis religionis,* in *Walter Hilton's Latin Writings,* 1:119–72.

21. See, for instance, Gardner, "Walter Hilton and the Mystical Tradition in England," 103–27, 112–13; and Hughes, "Walter Hilton's Direction to Contemplatives," 7.

22. *Walter Hilton's Latin Writings,* 1:144.

23. Ibid., 2:225.

24. Ibid., 2:237.

25. Ibid., 2:215, 228, 237, 403, 405, 411–12; and Clark, "Walter Hilton and Liberty of Spirit," 61–78.

26. *Walter Hilton's Latin Writings,* 2:216.

27. Ibid., 2:227.

28. Ibid., 2:232.

29. Ibid., 2:230.

30. Ibid., 2:227.

31. This "experiencia divini amoris," to which Hilton wishes to guide his friend, is not, as Clark and Taylor maintain, "synonymous with what Hilton elsewhere describes as *intellectus*" (*Walter Hilton's Latin Writings,* 2:397). In *De adoracione ymaginum* Hilton will speak in even more Bernardine terms of the "libro experiencie" (*Walter Hilton's Latin Writings,* 1:193).

32. *Walter Hilton's Latin Writings,* 2:242.448–61; *Origen: Spirit and Fire,* ed. von Balthasar, 270.

33. See Rahner, "Die Gottesgeburt," 333–418.

34. "It need not at all be the case that Hilton derived the doctrine from the Rhineland; it was a commonplace for the early Cistercians, who are so influential on Hilton in other respects" (*Walter Hilton's Latin Writings,* 2:415).

35. See Clark, "Walter Hilton in Defence of the Religious Life."

36. *Walter Hilton's Latin Writings,* 1:175; Joy Russell-Smith, "Walter Hilton and a Tract in Defence of the Veneration of Images," *Dominican Studies* 7 (1954): 180–214; see also Minnis, "Affection and Imagination," 359–61.

37. Augustine of Hippo, *De magistro,* 97ff.

38. Minnis, "Affection and Imagination," 361.

39. Hilton uses the word "excitar[e]," which has multiple traditional meanings (*Walter Hilton's Latin Writings,* 1:193). At the end of time the images will be obsolete, for "tunc videbimus eum sicuti est, facie ad faciem, transformati in ipsam ymaginem inuisibilis Dei de claritate fidei in claritatem visionis beate" (*Walter Hilton's Latin Writings,* 1:214).

40. *Walter Hilton's "Mixed Life"* [hereafter *Mixed Life*], ed. Ogilvie-Thomson, 11; the "Epistle on Mixed Life" is also printed in Windeatt, *English Mystics.*

41. On the lord as addressee, cf. Ellis, "Literary Approach to the Middle English Mystics," 109–15. Also see *Mixed Life,* ed. Ogilvie-Thomson, 10; cf. also Hussey, "Langland, Hilton, and the Three Lives," 132–50. For lay persons' relationship to *vita activa* and *vita contemplativa,* see also Ronald N. Swanson, *Religion and Devotion in Europe, c. 1215–c. 1515* (Cambridge: Cambridge University Press, 1995), 105–6, 125–26.

42. *Mixed Life,* ed. Ogilvie-Thomson, 66.

43. Ibid., 68.

44. *Of Angels' Song* survives in six medieval manuscripts and in Pepwell's printed edition of 1521. Only in the early sixteenth-century MS Bodley 576 and in Pepwell is the tract ascribed to Hilton; it is included in Horstmann's *Yorkshire Writers* 1:175–182; more recent editions are found in T. Takamija, ed., *Of Angels' Song: Edited from the British Museum MS Additional 27592,* Studies in English Literature 162, Engl. no. 1977 (Tokyo, 1977), 3–31, reprinted in *Two Minor Works of Walter Hilton* (Tokyo, 1980); and in R. Dorward, ed., with modern English trans., *Walter Hilton: Eight Chapters on Perfection* (Oxford: Fairacres, SLG Press, 1983). For a good survey of scholarly issues in these texts, see Lagorio and Sargent, "English Mystical Writings," 3074–82.

45. The text is quoted from Windeatt, *English Mystics,* 135.

46. Ibid., 133.

47. See Hammerstein, *Musik der Engel,* 83–88.

48. Brantley, *Reading in the Wilderness,* 241–47.

49. Windeatt, *English Mystics,* 133.

50. Watson already expressed some doubt about the conjecture that Hilton was criticizing Rolle (*Invention,* 261). He made further relevant comments in "Middle English Mystics," 539–65.

51. *Walter Hilton's Latin Writings,* 2:352.

52. Windeatt, *English Mystics,* 134.

53. Ibid., 136.

54. There are, however, no indications that Hilton examined, or edited, the translation.

55. Quotations are taken from *Scale of Perfection,* ed. Bestul, based on the early fifteenth-century codex, London, Lambeth Palace MS 472.

56. So far, no edition of *The Scale of Perfection* satisfies the most stringent scholarly criteria. Since there are some divergences in the text as transmitted in the most important manuscripts, it is very problematic to establish a text as intended by the author; in any case, editorial principles of this kind are regarded as obsolete by modern philologists. *Scale* 1 and *Scale* 2 have each been edited, from the manuscripts, in an unpublished dissertation: Barbara E. Wykes, ed., "An Edition of Book I of *The Scale of Perfection* by Walter Hilton" (PhD diss., Ann Arbor, MI, 1957); and Stanley S. Hussey, ed., "An Edition, from the Manuscripts, of Book II of Walter Hilton's *Scale of Perfection*" (diss., London, 1962). For overall interpretations of the *Scale of Perfection,* see Hughes, "Walter Hilton's Direction to Contemplatives"; Joseph E. Milosh, *"The Scale of Perfection" and the English Mystical Tradition* (Madison: University of Wisconsin Press, 1966); Knowles, *English Mystical Tradition;* Glasscoe, *English Medieval Mystics;* and the important article, previously mentioned, by Helen Gardner, "Walter Hilton and the Mystical Tradition in England."

57. Warren, *Anchorites and Their Patrons.*

58. Doerr, *Das Institut der Inclusen*, 52.

59. The *Scale* does mention the wearing of a hair shirt (*Scale* 2, chap. 20, 173), as does Margery Kempe.

60. It has been noted that the Christocentric tendency of *Scale* 2 is strengthened in the contemporary translation by Thomas Fishlake; see Hussey, "Latin and English in the *Scale of Perfection*," esp. 469–70; and Clark, "English and Latin in *The Scale of Perfection*," 205–12.

61. Putter, "Walter Hilton's *Scale of Perfection*," 37; Michael G. Sargent, "The Organization of the *Scale of Perfection*," in *MMTE* 2 (1982), 231–61.

62. *Walter Hilton's Latin Writings*, 1:167.

63. Ibid., 132.

64. This influence was asserted by Clark, in *Scale of Perfection*, ed. Clark and Dorward, 24.

65. See esp. Clark, "Augustine, Anselm and Walter Hilton," *MMTE* 2 (1982), 102–26; *Scale of Perfection*, ed. Clark and Dorward, 307; and Kennedy, *Incarnational Element*, 118ff.

66. Clark, in *Scale of Perfection*, ed. Clark and Dorward, 23; Clark excludes Aelred as further influence—which is, as will be seen, an unjustified exclusion—but rightly includes the Victorines.

67. *Walter Hilton's Latin Writings*, 2:227.

68. Clark, in *Scale of Perfection*, ed. Clark and Dorward, 23; more recently, also Hopf, *Der Weg*.

69. As we saw in the case of the *Cloud* author, it is also the ground of the soul (see Riehle, *Middle English Mystics*, chap. 11, 142–64).

70. *Scale of Perfection*, ed. Bestul, 1:51.

71. D. Baker, "Image of God," 35–60.

72. *Scale of Perfection*, ed. Bestul, 2:143; see Clark's important theological essay, "Image and Likeness in Walter Hilton," *DR* 97 (1979): 204–20.

73. von Balthasar, *Walter Hilton: Glaube und Erfahrung*, 6–8.

74. See also Ellen M. Ross, "Ethical Mysticism: Walter Hilton and *The Scale of Perfection*," *SM* 17 (1996): 160–84; I do not find Nicholas Watson's discussion of Hilton's concept of *imago Dei* convincing; he would even like to derive from it a hostility toward images. "Image" in the *imago Dei* is not simply a metaphor. Nor can I understand the following statement: *"The Cloud of Unknowing*... offers a brilliant reading of a problem in Book I of *The Scale of Perfection*: its failure to integrate the later chapters' account of the 'image of sin' with its earlier survey of the types of contemplative experience, which (far from resembling anything the *Cloud*-author would endorse) are indebted to Rolle's optimistic spirituality and do suggest the possibility of moving beyond this image" ("'Et Que Est Huius Ydoli Materia? Tuipse,'" 107–8).

75. See also Riehle, *Middle English Mystics*, 162; and Bernard McGinn, "Vere Tu Es Deus Absconditus: The Hidden God in Luther and Some Mystics," in *Silence and the Word: Negative Theology and Incarnation*, ed. Oliver Davis and Denys Turner (Cambridge: Cambridge University Press, 2002), 94–114.

76. McGinn, *Presence of God*, vol. 4, *Harvest*, 288; see also *Origen: Spirit and Fire*, ed. von Balthasar, 31.

77. See, e.g., the subject index of McGinn's *Flowering* (*Presence of God*, vol. 3).

78. Tarjei Park, "Reflecting Christ: The Role of the Flesh in Walter Hilton and Julian of Norwich," in *MMTE* 5 (1992), 23. This is emphasized too strongly by Baker, "Image of God."

79. Park, "Reflecting Christ," 23.

80. *Scale of Perfection,* ed. Bestul, 2:153.

81. Gunnel Cleve concludes, not quite correctly, that "there does not seem to be much room for the resurrection of the body in Hilton's theology" (*Basic Mystic Themes,* 80).

82. *De trinitate,* 12.12.

83. Recognized also by Hopf (*Der Weg,* 155), as opposed to Baker, "Image of God."

84. Windeatt, *English Mystics,* 133.

85. Ibid.

86. Cleve, *Basic Mystic Themes,* 48.

87. Ibid., 52.

88. "Prayer is one of the central concepts, if not the central concept, in Book I of *The Scale*" (ibid).

89. On prayer, see Heiler, *Prayer.*

90. Cleve, *Basic Mystic Themes,* 100; and *Scale of Perfection* 2, esp. chap. 42.

91. See the interesting article by S. J. McEntire, "The Doctrine of Compunction from Bede to Margery Kempe," *MMTE* 4 (1987), 77–90.

92. Cf. Karl-Heinz Steinmetz, "'Thiself a Cros to Thiself': Christ as *Signum Impressum* in the *Cloud*-Texts against the Background of Expressionistic Christology in Late Medieval Devotional Theology," in *MMTE* 7 (2004), 146.

93. Cf. Hopf, *Der Weg,* 154.

94. "The Christian lives, as it were, with a double character: a human, sinful and fallen one, and a divine, a restored and reformed one" (Cleve, *Basic Mystic Themes,* 41).

95. Hopf, *Der Weg,* 171.

96. G. Kittel, *Theological Dictionary of the New Testament,* 5 vols., trans. and ed. G. W. Bromiley (Grand Rapids, MI: Eerdmans Publishing, 1964ff.); see also *Middle English Dictionary,* ed. Kurath et al.

97. Cf. Hopf (*Der Weg,* 131), who also refers to McGinn.

98. This recalls Augustine, *Enarratio in psalmos,* 135.8; see also *Walter Hilton's Latin Writings,* 2:371.

99. See McGinn, *Presence* of God, vol. 4, *Harvest,* 281, and "Love, Knowledge and *Unio mystica* in the Western Christian Tradition," in *Mystical Union in Judaism, Christianity, and Islam: An Ecumenical Dialogue,* ed. Moshe Idel and Bernard McGinn (New York: Continuum, 1996), 59–86.

100. On this see the important chapter "Union with God by the Holy Spirit," in Gilson, *Mystical Theology of Saint Bernard,* 210–11.

101. See also, for instance, *Die Predigten des Heiligen Augustinus über den 1. Johannesbrief,* trans. and introduced by F. Hofmann, 3rd ed. (Freiburg: Herder, 1954), VII, VIII.

102. Cleve, *Basic Mystic Themes,* 49; see also Riehle, *Middle English Mystics,* 112–13. Cleve notes that "sight does not seem to cover the whole range of sensations contained in Hilton's descriptions of the 'reformyng in felyng': these sensations also cover experiences related to other senses. . . . A full record of the occurrences of 'felyng,' as it is used by Hilton, thus displays a multiplicity of notions" (*Basic Mystic Themes,* 102).

103. Hopf, *Der Weg*, 169–70.

104. Minnis, "Affection and Imagination," 352.

105. Ibid., 353–54.

106. William of St. Thierry, *Meditation* 12.14, in *William of St. Thierry*, vol. 1, *On Contemplating God, Prayer, Meditations*, trans. Sister Penelope CSMV, Cistercian Fathers Series 3 (Kalamazoo, MI: Cistercian Publications, 1977), 175.

107. This has to be conceded even by Clark, one of the keenest champions of the thesis that the *Cloud* author and Hilton developed two entirely different theologies ("Trinitarian Theology of Walter Hilton's *Scale of Perfection*, Book II," in Phillips, *Langland, the Mystics, and the Medieval Religious Tradition*, 130).

108. von Balthasar, *Walter Hilton: Glaube und Erfahrung*, 8.

109. In *Scale* 1 Hilton had advised the recluse against undertaking a pilgrimage to Jerusalem, on the grounds that Jesus was to be found within her and did not need to be sought in distant places. Bernard of Clairvaux had decisively adopted this position; see Dinzelbacher, *Bernhard von Clairvaux*, 285. Steinmetz frequently draws comparisons with Hilton in his investigation of the *Cloud* group of texts, *Mystische Erfahrung*.

110. Notwithstanding Clark's contrary opinion, the attempt to demonstrate a differing use of "luminous darkness" in *Cloud* and in Hilton risks splitting hairs (see *Scale of Perfection*, ed. Clark and Dorward, 46).

111. See Clark, "Walter Hilton and the Psalm Commentary *Qui Habitat*."

112. For a rather different interpretation, see Clark, "Lightsome Darkness," 95–109; see also Clark's later essay, "Augustine, Anselm, and Walter Hilton," *MMTE* 2 (1982), 102–26.

113. McGinn, *Presence of God*, vol. 2, *Growth*, 318. Like Hilton, Aelred did not write a commentary on the Song of Songs, but drew on its images in order to provide visual stimuli for devotion to Jesus, and allegorized them (ibid., 317ff.).

114. In a Latin letter he had already recommended the Bible as foundation and guideline; on this topic in general, see Beryl Smalley, *The Study of the Bible in the Middle Ages*, 3rd ed. (Oxford: Oxford University Press, 1983).

115. He also recalls explicitly the fourfold biblical exegesis, regarding the anagogical sense as the truly mystical level, because it encompasses the heavenly, or what is being accomplished in heaven, while what he calls the "mystical" interpretation refers to the meaning that relates to the *corpus mysticum* of the church of Christ (*Scale* 2:251).

116. Anne Hudson, *Lollards and Their Books* (London: Hambledon, 1985), 83; and Hudson, *The Premature Reformation: Wycliffite Texts and Lollard History* (Oxford: Oxford University Press, 1988; cf. also Clark, in *Scale of Perfection*, ed. Clark and Dorward, 64. I do not go into the discussion of so-called "vernacular theology," proposed above all by Nicholas Watson, which I consider highly problematic ("Censorship and Cultural Change").

117. Hughes, *Pastors and Visionaries*, 213.

118. Spencer, *English Preaching*, 178.

119. For a reference to the Lollards in this connection, see Wogan-Browne et al., *Idea of the Vernacular*, 149.

120. See also Annie Sutherland, "Biblical Citation and Its Affective Contextualization in Some English Mystical Texts of the Fourteenth Century" (PhD diss., Oxford 1999), 126–27; and Hopf, *Der Weg*, 78.

121. Hughes, *Pastors and Visionaries,* 366.

122. Ibid., 77.

123. von Nolcken, "The *Recluse* and Its Readers: Some Observations on a Lollard Interpolated Version of *Ancrene Wisse,*" in Wada, *Companion,* 192.

124. Angenendt, *Geschichte der Religiosität im Mittelalter,* 300.

125. This interpretation is not weakened by the recognition that Paul does not speak against keeping of slaves (Col 3:22).

126. See above chap. 7; see also, for instance, Ronald A. Knox, *Enthusiasm: A Chapter in the History of Religion* (Oxford: Collins, 1950); Lerner, *Heresy;* Eleanor McLaughlin, "The Heresy of the Free Spirit and Late Medieval Mysticism," *Mediaevalia et Humanistica* n.s. 4 (1973): 37–54; Gordon Leff, *The Dissolution of the Medieval Outlook* (New York: New York University Press, 1976); McGinn, "Mysticism and Heresy: The Problem of the Free Spirit," in *Presence of God,* vol. 4, *Harvest,* 48–79.

127. Clark already observed a certain connection, if a negative one, between Hilton and the Free Spirit movement: "Some of Hilton's careful teaching on the contemplative life—more especially in *Scale* 2, though there are traces in his minor works too—was sharpened by the perceived need to combat error and prevent any possibility of the misunderstanding of his own views" (Clark, "Walter Hilton and Liberty of Spirit," 61–78).

128. Clark's attempt to establish a difference between the *Cloud* author and Hilton in their use of the term "intention" is unjustified ("Intention in Walter Hilton," *DR* 97 [1979]: 72).

129. Especially on humility, see Robert Englert, "Monastic Humility: A Study of Humility in Bernard of Clairvaux and the Author of *The Cloud of Unknowing,*" *SM* 19 (1998): 36–44.

130. *Commedia,* Paradiso, III:85.

131. On Hilton's conformity to the church, see Ellen Ross, "Submission or Fidelity? The Unity of Church and Mysticism in Walter Hilton's 'Scale of Perfection,'" *DR* (1988): 134–44.

132. Steinmetz, *Mystische Erfahrung,* 61.

133. For a different reason, Watson already spoke of a recognizable ambiguity in Hilton: "He...shared many preoccupations with vernacular writers more radical than himself" (Watson, "'Et Que Est Huius Ydoli Materia? Tuipse,'" 97).

134. The author warns further against harboring a false sense of security on account of one's own visions and revelations; he considers it advisable, when St. Bridget is spoken of, to say nothing of her revelations.

135. Clark is clearly aware of this ("Walter Hilton and Liberty of Spirit").

9. The Singular Vision of Julian of Norwich

1. Duffy, *Stripping of the Altars,* 314.

2. Back cover of *Writings of Julian of Norwich,* ed. Watson and Jenkins; Thomas Merton had expressed a similar opinion, and given equal standing only to John Henry Newman (cited in John Swanson, "Guide for the Inexpert Mystic," in Llewelyn, *Julian: Woman of Our Day,* 75).

3. See Sarah Salih, "Julian's Afterlives," in McAvoy, *Companion to Julian of Norwich,* 208; following Alexandra Barratt, "How Many Children Had Julian of

Norwich? Editions, Translations and Versions of Her Revelations," in Bartlett, *Vox Mystica*, 27. See esp. Sarah Salih and Denise N. Baker, eds., *Julian of Norwich's Legacy: Medieval Mysticism and Post-Medieval Reception* (Houndmills-Basingstoke, UK: Palgrave, 2009).

4. Evelyn Underhill, *The Mystics of the Church* (New York: James Clarke, 1964), 127.

5. Cf. Jeffrey F. Hamburger and Robert Suckale, "Zwischen Diesseits und Jenseits—Die Kunst der geistlichen Frauen im Mittelalter," in *Krone und Schleier*, 32.

6. See esp. Warren, *Anchorites and Their Patrons;* Dunn, "Hermits, Anchorites and Recluses," 18–26; and Paulette L'Hermite-Leclercq, "La réclusion volontaire au Moyen Âge: Une institution religieuse spécialement féminine," in *La condición de la mujer en la Edad Media* (Madrid: Casa de Velázquez, 1986), 136–54.

7. Cf. the list in Tanner, *Church in Late Medieval Norwich*, 198ff.

8. On courtesy, see esp. M. Olson, "'God's Inappropriate Grace': Images of Courtesy in Julian of Norwich's *Showings*," *MQ* 20 (1994): 47–59.

9. All Julian quotations, and page and line references to them cited in the text, are taken from *Book of Showings*, ed. Colledge and Walsh.

10. Great importance is attached to this in mysticism in general, as in Gertrud of Helfta's *Herald of Divine Love* where the Lord says of her that there is great sweetness "in the wonderful condescension of God who raises a soul to heights proportioned to the humility into which it has been cast by the consideration of its own vileness!" She has "achieved greater knowledge and ardent love... by means of the gift of nobility, which is such a blessing that through it she reaches highest perfection by the direct route" (*Herald of Divine Love*, chap. 11, 71).

11. Peters, *Religiöse Erfahrung*, 30.

12. Ibid.; see also Barbara Newman, *The Life of Juliana of Mont-Cornillon* (Toronto: Peregrina), 1988.

13. M. J. Wright, "Julian of Norwich's Early Knowledge of Latin," *NM* 95 (1993): 37–45. In their edition, Colledge and Walsh made an important statement regarding Julian's learning: "She is at some pains... to present us with a misleading picture of herself as a simple and unlearned woman, the humble recipient of unmerited graces. Partly this was dictated by true Christian humility, partly by an exceptionally sound theology of grace, partly by a wholly comprehensible wish not unnecessarily to antagonize her critics by any parade of erudition. But she does not conceal... that the *sancta simplicitas* which was indeed hers in no way is incompatible with the intellectual profundity and subtlety which informs all that she writes" (quoted from Wright, ibid., 45). Nicholas Watson convincingly surmises that she did not dictate her book ("Composition," 674, n.). See also, more recently, Anneke B. Mulder-Bakker, ed., *Seeing and Knowing: Women and Learning in Medieval Europe, 1200–1550* (Turnhout: Brepols, 2004).

14. Two seventeenth-century manuscripts (Paris, Bibliothèque Nationale, MS Fonds anglais 40, and British Library, MS Sloane 2499) contain the entire longer version (LV). The short version (SV) is found only in British Library MS Add. 37790 (the famous Amherst MS) from the mid-fifteenth century. SV is a continuous text without emphasis on the separateness of the visions and without chapter divisions. On editorial questions and problems, see *Writings of Julian of Norwich*, ed. Watson

and Jenkins, 24–43. (The title is rather misleading, since the book contains just two versions of a single work.)

15. For instance, "the fyrste tyme when I sawe itte" (220.16) looks back to the past (cf. Watson, "Composition," 658). I do not agree with Watson's suggestion that the SV was written no earlier than 1382–88. Nor do I see any evidence that Julian delayed writing for fear of suspicions of Lollard associations.

16. Her term "souerayne techare" is an allusion to the theological tenet of Jesus as "inner teacher" (*Book of Showings,* ed. Colledge and Walsh, 222.43).

17. For detailed comparison of the two versions, see *Book of Showings,* ed. Colledge and Walsh, 18–25; Baker, *Julian of Norwich's "Showings";* Marion Glasscoe, "Visions and Revisions: A Further Look at the Manuscripts of Julian of Norwich," *Studies in Bibliography* 42 (1989): 103–20. Barry Windeatt, in his thoughtful comparison of the two versions, suggests that in the LV she overcomes earlier theological uncertainty and makes progress "from the newness and insecurity of her position at the time of her writing A [Amherst] toward the meditative assurance of S [Sloane]" ("Julian of Norwich and Her Audience," *RES* n.s. 28 [1977]: 3). However, this view is not quite convincing. As mentioned, in the SV Julian is already very confident, because she believes that her revelations come from God, and she wishes to take her fellow Christians with her, into her new knowledge: "And therfore I praye ȝowe alle for goddys sake, and cownsayles ȝowe for ȝowre awne profyt, that ȝe leve the behaldynge of the . . . synfulle creature, that it was schewyd vnto, and that ȝe myghtlye, wyselye, lovandlye and mekelye be halde god, that of his curtays love and of his endles goodnes walde schewe generalye this visyonn in comforthe of vs alle" (219.3ff.). There is therefore no reason, in my view, to speak of "anxiousness about the correct understanding of her material" (Windeatt, "Julian of Norwich and Her Audience," 3). In his recent and very perceptive comparison of the two versions Windeatt somewhat tones down this earlier statement ("Julian's Second Thoughts: The Long Text Tradition," in McAvoy, *Companion to Julian of Norwich,* 101–15). Watson concedes that the SV is "not the timid and youthful experiment . . . but rather a mature and carefully thought out attempt to articulate Julian's experience" ("Composition," 674). It never occurs to her (unlike Margery Kempe) that her visions could stem from a demonic seducer; rather she firmly maintains that she received them from God. Likewise, it should be taken as self-assurance rather than uncertainty (which would express itself differently) when her visions lead her to recognize that it is *God's will* that she should speak of his goodness. Yet undoubtedly, the theological understanding of the LV is characterized by greater clarity and order.

18. See also Riddy, "Julian of Norwich and Self-Textualization," 103.

19. Watson believes that she started on the LV from this date at the earliest, and that it was essentially a fifteenth-century work ("Composition," 680). Denise Baker sees in the development from SV to LV a transition from visionary to theologian (*Julian of Norwich's "Showings,"* 5).

20. Peters, *Religiöse Erfahrung,* 104. Windeatt goes too far in saying "the work has something of the effect, if not the aim, of a spiritual autobiography" ("The Art of Mystical Loving: Julian of Norwich," *MMTE* 1 [1980], 62).

21. Mystics, both male and female, quite frequently articulate such a request in the belief that sickness, as a form of co-suffering with Christ (*compassio*), brings about a special "sensibilization" for spiritual experience, or cleansing. Gertrud of

Helfta, for instance, speaks of the strengthening of the spirit through sickness; Mary explains to her: "'You have never received a more noble gift from my Son, which your preceding physical sickness has strengthened your spirit to receive as it should be received.'" (*Herald of Divine Love*, bk. 2, chap. 7, p. 105). Ernst Benz rightly equates this kind of sickness with the process of *exinanitio* (*Die Vision*, 27); see also Riehle, *Middle English Mystics*, 28.

22. See Jantzen, *Julian of Norwich*, 74–75. Cf. also Denise Baker, "The three metaphoric wounds of the third petition correspond to the three topics for meditation that Aelred of Rievaulx recommends in the final section of *De institutione inclusarum*. . . . The fact that Julian articulates all three goals of meditation—compassion, contrition, and longing for God—provides a clue to her state of mind, and perhaps her state of life, prior to the visionary experience" ("Julian of Norwich and Anchoritic Literature," 154).

23. McAvoy, "'For We Be Doubel of God's Making': Writing, Gender, and the Body in Julian of Norwich," in McAvoy, *Companion to Julian of Norwich*, 166–80.

24. "I know someone who bears a heavy coat of mail and a hair shirt. . . . All that is bitter seems sweet to him for our Lord's love. God knows it, he still cries to me in the sorriest manner, and says God forgets him because he has not sent him any great illness. . . . I also know a woman of the same sort, who endures little less" (*Ancrene Wisse*, ed. Savage and Watson, 188).

25. F. J. Wetz, ed., *Texte zur Menschenwürde* (Stuttgart: Reclam, 2011), 176.

26. The most important citation for Augustine's definition of visions is in J. Zycha, ed., *De Genesi ad litteram libri duodecim* 12.12, Corpus Scriptorum Ecclesiasticorum Latinorum, 28/1 (Vienna, 1894), 395–97; see also E. A. Petroff, ed., *Medieval Women's Visionary Literature* (New York: Oxford University Press, 1986); E. P. Nolan, *Cry Out and Write: A Feminine Poetics of Revelation* (New York: Continuum, 1994); F. Tobin, "Medieval Thought on Visions and Its Resonance in Mechthild of Magdeburg's *Flowing Light of the Godhead*," in Bartlett, *Vox Mystica*, 41–53.

27. Bazire and Colledge, *Chastising of God's Children*, 169ff. See also Kerby-Fulton, *Books under Suspicion*, 309ff.

28. Newman, "What Did It Mean," 7.

29. Ibid., 25.

30. Newman points out that, according to Alcher of Clairvaux, visions in general are not in reality corporeal, but merely images of bodies ("What Did It Mean," 11).

31. Julian alludes to this at the beginning of chap. 23, LV. The tradition of devotional images used for meditation will certainly have influenced her; cf. Hamburger, *Visual and the Visionary*.

32. For Julian, as for the *Ancrene Wisse* recluses before her, the whole of life signifies being crucified with Christ, in St. Paul's sense: a process of martyrdom and dying. She recognizes that "we be now in our lordes menyng in his crosse with hym in our paynes and in our passion dyeng" (378–79).

33. This is well observed by Aers in "Humanity of Christ," 89ff.

34. See Ellis and Fanous, "1349–1412: Texts," in Fanous and Gillespie, *Cambridge Companion to Medieval English Mysticism*, 141.

35. See Hamburger, *Visual and the Visionary*, 161–82.

36. Christopher Marlowe, *The Complete Plays*, ed. J. B. Steane (Harmondsworth, UK: Penguin, 1969), 5.2.156–57, p. 336.

37. Both the nonmimetic dimension of the wound and the combination with the riven heart occur in the earlier *Ancrene Wisse* (cf. chap. 4 above). The description of the wound in Christ's side contrasts strikingly with the "erotic" visualization, e.g. in Lutgart of Tongeren, that culminates in the kissing and caressing of the wound; Christ comes toward her on the cross and presses her mouth on his wound. The monk of Farne also has an erotically colored version of the motif ("Meditations of the Monk of Farne," ed. Farmer, 182). Earthy realism obtrudes in the Middle English versions of *Institutio inclusarum* when (in the MS Bodley 423 version) the woman reader is called on to penetrate the opening in Christ's side, from which blood and water are seeping, and conceal herself there like a dove in the rock (following an image from the Song of Songs) and savor the drops of his blood until her lips take on the hue of a scarlet hood (*Aelred of Rievaulx's "De institutione inclusarum,"* ed. Ayto and Barratt [MS Bodley 423], 22.865–66).

38. As in Julian, so also in Gertrud of Helfta there is no trace of the reification of the sacred heart of Jesus that occurs in the cult (Ruh, *Geschichte,* 2:322).

39. See, for instance, Glasscoe, "Means of Showing," 161.

40. See also Aers, "Humanity of Christ," 84 and 8; further, *Writings of Julian of Norwich,* ed. Watson and Jenkins, 7.

41. E. Benz was the first to recognize this; he spoke of the "transformation of the image vision into a didactic vision" (*Die Vision,* 152).

42. See also Aers, "Humanity of Christ," 84.

43. Watson pointed out that there is sometimes no clear dividing line between vision narrative and commentary, so that it may become almost impossible to distinguish between them ("Trinitarian Hermeneutic," 93); cf. also *Writings of Julian of Norwich,* ed. Watson and Jenkins, 8–9.

44. Watson rightly speaks of "theological thinking through images" ("Trinitarian Hermeneutic," 91).

45. Watson helpfully lists ample attestations of devout women commissioned by God to write ("Composition," 644), but he does not refer to a visionary's special relationship with her confessor; nor does he consider nuns' cooperation in producing a vita.

46. Peters, *Religiöse Erfahrung,* 121.

47. Ibid., 178.

48. Ibid., 129.

49. Ibid., 115.

50. Ibid., 122.

51. Ibid., 127.

52. Here I follow Ruh's account in *Geschichte,* 2:301–14.

53. Ibid., 2:296.

54. See Peters's seminal investigation in *Religiöse Erfahrung.*

55. Bazire and Colledge, *Chastising of God's Children,* 175. The text is based on Alphonse of Jaén's *Epistola solitarii ad reges* but largely suppresses Alphonse's positive approach, as Rosalynn Voaden has shown ("Rewriting the Letter: Variations in the Middle English Translation of the *Epistola solitarii ad reges* of Alfonso of Jaén," in *The Translations of the Works of St. Birgitta of Sweden into the Medieval European Vernaculars,* ed. Bridget Morris and V. M. O'Mara [Turnhout: Brepols, 2000], 170–85); see also Kerby-Fulton, *Books under Suspicion,* 309.

56. See Mulder-Bakker, *Lives of the Anchoresses.*

57. Riddy, "Julian of Norwich and Self-Textualization," 107.

58. Ibid., 118.

59. Peters, *Religiöse Erfahrung,* 109.

60. Ibid., 110.

61. Riddy, "Julian of Norwich and Self-Textualization," 106.

62. Kerby-Fulton, *Books under Suspicion,* 17.

63. See Voaden's important essay, "God's Almighty Hand: Women Co-Writing the Book," in Smith and Taylor, *Women, the Book and the Godly,* 1:55–65. However, Voaden does not deal with Julian in detail, and does not identify the differences between Julian and the "usual" women mystics; see also Newman, "What Did It Mean," 4–5; see also J. Johnson, "*Auctricitas*? Holy Women and Their Middle English Texts," in Voaden, *Prophets Abroad.*

64. Ruh, *Geschichte,* 2:123.

65. Ibid., 128.

66. Gertrude of Helfta, *Herald of Divine Love,* 88, n. 5; Winkworth notes that Gertrude would have completed the study of the trivium and quadrivium, yet "rather than referring to knowledge of God acquired through academic study, it [the text] suggests knowledge gained in prayer and contemplation."

67. *Mechthild von Magdeburg,* ed. Vollmann-Profe, 406, 809. Mechthild goes so far as to say "Now I lay aside all sorrow and ascend with St. Paul to the third heaven" (Nu leg ich allen kumber nider und var mit Sant Paulo in den dritten himmel, 108).

68. Ruh, *Geschichte,* 2:312.

69. They are not recorded *in extenso* by Voaden, the specialist in this field, in her *Prophets Abroad,* or in her "All Girls Together: Community, Gender and Vision at Helfta," in *Medieval Women in Their Communities,* ed. Diane Watt (Cardiff: University of Wales Press, 1997), 72–91.

70. "The female sex is banned by apostolic authority from teaching in public," quoted from Newman, "What Did It Mean," 41.

71. Mulder-Bakker, *Lives of the Anchoresses,* 98.

72. The passage regularly ignored occurs in Paul's first letter to the Corinthians (11:5); see *Stuttgarter Neues Testament,* 335.

73. Mechthild of Magdeburg, for instance, knew such doubts (*Mechthild von Magdeburg,* ed. Vollmann-Profe, 782); therefore she seeks reassurance (ibid., 844). Like Julian, Mechthild of Magdeburg does not set out to be a theological teacher (ibid., 834).

74. The final cause of her self-assurance is that she can cite the authority of Jesus as inner teacher; see Ritamary Bradley, "Christ the Teacher in Julian's *Showings:* The Biblical and Patristic Traditions," *MMTE* 2 (1982), 127–42.

75. Jantzen already pointed this out: "The influence of Bernard and the Cistercians was of course ubiquitous in fourteenth-century England" (*Julian of Norwich,* 63).

76. Cf. Baker, "Image of God," 40. Knowledge of self and knowledge of God coalesce.

77. See G. Vann, "Julian of Norwich and the Love-Longing of Christ," *Month* 160 (1932): 537ff.

78. Gertrud die Grosse, *Exercitia spiritualia,* 330; see also M. A. Schenkl, "'Sieh her auf mich!' Die Botschaft vom liebenden Gott," in Ringler, *Aufbruch,* 38–41.

79. Beauty is an important theme in Bernard's sermons on the Song of Songs.

80. Frederick C. Bauerschmidt speaks of "the intensely somatic character of her 'seeing' and 'knowing,'" in *Julian of Norwich and the Mystical Body Politic of Christ*, Studies in Spirituality and Theology 5 (Notre Dame, IN: University of Notre Dame Press, 1999), 50.

81. Hans Belting, *Bild und Kult. Eine Geschichte des Bildes vor dem Zeitalter der Kunst*, 7th ed. (Munich: C. H. Beck: 2011), 248.

82. Cf. also *Book of Showings*, ed. Colledge and Walsh, 57.

83. Aers, *Salvation and Sin*, 153.

84. On a detailed comparison with the Sudarium motif in Gertrud and Mechthild of Hackeborn see Hamburger, *Visual and the Visionary*, 351–62.

85. For an authoritative account of prayer, see Heiler, *Prayer*.

86. Brant Pelphrey speaks of "the nature of prayer as a free approach to God, to ask him for the gift of himself" (*Love Was His Meaning*, 219, 218).

87. Glasscoe: "This longing comes from God himself" (*English Medieval Mystics*, 242).

88. Pelphrey, *Love Was His Meaning*, 240, 235.

89. "One of her most important theological insights, which ought to be underlined in every Christian theology of prayer: *To pray at all is to will God's will*" (Pelphrey, *Love Was His Meaning*, 227).

90. Mieth, *Meister Eckhart*, 94.

91. Pelphrey, *Love Was His Meaning*, 229.

92. "We move beyond conscious prayer into simply 'being' with him" (ibid., 242); see also Bradley, "Julian of Norwich on Prayer," in Spätmittelalterliche geistliche Literatur in der Nationalsprache, ed. J. Hogg, AC 106, 2 vols. (1983–84), 1:136–54; and, in general, Heiler, *Prayer*.

93. See also Roland Maisonneuve, "The Visionary Universe of Julian of Norwich: Problems and Methods," *MMTE* 1 (1980), 86–98, and *L'Univers visionnaire de Julian of Norwich*, 267ff.

94. Walter Haug, "Das Gespräch mit dem unvergleichlichen Partner: Der mystische Dialog bei Mechthild von Magdeburg als Paradigma für eine personale Gesprächsstruktur," in *Das Gespräch*. Poetik und Hermeneutik 1, ed. Klaus Stierle and Rainer Warning (Munich: Fink, 1984), 251–79. Brad Peters's interesting essay touches on this theme, "Julian of Norwich and the Internalized Dialogue of Prayer," *MQ* 20 (1994): 122–30.

95. See Ritamary Bradley, "Christ, the Teacher in Julian's *Showings:* The Biblical and Patristic Traditions," *MMTE* 2 (1982), 127–42.

96. "Meditacio ad Crucifixum," in "Meditations of the Monk of Farne," ed. Farmer, 184.

97. See Stölting, *Christliche Frauenmystik*, 175, following McGinn, *Presence of God*, vol. 3, *Flowering*, 415–16, 233–34.

98. Exemplified by Gertrude of Helfta (*Legatus divinae pietatis, The Herald of Divine Love*) and her fellow nun Mechthild of Magdeburg (*Das fliessende Licht der Gottheit, The Flowing Light of the Godhead*); see Ruh, *Geschichte*, 2:275; also Watson, "Trinitarian Hermeneutic."

99. Pelphrey, *Love Was His Meaning*, 108.

100. Ibid., 108–9. Hadewych stresses that the *fruitio* of God means "the unfolding of unity into the three persons" (Ruh, *Geschichte*, 2:220); for Mechthild of Magdeburg it is the blissful tasting of love (ibid., 270).

101. Cf. Hide, *Gifted Origins*, 45.

102. Palliser, *Christ, Our Mother of Mercy*, 29.

103. Ibid., 30. The monk of Farne also insists that God can only be recognized in Jesus ("Meditacio ad Crucifixum," in "Meditations of the Monk of Farne," ed. Farmer, 173).

104. Hide, *Gifted Origins*, 47.

105. Hide speaks aptly of "an ontology of being-in-relationship" (*Gifted Origins*, 56).

106. *Mechthild von Magdeburg*, ed. Vollmann-Profe, 755.

107. Baker, *Julian of Norwich's "Showings,"* 44; cf. also Baker, "Image of God."

108. She has a predilection for threefold qualities of the soul as well as of the Trinity (cf. Watson, "Trinitarian Hermeneutic," 97–98); also John P. H. Clark, "Nature, Grace, and the Trinity in Julian of Norwich," *DR* 100 (1982): 203–20.

109. They are discussed in detail esp. in *De trinitate*, 12, and in *Confessiones*, X.viii.12–xxvi.37.

110. See Pelphrey's lucid account in *Christ Our Mother*, 170.

111. As Watson has shown, Julian overcomes medieval misogynist tendencies by relating "frailty" not only to women, but to mankind in general ("'Yf Wommen Be Double Naturelly,'" 24).

112. Hide, *Gifted Origins*, 84.

113. Steinmetz, *Mystische Erfahrung*, 190.

114. Her visions are permeated by a series of oppositions, above all by sorrow and joy, doubt and certainty, sickness and solace, fear and hope, depravity and purity, death and life (see also Glasscoe, "Means of Showing," 159).

115. Mechthild of Magdeburg similarly speaks of a natural relationship between the human being and God the Father (*Mechthild von Magdeburg*, ed. Vollmann-Profe, 781, 824).

116. Ruh, *Geschichte*, 2:67.

117. *Wohunge of Ure Lauerd* had already put forward this argument. Mechthild does not shrink from making extreme statements, any more than Julian does, and she does not think of submitting them to the scrutiny of theological dogmatics. She is not perturbed by the assertion of her contemporary Albertus Magnus: "To say that the soul is derived from the substance of God, is Manichaean heresy" (Ruh, *Geschichte*, 2:68). Angela of Foligno also maintains that everything has its being from God (ibid., 525).

118. Aers speaks of a "Plotinian turn" (*Salvation and Sin*, 162).

119. Mieth, *Meister Eckhart*, 83.

120. Baker gives one-sided emphasis to Julian's demand for knowledge of God as prerequisite for self-knowledge (*Julian of Norwich's "Showings,"* 109).

121. See Jantzen, *Julian of Norwich*, 140–41.

122. Ibid., 148.

123. There is a good article by J. Lang: "'Godly Wylle.'" More recently, Baker has perceptively revisited this problem in "The Structure of the Soul and the 'Godly Wylle' in Julian of Norwich's *Showings*," *MMTE* 7 (2004), 37–49; cf. also Hide, *Gifted Origins*, 80ff. Riehle, *Middle English Mystics*, 157–58.

124. Cf. Endre von Ivánka, "Apex mentis," in *Plato Christianus,* 315–51; and Uta Störmer-Caysa, *Einführung in die mittelalterliche Mystik,* 2nd ed. (Stuttgart: Reclam, 2004), 123–28.

125. Different ideas are conflated by Baker: "She derives her conception of the 'godly wylle' from the same discussions about *synderesis* and the related *scintilla* in the Augustinian and Pseudo-Dionysian mystical theology which influenced Eckhart" (Baker, *Julian of Norwich's "Showings,"* 45); cf. also J. Lang, "'Godly Wylle,'" 165–73.

126. Gertrude of Helfta, *Herald of Divine Love,* 3, chap. 74, 238.

127. A. M. Reynolds, "Julian of Norwich," in Walsh, *Pre-Reformation English Spirituality,* 205.

128. Jantzen, *Julian of Norwich,* 151.

129. Palliser rightly observes: "Julian equates neither flesh nor sensuality with evil" (*Christ, Our Mother of Mercy,* 53).

130. Baker, *Julian of Norwich's "Showings,"* 47.

131. See the important essay by Coiner, "'Homely' and the *Heimliche.*"

132. Gertrud die Grosse, *Exercitia spiritualia,* 308; Gertrud of Helfta, *Spiritual Exercises,* trans. G. Jaron and J. Lewis, Cistercian Fathers Series 49 (Kalamazoo, MI: Cistercian Publications), 1989; on Gertrud cf. also H. Gosebrink, "In der Sinne Achtsamkeit: Leib und Sinne in Gertruds 'Exercitia spiritualia,'" in Ringler, *Aufbruch,* 76–92.

133. See also Tarjei Park, "Reflecting Christ: The Role of the Flesh in Walter Hilton and Julian of Norwich," in *MMTE* 5 (1992), 17–37.

134. Robert E. Lewis, ed., *Innocent III. De miseria condicionis humane* (Athens: University of Georgia Press, 1978).

135. See J. M. Nuth, *Wisdom's Daughter: The Theology of Julian of Norwich* (New York: Crossroad Publication Co., 1991), 109.

136. Jantzen speaks of "all of our psychology and physicality as individual human beings... our existence as psychosomatic beings," *Julian of Norwich,* 142; see also Riehle, *Middle English Mystics,* 148.

137. Wilckens comments as follows on Paul's concept of the flesh in his letters to the Galatians and Romans: "'Flesh' is the human being as he experiences and conducts himself in daily life, with only himself to rely on.... It always means the whole person... the human being [is] 'flesh' with body and soul. According to Paul, flesh becomes evil when it withdraws into itself, relinquishes the connection with God, and seeks to harm fellow human beings" (*Das Neue Testament,* 677).

138. Jantzen, *Julian of Norwich,* 143.

139. Similarly in Gertrud of Helfta; cf. Hide, *Gifted Origins,* 25. Tarjei Park's approach is wide of the mark because he neglects this important tradition of the inner senses (*Selfhood and "Gostly Menyng" in Some Middle English Mystics: Semiotic Approaches to Contemplative Theology* [Lewiston, NY: Edwin Mellen Press, 2002]). By contrast, Palliser's *Christ, Our Mother of Mercy* is very useful on this subject.

140. Jantzen, *Julian of Norwich,* 145–46.

141. Ibid., 155.

142. Following Paul, Rom 8:22; *Das Neue Testament,* ed. Wilckens, 529.

143. 1 Cor 15:28.

144. See *DS,* s.v. "fruitio," col. 1548.

145. See Langer, *Christliche Mystik*, 323, 348, 390. For Meister Eckhart, God is wholly in every created being (Mieth, *Meister Eckhart*, 208).

146. See esp. Lichtmann, "'I Desyrede a Bodylye Syght.'"; Lichtmann notes that for Julian "the passage from an intellectual, non-integral faith to a thoroughly grounded experience is through bodiliness" (ibid., 14); Julian's bodily experience is "an epistemology of the divine" (ibid., 12); see also G. Brandolino, "'The Chiefe and Principal Mene': Julian of Norwich's Redefining of the Body in *A Revelation of Love*," *MQ* 22 (1996): 102–10.

147. Pelphrey, *Love Was His Meaning*, 70.

148. Ruh, *Geschichte*, 2:325; see also A. Sprung, "'We Never Shall Come out of Him': Enclosure and Immanence in Julian of Norwich's *Book of Showings*," *MQ* 19 (1993): 47–62.

149. Quoted from Biser, *Paulus*, 37.

150. *Mechthild von Magdeburg*, ed. Vollmann-Profe, 2:5.7–8; and Gertrude of Helfta, *Herald of Divine Love*, 2, chap. 16, 117.

151. See C. Cummings, "God's 'Homely' Love in Julian of Norwich," *Cistercian Studies* 13 (1978): 68–74; Anna Maria Reynolds, "'Courtesy' and 'Homeliness' in the *Revelations* of Julian of Norwich," *FCEMN* 5 (1979): 12–20.

152. Phil 1:11; cf. Wilckens's comment that God took his sons into his house (*Neues Testament*, 700); there is also an allusion—as in *Ancrene Wisse*—to 1 John 4:15.

153. See Coiner, "'Homely' and the *Heimliche*,"; 305–23.

154. Ruh, *Geschichte*, 2:260.

155. See, for instance, James Walsh, "God's Homely Loving: St. John and Julian of Norwich on the Divine Indwelling," *Month* 205 n.s. 19 (1958): 164–72.

156. Cf. Nicholas of Cusa, *Docta ignorantia* I:119. The notion of finding God in one point was current in the Middle Ages. It is related to a similarly widespread image of God as intelligible sphere: he is everything and encompasses everything. On this image in Mechthild of Magdeburg, see the commentary by Vollmann-Profe, *Mechthild von Magdeburg*, 825; also Stölting, *Christliche Frauenmystik*, 210.

157. Vincent Gillespie and Maggie Ross, "The Apophatic Image: The Poetics of Effacement in Julian of Norwich," in *MMTE* 5 (1992), 67; see also Cynthea Masson, "The Point of Coincidence: Rhetoric and the Apophatic in Julian of Norwich's *Showings*," in McEntire, *Julian of Norwich*.

158. See also Benz, *Die Vision*, 505–6.

159. Glasscoe, *English Medieval Mystics*, 224.

160. Gertrud die Grosse, *Exercitia spiritualia*, 58.

161. Cf. Reynolds: "Julian's joyfulness is all-pervasive.... Her vision of the Lord is itself a vision of joy," in Llewelyn, *Julian: Woman of Our Day*, 221; also P. M. Vinje: "Julian said that man's greatest joy stems from the sight of God's delight in him" (*An Understanding of Love according to the Anchoress Julian of Norwich* [Salzburg: Institut für Anglistik und Amerikanistik, 1983], 182).

162. *Das Neue Testament*, ed. Wilckens, 531. The theme is important for English mysticism as a whole. It occurs with comparable intensity in Rolle (e.g. *Melos amoris*, ed. Arnould, 6.9–10, 57.13, 85.27); it is least evident in Margery Kempe.

163. Pelphrey, *Love Was His Meaning*, 216; see also Domenico Pezzini, "The Vocabulary of Joy in Julian of Norwich," *Studies in Spirituality* 4 (1994): 94–115.

164. See also Pia Luislampe, "Gottes Antlitz hülle dich in Licht: Gott und Mensch in der Lichtmetaphorik Gertruds von Helfta," in Ringler, *Aufbruch,* 68.

165. Biser emphasizes in his New Theology that this theme goes even further than the doctrine of man made in God's likeness (*Gotteskindschaft*).

166. See also Gertrude of Helfta, *Herald of Divine Love,* 2, 19, 119.

167. On the history of the theme of God, or Jesus, as mother, cf. esp. A. Cabassut, "Une dévotion médiévale peu connue: 'La dévotion à Jesus notre mère,'" *Revue d'ascétique et de mystique* 25 (1949): 234–45; further, Ritamary Bradley, "Patristic Background of the Motherhood Similitude in Julian of Norwich," *Christian Scholar's Review* 8 (1978): 101–13; Caroline Walker Bynum, *Jesus as Mother: Studies in the Spirituality of the High Middle Ages* (Berkeley: University of California Press, 1982), esp. the chap. "Jesus as Mother and Abbot as Mother: Some Themes in Twelfth-Century Cistercian Writing," 110–69; she demonstrates impressively how widespread these metaphors were in the Bible and in patristic literature (e.g. in Origen and Augustine), and especially among the Cistercians, whose abbots were often compared with mothers, most frequently in Bernard's circle. See also M. L. Dutton, "Christ Our Mother: Aelred's Iconography for Contemplative Union," in Elder, *Goad and Nail,* 21–45. Biblical sources include Isa 49:1, 49:15, 66:11–13; Mt 23:37. Taking up this last citation, Anselm of Canterbury speaks in his *Monologion* of Jesus the mother, who revives the soul at her breast as the hen takes her chicks under her wing.

168. I mention only a selection of further studies with important insights: e.g. J. P. Heimmel, *"God Is Our Mother": Julian of Norwich and the Medieval Image of Christian Feminine Divinity,* Salzburg Studies in English Literature 92.5 (Salzburg: Institut für Anglistik und Amerikanistik, 1982); Patricia M. Vinje, *An Understanding of Love according to the Anchoress Julian of Norwich,* Salzburg Studies in English Literature 92.8 (Salzburg: Institut für Anglistik und Amerikanistik, 1983); Palliser, *Christ, Our Mother of Mercy;* Bradley, "Mysticism in the Motherhood Similitude"; Pelphrey, *Christ Our Mother;* McNamer, "Exploratory Image," 21–28; Innes-Parker, "Legacy of *Ancrene Wisse,"* with many examples in the chap. "The Mother-God," 158–65.

169. In his 20th sermon on the Song of Songs, *Sancti Bernardi opera* 1:115. The motif also occurs in Marguerite Porete's *Mirouer des simples âmes.*

170. On the "properties of motherhood" see McNamer, "Exploratory Image," 26.

171. See Bradley, "Julian of Norwich: Everyone's Mystic," 141 n.; Suso and Rolle revitalized this notion (*Book of Showings,* ed. Colledge and Walsh, 154; Newman, *God and the Goddesses*).

172. Gertrud die Grosse, *Exercitia spiritualia,* 337.

173. Colledge and Walsh draw attention to numerous biblical allusions (Vulgate text), especially to the Gospels, the letters of Paul and John, Hebrews, the Psalms, the book of Wisdom, Deutero-Isaiah (probably mediated indirectly). Annie Sutherland also cites many examples in "'Oure Feyth'"; she affirms that Julian's "scriptural familiarity was profound" (3), that she was familiar with "a wide spectrum of biblical doctrine" (10), and had "an intricate understanding of scriptural theology," but that her own approach was "theologically daring" (14). Sutherland stops short of a detailed comparison between Julian's theology and the Bible.

174. Cf. Reynolds, "Julian of Norwich," in Walsh, *Pre-Reformation English Spirituality,* 209; and Sutherland, "'Oure Feyth,'" 18.

175. In the First Letter to Timothy (2:14), however, it is said that the woman first let herself be seduced (*Das Neue Testament,* ed. Wilckens, 745).

176. Baker emphasizes that he displays "weakness rather than guilt" (*Julian of Norwich's "Showings,"* 99).

177. Hide, *Gifted Origins,* 118–19.

178. Glasscoe, "Means of Showing," 168–69.

179. See esp. Hugh of St. Victor in his little *De institutione novitiorum* concerning the monastery schoolboys' education (quoted in Joachim Bumke, "Höfischer Körper—Höfische Kultur," in *Modernes Mittelalter: Neue Bilder einer populären Epoche,* ed. Joachim Heinzle, insel taschenbuch 1513 [Frankfurt am Main: Insel, 1999], 80–90).

180. Glasscoe, "Means of Showing," 172.

181. John P. H. Clark: "Christ is a lineal descendant of Adam, and restores the humanity from which according to the flesh he is sprung—a humanity which in the sight of God was predestined to union with him." ("Predestination in Christ," 84).

182. *Das Neue Testament,* ed. Wilckens, 517; cf. Rom 5:5–6, 17.

183. Clark: "Augustine had contrasted the *cadere* of Adam with the *descendere* of Christ. Julian prefers to see them as inseparable in the mind of God, using one word 'fall' for both, and rejoicing that the *felix culpa* of Adam merited such a redeemer" (Clark, "Predestination in Christ," 83).

184. Likewise in the *Mirror of Simple Souls.* Similarly also in Meister Eckhart, in his great sermon on "Poverty of Spirit": "In God's self... where God is above all being and above every distinction, there was I myself, there I desired myself and saw myself (willing) to create this being (= myself). Therefore I am the cause of myself in my being, which is eternal, but not in my becoming, which is temporal. And thus I am unborn, and just as I am unborn, so I can never die. Unborn, I have always been, and am now, and shall be to all eternity" (Mieth, *Meister Eckhart,* 154).

185. Ruud, "Nature and Grace," 79–80.

186. Cf. Clark, "Predestination in Christ"; similarly in the *Mirror of Simple Souls.*

187. Ruh, *Geschichte,* 2:278.

188. Already taught by Origen (*De principiis,* 4.4.8. Origenes: *Vier Bücher von den Prinzipien,* ed. and trans. H. Görgemanns and H. Karpp. Texte zur Forschung 24. 3rd ed. (Darmstadt: Wissenschaftliche Buchgesellschaft, 1985), 808–9; cf. *St. Trudperter Hohelied,* ed. Ohly, 445.

189. This does happen in Mechthild (*Mechthild von Magdeburg,* ed. Vollmann-Profe, 754–55); and in the *St. Trudperter Hohelied,* ed. Ohly, 449.

190. *Mechthild von Magdeburg,* ed. Vollmann-Profe, 755; on the tenet that God would have become man even without the fall, cf. Ruh, *Geschichte,* 2:519.

191. E.g. Eduard Lohse, *Paulus,* 168.

192. Ruud, "Nature and Grace," 79.

193. Ringler, ed., in Gertrud die Grosse, *Exercitia spiritualia,* 345.

194. Fries, ed., *Handbuch theologischer Grundbegriffe,* 4:163, "Sünde"; cf. Baker, *Julian of Norwich's "Showings,"* 65; Ringler, ed., in Gertrud die Grosse, *Exercitia spiritualia,* 15–17; also J. Dale, "'Sin Is Behovely': Art and Theodicy in the Julian Text," *MQ* 25 (1999): 127–47.

195. Palliser, *Christ, Our Mother of Mercy,* 96.

196. Hide, *Gifted Origins,* 94.

197. Baker, *Julian of Norwich's "Showings,"* 94, 97.

198. Pelphrey, *Love Was His Meaning,* 256.

199. Baker, *Julian of Norwich's "Showings,"* 70.

200. Hide, *Gifted Origins,* 97.

201. Tugwell, *Ways of Imperfection,* 197.

202. Cf. Baker, *Julian of Norwich's "Showings,"* 70.

203. Hide, *Gifted Origins,* 98.

204. The gaining of "honor" through love is a Bernardine notion (see Dinzel-bacher, *Bernhard von Clairvaux,* 179). This is also taught by Mechthild, for whom man regains honor through God's incarnation and death on the cross (*Mechthild von Magdeburg,* ed. Vollmann-Profe, 780).

205. It is interesting that under "worshipe" the *MED* does not note the meaning "special acceptance [by God], loving care"; cf. Irene Leicht, "Die Vorstellung von Erlösung im theologischen Denken der Julian of Norwich," in *Denkmodelle von Frauen im Mittelalter,* ed. Béatrice Acklin-Zimmermann, Dokimion 15 (Freiburg, Switzerland: Universitätsverlag, 1994), 173–204.

206. In Palliser's words: "The 'token of sin' … is turned to worship and joy by the working of mercy and grace" (*Christ, Our Mother of Mercy,* 105). It seems to me that in talking of the necessity of sin Julian was influenced in some way by Origen, who asserted "it is necessary for there to be evil before there is virtue among human beings" (*Origen: Spirit and Fire,* ed. von Balthasar, 338–39).

207. Gertrud die Grosse, *Exercitia spiritualia,* 345.

208. Glasscoe: "The growth to spiritual maturity comes only by means of falling" (*English Medieval Mystics,* 254).

209. Fries, *Handbuch theologischer Grundbegriffe,* 4:166.

210. Tugwell, *Ways of Imperfection,* 200. Paul Molinari's *Julian of Norwich: The Teaching of a Fourteenth-Century Mystic* (London: Longman, 1958) is still useful for Julian's theology in general.

211. Aers, *Salvation and Sin,* 142ff., 170.

212. Hide, *Gifted Origins,* 82.

213. Cf. Brad Peters, "The Reality of Evil within the Mystic Vision of Julian of Norwich," *MQ* 13 (1987): 195–202, and "Julian of Norwich and Her Conceptual Development of Evil," *MQ* 17 (1991): 181–88; also D. F. Tinsley, "Julian's Diabology," in McEntire, *Julian of Norwich,* 207–37.

214. Cited from Ruh, *Geschichte,* 2:523; Marguerite Porete and Meister Eckhart were handed over to the Inquisition for such a statement (ibid.).

215. See Bernd J. Claret, ed., *Theodizee: Das Böse in der Welt* (Darmstadt: Wissenschaftliche Buchgesellschaft, 2007).

216. Eugen Biser in *Mensch und Spiritualität: Eugen Biser und Richard Heinzmann im Gespräch* (Darmstadt: Wissenschaftliche Buchgesellschaft, 2007), 34.

217. Jantzen speaks of a "message of healing" (*Julian of Norwich,* 124).

218. Eugen Biser, *Einweisung ins Christentum* (Düsseldorf: Patmos, 2004), 108.

219. Vincent Gillespie, "Vernacular Theology," in *Oxford Twenty-First Century Approaches to Literature: Middle English,* ed. Paul Strohm (Oxford: Oxford University Press, 2007), 403, following Nicholas Watson, who also sees Julian's work as a product of "vernacular religious culture" ("Julian of Norwich," in Dinshaw and Wallace, *Cambridge Companion to Medieval Women's Writing,* 220).

220. See the numerous footnotes and esp. the index in *Book of Showings,* ed. Colledge and Walsh; further, C. H. Hildesley, *Journeying with Julian* (Harrisburg, PA: Morehouse Publishing, 1993), 78; and Wai Man Yuen, *Religious Experience and Interpretation: Memory on the Path to the Knowledge of God in Julian of Norwich's "Showings,"* Feminist Critical Studies in Religion and Culture 1 (New York: Peter Lang, 2003), 79.

221. Jantzen sees her teaching embedded "in the teaching and practice of the patristic and monastic tradition" (*Julian of Norwich,* 97).

222. As previously mentioned, Sutherland draws attention to her "rumination" of biblical texts ("'Oure Feyth'"). For an overview of scholarly discussion, see D. F. Krantz, *The Life and Text of Julian of Norwich: The Poetics of Enclosure* (Bern: Peter Lang, 1997), 34–35.

223. Christopher Abbott's book on Julian's theology mentions Paul only in a footnote: Christopher Abbott, *Julian of Norwich: Autobiography and Theology,* Studies in Medieval Mysticism 2 (Woodbridge, UK: Boydell & Brewer, 1999).

224. See Wischmeyer, *Paulus;* further, the dissertation by I. Bendik, "Paulus in neuer Sicht? Eine kritische Einführung in die 'New Perspective on Paul,'" Judentum und Christentum 18 (Stuttgart: Kohlhammer, 2010).

225. The term is discussed, for instance, by Sanders, *Paul,* 58ff.

226. Wischmeyer, *Paulus,* 40.

227. Less so in Britain, according to Sanders, *Paul,* 154.

228. Augustine already recognized contradictions in the Bible and could not resolve them entirely. "He takes an admittedly obscure passage from Paul (1 Cor. 3:13–15) and sets it against other passages in which Paul speaks more clearly. The principle is this: difficult passages are to be interpreted in the light of passages whose meaning is certain" (Le Goff, *Birth of Purgatory,* 72). Llewelyn is only partially correct in saying "Julian's thought is thoroughly Pauline; indeed she appears to be soaked in his writngs" (in Llewelyn, *Julian: Woman of Our Day,* 6).

229. "Paul was not systematic...since he did not reconcile his responses to these multifaceted problems with one another.... He forces us, in fact, to pose an extremely serious question: must a religion, in addressing diverse problems, offer answers that are completely consistent with one another? Is it not good to have passionate hopes and commitments which cannot all be reduced to a scheme in which they are arranged in a hierarchical relationship?" (Sanders, *Paul,* 149).

230. Wischmeyer, "Themen paulinischer Theologie," in Wischmeyer, *Paulus,* 276.

231. Wischmeyer, "Römerbrief," ibid., 269.

232. Biser, *Paulus,* 210.

233. Ibid., 211.

234. Clark already noted that she does not use the term *iustificatio,* or develop a concept of justification by faith ("Time and Eternity," 267).

235. It is interesting that Gertrud of Helfta, comparable to Julian in many ways, does not entirely relinquish the idea of justification (Gertrud die Grosse, *Exercitia spiritualia,* 351).

236. Lohse, *Paulus,* 166.

237. Sutherland does not do full justice to Julian's theology when she asserts that a comparison should be made above all with Hebrews ("'Oure Feyth,'" 11).

238. In Gertrud, too, guilt is not "atoned" but "paid for" (Gertrud die Grosse, *Exercitia spiritualia,* 339).

239. See esp. Baker, *Julian of Norwich's "Showings,"* chap. 4.ii, 100ff.; and J. M. Nuth, "Two Medieval Soteriologies: Anselm of Canterbury and Julian of Norwich," *Theological Studies* 53 (1992): 611–45.

240. "Why God Became Man," in *Anselm of Canterbury: The Major Works,* ed. B. Davies and G. R. Evans, Oxford World Classics (Oxford: Oxford University Press, 1998), 282–90.

241. Bradley offers the best interpretation of this theological problem, in "Julian of Norwich: Everyone's Mystic," 142–51.

242. Gertrud die Grosse, *Exercitia spiritualia,* 268.

243. Bradley, "Julian of Norwich: Everyone's Mystic," 153; Hide, *Gifted Origins,* 59.

244. Gertrud die Grosse, *Exercitia spiritualia,* 345.

245. *Sancti Bernardi opera,* 2:93.

246. Baker, *Julian of Norwich's "Showings,"* 84.

247. Wilckens, *Theologie des Neuen Testaments,* II/1, 202.

248. Abbott offers too simple an explanation with his assertion that the motif of the Last Judgment is attenuated because Julian is writing for the advanced (*Julian of Norwich,* 175); for a more profound view, see Clark, "Predestination in Christ," 81.

249. *Anchoritic Spirituality,* ed. Savage and Watson, 171.

250. R. Miggelbrink, *Der zornige Gott* (Darmstadt: Wissenschaftliche Buchgesellschaft, 2002).

251. Wilckens, *Theologie des Neuen Testaments* II/1, 96.

252. For Origen's important comments on this, see *Origen: Spirit and Fire,* ed. von Balthasar, 349–50.

253. *Das Neue Testament,* ed. Wilckens, 532.

254. "NVMQVID INIQVITAS EST APVD DEVM? ABSIT!" Quoted in Flasch, *Logik des Schreckens,* 198–99; likewise with reference to Jacob and Esau (208–39). Other writers—such as the monk of Farne—disregard the problem and consider God's meting out of punishment and mercy just ("Meditacio ad crucifixum," in "Meditations of the Monk of Farne," ed. Farmer, 172).

255. Flasch, *Logik des Schreckens,* 201.

256. In sent. I d 41 E (quoted from Schiwy, *Birgitta von Schweden,* 32–33; with reference to Carl Andresen, *Handbuch der Dogmen- und Theologiegeschichte* I [Göttingen: Vandenhoeck & Ruprecht, 1982], 712).

257. Le Goff, *Birth of Purgatory,* 154–76.

258. *Mechthild von Magdeburg,* ed. Vollmann-Profe, 727; see also R. Harries, "On the Brink of Universalism," in Llewelyn, *Julian: Woman of Our Day,* 41–60.

259. The Norwich monk and subsequently cardinal Adam Easton (d. 1397) possessed a large collection of books, including works by Origen (Pantin, *English Church,* 175–81, esp. 181). Easton was, incidentally, an admirer of St. Bridget of Sweden and took an effective part in bringing about her canonization. "The fact that Easton so ardently defended St. Bridget shows that he was by no means a hidebound conservative and that he had sympathy with the mystical movements of his day" (Pantin, *English Church,* 180–81). See also Reynolds and Bolton Holloway, *Julian*

of Norwich; and Hans Urs von Balthasar, "Apokatastasis," *Trierer Theologische Zeitschrift* 97 (1988): 169–82.

260. Angenendt, *Geschichte der Religiosität,* 738.

261. Ibid.

262. Johann Wolfgang von Goethe, *Faust,* ed. Albrecht Schöne (Frankfurt am Main: Insel, 1999), 2:786–95.

263. Dieter Borchmeyer, *Richard Wagner: Ahasvers Wandlungen* (Frankfurt am Main: Insel, 2002), 308–34; Dieter Borchmeyer, *Drama and the World of Richard Wagner,* trans. D. Ellis (Princeton, NJ: Princeton University Press, 2003).

264. Walker Bynum, "Formen weiblicher Frömmigkeit im späteren Mittelalter," in *Krone und Schleier,* 127.

265. Jantzen, *Julian of Norwich,* 178.

266. Peter Dronke, "The Completeness of Heaven," in *Envisaging Heaven in the Middle Ages,* ed. Carolyn Muessig and Ad Putter (London: Routledge, 2007), 44–56.

267. Hide, *Gifted Origins,* 189. Watson rightly speaks of a "tantalizing near-equivalence" between "all shall be well" and "all shall be saved": "Julian assumes that, if Christ will make all things well, he has to do so by saving all humanity.... If Christ can promise that all shall be well... this is, she argues, because love... is the basis of God's nature" ("Visions of Inclusion,"164).

268. *Das Neue Testament,* ed. Wilckens, 541. Clark makes the apt comment: "She concludes with a hope of cosmic restoration that is in the spirit of the Apostle.... The thought that we are predestined to adoption in Christ from all eternity, and that mankind and indeed all creation are brought to their fulfilment in him, is of course Pauline (Eph 1:4–10)" ("Predestination in Christ," 88).

269. *Das Neue Testament,* ed. Wilckens, 542.

270. As Watson explains: "For Julian, as for Langland, the orthodox views of sin and punishment will hold true only until the end of time and will then... be transcended in an eternal reunion of God and his creation" ("Visions of Inclusion," 166).

271. Bradley, "Julian of Norwich: Everyone's Mystic," 157; Watson points to further instances of universal salvation in *Piers Plowman, The Book of Margery Kempe, Château d'Amour;* to this list could be added the morality play *The Castle of Perseverance,* which needs further investigation.

272. See Le Goff, *Birth of Purgatory,* 73.

273. See also R. E. Wright, "'The Boke Performyd': Affective Technique and Reader Response in the *Shewings* of Julian of Norwich," *Christianity and Literature* 36 (1987): 13–32.

274. Wilckens, *Theologie des Neuen Testaments,* II/1: *Das Fundament,* 57–60; he claims, however, that biblical discrepancies and contradictions must not simply be removed.

275. Watson, "Trinitarian Hermeneutic," 93.

276. J. P. H. Clark draws special attention to one of Tanner's research outcomes: he suggests that "an important reason for the lack of interest in Lollardy [in Norwich] was that the religion provided by the local Church was sufficiently rich and varied, and sufficiently tolerant towards what might be called the left wing of orthodoxy, as to cater for the taste of most citizens" ("Time and Eternity in Julian of Norwich," 273); see also Kerby-Fulton, *Books under Suspicion;* and for further

stimulating observations, Watson, "Julian of Norwich," in Dinshaw and Wallace, *Cambridge Companion to Medieval Women's Writing,* 210–21.

277. Kerby-Fulton, *Books under Suspicion,* 17.

278. E.g. "endlesshead"—*infinitas* (LV 303), "homelynesse"—*familiaritas* (LV 315). Julian's tendency toward formation of abstract nouns must surely be attributed to her striving for knowledge, and merits further investigation. There is an interesting parallel to this stylistic trait—and also to the combination of image and abstract noun—in Mechthild of Magdeburg (Ruh, *Geschichte,* 2:283), as well as in Hadewych's *Mengeldichten* [Mixed Poems] (Ruh, *Geschichte,* 2:187). Ruh considers that Hadewych's terminology and imagery suggest the influence of German mysticism (ibid., 188). Julian might have heard of the work of the aristocrat Hadewych, who, on her own account, had personal contacts with English recluses.

279. The same rhetorical elements recur (see esp. *Book of Showings,* ed. Colledge and Walsh, 49–52; and Maisonneuve, *L'Univers visionnaire de Julian of Norwich,* 381ff., who also draws attention to the "musical" effect of Julian's style brought about by these rhythms).

280. Pelphrey, *Love Was His Meaning,* 17–18.

281. Reynolds and Bolton Holloway, however, take the view that "Julian seems to have lived monastically in the world" (*Julian of Norwich,* 7).

282. This was surmised most recently by Watson and Jenkins (*Writings of Julian of Norwich,* 4). Other scholars have suspected that she had been a nun in some convent since girlhood (possibly the Benedictine nunnery of Carrow) and had received an exceptionally good basic education in Latin, holy scripture, and the arts (see, e.g., *Book of Showings,* ed. Colledge and Walsh, 1:43–59).

283. Cf. Pelphrey, *Love Was His Meaning,* 16.

284. This applies also to the arguments put forward by Watson ("Composition," 673 n.), who cites two inconclusive essays by Sister Benedicta [Ward]: "Julian the Solitary," in Kenneth Leech and Sister Benedicta, *Julian Reconsidered* (Fairacres, Oxford, 1988), 11–31; and Sister Benedicta, "Lady Julian and Her Audience: 'Mine Even-Christian,'" in *The English Religious Tradition and the Genius of Anglicanism,* ed. Geoffrey Rowell (Oxford: Oxford University Press, 1992), 47–63. Her reasoning as to why Julian cannot have been a nun is convincing.

285. Pelphrey, *Love Was His Meaning,* 18.

286. See chap. 5 above.

287. Doyle already considered it possible that Julian knew *Ancrene Wisse* (*Survey,* 233). Denise N. Baker's arguments, by contrast, are not persuasive when she asserts that there is no real evidence of Julian's knowledge of anchoritic literature, and that she presumably had not read Rolle's *Form of Living* or Hilton's *Scale of Perfection* ("Julian of Norwich and Anchoritic Literature," 153). There are in fact interesting echoes of *The Scale of Perfection.* On anchorites in Norwich, cf. Dunn, "Hermits, Anchorites and Recluses." He speaks of people who sacrifice their own youth to God of their own free will, and Julian of Norwich will have been one of them. Christ himself thanks her for her service and for her ascetic self-sacrifice—chiefly in her youth. Does not this, too, point toward an early start to her life as recluse?

288. Bradley is also of the opinion that "before her showings, Julian already possessed considerable spiritual maturity" ("Julian on Prayer," in Llewelyn, *Julian: Woman of Our Day,* 61). Lichtmann believes that Julian was already a recluse when

she received her revelations: "Her anchorage existence freed her to accept uncommon insights into the spiritual significance of the body" ("'I Desyrede a Bodylye Syght,'" 17). Likewise, Jantzen considers it not unlikely that she was already an anchoress when she received her visions, since "the depth and profundity of her prayer life and devotion to Christ...had been developed over some considerable time...it might well be thought that this points already to the life of deep devotion of a recluse" (*Julian of Norwich*, 24–25). Jantzen's interpretation is therefore preceded by a whole chapter on "The Life of an Anchoress."

289. S. Bhattacharji, "Independence of Thought in Julian of Norwich," *Word and Spirit* 11 (1989): 80.

290. E. Jenkins, "Julian's *Revelation of Love:* A Web of Metaphor," in McAvoy, *Companion to Julian of Norwich*, 183.

291. Benz, *Die Vision*, 181.

292. So Pelphrey, *Love Was His Meaning*, 18.

293. See the sketch of the *Ancrene Wisse* cell in Robert Hasenfratz, ed., *Ancrene Wisse*, 11.

294. Matarasso, *Cistercian World*, 233.

295. *Anchoritic Spirituality*, ed. Savage and Watson, 176–77.

10. Margery Kempe

1. *A Shorte Treatyse of Contemplacyon* (London, 1501). In 1521 Henry Pepwell published the text again, as part of a small collection of devotional texts, which led to Margery Kempe being known for four hundred years as "holy anchorite."

2. *Book of Margery Kempe,* ed. Meech and Allen, lxi.

3. See, for instance, Charity Scott-Stokes, "Margery Kempe: Her Life and the Early History of Her Book," 12–17; further, Margaret Gallyon, *Margery Kempe of Lynn and Medieval England* (Norwich, UK: James Clarke, 1995), 61; A. Goodman, *Margery Kempe and Her World* (Harlow, UK: Longman), 2002; and Parker, "Lynn and the Making of a Mystic," 55–73.

4. Further details in Parker, "Lynn and the Making of a Mystic," 56.

5. Scott-Stokes, "Margery Kempe," 21 and 17.

6. Staley, *Dissenting Fictions,* 3.

7. Christ wears a red silk robe in other female mystical texts, e.g. those of the nuns of Helfta.

8. Quotations are taken from *The Book of Margery Kempe* (abbreviated *BMK*), ed. Windeatt (Cambridge: D. S. Brewer, 2004); here p. 62. Page and line numbers cited parenthetically are from this source.

9. Readers have understandably puzzled over her mysterious indication of a grave sin in youth, before her marriage, and it has often been suggested that this involved sexual misconduct. Against such an assumption it has recently been objected that in this case she would have identified the sin, since her book is by no means prudish in matters of sexuality. In Scott-Stokes's opinion, the sin might have been related to sympathy for Lollard heresy, which would have been concealed because such connections were increasingly dangerous (Scott-Stokes, "Margery Kempe," 25).

10. *BMK*, ed. Windeatt (2004), 74.

11. Scott-Stokes, "Margery Kempe," 29.

12. On her spirituality, see esp. Bhattacharji, *God Is an Earthquake*, 87.

13. Scott-Stokes, "Margery Kempe," 30.

14. Ibid.

15. Cf. ibid., 33, quoting another woman's comparable reaction from Felix Fabri of Ulm (a late fifteenth-century pilgrimage record).

16. *BMK*, ed. Windeatt (2004), 209–10.

17. Herbers, *Jakobsweg*, 183.

18. Scott-Stokes, "Margery Kempe," 36.

19. Gibson, *Theater of Devotion*, 47.

20. *BMK*, ed. Windeatt (2004), 6. This, too, she sees as contributing to the martyrdom of the *imitatio Christi;* see also Arnold in Arnold and Lewis, *Companion*, 81.

21. Spearing, "Margery Kempe," in Edwards, *Companion to Middle English Prose*, 89; also J. K. Tarvers, "The Alleged Illiteracy of Margery Kempe," *Medieval Perspectives* 11 (1996): 113–24.

22. In *Scale* 1 it is said that whoever wishes to build churches, abbeys, etc., will be rewarded in heaven for his "good wil" (*Scale* 1:105); Jesus confirms to Kempe that she had precisely this will and intention (*BMK*, ed. Windeatt [2004], 364:6860–61). She also follows the admonition expressed in *Scale* 1 (chap. 70) to love the good and the evil.

23. Cf. Jenkins, "Reading and *The Book of Margery Kempe*," 113–28.

24. Cf. Scott-Stokes, "Margery Kempe," 23. Lochrie considers it proven that Margery could not read, since she needed to be alerted in her Trinity vision to the fact that her name was inscribed in the Book of Life ("The Book of Margery Kempe," 54); but this conclusion is by no means compelling, since she may have been too overcome by the vision in its totality to be looking for her own name.

25. Melissa Furrow, "Unscholarly Latin and Margery Kempe," in *"Doubt Wisely": Papers in Honour of E. G. Stanley*, ed. M. J. Toswell (London: Routledge, 1996), 240–51, esp. 249–50.

26. Uhlman, "Comfort of Voice."

27. See Coleman, "Aurality," 68–85.

28. Cf. also *Augustinus Confessiones. Bekenntnisse. Lateinisch-deutsch*, trans. Joseph Bernhart, 3rd ed. (Munich: Kösel, 1966), 250–51 and note.

29. See Coleman, "Aurality," 74.

30. Cf. also Jenkins, "Reading and *The Book of Margery Kempe*," 117.

31. On Margery in her social and economic position see the following excellent comments: Sheila Delany, "Sexual Economics, Chaucer's Wife of Bath, and *The Book of Margery Kempe*," *Minnesota Review* 5 (1978): 104–15, repr. in Delany, *Writing Woman: Women Writers and Women in Literature, Medieval and Modern* (New York: Schocken Books 1983), 76–92; Sarah Beckwith, "A Very Material Mysticism: The Medieval Mysticism of Margery Kempe," in *Medieval Literature: Criticism, Ideology, and History*, ed. David Aers (New York: Harvester, 1986), 34–57; David Aers, "The Making of Margery Kempe," in Aers, *Community, Gender, and Individual Identity*.

32. *BMK*, ed. Windeatt (2004), 199; P. H. Cullum rightly observes that her living in poverty was not a voluntary decision, and "it may well be that it was not until Margery visited Rome that she encountered a more radical practice of charity" ("'Yf Lak of Charyte,'" 190, 189).

33. Cullum, "'Yf Lak of Charyte,'" 190.

34. Scott-Stokes, "Margery Kempe," 38.

35. *BMK*, ed. Windeatt (2004), 21.

36. McGinn, *Presence of God*, vol. 3, *Flowering*, 238–39.

37. Cf. *BMK*, ed. Windeatt (2004), 30–31; see also esp. Salih, *Versions of Virginity*, 238–39.

38. E.g. in *Mechthild von Magdeburg*, ed. Vollmann-Profe, despite her nonerotic descriptions of unity with the Trinity.

39. See also esp. Salih's comment, *Versions of Virginity*, 230.

40. Cf. Biser in *Gotteskindschaft*.

41. Cf. esp. Duffy, *Stripping of the Altars*, 238–48.

42. *BMK*, ed. Windeatt (2004), chap. 28, 166–67; for text reference and indication of the motif's source in Bernard's exegesis of the Song of Songs, see Windeatt's note.

43. On the cult of the wounds in England see also Duffy, *Stripping of the Altars*, 238–48. It is interesting to observe in this context that in England no major case of stigmatization is known.

44. Bhattacharji, *God Is an Earthquake*, 130.

45. Edmund Colledge, "Margery Kempe," in Walsh, *Pre-Reformation English Spirituality*, 221.

46. Baker, Murphy, and Hall, *Late Medieval Religious Plays*, 182, 450.

47. Cf. esp. Duffy, *Stripping of the Altars*.

48. Glasscoe aptly observes with regard to Margery Kempe: "All human suffering became an icon of Christ's Passion" (*English Medieval Mystics*, 279).

49. See esp. Benke, *Gabe der Tränen*, 29–188; see also McEntire's useful chapter, "Walter Hilton and Margery Kempe: Tears and Compunction," in Lagorio, *Mysticism: Medieval and Modern*, 49–57; further, Mahoney, "Margery Kempe's Tears," in McEntire, *Margery Kempe*, 37–50.

50. See esp. McEntire, "The Doctrine of Compunction from Bede to Margery Kempe," *MMTE* 4 (1987), 77–90; and McEntire, *Doctrine of Compunction*.

51. This was also the subject of some of her discussions with Julian of Norwich; cf. Pelphrey, *Christ Our Mother*, 180–81. *Ancrene Wisse* already mentions the gift of tears (*Anchoritic Spirituality*, ed. Savage and Watson, 137).

52. Benke, *Gabe der Tränen*, 265–66. "More intensely than for her own sins Margery weeps for the wrongdoings of her fellow human beings and of the whole world. In this she perceives her actual mission. . . . In the form of vicarious weeping for the salvation of mankind, the Church, and the whole world, Margery serves the original Christian concern for solidarity in accomplishing the salvation of all" (Benke, *Gabe der Tränen*, 283); cf. also Susan Dickman, "Margery Kempe and the English Devotional Tradition," *MMTE* 1 (1980), 156–72.

53. Cf. Stölting, *Christliche Frauenmystik*, 248, 453, 458, 478, 493.

54. Benke, *Gabe der Tränen*, 265.

55. Ibid., 257.

56. Ibid., 264.

57. Ibid., 282.

58. Ibid., 267.

59. Suggested, e.g., by N. Hoppenwasser, "A Performance Artist and Her Performance Text: Margery Kempe on Tour," in Suydam and Ziegler, *Performance and Transformation*, 97–132. See also J. Boffey, "'This Is a Deed Bok, the Tother a Quick': Theatre and the Drama of Salvation in the Book of Margery Kempe," in Wogan-Browne et al., *Medieval Women*, 49–68; see also Denis Renevey, "Mystical Texts or Mystical Bodies? Peculiar Modes of Performance in Late Medieval England," in *Performance*, Swiss Papers in English Language and Literature 11, ed. Peter Halter (Tübingen: Günter Narr, 1998), 89–104.

60. Benke, *Gabe der Tränen*, 257, 264.

61. Glasscoe recognized this: "For Margery they were a sign that the Incarnation is not simply a historical event but an ever-present reality" (*English Medieval Mystics*, 278).

62. *Mechthild von Magdeburg*, ed. Vollmann-Profe, 728.

63. Quoted from Biser, *Paulus*, 147.

64. E.g., Benke, *Gabe der Tränen*, 282.

65. See Gibson, *Theater of Devotion*.

66. See D. L. Despres, "The Meditative Art of Scriptural Interpolation in *The Book of Margery Kempe*," *DR* 106 (1988): 256; also Despres, "Franciscan Spirituality: Margery Kempe and Visual Meditation," *MQ* 11 (1985): 12–18.

67. Atkinson, *Mystic and Pilgrim*, 134–37.

68. J. Huizinga, trans. R. J. Payton and U. Mammitzsch, *The Autumn of the Middle Ages* (Chicago: University of Chicago Press, 1996), 156–72; and Kieckhefer, *Unquiet Souls*.

69. McGinn, *Presence of God*, vol. 3, *Flowering*, 33.

70. See also Ruh, *Geschichte*, 2:83–90 McGinn's account is in some respects particularly successful (and he offers very detailed bibliographical references), but it is impaired by his misguided theory that the thirteenth century witnessed the beginning of a "New Mysticism" (*Presence of God*, vol. 3, *Flowering*, 12ff.). The history of medieval mysticism does not proceed in leaps and bounds: what we find is an intensification and enhancement of previous developments, rather than a decisive new beginning. Mystical *raptus* may occur frequently for women at this time, and last longer, perhaps days or weeks, but this does not introduce a fundamentally new quality into their mysticism; rather, it intensifies what was already there; cf. Dickman, "Margery Kempe and the Continental Tradition," and Dickman, "Shewing of God's Grace."

71. See Blume and Werner, *Elisabeth von Thüringen*, 2:110.

72. Geyer, *Maria von Oignies*, 145.

73. Spencer, *English Preaching*, 150.

74. On the reevaluation of the sermon, see esp. Ruh, *Geschichte*, 1:249–52.

75. Peters, *Religiöse Erfahrung*, 31.

76. Brown, *Three Women of Liège*, 284.

77. Ruh, *Geschichte*, 2:73.

78. Geyer, *Maria von Oignies*, 46; see also Brown, *Three Women of Liège*, 284–85.

79. McGinn, *Presence of God*, vol. 3, *Flowering*, 34–35; Geyer, *Maria von Oignies*, 46.

80. Ibid., 47.

81. Jenkins, without being aware of the parallel to Marie, affirmed: "The priest, at Margery's urging, seeks out works he would not otherwise have encountered, and

which she must have known by reputation or earlier experience. Over the course of their reading together, she therefore helps to increase both his intellect ('hys cynnyng') and his religious standing ('hys meryte')" ("Reading and *The Book of Margery Kempe*," 117). Dickman also recognized that Margery felt herself called by Christ to "teaching and preaching" ("Shewing of God's Grace," 174).

82. Proposed by Ellis, "Margery Kempe's Scribe," in Phillips, *Langland, the Mystics and the Medieval English Religious Tradition*, 161–75.

83. Cf. Stargardt, "Beguines of Belgium," 280.

84. Proposed by Spearing, "Margery Kempe," in Edwards, *Companion to Middle English Prose*, 90.

85. See Spearing, who on the one hand says that her relationship "is strongly eroticized throughout," but on the other hand draws attention to many parallels in female mysticism. He goes too far in reading into God the Father's promise to "schewyn þe my preuytes" a play on words, for sight of God's mysteries—often described in English mysticism as "privities"—is a theological topos that can be traced all the way back to Paul (ibid., 83–97).

86. Monika Rener, ed., *Die Vita der heiligen Elisabeth des Dietrich von Apolda*. *Veröffentlichungen der Historischen Kommission für Hessen* 53 (Marburg: N. G. Elwert Verlag, 1993), 66 and 70. For a shortened German version, see Rainer Kössling, ed. and trans., *Leben und Legende der heiligen Elisabeth: Nach Dietrich von Apolda*. Mit 14 Miniaturen der Handschrift von 1481 (Frankfurt am Main: Insel, 1997), 91.

87. See S. Tebruck, "Militia Christi—Imitatio Christi: Kreuzzugsidee und Armutsideal am Thüringischen Landgrafenhof zur Zeit der heiligen Elisabeth," in Blume and Werner, *Elisabeth von Thüringen*, 1:137–52, 137–38.

88. V. Honemann, "Die 'Vita Sanctae Elisabeth' des Dietrich von Apolda und die deutschsprachigen 'Elisabethleben' des Mittelalters," ibid., 1:422.

89. Ibid., 2:426, 428.

90. For the numerous parallels between *Revelationes* and *BMK*, see Barratt, "Virgin and the Visionary"; Barratt, "Margery Kempe and the King's Daughter of Hungary"; further, McNamer, *Two Middle English Translations*, 42–48 and n.

91. Barratt, "Virgin and the Visionary"; Barratt, "The Revelations of St Elizabeth of Hungary: Problems of Attribution," *Library*, 6th series, 14 (1992): 1–11; Barratt, "Margery Kempe and the King's Daughter of Hungary"; McNamer, *Two Middle English Translations*, 12.

92. See esp. Salih, *Versions of Virginity*, 16.

93. I. Würth concludes that "the Italian Rivelazioni [leave] no doubt but that the visionary concerned is St. Elizabeth of Thuringia" ("Marienvisionen der Hl. Elisabeth," in Blume and Werner, *Elisabeth von Thüringen*, 2:438).

94. Gabor Klaniczay, "Elisabeth von Thüringen und Ungarn," ibid., 1:173. For the Latin text, see L. Oliger, "Revelationes B. Elisabeth: Disquisitio critica una cum textibus latino et catalaunensi," in *Antonianum* 1 (1926): 24–83, and "Revelationes B. Elisabeth," in Addenda, *Antonianum* 2 (1927), 483ff. Indisputably, Elizabeth was close in spirit to Francis, but the hospital that she founded and directed has nothing to do with Franciscans.

95. Sheila Delany, ed. and trans., *Osbern Bokenham: A Legend of Holy Women* (Notre Dame, IN: University of Notre Dame Press, 1992).

96. C. Kolletzki, "'Über die Wahrheit dieses Buches': Die Entstehung des 'Liber Specialis Gratiae' Mechthilds von Hackeborn zwischen Wirklichkeit und Fiktion," in *"Vor dir steht die leere Schale meiner Sehnsucht": Die Mystik der Frauen von Helfta,* 2nd ed., ed. M. Bangert and H. Keul (Leipzig: Benno, 1999), 168.

97. E.g., Ruh, *Geschichte* 2:110.

98. Ute Stargardt, "The Influence of Dorothea von Montau on the Mysticism of Margery Kempe" (PhD diss., University of Tennessee, 1981), and Stargardt, "Beguines of Belgium"; cf. also Kieckhefer, *Unquiet Souls.* For the Latin text, see H. Westphal, *Vita Dorotheae Montoviensis Magistri Johannis Marienwerder* (Cologne: Böhlau, 1964).

99. Günter Grass, *Der Butt,* 3rd ed. (Darmstadt: Luchterhand, 1977), 209.

100. Stargardt, "Beguines of Belgium," 307; see also P. Hörner, *Dorothea von Montau: Überlieferung, Interpretation: Dorothea und die osteuropäische Mystik* (Frankfurt am Main: P. Lang, 1993); P. Dinzelbacher, *Christliche Mystik im Abendland,* 349–55; further, McGinn, *Presence of God,* vol. 4, *Harvest,* 353–55.

101. Stölting, *Christliche Frauenmystik,* 449.

102. Ruh, *Geschichte,* 2:502–9.

103. Ibid., 506.

104. Ibid., 521.

105. Ibid., 520.

106. See C. Mazzoni, *Angela of Foligno's "Memorial,"* trans. John Cirignano, Library of Medieval Women (Cambridge: D. S. Brewer, 1999); see also Carole Slade, "The Mystical Experience of Angela of Foligno and Margery Kempe," *Religion and Literature* 23 (1991): 109–26.

107. Middle English translation in C. Horstmann, ed., " Prosalegenden: Die Legenden des ms 114," *Anglia* 8 (1885): 119–34; Elizabeth of Spalbeek, ibid., 107–18. For a more recent critical edition, see J. N. Brown, *Three Women of Liège* (Elizabeth, 27–50; Christina, 51–84).

108. E.g. S. Dickman, "Margery Kempe and the Continental Tradition"; Atkinson, *Mystic and Pilgrim,* 157–94.

109. Ruh, *Geschichte,* 2:303.

110. Ibid., 2:306.

111. Ibid.

112. See Gertrud of Helfta, *Herald of Divine Love,* bk. 3, chap. 2ff., 157ff.

113. Ruh, *Geschichte,* 2:101–2.

114. For Birgitta's biography, see the detailed account by Schiwy, *Birgitta von Schweden;* also Bridget Morris, *St Birgitta of Sweden,* Studies in Medieval Mysticism 1 (Woodbridge, UK: Boydell Press, 1999); M. T. Harris and A. R. Kezel, eds., *Birgitta of Sweden: Life and Selected Revelations* (Mahwah, NJ: Paulist Press, 1990). For Middle English translations, see W. P. Cumming, ed., *The Revelations of Saint Birgitta,* EETS o.s. 178 (1929); and Ellis, *Liber Celestis.*

115. Barratt gives a detailed account of knowledge of Birgitta in England but cannot prove her influence on Margery ("Continental Women Mystics and English Readers," in Dinshaw and Wallace, *Cambridge Companion to Medieval Women's Writing,* 248–50).

116. Barry Windeatt, "1412–1534: Texts," in Fanous and Gillespie, *Cambridge Companion to Medieval English Mysticism,* 200.

117. Schiwy, *Birgitta von Schweden,* 215.

118. Ibid., 242.

119. Ibid., 221.

120. Ibid., 158.

121. Ellis, *Liber celestis,* 255; quoted from *BMK,* ed. Windeatt (2004), 199.

122. Schiwy, *Birgitta von Schweden,* 330.

123. Ibid., 41.

124. See Atkinson, *Mystic and Pilgrim,* 176–77, esp. for the interesting parallels between the sons of Birgitta and Margery (further parallels in *BMK,* ed. Windeatt [2004], 13).

125. See C. L. Sahlin, "Preaching and Prophesying: The Public Proclamation of Birgitta of Sweden's Revelations," in Suydam and Ziegler, *Performance and Transformation,* 69–96.

126. N. Hoppenwasser and S. Weaver had to concede this, although they make every effort (if unconvincingly) to prove that Margery modeled her life closely on Birgitta's, and even claimed her as spiritual mother ("Vox Matris: The Influence of St. Birgitta's Revelations on *The Book of Margery Kempe*—St. Birgitta and Margery Kempe as Wives and Mothers," in *Crossing the Bridge: Comparative Essays on Medieval European and Heijan Japanese Women Writers,* ed. B. Stevenson and Cynthia Ho [New York: Palgrave Macmillan, 2000], 72). There are enormous differences between the two women.

127. Cf. Gunnel Cleve: "St Bridget was the most important model for Margery Kempe" ("Margery Kempe: A Scandinavian Influence in Medieval England?" *MMTE* 5 [1992], 177); see also Jenkins, "Reading and *The Book of Margery Kempe,*" 125; N. Hoppenwasser, "The Human Burden of the Prophet: St Birgitta's Revelations and *The Book of Margery Kempe,*" *Medieval Perspectives* 8 (1993): 153–62; also N. K. Yoshikawa, "Margery Kempe's Mystical Marriage and Roman Sojourn: The Influence of St. Bridget of Sweden," *Reading Medieval Studies* 28 (2002): 39–57. The scribe of the second prologue notes that he began his work on the day after the feast of Mary Magdalen, i.e., July 23, which also commemorates the death of Birgitta of Sweden; if this were significant for the reader of *BMK,* there would be some direct reference to it in the text.

128. A. M. Hutchison, "Reflections on Aspects of the Spiritual Impact of St Birgitta, the Revelations and the Bridgettine Order in Late Medieval England," *MMTE* 7 (2004), 78.

129. K. Lochrie, "The Language of Transgression: Body, Flesh, and Word in Mystical Discourse," in *Speaking Two Languages: Traditional Disciplines and Contemporary Theory in Medieval Studies,* ed. A. J. Frantzen, SUNY Series in Medieval Studies (Albany: SUNY Press, 1991), 117.

130. See esp. Gibson, "St. Margery: The Book of Margery Kempe," in Gibson, *Theater of Devotion,* 47–65. According to K. J. Lewis, "The Book does everything it possibly can to present Margery as a saint, both in terms of her way of life and her intercessory powers" ("Margery Kempe and Saint Making in Later Medieval England," in Arnold and Lewis, *Companion,* 215). The hagiographic resonances are exaggerated by S. Fanous, who considers the entire *BMK* to be structured according to "hagiographic modes of discourse" ("Measuring the Pilgrim's Progress," ibid., 171). However, Fanous makes some interesting observations, e.g. on the conscious

selection of events to be reported, and the deliberate vagueness of some indications of time, intended to diminish the temporal concreteness of Margery's life and enhance the claim to sainthood (ibid., 168).

131. See the very useful study by Diane Watt, *Secretaries of God: Women Prophets in Late Medieval and Early Modern England* (Cambridge: D. S. Brewer, 1997); Ellen Ross observes how "the prophet motif runs through Kempe's autobiography" ("Spiritual Experience and Women's Autobiography," *Journal of the American Academy of Religion* 59 [1991], 543).

132. Windeatt, in Arnold and Lewis, *Companion,* 12.

133. S. Fanous, "Measuring the Pilgrim's Progress"; see also Yoshikawa's less persuasive "Veneration of Virgin Martyrs in Margery Kempe's Meditation: Influence of the Sarum Liturgy and Hagiography," in Renevey and Whitehead, *Writing Religious Women,* 177–95, which tries to prove a dominant influence of St. Katherine on Margery. It does not seem at all likely that there was a conscious stylistic intention to elevate Margery to national sainthood, since there is much that does not fit the hagiographic pattern.

134. I therefore do not agree with Gibson's view that Margery attained the pinnacle of her spiritual life with the St. Margaret miracle, the healing of an insane woman: "Margaret has come full circle by this miracle" ("St. Margery: The Book of Margery Kempe," in *Equally in God's Image: Women in the Middle Ages,* ed. Julia Bolton Holloway et al. [New York: Peter Lang, 1990], 158).

135. Useful earlier writings on autobiography include Georg Misch, *Geschichte der Autobiographie,* 4 vols., 3rd ed. (Frankfurt am Main: Klostermann, 1949–69); R. Pascal, *Design and Truth in Autobiography* (Cambridge, MA: Harvard University Press, 1960); J. Olney, *Metaphors of Self: The Meaning of Autobiography* (Princeton, NJ: Princeton University Press, 1972); P. Zumthor, "Autobiography in the Middle Ages," *Genre* 6 (1973): 29–48, and "Über die Entwicklung der Selbstbiographie im ausgehenden deutschen Mittelalter," in *Die Autobiographie,* ed. G. Niggl (Darmstadt: Wissenschaftliche Buchgesellschaft, 1989), 321–42, first printed in *Archiv für Kulturgeschichte* 14 [1919]: 193–213); see also Horst Wenzel, "Zu den Anfängen der volkssprachlichen Autobiographie im späten Mittelalter," *Daphnis* 13 (1984): 59–75.

136. Holdenried, *Autobiographie,* 97.

137. Ibid., 99.

138. Ibid., 91.

139. Ibid., 97.

140. Cf. *BMK,* ed. Windeatt (2004), 25–27.

141. See Lynn Staley Johnson, "The Trope of the Scribe and the Question of Literary Authority in the Works of Julian of Norwich and Margery Kempe," *Speculum* 66 (1991): 820–38; C. Glenn, "Author, Audience and Autobiography: Rhetorical Technique in *The Book of Margery Kempe," College English* 54 (1992): 540–53; Uhlman, "Comfort of Voice," 50–69; Staley, *Margery Kempe's Dissenting Fictions;* and Scott-Stokes, "Margery Kempe," 45–46.

142. Watson, "Making of *The Book of Margery Kempe,*" 404.

143. See on this the important essay by Uhlman, "Comfort of Voice"; R. C. Ross, "Oral Life, Written Text: The Genesis of *The Book of Margery Kempe,*" *Yearbook of English Studies* 22 (1992): 226–37.

144. E.g. Ross, "Oral Life, Written Text"; see also Spearing, "Margery Kempe," in Edwards, *Companion to Middle English Prose*, 83–97.

145. Watson, "Making of *The Book of Margery Kempe*," 397; Riddy, by contrast, sees the text as a social and collaborative product: "Text and Self in *The Book of Margery Kempe*," in Olson and Kerby-Fulton, *Voices in Dialogue*, 435–53.

146. Staley, *Margery Kempe's Dissenting Fictions*, 19–20, 22–23; Voaden, "God's Almighty Hand: Women Co-writing the Book," in Smith and Taylor, *Women, the Book and the Godly*, 55–65.

147. *"The Book of Margery Kempe": A New Translation, Contexts, Criticism*, trans. and ed. Lynn Staley (New York: W. W. Norton, 2001), 12.

148. Watson, "Making of *The Book of Margery Kempe*," 403.

149. Further attempts to maximize "textualization" include the rephrasing of colloquialisms as indirect speech, abbreviations, clerical peculiarities, personal comment.

150. On these examples, see Spearing, "Margery Kempe," 93.

151. Ibid.

152. There are other instances of careful clerical cooperation in the composition of such a text, e.g. in the *Offenbarungen* of Agnes Blannbekin (Wiethaus, *Agnes Blannbekin*, 8); the scribe participated with great reverence (Stölting, *Christliche Frauenmystik*, 462).

153. Windeatt, "1412–1534: Texts," in Fanous and Gillespie, *Cambridge Companion to Medieval English Mysticism*, 198.

154. Unlike in Julian, there is no suggestion in Margery that love of one's neighbor presupposes love of self; there is no evidence in *BMK* that she is willing to accept herself, in all her individuality and with all her contradictions. Instead she maintains her self-contempt as prerequisite for her spiritual practice.

155. N. K. Yoshikawa, too, observes: "By undergoing a similar psychological process as Julian did, Margery penetrates the meaning of the Incarnation" (*"Discretio Spirituum* in Time," 127).

156. This was recognized by Dickman, "Shewing of God's Grace," 175.

157. This brief doctrine of the Trinity is based on Augustine; see chap. 9 above; and John P. H. Clark, "The Trinitarian Theology of Walter Hilton's *Scale of Perfection*, Book Two," in Phillips, *Langland, the Mystics and the Medieval Religious Tradition*, 125; also Yoshikawa, *"Discretio Spirituum* in Time," 129–30.

158. The popular element in Margery's descriptions of the court of heaven is reminiscent of Mechthild of Hackeborn. She calls on Mary Magdalen, the apostles, martyrs, confessors, Katherine, Margaret, and all the holy virgins, the entire "retinue of heaven" (373:7084), to decorate the chamber of her soul as dwelling place for Jesus, and to welcome him. She stages a vivid enactment of the familiar Pauline mystical theme "Christ in me" (Gal 2:20). The vision culminates in the presence of the entire Trinity, cleverly differentiated theologically by each person sitting on his own symbolically colored cushion. There are reminiscences, too, of the vita of Marie d'Oignies, for whom the hagiographer stages "a unique gathering of the saints" as her life comes to an end: all the apostles are present as she receives extreme unction, and Christ himself holds the banner of victory at her feet.

159. Bhattacharji, *God Is an Earthquake*, 86–87.

160. See also Watson, "Visions of Inclusion"; Watson refers to her "Good Friday intercessions for the needy, including 'Iewys, Sara3inys, and alle fals heretikys,'"

152–53. For comparable inclusiveness in Mechthild of Magdeburg, see *Mechthild von Magdeburg,* ed. Vollmann-Profe, 762.

161. Watson sees this as an example of "vernacular theology," as in *Piers Plowman* and in Julian's *Revelation of Love* ("Visions of Inclusion," 152–53). More probably it exemplifies a tradition of women devoting themselves especially to intercession; their intercessory prayers were thought to be particularly effective.

162. The beguine Agnes Blannbekin was also tempted to engage in sexual activity; see Wiethaus, *Agnes Blannbekin,* 142. *Ancrene Wisse* goes all the way back to the desert mother Syncletica for an example.

163. Ez 18:23, 33:11; similarly in Marie d'Oignies, Gertrud of Helfta, and Agnes Blannbekin.

164. See esp. P. H. Cullum, "'Yf Lak of Charyte,'" 177–93.

165. D. Watt exaggerates the differences between Julian and Margery's attitudes ("Saint Julian of the Apocalypse," in McAvoy, *Companion to Julian of Norwich,* 73.

166. Yoshikawa merely surmises that Julian is citing Paul: "She probably knew the teaching of St Paul: 'Likewise the Spirit also helpeth our infirmity'" ("*Discretio Spirituum* in Time," 121).

167. Karma Lochrie, *Margery Kempe and Translations of the Flesh,* 88.

168. See Lochrie, "*Book of Margery Kempe.*"

169. Watson affirms the need for this but argues from too modern a perspective ("Afterwords," in "Making of *The Book of Margery Kempe*," 455).

170. See Michael Sargent, "The Self-Verification of Visionary Phenomena: Richard Methley's *Experimentum veritatis,*" in *Kartäusermystik- und mystiker,* vol. 2, AC 55, ed. James Hogg (Salzburg: Institut für Anglistik und Amerikanistik, 1981), 121–23.

171. Windeatt has listed the reasons why she cannot be a Lollard (*BMK* [2004], 95).

172. Cf. Janette Dillon's important chapter, "Holy Women and Their Confessors or Confessors and Their Holy Women?" in Voaden, *Prophets Abroad,* 115–40.

173. Staley, *Margery Kempe's Dissenting Fictions,* 8.

174. Dickman therefore overemphasizes Margery's criticism of "the clergy" ("Margery Kempe and the Continental Tradition").

175. Some of the themes Margery broaches are particularly likely to occur also in contemporary sermons, e.g. the central tenet of voluntarist ethics, that in God's eyes the will to do something counts as much as the action. Abelard was one of those who taught the primacy of intention over action, and the *Speculum virginum* emphasized the precedence of *animus* over *habitus* (cf. Küsters, *Der verschlossene Garten,* 206).

176. Voaden, *God's Words,* 134.

177. Geyer, *Maria von Oignies,* 48.

178. Duffy, *Stripping of the Altars.*

179. G. Holmstedt, ed., *Speculum christiani:* A Middle English Religious Treatise of the 14th Century, EETS o.s. 182 (1933), 21.

180. Allen, *Writings,* 190–91.

181. Salih, *Versions of Virginity,* 222; her discussion of this motif is excellent; see also Gunnel Cleve, "Semantic Dimensions in Margery Kempe's 'Whyght Clothys,'" *MQ* 12 (1986): 162–70, and Mary C. Erler, "Margery Kempe's White Clothes," *MAE* 62 (1993): 78–83.

182. See Roland Maisonneuve, "Margery Kempe and the Eastern and Western Tradition of the 'Perfect Fool,'" *MMTE* 2 (1982), 1–17; Glasscoe, *English Medieval Mystics,* 311; Benke, *Gabe der Tränen,* 275. R. Lawes looks at the psychology of Margery's "madness" in the light of fifteenth-century mentality, in "The Madness of Margery Kempe," *MMTE* 6 (1999), 147–67.

183. *BMK,* ed. Windeatt (2004), 339.

184. Ibid., 85.

185. Bede, *De muliere forti, PL* 91, cols. 1039–52. Richard Rolle also wrote a tract *De muliere forti.*

186. Cf. Lochrie, *"Book of Margery Kempe,"* 52–54.

187. Salih, *Versions of Virginity,* 180. Christ assures Margareta Contracta of Magdeburg: "The whole world will be revived by your heart, now and in future" (Ruh, *Geschichte,* 2:129).

188. Eugen Biser, *Einweisung ins Christentum,* 2nd ed. (Düsseldorf: Patmos, 1998), 331–32. Windeatt also observes, rightly, that Margery is "inwardly taught by Mary, Christ and God" (Arnold and Lewis, *Companion,* 8; cf. also *Book of Showings,* ed. Colledge and Walsh, Julian of Norwich, *Revelation of Love,* LV, 431).

189. Ruh, *Geschichte,* 2:506.

190. S. Rees Jones mistakenly sees the text not only as fiction, but also as a compilation by several contributors "to illustrate a series of threats to the authority of the clergy that needed to be recognized and accommodated in their pastoral work. It was, perhaps, a book written by clergy, for clergy, and about clergy." The book is said to be written by men, to show "what men wanted women to be" ("'A peler of Holy Cherch': Margery Kempe and the Bishops," in Wogan-Browne, Diamond, Hutchison, et al., *Medieval Women,* 391).

191. Hildegund Keul, *Mechthild of Magdeburg—Poetin, Begine, Mystikerin* (Freiburg: Herder, 2007), 152–53; and Ringler, *Aufbruch,* 14.

192. Langer, *Christliche Mystik,* 32.

193. See C. M. Waters, "Power and Authority," in Sarah Salih, ed., *A Companion to Middle English Hagiography* (Cambridge: D. S. Brewer, 2006), 70.

194. Riehle, *Middle English Mystics,* 11.

195. Ibid.

196. Colledge, "Margery Kempe," in Walsh, *Pre-Reformation English Spirituality,* 210.

197. Lochrie, *Margery Kempe and Translations of the Flesh,* 144.

198. See also the conclusion of Windeatt's introduction (*BMK,* 2004).

199. Benke, *Gabe der Tränen,* 284; for ostensible heterodoxy in Margery Kempe, see R. Shklar, "Cobham's Daughter: *The Book of Margery Kempe* and the Power of Heterodox Thinking," *MLQ* 50 (1995): 277–304.

200. See above all Atkinson, *Mystic and Pilgrim;* Aers, *Community, Gender, and Individual Identity;* Beckwith, *Christ's Body;* also Kathleen Ashley's article written from the viewpoint of cultural history, "Historicizing Margery: *The Book of Margery Kempe* as Social Text," *Journal of Medieval and Early Modern Studies* 28 (1998): 371–88.

201. R. Lovatt, "The Imitation of Christ in Late Medieval England," *Transactions of the Royal Historical Society,* 5th series, 18 (1968): 98.

11. Some Aspects of Popularizing Mysticism in Late Medieval England

1. See Renevey, "'Name Poured Out,'" 127–48. I cannot agree with all of Renevey's conclusions; e.g., the cult of the Name of Jesus is far less significant in Rolle than Renevey suggests, in agreement with widespread opinion (ibid., 133).

2. See Norman F. Blake, "Vernon Manuscript: Contents and Organization," in Pearsall, *Studies in the Vernon Manuscript*.

3. See esp. Margaret Deanesly, "Vernacular Books in England in the Fourteenth and Fifteenth Centuries," *MLR* 15 (1920): 349–58. Of fundamental importance is Doyle's "Survey"; see further Sargent, "Transmission"; Carol M. Meale, "'Alle the Bokes That I Haue of Latyn, Englisch, and Frensch': Laywomen and Their Books in Late Medieval England," in Meale, *Women and Literature in Britain*, 128–58; S. Groag Bell, "Medieval Women Book Owners: Arbiters of Lay Piety and Ambassadors of Culture," in *Women and Power in the Middle Ages*, ed. Mary Erler and Maryanne Kowaleski (Athens: University of Georgia Press, 1988): 149–87; Vincent Gillespie, "Vernacular Books of Religion," in *Book Production and Publishing in Britain, 1375–1475*, ed. Jeremy Griffiths and Derek Pearsall (Cambridge: Cambridge University Press, 1989), 317–44; Gillespie, "Anonymous Devotional Writings," in Edwards, *Companion to Middle English Prose*, 127–49; Mary C. Erler, *Women, Reading, and Piety in Late Medieval England*, Cambridge Studies in Medieval Literature (Cambridge: Cambridge University Press, 2002).

4. J. Catto, "Religion and the English Nobility in the Late Fourteenth Century," in *History and Imagination: Essays in Honour of Hugh Trevor Roper*, ed. Hugh Lloyd Jones, Valerie Pearl, and Blair Worden (London: Duckworth, 1981), 43–55.

5. Hilary Carey, "Devout Literate Laypeople and the Pursuit of the Mixed Life in Later Medieval England," *Journal of Religious History* 14 (1987), 361–83, 370.

6. Lagorio and Sargent, "English Mystical Writings," 3077.

7. Ibid., 3420–34.

8. Cf. J. P. H. Clark: "In practice it was recognized that every Christian life contains something of action and something of contemplation.... The consideration of the 'mixed life' as a distinct category had been stimulated by the advent of the Friars" ("Action and Contemplation in Walter Hilton," *DR* 97 [1979]: 265). Prior to Hilton, the problem of combining *vita activa* and *vita contemplativa* was looked at only with regard to clerics obligated to *cura pastoralis*, who necessarily had to combine contemplation with active duty (Walter H. Beale, "Walter Hilton and the Concept of 'Medled Lyf,'" *American Benedictine Review* 26 [1975]: 381–94).

9. *Mixed Life*, ed. Ogilvie-Thomson, 11; the "Epistle on Mixed Life" is also printed in Windeatt, *English Mystics*.

10. On the lord as addressee, cf. Ellis, "Literary Approach," 109–17.

11. *Mixed Life*, ed. Ogilvie-Thomson, 10; cf. also Hussey, "Langland, Hilton, and the Three Lives." For lay persons' relationship to *vita activa* and *vita contemplativa*, see also R. N. Swanson, *Religion and Devotion in Europe, c. 1215–c. 1515* (Cambridge: Cambridge University Press, 1995), 105–6, 125–26.

12. *Mixed Life*, ed. Ogilvie-Thomson, 68.

13. Ibid., 60.

14. Horstmann, *Yorkshire Writers,* vol. 1; and G. G. Perry, *Religious Pieces in Prose and Verse,* rev. ed., EETS o.s. 26 (1914); new ed., Blake, *Middle English Religious Prose,* 88–102; see also Christiania Whitehead, "Making a Cloister of the Soul in Medieval Religious Treatises," *MAE* 67 (1998): 1–29.

15. Cf. the excellent monograph by Gerhard Bauer, *Claustrum Animae.*

16. See the perceptive and well-informed study by Nicole Rice, "Spiritual Ambition and the Translation of the Cloister"; see also her book *Lay Piety and Religious Discipline in Middle English Literature.*

17. Bauer, *Claustrum Animae,* 44; Endre von Ivánka, *Plato Christianus,* 315–51; Hugh of Fouilloy (Hugo de Folieto), *De Claustro animae,* PL 175, 1017–1184

18. Rice, "Spiritual Ambition and the Translation of the Cloister," 239.

19. Blake, *Middle English Religious Prose,* 89.

20. Denis Renevey and Christiania Whitehead, eds., *The Book to a Mother* (Cardiff: University of Wales Press, 2000).

21. Jon Whitman, "Twelfth-Century Allegory: Philosophy and Imagination," in Copeland and Struck, *Cambridge Companion to Allegory,* 101–15.

22. Joachim Söder, "'In actibus nostris nulla sit discordia': Ganzheitlichkeit als cisterciensisches Prinzip," *ACist* 60 (2010): 79–90, 83.

23. See Nicole Randolph Rice, "Spiritual Ambition and the Translation of the Cloister."

24. Ibid., 232, quoting George Keiser, "'To Knawe God Almyghtyn': Robert Thornton's Devotional Book," *AC* 106.2 (Salzburg, 1984), 117.

25. M. Stallings-Taney, ed., *Meditaciones vite Christi,* CCCM 153 (Turnhout: Brepols, 1997); for the English version, see Isa Ragusa and R. B. Green, eds., *Meditations on the Life of Christ: An Illuminated Manuscript of the Fourteenth Century* (Princeton, NJ: Princeton University Press, 1961).

26. Aelred of Rievaulx, *De institutione inclusarum,* CCCM 1, 670. We have seen the importance of this spirituality for Margery Kempe; cf. also Denis Renevey, "Margery's Performing Body: The Translation of Late Medieval Discursive Religious Practices," in Renevey and Whitehead, *Writing Religious Women,* 197–216, esp. 202–4.

27. Michael G. Sargent, *Nicholas Love's "Mirror of the Blessed Life of Jesus Christ": A Critical Edition Based on Cambridge University Library Additional MSS 6578 and 6686,* Garland Medieval Texts 18 (New York: Garland, 1997).

28. Barbara Nolan, "Nicholas Love," in Edwards, *Middle English Prose,* 86; for important conference papers, see also Oguro, Beadle, and Sargent, *Nicholas Love at Waseda;* further, Ghosh, "Nicholas Love"; and Sargent, "Versions of the Life of Christ: Nicholas Love's *Mirror* and Related Works," *Poetica* 42 (for 1994): 39–70.

29. Sargent, *Nicholas Love's "Mirror,"* 10.

30. Ibid., 148–49.

31. Ibid., 10.25.

32. Ibid., 162.

33. Michael G. Sargent, ed., *Nicholas Love's "Mirror of the Blessed Life of Jesus Christ,"* 34.

34. Elizabeth Salter, ed., *Nicholas Love's "Myrrour of the Blessed Lyf of Jesu Christ,"* AC 10 (Salzburg: Institut für Englische Sprache und Literatur, 1974), 33.

35. Nolan, "Nicholas Love," 85.

36. For bibliographical references see ibid., 83.

37. Well summarized by Ghosh, "Nicholas Love," 62–63.

38. The various essays by E. Salter are still useful, listed by Nolan, "Nicholas Love," 95; see esp. Elizabeth Zeeman [Salter], "Nicholas Love—a Fifteenth Century Translator," *RES*, n.s. 6 (1955): 113–27.

39. See Beadle, "'Devoute ymaginacioun' and the Dramatic Sense in Love's *Mirror* and the N-Town Plays," in Oguro, Beadle, and Sargent, *Nicholas Love at Waseda,* 1–17; on the additional influence of Ludolf of Saxony, see Elizabeth Salter, "Ludolfus of Saxony and His English Translators," *MAE* 33 (1964): 26–35; see also David L. Jeffrey, "Franciscan Spirituality and the Rise of Early English Drama," *Mosaic* 8 (1975): 17–46.

40. R. M. Lumiansky and David Mills, eds., *The Chester Mystery Cycle,* 2 vols., EETS s.s. 3 (1974), 2:268.

41. Ibid., 394.

42. Sargent, *Nicholas Love's "Mirror,"* esp. lxvii; cf. also Gibson, who draws attention to the likelihood of this cycle's monastic provenance (*Theater of Devotion,* 126ff.).

43. Stephen Spector, ed., *The N-Town Play,* EETS s.s. 11 and 12 (1991), 1:331, 162ff.

44. Ibid., 391, 117.

45. See Hammerstein, "Himmelfahrt Mariä," in *Die Musik der Engel,* 232–34, 232.

46. Spector, *N-Town Play,* 1:401, 347.

47. Ibid., 409, 521.

48. Rosemary Woolf, *The English Mystery Plays* (London: Routledge, 1972), 288–89, 287; on the *N-Town Plays,* see also Gibson, *Theater of Devotion,* 126–35.

49. *Towneley Plays,* ed. England, 55.

50. Ibid., 218.

51. Ibid., 267.

52. Ibid., 341.

53. Ibid., 380.

54. Gibson points out that doubting Thomas, who wanted to touch Christ's wounds, was surprisingly transformed in late-medieval piety "into a positive emblem" (*Theater of Devotion,* 16); cf. also J. W. Robinson, "The Late Medieval Cult of Jesus and the Mystery Plays," *PMLA* 80 (1965): 508–14.

55. *Rolle: Prose and Verse,* ed. Ogilvie-Thomson, 50.

56. Alan J. Fletcher, "The N-Town Plays," in Beadle, *Cambridge Companion to Medieval English Theatre,* 164–67.

57. *Towneley Plays,* ed. England, 339.

58. *Macro Plays,* ed. Mark Eccles. All quotations are from this edition; a shortened version has also survived. Gibson mentions that Bury was a late-medieval center for religious plays (*Theater of Devotion,* 108ff.); see also Gibson, "Play of *Wisdom,*" also printed in Milla C. Riggio, *The 'Wisdom" Symposium: Papers from the Trinity College Medieval Festival* (New York: AMS Press, 1986), 39–66; further, Riggio, *The Play of Wisdom: Its Text and Contexts* (New York: Ams Press, 1986); Michael G. Sargent, "The Macro Play of *Wisdom* and the Fifteenth-Century Audience for Fourteenth-Century Mysticism," in *A Salzburg Miscellany: English and American Studies, 1964–84,* ed. James Hogg, Salzburg Studies in English Literature, Poetic Drama and Poetic

Theory 27/6, 2 (Salzburg: Institut für Anglistik und Amerikanistik, 1984), 145–57; Wolfgang Riehle, "English Mysticism and the Morality Play *Wisdom Who Is Christ*," in *MMTE* 1 (1980), 202–15; M. McGatch, "Mysticism and Satire in the Morality of *Wisdom*," *Philological Quarterly* 53 (1974): 342–62; Pamela M. King, "Morality Plays," in Beadle, *Cambridge Companion to Medieval English Theatre*, 240–64.

59. *Mixed Life*, ed. Ogilvie-Thomson, 15, 17, 21; Bestul also noted Hilton's presentation of Christ as exemplum of the "mixed life" ("Walter Hilton," in Dyas, Edden, and Ellis, *Approaching Medieval English Anchoritic and Mystical Texts*).

60. For a theological interpretation, see J. J. Molloy, *A Theological Interpretation of the Moral Play "Wisdom, Who Is Christ"* (Washington, DC: Catholic University of America Press, 1952).

61. W. K. Smart, *Some English and Latin Sources and Parallels for the Morality of "Wisdom"* (Menasha, WI, 1912), 86.

62. Gibson even writes that "a strong monastic presence...is a crucial context of the N-Town cycle and indeed of much of the religious drama of East Anglia...this monasticism...pervades East Anglian drama" ("Play of *Wisdom*," 127).

63. See the important remarks in Baker, Murphy, and Hall, *Late Medieval Religious Plays*, lxxi; further, the article by John C. Coldewey, "The Non-Cycle Plays and the East Anglian Tradition," in Beadle, *Cambridge Companion to Medieval English Theatre*, 189–210.

64. King, "Morality Plays," in Beadle, *Cambridge Companion to Medieval English Theatre*, 243–47; Cornelius, "Figurative Castle."

65. Richard W. Southern, *The Medieval Theatre in the Round*, 2nd ed. (London: Faber and Faber, 1975).

66. N. Crohn Schmitt, "Was There a Medieval Theatre in the Round? A Reexamination of the Evidence," *Theatre Notebook* 23 (1968–9): 130–42; (1969–70): 18–25, 24; repr. in *Medieval English Drama: Essays Critical and Contextual*, ed. Jerome Taylor and Alan H. Nelson (Chicago: University of Chicago Press, 1972), 292–315.

67. In this she follows Cornelius, "Figurative Castle"; see also Christiania Whitehead, *Castles of the Mind: A Study of Medieval Architectural Allegory* (Cardiff: University of Wales Press, 2003). In *Sawles Warde*, close in time to *Ancrene Wisse*, the soul is also symbolized as a castle.

68. Crohn Schmitt, "Was There a Medieval Theatre in the Round?" (quoted from reprint in Taylor and Nelson, *Medieval English Drama*, 300).

69. Ibid., 302.

70. Ibid., 301.

71. Ibid., 306.

72. On this point see esp. Innes-Parker, "Legacy of *Ancrene Wisse*."

73. *Anchoritic Spirituality*, ed. Savage and Watson, 137; cf. Augustine: "The more holy a man is, and the more he is filled with holy yearning, the more he weeps in prayer" (*De civ. Dei* 20.19); a key passage for the evaluation of spiritual tears in the patristic tradition occurs in the *Speculum Christiani*; such statements are often absorbed into vernacular texts. The well-known definition from the passage quoted ("Oratio lenit...") is followed by one of Bernard's characteristic images, depicting tears as the wine of angels, for they contain the odor of life, the savor of mercy and forgiveness. A sinner's tear torments the devil more than any torture (G. Holmstedt, ed., *Speculum Christiani: A Middle English Religious Treatise of the 14th Century*, EETS

o.s. 182 [1933], 215–16); see esp. the interpretation of the function of Margery Kempe's tears, in chap. 10 above.

74. Eccles, *Macro Plays,* xxxii–xxxiv; see also Vincent Gillespie and Maggie Ross, "'With Mekeness Aske Perseverantly': On Reading Julian of Norwich," *MQ* 30 (2004): 125–40.

75. K. Kerby-Fulton, "Piers Plowman," in Wallace, *Cambridge History of Medieval English Literature,* 533.

76. Ibid., 532; it is, however, not appropriate to list *Ancrene Wisse* under the general heading of "allegorical prose."

77. W. W. Skeat, ed., *The Vision of William concerning Piers the Plowman* (B-Text), EETS o.s. 38 (1869), 323ff.

78. Ibid., 180.

79. Ibid., 277.

Conclusion

1. *Elisabeth of Schönau: The Complete Works,* trans. and introduced by Anne L. Clark (Mahwah, NJ: Paulist Press, 2000), 126.

2. It may be interesting in this connection that in her Short Version Julian expressly refers to St. Cecilia, whose legend in Chaucer's "Second Nun's Tale" "demonstrates a relation between women as preachers and teachers in the late Middle Ages and the importance of lay devotion and education" (Richard Newhauser, "Religious Writing: Hagiography, *Pastoralia,* Devotional and Contemplative Works," in *The Cambridge Companion to Medieval English Literature, 1100–1500,* ed. Larry Scanlon [Cambridge: Cambridge University Press, 2009], 37–55, 43).

❧ BIBLIOGRAPHY

Primary Literature

Aelred of Rievaulx

Aelredi abbatis Rievallensis, Opera omnia. CCCM 1. *Opera ascetica.* Edited by A. Hoste and C. H. Talbot. Turnhout: Brepols, 1971.

Aelred of Rievaulx's "De institutione inclusarum": Two English Versions. Edited by John Ayto and Alexandra Barratt. EETS o.s. 287. London: Oxford University Press, 1984.

De institutione inclusarum. In *Opera omnia,* 1:637–82.

De speculo caritatis. Edited by C. H. Talbot. In *Opera omnia,* 1:3–161.

De spiritali amicitia. In *Opera omnia,* 1:287–350.

Liber de speculo caritatis, De spiritali amicitia, De institutione inclusarum, De Iesu puero duodenni, Dialogus de anima, Oratio pastoralis, and numerous sermons. In *Opera omnia,* CCCM 1.

The Mirror of Charity. Translated by Geoffrey Webb and Adrian Walker. London: A. R. Mowbray & Co., 1962.

A Rule of Life for a Recluse. Translated by Mary Paul Macpherson. In *Treatises and the Pastoral Prayer,* edited by David Knowles, 41–102. Cistercian Fathers Series 2. Kalamazoo, MI: Cistercian Publications, 1971.

Spiritual Friendship. Translated by Lawrence C. Braceland and edited by Marsha L. Dutton. Collegeville, MN: Cistercian Publications, 2010.

Ancrene Wisse

Anchoritic Spirituality: "Ancrene Wisse" and Associated Works. Edited and translated by Anne Savage and Nicholas Watson. Mahwah, NJ: Paulist Press, 1991.

Ancrene Riwle. Edited and translated by M. B. Salu. London: Burns & Oates, 1955; rev. ed., Exeter Medieval Texts and Studies: University of Exeter Press, 1990.

Ancrene Wisse. Edited by Robert Hasenfratz. TEAMS Middle English Texts. Kalamazoo MI: Medieval Institute Publications, 2000.

Ancrene Wisse: A Corrected Edition of the Text in Cambridge, Corpus Christi College, MS 402, with Variants from Other Manuscripts. Vol. 1. Edited by Bella Millett. EETS o.s. 325. Oxford: Oxford University Press, 2005.

Ancrene Wisse: A Corrected Edition of the Text in Cambridge, Corpus Christi College, MS 402, with Variants from Other Manuscripts. Vol. 2. Edited by Bella Millett. EETS o.s. 326. Oxford: Oxford University Press, 2006.

Ancrene Wisse: Guide for Anchoresses, a Translation. Translated by Bella Millett. Exeter Medieval Texts and Studies. Exeter: University of Exeter Press, 2009.

Ancrene Wisse: Parts Six and Seven. Edited by Geoffrey Shepherd. London: Thomas Nelson & Sons, 1959; rev. ed., Exeter Medieval Texts and Studies. Exeter: University of Exeter Press, 1991.

Ancrene Wisse: The English Text of the Ancrene Riwle. Edited from MS Corpus Christi College, Cambridge 402. Edited by J. R. R. Tolkien. EETS o.s. 249. London: Oxford University Press, 1962.

The English Text of the Ancrene Riwle. Edited from Cotton MS Nero A. 14. Edited by Mabel Day. EETS o.s. 225. London: Oxford University Press, 1952.

Anselm of Canterbury

Davies, Brian, and G. R. Evans, eds. *Anselm of Canterbury: The Major Works.* Oxford World Classics. Oxford: Oxford University Press, 1998.

The Prayers and Meditations of St. Anselm. Translated by Benedicta Ward. Foreword by R. W. Southern. New York: Penguin, 1973.

S. Anselmi Cantuariensis archiepiscopi opera omnia, Tomus Secundus. Edited by Franz S. Schmitt. Stuttgart-Bad Cannstatt: Frommann-Holzboog, 1968.

Athanasius. *The Life of Antony and the Letter to Marcellinus.* Translated by Robert C. Gregg. New York: Paulist Press, 1980.

Augustine of Hippo

De doctrina christiana. Edited and translated by R. P. H. Green. Oxford: Clarendon Press, 1995.

De doctrina christiana. PL 34, 15–122.

De magistro: "Against the Academicians" and "The Teacher." Translated by Peter King. Indianapolis: Hackett Publication Co., 1995.

Benedict's Rule: A Translation and Commentary. Edited by Terence G. Kardong. Collegeville, MN: Liturgical Press, 1996.

Bernard of Clairvaux

De diligendo Deo. Sancti Bernardi opera, vol. 3 (1963), 119–54.

On Loving God. Translated by Robert Walton. Cistercian Fathers Series 13B. Kalamazoo, MI: Cistercian Publications, 1995.

Sancti Bernardi opera. 8 vols. Edited by J. Leclercq, C. H. Talbot, and H. M. Rochais. Rome, 1957–77.

Sermones super Cantica Canticorum. Sancti Bernardi opera, vols. 1 and 2.

Sermons on Conversion. Translated by Marie-Bernard Saïd. Cistercian Fathers Series 25. Kalamazoo, MI: Cistercian Publications, 1981.

Sermons on the Song of Songs. Translated by Kilian Walsh and Irene Edmonds. 4 vols. Cistercian Fathers Series 4, 7, 31, 40. Kalamazoo, MI: Cistercian Publications, 1971–80.

Holy Bible

Biblia Sacra iuxta Vulgatam Clementinam. Edited by A. Colunga and L. Turrado. 4th ed. Madrid: Biblioteca de Autores Cristianos, 1965.
Das Neue Testament. Edited and translated by Ulrich Wilckens. Hamburg: Furche-Verlag, 1970.
Das Neue Testament und frühchristliche Schriften. Edited by Klaus Berger and Christiane Nord. Frankfurt am Main: Insel, 1999.
New Revised Standard Version Bible. Washington, DC: Division of Christian Education of the National Council of the Churches of Christ in the United States of America, 1989.
Zenger, Erich, ed. *Stuttgarter Altes Testament: Einheitsübersetzung mit Kommentar und Lexikon.* 3rd ed. Stuttgart: Stuttgarter Bibelanstalt, 2005.
———. *Stuttgarter Neues Testament. Einheitsübersetzung mit Kommentar und Erklärungen.* Stuttgart: Katholische Bibelanstalt, 2000.

Barratt, Alexandra, ed. *Women's Writing in Middle English.* New York: Longman, 1992.

Bonaventure

Bonaventure [pseud.]. "Stimulus amoris." *S. Bonaventurae opera omnia,* 12:631–703.
S. Bonaventurae opera omnia. 15 vols. Edited by A. C. Peltier. Paris, 1864–71.

Brown, Jennifer N., ed. *Three Women of Liège. A Critical Edition of and Commentary on the Middle English Lives of Elizabeth of Spalbeek, Christina Mirabilis, and Marie d'Oignies.* Medieval Women: Texts and Contexts, 23. Turnhout: Brepols, 2008.
Chaucer, Geoffrey. *The Riverside Chaucer.* Edited by Larry Benson. Boston: Houghton Mifflin, 1987.
The Chester Mystery Cycle. Edited by R. M. Lumiansky and David Mills. 2 vols. EETS s.s. 3 (1974).

The Cloud of Unknowing

The Cloud of Unknowing. Edited by Phyllis Hodgson. AC 3. Salzburg: Institut für Anglistik und Amerikanistik, 1982.
"The Cloud of Unknowing" and "The Book of Privy Counselling." Edited by Phyllis Hodgson. EETS o.s. 218 (1944). Repr., London: Oxford University Press, 1958.
"Deonise Hid Diuinite" and Other Treatises on Contemplative Prayer Related to "The Cloud of Unknowing." Edited by Phyllis Hodgson. EETS o.s. 231 (1955 for 1949). London: Oxford University Press, 1958.

Colgrave, Bertram, ed. and trans. *Two Lives of Saint Cuthbert: A Life by an Anonymous Monk of Lindisfarne and Bede's Prose Life*. Cambridge: Cambridge University Press, 1940.

Gertrud die Grosse. *Exercitia Spiritualia. Geistliche Übungen*. Edited and translated by Siegfried Ringler. Elberfeld: Humberg, 2001.

Gertrude of Helfta. *The Herald of Divine Love*. Translated and edited by Margaret Winkworth [books 1–3]. Classics of Western Spirituality. Mahwah, NJ: Paulist Press, 1993.

Gilbert of Hoyland

Gilbert of Hoyland, *Sermons on the Song of Songs*. Translated by Lawrence C. Braceland. 3 vols. Cistercian Fathers Series 14, 20, 26. Kalamazoo, MI: Cistercian Publications, 1978–79.

Hali Meiþhad

Hali Meiþhad. Edited by Bella Millett. EETS o.s. 284. London: Oxford University Press, 1982.

Walter Hilton

Of Angels' Song. In Windeatt, *English Mystics of the Middle Ages*.

The Scale of Perfection. Edited by Thomas Bestul. Kalamazoo, MI: Medieval Institute Publications, 2000.

The Scale of Perfection. Edited by John P. H. Clark and Rosemary Dorward. Mahwah, NJ: Paulist Press, 1991.

Walter Hilton's Latin Writings. Edited by John P. H. Clark and Cheryl Taylor. 2 vols. AC 124. Salzburg: Institut für Anglistik und Amerikanistik, 1987.

Walter Hilton's "Mixed Life." Edited by S. J. Ogilvie-Thomson. Salzburg Studies in English Literature. Elizabethan and Renaissance Studies 92:18. Salzburg: Institut für Anglistik und Amerikanistik, 1986.

Hugh of St. Victor. *De laude caritatis. PL* 176:968–76.

James of Milan. *Stimulus amoris*. Bibliotheca Franciscana Ascetica Medii Aevi, v. 4. Quaracchi,

John of Forde

John of Ford. *Sermons on the Final Verses of the Song of Songs*. Translated by Sister Wendy Mary Beckett. 7 vols. Cistercian Fathers Series 29, 39, 43–47. Kalamazoo, MI: Cistercian Publications, 1977–84. 1905.

Julian of Norwich

A Book of Showings to the Anchoress Julian of Norwich. Edited by Edmund Colledge and James Walsh. 2 vols. Toronto: Pontifical Institute of Medieval Studies, 1978.

Revelations of Divine Love (short text and long text). Translated by Elizabeth Spearing. Introduction and notes by A. C. Spearing. London: Penguin, 1998.

The Writings of Julian of Norwich: "A Vision Showed to a Devout Woman" and "A Revelation of Love." Edited by Nicholas Watson and Jacqueline Jenkins. University Park: Penn State University Press, 2006.

Margery Kempe

The Book of Margery Kempe. Edited and translated by Barry M. Windeatt. Harmondsworth, UK: Penguin, 1985.

The Book of Margery Kempe. Edited by Barry Windeatt. Cambridge: D. S. Brewer, 2004.

The Book of Margery Kempe. Edited by Sanford Brown Meech and Hope Emily Allen. EETS 212. London: Oxford University Press, 1940.

The Life of Christina of Markyate: A Twelfth Century Recluse. Edited and translated by C. H. Talbot. Rev. ed. by Samuel Fanous and Henrietta Leyser. New York: Oxford University Press, 2008.

Love, Nicholas. *The Mirror of the Blessed Life of Jesus Christ.* A Critical Edition Based on Cambridge University Library Additional MSS 6578 and 6686. Edited by Michael G. Sargent. New York: Garland 1992.

The Macro Plays: "The Castle of Perseverance," "Wisdom," "Mankind." Edited by Mark Eccles. EETS o.s. 262. New York: Oxford University Press, 1969.

Matarasso, Pauline, ed. *The Cistercian World.* London: Penguin, 1993.

Mechthild of Hackeborn. *The Booke of Gostlye Grace.* Edited by Theresa Halligan. Toronto: Pontifical Institute of Medieval Studies, 1978.

Mechthild von Magdeburg. Das Fliessende Licht der Gottheit. Edited by Gisela Vollmann-Profe. Bibliothek des Mittelalters 19. Berlin: Deutscher Klassiker Verlag, 2003.

Meditationes de vita Christi. Edited by M. Jordan Stallings-Taney. CCCM 153 (1999).

Millett, Bella, and Jocelyn Wogan-Browne, eds. *Medieval English Prose for Women from the Katherine Group and Ancrene Wisse.* Oxford: Clarendon Press, 1990.

Mirouer des simples âmes anienties. See Marguerite Porete.

The Mirror of Simple Souls. See Marguerite Porete.

Monk of Farne

Farmer, Hugh, ed. "The Meditations of the Monk of Farne." *Analecta Monastica. Textes et études sur la vie des moines au Moyen Age,* 4. Studia Anselmiana, 41, 141–245. Rome: Herder, 1957.

The Meditations of a Fourteenth Century Monk. Edited and introduction by Hugh Farmer. Translated by a Benedictine of Stanbrook. London: Darton, Longman & Todd, 1961.

The N-Town Play. Edited by Stephen Spector. 2 vols. EETS s.s. 11 and 12. Oxford: Oxford University Press, 1991.

Origen: Spirit and Fire; A Thematic Anthology of His Writings. Edited by Hans Urs von Balthasar. Translated by Robert J. Daly. Washington, DC: Catholic University of America Press, 1984.

Marguerite Porete

Doiron, Marilyn, ed. *Margaret Porete: "The Mirror of Simple Souls"; A Middle English Translation*, with appendix "The Glosses by 'M.N.' and Richard Methley to 'The Mirror of Simple Souls,'" by Edmund Colledge and Romana Guarnieri. Archivio Italiano per la Storia della Pietà 5. Roma: Edizioni di Storia e Letteratura, 1968.

Le mirouer des simples âmes. Édité par Romana Guarnieri / *Specvlvm simplicivm animarvm*, cura et studio P. Verdeyen. CCCM 69 (1986).

Marguerite Porete: "The Mirror of Simple Souls." Edited and translated by Ellen L. Babinsky. New York: Paulist Press, 1993.

The Prickynge of Love. Edited by H. Kane. Salzburg Studies in English Literature. Elizabethan and Renaissance Studies 92/10. Salzburg: Institut für Anglistik und Amerikanisitk, 1983.

Richard of St. Victor

Benjamin minor, PL 196, cols. 1–63; *Benjamin major, PL* 196, cols. 64–202.

The Twelve Patriarchs [Benjamin minor]; The Mystical Ark; Book Three of Trinity. Translated by Grover A. Zinn. Classics of Western Spirituality. New York: Paulist Press, 1979.

Richard Rolle

Boenig, Robert, ed. and trans. *Richard Rolle Biblical Commentaries: Short Exposition of Psalm 20, Treatise on the Twentieth Psalm, Comment on the First Verses on the Canticle of Canticles, Commentary on the Apocalypse*. Salzburg Studies in English Literature 92.13. Salzburg: Institut für Anglistik und Amerikanistik, 1984.

The "Contra amatores mundi" of Richard Rolle of Hampole. Edited by Paul F. Theiner. University of California Publications. English Studies 33. Berkeley: University of California Press, 1968.

De emendatione vitae. Eine kritische Ausgabe des lateinischen Textes von Richard Rolle. Mit einer Übersetzung ins Deutsche und Untersuchungen zu den lateinischen und englischen Handschriften. Edited by Rüdiger Spahl. Bonn: V&R unipress, 2008.

Emendatio vitae. Orationes ad honorem nominis Ihesu. Edited by Nicholas Watson. Toronto Medieval Latin Texts. Toronto: Pontifical Institute of Medieval Studies, 1995.

Horstmann, Carl, ed. *Yorkshire Writers: Richard Rolle, an English Father of the Church, and His Followers*. 2 vols. London, 1895–96, vol. 1.

Incendium amoris. Edited by Margaret Deanesly. Manchester: Manchester University Press, 1915.

Judica me Deus. Edited by John P. Daly. Elizabethan and Renaissance Studies 92.14. Salzburg: Institut für Anglistik und Amerikanistik, 1984.

Melos amoris. Edited by E. J. F. Arnould. Oxford: Blackwell, 1957.

The *"Officium et miracula" of Richard Rolle, of Hampole.* Edited by Reginald M. Woolley. London: SPCK, 1919.

The Psalter or Psalms of David and Certain Canticles, with a Translation and Exposition in English by Richard Rolle of Hampole (the English Psalter). Edited by H. E. Bramley. Oxford: Clarendon Press, 1884.

Richard Rolle de Hampole 1300–1349: Vie et oeuvres suiviés du Tractatus super apocalypsim. Edited by Nicole Marzac. Paris: Vrin, 1968.

Richard Rolle: Prose and Verse Edited from MS Longleat 29 and Related Manuscripts. Edited by S. J. Ogilvie-Thomson. EETS o.s. 293. London: Oxford University Press, 1988.

Richard Rolle's Comment on the Canticles (Super Canticum Canticorum). Edited by Elizabeth M. Murray. Unpubl. PhD diss., Fordham University, 1958 (English trans. in Boenig, *Richard Rolle: Biblical Commentaries*).

Richard Rolle's "Expositio super novem lectiones mortuorum": An Introduction and Contribution towards a Critical Edition. Edited by Malcolm Moyes. 2 vols. Salzburg Studies in English Literature: Elizabethan and Renaissance Studies 92:12. Salzburg: Institut für Anglistik und Amerikanistik, 1988.

"Rolle's Latin Commentary on the Psalms." Edited by Mary Louise Porter. Dissertation, Cornell University, 1929.

Super apocalypsim. See *Richard Rolle de Hampole,* ed. Marzac.

The *"Tractatus super psalmum vicesimum" of Richard Rolle of Hampole.* Edited and translated by James C. Dolan. Texts and Studies in Religion 57. Lewiston, NY: E. Mellen Press, 1991.

Das St. Trudperter Hohelied. Eine Lehre der liebenden Gotteserkenntnis. Edited by Friedrich Ohly. Bibliothek des Mittelalters 2. Bibliothek deutscher Klassiker 155. Berlin: Deutscher Klassiker Verlag, 1998.

A Talkyng of þe Loue of God. Edited by Salvina Westra. The Hague: Martinus Nijhoff, 1950.

A Talkyng of þe Loue of God. Edited by Carl Horstmann. In *Yorkshire Writers.* Vol. 2. London: Swan Sonnenschein, 1896.

Thomas of Hales

Love Rune. Edited by Susanna Greer Fein. In *Moral Love Songs and Laments.* TEAMS Middle English Texts Series. Kalamazoo, MI: Medieval Institute Publications, 1998.

The Towneley Plays. Edited by George England. EETS e.s. 71. Oxford: Oxford University Press, 1966.

William of St. Thierry

De natura et dignitate amoris. PL 184.

The Golden Epistle: A Letter to the Brethren at Mont Dieu. Translated by Theodore Berkeley. Kalamazoo, MI: Cistercian Publications, 1971.

Meditationen und Gebete. Edited by Klaus Berger and Christiane Nord. Frankfurt am Main: Insel, 2001.

Meditativae orationes. Translated by M.-M. Davy. Paris, 1934.

The Nature and Dignity of Love. Translated by Thomas X. Davis, introduction by David N. Bell. Kalamazoo, MI: Cistercian Publications, 1981.

The Works of William of St Thierry. Vol. 1, *On Contemplating God, Prayer, Meditations.* Translated by Sr Penelope. Cistercian Fathers Series 3. Shannon, 1971.

Windeatt, Barry, ed. *English Mystics of the Middle Ages.* New York: Cambridge University Press, 1994.

Wogan-Browne, Jocelyn, et al., eds. *The Idea of the Vernacular: An Anthology of Middle English Literary Theory.* University Park: Penn State University Press, 1999.

The Wohunge of Ure Lauerd. Edited by W. Meredith Thompson. EETS o.s. 241. London: Oxford University Press, 1958.

Secondary Literature

Aers, David. *Community, Gender, and Individual Identity: English Writing, 1360–1430.* New York: Routledge, 1988.

———. "The Humanity of Christ: Reflections on Julian of Norwich's *Revelation of Love.*" In Aers and Staley, *Powers of the Holy.*

———. *Medieval Literature: Criticism, Ideology and History.* Brighton, UK: Harvester, 1986.

———. *Salvation and Sin: Augustine, Langland, and Fourteenth-Century Theology.* Notre Dame, IN: University of Notre Dame Press, 2009.

Aers, David, and Lynn Staley. *Powers of the Holy: Religion, Politics, and Gender in Late Medieval English Culture.* University Park: Penn State University Press, 1996.

Alford, John A. "Biblical *Imitatio* in the Writings of Richard Rolle." *ELH* 40 (1973): 1–23.

Allen, Hope Emily. *English Writings of Richard Rolle, Hermit of Hampole.* Oxford: Oxford University Press, 1931.

———. *Writings Ascribed to Richard Rolle Hermit of Hampole and Materials for His Biography.* New York: MLA, and London: Oxford University Press, 1927.

Angenendt, Arnold. *Geschichte der Religiosität im Mittelalter.* Darmstadt: Wissenschaftliche Buchgesellschaft, 1997.

Anson, Peter. *The Call of the Desert: The Solitary Life in the Christian Church.* London: SPCK, 1964.

Arnold, J. H., and K. J. Lewis, eds. *A Companion to the Book of Margery Kempe.* Cambridge: D. S. Brewer, 2010.

Astell, Ann. "Feminine *Figurae* in the Writings of Richard Rolle: A Register of Growth." *MQ* 15 (1989): 117–24.

———. *The Song of Songs in the Middle Ages.* Ithaca, NY: Cornell University Press, 2000.

Atkinson, Clarissa W. *Mystic and Pilgrim: The Book and the World of Margery Kempe.* Ithaca, NY: Cornell University Press, 1983.

Baker, Denise Nowakowski. "Active and Contemplative Lives in Rolle, the *Cloud*-Author and Hilton." *MMTE* 6 (1999), 85–102.

———. "The Image of God: Contrasting Configurations in Julian of Norwich's *Showings* and Walter Hilton's *Scale of Perfection*." In *Julian of Norwich: A Book of Essays,* edited by Sandra McEntire, 35–60. New York: Garland, 1998.

———. "Julian of Norwich and Anchoritic Literature." *MQ* 19 (1993): 148–60.

———. *Julian of Norwich's "Showings": From Vision to Book.* Princeton, NJ: Princeton University Press, 1994.

Baker, Derek, ed. *Medieval Women.* Oxford: Blackwell, 1978.

Baker, Donald C., John L. Murphy, and Louis B. Hall Jr., eds. *The Late Medieval Religious Plays of Bodleian MSS Digby 133 and E Museo 160.* EETS o.s. 283. Oxford: Oxford University Press, 1982.

Barratt, Alexandra. "Margery Kempe and the King's Daughter of Hungary." In McEntire, *Margery Kempe,* 189–201.

———. "The Virgin and the Visionary in the Revelations of St. Elizabeth." *MQ* 17 (1991): 125–36.

Bartlett, Anne Clark, et al., eds. *Vox Mystica: Essays on Medieval Mysticism in Honour of Professor Valerie M. Lagorio.* Cambridge: D. S. Brewer, 1995.

Bauer, Gerhard. *Claustrum Animae: Untersuchungen zur Geschichte der Metapher vom Herzen als Kloster.* Munich: Fink, 1973.

Beadle, Richard. "'Devoute Ymaginacioun' and the Dramatic Sense in Love's Mirror and the N-Town Plays." In Oguro, Beadle, and Sargent, *Nicholas Love at Waseda,* 1–17.

———, ed. *The Cambridge Companion to Medieval English Theatre.* Cambridge: Cambridge University Press, 1994.

Beckwith, Sarah. *Christ's Body: Identity, Culture and Society in Late Medieval Writings.* New York: Routledge, 1993.

———. "A Very Material Mysticism: The Medieval Mysticism of Margery Kempe." In Aers, *Medieval Literature,* 34–57.

Beer, Frances. *Women and Mystical Experience in the Middle Ages.* Library of Medieval Women. Cambridge: D. S. Brewer, 1992.

Bell, David. *An Index of Authors and Works in Cistercian Libraries in Great Britain.* Cistercian Studies 130. Kalamazoo, MI: Cistercian Publications, 1992.

———. *What Nuns Read: Books and Libraries in Medieval English Nunneries.* Kalamazoo, MI: Cistercian Publications, 1995.

Benke, Christoph. *Die Gabe der Tränen. Zur Tradition und Theologie eines vergessenen Kapitels der Glaubensgeschichte.* Studien zur systematischen und spirituellen Theologie 35. Würzburg: Echter, 2002.

Benz, Ernst. *Die Vision: Erfahrungsformen und Bilderwelt.* Stuttgart: Klett, 1969.

Berman, Constance H. *The Cistercian Evolution: The Invention of a Religious Order in Twelfth-Century Europe.* Philadelphia: University of Pennsylvania Press, 2000.

Bhattacharji, Santha. *God Is an Earthquake: The Spirituality of Margery Kempe.* London: Darton, Longman & Todd, 1997.

Biser, Eugen. *Gotteskindschaft: Die Erhebung zu Gott.* Darmstadt: Wissenschaftliche Buchgesellschaft, 2006.

———. *Paulus: Zeugnis—Begegnung—Wirkung.* Darmstadt: Wissenschaftliche Buchgesellschaft, 2003.

Bitel, Lisa M. *Isle of the Saints: Monastic Settlement and Christian Community in Early Ireland.* Ithaca, NY: Cornell University Press, 1990.

Blake, Norman F., ed. *Middle English Religious Prose.* York Medieval Texts. London: Edward Arnold, 1972.

Blume, Clemens. *Hymnologische Beiträge.* Vol. 4. Leipzig: Olms, 1930.

Blume, Dieter, and Matthias Werner, eds. *Elisabeth von Thüringen. Eine europäische Heilige.* 2 vols. Petersberg: Michael Imhof Verlag, 2007.

Bradley, Ritamary. "Julian of Norwich: Everyone's Mystic." In Pollard and Boenig, *Mysticism and Spirituality,* 139–58.

———. "Metaphors of Cloth and Clothing in the Showings of Julian of Norwich." *Mediaevalia* 9 (1986 for 1983): 269–82.

———. "Mysticism in the Motherhood Similitude of Julian of Norwich." *Studia Mystica* 8, no. 2 (1985): 4–14.

Brantley, Jessica. *Reading in the Wilderness: Private Devotion and Public Performance in Late Medieval England.* Chicago: University of Chicago Press, 2007.

Brown, Peter. *The Body and Society: Men, Women, and Sexual Renunciation in Early Christianity.* New York: Columbia University Press, 1988.

Bruun, Mette Birkedal, ed. *The Cambridge Companion to the Cistercian Order.* Cambridge: Cambridge University Press, 2013.

Bryan, Jennifer. *Looking Inward: Devotional Reading and the Private Self in Late Medieval England.* The Middle Ages Series. Philadelphia: University of Pennsylvania Press, 2008.

Buchmüller, Wolfgang, G. *Die Askese der Liebe. Aelred von Rievaulx und die Grundlinien seiner Spiritualität.* Langwaden: Bernardus-Verlag, 2001.

Burton, Janet. *Monastic and Religious Orders in Britain, 1000–1300.* New York: Cambridge University Press, 1994.

Burton, Janet, and Julie Kerr. *The Cistercians in the Middle Ages.* Woodbridge, UK: Boydell Press, 2011.

Bynum, Caroline Walker. *Holy Feast and Holy Fast: The Religious Significance of Food to Medieval Women.* The New Historicism: Studies in Cultural Poetics. Berkeley: University of California Press, 1987.

———. *Jesus as Mother: Studies in the Spirituality of the High Middle Ages.* Berkeley: University of California Press, 1982.

Caie, Graham D., and Denis Renevey, eds. *Medieval Texts in Context.* London: Routledge, 2008.

Caldwell, E. "The Rhetorics of Enthusiasm and of Restraint in *The Form of Living* and *The Cloud of Unknowing.*" *MQ* 10 (1987): 9–16.

Caucci von Saucken, P., ed. *Santiago: L'Europa del pellegriaggio.* Milan: Jaca Books, 1993.

Chenu, M.-D. *L'éveil de la conscience dans la civilisation médiévale.* Montréal: Institut d'études médiévales, 1969.

Chewning, Susannah M., ed. *Intersections of Sexuality and the Divine in Medieval Culture: The Word Made Flesh.* Aldershot, UK: Ashgate, 2005.

———. *The Milieu and Context of the Wooing Group: Religion and Culture in the Middle Ages.* Cardiff: University of Wales Press, 2009.

Clark, John P. H. "English and Latin in *The Scale of Perfection:* Theological Considerations." *AC* 35/1. Salzburg: Institut für Anglistik und Amerikanistik, 1982.

————. *"The Cloud of Unknowing": An Introduction.* 2 vols. AC 119. Salzburg: Institut für Anglistik und Amerikanistik, 1995.

————. "Late Fourteenth-Century Cambridge Theology and the English Contemplative Tradition." *MMTE* 5 (1992), 1–16.

————. "The 'Lightsome Darkness': Aspects of Walter Hilton's Theological Background." *DR* 95 (1977): 95–109.

————. "Predestination in Christ According to Julian of Norwich." *DR* 100 (1982): 79–91.

————. "Richard Rolle as a Biblical Commentator." *DR* 104 (1986): 165–213.

————. "Richard Rolle: A Theological Re-assessment." *DR* 101 (1983): 108–39.

————. "Sources and Theology in *The Cloud of Unknowing." DR* 98 (1980): 83–109.

————. "Time and Eternity in Julian of Norwich." *DR* 109 (1991): 259–76.

————. "Walter Hilton and Liberty of Spirit." *DR* 96 (1978): 61–78.

————. "Walter Hilton and the Psalm Commentary *Qui Habitat." DR* 100 (1982): 235–62.

————. "Walter Hilton in Defence of the Religious Life and of the Veneration of Images." *DR* 103 (1985): 1–25.

Clay, Rotha Mary. *The Hermits and Anchorites of England.* London: Methuen, 1914.

Cleve, Gunnel. *Basic Mystic Themes in Walter Hilton's "Scale of Perfection" Book II.* Salzburg: Institut für Anglistik und Amerikanistik, 1994.

Coiner, Nancy. "The 'Homely' and the *Heimliche:* The Hidden, Doubled Self in Julian of Norwich's *Showings." Exemplaria* 5 (1993): 305–23.

Coleman, Joyce. "Aurality." In Strohm, *Middle English,* 68–85.

Colledge, Edmund, and Romana Guarnieri. "The Glosses by 'M.N.' and Richard Methley to 'The Mirror of Simple Souls,'" *Archivio italiano per la storia della pietà* 5 (Rome: n.p., 1968): 381–82.

Comper, Frances M. M. *The Life of Richard Rolle, together with an Edition of His English Lyrics.* London: Dent & Sons, 1928; reprint, New York: Barnes & Noble, 1969.

Constable, Giles. *The Reformation of the Twelfth Century.* Cambridge: Cambridge University Press, 1996.

Copeland, Rita. "Richard Rolle and the Rhetorical Theory of the Levels of Style." *MMTE* 3 (1984), 55–80.

Copeland, Rita, and Peter T. Struck, eds. *The Cambridge Companion to Allegory.* Cambridge: Cambridge University Press, 2010.

Cornelius, Roberta. "The Figurative Castle: A Study in the Medieval Allegory of the Edifice." PhD diss., Bryn Mawr College, 1930.

Cré, Marleen. "Women in the Charterhouse? Julian of Norwich's *Revelations of Divine Love* and Marguerite Porete's *Mirror of Simple Souls* in BL MS Add. 37790." In Renevey and Whitehead, *Writing Religious Women,* 43–62.

Cullum P. H. "'Yf Lak of Charyte Be Not Ower Hynderawnce': Margery Kempe, Lynn, and the Practice of the Spiritual and Bodily Works of Mercy." In Arnold and Lewis, *Companion,* 177–93.

Darwin, F. D. S. *The English Mediaeval Recluse.* London: SPCK, 1944.

de Ford, Sarah. "Mystical Union in the *Melos amoris* of Richard Rolle." In *MMTE* 1 (1980), 173–201.

————. "The Use and Function of Alliteration in the *Melos amoris* of Richard Rolle." *MQ* 12 (1986): 59–66.

Despres, Denise. *Ghostly Sights: Visual Meditation in Late Medieval Literature.* Norman, OK: Pilgrim Books, 1989.

Dickman, Susan. "Margery Kempe and the Continental Tradition of the Pious Woman." In Glasscoe, *MMTE* 3 (1984), 150–68.

————. "A Shewing of God's Grace: *The Book of Margery Kempe.*" In Pollard and Boenig, *Mysticism and Spirituality,* 159–76.

Dinshaw, Carolyn, and David Wallace, eds. *The Cambridge Companion to Medieval Women's Writing.* Cambridge: Cambridge University Press, 2003.

Dinzelbacher, Peter. *Bernhard von Clairvaux: Leben und Werk des berühmten Zisterziensers.* Darmstadt: Primus Verlag, 1998.

————. *Christliche Mystik im Abendland. Ihre Geschichte von den Anfängen bis zum Ende des Mittelalters.* Paderborn: Schöningh, 1994.

————. *Vision und Visionsliteratur im Mittelalter.* Monographien zur Geschichte des Mittelalters 23. Stuttgart: Hiersemann, 1981.

Dinzelbacher, Peter, and Dieter Bauer, eds. *Religiöse Frauenbewegungen und mystische Frömmigkeit im Mittelalter.* Köln: Böhlau, 1988.

Dobson, Eric J. "The Date and Composition of *Ancrene Wisse.*" *Proceedings of the British Academy* 52 (1966): 181–208.

————. *The Origins of "Ancrene Wisse."* Oxford: Clarendon Press, 1976.

Doerr, Otmar. *Das Institut der Inclusen in Süddeutschland.* Beiträge zur Geschichte des alten Mönchtums und des Benediktinerordens 18. Münster: Aschendorff, 1934.

Doyle, A. I. "Carthusian Participation in the Movement of the Works of Richard Rolle between England and the Other Parts of Europe in the Fourteenth and Fifteenth Centuries." *AC* 55, no. 2 (1981): 157–66.

————. "A Survey of the Origin and Circulation of Theological Writings in English in the 14th, 15th and early 16th Centuries with Special Consideration of the Part of the Clergy Therein." Unpublished PhD diss., Cambridge University, 1953.

Duby, Georges. *The Age of the Cathedrals: Art and Society, 980–1420.* Translated by E. Levieux and B. Thompson. Chicago: University of Chicago Press, 1981.

Duffy, Eamon. *The Stripping of the Altars: Traditional Religion in England, c.1400–c.1580.* 2nd ed. New Haven, CT: Yale University Press, 2005.

Duncan, T. G., ed. *Companion to the Middle English Lyric.* Cambridge: D. S. Brewer, 2005.

Dunn, F. I. "Hermits, Anchorites and Recluses: A Study with Reference to Medieval Norwich." In *Julian and Her Norwich: Commemorative Essays and Handbook to the Exhibition "Revelations of Divine Love,"* edited by F. D. Sayer, 18–26. Norwich: Celebrational Committee, 1973.

Dyas, Dee. "'Wildernesse Is Anlich Lif of Ancre Wununge': The Wilderness and Medieval Anchoritic Spirituality." In Dyas, Edden, and Ellis, *Approaching Medieval English Anchoritic and Mystical Texts,* 19–33.

Dyas, Dee, Valerie Edden, and Roger Ellis, eds. *Approaching Medieval English Anchoritic and Mystical Texts.* Cambridge: D. S. Brewer, 2005.

Edwards, A. S. G., ed. *A Companion to Middle English Prose*. Cambridge: D. S. Brewer, 2004.

——, ed. *Middle English Prose: A Critical Guide to Major Authors and Genres*. New Brunswick, NJ: Rutgers University Press, 1984.

Elder, E. Rozanne, ed. *Goad and Nail: Studies in Medieval Cistercian History*. Kalamazoo, MI: Cistercian Publications, 1985.

——, ed. *The Roots of the Modern Christian Tradition*. Vol. 2, *The Spirituality of Western Christendom*. Kalamazoo, MI: Cistercian Publications, 1984.

Elkins, Sharon K. *Holy Women of Twelfth-Century England*. Chapel Hill: University of North Carolina Press, 1988.

Ellis, Roger, ed. *The "Liber Celestis" of St Bridget of Sweden*. EETS o.s. 291. London: Oxford University Press, 1987.

——. "A Literary Approach to the Middle English Mystics." In *MMTE* 1 (1980), 99–119.

Ellis, Roger, and René Tixier, eds. *The Medieval Translator* 5. Turnhout: Brepols, 1996.

Fanous, Samuel. "Measuring the Pilgrim's Progress Internal Emphases in 'The Book of Margery Kempe.'" In *Writing Religious Women: Female Spiritual and Textual Practices in Late Medieval England,* edited by Denis Renevey and Christiania Whitehead, 157–76. Cardiff: University of Wales Press, 2000.

Fanous, Samuel, and Vincent Gillespie, eds. *The Cambridge Companion to Medieval English Mysticism*. Cambridge: Cambridge University Press, 2011.

Fanous, Samuel, and Henrietta Leyser, eds. *Christina of Markyate: A Twelfth-Century Holy Woman*. London: Routledge, 2005.

Fite, P. P. "To 'Sytt and Syng of Luf Langyng': The Feminine Dynamic of Richard Rolle's Mysticism." *SM* 14 (1991): 13–29.

Flasch, Kurt, ed. *Logik des Schreckens: Augustinus von Hippo: Die Gnadenlehre von 397*. Excerpta classica 8, 2nd ed. Mainz: Dieterich'sche Verlagsbuchhandlung, 1995.

——. *Meister Eckhart*. Munich: C. H. Beck, 2011.

Forman, Robert K. "Mystical Experience in the *Cloud* Literature." In *MMTE* 4 (1987), 177–94.

Gardner, Helen. "Walter Hilton and the Mystical Tradition in England." *Essays and Studies* 22 (1937), 103–27.

Gemünden, Petra von, Matthias Konradt, and Gerd Theissen., eds. *Der Jakobusbrief. Beiträge zur Rehabilitierung der "strohernen Epistel."* Münster: LIT, 2003.

Georgianna, Linda. *The Solitary Self: Individuality in the "Ancrene Wisse."* Cambridge, MA: Harvard University Press, 1981.

Geyer, Iris. *Maria von Oignies. Eine hochmittelalterliche Mystikerin zwischen Ketzerei und Rechtgläubigkeit*. Frankfurt am Main: Peter Lang, 1992.

Ghosh, Kantik. "Nicholas Love." In Edwards, *Companion to Middle English Prose,* 53–66.

Gibson, Gail McMurray. "The Play of *Wisdom* and the Abbey of St Edmund." *Comparative Drama* 19 (1985): 117–35.

——. *The Theater of Devotion: East Anglian Drama and Society in the Late Middle Ages*. Chicago: University of Chicago Press, 1989.

Gillespie, Vincent. "Cura Pastoralis in Deserto." In Sargent, *De cella in seculum,* 161–81.

————. "Dial M for Mystic: Mystical Texts in the Library of Syon Abbey and the Spirituality of the Syon Brethren." In *MMTE* 6 (1999), 241–68.

————. "Mystic's Foot: Rolle and Affectivity." In *MMTE* 2 (1982), 199–230.

————. "Postcards from the Edge: Interpreting the Ineffable in the Middle English Mystics." In *Interpretation: Medieval and Modern,* edited by Piero Boitani and Anna Torti. Cambridge: D. S. Brewer, 1993.

————. "Strange Images of Death. The Passion in Later Medieval English Devotional and Mystical Writing." In *Zeit, Tod und Ewigkeit in der Renaissance-Literatur,* I, edited by James Hogg, AC 117.1. 111–59 (Salzburg, 1987).

Gilson, Étienne. *The Mystical Theology of Saint Bernard.* Translated by A. H. C. Downes. London: Sheed and Ward, 1940; reprinted, Kalamazoo, MI: Cistercian Publications, 1990.

Glasscoe, Marion. *English Medieval Mystics: Games of Faith.* London: Longman, 1993.

————. "Means of Showing: An Approach to Reading Julian of Norwich." In *Spätmittelalterliche geistliche Literatur in der Nationalsprache.* AC 106.1. Salzburg: Institut für Anglistik und Amerikanistik, 1983.

Gleba, Gudrun. *Klosterleben im Mittelalter.* Darmstadt: Wissenschaftliche Buchgesellschaft, 2004.

Grabes, Herbert. *The Mutable Glass: Mirror Imagery in Titles and Texts of the Middle Ages and English Renaissance.* Translated by G. Collier. Cambridge: Cambridge University Press, 1982.

Grayson, Janet. *Structure and Imagery in "Ancrene Wisse."* Hanover, NH: University Press of New England, 1974.

Grundmann, Herbert. *Religious Movements in the Middle Ages: The Historical Links between Heresy, the Mendicant Orders, and the Women's Religious Movement in the Twelfth and Thirteenth Century.* Translated by Steven Rowan. Notre Dame, IN: University of Notre Dame Press, 1995.

Guilfoy, Kevin. "William of Champeaux." In *The Stanford Encyclopedia of Philosophy.* Winter 2012 edition. Edited by Edward N. Zalta. http://plato.stanford.edu/archives/win2012/entries/william-champeaux/.

Gunn, Cate. *"Ancrene Wisse": From Pastoral Literature to Vernacular Spirituality.* Cardiff: University of Wales Press, 2008.

Haas, Alois M. *Gottleiden? Gottlieben. Zur volkssprachlichen Mystik im Mittelalter.* Frankfurt am Main: Insel, 1989.

Hallier, Amédée. *The Monastic Theology of Aelred of Rievaulx: An Experiential Theology.* Shannon: Irish University Press, 1969.

Hamburger, Jeffrey. *The Visual and the Visionary: Art and Female Spirituality in Late Medieval Germany.* New York: Zone Books, 1998.

Hammerstein, Reinhold. *Die Musik der Engel. Untersuchungen zur Musikanschauung des Mittelalters.* Berne–Munich: Francke, 1962.

Hanna, R. "Rolle and Related Works." In Edwards, *Companion to Middle English Prose,* 19–31.

Heffernan, Thomas J., ed. *The Popular Literature of Medieval England.* Tennessee Studies in Literature 28. Knoxville: University of Tennessee Press, 1985.

Heiler, Friedrich. *Prayer: A Study in the History and Psychology of Religion.* Oxford: Oxford University Press, 1932.

Heimmel, Jennifer P. *"God Is Our Mother": Julian of Norwich and the Medieval Image of Christian Feminine Divinity.* Salzburg Studies in English Literature 92.5. Salzburg: Institut für Anglistik und Amerikanistik, 1982.

Herbers, Klaus. *Jakobsweg. Geschichte und Kultur einer Pilgerfahrt.* Munich: C. H. Beck, 2006.

Hide, Kerrie. *Gifted Origins to Graced Fulfillment: The Soteriology of Julian of Norwich.* Collegeville, MN: Liturgical Press, 2001.

Hodapp, William F. "Richard Rolle's Passion Meditations in the Context of His English Epistles: *Imitatio Christi* and the Three Degrees of Love." *MQ* 20, no. 3 (1994): 96–104.

Hogg, James, ed. *The Mystical Tradition and the Carthusians.* AC 130.5. Salzburg: Institut für Anglistik und Amerikanistik, 1996.

Holbrook, Sue Ellen. "Order and Coherence in *The Book of Margery Kempe.*" In *The Worlds of Medieval Women: Creativity, Influence, Imagination,* edited by Constance H. Berman, Charles W. Connell, and Judith Rice Rothschild, 97–110. Morgantown: West Virginia University Press, 1985.

Holdenried, Michaela. *Autobiographie.* Stuttgart: reclam, 2000.

Hollywood, Amy. *The Soul as Virgin Wife: Mechthild of Magdeburg, Marguerite Porete, and Meister Eckhart.* Notre Dame, IN: University of Notre Dame Press, 1995.

Hopf, Margarete. *Der Weg zu christlicher Vollkommenheit. Eine Studie zu Walter Hilton auf dem Hintergrund der romanischen Mystik.* Forschungen zur Kirchen- und Dogmengeschichte 95. Göttingen: Vandenhoeck & Ruprecht, 2009.

Hourlier, Jacques. "Saint Bernard et Guillaume de Saint-Thierry dans le 'Liber de Amore.'" In *S. Bernard théologien,* Actes du congrès de Dijon 15–19 septembre, Analecta sacri ordinis cisterciensis 9 (1953): 223–33.

Hughes, A. C. "Walter Hilton's Direction to Contemplatives." PhD diss., Pontifica Università Gregoriana, Rome, 1962.

Hughes, Jonathan. *Pastors and Visionaries: Religion and Secular Life in Late Medieval Yorkshire.* Woodbridge, UK: Boydell Press, 1988.

Hussey, Stanley S. "Langland, Hilton and the Three Lives." *RES* n.s. 7 (1956): 132–50.

———. "Latin and English in *The Scale of Perfection.*" *MS* 35 (1973): 456–76.

———. "The Rehabilitation of Margery Kempe." *Leeds Studies in English* n.s. 32 (2001): 171–94.

———. "Walter Hilton: Traditionalist?" In *MMTE* 1 (1980), 1–16.

Hutchison, Ann M. "What the Nuns Read: Literary Evidence from the English Bridgettine House, Syon Abbey." *MS* 57 (1995): 205–22.

Innes-Parker, Catherine. "The Legacy of *Ancrene Wisse:* Translations, Adaptations, Influences and Audience, with Special Attention to Women Readers." In Wada, *Companion to "Ancrene Wisse,"* 145–73.

Ivánka, Endre von. *Plato Christianus. Übernahme und Umgesgtaltung des Platonismus durch die Väter.* Einsiedeln: Johannes Verlag, 1964.

Jaeger, Stephen. *Ennobling Love: In Search of a Lost Sensibility.* Philadelphia: University of Pennsylvania Press, 1999.

Jantzen, Grace. *Julian of Norwich: Mystic and Theologian.* 2nd ed. New York: Paulist Press, 2000.

Jenkins, Jacqueline. "Reading and *The Book of Margery Kempe.*" In Arnold and Lewis, *Companion,* 113–28.

Jennings, Margaret. "Richard Rolle and the Three Degrees of Love." *DR* 93 (1975): 193–200.

Jones, E. A. "Langland and the Hermits." *Yearbook of Langland Studies* 11 (1997): 67–86.

Kasper, Clemens, and Klaus Schreiner, eds. *Zisterziensische Spiritualität: Theologische Grundlagen, funktionale Voraussetzungen und bildhafte Ausprägungen im Mittelalter.* St. Ottilien: EOS Verlag, 1994.

Kennedy, David G. *The Incarnational Element in Hilton's Spirituality.* Elizabethan and Renaissance Studies 92/3. Salzburg: Institut für Anglistik und Amerikanistik, 1982.

Kerby-Fulton, Kathryn. *Books under Suspicion: Censorship and Tolerance of Revelatory Writing in Late Medieval England.* Notre Dame, IN: University of Notre Dame Press, 2006.

Kerr, B. M. *Religious Life for Women, c. 1100–1350: Fontevrault in England.* Oxford: Oxford University Press, 1999.

Kieckhefer, Richard. *Unquiet Souls: Fourteenth-Century Saints and Their Religious Milieu.* Chicago: University of Chicago Press, 1984.

Knowles, David. *The English Mystical Tradition.* New York: Harper & Bros., 1961.

———. *The English Mystics.* London: Burns and Oates, 1927.

———. *The Evolution of Medieval Thought.* Baltimore: Helicon Press, 1962.

———. *The Monastic Order in England.* 2nd ed. Cambridge: Cambridge University Press, 1963.

———. *The Religious Orders in England.* 3 vols. Cambridge: Cambridge University Press, 1948–59.

Kratzmann, Gregory, and James Simpson, eds. *Medieval English Religious and Ethical Literature: Essays in Honour of G. H. Russell.* Cambridge: D. S. Brewer, 1986.

Krone und Schleier, Kunst aus mittelalterlichen Frauenklöstern. Ed. Kunst- und Ausstellungshalle der Bundesrepublik Deutschland, Bonn Ruhrlandmuseum Essen. Munich: Hirmer Verlag, 2005.

Kuczynski, Michael P. *Prophetic Song: The Psalms as Moral Discourse in Late Medieval England.* Philadelphia: University of Pennsylvania Press, 1995.

Küsters, Urban. *Der verschlossene Garten Volkssprachliche Hohelied-Auslegung und monastische Lebensform im 12. Jahrhundert.* Studia humaniora. Düsseldorfer Studien zu Mittelalter und Renaissance 2. Düsseldorf: Droste, 1985.

Lagorio, Valerie M., ed. *Mysticism: Medieval and Modern.* Salzburg: Institut für Anglistik und Amerikanistik, 1986.

Lagorio, Valerie, and Michael G. Sargent. "English Mystical Writings." In Hartung and Burke Severs, *Manual,* 9.2957–3592.

Lang, Judith. "The 'Godly Wylle' in Julian of Norwich." *DR* 102 (1984): 163–73.

Lang, Justin. *Die Mystik mittelalterlicher Christus-Johannes-Gruppen.* Ostfildern: Schwabenverlag, 1994.

Langer, Otto. *Christliche Mystik im Mittelalter. Mystik und Rationalität- Stationen eines Konflikts.* Darmstadt: Wissenschaftliche Buchgesellschaft, 2004.

Largier, Niklaus. *Die Kunst des Begehrens: Dekadenz, Sinnlichkeit und Askese.* Munich: C. H. Beck, 2007.

Lawrence, C. H. *Medieval Monasticism: Forms of Religious Life in Western Europe in the Middle Ages.* 3rd ed. New York: Longman, 2000.

Leclercq, Jean. *The Love of Learning and the Desire for God: A Study of Monastic Culture.* Translated by Catherine Misrahi. 3rd ed. Repr. 2003. New York: Fordham University Press, 1961.

Lees, Rosemary Ann. *The Negative Language of the Dionysian School of Mystical Theology: An Approach to the "Cloud of Unknowing."* AC 107. 2 vols. Salzburg: Institut für Anglistik und Amerikanistik, 1983.

Leff, Gordon. *Heresy in the Later Middle Ages: The Relationship of Heterodoxy to Dissent.* Manchester: Manchester University Press, 1999.

Le Goff, Jacques. *The Birth of Purgatory.* Translated by Arthur Goldhammer. London: Scolar Press, 1984.

Lehmann, Max. *Untersuchungen zur mystischen Terminologie Richard Rolles.* Jena: Gustav Neuenhahn, 1936.

Leicht, Irene. *Marguerite Porete—Eine fromme Intellektuelle und die Inquisition.* Freiburger theologische Studien 163, Freiburg im Breisgau, Basel, 1990.

Lerner, Robert E. *The Heresy of the Free Spirit in the Later Middle Ages.* Berkeley: University of California Press, 1972.

———. "New Light on *The Mirror of Simple Souls,*" *Speculum* 85 (2010): 91–116.

Leyser, Henrietta. *Hermits and the New Monasticism: A Study of Religious Communities in Western Europe, 1000–1150.* London: Macmillan, 1984.

Licence, Tom. *Hermits and Recluses in English Society, 950–1200.* Oxford: Oxford University Press, 2011.

Lichtmann, Maria R. "I Desyrede a Bodylye Syght: Julian of Norwich and the Body." *MQ* 17 (1991): 12–19.

Llewelyn, Robert, ed. *Julian: Woman of Our Day.* London: Darton, Longman & Todd, 1985.

Lochrie, Karma. "*The Book of Margery Kempe:* The Marginal Woman's Quest for Literary Authority." *Journal of Medieval and Renaissance Studies* 16 (1986): 33–55.

———. *Margery Kempe and the Translations of the Flesh.* Philadelphia: University of Pennsylvania Press, 1991.

Lohse, Eduard. *Paulus: Eine Biographie.* Munich: C. H. Beck, 1996.

Madigan, M. F. *The "Passio Domini" Theme in the Works of Richard Rolle: His Personal Contribution in Its Religious, Cultural, and Literary Context.* Salzburg Studies in English Literature, Elizabethan and Renaissance Studies. Salzburg: Institut für Anglistik und Amerikanistik, 1978.

Maisonneuve, Roland. *L'Univers visionnaire de Julian of Norwich.* Paris: Université de Lille, 1987.

Matter, E. Ann. *The Voice of My Beloved: The Song of Songs in Western Medieval Christianity.* Philadelphia: University of Pennsylvania Press, 1990.

Mayr-Harting, Henry. *The Coming of Christianity to Anglo-Saxon England.* 3rd ed. University Park: Penn State University Press, 1991.

McAvoy, Liz Herbert, ed. *Anchoritic Traditions of Medieval Europe.* Woodbridge, UK: Boydell Press, 2010.

———. *Authority and the Female Body in the Writings of Julian of Norwich and Margery Kempe.* Cambridge: D. S. Brewer, 2004.

———, ed. *A Companion to Julian of Norwich.* Cambridge: D. S. Brewer, 2008.

————, ed. *Rhetoric and the Anchorhold.* Cardiff: University of Wales Press, 2008.

McAvoy, Liz Herbert, and Mari Hughes-Edwards, eds. *Anchorites, Wombs, and Tombs: Intersections of Gender and Enclosure in the Middle Ages.* Religion and Culture in the Middle Ages. Cardiff: University of Wales Press, 2005.

McEntire, Sandra J. *The Doctrine of Compunction in Medieval Literature: Holy Tears.* Studies in Medieval Literature 8. Lewiston, NY: E. Mellen Press, 1990.

————, ed. *Julian of Norwich: A Book of Essays.* New York: Garland, 1998.

————, ed. *Margery Kempe: A Book of Essays.* New York: Garland, 1992.

McFarlane, Kenneth B. *Lancastrian Kings and Lollard Knights.* Oxford: Oxford University Press, 1972.

McGinn, Bernard, ed. *The Essential Writings of Christian Mysticism.* New York: Random House, 2006.

————, ed. *Meister Eckhart and the Beguine Mystics: Hadewijch of Brabant, Mechthild of Magdeburg and Margurite Porete.* New York: Continuum, 1994.

————. *The Mystical Thought of Meister Eckhart: The Man from Whom God Hid Nothing.* New York: Crossroad, 2001.

————. *The Presence of God: A History of Western Christian Mysticism.* 4 vols. New York: Crossroad, 1991–2008: vol. 1, *The Foundations of Mysticism: Origins to the Fifth Century* (1991); vol. 2, *The Growth of Mysticism: Gregory the Great through the 12th Century* (1994); vol. 3, *The Flowering of Mysticism: Men and Women in the New Mysticism—1200–1350* (1998); vol. 4, *The Harvest of Mysticism in Medieval Germany* (2008).

McGuire, Brian Patrick. *Brother and Lover: Aelred of Rievaulx.* New York: Crossroad, 1994.

————. *The Difficult Saint: Bernard of Clairvaux and His Tradition.* Kalamazoo, MI: Cistercian Publications, 1991.

McIlroy, Claire Elizabeth. *The English Prose Treatises of Richard Rolle.* Studies in Medieval Mysticism 4. Cambridge: D. S. Brewer, 2004.

McNamer, Sarah. "The Exploratory Image: God as Mother in Julian of Norwich's *Revelations of Divine Love.*" *MQ* 15 (1989): 21–28.

————. "The Origins of *Meditationes vitae Christi.*" *Speculum* 84 (2009): 905–55.

————, ed. *The Two Middle English Translations of the Revelations of St Elizabeth of Hungary.* Heidelberg: Carl Winter, 1996.

Meale, Carol M., ed. *Women and Literature in Britain, 1150–1500.* Cambridge Studies in Medieval Literature 17. 2nd ed. Cambridge: Cambridge University Press, 1997.

Melville, G., and A. Müller, eds. *Regula sancti Augustini: Normative Grundlage differenter Verbände im Mittelalter.* Publikationen der Akademie der Augustiner-Chorherren von Windesheim 3. Paring: Akademie der Windesheimer Kongregation, 2002.

Meyer, Ruth. *Das "St. Katharinenthaler Schwesternbuch": Untersuchung: Edition: Kommentar.* Münchener Texte und Untersuchungen zur deutschen Literatur des Mittelalters 104. Tübingen: Niemeyer, 1995.

Mieth, Dietmar. *Meister Eckhart. Mystik und Lebenskunst.* Düsseldorf: Patmos, 2004.

Millett, Bella. "The *Ancrene Wisse* Group." In Edwards, *Companion to Middle English Prose,* 1–17.

————. "The Audience of the Saints' Lives of the Katherine Group." *Reading Medieval Studies* 16 (1990): 128.

———. "The Genre of *Ancrene Wisse.*" In Wada, *Companion to "Ancrene Wisse,"* 29–44.

———, ed. *Hali Meiþhad.* EETS o.s. 284. Oxford: Oxford University Press, 1982.

———. "The Origins of *Ancrene Wisse:* New Answers, New Questions," *MAE* 61 (1992): 206–28.

———. "Woman in No Man's Land." In Meale, *Women and Literature in Britain,* 86–103.

Minnis, Alastair. "Affection and Imagination in 'The Cloud of Unknowing' and Hilton's 'Scale of Perfection.'" *Traditio* 39 (1983): 323–66.

Minnis, A. J., and A. B. Scott, eds., with assistance of D. Wallace. *Medieval Literary Theory and Criticism, c. 1100–c. 1375: The Commentary Tradition.* Oxford: Clarendon, 1988.

Morgan, Margery M. "A Treatise in Cadence." *MLR* 47 (1952): 156–64.

Morris, Colin. *The Discovery of the Individual.* New York: Harper & Row, 1972.

Mulder-Bakker, Anneke. *Lives of the Anchoresses: The Rise of the Urban Recluse in Medieval Europe.* Philadelphia: University of Pennsylvania Press, 2005.

Nelstrop, Louise, with K. Magill and B. B. Onishi. *Christian Mysticism: An Introduction to Contemporary Theoretical Approaches.* Burlington, VT: Ashgate, 2009.

Newman, Barbara. *From Virile Woman to WomanChrist: Studies in Medieval Religion and Literature.* Philadelphia: University of Pennsylvania Press, 1995.

———. *God and the Goddesses: Vision, Poetry, and Belief in the Middle Ages.* Philadelphia: University of Pennsylvania Press, 2003.

———. "What Did It Mean to Say 'I Saw'? The Clash between Theory and Practice in Medieval Visionary Culture." *Speculum* 80, no. 1 (2005): 1–43.

Nichols, John A. "Cistercian Nuns in Twelfth and Thirteenth Century England." In *Hidden Springs: Cistercian Monastic Women,* edited by John A. Nichols and Lillian Thomas Shank, 49–61. Kalamazoo, MI: Cistercian Publications, 1995.

Nichols, J. A., and L. T. Shank, eds. *Medieval Religious Women.* Vol. 1, *Distant Echoes.* Kalamazoo, MI: Cistercian Publications, 1984.

Oguro, Shoichi, Richard Beadle, and Michael G. Sargent, eds. *Nicholas Love at Waseda: Proceedings of the International Conference 20–22 July 1995.* Cambridge: D. S. Brewer, 1997.

Ohly, Friedrich. *Hohelied-Studien. Grundzüge einer Geschichte der Hoheliedauslegung des Abendlandes bis um 1200.* Wiesbaden: Franz Steiner, 1958.

Olmes, Antonie. *Sprache und Stil der englischen Mystik des Mittelalters unter besonderer Berücksichtigung des Richard Rolle von Hampole.* Studien zur englischen Philologie 76. Tübingen: Max Niemeyer, 1933.

Olson, Linda, and Kathryn Kerby-Fulton, eds. *Voices in Dialogue: Reading Women in the Middle Ages.* Notre Dame, IN: University of Notre Dame Press, 2005.

Ott, Karl August. *Der Rosenroman.* Erträge der Forschung 145. Darmstadt: Wissenschaftliche Buchgesellschaft, 1980.

Palliser, Margaret Ann. *Christ, Our Mother of Mercy: Divine Mercy and Compassion in the Theology of the "Shewings" of Julian of Norwich.* New York: De Gruyter, 1992.

Pantin, W. A. *The English Church in the Fourteenth Century.* Cambridge: Cambridge University Press, 1955. Repr., Toronto: University of Toronto Press, 1980.

———. "The Monk-Solitary of Farne: A Fourteenth-Century English Mystic." *English Historical Review* 59 (1944): 162–86.

Parker, Kate. "Lynn and the Making of a Mystic." In Arnold and Lewis, *Companion*, 55–73.

Pearsall, Derek, ed. *Studies in the Vernon Manuscript*. Woodbridge, UK: Boydell & Brewer, 1990.

Pelphrey, Brant C. *Christ Our Mother: Julian of Norwich*. Wilmington, DE: M. Glazier, 1989.

———. *Love Was His Meaning: The Theology and Mysticism of Julian of Norwich*. Salzburg: Institut für anglistik und Amerikanistik, 1982.

Peters, Ursula. *Religiöse Erfahrung als literarisches Faktum: Zur Vorgeschichte und Genese frauenmystischer Texte des 13. und 14. Jahrhunderts*. Tübingen: Niemeyer, 1988.

Phillips, Helen, ed. *Langland, the Mystics and the Medieval English Religious Tradition*. Cambridge: D. S. Brewer, 1990.

Pollard, William, and Robert Boenig eds. *Mysticism and Spirituality in Medieval England*. Cambridge: D. S. Brewer, 1997.

Price [Wogan-Browne], Jocelyn. "'Inner' and 'Outer': Conceptualizing the Body in *Ancrene Wisse* and Aelred's *De institutione inclusarum*." In *Medieval English Religious and Ethical Literature: Essays in Honour of G. H. Russell*, edited by Gregory Kratzmann and James Simpson, 92–208. Cambridge: D. S. Brewer, 1986.

Putter, Ad. "Walter Hilton's *Scale of Perfection* and *The Cloud of Unknowing*." In Edwards, *Companion to Middle English Prose*, 33–50.

Rahner, Hugo. "Die Gottesgeburt. Die Lehre der Kirchenväter von der Geburt Christi im Herzen der Gläubigen." *Zeitschrift für katholische Theologie* 59 (1935): 333–418.

Rahner, Karl. "Die Lehre von den 'geistlichen Sinnen' im Mittelalter. Der Beitrag Bonaventuras." In *Schriften zur Theologie* 12:137–72. Zürich: Benziger, 1975.

Raitt, Jill, ed. *Christian Spirituality: High Middle Ages and Reformation*. 2 vols. London: Routledge, 1987.

Renevey, Denis. "The Choices of the Compiler: Vernacular Hermeneutics in *A Talkyng of þe Loue of God*." In *The Medieval Translator. Traduire au Moyen Age* 6, edited by Roger Ellis, René Tixier, and Bernd Weitemeier, 232–53. Turnhout: Brepols, 1998.

———. "Enclosed Desires: A Study of the Wooing Group." In Pollard and Boenig, *Mysticism and Spirituality*, 39–62.

———. *Language, Self and Love: Hermeneutics in the Writings of Richard Rolle and the Commentaries on the Song of Songs*. Cardiff: University of Wales Press, 2001.

———. "Looking for a Context: Rolle, Anchoritic Culture and the Office of the Dead." In *Medieval Texts in Context*, edited by Denis Renevey and Graham D. Caie, 192–210. London: Routledge, 2008.

———. "Name above Names: The Devotion to the Name of Jesus from Richard Rolle to Walter Hilton's *Scale of Perfection* I," *MMTE* 6 (1999), 103–21.

———. "'The Name Poured Out': Margins, Illuminations and Miniatures as Evidence for the Practice of Devotions for the Name of Jesus in Late Medieval England." AC 130.9 (1996): 127–47.

Renevey, Denis, and Christiania Whitehead, eds. *Writing Religious Women: Female Spiritual and Textual Practices in Late Medieval England*. Toronto: University of Toronto Press, 2000.

Reynolds, Anna Maria, and Julia Bolton Holloway, eds. *Julian of Norwich: Extant Texts and Translation.* Florence: SISMEL, Edizioni del Galluzzo, 2001.

Rice, Nicole R. "Spiritual Ambition and the Translation of the Cloister: The Abbey and Charter of the Holy Ghost." *Viator* 33 (2002): 222–60.

———. *Lay Piety and Religious Discipline in Middle English Literature.* Cambridge: Cambridge University Press, 2009.

Riddy, Felicity. "Julian of Norwich and Self-Textualization." In *Editing Women: Papers Given at the Thirty-First Annual Conference on Editorial Problems, University of Toronto, 3–4 November 1995,* edited by Ann M. Hutchison, 101–24. Toronto: University of Toronto Press, 1998.

———. "'Women Talking about the Things of God': A Late Medieval Subculture." In Meale, *Women and Literature in Britain,* 104–27.

Riehle, Wolfgang. *The Middle English Mystics.* Translated by Bernard Standring. London: Routledge & Kegan Paul, 1981.

Ringler, Siegfried, ed. *Aufbruch zu neuer Gottesrede. Die Mystik der Gertrud von Helfta.* Ostfildern. Matthias Grünewald Verlag, 2008.

Robertson, Elizabeth. "An Anchorhold of Their Own: Female Anchoritic Literature in Thirteenth-Century England." In *Equally in God's Image: Women in the Middle Ages,* edited by Julia Bolton Holloway, Constance S. Wright, and Joan Bechtold, 170–83. New York: Peter Lang, 1990.

———. *Early English Devotional Prose and the Female Audience.* Knoxville: University of Tennessee Press, 1990.

———. "'Savouring Scientia': The Medieval Anchoress Reads *Ancrene Wisse.*" In Wada, *Companion to "Ancrene Wisse,"* 113–44.

Robinson, Joanne Maguire. *Nobility and Annihilation in Marguerite Porete's "Mirror of Simple Souls."* Albany: SUNY Press, 2001.

Rosof, P. J. F. "The Anchoress in the Twelfth and Thirteenth Centuries." In *Medieval English Women,* vol. 2, *Peaceweavers,* edited by J. A. Nichols and L. Thomas Shank, 123–44. Cistercian Studies Series. Kalamazoo, MI: Cistercian Publications, 1987.

Ruh, Kurt, ed. *Abendländische Mystik im Mittelalter. Symposion Kloster Engelberg 1984.* Stuttgart: Metzler, 1986.

———. *Geschichte der abendländischen Mystik.* Munich: C. H. Beck, 1990–99: vol. 1, *Die Grundlegung durch die Kirchenväter und die Mönchstheologie des 12. Jahrhunderts* (1990); vol. 2, *Frauenmystik und Franziskanische Mystik der Frühzeit* (1993); vol. 3, *Die Mystik des deutschen Predigerordens und ihre Grundlegung durch die Hochscholastik* (1996); vol. 4, *Die niederländische Mystik des 14. bis 16. Jahrhunderts (1999).*

Russell, Kenneth C. "The Gay Abbot of Rievaulx." *SM* 5 (1982): 51–64.

Ruud, J. "Nature and Grace in Julian of Norwich." *MQ* 19 (1993): 79–80.

Rygiel, Dennis. "Structures and Style in Rolle's *The Form of Living.*" *FCEMN* 4, no. 1 (1978): 6–15.

Salih, Sarah. *Versions of Virginity in Late Medieval England.* Cambridge: D. S. Brewer, 2001.

Sanders, Ed Parish. *Paul.* Oxford: Oxford University Press, 1991.

Sargent, Michael G. "Contemporary Criticism of Richard Rolle." In *Kartäusermystik und Mystiker* 1, AC 55: 160–205. Salzburg: Institut für Anglistik und Amerikanistik, 1981.

————, ed. *De cella in seculum: Religious and Secular Life and Devotion in Late Medieval England*. Cambridge: D. S. Brewer, 1989.

————. "*Le Mirouer des simples âmes* and the English Mystical Tradition." In Ruh, *Abendländische Mystik,* 443–65.

————. "The Transmission by the English Carthusians of Some Late Medieval Spiritual Writings." *Journal of Ecclesiastical History* 27 (1976): 225–40.

————. "What Kind of Writing Is *A Talkyng of þe Loue of God*"? In *The Milieu and Context of the Wooing Group,* edited by Susannah M. Chewning, 178–93. Cardiff: University of Wales Press, 2009.

Schiwy, Günther. *Birgitta von Schweden. Mystikerin und Visionärin des späten Mittelalters. Eine Biographie*. Munich: C. H. Beck, 2003.

Schulte, F. "Das musikalische Element in der Mystik Richard Rolles von Hampole." Unpubl. diss., University of Bonn, 1951.

Scott-Stokes, Charity. "Margery Kempe: Her Life and the Early History of Her Book." *MQ* 25 (1999): 9–67.

————. *Women's Books of Hours in Medieval England*. Library of Medieval Women. Woodbridge, UK: Boydell & Brewer, 2006.

Sells, Michael A. *Mystical Languages of Unsaying.* Chicago: University of Chicago Press, 1994.

Smedick, Lois. "Parallelism and Pointing in Rolle's Rhythmical Style." *MS* 41 (1979): 404–67.

Smith, Lesley, and J. H. M. Taylor, eds. *Women, the Book and the Godly.* Selected Proceedings of the St Hilda's Conference, 1993. 2 vols. Cambridge: D. S. Brewer, 1995.

Southern, Richard W. *The Making of the Middle Ages*. New Haven, CT: Yale University Press, 1961.

Spencer, Helen L. *English Preaching in the Late Middle Ages.* Oxford: Clarendon Press, 1993.

Squire, Aelred. *Aelred of Rievaulx: A Study*. Kalamazoo, MI: Cistercian Publications, 1981.

Staley, Lynn. *Margery Kempe's Dissenting Fictions*. University Park: Penn State University Press, 1994.

Stargardt, Ute. "The Beguines of Belgium, the Dominican Nuns of Germany, and Margery Kempe." In Heffernan, *Popular Literature,* 277–313.

Steinmetz, Karl-Heinz. *Mystische Erfahrung und mystisches Wissen in den Cloudtexten*. Berlin: Akademie Verlag, 2005.

Stölting, Ulrike. *Christliche Frauenmystik im Mittelalter. Historisch-theologische Analyse*. Mainz: Matthias- Grünewald- Verlag, 2005.

Strohm, Paul, ed. *Middle English*. Oxford: Oxford University Press, 2007.

Sutherland Annie. "'Oure Feyth Is Groundyd in Goddes Worde'—Julian of Norwich and the Bible." *MMTE* 7 (2004), 1–20.

Suydam, Mary A., and Joanna E. Ziegler, eds. *Performance and Transformation: New Approaches to Late Medieval Spirituality*. New York: St. Martin's Press, 1999.

Tanner, Norman P. *The Church in Late Medieval Norwich, 1370–1532*. Studies and Texts 66. Toronto: Pontifical Institute of Medieval Studies, 1984.

Thompson, E. Margaret. *The Carthusian Order in England*. Church Historical Society, n.s. 3. London: SPCK, 1930.

Thompson, Sally. *Women Religious: The Founding of English Nunneries after the Norman Conquest*. Oxford: Clarendon Press, 1991.

Tuck, J. Anthony. "Carthusian Monks and Lollard Knights: Religious Attitudes at the Court of Richard II." In *Studies in the Age of Chaucer*, Proceedings no. 1, 1984, 149–61.

Tugwell, Simon. *Ways of Imperfection: An Exploration of Christian Spirituality*. Springfield, IL: Templegate Publishers, 1985.

Turner, Denys. *Eros and Allegory: Medieval Exegesis of the Song of Songs*. Kalamazoo, MI: Cistercian Publications, 1995.

Uhlman, Diane R. "The Comfort of Voice, the Solace of Script: Orality and Literacy in *The Book of Margery Kempe*." *Studies in Philology* 91, no. 1 (1994): 50–69.

Ullmann, Walter. *The Individual and Society in the Middle Ages*. Baltimore: Johns Hopkins University Press, 1966.

Voaden, Rosalynn. *God's Words, Women's Voices: The Discernment of Spirits in the Writing of Late Medieval Women Visionaries*. Cambridge: D. S. Brewer 1999.

———. *Prophets Abroad: The Reception of Continental Holy Women in Late-Medieval England*. Cambridge: D. S. Brewer, 1996.

von Balthasar, Hans Urs, ed. *Walter Hilton: Glaube und Erfahrung (The Scale of Perfection)*. German translation of Middle English text by Elisabeth Strakosch. Lectio Spiritualis 10. 12. Einsiedeln: Johannes Verlag, 1966.

Wada, Yoko, ed. *A Companion to "Ancrene Wisse."* Cambridge: D. S. Brewer, 2003.

Waddell, Chrysogonus. "The Myth of Cistercian Origins: C. H. Berman and the Manuscript Sources." *Cîteaux: Commentarii Cistercienses* 51, nos. 3–4 (2000): 298–386.

Wallace, David, ed. *The Cambridge History of Medieval English Literature*. Cambridge: Cambridge University Press, 1999.

Walsh, James, ed. *Pre-Reformation English Spirituality*. New York: Fordham University Press, 1966.

Ward, Benedicta. *Miracles and the Medieval Mind*. Philadelphia: University of Pennsylvania Press, 1982.

Warren, Ann K. *Anchorites and Their Patrons in Medieval England*. Berkeley: University of California Press, 1985.

———. "The Nun as Anchoress: England, 1100–1500." In *Medieval Religious Women*, vol. 1, *Distant Echoes*, edited by John A. Nichols and Lillian Thomas Shank, 197–212. Kalamazoo, MI: Cistercian Publications, 1984.

Watson, Nicholas. "Censorship and Cultural Change in Late-Medieval England: Vernacular Theology, the Oxford Translation Debate, and Arundel's Constitutions of 1409." *Speculum* 70 (1995): 822–64.

———. "The Composition of Julian of Norwich's *Revelation of Love*." *Speculum* 68 (1993): 637–83.

———. "'Et Que Est Huius Ydoli Materia? Tuipse': Idols and Images in Walter Hilton." In *Images, Idolatry, and Iconoclasm in Late Medieval England*, edited by Jeremy Dimmick et al., 95–111. Oxford: Oxford University Press, 2002.

———. "The Making of *The Book of Margery Kempe*." In Olson and Kerby-Fulton, *Voices in Dialogue*, 395–434.

———. "Melting into God the English Way: Deification in the Middle English Version of Marguerite Porete's *Mirouer des simples âmes anienties*." In *Prophets Abroad*, edited by Rosalynn Voaden, 19–50. Cambridge: D. S. Brewer, 1996.

————. "The Middle English Mystics." In Wallace, *Cambridge History of Medieval English Literature,* 539–65.

————. "Misrepresenting the Untranslatable: Marguerite Porete and the *Mirouer des simples âmes." New Comparison* 12 (1991): 124–37.

————. *Richard Rolle and the Invention of Authority.* Cambridge Studies in Medieval Literature 13. Cambridge: Cambridge University Press, 1991.

————. "Richard Rolle as Elitist and Popularist: The Case of *Judica me."* In Sargent, *De cella in seculum,* 123–44.

————. "Translation and Self-Canonization in Richard Rolle's *Melos amoris."* In *The Medieval Translator: The Theory and Practice of Translation in the Middle Ages,* edited by Roger Ellis, 167–80. Cambridge: D. S. Brewer 1989.

————. "The Trinitarian Hermeneutic in Julian of Norwich's *Revelation of Love."* In McEntire, *Julian of Norwich,* 61–90.

————. "Visions of Inclusion: Universal Salvation and Vernacular Theology in Pre-Reformation England." *Journal of Medieval and Early Modern Studies* 27, no. 2 (1997): 145–87.

————. "'Yff Wommen Be Double Naturelly': Remaking 'Woman' in Julian of Norwich's *Revelation of Love." Exemplaria* 8 (1995): 1–34.

Wiethaus, Ulrike. *Agnes Blannbekin, Viennese Beguine: Life and Revelations.* Library of Medieval Women. Cambridge: D. S. Brewer, 2002.

————, ed. *Maps of Flesh and Light: The Religious Experience of Medieval Women.* Syracuse, NY: Syracuse University Press, 1993.

Wilckens, Ulrich. *Theologie des Neuen Testaments.* Bd. II *Die Theologie des Neuen Testaments als Grundlage kirchlicher Lehre.* Teilband I: *Das Fundament.* Neukirchen-Vluyn. Neukirchener Verlag, 2007.

Wilmart, André. "Le 'Jubilus' sur le nom de Jesus dit de Saint Bernard." *Ephemerides liturgicae* 57 (1943): 1–285.

Wischmeyer, Oda, ed. *Paulus: Leben—Umwelt—Werk—Briefe.* Tübingen: Francke, 2006.

Wogan-Browne, Jocelyn. *Saints' Lives and Women's Literary Culture.* Oxford: Oxford University Press, 2001.

Wogan-Browne, Jocelyn, Arlyn Diamond, Ann Hutchison, et al., eds. *Medieval Women: Texts and Contexts in Late-Medieval Britain.* Turnhout: Brepols, 2000.

Wogan-Browne, Jocelyn, et al., eds. *The Idea of the Vernacular: An Anthology of Middle English Literary Theory, 1280–1520.* University Park: Penn State University Press, 1999.

Yoshikawa, N. K. "*Discretio Spirituum* in Time: The Impact of Julian of Norwich's Counsel in the *Book of Margery Kempe." MMTE* 7 (2004).

Zaluska, Yolanta. *L'enluminure et le scriptorium de Cîteaux au XIIe siècle.* Brecht: Cîteaux, 1989.

Reference Works

"Ancrene Wisse," the Katherine Group, and the Wooing Group. Annotated Bibliographies of Old and Middle English Literature. Edited by Bella Millett. Cambridge: D. S. Brewer, 1996.

Dictionnaire de spiritualité ascétique et mystique. Doctrine et histoire. Fondé par M. Viller et al., continué par A. Derville et al. Paris: Beauschesne, 1932–95.

Fries, Heinrich, ed. *Handbuch theologischer Grundbegriffe*. Munich: Deutscher taschenbuch verlag, 1970.

Jolliffe, P. S. *A Check-List of Middle English Prose Writings of Spiritual Guidance*. Toronto: Pontifical Institute of Medieval Studies, 1974.

Lagorio, Valerie M., Michael G. Sargent, and Ritamary Bradley. "English Mystical Writings." Chap. 23 of Hartung and Burke Severs, *Manual of the Writings in Middle English*, 9:3051–68, 3411–25.

A Manual of the Writings in Middle English, 1050–1500. Edited by Albert E. Hartung and J. Burke Severs. Vol. 9. New Haven, CT: Connecticut Academy of Arts and Sciences, 1993.

Middle English Dictionary (MED). Edited by Hans Kurath et al. Ann Arbor: University of Michigan Press, 1952–2001.

❧ Index

Specific works with known authors may be located by checking entries at the authors' name, unless otherwise indicated. Page numbers in *italics* indicate illustrations.

purgatio, 84–85, 91, 103, 107, 110, 131, 154, 314n52

Raimondo da Capua, 175, 265
raptus. See ecstasy
Reformation and pre-Reformation stance, 173, 174, 196, 233, 278
Reginald of Durham, 8, 306n26
Regula heremitarum, 75, 76
religious drama, 288–95; *The Castle of Perseverance*, 292–95, *294*, 370n271; Chester plays, 288; *Christ's Resurrection*, 256; *Everyman*, 292; mystic themes in, 288–92; N-Town plays, 288–89, 290, 386n62; *Northern Passion*, 288; staging and performance practice, 292–93, *294;* Towneley plays, 289–90; *Wisdom Who Is Christ, or Mind, Will and Understanding* (Macro play), 290–92
resurrection of the body, 50, 103, 104, 186, 221, 228, 300, 353n81
Revelation, Book of, 67, 68, 88–91, 102, 117, 121, 130, 132, 327n149, 327n151
Richard II (king of England), 147, 149
Richard of St. Victor: *Ancrene Wisse* and, 51; *Cloud* texts and, 153, 158, 160, 161, 164, 345n68, 345n73, 346–47n103; *De quattuor gradibus violentae caritatis* (The Four Degrees of Fervent Love), 20, 83; *De trinitate*, 137; Hilton and, 183, 197; *The Mystical Ark*, 197; Rolle influenced by, 83, 325n118; *The Twelve Patriarchs (Benjamin Minor)*, 20, 153, 158, 160, 161, 345n68
Rievaulx Abbey, 15, 21
Rolle, Richard, xiv, xv, 70–134; on angels, 69, 97, 118, 126–30; apparent 13th-century gap between early English mystics and, 59; autobiographical material in works of, 107, 331n227; on Bible and biblical exegesis, 78–79, 88–89, 91, 95–96, 112, 131; on bodily resurrection, 50; Cistercians and, 305n10; classification, tendency towards, 334n281; *Cloud* texts and, 82, 90, 154, 155, 162, 165, 166–67, 169, 170; *cura pastoralis* of, 77, 86, 91; Greek, knowledge of, 71, 121, 129; heaven, experience of, 123, 335n307; Hilton and, 82, 176, 179–84, 188, 194, 329n177, 330n198, 349n7, 351n50, 359n59; influence of anchoritic idea in England and, 14; interiority of, 92, 299; John the Evangelist influencing, 67; Julian of Norwich compared, 85, 104, 117, 209, 220, 221, 225, 226, 236, 243;

Kempe and, 109, 121, 247, 252, 255, 268, 273, 275, 280; Latin, acquisition and use of, xv, 70, 80, 121, 133; life, education, and career of, 70–75, 298; literary and theological authority, development of, 75–80, 298; love as understood by, 82–84, 92–94, 96–97, 122, 134; Mary, veneration of, 87–88, 99–101, 327n142–43; mobility and exchange of ideas affecting, 298; monk of Farne and, 67, 69, 126, 325n117, 334n394; music, importance of, 71, 114–15, 123–30, *127*, 289, 329n183; mysticism of, 80–86; *Officium et miracula* of, 70, 72, 73, 75, 77, 91, 130, 275, 323, 329n178; "Oleum effusum nomen tuum" exegesis and Name of Jesus cult, 98, 99, 283, 383n1; originality/eccentricity of, 75; Pauline writings and, 82, 84, 89, 97, 99, 104, 123, 128, 134, 327n149, 335n307; *Philomena* (John of Howden) and, 311n54; portrait in *Desert of Religion* MS, *127;* sexual temptation of, 73–74, 87, 321n25, 328n157; on sitting posture, 80–81, *127*, 324n82; *A Talkyng of þe Loue of God* and, 60, 66; Vernon MS and, 60; on *vita mixta*, 284
Rolle, Richard, works of, 86–87; *The Bee*, 86; *Canticum amoris*, 86, 87–88; *The Commandment*, 83, 86; in compilations, 283; *Contra amatores mundi*, 83–84, 86, 101, 325n95, 325n100, 326n132, 334n297; *De Dei misericordia*, 86; *Desyre and Delit*, 86; *Ego dormio*, 75, 83, 86, 117–19; *Emendatio vitae*, 83, 86, 94, 106–9, 325n101, 326n122, 332n230; *Encomium nominis Iesu*, 98, 283; English Psalter, 86, 105, 106, 109–15, 133, 332n237; *Expositio super novem lectiones mortuorum*, 77, 85, 86, 101–5, 107, 132, 305n10, 321n36, 322n51, 331n214; *The Form of Living*, 75, 83, 86, 107, 109, 115–17, 119, 181, 331n227, 334n281, 371n287; *Ghastly Gladnesse*, 86; *Incendium amoris*, xv, 71, 72, 74, 77, 86, 91–97, 104, 107, 109, 118, 252; *Judica me Deus*, 74, 77, 86, 91, 322n49, 328n160; Lamentations of Jeremiah, commentary on, 321n16; Latin Psalter, 86, 105–6, 111, 113, 114; *Meditations on the Passion*, 68, 86, 119–21, 255, 290, 334n293; *Piers Plowman* and, 296; *Prick of Conscience* attributed to, 87; *Seven Gifts of the Holy Spirit*, 86; *Super apocalypsim*, 86, 88–91, 102, 105, 117, 121, 130; *Super canticum canticorum* (Comment on